In Health and Human Development Series

BEHAVIORAL PEDIATRICS
3RD EDITION

HEALTH AND HUMAN DEVELOPMENT SERIES

JOAV MERRICK, EDITOR

Adolescent Behavior Research: International Perspectives
Joav Merrick and Hatim A. Omar
2007. ISBN: 1-60021-649-8

Disability from a Humanistic Perspective: Towards a Better Quality of Life
Shunit Reiter
2008. ISBN: 978-1-60456-412-9

Complementary Medicine Systems: Comparison and Integration
Karl W. Kratky
2008 ISBN 978-1-60456-475-4

Pain in Children and Youth
Patricia Schofield and Joav Merrick
2008 ISBN 978-1-60456-951-3

Obesity and Adolescence: A Public Health Concern
Hatim A. Omar, Donald E. Greydanus, Dilip R. Patel and Joav Merrick
2009 ISBN 978-1-60456-821-9

Health and Happiness from Meaningful Work: Research in Quality of Working Life
Søren Ventegodt and Joav Merrick
2009 ISBN 978-1-60692-820-2

Behavioral Pediatrics 3rd Edition
Donald E. Greydanus, Dilip R. Patel, Helen D. Pratt and Joseph L. Calles, Jr.
2009. ISBN: 978-1-60692-702-1

In Health and Human Development Series

BEHAVIORAL PEDIATRICS
3RD EDITION

DONALD E. GREYDANUS
DILIP R. PATEL
HELEN D. PRATT
AND
JOSEPH L. CALLES, JR.
EDITORS

Nova Biomedical Books 2009
New York

NOTICE TO THE READER

The Publisher has taken reasonable care in the preparation of this book, but makes no expressed or implied warranty of any kind and assumes no responsibility for any errors or omissions. No liability is assumed for incidental or consequential damages in connection with or arising out of information contained in this book. The Publisher shall not be liable for any special, consequential, or exemplary damages resulting, in whole or in part, from the readers' use of, or reliance upon, this material.

Independent verification should be sought for any data, advice or recommendations contained in this book. In addition, no responsibility is assumed by the publisher for any injury and/or damage to persons or property arising from any methods, products, instructions, ideas or otherwise contained in this publication.

This publication is designed to provide accurate and authoritative information with regard to the subject matter covered herein. It is sold with the clear understanding that the Publisher is not engaged in rendering legal or any other professional services. If legal or any other expert assistance is required, the services of a competent person should be sought. FROM A DECLARATION OF PARTICIPANTS JOINTLY ADOPTED BY A COMMITTEE OF THE AMERICAN BAR ASSOCIATION AND A COMMITTEE OF PUBLISHERS.

Library of Congress Cataloging-in-Publication Data

Behavioral pediatrics / editors: Donald E. Greydanus ... [et al.]. -- 3rd ed.
    p. ; cm. -- (Health and human development)
 Includes bibliographical references and index.
 ISBN 978-1-60692-702-1 (hardcover : alk. paper)
 1. Behavior disorders in children. I. Greydanus, Donald E. II. Series: Health and human development series.
 [DNLM: 1. Child Behavior Disorders. 2. Adolescent. 3. Child Behavior. 4. Child. 5. Developmental Disabilities. WS 350.6 B4189 2009]
 RJ506.B44.B445 2009
 618.92'89--dc22
                        2008053077

Published by Nova Science Publishers, Inc. ✚ New York

Contents

Foreword   ix
   D. E. Greydanus, D. R. Patel, H. D. Pratt, and J. L. Calles

Preface   xv

Section I.   **Introduction**   1

Chapter 1   Introduction to Behavioral Pediatrics   3
                      Helen D. Pratt

Chapter 2   Behavioral and Psychological Assessment   9
                      Margo Adams Larsen and Erin Tentis

Section II.   **Developmental Disorders**   37

Chapter 3   Intellectual Disability   39
                      Dilip R. Patel and Joav Merrick

Chapter 4   Learning Disabilities   51
                      Helen D. Pratt and Donald E. Greydanus

Chapter 5   Speech-Language Disorders and Other Communication Problems   61
                      Nickola Wolf Nelson and Heather Kay Koole

Chapter 6   Autism Spectrum Disorders   79
                      Ahsan Nazeer

Chapter 7   Sensory Processing Disorders and Treatment: Occupational Therapy
                      Using a Sensory Integration Approach   101
                      Cindee Quake-Rapp and Ben Atchison

Chapter 8   Tic Disorders   121
                      Donald E. Greydanus and Artemis K. Tsitsika

Chapter 9   Enuresis   131
                      *Donald E. Greydanus, Alfonso Torres, Arthur Feinberg and
                      Cynthia Feucht*

Chapter 10   Encopresis   **147**
                    Dilip R. Patel, Helen D. Pratt and Cynthia Feucht

Section III.   **Disruptive Behavior Disorders**   **157**

Chapter 11   Attention-Deficit/Hyperactivity Disorder   **159**
                    Joseph L. Calles

Chapter 12   Oppositional Defiant and Conduct Disorders   **175**
                    Joseph L. Calles

Chapter 13   Aggressive Behaviors   **185**
                    Joseph L. Calles

Section IV.   **Mood Disorders**   **215**

Chapter 14   Major Depressive and Dysthymic Disorders   **205**
                    Joseph L. Calles

Chapter 15   Pediatric Bipolar Disorder   **219**
                    Amy E. West and Mani N. Pavuluri

Section V.   **Anxiety Disorders**   **237**

Chapter 16   Anxiety Disorders   **239**
                    Christopher K. Varley and Amy Henry

Chapter 17   Obsessive Compulsive Disorder   **255**
                    Amy Henry and Christopher K. Varley

Section VI.   **Sexuality**   **277**

Chapter 18   Childhood and Adolescent Sexuality   **265**
                    Donald E. Greydanus, Artemis K. Tsitsika, Lyubov A. Matytsina and
                    Antonio C. Sison

Chapter 19   Homosexual Attraction and Sexual Behavior in Adolescents   **297**
                    Donald E. Greydanus, Antonio C. Sison and Kristin W. Guilonard

Section VII.   **Special Issues**   **317**

Chapter 20   Suicidal Behavior in Children and Adolescents   **319**
                    Kimberly K. McClanahan and Hatim A. Omar

Chapter 21   Schizophrenia in Childhood and Adolescence   **349**
                    Gretchen R. Gudmundsen and Jon M. McClellan

Chapter 22   Personality Disorders and Adolescents: A Developmental Perspective   **369**
                    Helen D. Pratt

Chapter 23   Anorexia Nervosa and Bulimia Nervosa   **383**
                    Vinay N. Reddy and Lesley A. Reid

Chapter 24   Obesity   **405**
                    Vinay N. Reddy

Chapter 25   Substance Use and Abuse in Adolescents   **417**
                 Donald E. Greydanus and William J. Reed

Chapter 26   Abuse in the Child and Adolescent   **451**
                 Vincent J. Palusci and Margaret T. McHugh

Chapter 27   Sexual Offenders   **485**
                 Helen D. Pratt, Dilip R. Patel and Donald E. Greydanus

Chapter 28   Behavioral Aspects of Chronic Illness   **495**
                 Dilip R. Patel, Kristin Guilonard and Helen D. Pratt

Contributors   **501**

Index   **507**

In: Behavioral Pediatrics, 3rd Edition
Editor: Donald E. Greydanus et al.

ISBN 978-1-60692-702-1
© 2009 Nova Science Publishers, Inc.

Foreword

New York: Nova Science, 3 edition, 2009

D. E. Greydanus, D. R. Patel, H. D. Pratt, and J. L. Calles

Pediatrics (from two Greek words for child (pais) and healer (iatros) is the field of medicine concerned with infants, children and adolescents, their growth and development along with their prospect to achieve fill potentials as adults.

Abraham Jacobi (1830-1919), the father of American pediatrics and also the area of social pediatrics, is the name that comes up first to mind, when you think about pediatrics. This German Jewish physician graduated from the University of Bonn in 1851, but when he traveled to Berlin to take his state medical exams, he was arrested and held in prison for nearly two years on a charge of promoting political and social reform in the German revolution of 1848. He left Germany and arrived in New York later in 1853, where he practiced general medicine, surgery and obstetrics, but his early contributions to the New York Medical Journal helped establish the field of pediatrics. In 1857, Jacobi lectured on childhood diseases of the larynx at the College of Physicians and Surgeons, his first formal pediatric lecture and in 1860, he accepted a position as professor of infantile pathology and therapeutics at New York Medical College. This appointment signaled a turning point as it was the first pediatric medical position and launched pediatrics as an academic discipline in the United States and during his lifetime all major medical centers in the United States established pediatric departments. He also established the bedside clinical teaching method, a landmark in medical education. In 1865 he accepted the position of clinical professor of diseases of children at New York University Medical College and in 1870 the College of Physicians and Surgeons (Columbia University) appointed him professor of clinical pediatrics. He worked at almost every hospital in New York, but he concentrated on the Jews Hospital (later Mount Sinai Hospital), where he set up the first outpatient pediatric clinic in 1874. By 1878, the Jews Hospital had the first department of pediatrics in a United States general hospital.

But the fact is that already much earlier in time pediatrics had been the focus of several Persian physicians. In the 10th century, the famous Persian physician Rhazes (Muhammad ibn Zakariya Razi, 865-925) wrote the first book that we know about (diseases of children, one of his 184 publications) to deal with pediatrics as an independent field of medicine. His teacher Ali ibn Sahl Rabban al-Tabari (838-870), a moslem convert of Jewish decent, who produced the first encyclopedia of medicine, was also a pioneer in the field of child development, which was discussed in depth in his book "Firdous al-Hikmah" (Paradise of wisdom). The first work on pediatrics in the Western world was the Book of Children, published in 1545 by Thomas Phaer (1510-1560). The first Hospital for Sick Children in Great Ormond Street in London that we know about was founded in 1852 and still today considered as one of the best pediatric centers in the world.

So where and when does the field of behavioral pediatrics come into the picture? Some will go back to Charles Darwin (1809-1882), who in 1877 published his observations on his first child (A biographical sketch of an infant. Mind 1877;2:285-94) as a study of human behavioral development. This and his other work inspired and influenced other scholars, which again resulted in major progress in cognition, personality, intellegence testing, learning, psychoanalysis and animal research on human development. In Europe and in Scandinavia, where I grew up and was trained we would call this special field or area of interest for social pediatrics or even some would say that it is not a discipline, but rather a state of mind. In the 1980s this area in Europe (influenced a lot by the British discipline of community pediatrics) has developed into a field now called child public health involved with the organised efforts of society to develop public health policies to promote child and young people's health, to prevent disease in children and young people and to foster equity for children and young people, within a framework of sustainable development.

In the United States the Society for Developmental and Behavioral Pediatrics was founded in 1982 in order to improve the health care of infants, children, and adolescents by promoting research and teaching in developmental and behavioral pediatrics. This society of pediatricians and other professionals have worked to encourage research in developmental and behavioral pediatrics with an emphasis on psychosocial issues arising in the context of health care, to promote education in developmental and behavioral pediatrics, to raise questions and respond to issues that affect research, teaching, or program development in developmental and behavioral pediatrics and to promote an understanding of and particular interest in the social, educational and cultural influences on children. The work of this society and others resulted in the American Board of Pediatrics in 2002 to accept a subspecialty training in developmental and behavioral pediatrics.

The Journal of Developmental and Behavioral Pediatrics devoted to the developmental and psychosocial aspects of pediatric health care is now in 2009 in its 30th year of publication and this present textbook is now in its third edition.

The present book is a welcome addition to the field of behavioral pediatrics and it will be the textbook that will follow pediatricians interested in this field, in a career and subspecialty in behavioral pediatrics.

Professor Joav Merrick, MD, MMedSci, DMSc
Director, National Institute of Child Health and Human Development, Jerusalem,
Medical Director, Office of the Medical Director,
Division for Mental Retardation, Ministry of Social Affairs, Jerusalem, Israel and
Professor of Pediatrics, Kentucky Children's Hospital,
University of Kentucky, Lexington, United States.
E-Mail: jmerrick@internet-zahav.net. Website: www.nichd-israel.com

Foreword to Behavioral Pediatrics, Second Edition, 2006

When all's said and done, when the doors of the clinic or office close, the pediatrician, family doctor or nurse practitioner, will drive home to a late dinner all the time thinking about the social and behavioral challenges presented by his or her young patients that day. The "medical" decision making, diagnosis and treatment of the principal problems will, on the whole, have been easy in comparison to the social and behavioral problems presented by the patients. For most practitioners, behavioral training (the psychosocial in the biopsychosocial) occurred years ago. The practitioner may not be conversant with contemporary diagnosis, treatment, and psychological perspectives. So fortunately, within the pages of this volume you will find expert articulation of the behavioral and social dimensions of your challenging cases as well as an excellent presentation of child and adolescent psychological and psychiatric diagnosis and treatment.

There are a number of features of this carefully edited volume that I recommend to you the reader. The disciplinary "silos" of specialty and subspecialty are breached in a healthy way; the reader is presented with comprehensive coverage of behavior both normal and pathological in children and adolescents in clear prose written by experts from many disciplines. The writing avoids specialty jargon while clarifying key concepts. This book is an asset not only for those seeking a deeper understanding but those interested in becoming more engaged in diagnosis and treatment of their behavioral disordered young patients. Increasing involvement by primary care in such treatment is essential in my view if we expect that access to treatment for these relatively common conditions will be available.

More important than treatment is prevention. Primary prevention remains a "holy grail" awaiting more scientific discovery at least for the serious mental disorders but much is known about secondary prevention (reducing episodes of illness and morbidity) and tertiary prevention (reducing social disability). Prevention in many areas of behavioral health can be linked to healthy family behaviors, for example, it is clear that drug use and dependence (including smoking) in adolescents is less common in families that closely monitor their children's activities. The same can be said for other risky behaviors with damaging consequences to health and well being.

Family doctors, pediatricians, nurses, and other primary care providers function as sentinels in the community for much that is happening in our culture and, function, to use a current phrase, as "first responders." This volume can be a key resource for "first responders." The role of human behavior in illness and the human behavior illnesses is so widely prevalent that, as a psychiatrist and a dean, it won't surprise the reader to know that I hope and even expect a high level of behavioral sophistication in those who care for children and adolescents.

Robert Haggerty in his Foreword to the first edition provided a brief history of behavioral pediatrics and attempts a definition of behavioral pediatrics that might distinguish child psychiatry from behavioral pediatrics. Since the first edition of this book the American Board of Pediatrics (ABP) has recognized the subspecialty of Developmental and Behavioral Pediatrics. The American Board of Medical Specialties in the last several years supported the ABP's application for recognition and the provision of a subspecialty certificate. Behavioral pediatrics is here to stay. The boundaries of specialties may always be fuzzy. But the key question is not how child psychiatry and behavioral pediatrics are similar or different but 'are patients better served" to have both. I have no doubt that they are! Dr. Haggerty also emphasized the need for us to function in teams—certainly a challenge we have in medical schools—to create curricula that teach the provision of care in cross-professional teams. This well crafted volume covers behavioral pediatrics content and provides a context for effective team delivery of high quality behavioral care to children and adolescents.

Glenn C. Davis, MD
Former Dean
College of Human Medicine
Michigan State University

Foreword to Behavioral Pediatrics, First Edition, 1992

The origins of the term "behavioral pediatrics" are not clear, but we used it in the early 1970s at the University of Rochester to distinguish a program based in pediatrics from those based in child psychiatry. Most behavioral pediatrics programs involved child psychologists working with pediatricians. In the late 1970s the William T. Grant Foundation funded 11 Behavioral Pediatrics Programs in the United States aimed at educating pediatric residents about behavioral problems in children. These programs were modeled on a program begun earlier by Dr. Stanford Friedman at the University of Maryland. A key element of all was that they were based in pediatric departments rather than in child psychiatry. This created some confusion and concern, especially among child psychiatrists. I see little reason for conflict, since, although there is some overlap, the two fields deal with different aspects of child behavior, and the very large need cannot be met by child psychiatry alone.

At the end of the Foundation's 6 years of support of these 11 programs, more than 35 pediatric training programs in the United States had divisions of behavioral pediatrics, and the field seemed well on its way to maturity. This was followed by the organization of the

Behavioral Pediatric Society, and, in the late 1980s, by the adoption of the *Journal of Developmental and Behavioral Pediatrics* as the official journal of the Society. All that is left to create a new specialty is a textbook and subspecialty boards. With this textbook, the first of these steps is achieved, and the second, subspecialty boards, is now being proposed.

Some will object to a separate subspecialty of behavioral pediatrics. I take pride in being an academic general pediatrician, and I believe that this field includes adolescent medicine and behavioral pediatrics, as well as the area represented by the grandfather of these breakaway societies—the Ambulatory Pediatric Association. While I have had concerns about the separation of behavioral pediatrics from general pediatrics and from the other pediatric research societies, I do have some difficulty in consistency, since I was one of the original "breakaway pediatricians" who formed the Ambulatory Pediatric Association. Behavioral Pediatrics has come of age, and it deserves to be recognized as a separate subspecialty. The task is to integrate its knowledge and skills into the fabric of all pediatric training programs.

This book gives a comprehensive coverage of the current status of the field of behavioral pediatrics. It deals very well with the general principles, the skills needed for assessment, and the management of the majority of clinical syndromes. It is authored, appropriately, by a group of authors from many disciplines, including pediatrics and psychology, and it touches on the psychologic aspects of chronic physical disease as well as family problems, including divorce, which puts children at risk. This coverage is very much in the tradition of most medical texts—oriented to the individual and family, and causes and treatments of the problems. There is relatively little in this or any other textbook of pediatrics on the social, cultural, and environmental origins of problem behaviors, or on social policies that may be necessary to prevent or effectively manage many of these problem behaviors of children and youth: better jobs for their parents and a hopeful future for themselves, better education, reduction of discrimination, and social violence. And, at the level of therapy, group approaches, peer counseling, community support groups, and community empowerment are interventions that, I believe, the behavioral pediatrician will use more in the future, as well as the individual and family approach so well outlined in this book.

Since this text contains excellent chapters on schizophrenia and depression, which are usually considered to be the domain of child psychiatry, the question remains, how does behavioral pediatrics differ from child psychiatry? I offer my own idiosyncratic definition: "behavioral pediatrics is what the pediatrician does to diagnose, to treat, and most important, to prevent mental illness and problem behaviors in children." The field obviously overlaps with child psychiatry, but is still distinct. Some problems, such as teen pregnancy, failure to thrive, behavioral aspects of sports medicine, and sexually transmitted diseases, are rarely dealt with by child psychiatrists, and are clearly the province of the behavioral pediatrician. On the other hand, schizophrenia, autism, and severe depression, while they may—and should—be picked up by the pediatrician, must usually be treated by the child psychiatrist. Given that behavioral pediatrics is a multidisciplinary field and has some overlap with child psychiatry and other disciplines, productive relations between these disciplines still need to be worked out in many institutions. The challenge to the field of behavioral pediatrics is to learn to work effectively as a team, to develop advocacy skills to promote social policies that deal with the sociocultural causes of problem behaviors and, at the same time, develop the skills to relate to individual patients and their families and to diagnose and manage effectively those problems for which the pediatrician can become competent. This is a big order, but one that this book goes a long way toward helping to achieve. Unless pediatricians learn to deal effectively with these major problems, they will be unable to deal with most pressing and common problems faced by the children and their families today. With a textbook of its own, behavior pediatrics has come of age.

Robert J. Haggerty, MD
President
William T. Grant Foundation
Clinical Professor of Pediatrics
New York Hospital/Cornell Medical Center

In: Behavioral Pediatrics, 3rd Edition
Editor: Donald E. Greydanus et al.

ISBN 978-1-60692-702-1
© 2009 Nova Science Publishers, Inc.

Preface to the Third Edition

"The boundary between biology and behavior is arbitrary and changing. It has been imposed not by the natural contours of disciplines but by lack of knowledge."

Kandel, 1991

Children, adolescents and their families are presented with prodigious difficulties as they face the challenges of the 21st century. Our children pass through intricate developmental phases as they traverse through childhood and adolescence on their inevitable journey into adulthood. Since many parents face considerable challenges in their endeavors to help their children, many families turn to their primary care professionals for counsel in this regard. There are a limited number of books summarizing current concepts of behavioral pediatrics as defined by the first edition of this book: "what the clinician does to diagnose, to treat, and most importantly, to *prevent* mental illness in children and adolescents." We have compiled this updated information for various health care professionals who are seeking to provide comprehensive health care for our children and adolescents—pediatricians, family medicine physicians, internists, physician assistants, nurse practitioners, psychologists, social workers, health educators and others involved in the care of children and adolescents.

Much has evolved in this field since the publication of the first edition in 1992. Research in child and adolescent psychiatry, psychology, behavioral sciences, pediatrics, family therapy, individual therapy and related fields have led to new and exciting information. Advancements in psychopharmacology have led to an explosion of medications used to treat a wide variety of mental health disorders, including depression, anxiety, schizophrenia, disruptive behavioral disorders, eating disorders, attention-deficit/hyperactivity disorder (ADHD), and others.

Behavioral Pediatrics, 3rd edition is designed to provide the primary-care clinician with a practical guide to early recognition and intervention in the significant problems increasingly affecting the emotional health of children and adolescents. It is the hope of the editors of this edition that this updated information will be of considerable guidance to clinicians in helping to meet the complex needs of the children, adolescents, and families that they serve. Today, our families expect us to look at both the medical and mental health aspects which affect our children and teenagers.

Finis Coronat Opus

Donald E. Greydanus MD
Dilip R. Patel MD
Helen D. Pratt PhD
Joseph L. Calles Jr, MD

Section I. Introduction

In: Behavioral Pediatrics, 3rd Edition
Editor: Donald E. Greydanus et al.

ISBN 978-1-60692-702-1
© 2009 Nova Science Publishers, Inc.

Chapter 1

Introduction to Behavioral Pediatrics

Helen D. Pratt

Abstract

Primary care physicians typically are the point of access for children who manifest developmental or behavioral concerns. Office visits are equally divided between pediatrics, family medicine, and internal medicine. Physicians are charged with being the "Medical Home" for youth with special needs and developmental disabilities. The involvement of multiple clinicians in the care of youth can result in fractured care. Current standards of care encourage physicians to take the lead in coordinating that care and ensuring that the patient and his or her family are able to comply with the medical and behavioral regimes necessary for optimal outcomes. In this context adding the word "behavioral" to pediatrics is intended to convey the combination of behavior responses to specific conditions with the processes of child and adolescent growth and development (biological, genetic, physiological). Conditions that impact these areas include: Demographic data parental history of mental disorders, prison, SES) access to resources; family conflict; environmental data; exposure to trauma; violence; substances; and interpersonal relationships. The text is divided into seven major sections: Section I presents the introduction to the text and behavioral assessment, Section II covers developmental disorders. Section III addresses disruptive behavior. Section IV discusses mood disorders, while Section VII addresses special issues. Clinicians who learn to detect, diagnose, treat, refer and manage the complexities of problems presented by their pediatric patients are better able to provide quality care.

Introduction

As the point of access for children and adolescents who manifest developmental or behavioral concerns, primary care physicians can serve a vital role in detecting problems that may impact youth health and medical compliance. Often these physicians have the most routine contact with youth during their early years and have established trust and familiarity with the family. In their 'gatekeeper" role, they are often required by insurance plans to determine the appropriateness of a referrals to subspecialist or other mental health professionals. Most parents prefer to obtain an initial assessment of their child's behavioral or developmental status from the primary care physician they trust. Often they will more readily accept suggestions for intervention from the child's or adolescent's physician, rather than from an unfamiliar specialist.

Over the last several decades, there has been an increase in the *developmental* evaluation of infants and young children. This is due in part to federal legislation mandating provision of early intervention (EI) services for those in the 0-3- year age range, and early childhood education (ECE) programs for children ages 3 through 5 years. One reason for increased developmental evaluation is due to improved survival rates of infants and children at biological risk, and the increased probability of long-term sequelae. Early developmental evaluation is critical because timely identification of developmental problems affords the opportunity to implement early intervention.

Behavioral Pediatrics Defined

In this context adding the word behavioral to pediatrics is intended to combine a person's behavior/responses to specific conditions, process of child and adolescent growth and development (biological, genetic, physiological). Conditions that impact these areas are included: demographic (data parental history of mental disorders, prison, SES) access to resources, family conflict, environmental data, exposure to trauma, violence, and substances, and interpersonal relationships.

Infant, child, and adolescent development encompasses a) physical growth and maturation (including: gross motor development, fine motor development, agility as well as flexibility, strength, and endurance); b) neurological maturation; c) biological maturation (which includes hormonal changes); d) the development of several domains of function (visual motor, perceptual motor, cognitive, language, auditory, social/emotional); and e) the level of maturity and sophistication of the interaction between all of these areas. Normal development is dynamic, sequential, orderly, and time-dependent. There is considerable individual variation in the onset, rate, and progression of developmental milestones. Behavioral refers to the way in which these infants, children, adolescents and their families act and react to specific sets of conditions.

Behavioral pediatrics is a multi-discipline field and has some overlap with child psychiatry and other disciplines, productive relations between these disciplines still need to be worked out in many institutions. The challenge to the filed of behavioral pediatrics is to learn to work effectively in teams with the physician serving as lead clinician. The text is divided into seven major sections: Section I presents the introduction to the text and behavioral assessment. Section II includes chapters on developmental disorders (behavioral assessment, intellectual disabilities, physical disabilities and chronic disease, speech-language disorders, autism spectrum disorders, sensory processing disorder, tic disorders, elimination disorders). Section III addresses disruptive behavior (attention-deficit/hyperactivity disorder, oppositional defiant and conduct disorders, and aggressive behaviors. Section IV offers information on three of the most common mood disorders seen in the child and adolescent population (major depressive disorders and dysthymic disorders, bipolar disorders). Section V addresses anxiety disorders (anxiety disorders, obsessive-compulsive disorder). Section VI provides information on sexuality (childhood and adolescent sexuality, homosexual attraction and sexual behavior in adolescents). Section VII addresses special issues which include discussion on the following: Suicide in children and adolescents, schizophrenia in childhood and adolescence, personality disorders, eating disorders, and substance abuse disorders, child abuse and neglect, and youth sexual offenders.

Epidemiology

Approximately 20% of the pediatric population has some type of developmental or behavioral problem, and the prevalence is increased in lower socioeconomic status households. Almost 70% of office visits for youth are for non medical reasons.

The *Diagnostic and Statistical Manual, Fourth Edition* (DSM-IV-TR), 2000. is the primary source for diagnosing most behavioral and mental disorders. DSM-IV-TR is used throughout this text in the discussion of behavioral and mental illness. The better a physician knows the patient and or his or her family, the more likely he or she is to detect behavioral problems. Empirical studies have increased our understanding of the intricate and interwoven nature of both biological regulation and environmental factors that influence development. An appreciation of these issues complements one's clinical skills in the promotion of healthy development and in the diagnosis and treatment of childhood problems.

The authors of this text represent an array of clinicians who are experts in their respective fields. The primary contributors are physicians. These individuals are charged with being the "Medical Home" for youth with special needs and developmental disabilities. The involvement of multiple clinicians in the care of youth can result in fractured care. Current standards of care encourage primary care physicians to take the lead in coordinating that care and ensuring that the patient and his or her family are able to comply with the medical and behavioral regimes necessary for optimal outcomes.

The primary "medical home" physicians will come from primary care: Pediatrics, family medicine, and internal medicine, and internal medicine/pediatric (med/peds). Other physicians may serve as consultants and provide essential intervention, but their involvement is often time limited or directed at a specific need. Other physicians, who are a part of primary care, may be involved over the long term but offer specific service; they are: Adolescent Health, Adolescent Medicine, Behavioral Pediatrics, Behavioral Sciences, Sports Medicine, Cognitive Medicine, Child Protection, Nutrition, Nursing, Psychiatry, Psychology, Occupational Therapy, Social Work, Speech Pathology and Audiology.

Advancements in behavioral and psycho-therapy have led to more evidence based treatments for child and adolescent behavioral disorders. Clinicians are now expected to be culturally competent and provide access to care in the patient's primary language. Advances in psychopharmacology have led to an explosion of medication used to treat a wide variety of mental health disorders, including depression, anxiety, schizophrenia, disruptive behavioral disorders, eating disorders, attention-deficit/hyperactivity disorder (ADHD), and others. Physicians are charged with being the "Medical Home" for youth with special needs and developmental disabilities. The involvement of multiple clinicians in the care of youth can result in fractured care. Current standards of care encourage physicians to take the lead in coordinating that care and ensuring that the patient and his or her family are able to comply with the medical and behavioral regimes necessary for optimal outcomes.

Evaluation in Behavioral Pediatrics should always address the following domains of function: a) motor: fine/gross motor skills coordination and control), postural control; b) visual, c) auditory, d) cognitive, e) language, f) eye-hand coordination, g) social/emotional, h) integrative. Deficits in any one of these domains will have an impact on the function in all other domains. For example, a child who is developing normally in all areas except in the attention domain may not experience any adverse outcomes if he has above average intellectual functioning. However, if he has below average intellectual function and problems with selective and sustained attention, problems will occur. These problems may result in missed skill acquisition or misinterpretation of information or conditions in the environment. Special attention should be given to the patient's cultural norms, temperament in addition to the customary assessments. A child or adolescent's temperament will impact how he or she will respond to events and conditions in the environment or internal states. These traits are as listed in Table 1.

Understanding the patient's information on these dimensions will facilitate the clinician's ability to tailor treatment recommendations and optimize the likelihood of compliance.

Another factor affecting the prognosis for healthy patient outcomes is the level of resilience on the parent of the individual child or adolescent. Youth who have the following internal and external characteristics are said to be resilient: a) internal: a strong sense of Autonomy, feel socially competent, have good problems solving skills and hope or belief in the future; and b) external: a strong sense of family and community connectedness and peer acceptance and social support network, and have a safe environment in which to live.

Table 1. Temperament Traits

- Activity: active versus relaxed
- Rhythmicity: eating and sleeping habits regulated or unregulated
- Approach/withdrawal: friendly or shy
- Adaptability: routines or plans: a) adapts to changes or b) requires notification
- or c) planning or resist transitions
- Intensity: react strongly to situations, either positive or negative reacts with
- calmness or acceptance
- Mood: a) stable (even-tempered) or b) shifts or c) pessimistic, d) positive
- Persistence/Tenacity gives up when frustrated or keeps trying to solve a problem
- Execution: attends to stimulus at developmentally appropriate level or
- becomes distracted
- Distractibility: easily or not easily distracted from task;
- Attention: selective attention to shut out external stimuli
- Sensory threshold:; sensitivity textures oral tactile, auditory

---

Conclusion

Clinicians who learn to detect, diagnose, treat, refer and manage the complexities of problems presented by their pediatric patients are better able to provide quality care. Children who have difficulties with respect to the domains of function or have certain temperament traits may have difficulty with their academic, social, emotional, and cognitive development. The goal of intervention in behavioral pediatrics is to help these children develop resilience so that they can be as successful as they can be in their environments.

Bibliography

Alessi G. The family and parenting in the 21st century. *Adolesc. Med.* 2000; 11(1):35-50.

Anastasiow NJ. Implications of the neurobiological model for early intervention. In: Meisels SJ, Shonkoff JP, eds. *Handbook of Early Childhood Intervention.* New York: Cambridge University Press; 1990:196-216.

Bishaw A, Iceland J. Census 2000: Poverty: 1999 Brief. Washington DC: U.S. Department of Commerce Economics and Statistics Administration, U.S. Census Bureau. http://www.census.gov/prod/2001pubs/c2kbr01-8.pdf

Culbertson JL, Newman JE, Willis DJ. Childhood and adolescent psychologic development. *Pediatric Clinics of North America.* 2003; 50(4):741-64.

Gemelli R. *Normal Child and Adolescent Development.* Washington, DC: American Psychiatric Press; 1996.

Gesell AL. Maturation and infant behavior patterns. *Psychol. Rev.* 1929; 36:305-319.

Gushurst CA. Child abuse: behavioral aspects and other associated problems. *Pediatr. Clin. No Amer.* 2003; 50(4): 919-38.

Levine MD. Neurodevelopmental variation and dysfunction among school-aged children. In Levine MD, Carey WB, Crocker AC (Eds.). *Developmental-Behavioral Pediatrics,* 3rd ed. Philadelphia: W.B.Saunders; 1999, p. 520-35.

Lewis M Overview of infant, child and adolescent development. In Wiener JM editor. *Textbook of Child and Adolescent Psychiatry, second edition.* Washington DC: American Psychiatric Press, 1997, p. 39 -66.

Luthar SS, Cicchetti D. The construct of resilience: implications for interventions and social policies. *Dev. Psychopathol.* 2000;12(4):857-85.

Masten AS, Hubbard JJ, Gest SD, Tellegen A, Garmezy N, Ramirez M. Competence in the context of adversity: pathways to resilience and maladaptation from childhood to late adolescence. *Dev. Psychopathol.* 1999; 11(1):143-69.

Newman JE, Willis DJ. Childhood and adolescent psychologic development. *Pediatr. Clin. No Amer.* 2003; 50(4):741-64.

Pratt, H. D. (2002). Neurodevelopmental issues in the assessment and treatment of deficits in attention, cognition, and learning during adolescence. *Adolescent Medicine: State of the Art Reviews.* 13(3): 579-598.

Resnick MD: Protective factors, resiliency, and healthy youth development. *Adolesc. Med.* 2000; 11:157-164.

Sarnat HB. "Normal development of the nervous system." In: *Textbook of Pediatric Neuropsychiatry*. Eds: CE Coffey and RA Brumback. Washington DC: American Psychiatric Press, Inc.; 1998, pp. 26-36.

Shonkoff JP, Phillips D, eds. Youth, and Families Board on Children, Committee on Integrating the Science of Early Childhood Development, National Research Council. From Neurons to Neighborhoods: The Science of Early Childhood Development, National Institutes of Medicine. Washington, D.C.: Academy Press; 2000.

Spritz RA. Hospitalism: An inquiry into the genesis of psychiatric conditions in early childhood. *Psychoanal Study Child* 1945; 1:53-74.

Walsh F. Conceptualizations of normal family functioning. In Walsh F (ed): *Normal Family Processes*. New Your: Guilford Press; 1982, pp. 3-42.

Werry JS, Zametkin A, Ernst M. "Brain and behavior." In: *Child and Adolescent psychiatry. A Comprehensive Textbook,* 3rd Edition. Ed: M. Lewis, Philadelphia: Lippincott Williams and Wilkins, 2002; pp. 120-125.

In: Behavioral Pediatrics, 3rd Edition
Editor: Donald E. Greydanus et al.

ISBN 978-1-60692-702-1
© 2009 Nova Science Publishers, Inc.

Chapter 2

Behavioral and Psychological Assessment

Margo Adams Larsen and Erin Tentis

Abstract

Assessment of patient problems requires the clinician to understand that presenting problems represent a complex array of contributing factors. Behavior can be influenced by the environment through antecedent and consequential events, as well as be reflexive to physiological circumstances. Behavioral and psychological assessment can often assist the medical provider in more comprehensive investigation regarding behavioral, cognitive, and neuropsychological functioning of a patient.

Introduction

Assessment of patient problems requires the clinician to understand that presenting problems represent a complex array of contributing factors. A patient and his parent visits the physician's with a complaint that Johnny has a medical problem; the physician must consider that there maybe behavioral (cognitive, emotional, social, academic, etc.) contributors to the onset, frequency, intensity and duration of that problem. For example, Johnny is brought in for problems with attention in all major settings. The clinician can not assume that problems with attention are purely medical or behavioral but must engage in assessment actives that allow for an accurate diagnosis.

Definitions

Behavior can be influenced by the environment through antecedent and consequential events, as well as be reflexive to physiological circumstances. When either reflexes or antecedents and consequences are structured in a way that adversely impacts others much of the time and to a moderate to strong degree, the humans exhibiting them are typically referred for evaluation and assessment. This includes contributing factors, as well as developmental and family history factors, medical history factors, and social and functional factors. Thus, psychological assessment is a very broad assessment of an individual's functioning that encompasses specific and multiple behaviors. Behavioral assessment is often more specific and directed at particular symptoms or behaviors that are problematic for the individual or others with whom the individual must interact.

Behavioral Assessment

Behaviors theoretically serve at least four major functions: (1) to obtain attention, (2) to escape unpleasant experiences, (3) to receive something tangible (object), and (4) internal satisfaction (covert stimulation). It is important to operationally define a target behavior so that it is clear what behavior or response is of concern. To ensure a behavior has been identified, the "dead man's test" should be applied: if a corpse can engage in the operationally defined target behavior, then a behavior has not been defined. A typical complaint may involve too much of behaviors, leading parents to complain of children "not sitting still". The children are engaging in many behaviors, often excessive in frequency, intensity, and energy. Sitting still, however, is a task a corpse is quite good at, and therefore, not a behavior. Sitting calmly and playing quietly would be a better descriptor, as a corpse would have difficulty engaging in a play task. Thus, parents should be encouraged to strive to request an active behavior for which an appropriate consequence can be enforced.

Functional Analysis of Behavior

The most formal assessment of a target behavior involves the experimental manipulation of factors known to maintain behaviors. Very specific and detailed observational data is collected on the frequency of the target behavior in each of these five primary conditions: (1) while alone, (2) after a tangible reward, (3) following attention, (4) following a demand, or (5) while at play. These conditions are evaluated on several days or across several environmental manipulations (e.g., different teachers, different classrooms, and different times of day). The data are reviewed by the behavioral consultant who established the experimental manipulation. From such data a determination of the likely function of the behavior is made. This would be considered a highly formal means of assessing behavior.

A Functional Behavioral Assessment (FBA) is a component of education law that requires demonstration of the effectiveness of behavioral intervention in schools to be assessed and documented. While this assessment also provides behavioral data and information regarding effectiveness, it is assessing the outcomes of a behavior program in contrast to a Functional Analysis which assesses the maintaining factors related to the behavior itself. The reader interested in learning more about either of these procedures is referred to O'Neill, Horner, Albin, et al., (1997) and Hanley, Iwata, and McCord (2003).

Interviews

Behavior can be assessed in much less formal manners as well. Behavioral assessment more typically involves interviewing the child and adults of interest. Once an understanding or operational definition of the behavior of concern is accomplished, the examiner may conduct behavioral observations, ask the child or parent to keep data on the target behavior (i.e., track the behavior), or ask for general self-report measures to be completed. In addition, the examiner may also ask the parents to monitor events occurring just before the behavior (antecedents) and events occurring immediately following the target behavior (consequences) (as seen in Figure 1). Most medical providers commonly use less formal behavioral assessment techniques when interacting with patients. For example, tools like the Denver Developmental-II rely on both parent reports and demonstrated skills observed by an evaluator to provide an assessment of developmental accomplishment. Behavior observations of the patient can also be made, as well as assessing the outcomes of engaging in a behavior (i.e., measuring blood serum levels of a medication is an outcome measure of the behavior of taking a medication).

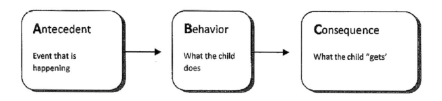

Figure 1.

Behavioral Observations and Recording

In terms of behavioral assessment of children, informal behavioral observations are often helpful. These less formal assessments can include the visual observation of the duration, start or stop time of a behavior, the frequency, the absence or occurrence of a behavior, the presence or absence of others (e.g., a parent) during the behavior, intensity of the behaviors, and various observations about the setting of a behavior (e.g., sensory experiences, location of the behavior).

Typically, behavioral observations will be conducted over various times and dates to help assess time of day or environmental factors. Behaviors of age and gender matched peers may also be tracked during the same observation times to assess a comparative sample from the same setting. The specific methods and approaches to this means of behavioral assessment approach are based on the type or topography of the target behavior. The major methods of recording the observations are summarized in Table 1.

Table 1. Major Methods of Recording Behavioral Observations

Outcome recording	Involves only sampling the product of the behavior and allows for assessment without actually having to observe the behavior itself. The complex behavior of dishwashing may not be observed, but may be measured by the number of clean dishes.
Event recording	Is used for behaviors that have a brief duration and a discrete beginning and end. The observer records an occurrence of the entire behavior, such as a speaker uttering the word "um".
Interval recording	Is used for a behavior without a definitive start or end, and that may last for long periods of time such as television watching or tantruming. The observation time is divided into discrete units (15 or 30 second intervals through one minute, for example), and the observer notes it the behavior occurred during any portion of the interval. For example, intervals of time spent in a chair during math class.
Time-sample recording	Is the same as interval recording but occurs over discontinuous intervals of time. This is typically used when conducting observation during the same time frame for multiple individuals (i.e., comparative sampling between age-matched peers participating in play or conversations).

When the child is asked to track the occurrence of the behavior (either in time, frequency, duration, intensity, or other experiential aspect of the behavior), this self-recording technique is referred to as awareness tracking/training. This procedure has been demonstrated to have a treatment effect at times, as increasing the awareness to the behavior can often result in a change in the behavior. Self-tracking is often linked to outcome measures in treatments so as to ensure a baseline level of the behavior prior to initiating treatment. For example, number of hairs pulled a day would be tracked by the child prior to initiating an intervention phase with the hair pulling behavior. Likewise, number of dry hours in a day may be tracked prior to implementing a behavior program to increase toilet usage during toilet training.

Psychological Testing in Primary Care Practice

In this growing age of managed care and required medical referrals, it is increasingly likely that children will be presenting to primary care with concerns related to academic progress and developmental delay, as well as general medical issues that may have implications for cognitive functioning. While schools must provide assessment once an Individual Education Plan (IEP) process has begun, often these services are inadequate for the referral question, not completed in a timely manner, or unable to provide the type of assessment required (i.e., neuropsychology assessment). It may even be the case that children with various medical conditions (e.g., head injury, spina bifida, cerebral palsy, diabetes, metabolic conditions, and brain tumors) are often referred for psychological assessment via primary or specialty care, long before the academic process is involved.

In addition, in many states, diagnoses for the disruptive behavioral disorders require a psychological or medical evaluation in order for a diagnosis to be accepted in the academic environment, and these cases tend to be referred to primary care or specialty clinics for diagnosis (e.g., Attention Deficit Hyperactivity Disorder). When a physician requires psychological information in order to provide appropriate care, referrals are made to psychologists. Referrals for evaluations that include the nature of the question (e.g., estimate cognitive functioning) as well as a release of medically related information pertinent for the psychologist to consider are most helpful. The remainder of this chapter will focus on aspects of the psychometric assessment that can aid the pediatrician or developmental specialist in understanding the tools used, the results obtained, and general recommendations or suggestions based on the findings from specific child-based psychological assessment measures.

As previously mentioned, behavioral assessment is a very important aspect of psychological assessment, and is typically the key component or basis for interpretation and the fundamental understanding of testing reports. While behavioral assessment findings may be located in the behavioral observations section of a report, the professional impression or interpretation based on these observations or findings will be located in the impressions section of a report, along with the diagnosis, if applicable.

Psychological Testing

When a collective group of behaviors are concerning for a child, and there is concern regarding developmental, cognitive, academic, adaptive, or behavioral/emotional functioning, referrals for psychological testing procedures are often made. These procedures provide more specific standardized behavioral assessments for a child that compared their behavior on various tasks to a very large normative sample, rather than to a single same age-gender matched peer. This type of assessment can also provide comparisons across domains for a single child's performance. Both behavioral assessment and psychological testing can compare a child's repertoire to their past performance as assessed in the same manner.

What Exactly is Psychological Testing?

A psychological test is a measure that has been empirically derived to assess the differences between one individual's performances compared to that of many other similar individuals, or between an individual's performance compared across situations. A psychological test generally has a standardized method of administration, requirements of training for those administering and interpreting the test, and has direct implications for the examinee's psychological, educational, or career-orientated functioning. Thus, Anastasi defined a psychological test as "an objective and standardized measure of a sample of behavior" (Anastasi, 1988;p. 23). Psychological assessments are used to predict how well an individual may perform given a certain set of circumstances, and in turn to predict or generalize to daily life (current and future) functioning for the examinee.

By definition, psychological tests have been standardized, meaning their validity (what they are measuring), reliability (consistency in measurement), method (manualized documentation so each administration is identical), and use (qualification of administrator) have been rigorously scrutinized prior to publication.

The *Mental Measurements Yearbook (MMY)* provides information regarding publisher, purpose of the assessment, and published reviews, on nearly every English-published psychological assessment. As well, the *Standards for Educational and Psychological Testing* provides information regarding the requirements for assessments to be considered empirically valid. Psychological tests are 'controlled' for the purposes of protection of the public, to increase validity and reliability, as well as to protect copyright and 'trade secrets'.

Variables Related to the Testing Circumstances

A psychological assessment requires many variables to be controlled to allow for the best assessment possible and increase the likelihood of a valid outcome. Specifically, evaluators must be trained and fully prepared in administering the procedures for the assessment, commonly referred to as a protocol. To be well prepared, the evaluator may need to memorize the entire protocol, ready various forms and materials that will be utilized, and be very familiar with the assessment procedures that are being applied. The testing conditions are also important. Most administration manuals specify how the materials should be presented, such as in a well lit, low-noise workspace with a table and chair of appropriate height to provide a comfortable atmosphere for the assessment. Any deviations from these basic expectations should be noted in the testing report, and should be considered by the report writer when interpreting the findings. Another aspect to the assessment is how the assessment is introduced to the examinee and how the examinee responds to the evaluator (rapport). Obviously, an assessment with an examinee who understands the reasons for the evaluation and who has a good working relationship with the evaluator is likely to result in more accurate estimates of functioning, and thus any deviations from the standardized procedure, again, should be noted in the report. Evaluator error is always possible, and should also be noted in the report if it occurred.

From the perspective of the child, anxiety related to the testing situation or to assessments in general may impact performance. As most psychological testing is done without parents present in the room, preparation for this situation is well advised for some children, particularly those who are young or shy. Generally, careful explanation regarding the current assessment will help alleviate worries and enhance performance. In situ assessment related to state of functioning (anxious vs. relaxed) and prompted coping skills are often useful in reducing anxiety during psychological assessment; however, as with other test circumstances, these should be documented in the report. For an individual who has recently (within the past year) been evaluated, re-testing may demonstrate improved performance due to learning and recollection of the test, resulting in an elevated performance than would be truly representative of the individual's daily functioning. Individuals who are sophisticated testers (e.g., are knowledgeable about testing or have taken test-taking courses) are likely to perform better than would be expected based on testing skills as opposed to their daily functioning skills in the domain being assessed. Psychological measures can be very sensitive and often can influence an individual's learning, such that retesting utilizing the same measure and materials within too close temporal proximity can confound the results and overestimate functioning for the examinee.

In general, unless a head injury or memory problems are apparent, a good guideline for reassessment is at least one year for psychological and neuropsychological assessments; however, assessment of mood, attention, or psychosocial aspects may be more frequent. Evaluators may choose to utilize comparative measures or alternative forms rather than repeating the same measure as well. Standardization of administration attempts to reduce the differences between examinees; however, the impact of the examinee on the assessment situation is often described in the behavioral observations section of the report, where characteristics thought to impact the test results are described (e.g., disruptive behavior throughout the assessment; wore glasses; required encouragement and motivation).

Ethical Concerns, Cautions, and Disposition of Assessment Results

The American Psychological Association (APA) Code of Ethics outlines a 'standard of care' for all practicing, licensed psychologists. Within this code are specific guidelines related to assessment and test results (Sections 9 and 4). An examiner must consider in his or her report all variables that might explain the findings, such as culture and educational exposure. As well, psychologists are to ensure the security of assessments, provide reports and full explanations of the assessment results to patients or their representative (e.g., parents), and provide raw data to appropriately informed requesting parties.

Confidentiality and sharing of test results are also guided by the APA Ethics Code (Sections 9 and 4). Psychologists have the utmost responsibility to maintain an individual's confidentiality and to ensure that no harm may come as a result of releasing their private information (e.g., test reports, raw scores). Reports are only released when the appropriate release forms are signed and are likely to only be released to professionals who will have an understanding and background in reviewing the report without disposition. Reports are generally not released to families unless a disposition meeting has been scheduled to fully review the results and findings.

Principles of Testing and Decoding the Psychological Report

A very brief review of principle and statistical concepts related to psychological assessment is warranted for a better understanding of the discussion of various assessments to follow. The reader may wish to refer to Figure 1 (below) to identify the concepts discussed below.

Norms

Norms broadly refer to the performance of the standardization sample on the same assessment. These may be broken down and presented in age-based groups, grade-based groups, gender-based groups, or some combination thereof. Norms are commonly used as a method of comparing the examinee's performance and functionality to that of the standardization group.

Statistical Concepts and the Bell Curve

The basis of most psychological assessments is a normal distribution, or the use of corrected statistical analyses to allow for extrapolation to the normal curve distribution of scores. This is also referred to as the Bell Curve, and represents the population frequency and distribution of scores for IQ, achievement, and functioning in a variety of domains (Figure 2).

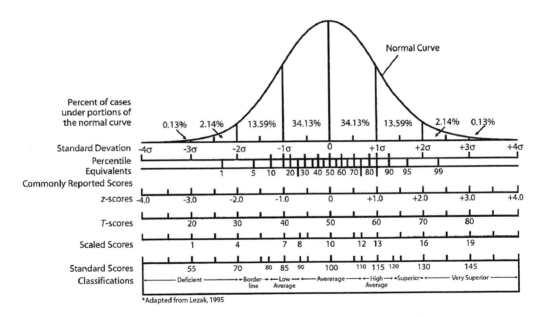

Figure 2.

All normal curve distributions have the following characteristics: 68.7% of the population falls between 1 standard deviation above and below the mean; 95.4% of the population falls between 2 standard deviations above and below the mean; and 99.7% of the population falls between 3 standard deviations above and below the mean. Standard deviation (SD) is a statistical measure of variability, while the mean (M) is a statistical measure of the average score. In considering deficits, generally 1.5 SD below the mean or greater (e.g., 2 SD below, 3 SD below) are cut-off points representing significant deviations from expected or typical performance, and reflective of a need for intervention. In contrast, an individual scoring at least 1.5 SD above the mean is thought to be gifted. The normal curve allows not only estimates of deviation based on where performance falls under the curve, but also translation of these data points into a variety of more frequently used, user-friendly 'scores'.

Percentiles

Percentiles are generally understandable and comparable by parents and non-professionals; however, it is important to understand that percentile units are not standard or equal. Thus, at the middle of the distribution, small differences in standard scores translate into great differences in percentiles, and at the extremes of a distribution, large differences in standard scores are required to have much difference in percentiles. Percentiles are utilized in providing relative position of an examinee's performance based on the normative sample.

Standard Scores

Standard scores are utilized more frequently as the method of summarizing or reporting an examinee's performance. Standard scores represent performance as a product of deviation from the mean based in standard deviation units, and can be translated into scores based upon the normative sample. Generally, in most psychometric assessments, standard scores have a mean of 100, and a standard deviation of 15. *Wechsler IQ* scores are reported as standard scores, such that a child who has an IQ value of 70 would fall 2 standard deviations below the mean and be classified with deficient intellectual abilities. On the *Wechsler* series assessments, as well as other tests, a scaled score is often used to describe performance on a subtest. Scaled scores are a form of standard score where the mean is 10 and the standard deviation is 3. A child is classified in the Very Superior range on *Block Design* form the *WISC-IV* by earning a subtest score of 18.

Other versions of comparative scores also exist. For example, another expression of the standard score is a *T*-score, for which the mean is 50 and the standard deviation is 10 points; a T-score of 45 falls in the normal range (i.e., within 1 SD below or above the mean of the normative sample). Yet another translation of standard scores are *z*-scores (refer to Figure 1), which are a product of calculation: obtained performance minus the mean of the normative sample, divided by the standard deviation of the normative sample. For *z*-scores, the comparative mean is expected to be 0, and the standard deviation is known to be 1. Thus, a student who has a *z*-score of -2 in preferred hand dexterity is performing 2 SD below the normative mean, and performance would be classified as deficient.

Confidence Intervals

Confidence Intervals are another method of providing information regarding a person's performance. In fact, this is commonly provided to demonstrate the non-static nature of assessment scores. Test reliability and error contribute to obtain performance scores being considered estimates of the individual's true performance. Confidence Intervals provide a range within which the true score is likely to fall, given a statistical confidence value (usually 90% or 95%). Thus, a *Wechsler IQ Index* score may be 90, but have a Confidence Interval Range from 85 to 95.

Grade Equivalence

It is important to understand the concept of grade-equivalence, particularly in achievement or academic testing. Grade-equivalence refers to the examinee's performance on the test, and the grade level of others who performed similarly. Grade-equivalence does not relate to the grade level of achieved performance on the test. For example, an individual in 5th grade who obtained a standard score of 85 may have a grade-equivalence of grade 4 on the assessment. This means that the level of performance for the individual was able to be achieved by all children in a 4th grade sample who took the same measure. It does not mean that the score of 85 was at a 4th grade work level. Grade equivalence is not considered a good basis for comparison as the concept is often misunderstood; in addition, grade equivalence does not take into account differences in instruction or inequality in grade units, and may have cast implications when utilized improperly.

Psychometric Testing Measures

A variety of standardized assessment measures have been developed to assess constructs of intellectual functioning, academic achievement, developmental progress, memory, and cognitive capacities. A brief description of areas of assessment and commonly used measures are reviewed. The information provided is not meant to be an endorsement of the tool, nor is the list exhaustive; however, most of the measures described below are generally considered to be reliable, valid assessment tools when utilized by a licensed professional. In the following pages, the reader will find an overview of several common psychological assessment tools, reviewed in categories relating to the psychological functions they are designed to assess.

Cognitive Assessment

Cognitive assessment tools (Table 2) estimate an individual's global cognitive functioning. These have typically been referred to as "IQ tests." However, testing theory and psychological assessment are now more sophisticated and "IQ tests" are comprised of multiple tasks or batteries. These batteries are able to assess multiple domains of cognitive functioning such as language skills, non-verbal performance abilities, mental agility, and memory.

Table 2. Cognitive Assessment Measures

Wechsler Preschool and Primary Scale of Intelligence – 3rd Edition (WPPSI-III) (Wechsler; Psychological Corporation)	2 years, 6 months – 7 years, 3 months	14 subtests; yields Full Scale, Verbal and Performance IQ scores
Wechsler Intelligence Scale for Children – 4th Edition (WISC-IV) (Wechsler; Psychological Corporation)	6 years – 16 years, 11 months	15 subtests; yields Full Scale IQ, Verbal Comprehension, Perceptual Reasoning, Working Memory, and Processing Speed Indices
Wechsler Adult Intelligence Scale – 3rd Edition (WAIS-III) (Wechsler; Psychological Corporation)	16 years – adulthood	14 subtests; yield Full Scale IQ, Verbal Comprehension, Perceptual Organization, Working Memory and Processing Speed Indices
Wechsler Abbreviated Scales of Intelligence (WASI) (Wechsler; Psychological Corporation)	6 years – adulthood	4 subtests; brief IQ screener; yields Full Scale, Verbal, and Performance IQ estimates
Mullen Scales of Early Learning (Mullen) (Mullen; AGS Publishing)	Birth – 68 months	5 subtests; yields Gross Motor, Visual Reception, Fine Motor, Receptive Language and Expressive Language scores
Stanford-Binet – 5th Edition (SB-V) (Roid; Riverside Publishing)	2 years – adulthood	10 subtests; yields Full Scale, Verbal, and Nonverbal IQ scores as well as 4 index scores

Measures like the *Wechsler Intelligence Scales* include standard scores for the various domains of functioning, and a score that provides an overall functioning estimate, or *Full Scale Intellectual Quotient*. In years gone by this *Full Scale* value was considered the intellectual quotient. Theories now put much less emphasis on this single number, and focus more on functioning in the various assessed domains.

Verbal Skills

Verbal skills are also evaluated (Table 3). These are the language skills thought to represent the functioning of the most dominant brain hemisphere in lateralized individuals. Assessment tools for this domain typically involve auditory or visual instructions, language-based assessment strategies, and focus on assessing receptive language, expressive language, and verbal memory functions if a comprehensive evaluation is conducted.

Table 3. Language Assessment Measures

Peabody Picture Vocabulary Test – 3rd Edition (PPVT-III) (Dunn and Dunn; American Guidance Services, Inc.)	2 years, 6 months – 90+	Assesses English receptive vocabulary skills
Expressive Vocabulary Test (EVT) (Williams; American Guidance Services, Inc.)	2 years, 6 months – 90+	Assesses English expressive vocabulary skills
Boston Naming Test – II (Goodglass and Kaplan; Pro-Ed, Inc.)	5 years through adult	Assesses expressive language skills and provides measures to evaluate assistance of phonological and multiple choice cues.

Nonverbal or Performance Skills

Nonverbal or performance skills (Table 4) are another domain area of psychological testing. Nonverbal skills are tasks that are thought to require no language in either the instruction, task process, or task response, which are considered to highlight the functioning of the non-dominant hemisphere in lateralized individuals.

Table 4. Performance Assessment Measures

Universal Test of Nonverbal Intelligence (UNIT) (Bracken and McCallum; Riverside Publishing Company)	5 years – 17 years, 11 months	6 subtests; no verbalizations required; yields Full Scale IQ, Memory, Reasoning, Symbolic, and Nonsymbolic Quotients
Comprehensive Test of Nonverbal Intelligence (CTONI) (Hammill, Pearson, Wiederholt; Pro-Ed, Inc).	6 years – 89 years	6 subtests; yields Nonverbal IQ, Picture Nonverbal IQ, and Geometric Nonverbal IQ Indices
Ravens Standard Progressive Matrices (Ravens; Harcourt Assessment, Inc.)	Child – adult norms	Assesses reasoning through pictures
Benton Judgment of Line Orientation (Benton; Psychological Assessment Resources, Inc.)	Child – adult norms	Measures visuospatial judgement

Assessment tools for this functioning domain include batteries that involve no language-based instructions (e.g., mimed), tasks that involve language instructions but no verbal responses (e.g., creating a block design to match a visual stimuli; copying a complex diagram), or tasks that utilize visual-based stimuli requiring a language-based response (e.g., determine a visual matched pair and state the letter of the matched stimuli). Memory functions can be assessed in non-verbal domains as well.

Executive Functioning

Executive functioning (Table 5) is another domain particularly of interest in individuals with attention and behavior regulation problems. The frontal lobe is thought to be involved heavily in organization, planning, and regulation of various behaviors, and is highly taxed on tasks that assess executive skills. These assessment tools emphasize attention, organization, short-term memory, mental shifting, and sustained mental focus.

Table 5. Executive Function Assessment Measures

Behavior Rating Inventory of Executive Function (BRIEF) (Gioia, et al; Psychological Assessment Resources, Inc.)	5 years-18 years	Parent-, Teacher-, and Self-(teenagers) report forms; assesses 7 areas of executive functioning, as well as 3 broad scores: Behavioral Regulation Index, Metacognition Index, and Global Executive Composite
Conners Continuous Performance Task – 2nd Edition (CPT-II) (Conners; Multi-Health Systems, Inc.)	Pre-school – Kindergarten (Kiddie CPT); 6 years – adulthood (CPT-II)	20-minute computer test to assess attention; tracks omission errors, commission errors, response times, and latency in responding
Test of Variables in Attention (TOVA) (Leark, et al; Universal Attention Disorders, Inc.)	6 years – 19 years	25-minute computer test to assess attention; yields omission errors, commission errors, response time, and variability in response time; 2 versions available – visual and auditory
Wisconsin Card Sorting Test (WCST) (Heaton, et al; Psychological Assessment Resources, Inc.)	6 years, 6 months – adulthood	Assesses abstract reasoning/problem-solving; yields information regarding errors, ability to learn abstractly, perseveration, and ability to shift and maintain set
Children's Categories Test (CCT) (Boll; Psychological Corporation)	Level I: 5 years – 8 years Level II: 9 years – 16 years	Nonverbal assessment of abstract reasoning
Tower of London (Culbertson and Zillmer; Psychological Assessment Resources, Inc.)	7 years – adult	Assesses visual problem solving skills including planning and organizing
Trail Making Test (Reitan; Reitan Neuropsychological Laboratory, Inc.)	5 years through adult	Assesses mental fluency as well as ability to shift set

These tasks challenge the workings of the frontal lobe and are typically found in neuropsychological assessments and assessments for attention-based disorders.

Memory Functions

Memory functions (Table 6) can be assessed in a variety of ways. Recall memory can involve free or cued/prompted responses, while recognition memory involves providing a verbal or visual stimuli and asking if it was one learned/seen before. In addition, memory can be assessed as a function of time. Immediate recall is assessed after a brief delay, such as 10 second exposure to the stimuli, and 5 second delay before recall. Delayed recall is assessed after a much longer delay, typically 30 minutes, and may occur after single review of materials or multiple repetitions of the target materials. These methods of memory assessment help determine aspects of memory that may be stronger or weaker comparatively. Some assessment tools will also add an element to purposefully assess impeded memory such as a distracter list. Both verbal and non-verbal (i.e., visual) memory can be assessed.

Table 6. Memory Assessment Measures

Children's Memory Scale (CMS) (Cohen; Psychological Corporation)	5 years – 16 years	Yields Immediate and Delayed scores for both Verbal Memory and Visual Memory, General Memory, Delayed Recognition, Learning, and Attention/Concentration
Wide Range Assessment of Memory and Learning – 2nd Edition (WRAML2) (Sheslow and Adams; Jastak Associates, Inc.)	5 years – adulthood	6 core and 4 optional subtests; yields Verbal and Visual Memory as well as Attention/Concentration scores; also has 4 Recognition Memory and 3 Delayed Recall subtests
Wechsler Memory Scale – 3rd Edition (WMS-III) (Wechsler; Psychological Corporation)	16 years – adulthood	6 core and 5 optional subtests; yields 3 domain scores: Immediate Memory, General Memory (delayed), and Working Memory
Rey Complex Figure Task (Meyers and Meyers; Psychological Assessment Resources, Inc.)	6 years – adulthood	Assesses visuospatial construction and visual memory; yields scores for Copy, Short-term Recall, Long-term Recall, and Recognition
California Verbal Learning Test – Children's Version (CVLT-C); California Verbal Learning Test – 2nd Edition (CVLT—II) (Dellis, et al; Psychological Corporation) Rey Auditory Verbal Learning Task (RAVLT) (Schmidt; Western Psychological Services)	CVLT-C: 5 years – 16 years CVLT-II: 16 years – adulthood RAVLT: 7 years – adulthood	All similar measures assessing ability to recall unrelated information in the form of word lists; generally yield scores related to learning ability, immediate recall, delayed recall, and recognition

Table 7. Neuropsychological Assessment Measures

Grooved Pegboard Test (Trites; Lafayette Instrument Company)	5 years – adulthood	Assesses fine-motor skills of hand-eye coordination & dexterity
Finger Tapping Test (Staff; Psychological Assessment Resources)	6 years – adulthood	Measures primary fine-motor functioning
Beery-Buktenica Test of Visual-Motor Integration (VMI) (Beery, Buktenica, & Beery; NCS Pearson)	2 years – 18 years	Assesses visual-motor integration, graphomotor production, & construction
Hooper Visual Organization Test (HVOT) (Western Psychological Services)	5 years – adulthood	Assesses visual processing & visual organization
Quick Neurological Screening Test-Second Edition (QNST-II) (Mutti, et al; Academic Therapy Publications)	5 years – 18 years	Assesses soft neurological signs associated with learning disabilities and other neurological conditions
Luria-Nebraska Neuropsychological Battery (LNNB) (Golden, et al; Western Psychological Services) Luria-Nebraska Neuropsychological Battery Children's Revision (LNNB-C) (Golden; Western Psychological Services)	Child Form: 8 years – 12 years Adult Form: 13 years – adulthood	Comprehensive neuropsychological battery
Halstead-Reitan Neuropsychological Test Battery – Composite Battery (HRNTB) (Reitan; Reitan Neuropsychological Laboratory, Inc.).	5 years – adulthood	Thorough neuropsychological battery
NEPSY (Korkman, et al; Psychological Corporation) (NEPSY-II coming in 2008)	3 years – 12 years	Assesses 5 domain areas: Attention/Executive Function, Language, Sensorimotor Functions, Visuospatial Processing, & Memory and Learning
Motor-Free Visual Perception Test – 3rd Edition (MVPT-3) (Colarusso & Hammill; Academic Therapy Publications)	4 years – late adulthood	Assesses visual perceptual processes in 5 areas: Spatial Relationships, Visual Discrimination, Figure-Ground, Visual Closure, & Visual Memory; does not require motor skills
Test for Auditory Processing Disorders In Children-Revised (SCAN – C); Adolescents and Adults (SCAN-A) (Keith; Harcourt Assessment, Inc.)	C: 5 years – 11 years A: 12 years – 50 years	Assesses auditory perception in several areas: Filtered Words, Auditory Figure-Ground, Competing Words, & Competing Sentences

Neuropsychological Measures

Specialized neuropsychological measures (Table 7) are utilized to assess the function of particular brain systems, and are typically conducted by assessing a function using two or more methods or tasks.

In addition, sensory functioning is typically assessed using neuropsychological tools that focus on one or more of the five sensory areas (i.e., visual, auditory, olfaction, gustatory, sensoimotor) and their integration and processing within the brain's neurocircuitry. For example, auditory and visual processing may be emphasized for individuals thought to have attentional disorders as these areas are fundamental to the comprehension and execution of instructions. Individuals with traumatic brain injury may require evaluation of all sensory areas to determine the nature and severity of injury or recovery.

Academic Assessments

Academic assessments (Table 8) examine achievement skills in the areas of reading, writing/spelling, and arithmetic, including basic knowledge (e.g., math facts or word reading), problem solving and higher order skills sets (e.g., essay writing), and the comprehension of these concepts. In addition, as grade levels increase, assessment tools are available for specific subject areas such as science, social studies, and geography. Brief measures as well as multi-concept measures are available. For individuals in high school, this assessment area may also include career and vocational interest and skill assessments.

Table 8. Academic Assessment Measures

Wide Range Achievement Test – 4th Edition (WRAT-4) (Wilkinson; Wide Range, Inc.)	5 years – adulthood	4 subtests: Sentence Comprehension, Word Reading, Spelling, and Math Computation
Bracken Basic Concepts Scale – Revised (BBCS-R) (Bracken; Psychological Corporation)	2 years, 6 months–8 years	Assesses knowledge of basic concepts learned during preschool and early elementary; 11 skills assessed
Wechsler Individual Achievement Test – 3rd Edition (WIAT-III) (Wechsler; Psychological Corporation)	4 years – 85 years	9 subtests; yields Composite scores for Reading, Mathematics, Written Language, and Oral Language
Woodcock-Johnson – III (WJ-III) (Woodcock, et al; Riverside Publishing)	2 years – adulthood	12 standard and 10 supplemental subtests; yields scores for Reading, Oral Language, Mathematics, Written Language, and Academic Knowledge

Developmental Assessments

Developmental assessments (Table 9) are utilized to estimate an individual's functioning compared to developmental constructs, concepts, and criterion. While likely most familiar to the medical provider for infants through preschool age, these tools have become increasingly utilized in the comprehensive assessment of children with any type of developmental delay such as Asperger's Syndrome, Autistic Disorder, or neurologically involved children. Age estimates are often used as comparative methods.

Table 9. Developmental Assessment Measures

Bayley Scales of Infant Development – 2nd Edition (Bayley) (Bayley; Psychological Corporation)	1 month – 42 months	Direct examination of the child; assesses mental, motor, and behavioral skills; cognitive, language, personal/social, and fine/gross motor skills also assessed
Vineland Adaptive Behavior Scales (Vineland); and Vineland Adaptive Behavior Scales – 2nd Edition (VABS-II) (Sparrow, et al; American Guidance Services, Inc.)	Birth – adulthood	Parent questionnaire or interview; yields General Adaptive Composite score and Communication, Daily Living Skills, Socialization, and Motor Skills Domain scores
Development Profile – 3 (DP-3) (Alpern et al; Western Psychological Services)	Birth – 155 months	Parent interview; also involves observation; assesses Physical, Adaptive, Social-Emotional, Cognitive, and Communication skills
Adaptive Behavior Assessment System – 2nd Edition (ABAS-II) (Harrison and Oakland; Harcourt Assessment, Inc.)	Birth – adulthood	Parent questionnaire or interview; separate forms for various age brackets; yields General Adaptive Composite score as well as Conceptual, Social, and Practical Domains; separate form for teachers
Ages and Stages Questionnaire (Squires, et al; Brookes Publishing Company)	4 months – 60 months	Parent-report form; used to screen/monitor 5 areas of development: Communication, Gross Motor, Fine Motor, Problem-Solving, and Personal-Social Skills; available in English, Spanish, French, and Korean
Denver Developmental 2nd Edition (Denver II) (Denver Developmental Materials, Inc.)	Birth – 6 years	Parent report form; screens a child's adaptive functioning compared to normal developmental expectations; English and Spanish versions

Behavioral Symptoms Assessment

Behavioral symptoms (Table 10) and behavioral functioning are assessed through interview, observation, and various standardized measures to augment the behavioral assessment procedures previously described. Comprehensive approaches would be recommended for children with behavioral problems in conjunction with behavioral assessment and the planning of behavioral programming.

Table 10. Behavioral Self-Report/Other-Report Measures

Child Behavior Checklist (CBCL) (Achenbach and Rescorla; University of Vermont Department of Psychiatry)	18 months – 18 years	Yields scores for 14 subscales as well as Internalizing, Externalizing, and Total Problems; corresponds to the Youth Self-Report (ages 11-18) and Teacher Report Form
Conners' Rating Scales – Revised (CRS-R) (Conners; Multi-Health System Inc.)	3 years – 17 years	Parent-, Self- (ages 12-17), and Teacher-report forms; yields 7 subscales and 7 index scores; emphasis on symptoms of ADHD
ADHD Rating Scales – IV (DuPaul, et al; Guilford Press)	5 years – 18 years	Separate parent and teacher report forms; yields 3 scores: Inattention, Hyperactivity/Impulsivity, and Total Score
Vanderbilt ADHD Diagnostic Rating Scale (Woraich, et al; Journal of Abnormal Child Psychology)	6 years – 12 years	Parent and teacher report forms; free to download; based on DSM-IV criteria for ADHD, ODD, and CD
Asperger Syndrome Diagnostic Scale (ASDS) (Myles, et al; Pro-Ed, Inc.)	5 years – 18 years	Parent, teacher, and professional questionnaire forms; yields diagnostic indicator and functioning in cognitive, maladaptive, language, social, and sensorimotor areas.
Childhood Autism Rating Scale (CARS) (Schopler, et al; Western Psychological Services)	2 years and older	Parent, teacher, professional questionnaire form; yields diagnostic indicator score based on over twenty areas of functioning.

Emotional Functioning Assessment

Emotional functioning (Table 11) is typically assessed through multiple methods, including self-report, parent/teacher report, and interview. There also are very specific tools utilized for specific symptom areas that are helpful when considering the diagnosis of anxiety disorders, obsessive compulsive disorders, depression, social skill deficits, and self-concept concerns.

Table 11. Emotional Assessment Measures

Piers-Harris Children's Self-Concept Scale – 2nd Edition (Piers and Herzberg; Western Psychological Services)	7 years – 18 years	Self-report form; yields 6 subscale scores and Total Score
Children's Depression Inventory (CDI) (Kovacs; Multi-Health Systems, Inc.)	7 years – 17 years	27-item self-report from; yields 5 subscale and Total Depression scores

Table 11. Continued

Suicide Ideation Questionnaire (SIQ) (Reynolds; Psychological Assessment Resources)	Adolescents, grades 7-12	Separate forms for junior high and high schools; screening tool for suicidal ideation
Revised Children's Manifest Anxiety Scale (RCMAS) (Reynolds and Richmond; Psychological Assessment Resources)	6 years – 19 years	37-item self-report form; yields Total Anxiety score as well as 3 subscales; also has a Lie scale
State-Trait Anxiety Inventory for Children (STAIC) (Spielberger; Mindgarden, Inc.)	Grades 4, 5, and 6	Self-report measure; 20 items assess State (fluctuating) anxiety, and 20 items assess Trait (consistent) anxiety
Roberts Apperception Test for Children – 2nd Edition (RATC) (McArthur and Roberts; Western Psychological Resources)	6 years – 18 years	Requires youth to create stories describing stimuli on cards presented to them; yields scores in several domains, including Available Resources, Problem Identification, Resolution, Emotion, Outcome, and Unusual or Atypical Response
Social Skills Rating Scale (SSRS) (Greshem and Elliot; American Guidance Services)	3 years – 18 years	Parent-, Teacher-, and Self-report forms; assesses 3 areas of social skills: Social Skill, Problem Behaviors, and Academic Competence

Table 12. Character Assessment Measures

Children's Personality Questionnaire (IPAT)	8 years – 12 years	Self-report objective measure; assesses several personality dimensions including shyness, assertiveness, and emotional stability
Louisville Behavior Checklist (Miller; Western Psychological Services)	4 years – 17 years	Parent-report objective measure
Minnesota Multiphasic Personality Inventory – Adolescent (MMPI-A) (Butcher, et al; National Computing Services, Inc.)	12 years – 18 years	Self-report objective measure; 478 items; yields scores related to response style/validity, drug/alcohol use, and psychopathology
Millon Adolescent Clinical Inventory (MACI) (Millon; National Computing Services)	13 years – 19 years	Self-report objective measure; 160 items; yields scores related to personality patterns, clinical syndromes, and response style/validity
Rorschach Inkblot Test (Exner; John Wiley and Sons)	5 years – adulthood	Projective measure; requires the individual to identify and describe perceptions on a stimulus card
Thematic Apperception Test (TAT) (Murray; Harvard University Press)	4 years – adulthood	Projective measure; requires the individual to create a story about a picture on a stimulus card; administered twice, on consecutive days

Personality Assessment

For the older adolescent, assessments of behavioral characteristics that may represent an emerging personality style (Table 12) are available. It should be noted that behavioral theory would suggest caution in the assessment of "personality" in individuals below the age of 18 years.

Psychological Assessment Report

In general, when psychological assessment has been conducted, a report should be generated. The report should include a review of the referral concerns, historical information for the child, a list of psychometric assessment tools used, current functioning status, behavioral observations, and specific scores related to any standardized assessment procedures conducted (this may be in a brief or comprehensive format). The report should provide a review of the individual's performance. There should be a dialogue discussing the impression of the findings related to the referral question, and provide a diagnosis when appropriate.

Psychological diagnoses are made based on the most current Diagnostic and Statistical Manual of Mental Disorders (DSM) which is published by the American Psychiatric Association. The current edition at the time of this publication is the *DSM-IV*. Diagnoses are made using a five axis system such that:

Axis I:	Transient Disorders (e.g., Anxiety Disorder; Major Depression)
Axis II:	Life-Long Disorders (e.g., Mental Retardation; Personality Disorders)
Axis III:	Medical Disorders that relate (e.g., Diabetes, Visual Processing Disorder)
Axis IV:	Areas of Functional Impact (e.g., family, school, development, health)
Axis V:	Global Assessment of Functioning (i.e., number 0-100 subjectively describing functioning level).

More than one diagnosis may be listed under a given axis. A diagnosis is required for billing and reimbursement purposes, as well as qualification for certain resources such as case management, school accommodations, and the like. Once a diagnosis is identified, recommendations typically will follow.

Recommendations in the report should reflect or respond to the initial consultation or referral questions, and may provide comprehensive management ideas for school, home, and professional treatment providers. Recommendations may include suggestions for referrals for further evaluation, therapeutic issues, behavioral interventions, and/or academic accommodations; specific ideas, recommendations, and suggestions for intervention, as well as resources for education and additional information may also be included.

Referrals

Following behavioral, psychological, or neuropsychological assessment there may be further aspects of the child's functioning that are of concern. For example, these assessments may have highlighted questions about audiological or visual functioning, fine or gross motor functioning, or social communication skills, resulting in referrals to specialty providers to further assess these functional areas. At times, these areas need to be evaluated prior to a psychological diagnosis being made. For example, finger agnosia, gait instability, and verbal memory problems may warrant a referral to a pediatric neurologist prior to a psychological or educational diagnosis being made that might erroneously identify attention deficit disorder versus a seizure disorder.

All psychological assessment assumes medical diagnoses are not responsible for impairments in performance, and thus, testing that highlights areas of significant weakness may simply have been overlooked prior to referral. Common referrals are to certified audiologists, vision specialists, occupational therapists, physical therapists, neurologists, and when complex neurochemical issues are potentially involved, pediatric psychiatrists. Some managed care companies do not reimburse for assessing learning disabilities, as this is a service that can be done within the school setting. As such, a recommendation for academic evaluation through the school district to assess for the presence and nature of a learning disability may be made. Additionally, if chemical dependency is an area of concern, a referral for a chemical dependency evaluation may be warranted. Most often, the psychologist would coordinate these referrals through the primary care provider.

Treatment Recommendations

Case Management

For children with significant difficulties, it may also be helpful to recommend *case management services,* if available. This service can be helpful in coordinating complex cases, multiple professional referrals, evaluations, and treatment plans, as well as serve as a helpful treatment team communication method. Mental health, medical, developmental disability, or chemical dependency is examples of case management services that may be available.

Therapy

If the child is diagnosed with a mental health disorder through a psychological evaluation, *therapy* may be recommended. The type of therapy – individual, family, or group therapy – may also be specified based on the nature of the difficulties, age of the child, and the like. For example, Applied Behavior Analysis might be recommended to address head-banging behaviors in a child with Autism, while individual therapy using cognitive-behavioral techniques might be suggested for a teen experiencing Major Depressive Disorder.

Behavioral interventions are often recommended for both school and home environments. Based on the assessment principles reviewed earlier, strategies and techniques for symptom reduction, skill attainment and utilization, as well as methods for improving adherence with treatment (medical and other) strategies will be reviewed briefly. Depending on age, developmental level, and needs of the child, school, and family, these strategies may include (but are not limited to):

Preteaching is a technique that communicates to the child the expectations for behavior and the consequences that can be anticipated if the child does or does not follow the expectations. This technique highlights the importance of communication regarding expectations and conveys in advance the antecedent, behavior, and consequences by stating this contingency clearly.

Positive feedback provides information, such as praise, to the child upon completion of their behavior. Labeled praise (e.g., "Good job hanging up your coat" rather than "Good job") is a specific form of praise that results in increasing desired behaviors. Encourage parents to praise any behavior that the child should repeat, from mundane, every-day task to less frequent or more difficult tasks. In addition to praise, positive feedback can include hugs, high-fives, or other forms of "celebration." Typically, it is recommended that children and teens receive positive feedback several times a day (e.g., at least hourly).

Star/sticker charts are generally is used as a reward system to increase behavior. Each age-appropriate target behavior is identified, and each occurrence earns the immediate reward of a star or sticker to place on a chart. At the end of the day, some charts may also allow these stars/stickers to be traded for another, "bigger" reward (e.g., TV time, a treat, an extra bedtime story). To increase efficacy, the chart should be reviewed with the child when the demonstration of the target behavior occurs; the adult attention from this process may increase the extent to which it is reinforcing. It is also important to establish at the bottom of the chart how many stars/stickers are needed to earn further privileges, such as an extra bedtime story. Finally, it is important to keep the number of target behaviors reasonable for age; if too many behaviors are identified, the child may become overwhelmed.

The token economy is a motivational technique that is based on reinforcement and punishment principles. The system involves rewarding the child's behavior with tokens that can be exchanged later for a secondary reinforcer (e.g., time alone with a parent or going to a movie). The tokens that are used can be tally marks, pennies, poker chips, stickers, tickets, or marbles. These items are collected when the child engages in the appropriate target behavior and are swapped for other pre-established rewards. If the child engages in an unwanted behavior, a token is returned to the parents.

Positive practice is a procedure that is based on positive reinforcement of a desired skill or behavior using repeated rehearsal of the skill or behavior. For example, a child who struggles with hanging up his coat could be repeatedly reinforced for practicing the behavior chain of opening the door, entering the house, removing his coat, and hanging it on a hook. The reinforcer would be immediately provided when the coat is hung on the hook, and would be given each time that the child completed the behavior correctly.

Time out is one of the most common consequences used by parents. Time out is a procedure whereby positive reinforcement is removed immediately following an unacceptable behavior, aiming to decrease future probability of the undesired behavior occurring. To be effective, time out must: (1) involve the child being removed to a situation that is void of stimulation; (2) involve a sense of loss of control on the child's part; and (3) not end until the child is calm and agreeable to comply with parental requests (either the initial request or restitution). The child must be removed from any type of stimulation: no parental attention (including eye contact), no parent lectures, no parent responses to questions, no parental touching of the child, no toys, no books, no games, and so forth. In the modern American family, this means that the child should not be sent to his/her room, because of the televisions, phones, computers, video games, and so forth that are typically found in the bedrooms of American children. Rather, the time out location should be one in which the child does not have access to anything that could potentially be reinforcing and the child has no control over the situation/location; in essence, it must be a boring situation for the child. Practical recommendations for the length of time out vary; however, generally the rule is 1 minute per year of age, up to 10 minutes. The child's behavior at the cessation of time out is what is *most* important, because the parent may inadvertently reinforce tantrum behavior by returning the child to the positive reinforcement environment immediately following another inappropriate behavior.

Removal of privileges tends to be a more effective strategy than time-out for children who are older than 10 years. *Grounding* is a more advanced time out for adolescents; rather than placing the child in time out, a privilege or item (eg, car, video game) is placed in time out. The key to these consequences is for parents to take away the privilege immediately, with a set duration, and consistently apply the same rule if the behavior occurs again.

A behavioral contract is a written agreement between the child and parent that explicitly identifies the target behaviors and the consequences (positive and negative) that are associated with each behavior. Behavioral expectations and their consequences should be written for all parties to review and refer to at any time (e.g., tape them inside a kitchen cabinet or post on the refrigerator). Contracting usually works well with older adolescents.

Ignoring involves eliminating the reinforcer (e.g., attention) for a previously reliably reinforced yet undesirable behavior. Ignoring must continue until the child has stopped the target behavior, or the behavior will be inadvertently strengthened. Ignoring includes the withdrawal of all attention, including verbalizations, sighs, eye contact, or body language. Of note, ignoring is not an appropriate strategy for unsafe behaviors.

Accountability for behaviors or choices can be a powerful intervention for many youth with behavioral struggles. Setting up school and home based behavioral programs that emphasize responsibility taking, establish well-defined consequences prior to poor choices, and that emphasize communication can positively impact behavior challenges.

Keys to Effective Behavioral Intervention

When establishing a behavioral intervention, such as those above, consistency, immediacy, and follow-through are important aspects to consider. A reinforcer or punisher should be implemented consistently by care providers. For example, in the situation of joint custody, it is recommended that both parents utilize the same strategies as well as support the other's decisions. A reinforcer or punisher should be provided immediately (within 3 to 5 seconds) following the undesired behavior to increase the likelihood that the child s able to link the behavior to the consequence. Finally, it is essential that the caregiver is able to follow-through with the stated consequence. If a parent is unable to provide a promised reward, an alternative should be provided. If the parent removes a privilege for one week but returns it after only three days, the child learns that the parent does not abide by their statements, and thus the consequence loses some effectiveness.

Academic Interventions

Oftentimes, the results of a psychological evaluation lead to recommendations for the academic setting, and may specifically address academic intervention related to curriculum, teaching and learning methods, as well as achievement levels. Depending on the area of weakness identified by the psychological evaluation, it may be recommended that the school establish an Individualized Education Plan (IEP) or a 504 Accommodations Plan (504). Typically, an IEP establishes goals related to learning disabilities, social deficits, speech struggles, and the like, while 504 plans establish accommodations related to physical deficits or a medical care plan. There are important distinctions to be aware of between these two academic intervention methods.

An *IEP* is an educational plan that structures specific goals for the child's needs based on the Individuals with Disabilities Education Act (IDEA) that sets national legal guidelines for education. IEPs address the learning services for children with special learning needs in various educational capacities, such as learning disabilities (e.g., need different curriculum for learning math), emotional disabilities (e.g., need a more structured class management approach that incorporates social and emotional learning tools in the curriculum), physical or other health impairments (e.g., need a computer to provide typed versus hand written responses, occupational therapy services, physical therapy services), speech and language problems (e.g., speech therapy services), or autism (e.g., behavior therapy in the educational setting).

A *504 Plan* is more global, and provides accommodations for a student under the Americans with Disabilities Act (ADA), which extends environmental and functional accommodations to individuals with disabilities. Therefore, a 504 Plan is appropriate for a child who needs wheelchair access, access to a school nurse for management of medication, or who needs to sit closer to the teacher or have an FM System installed in the classrooms. A 504 Plan will follow a child through elementary settings into college or the work place.

Other, more specific school interventions may also be a component of a child's IEP or 504 Plan. Some youth may benefit from participation in a *Social Skills Group*, which are often coordinated by a school social worker, counselor, or speech therapist. Additionally, many youth would benefit from *involvement in extra-curricular activities,* such as sport, clubs, youth groups, and the like. Such involvement allows the child to participate in age-appropriate activities, have fun, practice social skills, and build confidence/esteem.

As well, *specific classroom interventions* may be recommended, including suggestions for organization (e.g., color-coding folders, notebooks, and book covers; setting aside time weekly to organize desks, lockers, and backpacks), seating (e.g., seating the child near the teacher and/or away from high-traffic areas in the classroom), allowing the child to stand while doing desk work rather than requiring s/he be seated, frequent breaks, use of a behavior plan, and the use of day-planners. Other examples could include supporting material provided verbally with written information or providing notes ahead of time. Finally, for gifted students, it may be recommended that extra "challenge" questions be provided to keep the student interested.

Academic accommodations such as *time extensions or limits* may be identified for a student, along with implications for time and methods of testing. For example, it may be recommended that all testing be done in a quiet atmosphere away from the classroom, that the child be afforded time-and-a-half for test completion or that a child be assigned all the odd or even questions to reduce homework time to accommodate for a processing deficit.

Many youth with behavioral, emotional, or learning struggles at school could benefit from identifying a *supportive person* to whom they can turn at school. Seeking out the support of this identified person should not necessarily be contingent on behavior; at the same time, receiving the support should not serve to escape from or avoid academic tasks.

Establishing a *behavior plan* at school using the behavioral interventions previously identified may be helpful. It may also be helpful to match this behavior plan with one used at home to increase consistency across environments.

Involvement in an *after school homework program or tutoring sessions* may also be helpful for some students. While often this is an educational goal identified by an IEP, some parents may also choose to augment school services with private tutorial services where available.

Some children and teens may benefit from enrolling in an *alternative educational setting*. Some examples may include specialized special education programs, day treatment programs, sober high schools, or behavioral programs. When this is established, typically the IEP will either be written or transfer with the student and modified for the new setting. It is also important to know that children receiving extended medical care in hospital settings will typically have academic services available to them through the hospital's local school district.

Other Recommendations

Regardless of the diagnosis, a psychological evaluation should provide information regarding an individual's areas of strengths and needs. Based on these results, it will be important for parents, teachers, and other care providers in the child's life to have reasonable expectations for the child. It is essential that the child, family, and care providers have education regarding the child's diagnosis at a level that is understandable to them. In addition, explanation of recommendations will help motivate those involved to fully participate in the changes suggested. In general, it is most helpful to increase the communication between home and school, and between these environments and those of the treatment providers involved in the child's care.

It is helpful to continue to *monitor the child's difficulties*, whether related to learning, medical treatment response, emotional struggles, or behavior. Any changes in intensity, frequency, or quality should be addressed with teachers, therapists, doctors, or other treatment providers. At times, *re-evaluation* may be recommended after a designated period of time. Take, for example, a child who demonstrates symptoms of both ADHD and a learning disability. It is possible that the inattention and other ADHD symptoms are actually caused by the learning disability; as such, a re-evaluation to assess whether ADHD is truly present may be warranted if those symptoms continue after consistently addressing the learning disabilities for a significant period of time. In general, more comprehensive assessments are helpful in preparing for the major academic transitions of fourth grade (as learning to read changes to reading to learn), ninth grade, and high school graduation.

Establishing *safety plans* is recommended in instances when there is potential for unsafe behaviors. The safety plan could include identification of the unsafe behavior or its precursor behaviors, actions to take if the behavior occurs, and alternatives to the specific unsafe behavior (coping strategies). Behaviors addressed could include abusive situations, bullying, sexual behaviors, self-harm behaviors, suicidal or homicidal thoughts or plans, or aggressive acts.

If there is a family history of difficulties related to mental health, medical, or substance use illness, it may be recommended that the child, teen, or entire family participate in an *appropriate support/educational program*. For example, the family may be referred to Al-anon, Alateen, Students Against Destructive Decisions, National Alliance on Mental Illness, or other appropriate resource. Support groups for families such as Family-to-Family Network, Advocacy programs, and local disease specific support groups can be of great help in the education and adjustment phases to new diagnosis and treatment.

Some youth may benefit from involvement with a *mentorship program*, such a Big Brother/Big Sister. If Big Brother/Big Sister is not an option, alternatives may include teachers, coaches, advanced peers, or neighbors. In addition, high schools, colleges, or churches may have mentorship programs as well.

Oftentimes, it is recommended that parents seek out additional information regarding the diagnosis given to their child or to gain information regarding additional resources in the community. *Websites and books* are often recommended to meet this goal; however caution should be provided in evaluating the credibility of source of information (i.e., empirical versus anecdotal).

Conclusion

Behavioral and psychological assessment can often assist the medical provider in more comprehensive investigation regarding behavioral, cognitive, and neuropsychological functioning of a patient. These assessment procedures can often identify significant factors related to the individual's functioning that may not require medication intervention, but rather a cohesive plan of environmental changes that the physician can prescribe to improve functioning, relationships, and development. Teaming with a behavioral psychologist can benefit one's medical practice as well as patient outcomes.

References

AERA, APA, and NCME, *Standards for Educational and Psychological Testing*. 1999, Hanover, PA: Sheridan Press.

American's with Disabilities Act of 1990, in 42 USCA Section 12101 et seq. 1990.

Anastasi, A., *Psychological Testing - Sixth Edition*. 1988, New York: Macmillan Publishing Company.

APA, *Diagnostic and Statistical Manual of Mental Disorders: DSM-IV*. 4 ed, Ed. Task Force on DSM-IV). 1994, Washington, DC: American Psychiatric Association.

Ayllon, T., *How to Use Token Economy and Point Systems*. 2nd Edition ed. 1999, Austin, TX: PRO-ED.

Azrin, N.H. and V.A. *Besalel, How to use Positive Practice, Self-Correction, and Overcorrection*. 2nd Edition ed. 1999, Austin, TX: PRO-ED.

Friman, P. *Common Behavioral Problems*. in 13th Annual Spring Conference of the North Dakota Psychological Association. 2003. Fargo, ND.

Friman, P.C., *Time Out Guidelines for Parents, in common sense Parenting*, R.V. Burke and R.W. Herron, Editors. 1992, Boys Town Press: Boystown, NE. p. 101-103.

Hall, R.V. and M.L. Hall, *How to negotiate a Behavioral Con*tract. 2nd Edition ed. 1999, Austin, TX: PRO-ED.

Hanley, G.P., B.A. Iwata, and B.E. McCord, Functional Analysis of Problem Behavior: A Review. *Journal of Applied Behavior Analysis*, 2003. 36(2): p. 147-185.

Individual's with Disabilities Education Act (IDEA) 1997, in 20 USCA Section 1400(a). 1997.

Institute, B., ed. *The Fifteenth Mental measurements Yearbook*. ed. B.S. Plake, J.C. Impara, and R.A. Spies. Vol. 15. 2003, Buros Institute: Lincoln, NE.

Kaplan, H.I. and B.J. *Sadock, Synopsis of Psychiatry: Behavioral Sciences, Clinical Psychiatry*. 8th Edition ed. 1997, New York: Lippincott, Williams and Wilkins.

Lezak, M., *Neuropsychological Assessment*, 1995, New York: Oxford University Press, Inc.

Lovaas, O.I., *Teaching Developmentally Disabled Children: The ME Book*. 1981, Austin, TX: PRO-ED.

Miller, L.K., *Principles of Everyday Behavior Analysis. 3rd Edition* ed. 1997, Pacific Grove, CA: Brooks/Cole Publishing Company.

O'Neill, R.E., et al., *Functional Assessment and Program Development for Problem Behavior: A Practical Handbook*. 2nd Edition ed. 1997, Pacific Grove, CA: Brooks/Cole Publishing Company.

Patterson, G.R., *Living with Children: New Methods for Parents and Teachers*. 1972, Champaign, IL: research Press.

Patterson, G.R. and M. *Forgatch, Parents and Adolescents Living Together: Family Problem Solving*. 1989, Eugene, OR: Castalia Publishing Company.

Sattler, J., *Assessment of Children - Revised and Updated Third Edition*. 1992, San Diego: Jerome M. Sattler Publishing Inc.

Section II. Developmental Disorders

In: Behavioral Pediatrics, 3rd Edition
Editor: Donald E. Greydanus et al.

ISBN 978-1-60692-702-1
© 2009 Nova Science Publishers, Inc.

Chapter 3

Intellectual Disability

Dilip R. Patel and Joav Merrick

Abstract

Intellectual disability is characterized by deficits in cognitive and adaptive abilities that initially manifest before 18 years of age. In the United States, the prevalence of intellectual disability is estimated to be between 1 and 3 out of every 100 individuals in the general population. Most individuals have mild intellectual disability and the cause is generally not identified. A small percentage of individuals have severe deficits and who will need lifetime supports. The diagnosis of intellectual disability requires formal psychometric testing to assess the intelligence quotient and adaptive functioning. The management of individuals who have intellectual disability is based on providing general medical care, treatment of specific behavioral symptoms, early intervention, special education, and variable degrees of community based supports.

Introduction

Intellectual disability is now a more internationally accepted term used to describe deficits in cognitive and adaptive functioning. The term cognitive-adaptive disability is also used by some authors in this context. The evolution of the terminology from idiocy to mental retardation to intellectual disability is a reflection of a better understanding of the concept of cognition and cognitive deficits within the scientific and sociocultural contexts. Although intellectual disability is initially identified in infancy and early childhood years, it has life long implications for growth and development, education, ability to live independently, health care, find employment, and need for community based supports. In the United States various Federal and State laws provide the framework and funding for intervention services, educational services, and other support services for individuals who have intellectual disability. In addition to medical evaluation and management, the physician plays a vital role in facilitating and coordinating the overall long term management for individuals who have intellectual disability. This chapter reviews the definition, epidemiology, clinical features, diagnosis, and treatment of intellectual disability.

Definition

According to the American Association on Intellectual and Developmental Disabilities (AAIDD), intellectual disability "is a disability characterized by significant limitations both in intellectual functioning and in adaptive behavior as expressed in conceptual, social, and practical adaptive skills." The assessment of intellectual functioning and adaptive behavior must take into consideration the expectations based on individual's age and culture. The influence on cognitive assessment of sensory, motor, communication, or behavioral factors should also be appropriately considered in administration of assessment instruments, and interpretation of their results.

In the United States a widely used definition is the one from the Individuals with Disabilities Education Act that defines intellectual disability as "significantly sub-average general intellectual functioning, existing concurrently with deficits in adaptive behavior and manifested during the developmental period that adversely affects a child's educational performance."

According to the Diagnostic and Statistical Manual of Mental Disorders, 4th edition, text revision (DSM-IV-TR), intellectual disability (or mental retardation) is defined as an intelligence quotient (IQ) of approximately 70 or below on an individually administered standardized test of intelligence concurrent with deficits in adaptive functioning in two of the following areas: communication, self-care, home living, social or interpersonal skills, use of community resources, self-direction, functional academic skills, work, leisure, health, and safety. All definitions stipulate that the onset of disability must occur before the age of 18 years.

It is generally agreed that, although not perfect, appropriately measured IQ provides the best estimate of intellectual functioning. Based on the mean value for IQ of 100, the upper limit of 70 as the cut off represents the value that is two standard deviations below the mean. Because there a five point standard error of measurement, it is argued that a range of 70-75 should be considered as the upper limit of IQ as the cut off value for intellectual disability. Based on the typical bell shaped curve of distribution of IQ scores, raising the IQ score from 70 to 75 as the upper limit of cut off, will double the number of individuals with intellectual disability from 2.27% to 4.85% of the population. An individual with an IQ score of 75 with significant adaptive disability will be considered to have intellectual disability, whereas an individual with no adaptive disability and an IQ score of 65 may not be considered to have intellectual disability.

The severity of intellectual disability is further categorized based on intellectual functioning, adaptive functioning, and intensity of supports needed (Table 1). When the severity of intellectual disability cannot be reliably assessed, but there is a high level of confidence based on clinical judgment, a diagnosis of intellectual disability is made without specifying the severity.

Table 1. Classification of intellectual disability severity

Severity level	Percent of individuals who have intellectual disability	Intelligence quotient range	Intensity of supports needed in daily living activities such as school, work, or home.
Mild	85	From 50-55 to 70	Intermittent: Support on as needed basis, episodic or short-term
Moderate	10	From 35-49 to 50-55	Limited: Consistent over time, but time limited
Severe	4	From 20-25 to 35-40	Extensive: Regular, consistent, lifetime support. Regular support in at least one aspect such as school, work or home
Profound	1	Less than 20-25	Pervasive: High intensity, across all environments, lifetime, and potentially life-sustaining

[Based on American Psychiatric Association. DSM-IV-TR, 2000; American Association of Intellectual and Developmental Disabilities. Mental Retardation, 2002].

Epidemiology

The reported prevalence of intellectual disability reflects consideration of the definition used, method of ascertainment of the data, and the characteristics of the population studied. Based on the typical bell shaped distribution of intelligence in the general population and 2 standard deviations below the mean as a cut off point, approximately 2.5% of the population is expected to have intellectual disability. Most epidemiological studies consider those with an IQ score of 50 or less as having severe and those above that as having mild intellectual disability. Eighty five percent of individuals with intellectual disability have mild intellectual disability. The prevalence of severe intellectual disability has remained the same over several decades at 0.3%-0.5% of the population in the United States. Based on the United States National Center for Health Statistics 1997-2003 National Health Interview Survey, the prevalence of intellectual disability among children ages 5-17 years is estimated to be 7.5 per 1,000.

Intellectual disability is reported to be twice as common in males compared to females. The recurrence risk of intellectual disability in families with one previous child with severe intellectual disability is reported to be between 3% and 9%.

Mild intellectual disability is associated predominantly with environmental risk factors and a specific etiology can be identified in less than half of affected individuals. On the other hand, underlying biological or neurological etiology can be identified in more than two-thirds of affected individuals who have severe disability. The most common identified conditions in children with severe intellectual disability include chromosomal disorders, genetic syndromes, congenital brain malformations, neurodegenerative diseases, congenital infections, inborn errors of metabolism, and birth injury.

Clinical Features

Children who have intellectual disability can present with a wide range of initial clinical symptoms and signs depending up on the underlying cause and severity of the disability. Children who have severe intellectual disability generally present early and with clinical features of underlying condition. Children with mild intellectual disability generally do not have underlying identifiable etiology and present with developmental delay or behavioral symptoms and are identified relatively later. Common presentations of intellectual disability by age are summarized in Table 2. The age at which intellectual disability can be recognized depends on its severity (Table 3).

Other mental disorders (Table 4) are 3-4 times more common in children with intellectual disability compared to those that do not have intellectual disability. Children may present with behavioral symptoms of these disorders in addition to intellectual disability. In these children a dual diagnosis of intellectual disability and co-morbid mental disorder should be made if criteria for both are met.

Table 2. Common presentations of intellectual disability* by age

Age	Area of concern
Newborn	Dysmorphic syndromes, micorcephaly
	Major organ system dysfunction (e.g., feeding and breathing)
Early infancy (2-4 months)	Failure to interact with the environment
	Concern about vision and hearing impairments
Later infancy (6-18 months)	Gross motor delay
Toddlers (2-3 years)	Language delays or difficulties
Pre-school (3-5 years)	Language difficulties or delays
	Behavioral difficulty, including play
	Delays in fine motor skills: cutting, coloring, drawing
School age (older than 5 years)	Academic underachievement
	Behavior difficulties (attention, anxiety, mood, conduct, and so on)

*The word mental retardation from source is replaced with intellectual disability. [Used with permission from Shapiro B, Batshaw M. Mental retardation, In Kliegman RM, Behrman RE, Jenson HB, et al, eds. *Nelson Textbook of Pediatrics*, 18th edition. Philadelphia: Elsevier Saunders, 2007].

Table 3. Age at recognition of intellectual disability

Severity of intellectual disability	Most likely age at recognition
Mild	≥ 5-6 years
Moderate	3-5 years
Severe	≤3 years
Profound	≤2 years

Table 4. Conditions co-morbid with intellectual disability

Mental disorders
- Attention deficit/Hyperactivity disorder
- Mood disorders
- Pervasive developmental disorders
- Stereotypic movement disorder
- Anxiety disorders
- Obsessive compulsive disorder

Medical conditions
- Seizure disorders
- Hearing impairments
- Vision impairments
- Motor impairments
- Obesity
- Type 2 diabetes mellitus
- Gastroesophageal reflux disease

Behavioral symptoms
- Self-injurious behaviors
- Aggression
- Self-induced vomiting
- Sleep disturbances
- Challenging behavior

Diagnosis

Diagnosis is suspected based on the presenting symptoms. Next step is to obtain additional history (Table 5) followed by a complete general physical examination, dysmorphology examination, and neurological examination. By definition a diagnosis of intellectual disability requires individualized cognitive and adaptive testing by qualified examiners using standardized instruments (Table 6). Standardized testing should be age appropriate, take into account mental age of the child, and culturally sensitive. Appropriate accommodations should be made for any motor, behavioral or language variations. A work up should include compete audiological and vision evaluation in all children.

There is no consensus regarding the need to establish an etiological diagnosis in all children who have intellectual disability. Parents or other care givers are also divided in their need to know the cause of intellectual disability in their child. Factors that might guide the decision to pursue etiological diagnosis are summarized in Table 7 and some reasons offered by those who favor such an approach are summarized in Table 8.

In the absence of well defined clinical symptoms and signs, an extensive work up that includes genetic testing, neuroimaging, and metabolic testing, is needed to search for potential cause of intellectual disability. Such an extensive work up should preferably be undertaken in consultation with specialists with expertise in this field. The yield of these tests in identifying a cause varies depending up on presence or absence of associated symptoms and signs. Newborn screening programs generally identify major inborn errors of metabolism and the yield of metabolic testing done later in infancy and childhood is reported to be ≤1%. The yield of neuroimaging in detecting brain abnormality ranges from 33% to 63%. Abnormal findings on neuroimaging may or may not help in establishing a cause of intellectual disability. The yield of genetic testing in identifying a specific genetic condition ranges from 2% to 7%.

Table 5. Key elements of history

DETAILS OF PRESENTING SYMPTOMS
- Onset, duration, progression, severity of symptoms
- Current level of development and functioning as reported by parents or caregivers

PRENATAL
- Mother's and father's age at birth of the child
- Nature of prenatal care
- Previous pregnancies: number, term, preterm, abortions, living
- Multiple gestations
- Maternal weigh gain
- Fetal activity
- Maternal medical and obstetric complications
- Use of medications, drugs of abuse, alcohol, tobacco, radiation exposure
- Pre-natal maternal infections

PERINATAL
- Hospital or home delivery details
- Length of gestation
- Labor: spontaneous delivery, induced, vaginal, forceps, cesarian section
- Intrapartum monitoring, use of analgesia or anesthesia (epidural)
- Prolapse cord, breech, polyhydramnios, olighydraminos, prolonged rupture of membranes
- Maternal fever, toxemia, abnormal bleeding, abnormalities of placenta
- Meconium or foul-smelling amniotic fluid

NEONATAL
- Birth weight, height, head circumference
- Dubowitz score, small or large of gestational age
- Apgar scores, any resuscitation
- Duration of nursery stay
- Respiratory distress, assisted ventilation, apnea, seizures, sepsis, jaundice
- Blood type, Coomb's
- Congenital anomalies, feeding problems
- Brain imaging, laboratory testing

DEVELOPMENTAL
- Time and nature of initial parental concerns about development
- Any previous developmental evaluations
- Specific developmental diagnosis if any and at what age
- Early major milestone attainment

MEDICAL/ SURGICAL
- Major illnesses or surgeries
- Injuries and hospitalizations
- Procedures or investigations

FAMILY HISTORY
- Fetal wastage
- Unexplained infant or childhood deaths
- Parental and sibling health
- Medical conditions in family members: congenital, genetic, neurological, psychiatric, learning disorders, intellectual disability, speech and language disorders

PERSONAL/ SOCIAL HISTORY
- Parent occupation, socioeconomic status, level of education
- Primary caregiver, living situation, school functioning
- Any current services or therapies, early intervention or other special health services
- Extracurricular activities, family adjustment, school adjust ment
- Use of medications

REVIEW OF SYSTEMS
- Guided by presenting symptoms

Table 6. Selected standardized instruments

Measures of cognitive abilities

Instrument	Age range
Bayley Scales of Infant Development III	1-42 months
Wechsler Pre-School and Primary Scale of Intelligence	2 y 6 mo to 7 y 3 mo
McCarthy Scales of Children' Abilities	2 y 6 mo to 8 y 6 mo
Stanford-Binet Intelligence Scale (5th edition)	2 y to 85 y
Wechsler Intelligence Scale for Children (WISC-IV)	6 y to 12 y
Leiter International Performance Scale-Revised (Leiter-R)	2 to 21 y

Measures of adaptive abilities

Instrument	Age range
Vineland Adaptive Behavior Scale II (VBAS II)	Birth to 19 y
Adaptive Behavior Scales II (ABAS II)	Birth to 89 y
Scales of Independent Behavior-Revised (SIB-R)	Birth to 80 y
AAMR Adaptive Behavior Scales (ABS)	3 to 21 y

Table 7. Factors that may guide decision to pursue etiological diagnosis

Severity of intellectual disability
- Biologic cause can be found in 75% of individuals with severe intellectual disability

Presence or absence of disease specific symptoms and signs
- Disease specific features may indicate which tests to order

Parental decision as to future pregnancy
- If more children are planned, a pre-natal diagnosis and early appropriate intervention may be planned

Parental desire to know the cause of intellectual disability
- Varies. Some may want to know so that specific disease may be treated if treatment is available. Other may want to focus on services.

Table 8. Reasons offered in support of pursuing an etiological diagnosis

Associated complications can be anticipated
Specific cause may be treatable
Aid in the development of prevention strategies
Research is facilitated
Intervention can be planned for anticipated behavioral symptoms
Genetic counseling can be provided
Helps in long-term life planning

In children who have intellectual disability the predominant deficits are noted in cognitive abilities and language. Their social development is consistent with their mental age and generally there are no motor deficits. Children who have developmental language disorders or specific language impairments have predominant deficits in various aspects of language development whereas their social, motor, and cognitive development progresses typically. Children who have pervasive developmental disorders have predominant deficits in social and language or communication domains whereas their motor development is typical. In children who present with symptoms suggestive of intellectual disability, hearing and vision impairments should be ruled out. Conditions to be considered in the differential diagnosis of intellectual disability are listed in Table 9.

Table 9. Differential diagnosis

Developmental language disorders
Borderline intellectual functioning (IQ 71-84)
Pervasive developmental disorders
Hearing impairment
Visual impairment
Environmental deprivation
Dementia (rare)
Schizophrenia (rare)

Treatment

Children who have intellectual disability are best managed by an interdisciplinary team approach in the setting of a medical home. The physician should provide the general medical care similar to all children including preventive care according to established guidelines. Specific health maintenance guidelines are published by the American Academy of Pediatrics for several conditions (e.g., Down syndrome) associated with intellectual disability and can be accessed at www.aap.org.

The behavioral symptoms and co-morbid conditions seen in children and adolescents who have intellectual disability are managed most commonly by behavioral approaches. In select cases psychotropic medications are used. Depending up on the personal expertise of the child's physician this should preferably be done in consultation with a child psychiatrist. Various psychotropic medications used to manage behavioral symptoms include stimulants, antidepressants, mood stabilizers, and antipsychotics.

The physician should refer the child to community based agencies and programs for appropriate intervention services primarily depending on the age of the child. The physician should have ongoing communication with local agencies that provide such intervention services to the child and should facilitate and coordinate needed medical evaluations and specialist consultations.

Table 10. Severity of intellectual disability and adult age functioning

Level	Mental age as adult	Adult adaptation
Mild	9-11 y	Reads at 4th-5th grade level; simple multiplications/ divisions; writes simple letters, lists; completes job application; basic independent job skills (arrive on time, stay at task, interact with co-workers); uses public transportation; may qualify for recipes
Moderate	6-8 y	Sight-word reading; copies information e.g., address from card to job application; matches written number to number of items; recognizes time on clock; communicates; some independence in self-care; housekeeping with supervision or cue cards; meal preparation, can follow picture recipe cards; job skills learned with much repetition; uses public transportation with some supervision
Severe	3-5 y	Needs continuous support and supervision; may communicate wants and needs, sometimes with augmentative communication techniques
Profound	Less than 3 y	Limitations of self-care, continence, communication, and mobility; may need complete custodial or nursing care

[Used with permission from Shapiro B, Batshaw M. Mental retardation, In Kliegman RM, Behrman RE, Jenson HB, et al, eds. *Nelson Textbook of Pediatrics*, 18th edition. Philadelphia: Elsevier Saunders, 2007].

In the United States several Federal and State laws provide the framework and funding for intervention programs and educational services for children with developmental disabilities including those who have intellectual disabilities. The mainstay of overall management of young children (younger than three years of age) who have intellectual disability is early intervention services provided by local community agencies through the development and implementation of the Individualized Family Service Plan. For children and adolescents between the ages 3-16 years the main focus is on educational interventions, including special education, developed and implemented by the student's school district. This is called the Individualized Education Plan or the IEP. An Individualized Transition Plan is developed between 14 and 16 years of age that addresses the student's transition to adult services, vocational training, and independent living. After the completion of the high school the individual is supported by the Individualized Habilitation (Support) Plan that provides adult support services. The intensity of support services needed depends up on the severity of intellectual disability (Table 1). The adult outcomes and functioning of individuals with intellectual disability are summarized in Table 10.

Conclusion

Intellectual disability is defined as significant limitations in cognitive functioning characterized by an intelligence quotient of about 70 or below and concurrent deficits in adaptive functioning. The severity is classified as mild, moderate, severe, and profound, based on the IQ scores and the intensity of supports needed. Eighty five percent of individuals who have intellectual disability have mild deficits. Environmental factors are predominant risk factors for mild intellectual disability whereas biologic factors are predominant risk factors for severe intellectual disability. The age at initial presentation depends up on the severity of the deficits. Intellectual deficits can be identified in most children by 3 to 5 years of age. The diagnosis is based on clinical evaluation and psychometric testing for cognitive and adaptive functioning. The need to search for the cause of intellectual disability in all cases is debatable. The main strategies for management of individual who have intellectual disability are general medical care, treatment of co-morbid conditions, treatment of behavioral symptoms, special education, vocational training, and community based supports.

References

American Psychiatric Association. *Diagnostic and Statistical Manual of Mental Disorders*, 4th edition, Text Revision, Washington DC: American Psychiatric Association, 2000:41-48.

Calles JL Jr. Use of psychotropic medications in children and adolescents with cognitive-adaptive disabilities. *Pediar. Clin. North Am*. 2008;55(5):1227-1240

Centers for Disease Control and Prevention. At http://www.cdc.gov/ncbddd/dd/mr3.htm accessed 2008 August 30.

Curry CJ, Stevenson RE, Anghton D, et al. Evaluation of mental retardation: recommendations of a consensus conference. American College of Medical Genetics. *Am. J. Med. Genet.* 1997;72:468-477.

Kandel I, Schofield P, Merrick J. Aging and disability. *Research and clinical perspectives.* Victoria, BC: Int Acad Press, 2007.

Luckasson R, Borthwick-Duffy S, Buntix WHE, et al. *Mental Retardation: Definition, Classification, and System of Supports.* Washington, DC: American Association for Mental Retardation, 2002.

Moeschler JB, Shevell MI and Committee on Genetics: Clinical genetic evaluation of the child with mental retardation or developmental delays. *Pediatrics* 2006;117:2304-2316.

Pratt HD, Greydanus DE. Intellectual disability (mental retardation) in children and adolescents. *Prim. Care* 2007;34:375-386.

Rubin IL, Crocker AC, eds. *Medical care for children and adults with developmental disabilities.* Baltimore, Paul H Brookes, 2006.

Shapiro B, Batshaw M. Mental retardation, In Kliegman RM, Behrman RE, Jenson HB, et al, eds. *Nelson Textbook of Pediatrics*, 18th edition. Philadelphia: Elsevier Saunders, 2007.

Shevell MI, Ashwal S, Donley D, et al. Practice Parameter: Evaluation of the child with global developmental delay. *Neurology* 2003;60:367-379.

Shevell MI. Global developmental delay. *Pediatr. Clin. North Am.* 2008;55(5):1071-1084

VanKarnebeck CDH, Janswiejer MCE, Leenders AGE, et al. Diagnostic investigation in individuals with mental retardation: A systematic literature review of their usefulness. *Eur. J. Human Genet.* 2005;13:2-65.

In: Behavioral Pediatrics, 3rd Edition
Editor: Donald E. Greydanus et al.

ISBN 978-1-60692-702-1
© 2009 Nova Science Publishers, Inc.

Chapter 4

Learning Disabilities

Helen D. Pratt and Donald E. Greydanus

Abstract

Learning disabilities are a common problem seen in pediatric practice. Learning disabilities can affect various domains of cognitive functions and learning with significant impairments in academic achievement. The functional impairment can range from mild to severe. Learning disabilities are generally associated with many other behavioral symptoms. Early recognition and intervention have been shown to have significant impact in long term positive outcome for children and adolescents who have learning disabilities. These interventions include medical, behavioral and academic. This chapter reviews the definitions, epidemiology, clinical presentations and treatment of children who have learning disabilities.

Introduction

In many societies, the ability to successfully navigate the educational system means access to success, wealth, and power. In every educational system there is a subset of learners who are unable to engage in academic exercises because of deficits in sustaining attention, recalling and manipulating information, mastering specific cognitive processes, or demonstrating conceptual learning. These deficits may be the result of some type of intellectual, emotional, behavioral, physical, or environmental factor. Any combination of these factors can result in school failure.

Definition

"Learning disability" (LD) is not a diagnosis in the same sense as "chickenpox" or "mumps." Chickenpox and mumps imply a single, known cause with a predictable set of symptoms. Rather, LD is a broad term that covers a pool of possible causes, symptoms, treatments, and outcomes. Partly because learning disabilities can show up in so many forms, it is difficult to diagnose or to pinpoint the causes. And no one knows of a pill or remedy that will cure them.

The term "learning disability" only describes a constellation of symptoms and does not represent a group of independent symptoms, nor does it represent a single entity; therefore the term should be thought of as a label. Learning disability is defined as a discrepancy between the actual academic achievement of a student and that student's intellectual potential. Individuals who have learning disabilities (LD) experience seriously impaired functioning in one or more of the following areas: (1) reading (comprehension), (2) language (expression, comprehension), (3) written expression, (4) mathematics (calculation, reasoning), (5) sustained attention, and (6) goal directed behavior. Learning disability must be the primary cause of problems in functioning even in the presence of other disabilities (physical, mental, behavioral).

Many aspects of speaking, listening, reading, writing, and arithmetic overlap and build on the same brain capabilities. So it is not surprising that children can be diagnosed as having more than one area of learning disability. For example, the ability to understand language underlies learning to speak. Therefore, any disorder that hinders the ability to understand language will also interfere with the development of speech, which in turn hinders learning to read and write.

Epidemiology

Nearly 4 million school-age children have learning disabilities. Of these, at least 20 percent have a type of disorder that leaves them unable to focus their attention. The prevalence of reading disorder is estimated to be 2 - 8 % of school age children and is more common in males.

Clinical Features

Parents will often bring their child into the physician's office with concerns about their child's cognitive, language, attention, or behavioral development after noticing one or all of the following symptoms: intellectual deficits, delayed speech, problems with hearing, problems with coordination (clumsiness in walking, running, or manual dexterity), inability to sustain attention, poor visual-motor development (inability to track an object or to focus on an object or face), inability to follow instructions, academic failure, mild to severe emotional distress, and serious complaints about behavior from parents or teachers.

Parents most often will only ask for help with learning problems when they have been confronted by a family member or teacher about their child's difficulties. By this time in the process, the parents and teachers are often frustrated and may not be receptive to suggestions for rehabilitation. Parents who present with a child who has mild symptoms may be less able to articulate their concerns. They may describe their child as messy, unfocused, disorganized, unmotivated, clumsy, or odd. As their child grows up and the disability impacts the child's life in a more significant manner, teachers may describe him or her as a day dreamer, being zoned out, intentionally ignoring the teacher, or maybe even as being disturbed. Thus, a well-behaved, non-disruptive, polite child with an attention or language disorder may not come to the attention of the physician until a critical threshold of academic demand is reached.

The impact of abnormal development in the above domains can be severe enough to impede a child's or adolescent's ability to learn. It is important for clinicians to understand what role each domain plays in a child's or adolescent's ability to learn to communicate expressively, understand language, read, write, and calculate mathematical problems. Clinicians who know what an individual should be able to do (with allowance for variation) at a specific developmental level will be better prepared to detect problem learners. Not all learning problems are necessarily learning disabilities. Many children are simply slower in developing certain skills. Because children show natural differences in their rate of development, sometimes what seems to be a learning disability may simply be a delayed maturation. In order to be diagnosed as a learning disability, specific criteria must be met. Diagnosis is based on the predominant deficit sub-types. Specific learning disability are described and the clinical features are reviewed below.

Reading Disability (Dyslexia)

Impaired ability to read accurately or fully comprehend written words and text is called reading disability or dyslexia. The impairment must substantially interfere with academic achievement and result in performance that is substantially below that expected from the individual's age, intelligence, and educational level.

Children, who are poor readers, or have associated attention deficit-hyperactivity disorder symptoms, share a common generalized deficit in phonological processing and word recognition. One study found that when the investigators administered intellectual and reading assessments those children in the 1st through 5th grades with reading disabilities and attention deficit/hyperactivity-disorder (ADHD) had obtained Verbal IQ scores above 85 and word recognition scores below the 25th percentile.

Developmental Speech and Language Disability

Speech and language problems are often the earliest indicators of a learning disability. Children with developmental speech and language disorders have difficulty producing speech sounds, using spoken language to communicate, or understand what other people say. Depending on the problem, the specific diagnosis may be: a) Developmental Articulation Disorder -- Youth with this disorder may have trouble controlling their rate of speech, have problems with production ("wabbit" instead of "rabbit" and "thwim" for "swim."). Most youth outgrow this disorder by age 8 if they receive speech therapy; b) Developmental Expressive Language Disorder – These youth have problems with expressing themselves in speech; and, c) Developmental Receptive Language Disorder – difficulty in comprehending.

Children with developmental receptive language disorder have trouble understanding certain aspects of speech. It is as if their brains are set to a different frequency and the reception is poor. There's the toddler who doesn't respond to his name, a preschooler who hands you a bell when you asked for a ball, or consistently can't follow simple directions. Their hearing is fine, but they can't make sense of certain sounds, words, or sentences they hear. They may even seem inattentive. Using and understanding speech are strongly related, many people with receptive language disorders also have an expressive language disability.

Phonologic and language disorders are the most disruptive dysfunctions and are frequently the earliest signs in childhood that a serious disorder exists. Such deficits in phonological perception (i.e., the ability to process appropriately assembled sounds [incoming or outgoing] into meaningful information) cause particular havoc because such disability seriously impacts word decoding, word-recognition, and sequencing skills.

During attempts to read, these youth often focus undue emphasis on the critical process of attempting to decode the phonetic sounds of individual words. In doing so, however, they lose actual comprehension of the concepts that the words and groups of words convey which is the very purpose of the decoding. Organizational skills, sequential memory, and planning abilities are thus badly disrupted. This disruption in turn seriously affects both spoken and written receptive and expressive functioning. Female youth are somewhat less frequently identified with this group of disorders than are males.

Developmental Writing Diability

Writing, too, involves several brain areas and functions. The brain networks for vocabulary, grammar, hand movement, and memory must all be in good working order. So a developmental writing disorder may result from problems in any of these areas. For example, a child who is unable to distinguish the sequence of sounds in a word will have problems with spelling. A child with a writing disability, particularly an expressive language disorder, might be unable to compose complete, grammatically correct sentences.

Disorders of Written Expression

Disorder of written expression refers to an impaired ability to employ written language skills. The deficits cause the child to perform at a level that is substantially lower than those skills expected of that child based on age, intelligence, and education.

Developmental Arithmetic Disorder (Dyscalculia)

Developmental arithmetic disorder refers to an impaired ability to perform mathematical functions, specifically in the critical arenas of calculation, and of handling the step-wise logic of word-based problems. Calculation skill involves highly organized, sequential memory abilities, as well.

Arithmetic is a complex mental process that requires the student to recognize numbers, and symbols, memorizing facts such as the multiplication table, aligning numbers, and understanding abstract concepts like place value and fractions, and recall that information. Any of these may be difficult for children with developmental arithmetic disorders. Most students are also required to use fine and visual motor skills when performing academic work in mathematics. This means that problems in visual tracking and fine motor control, executive functions of planning and execution are also involved. Problems with numbers or basic concepts are likely to show up early. Disabilities that appear in the later grades are more often tied to problems in reasoning.

Motor Skills Disorder (Dysgraphia)

Motor skills disorders refer to coordination disorders that can lead to poor penmanship, as well as certain spelling and memory disorders. Problems with pincer grasp, fine motor control, and visual motor coordination can add to the student's inability to learn. Additionally, delays in acquiring motor skills that can affect the ability to learn, but do not meet the criteria for a specific learning disability are included in this category.

Specific Learning Disorder Not Otherwise Specified

Specific learning disabilities not otherwise specified refers to delays in acquiring language, academic, and motor skills that can affect the ability to learn, but do not meet the criteria for a specific learning disability: for example, difficulties telling time and poor sequencing abilities, visual perceptual reversals, or convergence insufficiency (www.convergenceinsufficiency.org).

Diagnosis

Students who perform substantially below grade level and obtain scores lower on standardized achievement tests (e.g., reading, mathematics, or written expression) may meet criteria for a learning disability. This disability must significantly interfere with the student's ability to function in the above subjects. Significant is defined as having standard scores on achievement tests which are more than 2 standard deviations below scores obtained in intelligence tests. Youth who have multiple impairments that produce the same outcome may also be diagnosed with a learning disability. Some associated problems include cognitive processing deficits, co-morbid mental disorders, general medical conditions, or the individual's ethnic or cultural background. The presence of a sensory deficit does not preclude diagnosis if the learning problems are in excess of those usually associated with the deficit.

Comorbid Conditions

While children with LD can manifest problems in attention and communication, those impairments may not be the primary result of a learning disorder. Problems in communication, language, behavior or emotions can also be significant enough to be diagnosed independently.

Distinction between LD and ADHD is often difficult because of overlapping features and ADHD often co-exists with LD. The shared symptoms include: distractibility, disorganization, impulsivity, poor social skills, poor frustration tolerance, impulsiveness, poor self-control, poor self-concept, and lack of self-esteem. Also children diagnosed with LD show higher rates of anxiety. Youth with learning disabilities, by contrast, characteristically demonstrate phonologic, logic, and language problems not seen in children with anxiety disorders.

Youth with learning disabilities may drop out of school (nearly 40%), be demoralized, have low self esteem, and suffer from social skills deficits. High drop out rates (roughly 1.5 times higher than for the general population), and learning deficits also limit later employment. Conduct, oppositional defiant disorders, ADHD, dysthymic disorders, major depressive disorders, and developmental language delays are each associated disorders (10 – 25%) with LD. Evidence suggests that developmental delays in language may occur in association with LD, especially reading disorder. LD may also be associated with a higher rate of developmental coordination disorder. Individuals with LD may have underlying abnormalities in cognitive processes (visual perceptual, linguist processes, attention, memory, combination of these); however, measure of these processes are generally less reliable and valid than other psycho-educational tests.

Table 1. Differential diagnosis of learning disabilities

- Normal academic variation in attainment
- Impairment in vision and hearing
- Mental retardation
- Pervasive developmental disorders
- Chromosomal anomalies/genetic disorders
- Neurological disorders
- Congenital malformations
- Inborn errors in metabolism
- Developmental disorders
- Severe toxic exposure
- Chronic mental illness
- Severe infectious illness
- Chronic disease
- Side effects of medication used to treat other conditions
- Psycho-emotional trauma
- Psychological trauma

LD is frequently found in association with a variety of general medical conditions, including, lead poisoning, fetal alcohol syndrome, and fragile x syndrome. Although genetic predisposition and perinatal injury and various neurological or general medical conditions may be associated with the development of LD, the presence of such conditions do not invariably predict an LD. Conditions to be considered in the differential diagnosis of learning disability are listed in Table 1.

Assessment

Assessment should always begin with a comprehensive general physical examination which includes a neurological screening exam, comprehensive medical history, mental status exam, and psychosocial history. A good psychosocial history will include developmental history (including prenatal, and birth data), history of unusual behaviors or habits, family history (including screening for history of mental illness, alcoholism, child abuse or spousal abuse, neglect, incarceration, learning disabilities, communications disorders, and attention disorders), and a thorough behavioral observation (minimum at school in several different activities or classes and in the physician's or psychologist's office; optimal evaluation would include the home setting). This data gathering should include three additional types of information on problem behaviors or issues: 1) the onset, frequency, duration, and intensity of problem issues or behaviors; 2) anecdotal information (parental and teacher observations); and 3) school records and teacher observations.

Psychological Evaluation

A qualified psychologist will administer several basic tests to determine if a child has a problem in a specific area that is significant enough to warrant a mental health diagnosis. Those tests can range from screening sessions to comprehensive examinations and include an assessment of intellectual ability (IQ) and function: behavioral, academic (math, reading, spelling, classroom behavior), language (expressive and receptive), neuropsychological (gross and fine motor, sequencing, visual motor, coordination and balance, hearing, and visual spatial), emotional (affective disorders), adaptive (social, emotional, independence, maturity), and personality (psychopathology) functioning. The decision to use a screening test versus a comprehensive test battery is governed by the type of questions the referring clinician asks at the time of referral and the severity of the child's problems. Only a few of these tests provide appropriate norms for individuals with different sociocultural backgrounds.

Consultation for Language, Motor, Vision and Auditory Deficits

Youth who evidence problems with vision should be referred to an ophthalmologist. Those with language or hearing delays should be referred to a speech pathologist and audiologist. Also, with gross or fine motor, coordination, balance or visual motor problems should be referred to an occupational therapist. Each of these individuals will conduct more comprehensive evaluations to identify specific deficits and provide treatment recommendations. Results from such evaluations will require the Clinician to organize clinical findings in a manner that will facilitate patient management and allow the physician to advocate on behalf of the child.

Treatment

The primary care clinician should identify and appropriately treat any underlying neurological or medical disorder, and assist in the medical management of comorbid disorders. Physicians who expect to effectively manage children with learning disabilities must collect relevant information which will allow them to arrive at an accurate diagnosis. This is a complex and time consuming venture that will require the input of multiple professionals, therefore, he or she must work at developing a network of healthcare professionals and educators in the community who can provide specific diagnostic evaluations, treatment recommendations and implement treatment interventions. Early diagnosis is very important for effective intervention and maximum academic success of the child. It is important to note that the underlying deficits of specific learning disabilities persist for life and any management plan must take a life span perspective starting from early childhood to workplace. The clinician should familiarize himself or herself with the specific laws pertaining to education of children with learning disabilities.

Specific learning disability will require specific individualized intervention strategies and in broad terms will encompass some form of remedial and accommodative interventions. During elementary and early school years remedial instructions play a key role in the management; for example, as in children with reading disability specific instructions in phonemic awareness, vocabulary, and comprehension, are integrated in the plan. During later years (secondary school and college years) the strategy shifts from remediation to accommodations such as allowing more reading time, allowing use of hand held computer devices or laptops, tape recorders, and recorded books. In children with specific problems with writing methods can be used that bypass writing such as recorded books, or prewritten assignments where the students has to only enter answers; occupational therapy for young children is also helpful.

Special education in each local school district is protected and regulated by strong legislative and judicial safeguards created by the Federal Education for All Handicapped Children Act (PL 94-142). The law provides for youth with disabilities severe enough to impair their ability to learn and function at age, grade, and developmentally appropriate levels. Educational systems must provide to those youth diagnosed with learning disabilities special accommodation. The special accommodations are generally managed by multidisciplinary teams (comprised of educators, school psychologists and social workers, the involved parents, speech therapist, occupational therapists and other specialists as necessary). School systems are usually very interested in having the youth's physician involved in the planning. Such planning activities are referred to as Individual Education Plans (IEPs) and the committee is referred to as the Individual Education Planning Committee. Youth who are suspected of having a learning disability are evaluated by the committee. The youth is then evaluated in the classroom and a decision is made as to whether testing (psychological, speech, occupational) should occur. Once the testing is completed, the results are evaluated to determine if the youth meets criteria for receiving special accommodation or if special education services are required. If the youth does not meet criteria to receive services from the school, parents can appeal or seek services and supports through the local or state Protection and Advocacy group. The clinician can also refer the child for independent evaluation to determine if the youth does indeed have multiple disabilities or problems more severe than the school determined. All clinicians should refer to their professional organization's policy statements dealing with children with learning disabilities.

Even though a learning disability do not disappear, given the right types of educational experiences, people have a remarkable ability to learn. The brain's flexibility to learn new skills is probably greatest in young children and may diminish somewhat after puberty. This is why early intervention is so important. Nevertheless, we retain the ability to learn throughout our lives. Because certain learning problems reflect delayed development, many children do eventually catch up. In regards to speech and language disorders, children who have an articulation or an expressive language disorder are the least likely to have long-term problems. For people with dyslexia, the outlook is mixed; however, an appropriate remedial reading program can help learners make great strides.

Conclusion

Findings indicate that students with severe learning disabilities can profit from instruction geared toward abstract higher order comprehension when it is designed according to their particular instructional requirements.

Early intervention improves outcomes for the majority of children with disorders of learning, attention and cognition. Impairment in the physical, language, sensory impairments, or mental domain are usually harder to diagnose prior to a child's entry into the school system, but they are easier to treat if diagnosed early. Children with more severe disorders are easier to detect, but children with milder disorders may not be easy to recognize. Delayed detection often results in greater problems in academic, social, emotional, and psychological functioning and even result in a child dropping out of school. Most authors agree that while individuals may never "outgrow" their disabilities, children with above average intellectual abilities often have the ability to compensate or master appropriate coping mechanisms that greatly minimize their overall negative outcomes. Parental attitudes and commitment, availability of resources, and the presence of associated neurological deficit or medical disorder can also significantly impact outcomes.

References

American Academy of Pediatrics: Committee on Children with Disabilities. Provision of Educationally-Related Services for Children and Adolescents with Chronic Diseases and Disabling Conditions Policy Statement. *Pediatrics*. 2000; 105(2): 448-451.

American Academy of Pediatrics, Committee on Children with Disabilities. The Pediatrician's Role in Development and Implementation of an Individual Education Plan (IEP) and/or an Individual Family Service Plan (IFSP), Policy Statement. *Pediatrics*. 1999; 104(1): 124-127.

Denckla, M. B. (1993). The Child with Developmental Disabilities Grown Up: Adult Residua of Childhood Disorders. *Neurologic Clinics*, 11 (1), 105-125.

Greydanus DE, Pratt HD, Patel DR: Attention deficit hyperactivity disorder across the life span. Disease a Month, March 2007

Greydanus DE, Patel DR, Pratt, HD (Eds.): Developmental Disabilities, Part II. *Pediatric Clinics of North America*, 2008; *55*(6): 1071-57; 55(6).

Lagae L. Learning disabilities: definitions, epidemiology, diagnosis and intervention strategies. *Pediatr. Clin. North Am.* 2008; 55(6):1259-1268

Lyon, G. R. Learning disabilities. *The Future of Children - Special Education for Students With Disabilities*, 1996;6 (1), 54-76.

Mason A, Pratt HD, Patel DR, Greydanus DE, and Yahya KZ. Psychology of Prejudice and Discrimination towards Persons with Disabilities. IN: JL Chin (Ed). *The Psychology of Prejudice and Discrimination*. Praeger Press, Inc. 2004.

Neuwirth S: *Learning disabilities*. Bethesda, MD: U.S. Department of Health and Human Services, Public Health Service, National Institutes of Health, National Institute of Mental Health, 1993. NIH Publication No. 93-3611. http://www.nimh.nih.gov/publicat/learndis.cfm#learn3

Pratt, H. D. (2002). Neurodevelopmental Issues in the assessment and treatment of deficits in attention, cognition, and learning during adolescence. *Adolescent Medicine: State of the Art Reviews. 13*(3): 579-598.

Pratt HD, Patel DR: Learning Disorders in Children and Adolescents. Behavioral Pediatrics: The Child and Adolescent. *Primary Care: Clinics in Office Practice*. 2007; 24(2): 361-374.

Pratt HD, Patel DR, Greydanus, DE: Learning disorders. In: Greydanus, D. E., Patel, D. R., Pratt, H. D. (Eds). (2006). *Behavioral Pediatrics, Vol. I & II, 2nd edition*, pp 143-160. New York: iUniverse.

Wilder AA, Williams J P. Students with severe learning disabilities can learn higher order comprehension skills. *Journal of educational psychology*. 2001; 93(2): 268-79.

In: Behavioral Pediatrics, 3rd Edition
Editor: Donald E. Greydanus et al.

ISBN 978-1-60692-702-1
© 2009 Nova Science Publishers, Inc.

Chapter 5

Speech-Language Disorders and Other Communication Problems

Nickola Wolf Nelson and Heather Kay Koole

Abstract

This chapter provides definitions, classifications, epidemiology, and diagnostic features for speech, language, and communication disorders. It includes a description of clinical features that should signal referral for full speech-language or hearing assessment from infancy through adolescence, and a brief introduction to treatment for disorders involving communication.

Introduction

Achieving competence with communication abilities—including listening, speaking, reading, and writing—is one of childhood's major developmental feats. Communication abilities not only are important in themselves, but as indices of the health of underlying neuromotor, cognitive, emotional, and psychosocial systems. Communication abilities also serve as critical tools for social, academic, and vocational success.

Definitions

Speech-language pathologists classify disorders broadly into categories of difficulty involving speech, language, communication, or feeding and swallowing. Speech disorders are classified further based on primary systems involved—speech sounds (articulation and phonology), voice, or fluency (stuttering). Language disorders are classified further in terms of relative effects on modalities (spoken or written; receptive or expressive), by language systems (phonology, morphology, syntax, semantics, and pragmatics), and increasingly, by language levels (sound, word, sentence, and discourse). In disorders involving communication in the broader sense, a child's speech and language may sound fairly normal from a phonological and syntactic perspective, but social-pragmatic difficulties may lead to problems of interpersonal communication, classified as pragmatic language impairment or social communication disorders. Developmental disability or acquired traumatic brain injury may lead to cognitive-communicative problems, affecting concept development and information processing, self regulation, and executive functioning. To understand relationships among diagnostic categories, it is helpful first to consider how speech, language, and communication develop and function typically.

Speech

Speech is a motor act. It involves the relatively smooth production of sequences of speech sounds representing words, phrases, and sentences through: (a) modification of respiratory processes (shortened inspiration and longer controlled expiration); (b) laryngeal control of voice onset and timing; (c) articulatory modulation of the oral cavity through adjustments of the jaw and tongue relative to the teeth, buccal surfaces, and hard palate; and (d) resonatory adjustments of the velopharyngeal mechanism. Pauses and revisions in speech production are perceived as normal unless they occur with unusual frequency and tension, prolongation, or repetition. Variations of voicing may be perceived as normal unless they result in loss of voice or chronic hoarseness (combined breathiness and tension), which may signal the presence of vocal nodules or some other structural interference with smooth voice production. Voice symptoms require medical diagnosis along with speech-language pathology assessment and intervention to reduce any abusive vocal behavior, such as yelling, singing, or talking with too much tension. Speaking is only one modality (others being written and sign language) into which language can be transformed for expressive communication.

Language

Language is a system of symbolic knowledge represented in the brain. Language knowledge is called on for both receptive and expressive communication. Whereas speech and communication both involve action and motor activity, language does not. *Speaking* and *communicating* both are verbs, but no one talks about "*languaging*."

Although language is not an action, it requires active processing. Peoples of the world speak thousands of languages and dialects, constantly evolving through geopolitical and sociological influences. Many of the world's languages have never been written down, but are contained only in the minds and communicative interactions of those who speak them. Whether spoken or written, linguists consider all the world's languages and dialects to be equally complex. All languages comprise five interrelated systems, the key defining concepts of which are summarized in Table 1.

Receptively, auditory or visual sensory input is transformed into neural information before it can be processed as meaningful language. Cranial nerves transport input to the brain.

Table 1. Five Language Systems

Phonology	The sound system of language is made up of phonemes and conventions for their combination.
Morphology	The system of smallest meaningful units of language; it includes both "free" morphemes, which can stand alone [e.g., *girl, eat, very*], and "bound" morphemes, which are affixed to other words and may be either derivational [e.g., *pre-, un-, non-, -able, -ation, -ology*] or inflectional [*-ed, -'s*].
Syntax	The grammatical system of language consists of conventions for organizing words into phrases, clauses, sentences, and complex sentences to convey causal, temporal, conditional, and other relationships.
Semantics	The meaning system of language comprises symbols for representing universal concepts, some of which are relatively concrete, such as agents, actions, and objects; and others more abstract, such as idioms and proverbs.
Pragmatics	The system of conventions for using language in socially appropriate ways, includes culturally influenced conventions for using intonation patterns, facial expressions, and other nonverbal supports for signaling true intentions, such things as humor, sarcasm, and intensity of purpose.

Most language processing is thought to occur in the peri-Sylvian area of the left hemisphere, but language interpretation involves broad cortical and subcortical contributions. The right hemisphere, in particular, is involved in inferring figurative and social meanings and interpreting nonverbal signals. While linguistic information is being received sequentially; it is decoded actively with parallel, synchronous processes that analyze and resynthesize linguistic and nonlinguistic components to construct literal and social meanings. Meanings may be concrete or abstract, direct or indirect. For example, a student might understand a teacher's irritated "Not now!" (with accompanying scowl) literally, as meaning to ask the question later. On a deeper level, the listener (and would-be speaker) also might get the indirect message that this teacher does not like being interrupted with questions. During the rapid pace of conversations, both partners must choreograph receptive-expressive moves, deciding moment-by-moment whether and how to respond and what to do with incoming information.

Expressively, individuals encode meanings that relate to prior messages and events to prepare to initiate or respond to a communication act. In verbal expression (spoken or written), language users employ neural systems strategically to transform ideas into linguistically encoded information, and then into physical reality. Speakers produce perturbations of the airstream, creating acoustic waveforms that represent words made up of morphemes and phonetic patterns that can be perceived auditorily; writers produce visual-spatial patterns that represent words made up of orthographic patterns (also representing morphemes and phonetic patterns) that can be perceived visually. In either case, language users encode concepts into linguistic forms and their physical representations by engaging speech production and/or grapho-motor (handwriting or typing) mechanisms.

Communication

Communication requires the cooperation of two communicative partners who use a combination of verbal (word-based) symbols and nonverbal (gestural and contextual) signals to co-construct meanings. One partner may talk, but unless another makes sense of the intended meaning, no communication has taken place. It also is possible to communicate meanings without words, but with a gesture or look that conveys intent. Motivated by intentions, people use verbal symbols (words) and nonverbal signals (proximity, gestures, eye gaze, facial expression) to affect other people's attention, understanding, feelings, or actions. Individuals also may use external self-talk and inner speech to communicate with themselves, supporting thinking and memory and regulating their attention, feelings, and actions.

DSM-IV Classification

The DSM-IV classification includes five disorders in which speech-language impairments are primary: *expressive language disorder* (315.31), *mixed receptive-expressive language disorder* (315.32), *phonological disorder* (315.39; formerly "developmental articulation disorder"), *stuttering* (307.0), and *communication disorder not otherwise specified* (307.9). This last category includes disorders that do not meet criteria for any specific communication disorder, such as a voice disorder. Language disorders also have implications for the acquisition of reading and writing. Thus, the DSM-IV diagnostic group of "Learning Disorders" (formerly known as "Academic Skills Disorders") is relevant as well, particularly *reading disorder* (315.00) and *disorder of written expression* (315.2).

Children and adolescents gain access to almost all other learning, formal and informal, through spoken and written language. Thus, it is not just acquisition of basic skills for reading and writing that may be affected, but also the secondary applications of language in all its modalities (listening, speaking, reading, and writing), and tertiary influences on other activities that use language for academic participation, social-interaction, and self-regulation. Even when children do not have communication *disorders*, they can improve their communication *abilities* as a means for supporting successful development in other areas, including healthy interpersonal relationships and images of themselves.

Speech, language, and communication development can be affected by essentially every other pediatric developmental disorder. Problems and delays in the development of communication skills can be the first signal that something else is wrong. Communication development (incorporating speech and language, and in many cases, feeding and swallowing) can be involved any time there is a sensory or motor impairment, intellectual disability (formerly called mental retardation), or emotional or behavioral disorder. Autism spectrum disorders, in particular, involve difficulty of social communication as a cardinal symptom. By definition, Asperger syndrome (called "Asperger disorder" in the DSM-IV-TR) must involve exclusion of language disorder as a central factor (signaled by single word production emerging by two years and communicative phrases by three years). Asperger syndrome nevertheless involves social communication difficulties that justify referral to a speech-language pathologist.

Epidemiology

Communication disorders are considered *primary* when there is no known cause to which they are attributable. They are considered *secondary* when they can be attributed to another primary (or "comorbid") condition such as autism, hearing impairment, general developmental difficulty, behavioral or emotional difficulty, or neuromotor impairment.

Prevalence estimates for LI based on epidemiological studies of the general population of Canadian and American children at the beginning of schooling have ranged from 3 to 13 percent. The current best estimate of specific language impairment (SLI) in the absence of comorbid hearing, intellectual, or neurological impairments is based on a comprehensive epidemiological study in Iowa and Illinois conducted in the 1990s. This study, known as the Epi-SLI study, revealed a prevalence rate of 7.4% (8% for boys and 6% for girls).

A national data base published by the U.S. Department of Education, Office of Special Education Programs (OSEP), for the Individuals with Disabilities Education Improvement Act (known as "IDEA") tracks data from state reports of children receiving special services by age and disability category. It does not, however, reflect dual or triple diagnoses. Thus, it is difficult to gauge the actual prevalence of speech-language impairments (and subtypes) at each age level. As children get older, they are more likely to be diagnosed with a related condition rather than speech-language impairment for school service delivery. When that occurs, speech-language impairment generally is considered secondary, which means that it becomes invisible to the federal unduplicated counting system. For example, in 2003, the national database showed the largest category for 3-year-olds to be the generic category of *developmental delay* (46% of all children identified), followed by *speech or language impairment* (39%). *Autism* (3%) formed the third largest category at age 3-years; with *specific learning disability* diagnosed in around only 1% of preschool children with disabilities. By age 6-years, only 6% of children with disabilities were identified as having *developmental delay*, 63% were identified with *speech or language impairment*, and 8% were found to have *specific learning disabilities*. By 16-years, *specific learning disabilities* made up the largest category (60%); at the same time, *speech or language impairment* dropped to 3% and was topped by *mental retardation* and *emotional disturbance* (both 12%) and other health impairments (8%). In 2003, *autism* was diagnosed in 1.3% of 16-year-olds with disabilities.

The National Research Council has reported that 80% of children with learning disabilities have a disability in reading, and a high proportion of these show difficulties in the area of phonological awareness, both forms of language impairment. Children with reading difficulties can be further classified by whether they demonstrate difficulties with the phonological aspects of language, affecting reading decoding but not listening comprehension, fitting the profile for dyslexia (36% of poor readers in one study of second graders showed this pattern); or problems with both reading decoding and listening and reading comprehension, fitting the profile for language impairment (another 36% of poor readers showed this pattern); or problems with listening and reading comprehension although able to read aloud the words on the page (15% showed this pattern). Children in the group with specific comprehension difficulties are sometimes diagnosed as having "hyperlexia." The diagnosis of hyperlexia is made when children learn to read aloud exceptionally early without instruction and also show minimal comprehension of what they read. Percentages of children fitting these varied reading profiles shift with time. By middle school, reading decoding problems remain only for those with the most severe forms of dyslexia or with intellectual disabilities, and more children show mixed disorders (involving both reading decoding and comprehension), or problems with comprehension that reflect general language weaknesses. These shifts reflect changes in response to education and intervention, and also changes in communicative contexts, particularly the higher language complexity demands in the curricular language of the upper grades.

Other disorders involve sensory and motor systems beyond those directly involved in speech and language development. *Dysarthria* is the term for motor speech disorders that involve broader neuromotor systems that affect eating and saliva control, as well as speech. In childhood, it is associated particularly with cerebral palsy, which is now estimated to occur in between 2 and 2.5 children per 1000 births. *Childhood apraxia of speech* (CAS), which involves speech control and coordination difficulties in the absence of difficulties involving feeding and oral-motor reflexes, has an estimated prevalence of about 1-10 children per 1,000. CAS (a somewhat controversial diagnosis) is the primary diagnosis for about 5 percent of children with speech-sound disorders (a newer term for articulation disorders). Children with the most severe forms of motor-speech production difficulty may require augmentative and alternative (AAC) supports to communicate. Some parents and professionals express concerns that AAC may interfere with the development of intelligible speech, but there is no evidence that it does. All children need to be able to communicate their intentions and ideas as a means to cognitive, social, and emotional health, and as a vehicle for learning language. AAC supports can provide essential access to all of these learning and relationship-building opportunities.

One to three infants per 1,000 are born deaf or hard of hearing each day in the U.S. That amounts to 33 babies per day when projected across the population of the country. Estimated prevalence figures suggest that about 3 million U.S. children currently are deaf and hard of hearing, and even more children fit this category if those with high-frequency and conductive loss are included. Early identification of hearing loss is so important that the U.S. Congress passed the Newborn Infant Hearing Screening and Intervention Act legislation in 1999 to authorize grants to states to provide Early Hearing Detection and Intervention (EHDI) programs so that newborns can be tested prior to leaving the hospital. Congress has reauthorized the grants since that time. As of 2007, 40 of the 50 United States had EHDI laws and five had voluntary compliance programs to screen the hearing of 95% or more of newborns, compared with only about 40% of infants being screened in 2000. Follow-up statistics show, however, that as many as one-third of babies who were identified in infant screening programs had not received complete diagnostic evaluations by three months of age, and less than half of infants who had been diagnosed were actually receiving early intervention services by the critical point of six months of age. Identification is not enough; an interdisciplinary effort is needed to support the process of follow-up and treatment.

Beyond motor or sensory impairments, general developmental delays or acquired disorder secondary to abuse and neglect and other forms of acquired brain injury can interfere with the development of speech, language, and communication. Diffuse insults to the central nervous system, such as those due to anoxia or traumatic brain injury, can have widespread and long lasting effects on cognitive-communication and literacy development. Each year, approximately 2 millions children and adolescents sustain central nervous system injuries as a result of falls, motor vehicle accidents, sports injuries, assaults, or abuse. Diffuse brain injury also is associated with self-regulatory issues and problems of attention and adjustment to school, including social-emotional issues, such as angry outbursts and low tolerance for frustration, making school placements problematic.

The terms *cognitive impairment* or *intellectual disability* are currently preferred by many advocacy groups to the use of the older DSM-IV terminology of *mental retardation*, with associated levels based largely on intelligent quotients (IQ). The prevalence of ID/MR between ages 5 and 65 years has been estimated to be approximately 1.5 million people, but prevalence estimates vary with definition. When based on statistical projections using the DSM-IV-TR criteria relative to the normal curve, approximately 2.5% of the population should be diagnosed with ID/MR on the basis of IQ scores. Of these, approximately 85% have mild functional limitations (IQ = 50-75); approximately 10% have moderate functional limitations (IQ = 35-50); approximately 3% have severe functional limitations (IQ = 20-35); and 1-2% have profound limitations (IQ < 20).

Other disorders that co-occur frequently with disorders of speech, language, and communication, are disorders of attention, emotion, and behavior. Some estimates place the prevalence of attention deficit disorders at from 2-7%. Language/literacy and communication difficulties also may occur in approximately 25% of children with emotional or behavioral disorders, although language deficits may go undiagnosed when behavioral disorders are primary.

In summary, epidemiological studies place the prevalence of specific language impairment at approximately 7% in children beginning school. When other forms of speech and communication disorders are considered, including those that co-occur with essentially every other developmental or acquired disability of childhood, the estimated prevalence for all communication disorders in childhood is 10-13%.

Clinical Features

Typical communication development provides a blueprint for guiding assessment processes and fostering normal development so that participation may be enhanced and disability prevented or reduced. Table 2 summarizes key features of developmental periods, as well as danger signs that all may not be going well.

Table 2. Developmental Markers and Danger Signs

Age/Stage	Developmental Benchmarks	Danger Signs
Infants/Toddlers (birth – 2;11 yrs)	• Responds to cuddling and quiets when needs are met • Engages in mutual eye gaze and synchronous interactions • Babbles canonically (*bababa, mamama*) • Responds to verbal and nonverbal signals, smiles reaches • Enjoys baby games (peekaboo, pattycake) • Finger point emerging around 10 mos • First words at around 1 yr • Vocabulary spurt around 18 mos • Combines 2 words by 24 months • Combines 3 words by 36 months	• Stiffens when held; cries when touched; feeding difficulties • Fails to meet parental eye gaze or engage in synchronous movement in first 3 mos • Few early sounds or reduction of babbling at around 8 months may signal hearing problems • Limited response to "baby talk" by 4 mos • Limited response to baby games at 10 mos • No finger point by 15 mos • No words by 18 mos • Less than 50 words by 24 mos • Few or no 2-word combinations by 24 mos • Few or no 3-word combinations by 36 mos
Preschoolers (3;0 to 5;11 yrs)	• Produces intelligible words with consonant-vowel patterns: CV, CVC, CVCV, CVCVC • Vocabulary continues to develop by leaps and bounds; can use abstract words for emotions by end of period; can play with the sound structure of words in rhymes, etc. • Sentence structure develops for expanding noun and verb phrases and for combining several ideas into one sentence by using connectors like *and, but, because.* • Play and pragmatic communication behaviors demonstrate increasing ability for symbolic representations and cooperating with peers to imitate adult communication scripts (talking on the phone, taking restaurant orders, doctor's office) • Emergent literacy for looking at books; retelling stories	• Phoneme/articulation repertoire is so limited that even caregivers cannot understand speech; produces mostly CV combinations (does not "close" syllables) • Vocabulary limited; difficulty responding to contextually supported Wh-questions (what, whose, where) at age 4 to 5 yrs • Cannot play with rhymes by age 4 to 5 yrs • Mean length of utterance of less than 3.5 words by 4 yrs • Mean length of utterance of less than 4.5 words by 5 yrs • Unresponsive to requests for information or action; limited expression of comments or questions (3 to 5 yrs) • Limited symbolic use of toys to create scenes; few coordinated actions or repetitive, nonsymbolic use of toys (e.g., spinning wheels, lining up cars without turning it into a meaningful game) • Limited interest in books; difficulty listening to or retelling stories

Table 2 – Continued

Age/Stage	Developmental Benchmarks	Danger Signs
Middle Childhood (6;0 to 10;11 yrs)	• Develops phonemic awareness for identifying initial and final sounds and the alphabetic principle for relating print symbols to speech sounds (around first grade); then orthographic awareness for relating syllable patterns to morphemes (e.g., silent –e rule; *-ough, -ight, -ing*) (by third grade) • Understands and formulates sentences with embedded and subordinated clauses representing complex temporal (*while, during*), causal (*because*), conditional (*if…then*), and logical (*whereas, however*) relationships (skills increase across grades) • Comprehends complex spoken and written texts (narrative and expository); retells, summarizes, and answers questions about them; produces stories and reports with mature organizational structures (skills increase across grades)	• Cannot identify the initial and ending sounds of words; has difficulty relating letters to speech sounds, and cannot generate intelligible spellings of CVC words by mid-first grade. • Restricted sentence length (average of less than 5 words); difficulty ordering words, with noun-verb agreement, awkward phrasing (any time) • Inadequate vocabulary for listening, speaking, reading, writing; inappropriate word choices; reliance on all-purpose words (*stuff, thing*); misunderstanding of academic relational words (*center, near, below, after*) (at grade level and lower) • Pragmatically inappropriate interactions with adults or peers; difficulty grasping subtle or indirect meanings; not accepted by peers • Difficulty with self-talk and self-regulation of attention and executive functions
Adolescence (11;0 to 20;11)	• Spells most words correctly; can read novel texts and figure out words and meanings from context, using word roots and morphological variation • Understands and produces complex sentences in spoken and written language • Develops skill for public presentation of formal oral and written discourse; revises and edits when writing; reads critically • Socially adept at forming new relationships, including with the opposite sex; varies communication style for academic, social, and vocational activities	• Ongoing difficulty with reading decoding, spelling, word analysis skills • Difficulty comprehending and producing complex sentences in spoken and written modalities • Pragmatically inappropriate interactions with adults or peers; difficulty grasping subtle or indirect meanings • Difficulty with self-talk and self-regulation of attention and executive functions

Infants, Toddlers, and Critical Foundations

As soon as they are born, babies seek out their parents' eyes and vice versa. This signals the beginning of healthy intimacy and attachment and a foundation upon which normal speech, language, and communication can be built. In the earliest stages of development, parents assign meaning to their babies' movements, moods, and noises, often interpreting them verbally, and responding to them as communicative. They follow their infants' gaze and comment on the objects of their children's attention. Gradually, infants learn to garner their parents' attention intentionally (e.g., by cooing or moving body parts and smiling when attention is achieved). They also learn to follow a parent's gaze to look at objects (e.g., the family dog) while the parent is talking about them. This supports the development of verbal concepts. The healthy baby also learns to draw parental attention to an object by reaching for it and looking at the parent and vocalizing. Gradually, these behaviors turn into the intentional finger point. The use of the finger pointing gesture and shift of eye contact between another's eyes and objects is considered a critical sign of intentional communication. If it remains absent after 12-15 months of age, it may be a symptom of risk for autism spectrum disorder or other cognitive-communicative impairment.

While the foundations of social communication are emerging, knowledge of the phonological system of language also is being shaped. Unless a hearing impairment interferes, a baby's babbling is narrowed from universal forms into the sound system of the family's native language over the first year of life. Canonical babbling (e.g., *bababa*, or *dadada*) should be clearly evident by around 8 months. If not, hearing may be suspect. Phonemes are combined into morphemes (meaningful units) when children learn to speak their first intelligible words to refer to things (e.g., *cookie, bottle, mama, dada*), actions (e.g., *up, bye bye, kiss*), or qualities (e.g., *hot, ucky*). These miraculous but commonplace developments occur with little deliberate effort or planning (but with much fanfare) in homes where infants receive adequate nurturing and when sensory and regulatory systems are adequate for infants to organize themselves, find contact and interaction with others pleasurable, and make sense of their external world and place within it.

At around two-years of age children begin to combine words into phrases. Toddlers who are producing fewer than 50 words and limited word combinations by 24 months meet criteria for a diagnosis of "late talker" (also called expressive language delay and specific language impairment-expressive). Many children who start out as late talkers appear to "catch up" by four or five years, especially if their problems are specifically expressive. Literature on late talkers, however, portrays a heterogeneous group, and the difficulty of predicting who will and will not "catch up" supports the need for referral for speech-language assessment and consultation, if not intervention. The general wisdom is that it is better to "watch and wait" (following speech-language assessment) rather than to "wait and see." If children's word production attempts are unintelligible, it is appropriate to provide intervention earlier rather than later. If eye contact and finger pointing and other signs of healthy nonverbal and social communication are absent, it is important not to wait, as absence of nonverbal communication is an important early appearing clinical feature of autism spectrum disorder.

Preschoolers and the Amazing Growth of Grammar

As children enter into daycare and relatively more formal preschool settings, their worlds expand, as does their knowledge of language and communication conventions. If all goes well, children learn to interpret the nonverbal communicative signals and to comprehend the language of adults other than their parents, to play with peers, and to represent more complex concepts in play. This is a time in which language knowledge explodes and grammatical foundations are laid. By the time children enter school they should be able to comprehend and produce complex sentences with embedding and subordination, as long as the vocabulary and underlying concepts are within their grasp. It is also a time when they should be playing with the sounds of words (in nursery rhymes and word play) and should be introduced to the alphabet and the sounds that letters make. These activities appear to contribute to *phonological awareness* (explicit knowledge that words are made up of speech sounds) which is an important predictor and precursor of the ability to learn to read and write. Parents should be encouraged to allow their children access to paper and writing utensils during the preschool period as well.

Childhood Years and the Development of Reading and Writing

The transition from home to school, which occurs at around 5 years, often means leaving more familiar communication settings for less familiar ones, and the degree of familiarity is often a function of socioeconomic level and cultural-linguistic match. Children move from situations in which much of the meaning, generally associated with social interactions, can be found in the nonverbal context, to situations in which academic meanings as well as social ones must be abstracted from the words (i.e., a shift from *contextualized* to *lexicalized* meanings).

Children need a well developed language system for knowing what to do in school and how to listen to and understand their teachers' instructional language. This includes narrative (stories) and expository (informational) discourse in books and other media. It also includes making friends and interacting with peers in play and cooperative learning contexts. Successful school-age children and adolescents learn to use self-talk for supporting idea development in internal and external thought. Self-talk also supports executive control for setting goals, organizing approaches to problem solving, maintaining attention to difficult tasks, stabilizing emotions while working through stressful situations, and evaluating outcomes.

Children with speech-language impairments are at high risk for difficulty learning to read. Those with speech impairments involving only articulation have lower risks, but kindergartners with difficulties involving phonological awareness and rapid naming of pictures or objects have increased risks for difficulty with written word recognition, and children with semantic-syntactic spoken language difficulties have increased risks for difficulty with reading comprehension. Children who demonstrate nonspecific language impairment in kindergarten (i.e., language delay accompanied by signs of developmental delay in broader systems) have high risk for literacy learning problems in second and fourth grade.

Adolescent Increases in Social, Academic, and Vocational Language Abilities

During adolescence, children undergo rapid changes in their physical, cognitive, and social-emotional development. They are becoming adults physically and developing the ability to use what Piaget called "formal thought" to reason out problems intellectually and entertain multiple points of view. Adolescents also are mired in the difficult business of figuring out their identities while negotiating the complexities of same and different sex relationships.

In the area of language learning, this is a time in normal development when abstract language use, higher cognitive functions, and executive control mechanisms are integrated and applied to solving the problems presented by social, academic, and vocational demands. Children with speech-language and communication difficulties need contextually based interventions to help them develop higher-level literate language abilities and social interaction sensitivities.

Diagnosis

When diagnosing communication disorders (the broadest categorical term), one of the first questions speech-language pathologists ask, along with the status of hearing, is the degree to which speech, language, and communication are relatively affected. Although deeply connected, aspects of speech, language, and communication may function somewhat independently. Discontinuity often signals disorder, but also may point to strengths available for facilitating activity and participation. As described previously, speech-language and communication abilities involve varying degrees of overlap not only with each other, but also comorbid conditions.

Speech Sound Disorder

In early childhood (ages 3- to 8-years), difficulty with speech sound production is likely to signal the need for communication assessment to parents and health care providers. Children whose primary difficulty is in the area speech sound production may be diagnosed as having *articulation impairment*. This diagnosis emphasizes difficulty with articulation function (i.e., accurate production of the desired sound with all its features). The newer DSM-IV diagnosis of *phonological disorder* emphasizes deficits with linguistic concepts of phonemes (e.g., treating /r/ and /l/ as members of the same phonological category with /w/). Because speech sound production ability is thoroughly intertwined with inner knowledge of linguistic phonology, the currently preferred diagnosis by speech-language pathologists is neither of these, but instead, *speech-sound disorder*. This term incorporates elements both of articulation and phonology without assuming dominance of either motor production or linguistic classification.

When children exhibit extreme difficulty with the motor control and coordination needed to articulate many different phonemes and sequence them smoothly in words, they may be diagnosed as having developmental, or childhood apraxia of speech (CAS). This diagnosis applies when word production is inconsistent and involves sequencing errors that increase in longer words and utterances and when oral-motor groping movements occur with imitation attempts.

Procedures for diagnosing speech-sound disorder varies with the child's age, but they often involve an inventory of the child's ability to produce all of the sounds of the language in all positions in words using a picture naming task, with comparison to standardized norms. Additional testing involves constructing an inventory of the child's "nonlinear" speech production skills in a sample of spontaneous speech at phrase levels, as well as in individual words. Hearing and oral-motor examinations are standard components of diagnostic procedures for speech-sound disorders.

Fluency Disorder

Fluency disorders are diagnosed by speech-language pathologists based on samples of spontaneous speech gathered in a variety of speaking contexts. Diagnosis is made when speech flow is characterized by atypical rate, rhythm, and repetitions of sounds, syllables, words, and phrases, possibly accompanied by excessive tension, struggle, and secondary mannerisms (e.g., eye blinks or foot tapping). The identification of stuttering is highest between a child's second and fourth birthdays, at which point girls and boys are approximately equally affected. Although many children show unassisted recovery from early abnormal difficulties with speech fluency, approximately 20-25% (3 times more boys than girls) continue to demonstrate abnormal types and amounts of dysfluency, requiring intervention.

Language Impairment and Learning Disability

The group of children with language-learning disabilities (LLD) includes children and adolescents with language impairment (LI), which is diagnosed by speech-language pathologists based on standardized language assessment instruments, parent input, and analysis of spontaneous language samples. Specific language impairment (SLI) is diagnosed when children's language abilities are below normal limits, but their cognitive abilities are within normal limits and there is a discrepancy between the two measures. The category of LI also includes children with nonspecific language impairment (NLI), which is diagnosed when cognitive skills and language abilities are both low, but still above the level for diagnosing ID/MR (i.e., with an IQ of ≥ 75). The official term for receiving federally mandated services under IDEA is "speech or language impairment" (S-LI).

When children experience excessive difficulty learning to read, they may be diagnosed as having reading delay or disability (RD) by psychologists and educational specialists, which qualifies them to receive special help at school, although not as part of special education. Increasingly schools are using "Response-to-Intervention" (RTI) programs to provide tiers of services that are individualized for children who are struggling to learn to read, in particular, but also for other learning and social difficulties. The official term for receiving federally mandated special education for disorders of listening, speaking, reading, writing, spelling, and mathematical reasoning is "learning disability" (LD). Diagnosis of LD is made by a team of specialists (often following three tiers of RTI services), including a school psychologist, learning disability specialist, and speech-language pathologist. Members of the team administer psychological tests to measure verbal and nonverbal IQ (usually administered by the school psychologist), academic achievement tests (usually administered by a teacher consultant who specializes in LD), and language tests (usually administered by a speech-language pathologist). Comprehensive assessment is needed, as no single instrument can be used to diagnose LD. It requires a pattern of difficulty that persists in spite of appropriate educational services and evidence of nonverbal cognitive ability within normal limits.

Autism Spectrum Disorders

Children with autism spectrum disorders (ASD) demonstrate language learning and use problems as core deficits. They can have difficulty with all aspects of speech, language, and communication development. A cardinal feature, however, is the presence of social-comprehension difficulties that make it difficult to infer the social meanings of language.

Specialized assessment tools and observational checklists are available for use by interdisciplinary teams with specialized expertise in diagnosing autism spectrum disorders. Speech-language pathologists play a role in interviewing parents and conducting careful observation of preverbal and nonverbal communication interactions, as well as conducting formal and informal language assessment. Diagnosis is based on symptoms observed in social communication contexts involving play, as well as in conversational interactions. Early identification is a goal so that intensive interventions can be provided as soon as possible. Family physicians and pediatricians can play an important role in remaining alert to early danger signs, such as problems with shared visual attention, lack of ability and apparent interest in soliciting the attention of others (e.g., by finger pointing), and slow or unusual language development (e.g., echolalia of the words of others in nonmeaningful ways, or early reading in the absence of social communication and interaction).

Treatment

Speech-language intervention services are provided by speech-language pathologists following diagnosis and comprehensive assessment of a child's or adolescent's individualized pattern of strengths and needs. Treatments vary based on the age, diagnosis, and specific needs of the child. Increasingly, speech-language pathologists are adopting the procedures of evidence-based practice that mirror those used in evidence-based medicine. Clinicians are limited, however, by the limited number of scientific studies of intervention practices and often must rely on authoritarian sources and their own clinical expertise. The need to consider family and client values and circumstances also plays a major role in the provision of services to children and families with communication disorders. Federal, state, and local policies also influence service delivery. The following brief overview describes some of the primary principles that guide intervention for disorders of speech, language, and communication, many of which could be encouraged by physicians in their interactions with families whose children are demonstrating risks for, or diagnosed, communication disorders.

An over-riding principle is to place communication effectiveness and completeness primary to speech or language "correctness." The first goal of intervention should be to help communicative partners show interest and attention to the child's objects of attention and ideas. This involves getting on the child's level, both literally and figuratively. Parents of infants and toddlers are encouraged to follow their child's gaze and comment on objects of interest. They are encouraged to match their child's level of language and to offer new models in meaningful contexts that are only a little more complex than what their child is currently saying. All toddlers and preschoolers need exposure to books, and interactions with books and talk about words can lead to higher level vocabulary and preparation for school. Parents should help their children focus on the meaning of the pictures before asking them to listen to the words being read aloud. Gradually, children will be able to listen to longer passages. Toddlers and preschoolers also should be encouraged and supported to use language in play, and to use their imaginations to create scenes with toy people, animals, and objects.

School-age children need to experience success in both social and academic settings. The principle of showing interest in children's thoughts and ideas remains important for encouraging higher level language development. When children show resistance to learning to read and write, their parents can tuck funny and loving notes under their bedroom doors or in lunch boxes and encourage their children to write back. They can seek books that attract their child's interests and take turns reading paragraphs and pages.

Formal language and literacy intervention practices for school-age children involve modeling and feedback focused on features of language that are missing or immature and just above the child's current developmental level. Children with phonological language weaknesses may require intensive explicit instruction in sound-symbol associations (phonics) that incorporates awareness of how sounds are made in the mouth. Children with social-interaction difficulties may require contextualized interventions in which the clinician works with peer partners as well as with the child with disability to make language-learning contexts more facilitative, along with explicit instruction in how to interact socially.

Interdisciplinary approaches are important to address complex communication needs. Children with autism spectrum disorders present particular challenges. Two primary approaches to intervention are based on behaviorist and social-interactionist theory. In approaches based on "applied behavioral analysis" (ABA), children are engaged in one-to-one sessions with explicit stimulus-response-reinforcement exchanges designed to teach discrete skills. In social interactionist approaches, the focus is on helping children learn the value of social interaction and meaning making through intensified interactions with communication partners. The evidence for these two approaches is interpreted differently by professionals depending on their theoretical preferences, but both appear to be effective with some children for teaching some skills at some levels of development.

Conclusion

Children in nurturing environments generally learn to regard communication as a successful and rewarding experience. If neurocognitive and caregiver nurturing resources are adequate, a child's speech-language abilities are likely to develop normally. Even when a child's central nervous system is not adequate to support normal speech motor-control or language and literacy learning, interdisciplinary assessments and interventions can capitalize on strengths, reduce impairments, and provide technological supports for reducing disability by increasing meaningful activity and participation.

Diagnosis of speech, language, and communication disorders is a complex process that varies with the age of the child and the nature of the disorder and any co-morbid conditions. Diagnosis and treatment of communication disorders justifies interdisciplinary input and collaboration, with family members playing a central role in both assessment and intervention.

References

American Psychiatric Association. *Diagnostic and Statistical Manual of Mental Disorders*, 4th edition, Text Revision (DSM-IV-TR). Washington, DC, American Psychiatric Association, 2000.

Catts HW, Fey M, Tomblin B, Zhang X. A longitudinal investigation of reading outcomes in children with language impairments. *J. Speech, Language, Hearing Research* 2002;45:1142–1157.

Catts HW, Hogan TP, Adlof SM. Developmental changes in reading and reading disabilities. In H. W. Catts and A. G. Kamhi (Eds.), *The Connections BetweenLanguage and Reading Disabilities*. Mahwah, NJ: Lawrence Erlbaum, 2005:25-40.

Greenspan SI: *The Growth of the Mind*. Reading, MA, Perseus Books, 1997.

Kelly DJ: A clinical synthesis of the "late talker" literature: Implications for service delivery. *Language, Speech, Hearing Services in Schools* 1998;29:76-84.

Nelson NW: *ChildhoodLanguage Disorders in Context: Infancy through Adolescence*, 2nd ed. Boston, MA, Allyn and Bacon, 1998.

Prelock PA. *Autism Spectrum Disorders: Issues in Assessment and Intervention*. Austin, TX: ProEd, 2006.

Tomblin JB, Records, NL, Buckwalter P, Zhang X, Smith E, O'Brien M Prevalence of specific language impairment in kindergarten children. *J. Speech, Language, Hearing Research*, 1997;40:1245–1260.

U.S. Department of Education, Office of Special Education Programs, Data Analysis System (DANS). Data Tables for OSEP State Reported Data based on the December 1, 2003 count, updated as of July 31, 2004. http://www.ideadata.org/ Accessed 10/14/04.

In: Behavioral Pediatrics, 3rd Edition
Editor: Donald E. Greydanus et al.

ISBN 978-1-60692-702-1
© 2009 Nova Science Publishers, Inc.

Chapter 6

Autism Spectrum Disorders

Ahsan Nazeer

Abstract

Autism that was initially described by Leo Kanner in his 11 case studies now appears to affect an estimated 3 per1000 children. Autistic Disorder itself belongs to a larger category of disorders classified as pervasive developmental disorders (*PDD)* or autism spectrum disorders (*ASD*) which also includes Asperger disorder, childhood disintegrative disorder, Rett's disorder and pervasive developmental disorder not otherwise specified (*PDD- NOS*). All these disorders have unique set of symptoms that are specific for each disorder but also share the core symptoms of social impairment, communication impairment and restricted, repetitive patterns of behaviors, among themselves. With the exception of Asperger disorder and PDD NOS, most of these disorders can be reliably diagnosed during infancy or early childhood.

In this chapter, we will present an overview of the types and the will address the diagnosis, differential diagnosis and management of autism spectrum disorders.

Introduction

Autism, a developmental disorder, the history of which spans well over 65 years has been conceptualized and understood in a variety of ways. Eugen Bleuler initially used "Autism" as a term in 1912 to describe the "self-absorption" or "withdrawal from reality" as one of the pathognomonic features of schizophrenia.

In 1943, Leo Kanner, an Austrian-American psychiatrist recounted eleven case studies in his seminal paper, "Autistic Disturbances of Affective Contact". He described these children to be born with out the ability to make social relationships and used the term "autism" to describe the psychopathology. Some of the characteristics features that he identified included: limited ability to develop relationships, language delays, aloofness, lack of imagination and persistence on sameness. Kanner was aware of the previous use of the word "autism" and its association with schizophrenia and though in later years he used the term "Early Infantile Autism" to describe the same set of characteristics but the use of the same term, which was initially used to describe adult schizophrenia, stirred significant controversies in the way autism was conceptualized for the next 20 years. Finally, in 1968, Michael Rutter identified four core symptom clusters of autistic disorder: social impairment, language disturbances, ritualistic behaviors and onset before 30 months of age, that were later adopted, with modifications and changes, by the Diagnostic and Statistical Manual of Mental Disorders (DSM) systems of classification. Diagnostic and Statistical Manual of Mental Disorders, Third Edition, Revised (DSM-III-R) in 1987 was the first to include autism as a separate diagnostic entity.

Definitions

Autism spectrum disorders (*ASD*) are characterized by impairment in social interactions, language deficits and ritualistic and repetitive behaviors with onset prior to 3 years of age. It is worth noting that the terms "pervasive developmental disorders" and "autism spectrum disorders" have more recently been used interchangeably. National Institute of Child Health and Human Development and educational facilities uses the term "autism spectrum disorder", while the Diagnostic and Statistical Manual identifies these disorders as "Pervasive Developmental Disorders". For the sake of continuity, in the following text we will use the term "autism spectrum disorders" to broadly classify these disorders.

DSM-IV-TR (text-revision) identifies five disorders under the broader category of pervasive developmental disorders (*PDD*) or autism spectrum disorders as listed in Table 1. These disorders though share the same core diagnostic criteria but have important differences. Because of this, it is important to diagnose a child with specific subtypes than using the broad category of PDD as a diagnostic entity.

Table 1. Autism spectrum disorders

Autistic Disorder
Asperger's Disorder
Childhood Disintegrative Disorder
Rett's Disorder
Pervasive Developmental Disorder NOS (not otherwise specified)

Autistic Disorder

In order to qualify for a diagnosis of autistic disorder, DSM-IV-TR requires impairment in social interactions (lack of social reciprocity, impairment in eye contact, failure to develop peer relationships), impairment in communication (delay in language acquisition, impairment in ability to initiate or sustain conversation, repetitive use of language), and stereotypic pattern of behavior (restricted pattern of interest, inflexible routines and repetitive motor mannerisms), all with onset prior to 3 years of age.

Asperger's Disorder

Asperger's disorder is a part of autism spectrum disorders in which impairment in social interactions and stereotypic patterns of behavior are present with *normal intelligence* and *relatively normal language development*. Individuals with Asperger's disorder do not have any clinically significant delays in language or cognitive development. In other words, this diagnosis is reserved for individuals who present with autistic features but are verbal and have normal IQ's. DSM-IV-TR describes language delays as single word use by age 2 years and phrases by 3 years of age.

Childhood Disintegrative Disorder (CDD)

CDD, also called Heller's syndrome, is a relatively rare disorder that presents with hallmark features of normal development till 2 years of age and then loss of social, intellectual and language skills by 3-4 years of age (by 10 years of age as per DSM-IV-TR). Affected individuals lose the acquired skills in play, language, self-care, bowel and bladder control. They appear autistic clinically but their histories suggest different trajectories to the current symptomatology.

Rett's Disorder

Rett's disorder is another autism spectrum disorder with distinctive history and presentation. Originally described in girls (as genetic mutation were believed to be too severe to be compatible with life in males) but now considered to be prevalent in boys also, this disorder presents with normal development till at least 6 months of age followed by deceleration in head growth, loss of social skills, mental retardation and characteristic hand-wringing movements.

Pervasive Developmental Disorder-Not Otherwise Specified (PDD-NOS)

DSM-IV-TR reserves this category for the individuals who presents with impairment in social interactions, communication skills or stereotypic behaviors but does not meet the full diagnostic criteria of autistic disorder, asperger's disorder, childhood disintegrative disorder and Rett's disorder. This is an evolving diagnosis and DSM does not provide any specific diagnostic criteria to help with diagnosis.

Multiplex Developmental Disorder (MDD)

MDD is a research category and is not included in the current version of DSM. It encompasses the individuals who display autistic features but also have symptoms of thought disorder including delusions and impaired reality testing. In other words, this category involves individuals who are at the junction of autism and schizophrenia.

Epidemiology

Because of the changes in diagnostic criteria over the last 10-15 years, there had been very few systematic studies to understand the epidemiology and prevalence of autism spectrum disorders. Some recent reports though have suggested that the prevalence of these disorders is on the rise. Fombonne (2005) in his review of 34 surveys, conducted in 14 countries, identified the median prevalence for autistic disorder to be at 13 per 10,000, Asperger's Disorder 2.6/10,000, Childhood disintegrative disorder 0.2/10,000 and PDD NOS to be at 20.8/10,000. However the cumulative prevalence of all PDD cases was at 36.6/10,000 with some new data suggesting it to be as high as 60-65 per 10,000 children.

In the United States, Center for Disease Control's Autism and Developmental Disabilities Monitoring Network reported an average incident of 6.6 per 1000 eight years old children. No precise explanation of the recent rise in the prevalence is known but theories range from more awareness in medical and general population to the broadening in diagnostic criteria. The mean male to female ration among studies was 4:1. This difference in sex ratio though disappears in children with moderate to severe mental retardation with male to female ratio of 2:1. Studies have failed to find a correlation between autistic disorders and race, geographical areas or social class. At this time there are no clear theories of what causes autism spectrum disorders; a higher rate of seizures and mental retardation among these individuals point towards biological factors.

Clinical Features

The clinical presentation of autism spectrum disorders is heterogeneous and depends upon the age of the patient, severity of symptoms and associated comorbidities. Despite this, the three core symptoms as described by DSM-IV and characteristic features of individual disorders usually lead to the diagnosis.

Impairment in Social Skills

Lack of social reciprocity remains to be one of the hallmark features of autism spectrum disorders. This impairment is evident even from early infancy and parents usually report a child who is "aloof" and does not like to be cuddled or touched. These infants do not seek human interactions or feel any joy in relationships. They do not come to parents with expectations to be cuddled or hugged and usually do not assume the anticipatory postures. They usually do not imitate the actions of parents, like, clapping hand, saying "bye bye" or playing social games like peek-a-boo. Infants as young as 6 months of age tend to avoid social stimuli and prefer non-social interactions. They tend to look at stationary inanimate objects instead of mom's eyes. Because their attachment with parental figures is impaired, they do not develop stranger anxiety. They do not respond to their names and studies have found that children who do not respond to their name by 12 months of age are at higher risk of developing autism as compared to the norms. It is because of this inability to respond that sometimes parents suspect that their child is deaf.

Researchers at CDC have emphasized certain warning signs in children at risk of developing autism spectrum disorders, as listed in Table 2.

"Impaired joint attention", is another hallmark symptom of autism in infancy. Briefly, *joint attention* is the phenomenon in which the child attends to the same object in the environment that his parents are attending to. Child then alters his gaze from the object to the parent and back to the object and then communicates with gestures and limited verbal skills. This is usually considered a pre-verbal phase of development and is important for language, communication and social development. This also reflects the child's understanding of his surroundings and his motivation to interact with others. Researchers have found deficits in joint attention to be one of the earliest sign of autism. Because of the heterogeneity in the age of diagnosis, the above-mentioned symptoms present as warning signs that justify closer follow up and further evaluation rather than the diagnostic symptoms.

As these children continued to grow, social deficits become starker. Inability to make the eye contact becomes more prominent. They continue to withdraw from social situations and show lack of interest in making friends. Some might develop friendships but because of their inflexible routines and their insistence on playing games by their own rules, these friendships usually do not last long.

These children also display lack of understanding of others' feelings and are at a loss in understanding social cues. This leads them to engage in socially inappropriate behaviors, for example, speaking with out thinking about the impact of their words, which further limit their friendships. This further leads to the development of depressive and anxiety disorder in early to later adolescent years.

Table 2. Warning signs in children at risk of developing autism spectrum disorders

Failure to respond to sounds during the first two months of life
Failure to initiate reciprocal behavior with parents by four months
Failure to start or initiate interactions with the parents at nine months of age. This includes exchanging smiles and imitating behaviors
Using parents' body parts as an extension of their own body, for example, using their hands to pick up toys

Impairment in Communication

Language delays are one of the most important reason for which parents seek medical help. This is also one of the hallmark symptoms of autistic disorder, though some times differentiation between autism and language disorders can be difficult with out formal speech and language testing. Speech and language development starts earlier in infancy and first 2-3 years are the most active time period for child to develop comprehensive speech and language abilities. Normally, children start babbling randomly around 3-4 months of age and start imitating parent's speech by 10-12 months. By 12 months most children can say 1-2 words and increase their vocabulary to 5-20 words by 18 months of age. Any lag in the above mentioned sequence constitutes language delays. For the sake of autistic disorder, DSM-IV defines language delays as the "inability to speak single word by 2 years and communicative phrases by 3 years of age".

Like other symptoms, speech and language abnormalities in autism are dependent upon the severity of the disorder. Deficits range from no speech and language abilities in severely autistic children to minimal abnormalities in articulation and pragmatics (social use of language) in individuals with mild form of autism. Children who can speak may have deviant language development. From infancy, they have abnormalities in babbling. Older autistic children can repeat other's phrases with out associating any meanings or emotions to it. In extreme cases this may lead parents to think that child is defiant and is doing this intentionally, which in-turn leads to further discord in the family who already is dealing with the stress of an autistic child. Pronoun reversal, when present, is another characteristic feature of deviant language development in autistic disorders. Others have difficulties with pragmatics or the correct social use of language. They say inappropriate things during conversations and have difficulty in understanding verbal and non-verbal clues. They also have difficulty in initiating and sustaining conversations. The quality of their speech is monotonous and sometimes chanting in nature. Because of the concrete nature of their speech and thought process, they have difficulty in understanding proverbs and metaphors. Their speech is factual and is limited to the content of the matter. Some children also display impaired pronunciation.

Abnormalities in language and communication are different in autism and in Asperger's disorder. Asperger's disorder is a part of the ASD that presents with normal intelligence and relative perseverance of speech and language. Even though these children do not present with language delays, their language displays characteristic abnormalities. Their speech is usually pedantic (dull, formal) in nature and monotonous. They have difficulties in understanding other's point of view and tend to talk in lecture format with rapid presentation of information that may or may not be relevant to the topic of discussion. These individuals also tend to talk in detail about the topics that they are interested in and have difficulties in understanding and explaining personal feelings. This leads to "one-sided-conversation" in which others do not feel like being listened to. Impairment in social skills further complicate their ways of communication and because of their flat facial affect, pedantic nature of speech and lack of eye contact, they are considered inappropriate in social gatherings. They usually do well in formal speech testing but reveal deficiencies in pragmatic use of language. Broadly, these impairments in communication further complicate the social interactions with peers and lead the autistic individuals to a down ward spiral.

Ritualistic Interests and Activities

Other than impairments in social interactions and communication, DSM-IV-TR requires at least one symptom from, "restricted pattern of interest, inflexible routines, repetitive motor mannerisms or preoccupations with a part of the object" to diagnose the autistic disorder.

"Restricted interests" constitute an important feature of autistic disorders. By around 2-5 years of age, children start engaging themselves in some form of ritualistic behaviors, but in most of the instances, these are neither fixed nor intense. Autistic children on the other hand engage themselves in behaviors that are intense in nature. They are time consuming and remain for extended periods of time. Some of these behaviors include, opening and closing a door multiple times, spinning toys, touching different objects and watching ceiling fan spinning. Children with Asperger's disorder usually have finer and sophisticated interests including preoccupations with computers, dinosaurs, trains and Roman mythologies. They spend extensive amount of time gathering information about their topics of interests and display behavioral dyscontrol problems if their parents or teachers ask them to focus on other subjects. These children usually enjoy these activities, likes to talk about them and feel motivated to continue pursuing these interests. This is in contrast to the obsessions in which individuals complete an act to avoid the unwanted thoughts and feelings. Some autistic individual though develop compulsions during the course of their illness and a specialty referral is usually warranted to differentiate these symptoms from other ritualistic behaviors.

Individuals with severe autistic symptoms usually present with more primitive ritualistic behaviors including hand flapping and walking on tiptoes. Some have multiple self-injurious behaviors including biting themselves and head banging.

Miscellaneous Symptoms

These symptoms are not part of the DSM-IV diagnostic criteria but are often found in clinical settings. Most frequently presenting symptoms among this category are the sensory sensitivities. Most children with ASD usually present with history of hypersensitivities to different sensory stimuli. Parents usually give history of sensitivities to shirt tags, certain type of fabrics, smells, sounds or bright lights. Some of these individuals also have higher pain thresholds and usually do not complain of pain even after serious injuries.

Gross and fine motor movements may be impaired in individuals with autistic disorders. Parents usually give history of poor performance in sports or being "clumsy in tasks that require coordination. Patterns of cognitive impairment can be different among the subgroups, with autistic disorders presenting with lower verbal IQ (VIQ) and higher performance IQ (PIQ), and Asperger's disorder showing reverse trend with higher VIQ then PIQ.

Along with the above core features, different disorders in autism spectrum present with some characteristics features that can help with the diagnosis. These features are described below.

Specific Features

Autistic Disorder

Symptoms of social impairment are usually evident from infancy when parents notice that the child does not like to be hugged and prefers to be in his own world. Around 10-12 months, language delays start becoming apparent and parents seek medical care for evaluation of hearing and vision. In severe cases speech is usually absent. Lorna Wing described the characteristic pattern of relatedness in these children as "aloof or passive". They also have cognitive impairment, behavioral dyscontrol issues and stereotypes. Most of these children are usually diagnosed before 3 years of age.

Asperger's Disorder

These children usually come to clinical attention after three years of age or more often during their 2nd or 3rd grade when the social difficulties start becoming apparent. By definition these children do not have any language delays or cognitive impairment. As mentioned above, their language is deviant and has characteristic pattern. Some of them have advanced speech acquisition. Their social deficits are mild and their interests are more refined and sophisticated.

Childhood Disintegrative Disorder (CDD)

Children with childhood disintegrative disorders develop age appropriate skills in verbal and non-verbal communication, play, social relationships by 2 years of age and then lose these skills before 10 years of age. A typical history is of a child with no developmental delays and achieving normal milestones by 2-3 years of age, suddenly started regressing by 3rd birthday. These individuals also started losing their intellectual abilities, even though this is not a diagnostic feature in DSM.

DSM-IV requires loss of skills in at least 2 of the following areas; language (ability to talk and to understand), adaptive behavior (ability to self care), play, bowel and bladder control and motor skills. Along with this, DSM-IV also requires impairment in at least 2 of the core symptoms of pervasive developmental disorders i.e. social interactions, communication and repetitive patterns of behavior. Even though CDD is sometimes is associated with lipid storage diseases, tuberous sclerosis and subacute sclerosing panencephalitis, in majority if cases extensive neurological work up fails to point to a specific pathology.

Rett's Disorder

Rett's disorder has also characteristic presentation. In this disorder children usually develop normally till 6 months of age and then they lose the previously acquired skills in socialization, language and motor skills. They also display characteristic features of "hand-wringing or hand washing" movements. Children have normal head circumference at birth and by 5 months, a deceleration is also noted. This disorder was thought to be present only in girls but there have been some recent reports of boys with this disorder.

Pervasive Developmental Disorder NOS

This category is used when there is impairment in communication; socialization with stereotypic patterns of behaviors, but the criteria does not meet for the diagnosis of above four disorders.

Diagnosis

Assessment

With the increase in prevalence and awareness of ASD, families are seeking more and more help for evaluation and treatment of their children. In this regard, primary care physicians are in a unique position as they have the opportunity to observe and identify any deviant symptoms from the infancy to late adolescent years. This early identification and intervention is the key for better long-term outcomes in these children.

On the other hand, for multiple reasons, early identification of autistic individuals has proven to be a challenge over years. A recent study from Center for Disease Control (CDC) showed a thirteen-month delay between evaluation of autistic children and their final diagnosis. This delay was universal across sex and racial lines. Study also found that initially these children were diagnosed with developmental delays and language disorders. Different organizations including American Academy of Pediatrics (AAP) and American Academy of Neurology (AAN) have established practice parameters to help the primary care physicians with early identification and diagnosis.

Broadly, assessment of autistic disorders includes multiple components and participation of multidisciplinary teams. Though, assessment are best done is specialized centers, it is important to maintain a high level of suspicion so that an early referral can be made.

Clinical and Developmental History

As mentioned in other parts of this text, autism and related disorders are characterized by impairment in three domains i.e. social interactions, communication deficits and repetitive and stereotypic behaviors. These symptoms are easier to elicit in school age children than in infants or preschool children. Studies have found impairments in verbal and non-verbal behaviors along with impairments in symbolic play to be the key features aiding in early diagnosis.

Deficits in school age children are more pronounced and some of the specific questions that can be asked about their social deficits are listed in Table 3, about communication are Table 4, about restricted interests and stereotypic behaviors in Table 5.

Table 3. Questions to assess social deficits

Able to relate with others (these individuals tend to be alone and do not appear to seek relatedness)
Ability to reciprocate affection and love by others
Number of friends and quality of friendships
Level of eye contact
Ability to understand other's emotions and feelings (Theory of mind)
Lack of socially appropriate facial expressions

Table 4. Questions to assess communication

History of language delays
Ability to communicate with others (because of the social issues, children with autism may not feel the need for interactions with others)
Ability to comprehend the speech
Difficulties with articulation and pronunciation
Immature use of grammar
Lack of empathy
Problems in social use of language
Echolalia
Pronoun reversals
Pedantic speech (speech that is focused on details, long-winded, one sided and in which individual keeps on talking about his favorite topic irrespective of the discussion at hand)

Table 5. Questions to assess restricted interests and stereotypic pattern of behavior

Hand flapping
Head banging
Touching things in systematic manner
Rocking
Walking on tip toes
Preoccupation with parts of object
Restricted interests that are abnormal in frequency and intensity (e.g. a 4 year old getting interested in the mechanical functioning of railroad steam engines and start gathering models and books about them)

Medical Assessment

Medical assessment is based on a thorough history (Table 6), focused physical examination (Table 7), and appropriate laboratory tests (Table 8), as indicated.

Table 6. Key points in medical history

Detailed pre-natal, birth and post-natal history of any medical complications
Complication during delivery
Family history
History of genetic transmission of diseases
History of ear infections
History of generalized viral ill or streptococcus throat (for PANDAS)
Chronic gastrointestinal problems (some studies have pointed towards an association between chronic GI infections and development of autism)
Vaccination history and response to vaccinations
Response to pain
History of seizures

Table 7. Key points in physical examination

Height and weight
Wood's lamp examination for tuberous sclerosis
Hearing evaluation
Visual acuity
Increased head circumference (Non specific sign but initially pointed out by Kanner and later by others)
Detailed neurological examination to review any localized deficits
Soft neurological signs including fine and gross motor impairment (clumsiness that some authors have suggested to be a symptom of Asperger's disorder)

Table 8. Laboratory tests

Basic tests including complete blood count, basic metabolic panel
Fasting lipid and glucose levels (as baseline incase of psychopharmacological interventions are required)
Urinanalysis
Electrocardiogram
Electroencephalogram. Studies have found about 30% of the autistic population to have seizure disorders. Most common variety is of complex partial seizures. Other important consideration to perform an EEG is Landau-Kleffner syndrome (a disorder in which children lose speech at 2 years of age because of epileptiform discharges in language areas)
Chromosomal analysis for karyotyping and Fragile-X
Magnetic resonance imaging studies of the brain
Hearing and vision testing

Autism Rating Scales

Depending on the age of the patient and setting of administration, numerous rating scales are available to help with the diagnosis. Some are appropriate for primary care settings, while others require formal training to administer, and are summarized in Table 9.

Table 9. Autism rating scales

Checklist for Autism in Toddlers (*CHAT*)	Appropriate for a quick screen (<5 minutes), this test can be administered to children ages 18-24 months and is suitable for primary care settings. Section A of this test is self-administered while the section B is for behavioral observations by the physician. Studies have shown this test to have limited sensitivity with values ranging between 0.18-0.40 and a specificity of 0.98.
Modified Checklist for Autism in Toddlers (*M-CHAT*)	Appropriate for the primary care physician's office, this test was designed to improve the sensitivity of CHAT. In this questionnaire physician's observation part from original CHAT was removed and was replaced by 14 self reported (by parents) questions about core symptoms of autism. This questionnaire was found to have better sensitivity (0.85) and specificity (0.93).
Childhood Autism Rating Scale (*CARS*)	This is a 15-item questionnaire that is observer rated and is widely use all over the world. Total time to completion is about 30 minutes and it reliably differentiates children with autism from the ones with other developmental disabilities. This also includes severity scales and some times used to assess the effectiveness of treatment interventions. This scale can be administered to the children older than 2 years and carries a sensitivity ranging from 0.92-0.98 and a specificity of 0.85.
Autism Behavior Checklist (*ABC*)	This is a 57-item questionnaire that can be completed by the parents or teacher and rate symptoms on 5 domains that includes: sensory, relation, body and object use, language and social and self help. It can be used for children 18 months of age or above and carries a sensitivity of 0.38-0.58 with a specificity of 0.76-0.97.
Social Communication Questionnaire (*SCQ*)	SCQ is a 40-item questionnaire that is based on Autism Diagnostic Interview-Revised and is usually administered to children 4 years and older. Though this was originally used for epidemiological research, this can easily be used in the primary care settings. This is a cost effective instrument with a sensitivity of 0.85-0.96 and a specificity of 0.80. Cut-off scores of >14 carry a positive predictive value of greater than 90%.
Autism Diagnostic Observation Schedule (*ADOS*)	Suitable to use in specialized settings, ADOS consists of 4 modules with each requiring about 30 minutes to complete. This is a semi-structured assessment that accesses the child's play, communication and social interactions. This is increasingly being used in research settings and in multidisciplinary centers for autism.

Speech and Language Testing

Speech and language impairment is closely tied to deficits in social interactions in autistic individuals. Abnormalities range from meaningless echolalic speech to fluent speech that is marred with articulation, pronunciation and noun reversal problems. Speech pathologist evaluates child's mechanics of speech, including the syntax (language form), pragmatics (social use of language) and semantics (contents of speech). Strengths and weaknesses are noted and a comprehensive plan for speech therapy is complied.

Neuropsychological Assessment

A thorough neuropsychological assessment is the mainstay of the assessment of children with autism spectrum disorders. These individuals have multiple cognitive and neuropsychiatric deficiencies including sensorimotor issues, limited verbal intelligence but strong non-verbal problem solving and visual-spatial skills. Autistic children also display others deficits including impaired executive functioning, mental retardation and learning disabilities. Psychological testing delineates areas of strength and weakness and help in the development of sound educational plan.

Educational Assessment

Educational assessment usually takes place in the schools where the child is enrolled. Along with using above scales, specific focus is also given to access the child's abilities in arithmetic, reading, writing and other areas of day-to-day functioning.

Occupational Assessment

Occupational assessment is focused on identifying child's strengths and skills in different domains including self-care, play and safety. Sensory integration problems are noted and appropriate treatments instituted. Autistic children tend to be "clumsy" with crude fine and gross motor abilities. This is another area which is addressed in occupational therapy.

Psychiatric Interview

A detailed psychiatric interview by a pediatric psychiatrist interested in autistic disorders is another tenet of a thorough assessment. Autism spectrum disorders are associated with significant psychiatric co-morbidity including ADHD, depression and anxiety disorders. There are reports of emerging psychosis and bipolar disorders in this population. Estimates of comorbidities ranges from 20% to 60% in some studies. A thorough psychiatric evaluation usually identifies these problems areas and help with the long term management.

Differential Diagnosis

Reactive Attachment Disorder (RAD)

Children with RAD also presents with impaired attachments with social figures before 5 years of age. These impairments though arise from the intense abuse, neglect and abandonment that these children suffer from their caregivers. Broadly, symptoms appear to be autistic in nature but the previous history of neglect and improvement in symptoms after placement in nurturing environment are the differentiating features.

Intellectual Disability

Children with autism usually have varied degree of cognitive impairment but not all the children with mental retardation display autistic features. In autism, history is usually positive for impaired social interactions and delays in language while achieving other developmental milestones. In some case the development is normal till 2 years of age with the late appearance of autistic features. In mental retardation, there is usually a global delay in almost all areas of development. Children with mental retardation are usually social and do not display the typical lack of social reciprocity that is the hallmark symptom of autistic disorders.

Schizophrenia

Early (EOS) and very early onset (VEOS) schizophrenia is some times confused with autism. Here, the clinical history again is the key. Autistic children usually do not present with delusions or hallucinations, which are one of the characteristic symptoms of schizophrenia. Autism is usually diagnosed before 3 years of age while the schizophrenia symptoms appear in early to late adolescence. Social functioning is also impaired in autistic children from an early age. This usually is not the case in children with schizophrenia. Though there are some deficits in their functioning before diagnosis, parents usually give history of adequate functioning till early adolescence when the disorganized thoughts and behaviors start appearing. Autistic children usually have associated mental retardation, while schizophrenia patients have normal cognitions at the start of the disease.

Obsessive-Compulsive Disorder (OCD)

Ritualistic interests of autistic children can present as obsessions or compulsions but in contrast to OCD, these rituals do not cause any distress to the individuals. Individuals with OCD engage in compulsions to avoid any unforeseen incidents and to avoid the thoughts, while autistic individuals engage in behaviors for self-stimulatory reasons.

Bipolar Disorder

Behavioral disruptions of autistic children can sometimes mimic inherent irritability and impulsivity of the bipolar disorder patients. Autistic individuals tend to maintain routines and any disruption in these routines make them irritable and aggressive. These symptoms at times can present with rapid mood fluctuations and temper tantrum that can be mistaken as "bipolarity". However, these two disorders are very different in their history and presentation. Bipolar disorders can be sometimes be difficult to diagnose in children but the presence of grandiosity, hypersexuality, talkativeness and lack of sleep are four symptoms that can help with the diagnosis with reasonable certainty. Bipolar patients also lack the impairment in social reciprocity that is the hallmark of the autistic disorders. Onset of the bipolar disorders also differs significantly than autistic disorders.

Selective Mutism

Preferential speaking of the children with selective mutism can some times be confused with autistic disorder. Children with selective mutism usually deal with underlying anxiety disorder and tend to speak with either only the immediate family members or the people of their liking. This may cause some impairment in their social functioning but developmental history usually reveals normal language development and normal patterns of relations. Other associated symptoms of autism, including intense focus of interests and ritualistic behaviors are also absent.

Treatment

Goals of treatment are listed in Table 10. To achieve these goals, the interventions mostly remained to be behavioral and educational. Psychopharmacology is an important constituent of the treatment planning but only after careful evaluation and identification of target symptoms that this needs to be instituted.

Because of highly individualized nature of this disorder, treatments also need to be individualized with focus on the community resources, family support and the age of the child. In most of the cases, limited community resources usually is the limiting factor, but with the increase in awareness of this disorder most communities are enjoying professionals who are interested in working with the autistic children. Following are some of the specific treatments and the strategies used to manage these individuals.

Table 10. Goals of treatment

Improvement in the core deficits of the autistic spectrum including language and social deficits
Improvement in academic functioning
Focus on long term rehabilitation
Treat psychiatric comorbidities
Treat behavioral problems
Help integrate the children in their communities
Support families and manage the stress
Psychopharmacology to target behavioral symptoms

Psychosocial Interventions

Psychosocial interventions are the mainstay of the management of autistic disorders.

Social Skill Training

Social skill deficits are the core of autism spectrum disorder with lack of social reciprocity being the hallmark symptom. As noted above, these individuals have an inability to understand other's point of view and struggle to modulate their behaviors in different settings.

Social skill training is mostly provided in school in 30 minutes twice weekly sessions and the basic tenants of this therapy include role playing, modeling and coaching. Children are taught the basic underpinnings of social functioning that include, proper eye contact, postures, gestures, flexible responses to different situations, monitoring the modulations in voice and engagement in reciprocal conversations. As these individuals lack the theory of mind, they also learn to decipher the nonverbal behaviors of others including proper perception of others' emotional responses (thought and feeling activities).

Speech Therapy

Speech therapy is one of the integral pieces of the overall treatment of children with autism spectrum disorders and aims to target all aspects of communication including verbal and non-verbal modes of communication. Impairment in communication also impairs the ability to socialize with the peers and family. These impairments vary widely and speech therapy programs are usually case specific and range from help with articulation to Picture Exchange Communication Systems (*PECS*) for children who are non-verbal.

Speech therapists work with children in different settings including home visits to consultation in schools. Therapies are usually structured and have specific goals with aim to facilitate communication in different settings. Successful programs also involve the family and teachers to support the child in this work. Some of the approaches that are used in speech therapy are, discrete trail training (based upon learning theory that focus on behaviors), peer mentors (age appropriate children who interact with autistic children for socialization and modeling), sign language (use of hand movements to communicate) and story scripts (use of stories to teach social and other skills).

Occupational Therapy

Occupational therapy is another important piece of comprehensive treatment planning and is used to address sensory issues, coordination, and life skills (Table 11).

Table 11. Role of occupational therapy

Sensory integrations disorder	Sensory integration issues (sensitivities to touch, light, smells, noise etc.) are inherent in autistic children and are a source of distress for them and for the families. Occupational therapists use different techniques to provide sensory input to all senses which in-turn leads to a gradual learning process that help mature the nervous system.
Developmental co-ordination disorder	It is a common knowledge that children with autism have deficient fine and gross motor skills. Occupational therapists encourage the child to participate in games, help them with their motor coordination and also works with families to help them better understand the symptoms.
Life skills	Another area of work is to improve the basic life skills including self care, dressing, structuring daily activities and thereby elevating the self-esteem of these individuals.

Support Groups

Support groups are usually targeted towards family with goals to share information, providing hope, advocacy, problem solving and to improve the parents' psychological well-being. Different autism support groups are available in communities and also via the Internet. Some of them include, Autism Speaks, Autism Society of America (*ASA*), Asperger Syndrome and High Functioning Autism Association (*AHA*) and National Association of Autism (*NAA*).

Vocational Training and Rehabilitation

Vocational rehabilitation programs provide services for autistic and other individuals with disabilities to help them maintain an independent or semi-independent life. Counselors help with job finding that is appropriate for individual's interest and help with the placement. They also provide continued support and crisis management to help continue the employment.

Family Counseling

Caring for an autistic child is stressful and creates unwanted stress in the immediate and extended family. Aggressive behaviors towards the family members also lead to safety issues. Functioning and bonding of the other members of the family gets disturbed in unpredictable ways, which causes frustrations and sense of anger in siblings. Parents' by themselves deal with sense of loss of a healthy child with resultant grief issues. Family therapy focuses on these emotions by providing education, support and skills to manage day-to-day stress.

Behavioral Interventions

Applies Behavioral Analysis (ABA) is a behavioral planning strategy that is based on the learning theory to help learn, maintain and utilize appropriate behaviors in different settings. Studies have shown ABA to be the best evidence-based treatment available for autism. It is an intensive treatment that uses one to one interactions and requires individuals to be in therapy for 36-40 hours per week. Studies have also shown improvement in social functioning and in some cases IQ levels after the ABA.

In ABA, first a maladaptive behavior is identified. Then, a detailed analysis of the precedents of the behavior, behavior itself and consequences are conducted. These elements are then targeted and modified to make change in the behavior. In ABA individual's behaviors is influenced by rewards and negative behaviors are ignored or changed systematically. Later the rewards are removed to help self sustain the desired behaviors. The rewards/reinforces are then used to teach a new behavior to the individual. "Discrete trial training (*DTT*)" is another intervention that is used extensively in ABA.

Educational Interventions

Treatment and education of autistic and communication handicapped children *(TEACCH)*.

TEACCH is probably the most well known educational program for the children with autism. Developed by Eric Schoppler, this program uses the concept of "culture of autism" to better understand the autistic children and to provide them with fulfilling educational experience. Briefly, "culture of autism" consists of the understandings that autistic children have preference to visual presentation of material, have difficulty social aspects of communications, tend to prefer structured routine and have preferred activities and have problems in attention. By using this understanding, TEACCH strives to accomplish the long terms goals of improved psychosocial functioning.

Structured Teaching

This is an intervention that is being used in TEACCH programs and stresses to develop an individualized plan for each child with the involvement of the family. Focus is more on the environment in which the children learn rather than the way they learn the material. Assumptions are that as autistic children like structure in their lives, the teaching also needs to be done in the structured environment, for it to be effective and to promote healthy behaviors.

Social Stories

Basically a part of the social skill training, this strategy is used to teach the social rules to the child in a story telling format. This technique is also sometimes used in speech therapy programs.

Pharmacological Interventions

Autism is a complex disorder with varied presentations and significant medical and psychiatric comorbidities. Till now, there is no cure and the above-mentioned treatments are usually focused to improve the long-term psychosocial outcomes. At times, comorbid symptoms including aggressions, hyperactivity, inhibition and anxiety, dominate the clinical picture, making it difficult to get benefit from psychosocial and educational interventions. It is during these times that psychopharmacology is used to maintain the safety of the patient and to target the associated pathological behaviors.

Aggression (Irritability, Impulsivity, Self-Injurious Behaviors)

Self harm and harm to others is one of the foremost symptoms that indicate pharmacotherapy. Medications though are very effective in managing these symptoms; it is prudent to take a thorough history and to do a careful physical examination to rule out any other underlying treatable pathology, including hunger, pain, dehydration and urinary tract infections. In these cases the treatment is usually directed towards the underlying cause. Sometimes interpersonal problems, limit settings, family dysfunction and improperly high expectations can trigger these behaviors. It is during these times that behavioral treatments and parent management therapy is usually the cornerstone of the treatment. This is done while maintaining the safety of patient in their home. It is only after this evaluation that a psychopharmacological agent should be considered to target the iatrogenic aggression.

Both typical and atypical antipsychotic agents have proven to be useful in managing irritability, impulsivity and aggressive behaviors in autistic children. Typical antipsychotics (Haldol, Thorazine, Melleril) usually act on the dopamine system to target these behaviors. These are relatively safe medications but have immediate and long-term side effects that outweigh their benefits. In the short term these medications are more prone to cause sedation while long-term side effects include tremors and other movement disorders. These medications are still sometimes used if patient do not respond to newer atypical medications or in some long-term residential facilities.

Among atypical antipsychotic, Risperdal (risperidone) is the only antipsychotic that is approved by FDA for the treatment of "irritability" in autistic children. "Irritability" is a broader heading under which FDA has included aggression and tamper tantrums. Others medications in this category include ziprasidone, aripripazole, olanzapine, quetiapine and clozapine. As a category these medication can cause metabolic syndromes and it is recommended to obtained baseline height, weight, BMI, waist circumference, fasting lipid and glucose level along with an EKG.

Mood Disorders (Depression, Agitation, Disinhibition)

Mood disorders are prevalent in general population and usually presents with depressed or elevated moods. Depression usually presents differently in individuals with autistic disorder than in other population. Autistic children may not be able to explain the loss of appetite, loss of enjoyment in activities that they used to enjoy or fatigue, but the family members usually notice increasing irritability, withdrawal, deterioration in functioning, increase in rituals and regression in different area. Bipolar disorder has traditionally been difficult to diagnose in autistic children and sometimes their aggression is misleadingly labeled as bipolar disorder. Chronological history of development of symptoms, family history of bipolar disorder and in vague cases consultation by a pediatric psychiatrist will clarify the diagnosis.

Treatment of these disorders in autistic population is essentially similar to non-autistic population. Depressive symptoms usually respond well to trail of SSRI. These patients though are more prone to the side effects including worsening irritability and aggression. Special focus should also be placed on the emergence of hypomanic symptoms after the trial. Guidelines to treat the depression in non-autistic individuals can be followed with a second trail of SSRI incase of 1st failed trial and using augmentation or combination treatments for refractory depression.

Treatment of bipolar disorders is usually focused on maintaining the safety of the patients, assessing the severity of manic or hypomanic symptoms and considering the possibility of hospitalization. Atypical antipsychotics, lithium carbonate and sodium valproate are usually the first choices.

Anxiety Disorders (Compulsions, Rituals, Phobias, Repetitive Behaviors)

Anxiety disorders are common in autistic individuals and are easier to diagnose in the high functioning individuals because of preserved verbal abilities. Autistic children have ritualistic behaviors that are some times difficult to differentiate from obsessive-compulsive disorder. Autistic children usually cannot verbalize their obsessions and their ego dystonic nature, however they present with worsening of their rituals. This is the key diagnostic point that differentiates core rituals of autism from the comorbid OCD. SSRI medications are usually the main stay of the treatment. Some studies also suggest the use of Risperdal for the treatment.

Post Traumatic Stress Disorder (PTSD) also is being recognized in autistic population. There is usually a history of traumatic event in the past with additional symptoms of regression in life skills, language, avoidance and impaired sleep. Treatment is multidisciplinary and usually the combination of psychotherapy with SSRI's work well for these children.

Other anxiety disorders including panic attacks, generalized anxiety disorder and social anxiety disorders respond well to the SSRI treatment.

Psychotic Disorders (Hallucinations, Agitation, Aggression, Delusions)

There are few case reports of comorbid psychotic disorders in autistic children. Though both typical and atypical antipsychotic medication will target these symptoms, looking at the complexity of differential diagnosis between these two conditions, it is recommended to consult pediatric psychiatrist for the evaluation and management.

ADHD (Hyperactivity, Impulsivity, Inattention)

Hyperactivity and inattentive symptoms are usually associated with autistic disorder but multiple other disorders including depression and anxiety can also present with inattention and other behaviors that looks like ADHD. It's by ruling out other disorders that a diagnosis of ADHD can be made with certainty in this population. Treatment usually remains to be via behavioral management and stimulant medications. Alpha agonists are also commonly used, as some children with autism are unusually sensitive to stimulant medications.

Conclusion

With the increase in prevalence and parental awareness of autism spectrum disorders, it is becoming more and more important to diagnose these disorders at an early age. This early diagnosis will set the stage for better educational and behavioral interventions that can be provided at the critical junctures of the development. Maintaining a high level of suspicion and awareness with the early warning signs usually provide the highest yield in the primary care setting. In vague cases, a referral to specialty services is warranted and should be done in consultation with the parents.

References

American Academy of Pediatrics Committee on Children With Disabilities. The pediatrician's role in the diagnosis and management of autistic spectrum disorder in children. Pediatrics, 2001; 107(5): 1221-1226.

American Psychiatric Association. *Diagnostic and statistical manual of mental disorders*: DSM-IV-TR (*fourth edition, text revision*). Washington DC: American Psychiatric Association, 2000.

Baron-Cohen S, Wheelwright S, Cox A, et al. Early identification of autism by the Checklist for Autism in Toddlers (CHAT), *J R Soc Med* 2000;93:521-525

Butter, E. M., Wynn, J., Mulick J. A. (2003). Early intervention critical to autism treatment. *Pediatric Annals,* 32, 677-684

Campbell, M., schopler, E., Cueva, J. E., Hallin, A. (1996) Treatment of autistic disorder. *Journal of the American Academy of Child and Adolescent psychiatry,* 35, 134-143

Center for Disease Control and Prevention: Autism information center. *http://www.cdc.gov/ncbddd/autism/symptoms.htm*

Cohen DJ, Volkmar FR, eds. *Handbook of autism and pervasive developmental disorders, 2nd ed.* New York: Wiley, 1997:767-795

Donnellan, A. (1985) *'Classic Readings in Autism'* Teachers College Press.

Filipek PA, Accardo PJ, Ashwal S, Baranek GT, Cook Jr. EH, Dawson G, Gordon B, Gravel JS, Johnson CP, Kallen RJ, Levy SE, Minshew NJ, Ozonoff S, Prizant BM, Rapin I, Rogers SJ, Stone WL, Teplin SW, Tuchman RF, Volkmar FR. Practice parameter: screening and diagnosis of autism. Neurology, 2000; 55: 468-479.

Fombonne E (2005), Epidemiology of autistic disorder and other pervasive developmental disorders. *Journal of Clinical Psychiatry* 66 Suppl 10: 3-8.

Ghaziuddin, M. (2005) *'Mental Health Aspects of Autism and Asperger Syndrome'* Jessica Kingsley Publishers.

Ghaziuddin M, Weidmer-Mikhail E, Ghaziuddin N (1998), Comorbidity of Asperger syndrome: a preliminary report. *Journal of Intellectual Disability Research* 42: 279-83.

Greenspan SI, Brazelton TB, Cordero J, Solomon R, Bauman ML, Robinson R, Shanker S, Breinbauer C (2008), Guidelines for Early Identification, Screening, and Clinical Management of Children With Autism Spectrum Disorders. *Pediatrics* 121: 828-830.

Karen Bowen D, Richard MG (2004), Understanding Asperger Disorder: A Primer for Early Childhood Educators. Early Childhood Education Journal V32: 199-203.

Kanner, L. (1943), Autistic disturbances of affective contact. *Nervous Child,* 2, 217-50.

Mesibov, G, Shea, V, Schopl, E (2004) The TEACCH Approach to Autism Spectrum Disorders. Springer, 2004

Myers SM, Johnson CP, the Council on Children With D (2007), Management of Children With Autism Spectrum Disorders. *Pediatrics* 120: 1162-1182.

National Research Council. (2001). *Educating Children with Autism.* Committee on Educational Interventions for Children with Autism. Washington, DC: National Academy Press

Posey DJ, McDogle CJ, eds. *Treating Autism Spectrum Disorders: Child and Adolescent Psychiatric Clinics of North America,* 2008;17(4):713-932.

Rapin I, Tuchman: Autism. *Pediatr. Clin. North* Am., October 2008, In Press.

Stewart ME, Barnard L, Pearson J, Hasan R, O'Brien G (2006), Presentation of depression in autism and Asperger syndrome: a review. *Autism* 10: 103-16

Tidmarsh L, Volkmar FR (2003), Diagnosis and epidemiology of autism spectrum disorders. Canadian Journal Of Psychiatry. *Revue Canadienne De Psychiatrie* 48: 517-525.

Tsatsanis KDP, Foley CBA, Donehower CBA Contemporary Outcome Research and Programming Guidelines for Asperger Syndrome and High-Functioning Autism. SO - *Topics in Language Disorders Asperger Syndrome and High-Functioning Autism: Addressing Social Communication and Emotional Regulation. October/November/December* 2004;24(4):249-259.

Wing L (1981), Asperger's syndrome: a clinical account. *Psychological Medicine* 11: 115-29.

Wing L (1997), The autistic spectrum. *Lancet* 350: 1761-1766.

Woods JJ, Wetherby AM (2003), Early Identification of and Intervention for Infants and Toddlers Who Are at Risk for Autism Spectrum Disorder. *Lang Speech Hear Serv. Sch.* 34: 180-193.

Xue M, Brimacombe M, Chaaban J, Zimmerman-Bier B, Wagner GC (2008), Autism Spectrum Disorders: Concurrent Clinical Disorders. *J. Child Neurol.* 23: 6-13.

In: Behavioral Pediatrics, 3rd Edition
Editor: Donald E. Greydanus et al.

ISBN 978-1-60692-702-1
© 2009 Nova Science Publishers, Inc.

Chapter 7

Sensory Processing Disorders and Treatment: Occupational Therapy Using a Sensory Integration Approach

Cindee Quake-Rapp and Ben Atchison

Abstract

The definition and typologies of SPD described in this chapter are those that have been incorporated in both the ICDL-DMIC and DC: 0-3R classification systems as well as the classification proposed for inclusion in the revised edition of the DSM-IV which is due for publication in 2012. A discussion of definitions is followed by a description of the clinical features, including signs and symptoms for each type of SPD. A comprehensive review of standardized and non standardized instruments used to diagnose SPD is provided, followed by a presentation of intervention referred to as occupational therapy use of a sensory integration approach (OT-SI).

Introduction

This chapter begins with a comprehensive definition of Sensory Processing Disorders (SPD) and descriptions of associated typologies derived from accepted classification systems of the Interdisciplinary Council on Developmental and Learning Disorders-Diagnostic Manual for Infancy and Early Childhood (ICDL-DMIC) (ICDL, 2005) and the Diagnostic Classification of Mental Health and Developmental Disorders of Infancy and Early Childhood, Revised (DC: 0-3R). The publication of these classification systems in these diagnostic manuals has provided important steps toward the legitimacy of SPD as a relevant and meaningful diagnosis that can be effectively treated with appropriate intervention by qualified clinicians. Additionally, in January 2007, a first-stage application was submitted to the DSM-V Committee of the American Psychiatric Association by the Sensory Processing Disorders Network Task Group to include SPD as a distinct diagnosis in the revision of the

Diagnostic and Statistical Manual of Mental Disorders IV-TR (DSM-IV). As of March, 2008, a response was forwarded by the chair of the DSM committee to the SPD workgroup which outlined specific evidence needed for inclusion, indicating at the very least serious consideration for the proposal.

Definitions

The concept of a sensory processing disorder was first identified by Ayres (1963), an occupational therapist and neuroscientist. Based on empirical studies of child behavior and her extensive study and knowledge of neural science, Ayres developed a framework to explain the relationship between sensory processing and behaviors associated with learning disabilities as well as developmental and emotional problems. Detailed in her classic textbook, Sensory Integration and Learning Disorders, Ayres described sensory integration dysfunction and associated syndromes. These syndromes were based on factor analysis studies of her first test battery, the Southern California Sensory Integration Tests (SCSIT) (1972b) and later refined as patterns of dysfunction, based on studies of the Sensory Integration and Praxis Tests as well as a standard set of clinical observations that she developed as part of the diagnostic regimen. While she was often erroneously accused of being dogmatic about the validity of sensory integration theory, Ayres consistently urged refinement of her theoretical postulates. This philosophy was stated clearly in her first textbook: "Just as the continued production of research results in constantly changing neurological concepts, so also will this theory need to undergo frequent revision" (1972a). Ayres consistently stated, throughout her many publications as well as national and international professional lectures, that evolution of sensory integration theory and treatment approaches were both necessary and ethical to find the best answers to explaining and treating disorders attributed to sensory processing problems. She held the highest standards regarding the need to "search for truth", which is, of course, the foundation of all legitimate evidence based practice.

In a seminal article titled, *Concept Evolution in Sensory Integration: A Proposed Nosology for Diagnosis*, Miller, Anzalone, Lane, Cermak, and Osten (2007) summarized the efforts by scholars to continue refinement of the theory, diagnosis, and treatment of what has been historically referred to as sensory integration dysfunction and sensory integration treatment. Following two years of deliberation among scholars in occupational therapy, consensus was reached on the need for separation of the terms associated with the theory, diagnosis and treatment of sensory processing disorders. As noted by Miller et. al. (2007) significant studies by many theorists and researchers such as Degangi, (2000); Dunn, (2001) and Mulligan (1998) led to a proposed taxonomy that uses the term sensory "processing" rather than sensory "integration" to describe the diagnosis of sensory-based learning and behavioral problems. This decision largely emerged from the reality that sensory "integration" is used more commonly by neuroscientists to describe a cellular process of sensory integration. The divergence of terms allows for a more clear differentiation among the theory (sensory integration theory), the disorder (sensory processing disorder SPD) and the intervention (occupational therapy using a sensory integration approach SI-OT).

Clinical Features

Sensory processing includes the detection, registration, and modulation of sensory modalities and ultimately, the organization of sensory information by the central nervous system to allow for an adaptive response that is meaningful and relevant to a given situation. It is hypothesized that children who demonstrate sensory processing disorders experience errors in the interpretation of sensory information in the brain. While all humans experience interpretation errors in sensory processing, it is the lack of habituation and adaptation to these errors that results in chronic expressions of poorly organized, maladaptive responses. Thus, the need to provide intervention is only recommended when sensory processing difficulties results in behaviors that interfere with normal function in school, play, self care and other daily occupations of a child. There are three identified patterns or categories of SPD, each with a subtype as described below and illustrated in Figure 1.

Sensory Processing Disorder (SPD) A Proposed Nosology

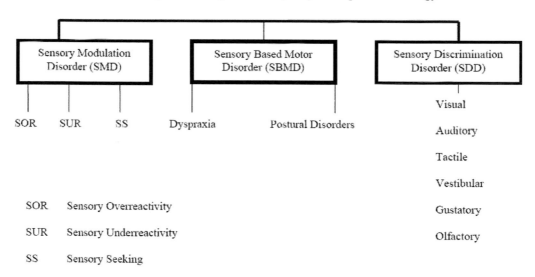

Figure 1. Sensory Processing Disorder: A Conceptual Model. From "Concept evolution in sensory integration: A proposed nosology for diagnosis by L. J. Miller, M. Anzalone, S. Lane, S. Cermak,& E.Osten, 2007. *American Journal of Occupational Therapy*, 61, 2. p 137. Copyright 2007 American Occupational Therapy Association. Used with permission of publisher.

Pattern 1: Sensory Modulation Disorder (SMD)

Sensory modulation refers to the process that takes place in the central and autonomic nervous system in response to internal and external sensory stimuli. Alterations in physiologic responses reflect activation of the interoreceptors, proprioceptors and exteroreceptors which are evidenced by laboratory measures and behavioral observations. A disorder in sensory modulation occurs when there is difficulty in the grading of responses to the quality, or nature of the stimulus as well as the quantity of sensory stimuli, resulting in maladaptive responses. There are three subtypes within SMD including Sensory

Overresponsivity (SOR), Sensory Underresponsivity (SUR), and Sensory Seeking (SS). Each is unique in terms of the level of reactivity to sensory thresholds as illustrated in Table I.

Table 1. Sensory Thresholds and Corresponding Behavior

	LOW	HIGH
Threshold Level	Increased Sensitivity	Decreased Sensitivity
	Over-responsivity	Under-responsivity
Reactions in accordance with threshold	Hyper-reactive	Hypo-reactive
Behaviors observed in effort to counteract threshold	Sensory avoider	Sensory Seeker

From "The sensory profile users manual" by W. Dunn 1999. The Sensory Profile Manual, Copyright 1999. The Psychological Corporation. Used with permission of publisher.

Subtype 1: Sensory Overresponsivity (SOR)

This subtype is characterized by responses to stimuli that are more intense or have a longer duration than typically expected and may occur in only one or among multiple sensory modalities. It is described by Dunn (1999) as behaviors that reflect active avoidance to certain stimuli as well as hypersensitivity to stimuli that is perceived to be offensive or unpleasant. Often times, the behaviors that children demonstrate are considered to be of a willful nature because the response sets are often context dependent. For example the same type of auditory stimulus that sets off an adverse behavioral reaction in the classroom but is not observed at home will often lead to the conclusion that the child can control the behavior when in fact it is automatic and unconscious. At home, the child may have more control of an auditory stimulus where, in the classroom, the same stimulus occurs without expectation. Repetition of this unexpected stimulus can create a cumulative effect, resulting in a range of aggressive reactions to complete avoidance or shutdown in the stimulus environment. Miller and her colleagues (1999) demonstrated in a laboratory model that activation of the sympathetic nervous system is a marker of SOR, specifically noted in exaggeration of the fight or flight responses typically experienced in stressful situations. Persons with SOR often demonstrate inflexibility, hypervigilance, and tend to be difficult to console when they are in "overresponsive" mode. SOR is often seen in children with autism, fragile X syndrome, attention deficit hyperactivity disorder and mood disorders. The SOR subtype is not always exclusive of other sensory modulation disorders such as sensory seeking, sensory discrimination and dyspraxia.

Subtype 2: Sensory Underresponsivity(SUR)

Children who experience SUR experience challenges in the feed-forward mechanism of the central nervous system, lacking a central predictive set of actions in given situations. It is as if there is a lack of ability to detect incoming sensory information, which is often misinterpreted as the child having "lazy" tendencies and unmotivated. As an infant, the child with SUR is often considered to be "an easy baby" or "good baby" because he or she may make minimal demands on the caregiver. When developmental expectations of exploratory behavior and spontaneity in reciprocal interaction emerge, it is clear that the child's arousal level is low. This hypoarousal state leading to a lack of natural, exploratory sensory behavior may be manifested in inefficient tactile and proprioceptive sensory responses which are typically robust in developing infants and toddlers. It is soon discovered that the child with SUR requires more intense and extended duration of sensory stimuli to reach an optimal level of arousal. Most caregivers will intuitively "turn up the volume" of sensory stimuli to address this behavior. A child with SUR often demonstrates difficulty with sustained task performance as the lack of a consistent interaction with sensory input leads to sensory discrimination disorders, dyspraxia, or both.

Subtype 3: Sensory Seeking/Craving (SS)

There is consistent evidence in the human growth and development literature, including teratologic study, that humans seek sensory input to make meaning of the external environment. Children with the SS subtype of sensory modulation disorders seek sensory input with an approach that results in erratic, disorganized behavior. The child in the physician's office who wants to touch the reflex hammer, stethoscope and other available items within reach is different than the child who runs about the office, turning things over and generally creating concern among those in the room. The behavior appears to be impulsive, unsafe, and boundary-free and the child will energetically engage in physical actions that add to their craving for sensory input. Often times, this child is considered to be "fearless" as they engage in constant spinning, jumping, running into objects with a "crashing and bashing" approach. When the necessary boundaries are enforced and thus unable to meet sensory needs, children with SS may become highly agitated and explosive. With extreme cases, the ability to learn is compromised, interpersonal relationships become very difficult to sustain, and activities of daily living are disrupted.

Pattern 2: Sensory Based Motor Disorder (SBMD)

Subtype 1: Postural Disorder (PD)

Those body functions that are dependent on smooth and efficient processing of vestibular and kinesthetic input are often disrupted among children with SPD, resulting in difficulty with maintaining normal postural tone. Smooth control of movement and endurance may be compromised, particularly in anti-gravity activity. Poor balance between agonist and antagonist muscle groups, poor balance reactions in both static and dynamic challenges, poor weight shifting and trunk mobility, as well as deficits in smooth oculomotor control may be present in children with SBMD. Children with either sensory seeking or underresponsivity may demonstrate behaviors associated with SBMD. The arousal level of the person, whether it is SOR or SUR may result in postural control problems as well as dyspraxia. The child who typically maintains a slumped position while attempting to complete a handwriting task and quickly losing a sustained effort to do so is typical of a child with this pattern of sensory processing disorder.

Subtype 2: Dyspraxia

Dyspraxia is the inability to plan unfamiliar or novel tasks, resulting in a clumsy, awkward adaptive response. The key idea here is that the task is novel. Asking a person to perform a task that is done routinely, such as buttoning a button on a shirt would be an evaluation of fine motor coordination and not motor planning ability. When attempting a motor task that is not in one's repertoire of acquired skills, the person with dyspraxia will demonstrate significant awkwardness in the use of hands and body to perform the task. It is clearly a sensory based problem in that persons with dyspraxia appear to be unsure of where their body is in space and may have difficulty with timing, grading, and executing movement to complete the task with success. Most people have experienced the awkwardness of learning new dance steps. After a series of repetition, a more accurate use of the body is felt and observed in most individuals. It is true, of course, that some of us will never learn to dance! That, however, may be tied to a lack of interest rather than poor somatosensory processing. Usually, there are other motor planning challenges that one can succeed in, unless dyspraxia prevents success in every new motor activity attempted. Many children with dyspraxia are creative, highly verbal and are safe when engaged in fantasy games that don't require "doing" something specific. Children with dyspraxia often prefer passive activity such as watching television, playing on computers, or reading to the exclusion of any activities that challenge motor planning abilities. The fear that emerges when being required to participate in physical education activities at school or other settings is real for a child. This may result in repeated feelings of failure, leading to significant impairment of confidence and self esteem.

Pattern 3: Sensory Discrimination Disorder (SDD)

Sensory discrimination disorders are reflected by difficulty with qualitative processing of sensory stimuli. It is not uncommon to have a combination of strengths and weaknesses in sensory discrimination which leads to the idea that one is a "visual" or "auditory" learner or learns best "by doing." Commonly, descriptions of sensory discrimination and assessments emphasize visual, auditory and tactile perception. Visual discrimination includes such skills as pattern recognition and visual-spatial analysis. Pattern recognition problems include difficulty in the recognition of differences in similar shapes such as ovals vs circles or in the reversal of letters and numbers that persists after the age of six. Problems in visual spatial analysis is observed in attempts to solve simple puzzles, replicating simple designs, and can ultimately impact on the ability to adequately develop handwriting skills. Auditory discrimination includes the ability to differentiate similar sounds such as b and d and words such as with and which, while tactile perception is often described as the ability to identify an object with vision occluded, using the integration of tactile and visual discrimination to do so, such as reaching into ones pocket and retrieving a quarter, rather than a penny, for the parking meter.

A unique feature of the SDD classification in a SPD model is the inclusion of the somatic senses, which includes proprioceptive and vestibular discrimination and referred in sensory processing language to as somatosensation. Normal somatosensation provides for a foundational body scheme which Ayres (1972) classically described as (1972) the "blue print for movement", enabling adequate processing of feed-forward skills for planning movement and postural stability. The awareness of where one's body is in space in relation to the external environment, and the excursion, speed, precision, and gradation of movement needed to complete a motor task is a function of somatosensory discrimination. Children who experience SOR as well as SUR may have difficulty with this aspect of sensory discrimination which can create difficulties in body scheme and motor planning.

Epidemiology

The estimated rates of sensory processing disorders among children with a variety of identified disabilities have been reported to be as significant as 40-88%. In an interesting study conducted by two pediatricians, Eide and Eide (2004), they reported that 52% of the children seen in their practice had signs of SPD severe enough to contribute to their learning difficulties and among that sample, 70% were under the age of ten. These studies, and others, have included children who were being treated for a variety of disorders and are consistent with hypothesized prevalence rates for these populations. However, only a few studies to date have prevalence rates among the typical population. Ahn, Miller, Milberger, and McIntosh (2004) employed a standardized survey of parent perceptions (Short Sensory Profile) to identify behaviors indicative of SPD. Of their sample of 703 surveys, 13.7 % met screening criteria for sensory processing disorders. Goldsmith, Van Hulle, Arneson, Schreiber, and Gernsbacher (2006) found similar prevalence rates in a pilot project which studied a sample of twins. Clearly, further studies that examine children not as yet referred or identified as having a SPD will provide necessary support for early screening, and if identified, early intervention.

Etiology of Sensory Processing Disorders

It is generally recognized that children with autism, Asperger's syndrome, attention deficit hyperactivity disorder (ADHD), learning disabilities, and Fragile X syndrome, experience disruption in sensory processing. While studies indicate that sensory processing disorders are found in up to 70% of children who are considered learning disabled by schools, the problems of SPD are not confined to children with learning deficits. SPD is evident in all age groups, as well as intellectual levels and socioeconomic groups.

There is minimal empirical evidence to determine the cause or etiology of sensory processing disorders based on human studies, although emerging evidence exists that SPD reduces a child's ability to engage in social interaction, self-care, learning, and play. Researchers are currently looking at animal and primate models to determine causative factors of SPD due to limitations in methodology in human studies. Factors that may contribute to SPD include pre and postnatal stressors, deficits in neurodevelopment, and environmental deprivation.

The tactile, visual, auditory, and somatosensory systems are not mature at birth and considerable modifications take place postnatally. During infancy, connections between sensory neurons continue to be established and sensory systems have the capacity to make functionally appropriate adjustments in neural pathways. Recent experimental studies have demonstrated that early exposure to environmental events that provoke sensory stimuli or spontaneous activity can influence the maturation of neuronal circuits. Studies have also shown that early developmental exposure to sensory rich experiences is necessary in neuronal development and brain plasticity. Sensory deprived animals prevent substantial loss of synapses that occurs in typically growing animals and in order for learning to occur, the brain's neurons have to be pruned. An unfortunate example of sensory deprivation in children was apparent in Eastern European orphanages where poor developmental and behavioral outcomes resulted from impoverished environments that did not provide adequate conditions for typical sensory development to occur. Many of these children were adopted by families from the United States who were unaware of the severe developmental delays and SPD resulting from a low caregiver to child ratio of 1:10-20. It has been reported that institutionalized infants receive only 18% as much holding, rocking, and tactile stimulation as infants living with families. One study found that children adopted from Romanian orphanages in the 1990's had significantly smaller brains than normal children.

Prenatal stress, alcohol exposure, and early postnatal lead exposure have been found to impact sensory processing in primates. Studies of humans have shown that maternal stress hormones can cross the placental barrier resulting in altered neurotransmitter activity producing abnormal sensory modulation in offspring. Sensory deprivation or any form of maltreatment or neglect produces either sensory- overresponsiveness, a persistent fear response and constant hyper-arousal, or, a dissociative, under responsive "surrender" response. Henry, Sloan, and Black-Pond (2007), found that children who had prenatal exposure to alcohol along with postnatal abuse had severe neurodevelopmental deficits in language, memory, visual processing, motor skills, attention, and behavior. Atchison (2007) reported significant sensory modulation disorders among the same population.

Diagnosis

Diagnostic Validity and Assessment of SPD

SPD is considered to be a diagnosis of exclusion. There are many causes of maladaptive behaviors such as chronic medical conditions, neurological disorders, genetic conditions and psychiatric disorders. SPD can exist in isolation or co-exist with other medical and psychological conditions that impede function. Children with SPD have difficulty grading the degree, nature, and intensity of sensory stimuli with developmentally appropriate attention and emotional responses.

According to Reynolds and Lane (2007), the incidence of SPD in diagnostic populations is 30% and is estimated to be close to 100% in children with autism. These estimates are based on behavioral rather than physiologic measures and do not differentiate between children who are over or under responsive to sensory stimulation.

A discrete measure of brain mechanisms in children with SPD is electroencephalography (EEG). Davies and Gavin (2007) found that processing of auditory stimuli was different in children with SPD compared to normally developing children using EEG techniques. In addition, the authors state that functional neuroimaging is a more accurate measure of processing of sensory stimuli by the brain than peripheral measures such as electodermal activity and heart rate that assess an individual's reaction to their environment. Similar evidence supporting the use of electrophysiologic measures in comparing differences in sensory responsiveness between children with SPD and normally developing children was found by Hong et.al, 2007, and Parush, Sohner, Steinberg, and Katitz, 2007.

Table 2. Behaviors often associated with sensory processing disorder

Sensory Over-Responsive signs - bothered by:
- Textures on body, face, hands, or feet, having hair or nails cut; hair combed
- Background noise, loud, unexpected sounds, fragrances
- Playing on swings and slides, being upside down
- Bright lights or sunshine

Sensory Under-Responsive signs
- Doesn't feel pain, doesn't notice when someone touches him
- Doesn't like physical activities; prefers sedentary activities
- Slow or unmotivated and unaware of what's going on around him
- Unaware of body sensations such as hunger, hot or cold or need to use toilet

Sensory-Seeking signs
- Is on the move constantly, crashing, bashing, and is unable to sit still
- Constantly touches objects and/or intrudes on people
- Seems unable to stop talking and takes excessive risks
- Often licks, sucks, chews smells or tastes objects

Dyspraxia/Motor Planning Problem signs
- Difficulty learning new motor activities or those that require more than one step
- Is clumsy, awkward, and/or accident-prone, tripping or bumping into other people
- Takes a long time to write things down and to do self-care activities like dressing
- Has difficulty organizing personal spaces or playing with small objects

Postural Disorder signs
- Has poor muscle tone, seems weak, slumps when sitting or standing
- Has difficulty crossing the middle of his body to complete a task
- Has poor balance and falls over easily, sometimes even when seated
- Has poor endurance and gets tired easily

Sensory Discrimination Disorder signs
- Difficulty knowing what is in his hands or telling what is touching him
- Judging how much force is required for a task
- Identifying and distinguishing between different sounds or letters
- Organizing writing on a page, e.g., spacing between letters or words

From "Signs and Symptoms of SPD, 2006, by the STAR Center and KID Foundation, Copyrighted 2006. Used with permission of author.

According to Lucy Jane Miller, author of Sensational Kids: Hope and Help for Children with Sensory Processing Disorder (2007), there are common behavioral observations that can assist parents, teachers, and health care practitioners to determine if a child would benefit from further evaluation of SPD. Those are listed in Table 2.

The most common measures of behavioral responses to sensory stimulation are survey instruments such as the Sensory Profile, the Infant-Toddler Sensory Profile, the Adolescent-Adult Sensory Profile, the Sensory Over-responsivity Inventory and the Sensory Processing Measure. These instruments can categorize a child's' dominant behavioral pattern in the areas of sensory seeking, sensory avoiding, sensory sensitivity, or low sensory registration based on self or parent report of behavioral reactions to touch, visions, sound, taste, smell, and movement. Standardized assessments used to measure dyspraxia , postural disorders , and sensory discrimination include the gold standard Sensory Integration and Praxis Test, the DeGangi-Berk Test of Sensory Integration and the Test of Sensory Functions in Infants.

See Table 3 for specific information on these various measures.

Treatment

Ayres first proposed a theory of sensory integration in 1965. A neuroscientist and an occupational therapist, she also created the initial framework for intervention, which has evolved to be termed occupational therapy using a sensory integration approach abbreviated as OT-SI. The principles, as well as specific applications of intervention, have evolved over 40 years with these grounded elements firmly in place:

1. Intervention is focused on engagement in child-directed, sensory-enriched experiences that are individually designed to address each child's specific sensory needs.
2. By providing the "just-right challenge", the occupational therapist seeks to facilitate the child's inner drive to engage in developmentally appropriate, sensory based activities.
3. The artful, yet practical adjustment of the sensory qualities of the external environment is engineered to enable the child to overcome the varies sensory processing challenges that interrupt "the ability to participate in daily life activities, including social participation and school tasks."

When an occupational therapist receives a referral from a child's physician for assessment to rule out SPD, the necessity for intervention is not decided based on whether a child demonstrates a sign or symptom of SPD. Rather, OT-SI should only be initiated if the child has difficulty with participation and engagement in necessary and meaningful occupations such as school, play, and activities of daily living. . The fact is that most individuals can describe one or more defensive reactions to a variety of sensory stimuli yet most will create strategies to support these challenges.

Table 3. Measures of SPD and Sensory Responsiveness Indicators

Tool	Description	Author	Population Characteristics	Norms
Sensory Profile	A caregiver questionnaire that includes a 125 item profile of 9 measures describing a child's response to various sensory experiences. A short version (38 items) is also available. • Sensory Seeking • Emotionally Reactive • Low Endurance/Tone • Oral Sensory Sensitivity • Inattention/Distractibility • Poor Registration • Sensory Sensitivity • Sedentary • Fine Motor/Perceptual	Winnie Dunn, PhD., OTR, FAOTA, 1999	Children 3-10 years of age	Classification system based on normative information.
Infant-Toddler Sensory Profile	The *Infant/Toddler Sensory Profile-Clinical Edition* is an observational tool to determine an infants sensory processing patterns. A caregiver questionnaire is completed concurrent while evaluating the infant/toddler. • General Processing • Auditory Processing • Visual Processing • Tactile Processing • Vestibular Processing • Oral Sensory Processing	Winnie Dunn, PhD, OTR, 2002	Birth to 36 months	Standardized with 598 cases, 100 per age range.

Table 3. (Continued)

Tool	Description	Author	Population Characteristics	Norms
Adolescent and Adult Sensory Profile	Adolescent/ Adult Sensory Profile is a self reporting questionnaire which measures responses to sensory events in everyday life. There are 60 items in the profile. The Adolescent/ Adult Sensory Profile yields four scores which correspond to the four quadrants of sensory processing proposed in Dunn's model of sensory processing, i.e., sensation seeking, sensation avoiding, sensory sensitivity and low registration.	Catana Brown, PhD, OTR, and Winnie Dunn, OTR, PhD.,2002.	11 years and older	Classification system based on normative information
Sensory Processing Measure	The Sensory Processing Measure provides an overview of children's sensory functioning at home, at school, and in the community. Recognizing that sensory processing problems often manifest differently in different environments, this set of three integrated rating scales assesses sensory processing, praxis, and social participation in elementary school children. The SPM provides norm-referenced standard scores for two higher level integrative functions and 5 sensory areas: • Social Participation • Vision • Hearing • Touch • Body Awareness (proprioception) • Balance and Motion (vestibular function) • Planning and Ideas (praxis) • Total Sensory Systems	Home Form by L. Diane Parham, Ph.D., OTR/L, and Cheryl Ecker, M.A., OTR/L Main Classroom and School Environments Forms by Heather Miller Kuhaneck, M.S., OTR/L, Diana A. Henry, M.S., OTR/L, and Tara J. Glennon, Ed.D, OTR/L, 2005	5 to 12 years	Based on a nationally representative sample of 1,051 children. Additional data were collected on a clinical sample of 325 children.

Table 3. (Continued)

Tool	Description	Author	Population Characteristics	Norms
Sensory Over-Responsivity Scales	This scale is designed to identify Sensory Over-Responsivity in Children and Adults. This in progress study provides preliminary support for the reliability and validity of a performance assessment and a caregiver/self-report inventory of the Sensory Over-Responsivity (SOR)	Lucy J. Miller, Ph.D., OTR Sarah A. Schoen, Ph.D., OTR, and Kathy E. Green, PhD,. A pilot Study of the Sensory Over-Responsivity Scales: Assessment and Inventory, *American Journal of Occupational Therapy*, July/August 2008, 62,(4). 393-406	Children and Adults	Data were collected on ~200 individuals with and without SOR, from three to 55 years of age
Sensory Integration and Praxis Test	The SIPT is a set of 17 standardized tests which measure aspects of sensory processing of perception and praxis, the ability to form an idea about an action, plan the action and execute it.	Ayres, 1989	4 to 8 years	Normed on 2,000 children in all eight census districts in the United States and Canada.
De Gangi-Berk Test of Sensory Integration	The De Gangi Berk Test of Sensory Integration has 36 items measuring overall sensory integration as well as three clinically significant subdomains: Postural Control, Bilateral Motor Integration, and Reflex Integration.	Georgia A. DeGangi, Ph.D., OTR and Ronald A. Berk, Ph.D, 1983	3 to 5 years	The TSI effectively differentiates normal and developmentally delayed children. When used as the basis for screening decisions ,total scores demonstrate an 81% accuracy rate, with a false normal error rate of only 9%.
Test of Sensory Functions in Infants	Offers an objective way to determine whether -and to what extent -an infant has sensory processing deficits • Reactivity to Tactile Deep Pressure • Visual Tactile Integration • Adaptive Motor Function • Ocular Motor Control • Reactivity to Vestibular Stimulation	Georgia A. DeGangi, Ph.D., OTR and Stanley M. Greenspan, MD, 1989	4 to 18 months	Normed on 344 infants.

OT-SI clearly requires a contextual based, clinical reasoning process rather than a set of fixed protocols as might be appropriate and necessary in treatment of other pediatric disorders. Miller devised an excellent scheme for considering the needs of a child who has SPD. In this scheme, known by the acronym STEP-SI, a series of questions guides the therapist, caregivers, teachers and others who are central to the success of enabling the child to obtain adaptive sensory processing abilities. This is illustrated in Table 4.

The efficacy of OT-SI has been scrutinized since Ayres first described her theoretical postulates and intervention ideas. Of the studies that have been published in the last 40 years, approximately one half of those have demonstrated favorable outcomes from OT-SI. Additionally, there have been two meta-analysis completed yet one, which indicated that intervention yielded minimal effect was noted to have significant methodological errors.

In the March/April 2007 issue of the American Journal of Occupational Therapy, a group of scholars published a seminal article on the status of research on OT-SI and in particular, to assess the validity of known research with regard to fidelity. The outcome of their inquiry resulted in the identification of core elements of sensory integration intervention.

Table 4: Dimensions of the STEP-SI Clinical Reasoning Intervention Model

STEP-SI Dimension		Description
S	Sensation	Sensory modalities: tactile, vestibular, proprioception, auditory, vision, taste, olfaction, oral input, and respiration
T	Task	Qualities of sensation: Duration ,frequency, complexity, and rhythmicity
E	Environment	Organization, complexity, demand for skill, demand for sustained attention, level of engagement, fun, motivation, and purposefulness (based on standard task analysis)
P	Predictability	Novelty, expectation, structure, routine, transitions, and congruency; Level of control by child or practitioner and control of events and routines
S	Self-monitoring	Moving the child from dependence on external cues and supports to self directed and internally organized ability to modify own behavior and manage challenges
I	Interaction	Interpersonal interaction style, including response to supportive, nurturing styles versus more challenging, authoritative styles, locus of control (practitioner guided vs child directed);and demands of expectations for engagement (passive awareness to active collaboration).

From "Use of Clinical Reasoning in Occupational Therapy: The STEP-SI Model of Intervention of Sensory Modulation Dysfunction", by L. Miller, J. Wilbarger, T. Stackhouse, S. Trunnel, 2002. p. IN: Bundy, A, Lane, S, and Murray, E (Eds) Sensory Integration: Theory and Practice. Copyright 2002, F.A. Davis. Used with permission of author.

These elements included two classifications: structural and process elements and essentially laid the groundwork towards establishing core components that need to be addressed in outcomes research of OT-SI. The core elements of the intervention process as illustrated in Table 5 provide a helpful understanding of the expected behaviors and attitudes of the therapist who is providing an OT-SI approach.

Table 5. Core Elements of Sensory Integration Intervention Process

Core Process Elements	Description of Therapist's Behavior and Attitude
Provide sensory opportunities	Presents the child with opportunities for various sensory experiences, which include tactile, vestibular, and/ or proprioceptive experiences; intervention involves more than one sensory modality.
Provide just-right challenges	Tailors activities so as to present challenges to the child that are neither too difficult nor too easy, to evoke the child's adaptive responses to sensory and praxis challenges.
Collaborate on activity choice	Treats the child as an active collaborator in the therapy process, allowing the child to actively exert some control over activity choice does not predetermine a schedule of activities independently of the child.
Guide self-organization	Supports and guides the child's self-organization of behavior to make choices and plan own behavior to the extent the child is capable; encourages the child to initiate and develop ideas and plans for activities.
Support optimal arousal	Ensures that the therapy situation is conducive to attaining or sustaining the child's optimal level of arousal by making changes to environment or activity to support the child's attention, engagement, and comfort.
Create play context	Creates a context of play by building on the child's intrinsic motivation and enjoyment of activities; facilitates or expands on social, motor, imaginative, or object play.
Maximize child's success	Presents or modifies activities so that the child can experience success in doing part or all of an activity that involves a response to a challenge.
Ensure physical safety	Ensures that the child is physically safe either through placement of protective and therapeutic equipment or through the therapist's physical proximity and actions.
Arrange room to engage child	Arranges the room and equipment in the room to motivate the child to choose and engage in an activity.
Foster therapeutic alliance	Respects the child's emotions, conveys positive regard toward the child, seems to connect with the child, and creates climate of trust and emotional safety.

From: Parham, L. D., Cohn, E. S., Spitzer, S., Koomar, J. A., Miller, L. J., Burke, J. P., et al. (2007). Fidelity in sensory integration intervention research. *American Journal of Occupational Therapy, 61,* 216 -227. Copyright 2007 American Occupational Therapy Association. Used with permission of publisher.

Conclusion

Sensory processing refers to the detection, registration, and modulation of sensory modalities, and the organization of sensory information by the central nervous system to allow for an adaptive response that is meaningful and relevant to a given situation. The estimated rates of sensory processing disorders among children with a variety of identified disabilities have been reported to be as significant as 40-88%. Clearly, the community of occupational therapists who specialize in OT-SI understand the need to not only implement and disseminate outcome studies to legitimize this approach, but to do so with sound fidelity instrumentation that will enable refinement of intervention, leading to improved outcomes for children with SPD.

References

Adrie, J., Lenoir, P., Martieneau, J. Perrot, A., Hameury, L., Larmande, C., et al. Blind ratings of early symptoms of autism based upon family home movies. *Journal of American Academy of Child and Adolescent Psychiatry*, 1993; 32(3): 617-626.

Ahn, R., Miller, L., Milberger, S., McIntosh, D. Prevalence of parents' perceptions of sensory processing disorders among kindergarten children. *American Journal of Occupational Therapy,* May-June, 2004;58(3): 287-93.

American Psychiatric Association. Diagnostic and statistical manual of mental disorders.(DSM-IV-TR). 2002, Washington, DC: Author.

Atchison, B. Sensory modulation disorders among children with a history of trauma: a frame of reference for speech pathologists. *Journal of Language, Speech, and Hearing Services in Schools*, American Speech and Hearing Association, 2007.

Ayres, A.J., Eleanor Clarke Slagle. Lecture: The development of perceptual motor abilities: a theoretical basis for treatment of dysfunction. *American Journal of Occupational Therapy,* 1963;27: 221-225.

Ayres, A.J. Sensory *Integration and learning disorders*. 1972a, Los Angeles: Western Psychological Services.

Ayres, A.J. *Southern California Sensory Integration Tests*. 1972b, Los Angeles: Western Psychological Services.

Ayres, A.J. *Sensory Integration and Praxis Tests*. 1989, Los Angeles: Western Psychological Services.

Baranek, G.T., Chin, Y.H., Greiss-Hess, L.M., Yankee, J.G., Hatton, D.D., Hooper, S.R. Sensory processing correlates of occupational performance in children with fragile X syndrome: preliminary findings. *The American Journal of Occupational Therapy*, 2002; 56(5): 538–546.

Brown, C., Dunn, W. *Adolescent/Adult Sensory Profile*. 2002, San Antonio, TX: The Psychological Corporation.

Brown, C., Cromwell, R.L., Filion, D., Dunn, W., Tollefson, N. Sensory processing in schizophrenia: missing and avoiding information. *Schizophrenia Research,* 2002;55(1–2): 187–195.

Casler, L. Supplementary auditory and vestibular stimulation: Effects on institutionalized infants. *Journal of Experimental Child Psychology*, 1975;19: 456-463.

Child Welfare Information Gateway. Available online at www.childwelfare.gov /pubs/focus/earlybrain/index.cfm.References, 2001.

Dahlgren, S., Gilberg, C. Symptoms in the first two years of life: a preliminary population study of infantile autism. *European Archives of Psychiatry and Neurological Science*, 1989; 38(3): 169-174.

Davies, P.L., Gavin, W.J. Conceptualizing and identifying sensory processing issues-validating the diagnosis of sensory processing disorders using EEG technology. *American Journal of Occupational Therapy*, 2007;61: 176-190.

DeGangi, G.A. *Pediatric disorders of regulation in affect and behavior:A therapist's guide to assessment and treatment*. 2000, San Diego, CA: Academic Press.

DeGangi, G.A., Greenspan, S.I. *Test of Sensory Functions in Infants (TSFI)* 1989, Los Angeles: Western Psychological Services.

DeGangi, G.A., Berk, R.A. *DeGangi-Berk Test of Sensory Integration (TSI)* 1983, Los Angeles: Western Psychological Services.

Dunn, W. *The sensory profile: users manual*. 1999, San Antonio, TX: The Psychological Corporation.

Dunn, W. Eleanor Clarke Slagle Lecture-The sensations of everyday life: Empirical, theoretical, and pragmatic considerations. *American Journal of Occupational Therapy*, 2001;55: 608-620.

Dunn, W. *Infant/Toddler Sensory Profile*. 2002, San Antonio, TX: The Psychological Corporation.

Eide, B., Eide, F. DSI in a learning disorders clinic. SI Focus, Grubb, M.S., Thompson, I.D. The influence of early experience on the development of sensory systems. *Current Opinions in Neurobiology*, 2004;14: 503-512.

Henry, J., Sloane, M., Black-Pond, C. Neurobiology and neurodevelopmental impact of childhood traumatic stress and prenatal alcohol exposure. *Language, Speech and Hearing Services in the Schools*, 2007;38: 99-108.

Interdisciplinary Council on Development and Learning Disorders. Diagnostic manual for infancy and early childhood: mental health, developmental, regulatory-sensory processing and language disorders and learning challenges. (ICDL-DMIC). 2005, Bethesda, MD: Author.

Kientz, M., Dunn, W. A comparison of the performance of children with and without autism on the sensory profile. *American Journal of Occupational Therapy*, 1997;51: 530-537.

Kuhaneck, H., Henry, D., Glennon, T. *Sensory Processing Measure: Main Classroom and School Environment From. 2005,* Los Angeles: Western Psychological Services.

Lin, S., Cermak, S., Coster, W., Miller, L. Sensory integration, sensory modulation, and growth predictors of attention and behavioral difficulties in post-institutionalized adopted children. In preparation.

Lin, S., Cermak, S., Coster, W., Miller, L. The relation between length of institutionalization and sensory integration in children adopted from Eastern Europe. *American Journal of Occupational Therapy,* 2005;59: 139-147.

Liss, M., Saulnier, C., Fein, D., Kinsbourne, M. Sensory and attention abnormalities in autistic spectrum disorders. *Autism,* 2006;10(2): 155–172.

Mangeot, S.D., Miller, L.J., McIntosh, D.N., McGrath, J., Simon, J., Hagerman, R., Goldson, E. Sensory modulation dysfunction in children with attention-deficit-hyperactivity disorder. *Developmental Medicine and Child Neurology*, 2001;43: 399–406.

Miller, L.J. Sensational kids: Hope and help for children with sensory processing. *Disorder.* 2007, New York: G.P. Putman's Sons.

Miller, L.J., Schoen, S.A, Green, K.E. A pilot Study of the Sensory Over-Responsivity Scales: Assessment and Inventory. *American Journal of Occupational Therapy,* July/August, 2008; 62 (4): 393-406

Miller, L.J., Schoen, S., James, K., Schaaf, R. Lessons learned: A pilot study on occupational therapy effectiveness for children with sensory modulation disorder. *American Journal of Occupational Therapy*, March/April, 2007; 61(2): 161-169.

Miller, L.J., Reisman, J. E., McIntosh, D.N., Simon, J. An ecological model of sensory modulation. In S. Smith Roley, E. Blanche, R.C. Schaaf (Eds.), *Understanding the nature of sensory integration with diverse populations* (pp. 57–82). 2001, San Antonio, TX: Therapy Skill Builders.

Miller, L.J., McIntosh, D.N., McGrath, J., Shyu, V., Lampe, M., Taylor, A.K., Tassone, F., Neitzel, K., Stackhouse, T., Hagerman, R. Electrodermal responses to sensory stimuli in individuals with fragile X syndrome: A preliminary report. *American Journal of Medical Genetics,* 1999;83: 268-279.

Mulligan, S. Patterns of sensory integration dysfunction. A confirmatory factor analysis. *American Journal of Occupational Therapy*, 1998;52: 819-828.

Ornitz, E., Guthrie, D., Farley, A. The early development of autistic children. *Journal of Autism and Childhood Schizophrenia*, 1977;7(3): 207-229.

Parham, L.D, Cohn, E., Spizwer, S., Koomar, J.A, Miller, L.J., Burke, J. P., et al. Fidelity in sensory integration intervention research. *American Journal of Occupational Therapy*, 2007;61: 216-227.

Parham, D., Ecker, C. *Sensory Processing Measure: Home Form. 2005*; Los Angeles: Western Psychological Services.

Parush, S., Sohmer, H., Steinberg, A., Kaitz, M. Somatosensory function in boys with ADHD and tactile defensiveness. *Physiology and Behavior*, 2007; 553–558.

Perry, B.D., Pollard, D. Altered brain development following global neglect in early childhood. *Society for Neuroscience: Proceedings from Annual Meeting*, 1997, New Orleans.

Perry, B.D., Pollard, R.A., Blakely, T.L., Vigilante, D. Childhood trauma, the neurobiology of adaptation and use-dependent development of the brain: how states become traits. *Infant Mental Health Journal*, 1995;16(4): 271-291.

Reeves, G., Cermak, S. Disorders of Praxis. In A. C. Bundy, S.J. Lane, E. Murray, (Eds). *Sensory Integration Theory and Practice*, 2nd Ed. F.A. Davis: 2002, Philadelphia.

Reynolds, S., Lane., S.J. Diagnostic validity of sensory over-responsivity: a review of the literature and case reports. *Journal of Autism and Developmental Disorders*, 2008; 38(3): 516- 530.

Schneider, M.L, Moore, C.F, Gajewski, L.L., Laughlin, N.D.K., Larson, J.S., Gay, C.L., Roberts, A.D., Converse, A.K., DeJesus, O.T. Sensory processing disorders in nonhuman primate model: Evidence for occupational therapy practice. *American Journal of Occupational Therapy*, 2007;61: 247-253.

Sensory Processing Disorder Network. Advocacy: DSM-V Intitiative. Retrieved May 13, 2008, http://209.169.7.42/dsmv.html.

Talay-Ongan, A., Wood, K. Unusual sensory sensitivities in autism: A possible crossroads. *International Journal of Disability, Development, and Education*, 2000; 47: 201-212.

Vargas, S., Camilli, G. A meta-analysis of research on sensory integration treatment. *American Journal of Occupational Therapy*, 1999;53: 189-198.

Zero to Three. *Diagnostic Classification of Mental Health and Developmental Disorders of Infancy and Early Childhood* (DC:0-3). Zero to Three: 2005, Washington, D.C.

Zuo, Y., Yang, G., Kwon. E, Gan, W.B. Long-term sensory deprivation prevents dendritic spine loss in primary somatosensory cortex. *Nature,* 2005;436: 261-5.

In: Behavioral Pediatrics, 3rd Edition
Editor: Donald. E. Greydanus et al.

ISBN 978-1-60692-702-1
© 2009 Nova Science Publishers, Inc.

Chapter 8

Tic Disorders

Donald E. Greydanus and Artemis K. Tsitsika

Introduction

One theory regarding etiology of tics involves central nervous system (CNS) circuitry dysfunction linking various CNS areas, such as the frontal lobe, thalamus, striatum, and globus pallidus. A more recent and controversial theory looks at the potential role of Group A beta-hemolytic streptococcal infection leading to conditions called PANDAS (Pediatric Autoimmune Neuropsychiatric Disorders Associated with Streptococci).

Definition

Tic or habit spasms are movements that are sudden, brief, highly stereotyped, involuntary, and purposeless. Tics are usually listed as motor tics, vocal tics, and, a rare third type, sensory tics. Tic disorders, based on the American Psychiatric Association's Diagnostic and Statistical Manual of Mental Disorders, 4th edition, Text Revision [DSM-IV-TR], are divided into *transient tic disorder*, *chronic motor/vocal tic disorder*, *Tourette's syndrome*, and *tic disorder not otherwise specified*. The onset for all tic disorders must be before age 18 years, not to be explained by any underlying disorder such as substance abuse or illnesses (e.g., Huntington's disease or post-viral encephalitis).

Transient Tic Disorder

Transient tic disorder is characterized by single or multiple motor and/ or vocal tics that last for at least 4 weeks, but not longer than 12 consecutive months.

Chronic Motor or Vocal Tic Disorder

Chronic motor or vocal tic disorder is characterized by single or multiple motor or vocal tics, but not both, present at some time during the illness. Tics last longer than a year with no period free of tics exceeding three months.

Tourette's Disorder

Tourette's disorder is characterized by multiple motor tics and one or more vocal tics that last longer than a year with no period free of tics exceeding three months.

Tic Disorder Not Otherwise Specified

Tic disorders that do not meet all the criteria to be classified as Tourette's syndrome, transient tic disorder or chronic motor or vocal tic disorder, are classified as tic disorder not otherwise specified.

Epidemiology

Transient tic disorder is noted in 4% to 20% of children, including young adolescents. There is a 2-3:1 male to female ratio and often a positive family history for tics. Voluntary suppression of these tics may occur for minutes to hours, and stress may worsen these tics. There may be eye blinking, shoulder shrugging, facial grimacing and others. Vocal tics are not present and multiple motor tics may occur in uncommon situations. The tics usually disappear spontaneously, often within weeks of their onset.

Chronic motor tic disorder (*chronic tic disorder*) is noted in 1%-2% of the general population and may be related to Tourette's syndrome; a positive family history is often found and the etiology is related to central nervous system dopamine metabolism dysfunction. *Gilles de la Tourette's syndrome* (*Tourette's syndrome*) is noted in 5 per 10,000 and is ten times more common in children versus adults. There is a 3-4:1 male to female ratio and its onset is usually between 2 and 15 years of age; the average age of onset is 7 years and, by definition, the end age of onset is age 21. There is often a positive family history for tic disorder, Tourette's syndrome, and/or chronic tic disorder.

Clinical Features

A wide variety of tics are noted in Tourette's syndrome (Table 1). Motor tics usually start before vocal tics and a single tic is the presenting symptom in 50%; multiple tics are also seen in 50% of patients. The presenting tic is the eye tic in 37%, the head tic in 16%, and a vocal tic in 18%. Coprolalia is the presenting feature in 0.1%, though one-third of patients with Tourette's syndrome eventually develop this classic swearing feature. A sensory tic is noted in 3% in which an unpleasant sensation develops about a joint or muscle group that is relieved with a tic. Voluntary suppression of tics is characteristic for a brief period of time; however, a feeling of unpleasantness develops, leading to the tic. Table 2 lists conditions associated with Tourette's Syndrome.

Table 1. Tics Noted in Tourette's Syndrome

Simple or complex tics involving	Head
	Neck
	Trunk
	Extremities (upper or lower)
Motor Tics	Eye blinking
	Lip smacking
	Shoulder shrugging
	Head Tossing
	Grimacing
	Others
Simple Vocal Tics	Coughing
	Grunting
	Shouting
	Crying
	Barking
	Throat clearing
	Sniffing
Complex Vocal Tics	Echolalia (repeating words)
	Palilalia (repeating the last sound)
	Coprolalia (swearing)

Table 2. Conditions Associated with Tourette's Syndrome

Condition	Frequency (estimated %)
Attention-deficit/hyperactivity disorder	50-60
Obsessive-compulsive disorder	25-50
Other anxiety disorders	30-40
Mood disorders	30-40
Learning disorders (± ADHD)	20-30
Disruptive behavior disorders	Common, but more related to ADHD
Explosive anger ("rage"), including intermittent explosive disorder	Common, related to ADHD and mood disorders
Substance-use disorders	Unknown, but increases with age
Pervasive developmental disorders	Unknown, but likely low

For example, attention-deficit/hyperactivity disorder (ADHD) is noted in 30% to 50% of children and adolescents with Tourette's syndrome; obsessive-compulsive disorder is found in 30% to 60%. Patient education about Tourette Syndrome can be obtained at the web site of the Tourette Syndrome Association from the United States at http://www.tsa-usa.org.

Diagnosis

The diagnosis is made in the patient with classic features. Table 3 provides a differential diagnosis of involuntary muscle movements. Tics are not the result of stimulants or illnesses, such as Huntington's disease or post-viral encephalitis.

Table 3: Involuntary Muscle Movements*

Athetosis	Slow, sinuous, writhing, involuntary movement that most frequently involves distal extremities; frequently increased by voluntary movements.
Ballismus	Wild, flinging, coarse, irregular, involuntary movements beginning in proximal limb muscles.
Chorea	Rapid, irregular, non-repetitive, sudden movement that may involve any muscle or muscle group; these movements generally interfere with voluntary movements.
Dystonia	Slow, twisting, involuntary movements associated with changes in muscle tone; movements generally involve trunk and proximal extremity muscles.
Myoclonus	Involuntary rapid, shock-like muscular contractions that are generally non-repetitive; can be increased by voluntary actions.
Spasm	Slow and prolonged involuntary contraction of a muscle or group of muscles.
Tic	Involuntary, repetitive movement of related groups of muscles; movements do not interfere with voluntary muscle movements.
Tremor	Involuntary movement that may be a slow or rapid vibration of the involved body art; tremors may get worse with movement (intentional tremor) or may occur only at rest.

*Used with permission from S Kuperman, Tic disorders in children and adolescents. In: Behavioral Pediatrics. DE Greydanus and ML Wolraich, eds, New York: Springer-Verlag, 1992, Chap. 33, p. 452.

Treatment

Tic disorders often require a wide range of treatment from education of the patient to intensive behavioral therapy to use of psychotropic medications. Transient tic disorder often disappears spontaneously within one year, often within several weeks. Thus, specific medical management is usually not necessary, unless tic progression develops in unusual situations.

Pharmacotherapy

Chronic motor tic disorder and Tourette's syndrome typically require the use of psychopharmacologic agents (Table 4) that traditionally have included haloperidol, pimozide, and clonidine. A variety of other medications have been used to ameliorate tics, but with less anecdotal and research support.

Table 4. Medications used in persons with Tourette's syndrome and comorbid disorders, and ages at which use may be appropriate

Class	Agent (A-C) ‡	Doses*	Ages**
Antipsychotics			
First-generation			
Phenothiazines	Fluphenazine (B)	1.5-10 mg/d	≥ 18
Butyrophenones	Haloperidol (A)	1-4 mg/d	≥ 18; ≥ 3†
Other	Pimozide (A)	0.05-0.2 mg/kg/d	≥ 12
Second-generation	Risperidone (A)	0.25-2 mg, 1-2x/d	≥ 18
	Ziprasidone (B)	5-40 mg/d	≥ 18
Partial DA agonist	Olanzapine (C)	2.5-12.5 mg/d	≥ 18
	Quetiapine (C)	25-150 mg/d	≥ 18
	Aripiprazole (C)	10-20 mg/d	≥ 18
Alpha-agonists	Clonidine (B)	0.05-0.3 mg/d	≥ 12
	Guanfacine (B)	0.5-1 mg, 3x/d	≥ 12
Anticonvulsants	Topiramate	50-200 mg/d	≥ 2
	Levetiracetam	1-2 g/d	≥ 16
Antidepressants			
SSRIs (for OCD)	Fluoxetine (A)	10-60 mg/d	≥ 7
	Sertraline (A)	50-250 mg/d	≥ 6
	Fluvoxamine (A)	50-350 mg/d	≥ 6
	Paroxetine (B)	10-60 mg/d	≥ 18
	Citalopram (B)	20-60 mg/d	N/A
	Escitalopram (B)	10-20 mg/d	N/A
Other (for ADHD)	Atomoxetine	0.5-1.2 mg/kg/d	≥ 6
DA receptor agonists	Pergolide (B)	0.1-0.4 mg/d	≥ 18
Muscle relaxants	Baclofen (C)	5-20 mg, 3x/d	≥ 12
Miscellaneous	Nicotine patch (C)	7-21 mg/d	≥ 18
	Mecamylamine (C)	2.5-7.5 mg/d	≥ 18
	Tetrabenazine (C)	12.5-25 mg, 1-3x/d	≥ 18

Psychostimulants: See Chapter 5 for details

‡Empirical support categories (see "Psychopharmacology" for a description)
*Dosing is clinically-based, unless stated otherwise.
**Ages (years) are for FDA-approved indications (see Table 2-x, Chapter 2, for details); use for other indications and/or at other ages is based on clinical judgment.
† For "severe behavioral problems."
DADopamine.

Most of the medications listed in Table 4 are followed by the empirical research designation letters A, B, or C. Category A denotes good supportive evidence for efficacy and safety (based on ≥ 2 randomized, placebo-controlled studies); Category B denotes fair supportive evidence (based on a minimum of one placebo-controlled study); and Category C represents minimal supportive evidence, based on less rigorous sources (such as open-label studies, case reports, etc.).

Alpha Agonists

This group of medications helps reduce adrenergic outflow from the CNS; how this lowers tic activity is uncertain. Clonidine is a presynaptic, central-acting alpha$_2$ adrenergic agonist that is used by to improve tic symptoms. Its daily dose range is 0.05 to 0.3 mg/day; depending on its use, clonidine is provided 2 to 4 times a day or only at bedtime. Guanfacine is an alpha$_{2A}$ adrenergic agonist related to clonidine, and is also used to reduce tic frequency. Its daily dosage range is 0.5 mg to 1 mg, three times a day.

Common side effects of alpha agonists include dry mouth, drowsiness, dizziness, constipation, and sedation. Children may experience orthostatic hypotension, but it is uncommon. Children may be more susceptible to the rebound hypertension associated with the abrupt discontinuation of the alpha agonist. There are no known specific contraindications to their use.

These medications are suggested as the first-line agents when pharmacotherapy is needed to treat the tics of Tourette's syndrome. Clonidine is also used as an alternative or adjunctive medication to stimulants for ADHD, and to help with post-traumatic stress disorder as well as severe aggressiveness with conduct disorder or oppositional defiant disorder. Gradual build-up and withdrawal when using clonidine are recommended; rapid withdrawal may lead to rebound hypertension. Sedation is a major limiting factor in using clonidine.

Guanfacine use may result in less blood pressure problems and sedation than seen with clonidine. Adverse reactions are similar to clonidine, but there may be more agitation and headaches, so patients should be monitored closely.

When prescribing clonidine, take some baseline data (blood pressure, pulse, blood sugar, ECG); follow this data on a regular basis, including a repeat ECG every 6 months. A few cardiac-related deaths have been reported in children and adolescents taking both methylphenidate and clonidine simultaneously. No specific laboratory testing is required when using alpha-agonists.

Antipsychotics

If tics are severe and/or bothersome to the patient, and have not responded to the alpha agonists and/or behavioral interventions, a trial of an antipsychotic is warranted (Greydanus, 2008). It is unclear exactly how the antipsychotics work in reducing the tics of Tourette's syndrome and other tic disorders. However, it is presumed that a major part of the mechanism involves dopamine blockade of post-synaptic receptors somewhere in the cortico-striatothalamic-cortical circuitry. Even with aggressive treatment, complete tic suppression may not be possible; thus, *reduction* in tic frequency may be the management goal along with education about the tic disorder itself.

Two common medications which have traditionally been used for tic suppression are *haloperidol* and *pimozide*, but *risperidone* has become more popular in the past decade. No matter which agent is chosen, a general rule in using these agents in children and adolescents is to start with a low dose and titrate slowly upwards to seek the best balance between tic amelioration and minimization of adverse effects.

Approximately one fourth of patients who are placed on haloperidol experience a 70% reduction in tics at a dose that avoids major side effects; 50% note a reduction in tics only at a dose that leads to major side effects, and 25% do not respond to haloperidol at all. Pimozide can lead to a 70% to 80% reduction in tics, often without development of serious side effects. Risperidone has been used to suppress tics at an oral dose that ranges from 0.25 mg a day to 2 mg twice a day.

For haloperidol, one should start with 0.25 mg each day, and increase to 2 mg, two times per day orally, as tolerated. Although higher doses may be used (e.g., 5 mg twice daily), tics generally respond to doses lower than those used to treat psychosis. For pimozide, starting with 1 mg daily and increasing up to 4 mg two times per day is one approach. A safer strategy may be to dose by weight, 0.05-0.2 mg/kg/d, with dosing not to exceed 10 mg daily. Dosing for risperidone is similar to that of haloperidol.

The antipsychotics haloperidol, pimozide, and risperidone are most effective at treating the tics of Tourette's syndrome. They are also the most likely to cause extrapyramidal symptoms (EPS) and neuroleptic malignant syndrome (NMS). Other side effects include lethargy and cognitive impairment. Pimozide can also prolong the QTc interval. The atypical antipsychotics (AA) risperidone, quetiapine, and olanzapine (in increasing order) tend to cause weight gain, and all of the AAs can elevate blood glucose to varying degrees. With the exception of quetiapine and aripiprazole, the newer antipsychotics used in Tourette's syndrome can elevate serum prolactin. Haloperidol and fluphenazine are contraindicated in patients with blood dyscrasias, hepatic disease, subcortical brain damage, and mental obtundation.

Pimozide should not be used in tic disorders other than Tourette's syndrome. Concurrent use with stimulant medications is discouraged if there is suspicion that the stimulant, and not Tourette's, is the cause of these tics. Pimozide should not be used with any other medications that may combine to prolong the QTc interval, including thioridazine, chlorpromazine, nefazodone, fluvoxamine, fluoxetine, sertraline, ziprasidone, and citalopram.

The patient's height, weight, and BMI (body mass index) should be measured before starting antipsychotic medications and at each subsequent visit. Blood pressure and pulse should be checked at baseline, and then at least every 3 months. Fasting glucose and lipids should be measured before starting treatment, after 3 months, and then every 6 months thereafter. A baseline examination for extrapyramidal signs should be recorded, and re-checked during dosage escalations, and once every 3 months after that. The use of the pimozide or ziprasidone requires baseline and follow-up ECGs, particularly during dosage titrations. Prolactin should be checked at any point, especially if menstrual problems develop.

Other

Other medications used in the treatment of tic disorders include dopamine receptor agonists, muscle relaxants, and anticonvulsants. These are not considered first line treatment for tic disorders and their use should be considered in selected cases in consultation with experts in child psychiatry or pediatric neurology. Obsessive-compulsive symptomatology may be noted in half of children and adolescents with Tourette's syndrome; medication used for these symptoms include clomipramine (tricyclic antidepressant) and other antidepressants, such as the selective serotonin reuptake inhibitors (SSRIs), including fluoxetine, sertraline, and fluvoxamine.

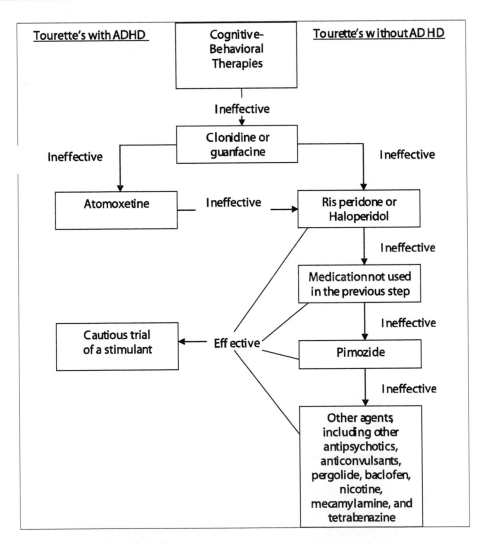

Figure 1. Treatment algorithm for Tourette's syndrome, with/without ADHD. [Modified with permission from Greydanus DE, Tsitsika AK. Tic disorders in children and adolescents, In Greydanus DE, Calles JL Jr, Patel DR. Pediatric and Adolescent Psychopharmacology. Cambridge, UK: Cambridge University Press, 2008:223-240].

Use of Stimulants

ADHD is found in 50% or more of patients with Tourette's syndrome. Children and adolescents with both ADHD and Tourette's may be given both stimulant medications (if effective) and anti-tic medications (such as pimozide or haloperidol), if tics develop. Research does not suggest that stimulant medications cause Tourette's; however, these medications should be used in a "start low and go slow" manner.

Their use in patients with Tourette's should be approached with caution. If the tics are worsened by the stimulant drugs, other anti-ADHD medications that do not typically worsen tics may be tried; these include alpha$_2$ agonists (such as clonidine or guanfacine) or atomoxetine, a selective norepinephrine reuptake inhibitor. Atomoxetine is given at an oral dose ranging from 0.5-1.2 mg per kilogram per day. The U. S. Food and Drug Administration (FDA) has given atomoxetine a black box warning due to a rare adverse effect of severe liver toxicity. The antidepressant bupropion may improve the symptoms of ADHD, but may also worsen tics.

Conclusion

The safe and effective treatment of Tourette's disorder, and other tic disorders, is based on a logical hierarchy of interventions, from cognitive and behavioral therapies to pharmacologic agents. Figure 1 illustrates one example of a treatment algorithm; other approaches may be found in the medical literature.

References

Bloch MH, Peterson BS, Scahill L et al: Adulthood outcomes of tic and obsessive-compulsive symptom severity in children with Tourette Syndrome. *Arch Pediatr. Adolesc. Med*. 2006; 160: 65-69.

Cohen DJ, Young JG, Nathanson JA, Shaywitz BA. Clonidine in Tourette's syndrome. *Lancet* 1979;2:551-553.

Delgado MR, Albright AL. Movement disorders in children: Definitions, classifications and grading systems. *J. Child Neurol*. 2003;18 Suppl 1:S1-S8.

Diagnostic and Statisical Manual of Mental Disorders, DSM-IV 4th ed. Washington, DC: American Psychiatric Association. *Tic Disorders*. 100-105, 2000.

Edgar, TS. Oral pharmacotherapy of childhood movement disorders. *J. Child Neurol*. 2003;18 Suppl 1:S40-S49.

Gaffney GR, Perry PJ, Lund BC, Bever-Stiller KA, Arndt S, Kuperman S. Risperidone versus clonidine in the treatment of children and adolescents with Tourette's syndrome. *J. Am. Acad. Child Adolesc. Psychiatry* 2002;41:330-36.

Gilbert D. Treatment of children and adolescents with tics and Tourette syndrome. *J. Child Neurol*. 2006;21:690-700.

Greydanus DE, Pratt HD. Attention-deficit/hyperactivity disorder in children and adolescents: Interventions for a complex costly clinical conundrum. *Pediatr. Clin. No Am.* 2003;50:1049-1092.

Greydanus DE, Van Dyke DH. "Neurologic Disorders." In: *Essential Adolescent Medicine* Eds: DE Greydanus, DR Patel, HD Pratt. NY: McGraw-Hill Medical Publishers, Ch. 13:235-279, 2006.

Greydanus DE, Pratt HD, Patel DR: Attention deficit hyperactivity disorder across the lifespan. Disease-A-Month 2007; 53 (2); 65-132.

Greydanus DE, Tsitsika AK: "Tic disorders in children and adolescents" In: Greydanus DE, Calles, Jr. JL, Patel DR: *Pediatric and Adolescent Psychopharmacology.* Cambridge, England: Cambridge University Press, ch. 12: 223-240, 2008.

Greydanus DE, Feinberg AN, Patel DR, Homnick DN (eds): *The Pediatric Diagnostic Examination.* NY: McGraw-Hill Medical Publishers, pages 371 and 616, 2008.

Johnson MV: "Tics" In: *Nelson Textbook of Pediatrics*, 17th Ed. Eds: RM Kliegman, RE Behrman, HB Jenson, BF Stanton. Philadelphia, PA: Saunders/Elsevier, ch. 597.4:2493, 2007.

Kuperman S. Tic disorders in the adolescent. Adolesc Med 2002;13:537-551. Jankovic J. Tourette's syndrome. *N. Engl. J. Med.* 2001;345:1184-1192.

Leckman JF. Tourette's syndrome. *Lancet* 2002;360:1577-1586.

Pina-Garza JE. "Tic disorders in children and adolescents" In: *Behavioral Pediatrics*, 2nd Ed.,Eds: DE Greydanus, DR Patel, HD Pratt. NY : iUniverse, Ch 19: 497-507, 2006.

Rampello L, Alvano A, Battaglia G, Bruno V, Raffaele R, Nicoletti F. Tic disorders: from pathophysiology to treatment. *J. Neurol.* 2006;253:1-15.

Sallee FR, Nesbitt L, Jackson C, Sine L, Sethuraman, G. Relative efficacy of haloperidol and pimozide in children and adolescents with Tourette's disorder. *Am. J. Psychiatry* 1997;154:1057-62.

Sanger TD. Pathophysiology of pediatric movement disorders. *J. Child Neurol.* 2003;18 Suppl 1:S9-S24.

Scahill L, Erenberg G, Berlin CM Jr, Budman C, Coffey BJ, Jankovic J, et al. Contemporary assessment and pharmacotherapy of Tourette syndrome. *NeuroRx* 2006;3:192-206.

Snider LA, Swedo SE: PANDAS: Current status and directions for research. *Mol. Psychiatry* 2004; 9: 900-7.

Swedo SE, Leonard HL, Rapport JL: The pediatric autoimmune neuropsychiatric disorders associated with streptococcal infections (PANDAS) Subgroup. *Pediatrics* 2004;113: 907-11.

Tourette Syndrome Study Group. Treatment of ADHD children with tics: a randomized controlled trial. *Neurology* 2004;58:527-536.

Wehr AM, Namerow LB. Citalopram for OCD and Tourette's syndrome. *J. Am. Acad Child Adolesc. Psychiatry* 2001;40:740-741.

In: Behavioral Pediatrics, 3rd Edition
Editor: D. E. Greydanus et al.

ISBN 978-1-60692-702-1
© 2009 Nova Science Publishers, Inc.

Chapter 9

Enuresis

Donald E. Greydanus, Alfonso Torres, Arthur Feinberg and Cynthia Feucht

Abstract

Incontinence disorders are an important group of problems clinicians manage in children and adolescents. This chapter reviews the physiology of micturition, the epidemiology of enuresis, general clinical approach to enuresis, laboratory evaluation, and general principles of management.

Introduction

Physiology of Micturition

Normal function of the lower urinary tract relies on the complex coordination of a number of inhibitory and stimulatory inputs. These inputs, both automatic and volitional in nature, originate in the central nervous system and travel over nerves of the peripheral nervous system to specific end organs. Continence relies heavily on the integrity of the autonomic nervous system. Intentional bladder emptying requires that input from the cortex be transmitted to somatic peripheral nerves and be integrated with appropriate changes in the basal state of the autonomic nervous system. While a number of supraspinal inputs and local reflex mechanisms contribute to the fine tuning and full conscious control of micturition, a more simplified approach may facilitate the present discussion.

Urine Storage

As the bladder fills and stretches, a mechanism to prevent urination must be in place. Afferent impulses travel through the pelvic nerves to the spinal column and result in a synapse with efferent neurons in two places: 1) With alpha motor neurons (at the same level) in the anterior horn of the spinal gray matter, sending excitatory impulses via the pudendal nerve to the striated muscle of the external urethral sphincter (contraction of the urethral sphincter); 2) After ascending briefly near the site of entry into the spinal column with cell bodies of the lumbar intermediolateral cell column (site of sympathetic outflow), sending impulses via the hypogastric nerve to inhibit detrusor (bladder) contraction and facilitate contraction of the smooth muscle of the internal urethral sphincter.

Bladder Sensation

While afferent fibers that run through the pelvic nerve are part of the involuntary reflex described above, the message regarding bladder distention is also carried up through the spinal cord to the cortex where the sensation of bladder fullness is realized.

Voiding Mechanism

Afferent fibers carry the message of bladder distention not only to the cortex, but also to the pontine micturition center in the brainstem. Synapses here give rise to interneurons that 1) stimulate contraction of the detrusor muscle and 2) inhibit firing of neurons that facilitate urethral sphincter contraction. Bladder emptying then follows. This reflex, however, is governed by input from the cortex, hypothalamus, and other supraspinal structures. Thus, voluntary control requires the integrity of structures above the level of the brainstem.

Normal Development

Bladder control is a developmental, as well as a social milestone that in the *Western* world, parents and society expect the child to achieve by 5 years of age. There is a chronologic progression of bladder control that matures with the individual's age. Voiding in fetuses and infants is an automatic process triggered by bladder distention to functional capacity. Voluntary control is clearly not present in infancy and urination occurs frequently in the newborn. Frequency diminishes during the first 12-24 months of life and awareness of the sensation of bladder fullness develops. Willful retention normally develops and appears to be practiced before voluntary voiding is mastered. Day time bladder control is obtained earlier than night time bladder control. The term *enuresis* is used in reference to the involuntary voiding by a child who has reached an age in which bladder control is expected.

It is now clear that the traditional concept that voiding in the fetus and in the infant is simply a sacral, automatic response to bladder distention is an oversimplification. Intrauterine voiding is more frequent when the fetus is awake, as demonstrated by ultrasound and can be triggered by other stimuli such as vibration or auditory stimulation indicating the participation of higher neurologic centers in the process even at these early states of development. In newborns, during sleep, the bladder is quiescent and there is no detrusor activity. When the bladder is distended, there is electroencephalographic evidence of cortical arousal. Such evidence along with animal studies indicate a complex fetal and postnatal development of bladder functions simultaneously at different levels.

After the normal diuresis observed in the first day, the number of voiding decreases to a few times a day in the first week of life only to increase up to around one per hour by the first month of life; then it decreases to 10 to 15 times a day by six months. By 2 to 3 years, the frequency of voiding is 8 to 10 times a day and by 12 years of age, the frequency is similar to that of an adult. The bladder capacity can be estimated by several formulas including the frequently used Hjalmas' formula: *bladder capacity in ml = 60 + (age in years X 30)*. The evaluation of the bladder capacity by non-invasive methods, such as ultrasonography, has practical implications for the treatment of enuresis, as noted later.

Definitions

The American Psychiatry Association's *Diagnostic and Statistical Manual for Mental Disorders, 4th edition, Text Revision (DSM-IV-TR)* defines enuresis as repeated intentional or involuntary voiding of urine into bed or clothes, with a frequency of at least 2 times a week for not less than 3 consecutive months or associated with significant social or academic impairment; the child should be 5 years of age or older (or of equivalent developmental level); also, the voiding behavior is not due to underlying medical conditions or physiologic effect of any substance. The International Children's Continence Society terminology related to enuresis is listed in Table 1.

Table 1. International Children's Continence Society Terminology

Enuresis	Intermittent incontinence of urine while sleeping
Enuresis, monosymptomatic	Enuresis without any (other) lower urinary tract symptoms
Enuresis, non-monosymptomatic	Enuresis with (other) lower urinary tract symptoms
Enuresis, primary	Enuresis in a child who has previously been dry for less than 6 months
Enuresis, secondary	Enuresis in a child who has previously been dry for at least 6 months

Based on Neveus T, von Gontard A, Hoebeke P, et al. The standardization of terminology of lower urinary tract function in children and adolescents: Report from the Standardization Committee of the International Children's Continence Society. J Urology 2006;176:314-324.

Epidemiology

By 2 1/2 years of age 90% of the girls and 80% of the boys know the need to micturate. Certainly by 3 years of age, boys and girls, with help and understanding, are able to be dry during the day. By 3-5 years of age 75% of the children will obtain night time bladder control. By 5 years of age between 15 to 20% of children will continue to have nocturnal enuresis. The number decreases to around 7% by 10 years of age. Approximately 3%-4% have enuresis by 12 years of age. The incidence of nocturnal enuresis continues to decline so that by 15 years of age and older still, about 1% of individuals will continue to have nocturnal enuresis. Sixty percent of the cases have been present from early childhood without interruption. Approximately 40% are "secondary", developing 3 to 6 months after the appearance of continence. Ninety percent of the cases of enuresis present only at night (nocturnal enuresis). Diurnal enuresis occurs more commonly in females while nocturnal enuresis is noted more commonly in males.

Clinical Features

Parents generally bring the child for evaluation because of bed wetting. Bed wetting may or may not be associated with day time incontinence or other behavioral symptoms.

History

The history should include specific questions regarding the frequency and severity of the enuresis. The parents may be able to answer the clinician's questions for the shy or embarrassed younger child. They will also be able to tell you if the child has ever been continent, thereby differentiating between *primary* and *secondary* enuresis. Questions that help differentiate between isolated nocturnal enuresis and incontinence in children are listed in Table 2.

Table 2. Questions that Help Differentiate Between Isolated Nocturnal Enuresis and Incontinence

---

1. The severity of the daytime voiding is evaluated by the size of the wet spot in the clothing.
2. Is the length of time between voiding greater than or less than 30 minutes?
3. Is the frequency of voiding more than 8 times during the day time?
4. Is the frequency of voiding during the day less than three times?
5. Is the child unable to hold back urine?
6. Does the child squat down or squeeze to hold back urine?
7. Does the child strain when voiding?
8. Does the child have an interrupted, staccato or weak stream? Keeps on dribbling?
9. Has periods when urinating is painful?
10. Once had blood in the urine?

11. Once had a urinary tract infection?
12. Gets out of bed at night to drink regularly?
13. Has a day without defecation? Does the child soil the underwear with feces?
14. Only a wet spot in bed (not a soaking wet bed)?
15. Has he/she been wetting the bed since infancy?
16. Has he/she been dry for at least 6 months in a row?
17. When were other children in the family older than 6 years dry?
18. When were the parents dry?
19. What has been done to stop the bed wetting?
20. How wet is he/she at night?
21. How many times does he/she wet at night?
22. Is the child easy to rouse at night?
23. How is the child doing in school?
24. Are there problems at school or at home?
25. Is the child also wet during the day?
26. If the child is wet during the day time: since when has he/she been wet during the day?
27. How does the wetting during the day relate to interrupting play? Laughing, giggling?
28. How wet is he/she during the day?

Physical Examination

A complete physical examination should be done with particular emphasis on the genitourinary exam (external genitalia, palpation of bladder, odor of urine), neurologic examination (sensory and motor function of the lower extremities, reflexes, anal wink, fundoscopic eye exam for increased intracranial pressure), and musculoskeletal examination (spinal abnormalities such as tufts of hair, hemangiomas, masses, scoliosis, and lower extremity abnormalities [clubfoot, tone or gait abnormalities]). The abdominal examination includes evaluation of the flanks for enlarged kidneys, enlarged bladder or masses, and severe constipation, the gluteal areas and back looking for asymmetry or midline defects.

Diagnosis

Diagnosis of enuresis is primarily based on a detailed history and physical examination (Greydanus, Feinberg, Patel, Homnick, 2008). Laboratory studies are indicated based on findings of the history and physical examination to exclude any underlying organic causes for enuresis.

Urinalysis and urine cultures are necessary; infection must be considered and ruled out. Other studies including renal and bladder ultrasonography or VCUG (voiding cystourethrogram) are to be requested only when clearly indicated. Imaging studies are seldom indicated for monosymptomatic nocturnal enuresis, but may be valuable in patients with significant dysfunctional voiding or associated with neurologic abnormalities. Usually the nocturnal enuresis resolves itself once the day time voiding problem has been successfully treated.

Most children with monosymptomatic enuresis do not require image studies and cystometrographic studies are of no additional value in the evaluation and management of these patients. Cystomethographic evaluation as well as imaging studies are reserved for patients that have symptomatic enuresis, recurrent UTI or evidence of neurological compromise (Greydanus, 2006; 2008). Patients with Hinman syndrome or those with suspected motor neuron abnormalities should undergo thorough neurologic evaluation. It is often recommended that patients with the Hinman syndrome (non-neurogenic neurogenic bladder) also under go a psychiatric evaluation.

Treatment

In evaluating the enuretic child, the physician must know how to answer two crucial questions: *When* to treat, and *how* to treat? Nocturnal enuresis in children has traditionally motivated very little interest in terms of research, evaluation, and treatment. This attitude is based on the observation that treatment is not always curative and most children with nocturnal enuresis will, with time, outgrow their condition. However, it had become increasingly evident that children with enuresis suffer from lack of self-esteem and embarrassment, potentially leading to stress and depression. It has been demonstrated that when the enuresis is successfully treated, the self-esteem of the child is normalized. Failure of treatment is associated with increasing stress and anger. Low self-esteem is a risk for psychiatric disorders and problems with social adjustment. Treatment needs to be instituted early, when the child expresses the desire to be dry at night.

Treatment of Nocturnal Enuresis

Though the timing for initiation of active treatment is variable, most physicians and families are comfortable starting treatment when the child is around 5 years of age. However, the most important consideration is the time when the child is ready to receive treatment. In the United States there are several well accepted treatments for monosymptomatic nocturnal enuresis. These include:

1. Conditioning with a Bell-Pad alarm.
2. The use of the vasopressin derivative, oral DDAVP
3. Tricyclic medications (imipramine).
4. The use of a detrusor relaxant, in cases of reduced bladder capacity or detrusor instability.

It is important to obtain the cooperation of the patient and the family for the treatment of enuresis to be successful. The family and child need to be educated at the appropriate level of communication and the use of visual aids about the causes of enuresis, how the different methods of treatment work, and the side effects of medications. The goals of the treatment need to be clearly established. It is important to encourage the child to keep a chart of dry and wet nights. Parents need to support and praise the achievement and efforts of the child. Criticism and punishment for wet nights should be avoided.

Non-Pharmacologic Methods

Most pharmacologic treatment of enuresis is combined with one of several *behavior modification programs* in order to improve bladder capacity and sphincter control. A number of operant conditioning devices are available, such as the Enurotone. The Bell-Pad conditioning devise is based on the principle that urine will complete an electric circuit that triggers an alarm. The patient learns to awaken to the sensations of bladder fullness and micturition and rises to complete voiding on a voluntary basis.

The newer models of these systems are safe and relatively inexpensive. The use of the *conditioning device* is associated with a change in the awakening response by EEG, as well as a significant increase in the nocturnal bladder capacity in those patients that become dry. The success rate of this treatment is over 70%, and is clearly related to the patient's age, with better results obtained in children 7 years and older. It is necessary to continue treatment until the child is dry for one month and s/he is able to tolerate normal fluid intake. Relapses are less frequent with this method of treatment. In case of a relapse, treatment with the alarm may be restarted.

Bladder retention exercises have been employed with occasional success. The patient is instructed to try to hold his or her urine for increasingly longer periods of time after experiencing the urge to micturate. Some individuals respond to a timed voiding program in which they learn to void "by the clock" every two hours rather than waiting for a sensation of fullness which may come too late. Fluid restriction in the evening and rousing the patient to void when the last family member goes to bed may be helpful. However, these adjunctive measures alone are generally futile in themselves.

Current thinking often concludes that counseling, per se, will *not* ameliorate enuresis, but is helpful in improving secondary emotional distress. Hypnosis, dietary manipulations, allergy therapies and other treatments have been suggested, but controlled studies are needed to confirm the effectiveness of these concepts as potential management tools. Reassurance that enuresis does not adversely affect sexual function is an important component of counseling for enuretic teenagers. If the child snores and has enlarged adenoids, adenoidectomy may correct the enuresis.

Table 3. Drugs Used in Neurogenic Bladder Dysfunction

Bladder Dysfunction	Drug	Mechanism	Dosage	Comments
Impaired Urine Storage				
Decreased Bladder Capacity	Proprantheline	Anticholinergic	2-3 mg/kg/day divided every 4-6 hrs & at bedtime	Administer 30 minutes before meals & at bedtime
	Flavoxate	Direct smooth muscle relaxation	6-12 yrs: 100-200mg at bedtime >12 yrs: 100-200mg 3-4 times daily	Administer 1 hour before or 2 hours after a meal
	Oxybutynin	Anticholinergic	Immediate release: 1-5 yrs: 0.2 mg/kg/dose 2-3 times daily >5 yrs: 5mg twice daily; maximum 15mg/day Extended release: ≥6 yrs: 5mg daily; increase in 5mg increments to maximum of 20mg daily	Administer on an empty stomach for immediate release formulation
	Tolterodine	Anticholinergic	Immediate release: 0.1 mg/kg/day in 2 divided doses	May require lower doses if patient concurrently taking CYP 450 3A4 inhibitors
	Hyoscyamine	Anticholinergic	Drops <2 yrs: 2.3kg: 3 drops every 4h as needed (max. 18 drops) 3.4kg: 4 drops every 4h as needed (max. 24 drops) 5kg: 5 drops every 4h as needed (max. 30 drops) 7kg: 6 drops every 4h as needed (max. 36 drops) 10kg: 8 drops every 4h as needed (max. 48 drops) 15kg: 11 drops every 4h as needed (max. 66 drops)	Oral drop concentration: 0.125 mg/ml Elixir concentration: 0.125mg/5ml Administer before meals

Table 3. (Continued)

Bladder Dysfunction	Drug	Mechanism	Dosage	Comments
			2-12 yrs: 0.25-1ml every 4h as needed (max. 6ml/day) >12 yrs: 1-2ml every 4h as needed (max. 12ml/day) Elixir: 2-12yrs: 10kg: 1.25ml every 4h as needed (max. 30ml/day) 20kg: 2.5ml every 4h as needed (max. 30ml/day) 40kg: 3.75ml every 4h as needed (max. 30ml/day) 50kg: 5ml every 4h as needed (max. 30ml/day) >12 yrs: 5-10ml every 4h as needed (max. 60ml/day) Oral/Sublingual: 2-12 yrs: 0.0625-0.125mg every 4h as needed (max. 0.75mg/day) >12 yrs: 0.125-0.25mg every 4 hours as needed (max. 1.5mg/day) Extended release: 2-12 yrs: 0.375mg every 12h >12 yrs: 0.375-0.75mg every 12h (max. 1.5mg/day)	

Table 3. (Continued)

	Drug	Mechanism	Dosage	Comments
	Desmopressin	Enhanced water reabsorption in the kidneys	Oral: ≥6 yrs: 0.2mg at bedtime; maximum 0.6mg daily	Restrict fluid intake 1 hour prior to dose until the following morning or for at least 8 hours after administration Intranasal no longer indicated for primary nocturnal enuresis due to multiple reports of hyponatremia-related seizures
Bladder Dysfunction	Drug	Mechanism	Dosage	Comments
Decreased Outflow Resistance	Imipramine	Anticholinergic & Sympathomimetic	6-12 yrs: 10-25mg at bedtime; maximum 50mg/day >12 yrs: 10-25mg at bedtime; maximum 75mg/day	Administer 1 hour prior to bedtime May increase by 25mg increments each week Overdose can be fatal
Impaired Bladder Emptying				
Increased Bladder Capacity	Bethanechol	Cholinergic	0.3-0.6 mg/kg/day divided in 3-4 doses	Administer 1 hour before or 2 hours after meals
Increased Outflow Resistance	Phenoxybenzamine	Alpha-adrenergic antagonist	0.6-1.5 mg/kg/day	
	Doxazosin	Alpha$_1$-adrenergic antagonist	Immediate release: <50kg: 0.5mg at bedtime	Dose may be titrated to effect

Pharmacologic Treatment

Desmopressin

DDAVP is a derivative of AVP. It is frequently used for the treatment of monosymptomatic nocturnal enuresis. The rational for the use of this medication is the observation that in some patients with nocturnal enuresis, the nocturnal levels of AVP are low, the osmotic pressure is low, and the urine volume is large in relation to the nocturnal bladder capacity resulting in bladder overflow and enuresis.

The dosage guideline is summarized in Table 3. The therapeutic response usually occurs during the first 48 hours. One has to be careful and clearly advise the parents and the patient about the importance of limiting the fluid intake during the evening. Symptomatic hyponatremia, including seizures has been reported in patients on DDAVP that do not limit fluid intake. The treatment is continued until the patient remains dry at night for 4-6 weeks; then, the dose is gradually decreased. The therapeutic response is greater than 70% and the relapse rate as high as 40%. The medication may be restarted in cases of relapse.

For monosymptomatic patients with nocturnal enuresis that have failed to respond to maximal doses of desmopressin, the addition of a long acting anticholinergic medication results in improvement in the risk of bed wetting by 66% compared with controls (Austin, 2008). Patients with nocturnal enuresis associated with low bladder capacity as assessed by ultrasound respond better to treatment with a combination of desmopressin and a long acting anticholinergic medication than with desmopressin alone. Patients with normal bladder capacity as assessed by ultrasound who are treated with desmopressin alone have a positive response to this treatment; those children with a large bladder capacity benefit from treatment with desmopressin, and utilization of a double voiding technique and scheduled voiding.

Tricyclic Antidepressants

Tricyclic antidepressants (TCAs), particularly imipramine pamoate, are classic medications in the treatment of children with enuresis. The dosage of imipramine is summarized in Table 3. The clinical effects may be seen within 1-2 weeks of therapy initiation. The drug has anticholinergic effects that have been associated with urinary retention, delayed micturation, and dilatation of the urinary tract. The use of TCAs has been associated with arousal changes in the EEG. The medication has also been implicated in an increase in the secretion of anti-diuretic hormone (ADH). The use of DDAVP and imipramine as a combination medication for treatment of enuresis should be avoided. Other side effects with TCAs include severe cardiac arrhythmias with accidental overdose or suicide attempts. Granulocytopenia and bone marrow suppression have also been described.

When the patient responds and remains dry for 2 weeks or more, the medication is given every other day, and then decreased or discontinued. The response rate is between 43-80%. Because of the severity of complications with overdose (including cardiac arrhythmias), the medication needs to be prescribed in small quantities and a responsible adult needs to give the medication to the patient. It should not be used in the child or adolescent who is at risk for suicide.

Oxybutynin

Some of the children who have nocturnal enuresis may also have daytime voiding syndrome (DVS). These symptoms include urinary frequency, urgency, urge incontinence, and urine withholding. Many of these children have developed poor toilet habits, resulting in abnormal patterns of defecation, including severe encopresis. Many of these children also have recurrent urinary tract infections as well as daytime and nighttime bladder control problems. Addressing the psychological factors involved in these situations as well as developing a program of bladder-bowel retraining and treatment of urinary tract infections is also important in the management.

Children with nocturnal enuresis and daytime voiding symptoms without urinary tract infections are otherwise asymptomatic. The treatment should be directed, initially, to the daytime enuresis with a program that involves timed voiding every 2 hours and anticholinergic medications such as oxybutynin; this may be given as a single nighttime dose or as frequently as twice or three times daily for daytime enuresis associated with an unstable bladder. Children should be alerted to the common side effects of anti-cholinergic medications, including sedation, constipation, dry mouth, flushing, and others. It is important to avoid over-heating on hot days.

Another antimuscarinic medication, in addition to oxybutynin, is tolterodine that has been used to treat enuresis including nonneurogenic daytime urinary incontinence and for enuresis when oxybutynin has failed. Side effects include blurred vision, constipation, abdominal pain, and others. Newer antimuscarinics that may be useful as determined by more research includes darifenacin and solifenacin. Drugs used in various disorders of voiding are listed in Table 3.

Conclusion

Enuresis is a common problem seen in pediatric practice. Although most children tend to have decreasing frequency of nocturnal episodes of bed wetting as they get older, some need active management because of the impact of enuresis on their academic and social functioning. Diagnosis of enuresis is primarily based on clinical evaluation. Behavioral management is effective in many children. Some children who do not respond adequately to behavioral management will benefit from the addition of pharmacotherapy. Desmopressin, imipramine, and oxybutynin are the most widely used drugs. Most children have an excellent prognosis.

Acknowledgment

This chapter is modified and updated with permission from Greydanus DE, Torres AD, O'Donnel DM, Feinberg AN. Enuresis: Current concepts. Indian J Pediatr 1999;66:425-438.

References

Aikawa T, Kasahara T and Uchiyama M: The arginine-vasopressin secretion profile of children with primary nocturnal enuresis. *Eur. Urol.* 33 Suppl 1998; 3: 41-4.

Austin PF, Richey ML: Dysfunctional voiding. *Pediatr. Rev.* 2000; 21: 336-341.

Austin PF, Ferguson G, Yan Y et al: Combination therapy with desmopressin and an anticholinergic medication for nonresponders to desmopressin for monosymptomatic nocturnal enuresis: A randomized, double-blind, placebo-controlled trial. Pediatrics 2008; 122 (5): 1027-32.

Ayan S, Kaya K, Topsakal K et al: Efficacy of tolterodine as a first-line treatment for non-neurogenic voiding dysfunction in children. *BJU Int* 2005; 96: 411-414.

Azhir A, Ghessari A, Fragzadegan Z, Adebi A: New treatment protocol for primary enuresis in children according to ultrasound bladder measurements. Saudi Med J 2008; 29 (10): 1475-9.

Boris NW, Dalton R: "Enuresis (Bed-wetting)" In: *Nelson Textbook of Pediatrics*, 18th Ed., Eds: RM Kliegman, RE Behrman, HB Jenson, RF Stanton. Philadelphia, PA: Saunders/Elsevier. Ch. 22.3: 113-115, 2007.

Butler RJ, Golding J, Northstone K: ALSPAC Study Team: Nocturnal enuresis at 7.5 years old. Prevalence and analysis of clinical signs. *BJU Int* 2005; 96: 404-410.

Cain MP, Wu SD, Austin PF, Herndon CD, Rink RC. Alpha blocker therapy for children with dysfunctional voiding and urinary retention. *J. Urol.* 2003;170:1514-1517

Chiozza ML, Plebani M. Evaluation and antidiuretic hormone before and after long term treatment with desmopressin in a group of children. *Br. J. Urol.,* 1998; Supp 3: 53-55.

Donaghue MB, Latimer ME, Pillsbury HL, Hertzog L: Hyponatremic seizures in a child using desmopressin for nocturnal enuresis: *Arch. Pediatr. Adoles Med.* 1998; 152(3): 290-292.

Eiberg H, Berendt I and Mohr J: Assignment of dominant inherited nocturnal enuresis (EUR 1) to chromosome 137. *Nature Genetics* 1995; 10: 354-356.

Evans JHC: Evidence-based management of nocturnal enuresis. *Br. Med. J.* 2001; 323: 1167-69.

Feldman AS, Bauer SB: Diagnosis and management of dysfunctional voiding. *Curr. Opin. Pediatr.* 2006; 18: 139-147.

Fergusson DM and Horwood LJ: Nocturnal enuresis and behavioral problems in adolescence: A 15-year longitudinal study. *Pediatrics* 1994; 94:662-668.

Firooze F, Batniji R, Aslan AR e t al: Resolution of diurnal incontinence and nocturnal enuresis after adenotonsillectomy in children. *J. Urol* 2006; 175: 1885-1888.

Fritz G, Rochney R: Work Group on Quality Issues: Summary of the practice parameter and treatment of children and adolescents with enuresis. *J. Am. Acad. Child Adolesc. Psychiatr.* 2004; 3: 123-5.

Friman PC, Handwerk ML, Swearer SM et al: Do children with primary nocturnal enuresis have clinically significant behavior problems? *Arch. Pediatr. Adolesc. Med.* 1998 152:537-9.

Ghoniem GM and Sakr MA: Bladder dysfunciton syndromes. *State of the Art Reviews*: *Adolescent Medicine* 1996; 7(1): 35-46.

Glazener CM, Evans JH, Petro RE: Tricylcic and related drugs for nocturnal enuresis in children. *Cochrane Database Sys Rev 3*: CD002117, 2003.

Goessl C, Sauter T, Michael T, Berge B, Staehler M, Miller K. Efficacy and tolerability of tolterodine in children with detrusor hyperreflexia. *Urology* 2000;55(3):414-418.

Greydanus DE and Torres AD: "Genitourinary and renal disorders": In: *Adolescent Medicine*, Third Edition. Stamford, CT: Appleton and Lange, ch 13:220-241, 1997.

Greydanus DE, Torres AD, Wan JH: "Genitourinary and renal disorders" In: *Essential Adolescent Medicine*. Eds: DE Greydanus, DR Patel, HD Pratt. Ch 16: 329-359, 2006.

Greydanus DE, Feinberg AN, Patel DR, Homnick DN (eds): *The Pediatric Diagnostic Examination*. NY: McGraw-Hill Medical Publishers, pages 616, 663, 684, 2008.

Greydanus DE, Calles Jr. JE, Patel DR: *Pediatric and Adolescent Psychopharmacology: A Practical Manual for Pediatricians*. Cambridge, England: Cambridge University Press, 301 pages, 2008.

Hagglof B, Andren O, Bergstrom E et al: Self-esteem in children with nocturnal enuresis and urinary incontinence: Improvement of self-esteem after treatment. *Eur. Urol.* 1998; 33 Suppl 3:16-19.

Hinman F: Non-neurogenic bladder (the Hinman syndrome) fifteen years later. *J. Urol.* 1991; 136:769.

Hjalmas K: Urodynamics in normal infants and children. Scand J Urol Nephrol Suppl 1988; 114: 30-37.

Humphreys MR, Reinberg YE: Contemporary and emerging drug treatments for urinary incontinence in children. *Paedatr Drugs* 2005; 7:151-162.

Kawauchi A, Imada N, Tanaka Y et al: Effects of systemic treatment based on overnight simultaneus monitory of electroencephalogram and cystometry. *Eur. Urol.* 1998, 33: supp 3: pp. 58-61.

Kilic N, Balkan E, Akgoz S et al: Comparison of the effectiveness and side-effects of tolterodine and oxybutynin in children with detrusor instability. *Int. J. Urol.* 2006; 13: 105-8.

Kuznetsova AA, Natochin YV and Papayan AV: Osmo-regulatory function of the kidney in enuretic children. *Scand. J. Urol. Nephrol.* 1998; 32:132-7.

Lane W, Robson M: Current management of nocturnal enuresis. *Curr. Opin. Urol.* 2008; 18: 425-430.

Lexi-Comp, Inc. (Pediatric Lexi-Drugs®). Lexi-Comp.; September 11, 2008.

Loening-Baucke V: Urinary incontinence and urinary tract infections and their resolution with treatment of chronic constipation in children. *Pediatrics* 1997; 100 (2): 228-232.

Mikkelsen EJ: Enuresis and encopresis: Ten years of progress. *J. Am. Acad. Child Adolesc. Psychiatr.* 2001; 40: 1146.

Miranda B, Bertraud JE Arano: Efficacy of oxybutyin chloride in children with vesicouretral reflux an detrusor instability. *Ann. Eur. Pediatr.* 1997; 47(3): 251-257.

Moffatt MS: Nocturnal enuresis: Psychologic implications of treatment and nontreatment. 1989; *J. Pediatr.* 114:697.

Neveus T, Lackgren G, Stenberg A et al: Sleep and night-time behaviour of enuretics and non-enuretics. *Br. J. Urol.* 1998; 81 Suppl 3:67-71.

Neveus T, von Gontard A, Hoebeke P, et al. The standardization of terminology of lower urinary tract function in children and adolescents: Report from the Standardisation Committee of the International Children's Continence Society. *J. Urology* 2006;176:314-324.

Nijman R: Role of antimuscarinics in the treatment of nonneurogenic daytime urinary Incontinence in children. *Urol.* 2003; 63: 45-50.

Odersson AF, Jorgensen TM: Changes in nocturnal bladder capacity during treatment with the bell and pad for monosymptomatic nocturnal enuresis. *J. Urol.* 1998; 160(1): 166-169.

Ohel G, Haddad S, Sanueloff A: Fetal urine production and micturition and fetal behavior state. Am J Perinatol 1995; 12: 91-2.

Palmer LS, Franco I, Rotario P et al: Biofeedback therapy expedites the resolution of reflux in older children. *J. Urol.* 2002; 168: 1699-1703.

Pennesi M, Pitter M, Bordugo A et al: Behavioral therapy for primary nocturnal enuresis. *J. Urol.* 2004; 171: 408-410.

Reiner WG. Pharmacotherapy in the management of voiding and storage disorders, including enuresis and encopresis. *J. Am. Acad. Child Adoles. Psychiatry* 2008;47(5):491-8.

Robson WL, Leung AK, Van Howe E: Primary and secondary nocturnal enuresis: similarities in presentation. *Pediatrics* 2005; 115: 956-9.

Schulman S, Stokes A, Salzman PM: The efficacy and safety of oral desmopressin in children with primary nocturnal enuresis. *J. Urol.* 2001; 166: 2427-31.

Schwab M. and Ruder J: Hyponatremia and cerebral convulsion due to DDAVP administration in patients with enuresis nocturnia or urinary concentrating testing. *Eur. J. Pediatr.* 1997; 156(8):668.

Sher PK, Reinberg Y, Yuri Reinberg: Successful treatment of giggle incontinence with methylphenidate. *J. Urol.* 1996; 156 :656-658.

Stenberg A and Läckgren G: Desmopressin tablets in the treatment of severe nocturnal enuresis in adolescents. *Pediatrics* 1994; 94:841-6.

The Arginine Vasopressin Secretion Profile in children with primary nocturnal enuresis. *Eur. Urol.* 1998; 33: Suppl 3, 41-44.

Thumfart J, Roehr CC, Kapelari K e tal: Demopressin associated symptomatic hyponatremic hypervolemia in children. Are there predictive factors? *J. Urol.* 2005; 174: 294-8.

Van de Walle JG, Bogaert GA, Mattson S et al: A new fast-melting oral formulation of desmopressin: A pharmacodynamic study in children with primary nocturnal enuresis. *BJU Int* 2006; 97:603-9.

Von Gontard A, Neveus T. *The Management of Disorders of Bladder and Bowel Control in Childhood.* London, UK: Mac Keith Press, 2006.

Yagei F, Kibar Y, Akay O et al: The effect of biofeedback treatment on voiding and urodynamic parameters in children with voiding dysfunction. *J. Urol.* 2005; 174: 1994-97.

Zimmer EZ, Chao CR, Guy GP et al: Vibroacoustic stimulation evokes human fetal micturition. Obstet Gynecol 1993; 81: 178-80.

In: Behavioral Pediatrics, 3rd Edition
Editor: Donald E. Greydanus et al.

ISBN 978-1-60692-702-1
© 2009 Nova Science Publishers, Inc.

Chapter 10

Encopresis

Dilip R. Patel, Helen D. Pratt and Cynthia Feucht

Abstract

Functional fecal incontinence or encopresis is a common condition seen by pediatricians and other health care practitioners who see children. Encopresis refers to the passage of feces in inappropriate places. There is a high prevalence of associated behavioral symptoms in children who have encopresis. Treatment involves patient and family education, behavioral strategies for stool regulation, disimpaction of stool in children who have constipation, and long term maintenance of regular bowel habits. This chapter reviews the definition, epidemiology, clinical presentation, and treatment of children who have encopresis.

Introduction

The majority of children are successfully toilet trained by 3 to 4 years of age. There seems to be a wide range of practices and attitudes of child rearing and bowel training in different cultures. Whiting studied child rearing practices in different cultures and noted that bowel training in most cultures was primarily a function of mothers. Regardless of the method used, the most children achieved bowel control at about the same age suggesting a significant role of maturational factors. The study included a primitive Kenyan community, an Indian farming community, a Japanese rural community, and a United States urban community.

Definition

Based on the International Classification of Diseases, 10th edition, of World Health Organization and the American Psychiatric Association Diagnostic and Statistical Manual of Mental Disorders, 4th edition, Text Revision, encopresis, (functional fecal incontinence), is characterized by the following:

- Repeated, voluntary and involuntary passage of feces in inappropriate places by a child who is chronologically at least 4 years old (or of equivalent mental age or developmental level).
- At least one such event must occur every month over a period of 3 months (per DSM-IV-TR) or 6 months (per ICD-10).
- There is no underlying organic cause for the fecal incontinence.
- In primary encopresis the longest period without fecal incontinence is shorter than 6 months, whereas it is 6 months or longer in secondary encopresis.
- Functional fecal encopresis may or may not be associated with constipation.

Functional constipation can result from either intentional or unintentional withholding of stool. Withholding of stool leads to retention of stool in the rectum. The water is further absorbed and the stool becomes firm and hard, which is difficult and painful to pass, further leading to withholding by the child. As the rectum continues to accommodate increasing amount of stool mass the rectal walls are stretched and the urge or the sensation to defecate is diminished or lost, further leading to retention. When the mass is large enough, the anal sphincter loses competency and there is leakage of unformed or watery stool around the impacted mass, which is not under the control of the child, leading to fecal soiling.

Epidemiology

Encopresis is 3 to 6 times more common in boys than in girls. The prevalence at age 4 is estimated to be between 2% and 8% in boys and between 1% and 3% in girls. The prevalence from preschool years through early adolescence is reported to be 2%-4% in boys and 1%-2% in girls. It is most prevalent between age 3 and 7 year.

Clinical Features

Because the child may be embarrassed from fecal soiling, he or she may not bring it to the attention of the parents and the problem continues to worsen. Parents may also find it difficult to share the information with anyone including the physician, and may feel guilty for failing to adequately toilet train their child. This may create tension within the family. The child may refuse to go to school. He or she may be teased by other children. This may result in isolation and adjustment problems for the child. The child may be at an increased risk for punishment and physical abuse because parents may not understand the fact that this is not the child's fault. The parents may assume that the child is defiant.

Infants and pre-school children may present with a history of gradually worsening constipation and withholding maneuvers. The infant may extend the body and contract the anal and gluteal muscles. The toddler may stand on toes, hold legs stiff, cross the legs, or rock back and forth. The school age child may have the problem for some years at the time of the detection. The child may have fecal incontinence one or many times per day everyday or intermittently with periods of no stools or soiling. Such periods generally follow passage of a large bowel movement. The child may deny foul odor and may hide the soiled clothes. Children may also present with intermittent acute moderate to severe abdominal pain or chronic non-specific abdominal pain preceding the passage of a large bowel movement. Some children may present with non-specific symptoms of headaches, and not feeling well. There is associated enuresis in 20-30 % of children with encopresis and in approximately 10 % of girls there is associated urinary tract infection.

Diagnosis

Diagnosis is primarily based on history and physical examination. Extensive laboratory investigations are not routinely indicated. Specific tests may be indicated based on the findings on history and physical examination to rule out organic etiology. A urinary analysis and plain film of the abdomen are useful initial studies. Barium studies of the bowel, anorectal manometry, endoscopy, and biopsy may be indicated in some children to exclude organic causes of fecal incontinence.

The history should specifically include information on usual pattern of bowel habits, and character, odor, consistency, and amount of stool. Passage of recurrent, small pellet like stool suggests incomplete evacuation, whereas intermittent massive stools are suggestive of functional fecal retention. Age of the child at the time of onset of the encopresis may be difficult to ascertain as initially the child may not tell parents, and later parents may be reluctant to seek medical advice. A thorough dietary history should be obtained. The family may be experiencing significant stress, and it is essential to assess parental emotions, family functioning, and how parents are dealing with the child. The general examination should include the growth and developmental parameters, height and weight progression, and signs of malnutrition. Specific attention to abdominal examination should include evidence of distention, mass, and bowel sounds. Look for local lesions such as anal fissures, and evidence of streptococcal anusitis, and elicit anal wink. Note position of the anus. Perform a rectal examination and specifically note sphincter tone and feel for the stool.

The prevalence of other behavioral disorders is significantly higher in children who have encopresis. The most common co-morbid behavioral disorders seen in children with encopresis are oppositional defiant disorder, attention deficit hyperactivity disorder, separation anxiety disorder, and depression. A high association between encopresis and sexual abuse has been reported. Encopresis has been reported in between 20% and 30% of children who have learning disability; more severe the disability higher the prevalence.

Treatment

Before instituting the treatment regimen for encopresis any specific organic obstructive or non-obstructive etiology for chronic constipation should be ruled out based on history, physical examination, and appropriate investigations. One may need to consult a pediatric gastroenterologist or surgeon in complex cases. Most treatment options require starting with an absence of any impactions.

Education

Education of the family is the essential first step in the overall management of the encopresis. The information which should be included in this process is listed in Table 1.

Table 1. Elements of Family Education

1. Treatment may take many months of continued efforts.
2. Fecal soiling is involuntary and not child's fault.
3. Disimpaction of stool and complete evacuation of rectum must be achieved.
4. Long term use of laxatives in children will not lead to dependence.
5. The most common cause of relapse is discontinuation of laxative regimen too soon.
6. Medical treatment is essential in all cases. Behavioural treatment is ineffective when used by itself.
7. Punishment of the child and forceful or coercive toilet training does not work and should not be attempted.

General Measures

General measures should be implemented to achieve stool regulation. These include adequate fluid intake, and appropriate modification of the diet that include high fiber intake, and behavioral measures.

Behavioral Measures

Most patients referred for behavioral or biofeedback therapies have failed to obtain bowel control from other treatment interventions (e.g. laxatives, suppositories, enemas, education, dietary changes, or toilet training). Prerequisites for treating children with behavioral interventions or biofeedback for fecal incontinence are listed in Table 2. Both behavioral and biofeedback interventions are most effective when used as adjuncts to the medical treatment. Children with a history of treatment failures may require psychological interventions to address specific fears and toilet phobias.

Table 2. Pre-requisites for Behavioral Interventions or Biofeedback

- Intact sphincter function
- Freedom from impaction
- Ability to follow instructions
- Ability to discriminate rectal sensations
- Motivation to learn fecal control
- Parental motivation to teach toileting skills

Clinicians rely heavily on parental data collection to measure treatment outcomes in a child's control of feces, bowel habits, and fecal staining. Parents are asked to complete survey instruments, participate in face-to-face or telephone interviews, and maintain behavioral charts or diaries (recording data on the presence/absence and intensity of pain at elimination, food intake, and number of laxatives or enemas required to prevent or eliminate constipation).

Behavioral treatment of fecal incontinence requires the clinician to maintain a good working relationship with parents and their children to access information and enlist cooperation for treatment interventions and data collection. The most effective behavioral approaches combine education, toilet training, incentive programs, and a punishment procedure. They focus on teaching parents to administer the program and record data (see Table 3). These techniques are time intensive for parents but are inexpensive and do not rely on technology.

Table 3. Enhanced Toilet Training

Incentive programs are designed according to the developmental stage and motivational level of child. The goal is to reward child for spontaneous trips to the toilet and for having clean pants. Children are shown how to appropriately strain to defecate using a structured procedure.

Structured Toilet Time: 15 to 30 minutes after meal the child is required to sit on the toilet for a 12 minute session
- During the first four minutes the child is encouraged to practice tensing and relaxing his or her external and sphincter. This procedure is designed to help the child localize control of and fatigue the sphincter and to mechanically stimulate the rectum.
- The second four minutes is designed to desensitize the child to toilet sitting. Parents are taught how to engage their child in fun activities (those that motivate the child-- being read to or playing games)
- The last four minutes are spent encouraging the child to strain and attempt to have a bowel movement.

Reward/Response Cost System
- Parents provide rewards for their child when he engages in specific activities that lead to appropriate control of feces (i.e. clean pants, defecating in the toilet, drinking water, asking to go to the toilet, etc)
- Parents make the child wash or assist in washing his or her soiled underpants and to clean his or her own soiled body.

Disimpaction

The next step in children who have encopresis with constipation is to achieve complete evacuation of the bowels. Disimpaction of the fecal mass can be achieved by several methods and may take from 2 to 5 days. Initially polyethylene glycol (PEG) given orally should be tried (Table 4). If oral PEG fails to achieve disimpaction, rectal enemas containing phosphates such as sodium hydrogen phosphate and sodium monohydrogen phosphate are administered.

Table 4. Laxative Drugs for Disimpaction

Laxative	Dosage	Comments
Rectal Administration		
Mineral oil	6ml/kg up to 120 ml	
Sodium biphosphate enema	3-6 ml/kg up to 135ml maximum (age ≥ 2 yrs)	Usual 1-2 per day for 1-2 days May result in metabolic abnormalities
Bisacodyl suppository	5-10mg 1-2 doses per day (age ≥ 2 yrs)	May be used up to 4 days
Glycerin suppository	Infant: 1 gm Children: 2gm	Safe for use in infants
Milk-of-molasses	200-600ml	1:1 concentration
Oral/Nasogastric Administration		
Mineral oil	15-30ml/year of age (240ml maximum) daily for 3 days	Do not use in infants <12 mos Can mix with chocolate milk or ice cream to improve taste
Polyethylene glycol with electrolytes	25ml/kg/hr (1000ml/hr maximum) by nasogastric OR 20ml/kg/hr for 4 hours/day orally	Taste and administration may be challenging
Polyethylene glycol 3350	1-1.5 g/kg/day for 3 days	Lack of taste
Bisacodyl tablets	5-15mg per dose (age ≥ 2 yrs)	
Senna syrup	2-5 yrs: 2.5-3.75ml daily (max 3.75ml 2x/day) 6-12 yrs: 5-7.5ml daily (max 7.5ml 2x/day)	Give at bedtime for once daily administration
Pulsed Irrigation-enhanced Evacuation		
Warm water	5 gallons of warm water over 25 minutes as automated small pulses of 25ml lasting a few seconds	Alternate with gravity drainage of feces & water into a sealed bag

The child may have to be hospitalized. In most children 1 -2 enemas will achieve disimpaction. Excessive use of hypertonic phosphate enema may cause hypernatremia, hypokalemia, hypovolemia, and dehydration. Soap water enema should be avoided as this may result in perforation and necrosis of the bowel. Tap water enemas may cause water intoxication, hyponatremia, and seizures, and should be avoided. If oral PEG and rectal phosphate enemas fail to achieve disimpaction and bowel evacuation other methods are considered preferably in consultation with a pediatric gastroenterologist (Table 4).

Maintenance

Once disimpaction and complete evacuation is achieved the next step in the treatment is to prevent reaccumulation of the stool. This is achieved by regular use of stool softeners and laxatives (Table 5). The most widely used and recommended laxatives are PEG and lactulose.

The goal of this phase is to allow sufficient time for the colon to return to normal caliber and tone. This may take up to 6 months or longer. In addition to the use of laxatives, dietary fiber should be appropriately increased. One can also use fiber supplements containing cellulose, psyllium, or polycarbophil. Use of laxatives and stool softeners may have to be continued for months in order to maintain regular bowel movements and prevent reaccumulation of stools. The child should be followed regularly in the office. Relapses may occur and evacuation may be needed with use of enemas.

Table 5. Stool Softeners and Laxatives for Maintenance Therapy

Laxative	Dosage	Comments
Barley malt extract	2-10ml per 240ml of milk or juice	Can be used in infants
Karo syrup	5-10ml in 60-120ml of milk or water	Can be used in infants
Lactulose	Age > 6mos: 1-3ml/kg/day in 2 divided doses	
Sorbitol (70% solution)	Age > 6mos: 1-3ml/kg/day in 2 divided doses	May be mixed with prune, pear or apple juices
Mineral oil	Age > 1 yr: 1-3 ml/kg/day in 1-2 divided doses	Avoid use in infants due to risk of aspiration Do not give with docusate
Magnesium hydroxide (milk of magnesia)	Age 2-5 yrs: 5-15 ml/day Age 6-11 yrs: 15-30 ml/day Age ≥ 12 yrs: 30-60 ml/day	Administer in 1-2 divided doses Increased risk of electrolyte abnormalities in infants & renal dysfunction
Polyethylene glycol 3350	0.5-1.5 gm/kg/day	Mix with water or juice Well tolerated
Docusate sodium	Age ≤ 3 yrs: 10-40 mg/day Age 3-6 yrs: 20-60 mg/day Age 6-12 yrs: 40-120 mg/day	Can cause rash, bitter taste and throat irritation Do not give with mineral oil

The child should be weaned from laxative regimen gradually at the same time. The child should be encouraged to sit on toilet after breakfast or evening meal to take advantage of the gastrocolic reflex. This should be a positive experience for the child and should not be a struggle and child should not be coerced or forced.

Biofeedback

Biofeedback therapy may consist of using a probe with a balloon on the end. It is inserted into child's anus (manometric procedure). The probe is designed to create, maintain, and measure the amount of pressure a patient can exert on the inflated balloon when it is inserted into the anus (requires hospitalization for one week for treatment which is administered 2 times a day).

A less invasive procedure attaches electrodes to the exterior of the anus to measure pressure. These devices are connected to transducers that are connected to a computer. The computerized equipment is used to present visual images designed to teach patients to easily learn how to voluntarily squeeze their anal sphincter and recognize associated physiological sensations. The child may be required to contract or relax the sphincter muscle to control a visual image on the computer's monitor screen. He or she might be asked to catch an egg and then drop it into a basket that is moving along the bottom of a computer monitor screen by contracting and relaxing his sphincter muscles.

To teach the patient how to generalize this skill to controlling his or her sphincter muscle, he or she might be shown a circle that expands and contracts with the relaxation and contraction of the patient's anal sphincter. The visual images on the computer are combined with auditory instructions from the clinician who conducts the training. Children are able to improve voluntary sphincter function and rectal sensation using similar procedures and can learn to master the process within 15 to 20 minutes.

Biofeedback used alone is not considered to be an effective adjunctive therapy for treating functional encopresis. Prognosis for successful treatment using behavioral interventions or biofeedback is worse for those children who have a long history of fecal incontinence or suffer from severe constipation. The longer a child has been incontinent or constipated, the longer it will take for him or her to respond to treatment and maintain therapeutic gains (no fecal staining, fecal incontinence or constipation) Treatment is considered effective when the child has been "clean" for 6 months.

Conclusion

Encopresis is a common condition seen in children. It can be effectively treated in most children; however, during the treatment relapses are not uncommon. The most common reason for relapse is discontinuation of maintenance regimen prematurely. In children, long term use of laxative regimen has been shown to cause no significant side effects or result in habit formation. Various studies show that 50 - 60 % of children will achieve acceptable bowel control free of incontinence within 12 months, and up to 80 % will do so by 2 years of treatment. A few children will require continued treatment for more than 2 years.

Acknowledgement

This chapter is modified and updated with permission from Patel DR, Pratt HD: Encopresis. *Indian Journal of Pediatrics*. 1999;66:439-446.

References

Abi-Hanna A, Lake AM: Constipation and encopresis in childhood. *Pediatrics in Review*, 1998;19(1):23-30.

American Psychiatric Association: Elimination disorders: *Encopresis, Diagnostic and Statistical Manual of Mental Disorders*, 4th edition, Text Revision, 2001.

Bell E. Pediatric ambulatory care. In: Schumock G, Brundage D, Chapman M, et al, eds. *Pharmacotherapy Self-Assessment Program*, 5th ed. Chronic Illnesses IV and Pediatrics. Kansas City, MO: American College of Clinical Pharmacy, 2006:137-174.

Brazzelli M, Griffiths P. Behavioural and cognitive interventions with or without other treatments for the management of faecal incontinence in children. *Cochrane Database Syst Rev*. 2006;19(2):CD002240.

Cox DJ, Sutphen J, Ling W, Quillian W, Borowitz S: Additive benefits of laxative, toilet training, and biofeedback therapies in the treatment of pediatric encopresis. *Journal of Pediatric Psychology*. 1996;21(5): 659-670.

Culbert TP, Banez GA. Integrative approaches to childhood constipation and encopresis. *Pediatr. Clin. North Am*. 2007;54(6):927-47.

Iwata G., Nagashima IM, Fukata R: New biofeedback therapy in children with encopresis. *European Journal of Pediatric Surgery*. 1995;5:231-234.

Loening-Baucke V: Biofeedback training in children with functional constipation: A critical review. *Digestive Diseases and Sciences*. 1996;41(1): 65-71.

Loening-Boucke V: Encopresis and soiling. *Pediatric Clinics of North America*. 1996;43(1):279-98.

Murphy MS, Clayden G: Constipation, pp 293-321, In Walker WA et al (Eds): *Pediatric Gastrointestinal Disease*, 2nd ed, 1996, Mosby-Yearbook, St Louis, USA.

Neveus T, von Gontard A, Hoebeke P, et al. The standardization of terminology of lower urinary tract function in children and adolescents: Report from the Standardisation Committee of the International Children's Continence Society. *J. Urology* 2006;176:314-324.

Reimers TM: A biobehavioral approach toward managing encopresis. *Behavior Modification*. 1996; 20(4):469-479.

Reiner WG. Pharmacotherapy in the management of voiding and storage disorders, including enuresis and encopresis. *J. Am. Acad. Child Adolesc. Psychiatry* 2008;47;5:491-497.

Udani PM: Constipation In Udani PM (Ed): *Textbook of Pediatrics*, pp 2675-82, 1991 Jaypee
   Brothers Medical Publishers, New Delhi, India.

van der Plas RN, Benninga MA, Taminiau JAJM, Buller HA: Treatment of defecation
   problems in children: The role of education, de-mystification and toilet training.
   European *Journal of Pediatrics*. 1997;156:689-692.

von Gontard A, Neveus T. *The Management of Disorders of Bladder and Bowel Control in
   Childhood.* Cambridge, UK: Cambridge University Press, 2006.

Section III. Disruptive Behavior Disorders

In: Behavioral Pediatrics, 3rd Edition
Editor: Donald E. Greydanus et al.

ISBN 978-1-60692-702-1
© 2009 Nova Science Publishers, Inc.

Chapter 11

Attention-Deficit/Hyperactivity Disorder

Joseph L. Calles

Abstract

Attention-deficit/hyperactivity disorder is common in the general population and is over-represented in general pediatric practice. This chapter will review how the disorder is defined, how it is diagnosed, what comorbid conditions are commonly associated with it, and how it is treated.

Introduction

Attention-deficit/hyperactivity disorder (ADHD) is a neurobehavioral disorder that is routinely encountered in clinical pediatric practice. It can be highly variable in terms of symptoms, impact on functioning, comorbid conditions, and persistence into adulthood. Despite its common nature, ADHD can still be problematic to pediatricians in terms of assessment and treatment.

Definition

The core symptoms of ADHD have traditionally been divided into three categories: (1) *inattention*; (2) *impulsivity*; and, (3) *hyperactivity*. These features can be seen in any child or adolescent, so in order to differentiate the clinical disorder from normality, symptoms must be present for *at least 6 months*; in addition, the following conditions must be met: (1) symptoms must be *maladaptive*, i.e. must impair functioning vs. just being bothersome; (2) symptoms must be *developmentally inappropriate*, i.e. would be consistent with a much younger age; (3) symptoms must be present, to a significant degree, *before the age of 7 years*;

(4) symptoms are *displayed in more than one setting*, i.e. not just at school or just at home; and, (5) the symptom complex *does not occur exclusively* with another disorder, nor is it *better accounted for* by another disorder. Regarding the age of onset criterion, some ADHD experts have argued that the cutoff of 7 years-of-age is not supported by empirical data, and that ADHD should be considered a disorder that can develop *anytime* during childhood.

In the current diagnostic system of the DSM-IV-TR (American Psychiatric Association, 2000), there are four types of ADHD: Combined (ADHD-C), Predominantly Inattentive (ADHD-I), Predominantly Hyperactive-Impulsive (ADHD-H), and Not Otherwise Specified (ADHD NOS). Table 1 describes the features of each ADHD subtype.

Table 1. DSM-IV-TR ADHD Subtypes and Associated Symptoms

Combined type (ADHD-C)	• 6* symptoms of inattention
	• $\geq 6*$ symptoms of hyperactivity-impulsivity
Predominantly Inattentive (ADHD-I)	• 6* symptoms of inattention
	• < 6* symptoms of hyperactivity-impulsivity
Predominantly Hyperactive-Impulsive (ADHD-H)	• 6* symptoms of hyperactivity-impulsivity
	• < 6* symptoms of inattention
Not Otherwise Specified (ADHD NOS)	Prominent symptoms of inattention and/or hyperactivity-impulsivity that do not meet full diagnostic criteria for any ADHD type

* Out of a total of 9 possible symptoms in each of the two clusters.

Epidemiology

The prevalence rates reported for ADHD vary greatly around the world. There are several factors that seem to account for the variability: (1) Diagnostic criteria utilized, i.e. the prevalence of ADHD is higher in newer studies that used DSM-IV vs. older studies that used DSM-III or DSM-III-R; (2) Source of information , i.e. teachers report higher rates of ADHD symptoms than do parents; (3) Impairment status, i.e. prevalence rates of ADHD are higher when functional impairment is excluded as a diagnostic criterion; and, (4) Geographic location, e.g. greater congruence between American and European studies vs. greater incongruence between American studies and those from developing countries. Taking all of these issues into consideration, the overall prevalence world-wide of ADHD has been calculated as 5.29%.

Prevalence rates of ADHD also vary based on individual characteristics. For example, studies have consistently shown that the ratio of boys-to-girls with ADHD is about 2:1. In clinical settings ADHD-C is the most commonly encountered type, whereas in community studies ADHD-I is the most common type (representing about one-half of the ADHD sample). The ADHD-H type is primarily seen in the preschool age group, with steady declines into adolescence; conversely, the ADHD-I type is uncommon in preschoolers, very common in adolescents. There are inconsistent findings regarding age at first diagnosis of ADHD, but affected younger children seem to be more readily recognized, especially when they begin school. Finally, the true prevalence of ADHD in children from minority and under-represented groups is difficult to gauge, in that the parents of those children tend to deny, minimize or normalize ADHD-like behaviors, whereas the teachers of those children tend to over-report symptoms.

Clinical Features

The types and ratios of ADHD symptoms not uncommonly change over time, and depend to some extent on the child's developmental level. The following clinical ADHD descriptions are divided into three broad age categories: preschoolers (3-5½ years); school-age (6-12 years); and adolescents (13-18 years).

ADHD in Preschoolers

The parents of young children with ADHD usually report a long history of fairly dramatic symptoms. Hyperactivity and impulsivity dominate the clinical picture. Excessive activity is expressed motorically, and the children are described as if they have a "motor running" inside of them, are in motion "non-stop" and "can't sit still," or "wear everyone out," including other children. Verbal activity is also excessive, and the children may be called "chatterboxes" or "motormouths," and may ask questions incessantly, even about things that they already know the answers to. They find it difficult to stay in their seats beyond brief periods of time, and family members may report that the children eat while standing up or walking in place at the table (in extreme cases the parents may follow the children around and put the food into their mouths!). In the daycare or preschool setting young children with ADHD exhibit similar motor and verbal activities. They often cannot participate in calmer indoor activities, such as coloring or putting puzzles together. They may have trouble settling down during rest periods, and many will not take a nap. They may monopolize classroom discussions or interfere with stories being read by the teacher. Even outdoor play may be problematic, as the children tend to be excitable, aggressive and difficult to re-direct.

If the hyperactivity weren't enough for the caring adults to deal with, young ADHD children also demonstrate impulsivity, i.e. the spontaneous motor or verbal actions that are expressed without regard for their appropriateness or their potential for being disruptive- or even dangerous. These children have been known to climb to high places, find themselves in precarious situations (e.g. being trapped), or run into traffic, all without regard to their own safety. They are careless in their play, such that injuries are more common in young children with ADHD vs. in those without it. The injuries themselves are not the routine "bumps and bruises" of childhood. Lacerations that require suturing, long bone fractures, concussions, burns, and ingestions of toxic substances are over-represented in this group of children.

All young children have relatively short attention spans (minutes at a time), but those with ADHD may only be able to sustain focus for seconds. Their interest in things also lasts only briefly, and they seem to require near-constant attention and stimulation. The combination of hyperactivity, impulsivity and inattention alienates peers and "burns out" caregivers. In addition, the associated low frustration tolerance, irritability and tendency towards aggression make it difficult for parents to take the children into public settings. They may tantrum in stores, become disruptive in restaurants, and may be "kicked out" of daycare and preschool. If the parents themselves share similar characteristics (or even have ADHD), their level of frustration and anger could rise to the point that physical punishments are used, placing the children at risk of being physically abused.

Biological rhythms may also be disturbed. Sleep onset may be delayed for up to hours and there may be frequent awakenings during the night; sometimes the children will not fall back asleep. Despite the low quantity of sleep, ADHD children may still awaken very early in the morning. The parents' sleep will also be disrupted, as they will get up to monitor the children and try to prevent injuries or other damages (such as playing with the stove and starting a fire). Appetite can be quite variable. Some ADHD children are picky and may eat only enough to briefly eliminate hunger pains; other children may eat large amounts of food, even to the point of feeling sick. There may be delays in attaining bladder control, and bedwetting may occur.

ADHD in School-Age Children

As ADHD children transition into elementary education their inattentive symptoms become more pronounced. Studies in this age group consistently show that one-half of all ADHD children meet criteria for ADHD-I. However, the diagnosis can be missed if the inattention is not accompanied by obvious hyperactivity or impulsivity, as the cognitive symptoms may be relatively subtle when compared to the motor and verbal symptoms. It is the poor attention span and easy distractibility that contributes to the poor academic functioning seen in most ADHD children. Disorganization is often a related feature. These children tend to "lose" things, such as classroom assignments, textbooks, pencils and other supplies, money, articles of clothing, etc. Their personal areas- desks, bins, lockers, etc. - are like "black holes," i.e. everything goes into them and nothing seems to come out again.

When hyperactivity and/or impulsivity are prominent, as in ADHD-H or ADHD-C, the children display disruptive behaviors, such as talking to peers during work periods, getting out of their seats without permission (frequently visiting the pencil sharpener seems to be a favorite), and blurting out answers to questions without raising their hands. In more extreme cases children may fall out of their seats, crawl around on the floor or under their desks, physically touch classmates or their belongings, or engage in play activities when they are supposed to be working. They find it difficult- or even impossible- to read quietly to themselves or to work independently. Children may be forced to sit close to teachers in order to be redirected more readily. Sometimes children are isolated away from peers in an attempt to reduce environmental stimulation; this may be in a back corner of the classroom, or even outside in the hallway. When classroom management strategies fail, ADHD children may be sent to the office. A persistent pattern of losing classroom time may prompt a referral to a smaller, self-contained classroom setting.

In addition to formal academic learning, schools also provide the opportunity for social learning. ADHD children also struggle in the social realm. There is a correlation between hyperactive/impulsive symptoms and being disliked by peers, which in turn may be related to socially inappropriate behaviors. ADHD children can be very impatient, and may alienate other children by not being able to wait their turns or follow the rules during games.

The behaviors demonstrated at school are mirrored at home. Family routines may be disrupted by the children's ADHD symptoms. Parents describe night times and mornings as being especially problematic. At night the children may have difficulty settling down (e.g. stopping play) and getting ready for bed, leading to "battles." In the morning there may be struggles in getting the children out of bed, and once up they may need frequent reminders or even assistance in getting ready for school (e.g. the children who are supposed to be brushing their teeth may be found watching TV). An especially common area of conflict centers on homework. ADHD children may not bring their books and assignments home, procrastinate in getting their work started, are easily distracted while working, may rush through their work (in order to get back to playing), and may not study for tests. Parents may have to sit with the children to keep them on task, and some parents may even do the work for the children to reduce their own time commitment and level of frustration. The issues related to homework may also be seen in chores, which can be "forgotten," sloppily rushed through, or even refused to be done by the children.

ADHD in Adolescents

During adolescence there is a tendency for the hyperactivity and impulsivity of ADHD to attenuate. Despite that apparent change for the better, the majority of adolescents with ADHD will still meet the DSM-IV-TR criteria for the disorder, will still have some functional impairment, and will still benefit from treatment. Although calmer in the classroom, these adolescents may continue to be inattentive, off-task, distractible, forgetful and disorganized. Grades may stay low or drop from previous levels. Interest in- and motivation for- school may be low, with associated poor academic effort. Faced with ongoing frustration and poor performance in the classroom, adolescents with ADHD may start skipping school, and are at high risk of dropping-out before graduating.

The adolescents with ADHD may fare no better at home. As they are now older but no more responsible than when younger, arguments with parents may increase and escalate even to the point of physical confrontations. The previously overactive children may now be sluggish and "lazy" teenagers, refusing to interact with their families and do their fair share of chores. Their mode of dress may become slovenly and personal hygiene may be neglected, most likely due to forgetfulness, but possibly secondary to comorbid psychiatric issues (see the next section on "Diagnosis"). This is the time of life when driver's training begins, yet parents may not trust that their ADHD adolescents are cognitively or emotionally ready to assume that level of responsibility. This presents families with one more issue over which to argue.

Socially, the adolescent with ADHD may continue to struggle with being accepted by peers. Conversely, they may start developing friendships, but these are commonly with adolescents who are also disinterested, unmotivated or troubled in some way. The risk of becoming involved in drug and/or alcohol use increases at this time. Their future goals may be vague, unrealistic (e.g. wanting to go to college as they're failing in high school), or non-existent. For families at this stage of their evolution, there are three possible responses to the situation: (1) Increasing their efforts to secure educational and therapeutic help for their ADHD adolescents; (2) Acquiescing to the adolescents, who essentially become "free boarders" in the home; or, (3) Expelling the adolescents once their legal obligations to care for them are met.

The following section will discuss other clinical conditions that can mimic or co-exist with ADHD.

Diagnosis

The first question to ask when presented with a child or adolescent who is inattentive, hyperactive and/or impulsive is whether or not the symptoms are due to the direct effects of substances of abuse. Table 2 lists the classes of drugs which can be obtained both legally and illegally, and which can produce ADHD-like effects. Drugs which stimulate the CNS, such as amphetamines and cocaine, can cause motor/verbal over-activity and risk-taking that mimic hyperactivity and impulsivity, respectively. Conversely, when those drugs wear-off the person may have slowed mentation that can look like inattention. Drugs which suppress the CNS, such as anxiolytics and opiates, can make people less aware of their environments and can look like inattention; the removal of those agents can cause agitation that looks like hyperactivity.

The second question to ask is whether the ADHD-like symptoms are due to the direct effects of a medical illness or of prescription medications. Table 3 lists some of the more common medical conditions that may present with features of ADHD, especially inattention and mental disorganization.

The third question to ask is whether the inattention, hyperactivity and/or impulsivity can be better accounted for by another psychiatric disorder. Table 4 lists the psychiatric diagnoses that may share features with or mimic ADHD (the reader is asked to consult the other chapters in this book for details on the diagnosis of non-ADHD psychiatric disorders).

Table 2. Substance-related* Differential Diagnosis for ADHD

- Alcohol
- Amphetamines
- Anxiolytics
- Caffeine
- Cannabis
- Cocaine
- Hallucinogens
- Inhalants
- Opiates

* Intoxication and/or withdrawal effects.

Table 3. Medical Differential Diagnosis for ADHD

Neurologic disorder	Seizure disorders
	Traumatic brain injury
	Encephalitis
	Sleep disorders
Endocrine disorders	Hypothyroidism
Metabolic disorders	Diabetes mellitus
Hematologic disorders	Anemia
Cardiovascular disorders	Congenital heart disease
Gastrointestinal disorders	Celiac disease
Renal disorders	Chronic renal failure
Pulmonary disorders	Asthma
Gynecologic disorders	Premenstrual syndrome
Infectious diseases	Epstein-Barr virus infection
	Cytomegalovirus infection
	HIV infection
	Lyme disease
Toxicologic disorders	Lead poisoning
	Carbon monoxide poisoning (chronic)
Sensory disorders	Hearing impairment
	Vision impairment
Nutritional disorders	Malnutrition
Medical treatments	Brain irradiation
	Cancer chemotherapy
Medications	Antiepileptic drugs
	Corticosteroids
	Beta-adrenergic agonists
	Antibiotics
	Antidepressants
	Antipsychotics
	Lithium
	Benzodiazepines

Lastly, even when the diagnosis of ADHD can be made with certainty (see the end of this section), the clinician should look for and rule-out comorbid psychiatric disorders, the prevalence of which has been estimated at between 50% and 90% in ADHD patients. The importance of identifying other psychiatric issues is in their relevance to treatment and prognosis. The conditions that most commonly coexist with ADHD are:

- *Other disruptive behavior disorders: Oppositional defiant disorder (ODD) and Conduct disorder (CD).* In younger patients with ADHD, 30%-60% will have ODD, 20%-30% will have CD, and about 50% will have ODD and/or CD.

- *Major depressive disorder (MDD)*. Having ADHD greatly increases the risk for developing depression in both males and females. Between 5% and 40% of ADHD patients will also be depressed.
- *Bipolar disorder*. There is somewhat of a bidirectional association between ADHD and bipolar disorder, in that 10%-22% of ADHD patients will eventually meet criteria for bipolar illness, while patients who are diagnosed with bipolar disorder will also have ADHD 29%-98% of the time.
- *Anxiety disorders*. In the primary pediatric setting about 50% of children with ADHD also have an anxiety disorder; conversely, 20% of children with an anxiety disorder have comorbid ADHD.
- *Tic disorders*. Large-scale epidemiological surveys have found that 50% of those with a tic disorder meet criteria for ADHD. Conversely, about 20% of those with ADHD will have some type of tic disorder.
- *Substance-use disorders (SUD).*There has been some debate regarding whether or not ADHD is an independent risk factor for the development of SUD. It seems fairly clear now that patients with ADHD are at greater risk of developing SUD if they are also comorbid for CD or bipolar disorder.
- *Learning disorders*. The academic struggles of children with ADHD could very well derive from their inattention and disorganization. However, learning disorders may coexist in as many as 70% of students with ADHD.
- *Enuresis*. Several studies have reported rates of enuresis in children with ADHD from 21% to 32%, an up to 6-fold increase compared to controls. Family studies have shown, however, that both conditions are transmitted independently of each other.
- *Sleep disorders*. Almost 50% of parents of ADHD children report that the youngsters have difficulty falling asleep and staying asleep. In addition, up to 25% will have sleep-disordered breathing and up to 36% will have excessive limb movements, including restless legs syndrome.
- *Eating disorders*. When compared to controls, girls with ADHD-C and ADHD-I have higher rates of body dissatisfaction and engage in more binge-purge behaviors. The ADHD-C girls also have higher rates of eating pathology than do the ADHD-I girls, likely related to a higher degree of impulsivity.

The Diagnostic Process for ADHD. This should begin with the taking of a thorough history of symptoms and behaviors, and how they are affecting development and functioning (see the Calles reference for a detailed description of the psychiatric examination). ADHD symptoms occur in a least two settings, so feedback will need to be obtained from family members as well as those outside the home (e.g. daycare, preschool, school, youth group, etc.). The information received will be most helpful if it is in two formats: structured, formal feedback as elicited by ADHD questionnaires and rating scales (available at the NICHQ website; registration is free); and, unstructured narratives, such as notes from teachers. In patients who are of school-age their report cards should be reviewed. As previously noted regarding Tables 2-4, the interview process should inquire about substance abuse, medical illnesses, medications, and non-ADHD psychiatric symptoms. Sometimes the data is equivocal and the diagnosis unclear. In that case the patient should be referred to a psychologist colleague for more formal testing procedures, such as computerized evaluation of attention and impulse control.

Table 4. Psychiatric Differential Diagnosis for ADHD

Developmental disorders	Mental retardation
	Learning disorders
	Communication disorders
	Pervasive developmental disorders
Disruptive behavior disorders	Oppositional defiant disorder
	Conduct disorder
Tic disorders	Tourette's disorder
Psychotic disorders	Schizophrenia
	Brief psychotic disorder
Mood disorders	Major depression
	Dysthymic disorder
	Bipolar disorder
	Cyclothymic disorder
Anxiety disorders	Panic disorder
	Social phobia
	Obsessive-compulsive disorder
	Post-traumatic stress disorder
	Generalized anxiety disorder
Dissociative disorders	Dissociative amnesia
	Dissociative fugue
Eating disorders	Anorexia nervosa
	Bulimia nervosa
Adjustment disorders	With depressed mood
	With anxiety
	With mixed anxiety and depressed mood
Other disorder(s)	Reactive attachment disorder

Once the diagnosis of ADHD is established, an individualized treatment approach is discussed with the patient and his/her caregivers, keeping in mind potential barriers to effective treatment, such as a history of non-compliance, restrictive insurance formularies, hypersensitivity to medications, psychiatric comorbidity, and/or medical conditions or medications that may limit or interfere with the use of ADHD medications.

Treatment

The cornerstone of treatment for ADHD is the stimulant medications, which have the highest rates of efficacy of all the psychotropic medications used for ADHD. If there are no comorbid psychiatric disorders, and after educating the patient and his/her caregiver(s) about available treatments, pharmacotherapy is initiated using either methylphenidate (MPH) or an amphetamine preparation, such as mixed amphetamine salts (MAS) or dextroamphetamine (DEX), depending on patient characteristics and clinical needs, as well as clinician and caregiver preferences. Starting doses and titration schedules for MPH, MAS, and DEX are given in Tables 5, 6 and 7, respectively (the methamphetamine preparation Desoxyn is not a first-line agent, and some physicians and/or caregivers may be hesitant to use it at any time, given its association with the street drug of abuse "meth.").

Table 5. Methylphenidate (MPH) Preparations: Racemic Mixture (*d- and l-* isomers)

Trade name	Forms (mg)	Start (daily)	Dosing Schedule Titration/wk†	Max./d	Duration of effect (hrs)
Ritalin (and generics)	Tabs [S] (5,10,20)	5 mg, 2-3x	5-10 mg	60 mg	3-4
Methylin	Tabs [S] (5,10,20) Tabs [C] (2.5,5,10) Solution: 5 mg/ml or 10 mg/ml	5 mg, 2-3x	5-10 mg	60 mg	4-8
Ritalin SR	Tabs [SR] (20)	20 mg in the morning	20 mg	60 mg	6-8
Metadate ER	Tabs [ER] (10,20)	10 mg in the morning	10 mg	60 mg	4-8
Methylin ER	Tabs [ER] (10,20)	10 mg in the morning	10 mg	60 mg	4-8
z	Caps* [ER] (10,20,30)	20 mg in the morning	20 mg	60 mg	4-8
Ritalin LA	Caps* [LA] (10,20,30,40)	10 mg in the morning	5-10 mg	60 mg	4-8
Concerta	Tabs [ER] (18,27,36,54)	18 mg in the morning	18 mg	72 mg	8-12
Daytrana	Patch [TD] (10,15,20,30)	10 mg, 2 hrs before effect needed; remove 9 hrs later	10 mg	30 mg	12

Legend: [S]= scored; [C]= chewable; [SR]= sustained release; [ER]= extended release; [LA]= long acting; [TD]= transdermal; *= may be sprinkled onto soft food; †= may use a 2nd PM dose.
Adapted, with permission, from Greydanus, et al. (see reference).

Table 6. Amphetamine Preparations: Mixed Salts [MAS] and Methamphetamine

Trade name	Forms (mg)	Dosing Schedule Start (daily)	Titration/wk	Max./d	Duration of effect (hrs)
Adderall (and generics) [MAS]	Tabs (5, 7.5, 10, 12.5, 15, 20, 30)	5-10 mg, 1-2x	5-10 mg	40 mg	4-6
Adderall XR [MAS]	Caps* [ER] (5, 10, 15, 20, 25, 30)	5-10 mg in the morning	5-10 mg	30 mg	8-12
Desoxyn†	Tabs (5)	5 mg, 1-2x	5 mg	25 mg	4-6

Legend: [ER]= extended release; *= may be sprinkled onto soft food.
†= not a first-line agent (see text for comments).
Adapted, with permission, from Greydanus, et al. (see reference).

Table 7. Amphetamine Preparations: Racemic Isolate (*d-* isomer only)

Trade name	Forms (mg)	Dosing Schedule Start (daily)	Titration/wk	Max./d	Duration of effect (hrs)
Dexedrine (and generics)	Tabs (5)	5 mg, 1-2x	5 mg	40 mg	4-6
Dextrostat (and generics)	Tabs [S] (5,10)	2.5-5 mg, 1-2 x	5 mg	40 mg	4-6
	Caps [ER] (5,10,20)	5 mg, 1-2x	5 mg	40 mg	4-6
Dexedrine Spansule	Spansules* (5,10,15)	5 mg in the morning	5 mg	45 mg	6-10
Vyvanse	Caps** (20,30,40,50,60,70)	20-30 mg in the morning	10-20 mg	70 mg	12

Legend: [S]= scored; [ER]= extended release; *= may be sprinkled onto soft food;
**= may be opened and mixed with water.
Adapted, with permission, from Greydanus, et al. (see reference).

Most patients with ADHD will usually respond to stimulants. Current treatment algorithms (e.g. in Pliszka, et al., 2006) recommend that if the first agent chosen (e.g. MPH) is ineffective or intolerable, that the second agent be one not chosen initially (e.g. MAS or DEX). If for some reason neither MPH nor amphetamines are effective or well-tolerated, then the next recommended choice would be atomoxetine, a non-stimulant, selective noradrenergic reuptake inhibitor that is approved for use in ADHD. Dosing is based on weight, and the initiation and titration details are listed in Table 8. Atomoxetine, although not as effective as the stimulants, has reasonable efficacy and may work well in some patients who have failed stimulant trials.

In the event of a failed trial of atomoxetine, the clinician is faced with several treatment options. The next choice could be one of the following: (1) atomoxetine plus a stimulant; (2) bupropion; (3) a tricyclic antidepressant (TCA); or, (4) dexmethylphenidate. Failure of these interventions would lead to the last step, that of using either clonidine or guanfacine. Table 8 does not include the TCAs; in my opinion it would be rare to have to use them, given the availability of newer agents that are safer and more effective. Dexmethylphenidate is the *d*-isomer of MPH (see Table 9). I have found it useful in patients who have been partial responders to MPH at doses so high that it precludes further dosage increases.

Table 8. Non-stimulant Agents

Trade name (generic)	Forms (mg)	Start (daily)	Dosing Schedule	
			Titration	Maximum/d
Strattera (atomoxetine) [SNRI]	Caps (10, 18, 25, 40, 60, 80, 100)	≤ 70 kg: 0.5 mg/kg >70 kg: 40 mg	≤ 70 kg: After at least 3 days increase to target of 1.2 mg/kg/d, given once or divided >70 kg: After at least 3 days increase to target of 80 mg/d given once or divided	≤ 70 kg: 1.4 mg/kg or 100 mg, whichever is less >70 kg: 100 mg
Wellbutrin (bupropion) [DNRI]	Tabs (75, 100)	3 mg/kg or 75-150 mg, whichever is lower	After at least 3 days can increase to 100 mg, 2x/d	100 mg, 3x/d, with at least 6 hrs between doses
Wellbutrin SR	Tabs (100, 150, 200)		After at least 3 days can increase to 150 mg, 2x/d	150 mg, 2x/d, with at least 8 hrs between doses
Wellbutrin XL	Tabs (150, 300)		After at least 3 days can increase to 300 mg, 1x/d	300 mg, 1x/d, with at least 24 hrs between doses
Catapres (clonidine) [α-2 agonist]	Tabs (0.1, 0.2, 0.3)	0.025-0.05 mg at bedtime	Every 3-5 days can increase by 0.05 mg, 1-3x/d	0.3-0.4 mg, divided 3-4x/d
Catapres-TTS (numbered 1, 2 and 3)	Transdermal patch (0.1, 0.2, 0.3)*	TTS-1 (0.1 mg/d) worn for 1 week intervals	After 1-2 weeks at each strength may increase to the next size up	TTS-3 (0.3 mg/d) worn for 1 week intervals
Tenex (guanfacine) [α-2 agonist]	Tabs (1, 2)	0.5-1 mg morning or evening	Every 3-5 days can increase by 0.5-1 mg, 1-2x/d	2-4 mg, divided 2-3x/d
Provigil (modafinil)	Tabs (100, 200)	50 mg days 1 and 2	100 mg days 3-7 200 mg days 8-14, 300 mg days 15-21 400 mg day 22+	< 30 kg: 300 mg ≥ 30 kg: 400 mg

Legend: SNRI= selective norepinephrine reuptake inhibitor; DNRI= dopamine and norepinephrine reuptake inhibitor; *= amount delivered daily.

The combination of atomoxetine and a stimulant should be approached cautiously, given the theoretical synergistic effects they can have on the cardiovascular system. I am much more likely to use an alpha agonist earlier in the treatment sequence, especially if hyperactivity is severe, or if stimulants or atomoxetine worsen the ADHD symptoms, or provoke irritability or aggression. An off-label alternative to the stimulants is modafinil, a wakefulness-promoting agent used for narcolepsy; this agent came close to getting FDA approval for use in ADHD, but failed after a report of it causing the Stevens-Johnson syndrome. Another drawback is that modafinil is quite expensive, and insurance carriers may not be willing to pay for its use in ADHD.

Table 9. Methylphenidate (MPH) Preparations: Racemic Isolate (*d*- isomer only)

| Trade name | Forms (mg) | Dosing Schedule | | | Duration of effect (hrs) |
		Start (daily)	Titration/wk	Max./d	
Focalin (dexMPH)	Tabs [S] (2.5,5,10)	2.5 mg, 1-2x	2.5 mg‡	30 mg	4-5
Focalin XR	Caps* [ER] (5,10)	5 mg in the morning	5 mg†	30 mg	8-12

Legend: [S]= scored; [ER]= extended release; *= may be sprinkled onto soft food; ‡= may use a 3rd PM dose; †= may use a 2nd PM dose.
Adapted, with permission, from Greydanus, et al. (see reference).

Treating ADHD in the Presence of Comorbid Conditions

At first glance this may seem like a daunting clinical task. My approach is relatively simple: first treat the disorder that is causing the most distress, is causing the most functional impairment, is the most likely to progress more quickly, and/or is associated with the worst outcome if left untreated. For example, in a child or adolescent with both ADHD and MDD, treating the depression would take priority, as the worst outcome for not treating the depressed mood (i.e. suicide) would be more serious than the worst outcomes associated with not treating the ADHD, at least in the short-term. Some experts recommend treating the ADHD first, as associated problems (e.g. depression or anxiety) may improve coincidentally with the improvement in ADHD. An argument can be made against that strategy, as it's also possible that the other problems- e.g., depression, anxiety, anger, mania and tics- could be exacerbated by the medications used to treat ADHD.

The reader is advised to consult the other chapters in this book for specific treatment recommendations for the other major psychiatric disorders seen in children and adolescents.

Medication Side Effects

The adverse effects associated with medications for ADHD are usually transient and not severe. The most common side effects from the stimulants are headaches, stomachaches, decreased appetite, insomnia and irritability. Atomoxetine tends to produce more gastrointestinal (GI) symptoms than do the stimulants and may also cause fatigue. Bupropion causes side effects similar to the stimulants, but generally to a greater degree. The alpha agonists mostly cause sedation, which is why they are started at nighttime. The side effects from modafinil commonly derive from the GI and nervous systems. More serious adverse effects are listed in Table 10.

As can be seen in Table 10, although not common, the medications used for ADHD can have effects on the cardiovascular system; this is especially of concern in those with pre-existing cardiac abnormalities or other cardiac risk factors, such as a positive family history. All children who are to be started on ADHD medications should have baseline pulse and blood pressure recorded, and those parameters should be monitored at each visit.

Table 10. Uncommon or Serious Side Effects of ADHD Medications

Medications	Adverse effects
Stimulants (MPH, MAS, DEX, dexMPH)	Weight loss
	Growth suppression
	Bruising
	Muscle damage
	Dyskinesia
	Hallucinations
	Mania
	Exacerbation of tics
	Increased heart rate and blood pressure
	Sudden cardiac death (in patients with clinically significant structural cardiac abnormalities, cardiomyopathy, or heart rhythm abnormalities)
Atomoxetine	Weight loss
	Suicidal ideation
	Mania
	Hepatotoxicity
	Seizures
	Increased heart rate and blood pressure (mostly diastolic)
Bupropion	Suicidal ideation
	Mania
	Seizures
	Increased blood pressure
Alpha agonists (clonidine, guanfacine)	Orthostatic hypotension
	Rebound hypertension
	Cardiac arrhythmias
Modafinil	Increased heart rate and blood pressure

MPH= methylphenidate; MAS= mixed amphetamine salts; DEX= dextroamphetamine; dexMPH= dexmethylphenidate.

Conclusion

This chapter has reviewed attention-deficit/hyperactivity disorder (ADHD) in terms of definition, epidemiology, diagnosis, comorbidity and treatment. It is hoped that the information contained herein will be helpful to pediatricians who are seeing ADHD patients in their practices. Further information can be found in the bibliographic references.

References

American Psychiatric Association. Diagnostic and Statistical Manual of Mental Disorders, Fourth Edition, *Text Revision*. Washington, DC, American Psychiatric Association; 2000.

Barkley RA, Biederman J. Toward a broader definition of the age-of-onset criterion for attention-deficit hyperactivity disorder. *J. Am. Acad. Child Adolesc. Psychiatry* 1997;36(9):1204-10.

Calles JL. The Psychodiagnostic Examination. In: Greydanus D, Feinberg AN, Patel DR, Homnick DN. *Pediatric Diagnostic Examination*. New York, NY: McGraw-Hill Professional; 2007:599-627.

Gaub M, Carlson CL. Behavioral characteristics of DSM-IV ADHD subtypes in a school-based population. *J. Abnorm. Child Psychol.* 1997;25(2):103-111.

Greydanus DE, Feucht C, Tzima-Tsitsika E. Attention deficit/hyperactivity disorder. In: Greydanus DE, Calles JL Jr, Patel DR. *Pediatric and Adolescent Psychopharmacology: A Practical Manual for Pediatricians*. Cambridge, UK: Cambridge University Press; 2008:77-102.

Hervey-Jumper H, Douyon K, Falcone T, Franco KN. Identifying, evaluating, diagnosing, and treating ADHD in minority youth. *J. Atten. Disord.* 2008 Mar;11(5):522-8. Epub 2008 Jan 11.

Himpel S, Banaschewski T, Heise CA, Rothenberger A. The safety of non-stimulant agents for the treatment of attention-deficit hyperactivity disorder. *Expert Opin. Drug Saf.* 2005;4(2):311-21.

Kunwar A, Dewan M, Faraone SV. Treating common psychiatric disorders associated with attention-deficit/hyperactivity disorder. *Expert Opin. Pharmacother.* 2007 Apr;8(5):555-62.

Manos MJ, Tom-Revzon C, Bukstein OG, Crismon ML. Changes and challenges: managing ADHD in a fast-paced world. *J. Manag. Care Pharm.* 2007 Nov;13(9 Suppl B):S2-S13.

Naglieri JA, Goldstein S. The role of intellectual processes in the DSM-V diagnosis of ADHD. *J. Atten. Disord.* 2006;10(1):3-8.

NICHQ: National Initiative for Children's Healthcare Quality. Caring for Children with ADHD: A Resource Toolkit for Clinicians. Available at: http://www.nichq.org/ NICHQ/Topics/ChronicConditions/ADHD/Tools/ADHD.htm. Accessed July 31, 2008.

Pelham WE Jr, Fabiano GA, Massetti GM. Evidence-based assessment of attention deficit hyperactivity disorder in children and adolescents. *J. Clin. Child Adolesc. Psychol.* 2005;34(3):449-76.

Pliszka S; AACAP Work Group on Quality Issues. Practice parameter for the assessment and treatment of children and adolescents with Attention-Deficit/Hyperactivity Disorder. *J. Am. Acad. Child Adolesc. Psychiatry* 2007;46(7):894-921.

Pliszka SR, Crismon ML, Hughes CW, et al. The Texas Children's Medication Algorithm Project: Revision of the algorithm for pharmacotherapy of Attention-Deficit/Hyperactivity Disorder. *J. Am. Acad. Child Adolesc. Psychiatry* 2006;45(6):642-657.

Polanczyk G, de Lima MS, Horta BL, Biederman J, Rohde LA. The worldwide prevalence of ADHD: a systematic review and metaregression analysis. *Am. J. Psychiatry* 2007 Jun;164(6):942-8.

Posner K, Melvin GA, Murray DW, et al. Clinical presentation of attention-deficit/hyperactivity disorder in preschool children: the Preschoolers with Attention-Deficit/Hyperactivity Disorder Treatment Study (PATS). *J. Child Adolesc. Psychopharmacol.* 2007 Oct;17(5):547-62.

Skounti M, Philalithis A, Galanakis E. Variations in prevalence of attention deficit hyperactivity disorder worldwide. *Eur. J. Pediatr.* 2007;166(2):117-123.

Vitiello B. Understanding the risk of using medications for attention deficit hyperactivity disorder with respect to physical growth and cardiovascular function. *Child Adolesc. Psychiatric. Clin. N Am.* 2008;17:459-474.

Wolraich ML, McGuinn L, Doffing M. Treatment of attention deficit hyperactivity disorder in children and adolescents: safety considerations. *Drug Saf.* 2007;30(1):17-26.

In: Behavioral Pediatrics, 3rd Edition
Editor: Donald E. Greydanus et al.

ISBN 978-1-60692-702-1
© 2009 Nova Science Publishers, Inc.

Chapter 12

Oppositional Defiant and Conduct Disorders

Joseph L. Calles

Abstract

The disruptive behavior disorders known as Oppositional defiant disorder and Conduct disorder are well-known in psychiatric and legal settings. What is less recognized is that patients seen in general pediatric settings can exhibit behaviors that are consistent with those diagnoses, yet they can be missed or attributed to other conditions. This chapter will describe the features of Oppositional defiant disorder and Conduct disorder and discuss their treatment.

Introduction

Every pediatrician has seen them: the younger patients who are resistant, provocative, challenging and/or hostile. They tend to be non-compliant with your recommendations, can be non-communicative, and divert an inordinate amount of time and energy away from other patients. They are described by their tired and frustrated parents as being the same way at home and sometimes at school. Children and adolescents with Oppositional defiant disorder and Conduct disorder are easy to dislike. The clinical task is to not only document the behaviors, but to look beyond them and to make sure that other psychopathology is not being missed. Following is a description of the epidemiology, core features, and treatment recommendations of both disorders.

Definition

Oppositional defiant disorder (ODD) is characterized by a pattern of angry resistance on the part of a child or adolescent to rules, requests or expectations initiated by authority figures (i.e. parents, teachers, coaches, etc.) of at least 6-months duration. The anger can be expressed directly through arguments or willful annoyance of others; its indirect expression can take the form of vindictiveness ("payback"). The behavior is usually confined to the home, and may never be displayed in other settings, although it is not uncommon to see ODD children "tantrum" in public settings when they don't get what they want.

Conduct disorder (CD) describes a set of behaviors (1 of at least 6-months duration, 3 of at least 12-months duration) that are more serious, in intentions and consequences, than those seen in ODD. In addition to rules, children and adolescents with CD violate the basic rights of other living beings (people, pets) and violate basic societal norms, i.e. laws. Covert symptoms (e.g. stealing) may never be discovered; overt symptoms (e.g. fighting) are difficult to ignore.

Epidemiology

Prevalence studies of ODD and CD can produce data that are quite variable and contradictory. Results can be influenced by the populations sampled, the ages and developmental levels of the subjects, and diagnostic criteria and/or instruments used.

Oppositional Defiant Disorder

Although the data are scant regarding ODD in very young children, one study found that in children ages 3 to 5 years referred to a psychiatric specialty clinic for preschool behavior problems, ODD symptoms were seen in 31.7% to 95.9% (as compared to 2% to 46% in the non-referred comparison group). The actual rates of ODD diagnosis in the two groups were 65.9% vs. 8.0%, respectively.

It is unclear whether increasing age affects the prevalence of ODD in the general population, although there does seem to be a decrease over time. That said the rate of ODD symptoms stays fairly steady as children get older if there is significant overlap with CD symptoms.

Conduct Disorder

The preschool study that looked at ODD symptoms also investigated the presence of CD symptoms, which were highly variable but significant in the referred population, ranging from 1.6% to 61.0% (but ≤ 20.0% in the non-referred sample). The rate of CD diagnosis in the two groups was likewise discrepant, made in 55.3% vs. 8.0%, respectively.

The relationship between aging and CD is more certain than that of ODD and aging, at least as far as the CD behaviors that are also seen in juvenile delinquents. There seems to be an increase of covert (non-aggressive) conduct behaviors, a decrease in minor aggression (e.g. fighting), and an increase in major aggression (e.g. rape and murder) into and through adolescence.

Clinical Features

Oppositional Defiant Disorder

As mentioned earlier, children and adolescents with ODD have major issues with rules and authority figures. In some sense ODD behaviors are an exaggeration and a prolongation of the normal developmental resistance seen in toddlers ("the terrible twos"), and parents often tell us that their ODD child has been "stubborn from the beginning." The tantrums that begin in early life are disruptive to the family, and also cause concern of inadvertent injury to the child. As the child gets older, bigger, and stronger, the concern of injury to family members develops. Even though the child or adolescent may not have been, or may never be, physically aggressive towards others in the home, it is the *possibility* of violence that often keeps parents from disciplining in ways that they would ordinarily use (thus reinforcing the behavior; see the "Treatment" section below).

It is almost guaranteed that the ODD child or adolescent will become angry when their wishes, desires, or expectations are frustrated (in other words, when they are told "no"). He/she will often react by yelling, swearing, or threatening to harm others (or occasionally himself/herself). The adults may be accused of "not caring" or "not understanding" their child, and they may be unfavorably compared to friends' parents, who reportedly let their children "do what they want." The other common cause of conflicts is when the children or adolescents do not follow through on what is expected of them (e.g. chores; homework). This is often compounded by their lying to avoid the task itself ("I didn't have any homework"), or to avoid the consequences for not doing the task ("I didn't cut the grass because the mower is broken"). Lying can also be combined with blame, such that the work that is not done is made to seem the fault of the parent, not the child ("You didn't tell me that you wanted it done today!").

Youth with ODD resent being called on their behaviors and having negative consequences. They may engage in spiteful behaviors that range from the relatively trivial (e.g. coming home late, thus missing their doctor's appointment) to the potentially more serious (e.g. making false accusations of parental abuse).

Conduct Disorder

The behaviors evidenced by youth with CD can be divided into four basic categories: (1) aggression towards other living creatures; (2) aggression towards property; (3) lying or stealing; and, (4) "status" offenses, such as running away from home or truancy from school (both of these starting before age 13 years, per diagnostic criteria). All of these behaviors are cause for concern, but some- the ones that are also illegal- are absolutely frightening.

Boys with CD like to fight and can do so with minimal-to-no provocation. Some of them have a high tolerance for pain, so their own discomfort may not stop them from hurting someone to the point of serious injury (e.g. fractured jaw), unconsciousness, or even death. They also don't like to lose, so they may employ weapons during a fight, thus increasing the potential of damage to others. The threat of violence can also be used to steal money (e.g. armed robbery) or to sexually violate someone, i.e. rape. The hurting of others for pleasure can extend to animals, with the possible end-result being the death of the animal. One of the more bothersome aspects of CD is that some youth with it seem to have no remorse for their harmful acts, and may even rationalize them ("He deserved it because he was disrespecting me").

Some boys also engage in destructive behaviors "for the fun of it," or because they're "bored." Arson is the most serious and dangerous manifestation of this, but malicious destruction of property- breaking windows, painting graffiti, tearing up landscaping- can lead to large repair bills for the owners.

Boys and girls with CD may both lie and steal to get what they want. Boys tend to use more extreme methods, such as breaking and entering ("BandE") into buildings or stealing a car (grand theft auto, aka "GTA"). Girls tend to employ more subtle techniques, such as shoplifting, running up large bills on a parent's credit card, or manipulating male friends to steal for them.

Running away and skipping school are ways for the CD child or adolescent to avoid responsibilities and to seek out excitement. They also place the person at risk of getting involved in dangerous activities, such as unprotected sex or substance use, criminal behaviors, or becoming victims of violence themselves.

Diagnosis

Oppositional Defiant Disorder

The identification of ODD is usually straight-forward, based on observable behavioral criteria; however, two cautions are necessary in that regard. The first is that oppositional behaviors may derive from other psychiatric disorders, may be a transient response to stressors, or may be part of normal developmental stages (Table 1). The second is that ODD usually does not exist in isolation from other psychiatric disorders, so it is important to search for and identify other potentially treatable comorbid conditions.

The most common disorder comorbid with ODD is Attention-deficit/hyperactivity disorder (ADHD). The presence of hyperactive-impulsive symptoms actually predisposes to the development of ODD; in one study of 3-7 year-olds with combined type ADHD, a full 60% also met criteria for ODD. Therefore, when either ADHD or ODD is diagnosed, the clinician should always rule-out the presence of the other (see Chapter 10, "Attention-deficit/hyperactivity disorder" for more information).

Table 1. Other conditions that may present with oppositional/defiant behaviors

Normal toddlerhood or early adolescence
Disruptive behavior disorders (other than ODD)
- Attention-deficit/hyperactivity disorder
- Conduct disorder

Mood disorders
- Major depressive disorder
- Dysthymic disorder
- Bipolar disorder

Psychotic disorders
Substance-use disorders
Adjustment disorders
Communication disorders
Developmental disorders (including Mental retardation)
Medical disorders, especially neurologic disorders

Clinically-referred patients with ODD also have significant rates of comorbid Major depressive disorder (MDD), Bipolar disorder (BD), and multiple anxiety disorders (MA) when compared to patients with psychiatric disorders other than ODD (or CD). When the group with other diagnoses was assessed, high rates of ODD were found in those with ADHD, MDD, BD, Pervasive developmental disorders, MA, Tourette's disorder, and Language disorders.

Conduct Disorder

The same cautions noted for ODD, regarding conditions that may mimic or be comorbid with the disorder, also apply to CD. In addition to the conditions listed in Table 1, another differential is Child or Adolescent Antisocial disorder, which is characterized by isolated (not pervasive) conduct problems that do not meet criteria for CD or Adjustment disorder.

Conduct disorder is highly comorbid with any disorder of mood, anxiety (except agoraphobia), impulse control, or substance use when compared to the general population. Conduct disorder is likely to develop before mood disorders about 70% of the time and before substance use disorders almost 89% of the time. Conversely, CD is more likely to develop after other impulse control disorders (i.e. ADHD and/or ODD) about 23% of the time. The temporal relationship between CD and anxiety disorders is mixed, with CD occurring after specific and social phobias but before all the other anxiety disorders about 32% of the time.

Diagnostic Dilemmas

In the current DSM-IV-TR, the diagnosis of ODD cannot be made if criteria are met for CD. This can be quite frustrating for the clinician, as real-world experience tells us that the two disorders often coexist. Research data confirms that there is a high degree of overlap. For example, in a longitudinal community study the majority of boys with CD also showed oppositional features, and one-quarter met full criteria for ODD. Interestingly, among the girls that were assessed, there was a stronger degree of overlap, with slightly over one-half of the girls with CD also meeting full ODD criteria. There was a reverse correlation between ODD and CD symptoms, in that 57% of boys and 55% of girls with ODD also evidenced substantial (but sub-diagnostic) levels of CD symptomatology.

Psychodiagnostic Assessment

Given the high degrees of comorbidity in both ODD and CD, and the high degree of overlap between ODD and CD symptoms, accurately identifying all of the Axis I disorders in any given patient can be challenging. The task can be nearly impossible if the patient and parent/guardian are unreliable historians. The use of standardized questionnaires and rating scales, structured or semi-structured interviews, validated observation protocols, and/or age-appropriate psychological testing can often be helpful in answering difficult clinical questions. As many of these methods require both time and specialized training, the pediatrician should enlist the consultative skills of, or refer to, a clinical psychologist as soon as possible (see Chapter 2, "Assessment").

Treatment

Oppositional Defiant Disorder

Good outcomes in the treatment of ODD are predicated on comprehensive evaluation and individualized interventions. The American Academy of Child and Adolescent Psychiatry has issued practice parameters in this regard, which are summarized in Table 2. The treatment plan will likely include psychological care of the child and family, pharmacologic treatment of the child, school-based interventions, and, in more serious cases, out-of-home placement.

An essential component of the treatment plan is some form of parent management training (PMT), which is based in the sound behavioral principles of: (1) reducing positive reinforcement of the undesirable behaviors (also called extinction, or the "starving" of the negative behaviors, e.g. ignoring a tantrum); (2) increasing reinforcement of desirable behaviors (i.e. paying attention to positive behaviors, or "catching them when they're good"); (3) using age-appropriate consequences that fit the behaviors (e.g. a "reward" for a younger child could be more time spent with the parent, whereas for the older child it could be having more time to pursue his/her interests. For "punishments" the younger child could be timed-out, whereas for the older child it could be the loss of privileges); and, (4) responding in a consistent and non-arbitrary manner, as soon as possible after the observed behaviors.

There are two circumstances in which the use of medications in ODD patients would be appropriate. The first is if there are clearly identified comorbid conditions that are amenable to pharmacotherapy, such as ADHD and MDD. The second is when the disruptive behaviors are unchanged or worsening despite good behavioral efforts (the selection and use of medications for aggressive behaviors is discussed in Chapter 12). The clinician needs to remember that medications should never be the only treatment used in patients with ODD.

Table 2. Recommendations for the evaluation and treatment of ODD

1. Establishment of therapeutic alliances with the child and family.
2. Cultural issues need to be considered in diagnosis and treatment.
3. Assessment includes information obtained directly from the child and from the parents regarding the core symptoms, age of onset, duration of symptoms, and degree of functional impairment.
4. Consider significant comorbid psychiatric conditions when diagnosing and treating ODD.
5. Include, if needed, information obtained independently from multiple outside informants.
6. Specific questionnaires and rating scales may be useful in evaluating for ODD and for tracking progress.
7. Develop an individualized treatment plan based on the specific clinical issues.
8. Choose a parent intervention based on empirically tested behavioral programs.
9. Medications should be used as adjuncts, for symptomatic treatment, and to treat comorbid conditions.
10. Intensive and prolonged treatment may be necessary if ODD is unusually severe and persistent.
11. Certain interventions (such as "boot camps") are not effective, and should be avoided, as they may worsen some behaviors.

Conduct Disorder

The approach to the treatment of CD is similar to that of ODD, beginning with good history-taking and mental status examination. Particular attention is paid to signs and symptoms that could indicate comorbid conditions.

For mild-moderate CD problems, it is reasonable to start with PMT (as was previously discussed for ODD), although it is unclear if the positive outcomes demonstrated in research settings can be effectively translated to the "real world" of clinical practice. For more severe conduct symptoms, such as violent behavior, parents are encouraged to utilize law enforcement interventions, including the filing of formal charges against the youth when appropriate to do so. If the child or adolescent is incarcerated, the parents are advised to not bail-out their son or daughter, as the loss of freedom is a natural consequence of his/her inappropriate and illegal actions. Depending on how unsafe the parents and/or siblings feel when the offending youth is at home, alternative living situations may have to be arranged before he/she is released.

If comorbid conditions are diagnosed they are treated following the protocols discussed elsewhere in this book (e.g. Chapter 10 for ADHD; Chapter 13 for depressive disorders). In the absence of clearly identified comorbid psychiatric disorders and/or response to behavioral psychotherapy, medication may still be an option.

Lithium and risperidone have been shown to reduce CD symptoms across several measures of behavior and mood; their use requires ongoing monitoring for potentially serious side effects. The psychostimulants, atomoxetine, valproic acid, and the selective serotonin reuptake inhibitors (SSRIs) have also shown promise in treating CD symptoms, but larger, well-controlled research studies demonstrating efficacy are needed before routine use of these agents can be recommended (see Chapter 12, "Aggressive behaviors," for details).

Conclusion

The successful diagnosis and treatment of patients with ODD and CD is dependent on ruling-out comorbid psychiatric disorders and initiating multidisciplinary interventions that can include parent training, psychotropic medications, and the legal system. The primary pediatrician can serve as the gateway through which patients and their families can be directed to the necessary community resources. The pediatrician may also choose to prescribe and manage the patients' medications (see the relevant chapters in this book).

References

American Academy of Child and Adolescent Psychiatry. Practice parameter for the assessment and treatment of children and adolescents with Oppositional Defiant disorder. *J. Am. Acad. Child Adolesc. Psychiatry* 2007;46(1):126-141.

American Psychiatric Association. Diagnostic and Statistical Manual of Mental Disorders, Fourth Edition, Text Revision. Washington, DC, American Psychiatric Association; 2000.

Burns GL, Walsh JA. The influence of ADHD-hyperactivity/impulsivity symptoms on the development of oppositional defiant disorder symptoms in a 2-year longitudinal study. *J. Abnorm. Child Psychol.* 2002;30(3):245-56.

Greene RW, Biederman J, Zerwas S, Monuteaux MC, Goring JC, Faraone SV. Psychiatric comorbidity, family dysfunction, and social impairment in referred youth with Oppositional Defiant Disorder. *Am. J. Psychiatry* 2002;159(7):1214-1224.

Ipser J, Stein DJ. Systematic review of pharmacotherapy of disruptive behavior disorders in children and adolescents. *Psychopharmacol* 2007;191:127-140.

Kadesjo C, Hagglof B, Kadesjo B, Gillberg C. Attention-deficit-hyperactivity disorder with and without oppositional defiant disorder in 3- to 7-year-old children. *Dev. Med. Child Neurol.* 2003;45(10):693-99.

Keenan K, Wakschlag LS, Danis B, Hill C, Humphries M, Duax J, et al. Further evidence of the reliability and validity of DSM-IV ODD and CD in preschool children. *J. Am. Acad. Child Adolesc. Psychiatry* 2007;46(4):457-468.

Loeber R, Burke JD, Lahey BB, Winters A, Zera M. Oppositional defiant and conduct disorder: a review of the past 10 years, *Part I. J. Am. Acad. Child Adolesc. Psychiatry* 2000;39(12):1468-1484.

Maughan B, Rowe R, Messer J, Goodman R, Meltzer H. Conduct disorder and oppositional defiant disorder in a national sample: developmental epidemiology. *J. Child Psychol. Psychiatry* 2004;45(3):609-621.

Nock MK, Kazdin AE, Hiripi E, Kessler RC. Prevalence, subtypes, and correlates of DSM-IV conduct disorder in the National Comorbidity Survey Replication. *Psychol. Med.* 2006;36(5):699-710. Epub 2006 Jan 26.

Rowe R, Maughan B, Pickles A, Costello EJ, Angold A. The relationship between DSM-IV oppositional defiant disorder and conduct disorder: findings from the Great Smoky Mountains Study. *Journal of Child Psychology and Psychiatry* 2002;43(3):365-373.

van de Wiel N, Matthys W, Cohen-Kettenis PC, van Engeland H. Effective treatments of school-aged conduct disordered children: recommendations for changing clinical and research practices. *Eur. Child Adolesc. Psychiatry* 2002;11:79-84.

In: Behavioral Pediatrics, 3rd Edition
Editor: Donald E. Greydanus et al.

ISBN 978-1-60692-702-1
© 2009 Nova Science Publishers, Inc.

Chapter 13

Aggressive Behaviors

Joseph L. Calles

Abstract

Aggressive behaviors are commonly seen in pediatric patients. The behaviors can be caused by medical, substance-related and/or psychiatric disorders. This chapter will discuss aggression in terms of its definition, epidemiology, clinical features, various etiologies, and treatments.

Introduction

Aggression- behavior that is hostile, threatening and attacking- has increasingly become a common clinical problem. Although aggression can be either verbal or physical, and the physical expression of aggression can be towards property or person, it is aggressive behavior directed towards people (i.e. violence) that generates the most concern from family members, school personnel, and the community at large. It also may cause a certain degree of discomfort for us clinicians, as our backgrounds and training to help people runs counter to the described hurtful and sometimes cruel behaviors perpetrated by some of our patients.

The pediatrician presented with an aggressive younger patient tends to ask two clinical questions: Why is this person behaving this way? What can I do to help? The purpose of this chapter is to guide the clinician in ways to assess the problem and to initiate a rational treatment plan.

Definition

We equate aggression with actions that are threatening or attacking, but there are also cognitive and affective components to the behaviors (see "Clinical Features" below). As we cannot know exactly what a person is thinking or feeling (unless he or she tells us), the clinical focus on aggressive behaviors is important for two reasons. The first is that we can actually experience the other person's aggressive acts with our own senses, e.g. hearing verbalized threats or seeing assaultive acts. The second is that the people on the receiving end of the aggression are likely to be injured emotionally and/or physically.

Aggression is the end result of a process that begins with some type of provoking event- internal or external- that leads to overwhelming angry thoughts and/or feelings that are eventually expressed in words and/or actions (Figure 1).

The outward expression of anger, i.e. aggression, is usually described in terms of a hierarchy, with the least dangerous level being verbal, such as threats to harm someone (the old saying "sticks and stones may break my bones, but words will never harm me" comes to mind) and the most dangerous level being the harming of a person (Figure 2).

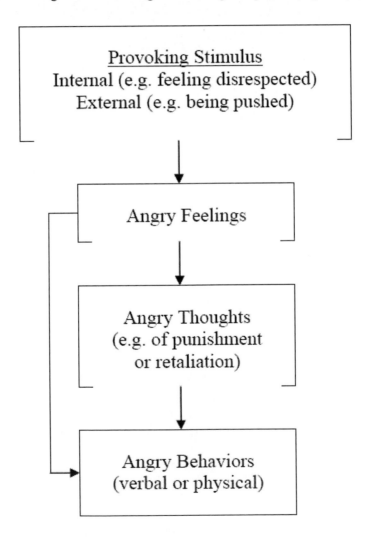

Figure 1.

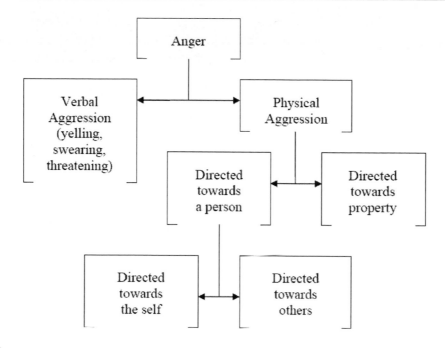

Figure 2.

In that regard, harming oneself is taken seriously, but harming someone else is taken even more seriously- as evidenced by the fact that most people who injure themselves are taken to a hospital, whereas most people who injure others are taken to jail! Multiple types of aggression will often be expressed simultaneously when people become extremely angry.

The sequence in Figure 1 is not quite complete, in that aggression that starts with uncontrollable anger (as noted) can be called *reactive*, i.e. feelings override thinking. There is another type of aggression, called *proactive*, wherein thinking overrides (at least temporarily) feelings, i.e. the aggression can be delayed and planned for (often called "payback"). This chapter is only considering reactive aggression; see the previous chapter on "Oppositional Defiant and Conduct Disorders" for more on proactive aggression.

Epidemiology

Every two years, the Centers for Disease Control and Prevention (CDC), of the U.S. Department of Health and Human Services, conduct their national Youth Risk Behavior Surveillance (YRBS); the last complete data available are for the year 2007. In that survey, representative samples of public school students in grades 9-12 were carefully questioned about various risk behaviors. Regarding those behaviors that have direct relevance to violence, the following statistics were reported for *the year preceding the survey*: of all students, 35.5% had been in at least one fight, 4.2% had been in at least one fight that led to an injury that required medical intervention, 12.4% had been in at least one fight on school property, and 9.9% had experienced dating violence. In the *preceding 30 days*, of all students, on at least one occasion 18.0% had carried a weapon, 5.2% had carried a gun, 5.9%

had carried a weapon on school property, and 7.8% of students had been threatened or injured with a weapon on school property. These data demonstrate that aggressive, violent, dangerous, and potentially lethal behaviors are- unfortunately- rather common in the lives of American youth.

Informal surveys suggest that aggressive behaviors are presenting more commonly in pediatric care settings, straining resources and generating fear and frustration on the part of clinicians.

Clinical Features

The presentation and course of aggression is quite variable, and depends on several factors:

Age of Onset

It appears that the use of aggression to deal with frustration, or to solve problems, is quite natural. By the age of 17 months most children display some physical aggression towards family members. It is the responsibility of the caregiving environment to model appropriate anger management. What happens when that guidance is lacking? Children who start out with high levels of aggression, which persists over time, are at greater risk of developing disruptive behavior disorders. Early-onset aggression is also more predictive of serious antisocial behavior into adulthood, even more so than are adolescent-onset aggressive behaviors.

Gender

Before adolescence, boys consistently display more physical aggression than do girls; however, that is not to say that girls cannot be aggressive. Girls tend to engage in what is called *relational* aggression, which involves the use of criticism, negative rumors and social ostracism to hurt female peers. During adolescence there appears to be an increase in physical aggression in both males and females. In more recent years the rate of increase of serious aggressive acts (e.g. assaults) in adolescent females has been much greater than that seen in adolescent males; the cause is likely multifactorial in nature.

Intelligence

In general, the lower a person's intellectual capability, the higher the risk for becoming aggressive. This probably derives from a combination of factors, including decreased/absent language skills, concrete thought processing, poor frustration tolerance, inability to delay gratification, and- depending on the nature of the intellectual impairment- the presence of seizure activity and psychiatric disorders.

Setting

Some aggressive behaviors may be confined to specific locales, e.g. fighting only at school or *being* destructive only at home. In general, the more places that aggression is displayed the more serious the problem.

Context

Aggression always derives from some type of interpersonal conflict. Its expression can be immediate (e.g. hitting someone after being pushed) or delayed (e.g. destroying a room at home following an argument at school). The quality and quantity of aggression can be modified by the social context within which it occurs. For example, peer pressure may influence a child to override his/her internal prohibition to fight. There is also a bidirectional relationship between aggression and peer rejection, i.e. an increase in one increases the likelihood of the other. In general, the more impersonal the trigger of aggression the more serious the problem. A chilling example of this is a boy who seriously injured another boy- a stranger- just because he "didn't like the way he looks."

Cognitions

What we tell ourselves is often more important than what others tell us, at least in regards to aggression. Making random eye contact with someone is usually unremarkable for most people. For people who have problems with anger dyscontrol, that act could be interpreted as a threat or a challenge, greatly increasing the probability that a verbal, or even physical, exchange will ensue. The aggression-prone individual is at high risk of perceiving the words and gestures of others as negative and personal; possible impressions are that the other person is being rude, disrespectful, or has "bad intentions."

Affective State

That there is a correlation between degree of anger and level of aggression seems fairly intuitive. Some people describe anger so intense that they "blackout," i.e. that they have little to no recall for their behavior, which can include serious property destruction or injury towards others (one adolescent male told me that, if people observing him hadn't pulled him off the other boy, "I probably would've killed him").

Past Outcomes

Every human event or situation has a behavioral element to it. Even in cases clearly involving psychiatrically-impaired individuals, how the environment (i.e. other people) responds to someone's aggressive behaviors will tend to either increase or decrease the probability of future episodes. An example is a family wherein their adolescent member assaults other members of the family and/or causes extensive property damage. Calling the police and filing criminal charges is likely to reduce the probability of similar future events. Conversely, having no negative consequences is likely to increase the odds of future episodes.

Degree of Impulsivity

Impulsivity- the tendency to act before thinking- is a risk factor for the reactive type of aggression. Some psychiatric conditions are associated with impulsivity and reactivity, and as such are risk factors for aggression (see "Diagnosis" below).

Degree of Control

The right amount of self-control can help an individual to avoid conflict, or to minimize it should it occur. People who are over-controlled may under-react to a conflictual situation. Depending on the other person's response style (i.e. impulsive vs. controlled), things may escalate in-part to try and elicit a reaction from the over-controlled individual. This may be part of the dynamic for a person who tends to be bullied, and who in turn is more likely to be a bully.

Diagnosis

Aggression is not a diagnosis, but a symptom of a medical, substance-related and/or psychiatric disorder. Table 1 lists some of the more common conditions associated with aggressive behaviors.

Medical Disorders

The assessment of aggression begins with identifying medical problems that may be the source of irritability and anger that leads to aggressive behaviors; common conditions include:

Table 1. Disorders associated with aggressive behaviors

Medical
Seizure disorders
Traumatic brain injury
Encephalitis/meningitis
Sensory impairments
Developmental disorders:
    Fetal alcohol syndrome
    Fragile X syndrome
    Prader-Willi syndrome
    Tuberous sclerosis complex
    Smith-Magenis syndrome
    Cri du chat syndrome
Substance-related (see Chapter 23)
    Alcohol abuse/dependence: Intoxication or withdrawal
    Anxiolytic abuse/dependence: Intoxication or withdrawal
    Cannabis abuse/dependence: Withdrawal
    Stimulant abuse/dependence: Intoxication
Psychiatric
Intellectual disabilities (see Chapter 3)
Autistic spectrum disorders (see Chapter 6)
Speech-Language disorders (see Chapter 5)
Disruptive behavior disorders
    Attention-deficit/hyperactivity disorder (see Chapter 10)
    Oppositional defiant disorder (see Chapter 11)
    Conduct disorder (see Chapter 11)
Mood disorders:
    Major depressive disorder (see Chapter 13)
    Bipolar disorder (see Chapter 14)
Anxiety disorders (see Chapter 15):
    Post-traumatic stress disorder
    Social anxiety disorder
    Separation anxiety disorder
Psychotic disorders (see Chapter 20)
Tic disorders (see Chapter 8)
Intermittent explosive disorder
Personality disorders (see Chapter 21):
    Borderline personality disorder (mostly females)
    Antisocial personality disorder (mostly males; not diagnosed before age 18)
    Paranoid personality disorder (mostly males)

Adapted, with permission, from Greydanus, et al. (see reference).

- *Seizure disorders.* It has been appreciated for some time that seizure disorders can manifest as emotional disturbances, including aggressive behaviors. Much of the medical literature has focused on seizure foci in the temporal lobes, but reports of seizure-related aggression have also been related to epileptogenic activity in the frontal lobes and in benign epilepsy of childhood with centrotemporal spikes. It is the interictal period- not during the times immediately surrounding the seizures- when aggressive behaviors are likely to be displayed. An additional risk factor for aggression in those with seizure disorders is their high rate of psychiatric comorbidity, which itself increases the risk for aggressive behaviors (see "Psychiatric disorders" below).

- *Traumatic brain injury* (TBI). Non-fatal head injuries are over-represented in people under the age of 19 years, especially males. Serious neuropsychiatric sequelae of TBI- including aggression- are related to factors such as age (hyperactivity and aggressiveness increase as the children get older), severity of injury, premorbid psychiatric status (e.g. the rate of *pre-injury* attention-deficit/hyperactivity disorder (ADHD) is quite high in TBI patients), and the development of seizures.
- *Encephalitis.* Infection-related inflammation of the brain has high morbidity and mortality associated with it. Especially problematic is encephalitis secondary to Herpes simplex virus (HSV), which has a predilection for the temporal lobes. As a result, post-HSV encephalitis patients- 50% of whom are children and young adults- can develop a myriad of neurobehavioral problems, including aggression. The psychiatric symptoms may be associated with seizure activity, which is a sequela of the encephalitis in almost one-half of the patients.
- *Sensory impairments.* Most of the literature on the presence of psychopathology in children with sensory impairments has focused on those with deafness, either as the primary sensory disorder or as part of multiple physical impairments. Internalizing disorders (e.g. anxiety or depression) are more common in deaf children than are externalizing disorders (e.g. conduct disorder), but both types are higher than in the hearing population, and the former may predispose to the latter. Aggressive behaviors in deaf children should be assumed to derive from factors *not* directly related to the deafness, except perhaps from the frustration associated with impaired communication ability.

Developmental Disorders (DD)

The practicing pediatrician will encounter children with a multitude of DD, many of which will have behavioral disturbances- including aggression- as part of the clinical picture.

Common DD with high rates of aggressive behaviors (expressed towards self or others) are:

- Fetal alcohol syndrome
- Fragile X syndrome
- Prader-Willi syndrome
- Tuberous sclerosis complex
- Smith-Magenis syndrome

Substance-Related Disorders

The next step in the evaluation process is the ruling-out of drug and/or alcohol problems that may be provoking anger and aggression. The previously mentioned YRBS (from the CDC) found that in 2007, of all American high school students- males and females- surveyed, 75% had tried alcohol at least once in their lifetimes, 44.7% had recently used alcohol, and 26% had episodic heavy drinking. In the same survey, 38.1% had tried marijuana (cannabis) at least once in their lifetimes and 19.7% were current users. Finally, regarding stimulating drugs, 7.2% had lifetime and 3.3% had current cocaine use, and 4.4% had lifetime methamphetamine use (the figure for current use was not included). These numbers highlight the importance of exploring substance-use as a possible factor in aggressive behavior.

The most common substance-use disorders associated with anger and aggression are:

- *Alcohol intoxication and withdrawal.* Some people who become intoxicated on alcohol can become angry and disinhibited, which can lead to assaultive and destructive behavior (the "mean drunk"). In those who develop alcohol dependence, withdrawal can include agitation and irritability, which can also lead to aggression, especially if their attempts to procure alcohol are thwarted (i.e. the person who tries to stop them becomes the target).

- *Anxiolytic intoxication and withdrawal.* It's amazing how readily younger people can acquire prescription anxiolytics that have been diverted from legitimate use. Although generally not as common nor as severe as alcohol-related problems, similar behaviors can be seen in younger people who are under the influence of, or withdrawing from, anxiolytic medications.

- *Cannabis (marijuana) withdrawal.* Agitation and aggression related to cannabis intoxication is uncommon. Its ability to calm someone makes its use attractive to those who are predisposed to anger and aggression, i.e. they tend to "self-medicate" with marijuana. A problem arises when the young person cannot obtain or otherwise use cannabis to calm themselves down, e.g. if they are getting drug tested while on probation. Cannabis withdrawal is better thought of as the recurrence of the underlying aggressive tendencies that the person has been suppressing with the cannabis use.

- *Stimulant intoxication.* Both cocaine and methamphetamine (as well as other similar drugs) are powerful stimulants of the CNS. Depending on the amounts used, the social context, and the user's psychological makeup, stimulants may not promote euphoria or a sense of wellbeing, but instead may lead to irritability, anger, paranoia and hostility. The intoxicated person may respond to the negative emotional state with acts of aggression. Similar to the anxiolytics, prescription stimulants that are prescribed for ADHD are increasingly being diverted for recreational use.

Psychiatric Disorders

The assessment of aggressive behaviors is completed by ruling-out psychiatric disorders (see the other chapters in this book for guidance in the diagnosis and treatment of specific psychiatric conditions). The following disorders can include aggression as part of their symptom pictures:

- *Intellectual disabilities.* As mentioned previously, people with intellectual impairment are at higher risk for expressing negative emotional states as aggressive behavior. Although the lower the intelligence the more obvious the problem, younger people with mild mental retardation, borderline intellectual functioning, or even low normal intelligence may be missed, i.e. their cognitive limitations may not be appreciated. In my experience intellectual testing is greatly under-employed in both school and clinical settings.
- *Autistic spectrum disorders* (ASD). Younger people with ASD have difficulties in the areas of communication and socialization, and commonly also have intellectual difficulties. Due to their unusual behaviors, they may be targeted by other children, especially at school. The ensuing confusion and frustration may be expressed in any form of aggression, including self-injury. Higher functioning individuals with ASD may not be recognized as such when younger; fortunately, better public awareness is making this oversight less common.
- *Speech-Language disorders.* We have a saying in our adolescent program that "Those who don't talk, act." Clearly, those for whom the ability to express themselves verbally is compromised or absent are more likely to behaviorally act out negative emotional states, such as frustration or anger. The importance of developmental screening and early referral for speech-language evaluation cannot be overstated, especially in children with aggressive behaviors and delayed language milestones.
- *Disruptive behavior disorders.* This group includes ADHD, oppositional defiant disorder (ODD) and conduct disorder (CD). There is high overlap between ADHD and the other two disorders. They all have various degrees of physical impulsivity and emotional lability, poor frustration tolerance, and lack of awareness of- or concern for- how their behaviors affect those around them. Given that those with ODD and CD come into conflict with authority figures, their aggressive behaviors not uncommonly lead to contact with the legal system, especially in the case of CD. Children and adolescents with ADHD, ODD and/or CD also have high rates of other psychiatric disorders, which must be ruled-out by the physician.
- *Mood disorders.* Depression can be experienced by young people not only as sad, but also as mad. The anger and irritability can be so severe that aggression may not be limited to self-injury. Depressed children and adolescents may get into fights with others or may become destructive. At the other end of the mood spectrum, youngsters with bipolar disorder in the manic or hypomanic phase may not experience elation, but instead may be irritable, angry and aggressive.

- *Anxiety disorders.* Children with *post-traumatic stress disorder* (PTSD) may act out recalled past traumas in aggressive ways. The trigger can be a nightmare, a re-living experience ("flashback"), or a reminder of the traumatic event(s) (e.g. people who look like the persons who hurt them). The aggression can look unprovoked or retaliatory, but is actually defensive in nature. Younger people with *social anxiety disorder* may become aggressive as a way of not going to, or getting out of, social situations that are too anxiety-provoking for them. Children with *separation anxiety disorder* may also fight to avoid being separated from the primary caregivers; conversely, they may attack- punish, if you will- the caregivers when reunited with them.

- *Psychotic disorders.* Psychosis in younger people is not very common; in fact, early-onset schizophrenia is rare. If psychosis is present, the affected youngster may become aggressive due to command hallucinations telling him/her to hurt people, or due to paranoid delusions that make the youngster feel threatened by others, or due to general mental disorganization and confusion that increases frustration and agitation.

- *Tic disorders.* Tourette disorder or syndrome (TS) is the prototypical tic disorder and has a high rate of psychiatric comorbidity, especially with ADHD, obsessive-compulsive disorder, and ODD. TS is also associated with episodic outbursts of anger and aggression called "rage attacks," which are not due to any specific etiology. They are usually sudden in onset, are very intense, can be violent, and may even be provoked by minor conflicts.

- *Intermittent explosive disorder* (IED). Similar to the aggressive outbursts of TS patients, the anger episodes of those with IED can be quite sudden reactions to even minimal provocation, can be quite severe and frightening, and can have serious consequences. This is a diagnosis of exclusion, as the symptoms should not be better accounted for by medical, substance-use or other psychiatric disorders. In our experience, many patients with IED will self-medicate with cannabis, which puts them at risk for increased aggression should they no longer be able to use the drug.

- *Personality disorders.* The DSM-IV-TR (American Psychiatric Association) allows for the diagnosis of personality disorders (except antisocial personality disorder) in those under 18 years, providing that the clinical features have been present for at least 1 year, and are "pervasive, persistent," and not limited to a specific stage of development nor part of an Axis I disorder. The most common personality disorder that we encounter in the adolescent psychiatry program is borderline personality disorder (BPD). Young people with BPD tend to express aggression as self-injury, but they also commonly get into physical altercations with others (especially family members) and can be destructive (e.g. "trashing" their bedrooms). Since BPD in younger people can be comorbid with other psychiatric and substance-use disorders, the clinician should rule-out other etiologies before attributing the aggression to the BPD.

Treatment

Some general comments are in order before discussing the treatment of aggression associated with specific disorders. *Firstly*, as aggression is expressed behaviorally, intervention should include a plan based on a thorough behavioral assessment. *Secondly*, safety will be the primary consideration in the selection of a therapeutic intervention. A certain medication may seem like the logical first choice (e.g. an antidepressant for a depressed, angry child), but there may be a high likelihood of making the symptoms worse (e.g. if there are risk factors for bipolar disorder, the antidepressant could provoke the emergence of mania). *Thirdly*, in the presence of multiple disorders which may all be contributing to the aggression, the initial target for treatment should be the disorder that will have the worst prognosis if left untreated. *Fourthly*, unless the aggressive behaviors are so severe that rapid sedation is warranted (e.g. in an emergency department or inpatient unit), medications should be started singly, in low doses, and titrated slowly. The ideal goals should always be to avoid or minimize polypharmacy, and to use the lowest effective dosages (vs. always increasing dosages to "usual" or maximum amounts). *Lastly*, whenever possible and when available, treatments should follow evidence-based guidelines and algorithms.

Medical Disorders

If the treatment of the medical condition is maximized and aggressive behaviors are still present, it is possible that there may be unidentified, comorbid psychiatric disorders that are the source of the aggression. Those should be sought out and treated.

- *Seizure disorders*. When there is clinical and EEG evidence that seizures have been controlled, the next step is to treat comorbid psychiatric disorders, such as depression, anxiety or psychosis. Psychotropic agents can be safely used in patients with seizure disorders, provided that dosing is done with caution.
- *Traumatic brain injury* (TBI). In the absence of seizure activity, the treatment of TBI-associated aggression can start with an alpha-2 agonist (clonidine or guanfacine) or a beta-blocker (propranolol or metoprolol). Pulse and blood pressure should be monitored closely. If not effective, anti-epileptic drugs (AED) or selective serotonin reuptake inhibitor (SSRI) antidepressants can be tried (I tend to favor using AED first, unless there are depressive features). Some groups have reported that the antiviral and anti-Parkinson drug amantadine can reduce agitation and aggression in post-TBI patients.
- *Encephalitis*. There is little in the medical literature to guide the use of psychotropic agents for aggressive behaviors related to encephalitis. However, given the propensity for the HSV to affect the temporal lobes and create seizure foci, it is reasonable to use AED and avoid medications with the potential to lower the seizure threshold, especially the mood stabilizer lithium and the antidepressant bupropion.
- *Sensory impairments*. In addition to treating psychiatric disorders in hearing-impaired children, it is very important that any communication deficits be addressed.

Medications will not make up for a deaf child's inability to express their thoughts and feelings.

Developmental Disorders (DD)

The pharmacologic treatment of aggression in DD is based on the presence of comorbid psychiatric and medical disorders. What follows are reasonable strategies for the use of psychotropic medications in select DD.

- o Fetal alcohol syndrome (FAS). Children and adolescents with FAS can have IED-like aggressive outbursts. As the prevalence of seizure disorders is not high in FAS, treatment can begin with lithium. If lithium is not effective, AED may be tried next. If the AED are ineffective or not tolerated, a trial of risperidone or a beta-blocker can be considered.
- o Fragile X syndrome (FXS). Individuals with FXS can also present with symptoms of IED. Unlike in FAS, the incidence of seizure disorders is significant (15%-20%) in FXS. Therefore, treatment should begin with AED, followed by lithium. The last step would be a beta-blocker or any atypical antipsychotic (AA) except for clozapine, which lowers the seizure threshold.
- o Prader-Willi syndrome (PWS). Children with PWS have a fair amount of anxiety and obsessive-compulsive features. Treatment may begin either with AED or SSRI. The next step would to use what was not tried initially. Finally, if the AED and SSRI are ineffective, buspirone or an AA may be used.
- o Tuberous sclerosis complex (TSC). Patients with TSC have high rates of seizure disorders (80% of patients), so the primary treatments for aggressive behaviors are the AED. There is also a significant rate of ADHD symptoms in those with TSC, so if the aggression is not responding to the AED, a trial of a stimulant would be indicated.
- o Smith-Magenis syndrome (SMS). This disorder is also associated with high rates of seizure disorders (25%-50%) and ADHD symptoms. Treatment should begin with AED, followed by SSRI (as much of the aggression may be self-directed, possibly due to deficient serotonin). For prominent ADHD features a stimulant may be used. Non-responsive cases may need to be treated with an AA.

Substance-Related Disorders

The primary intervention for young patients with drug and alcohol problems is formal substance abuse treatment, which usually involves individual, group, and family psychotherapy. If the substance abuse is secondary to another disorder, that problem should be identified and treated. If psychosocial interventions are not effective, patients may need to be evaluated for pharmacologic agents that may reduce drug/alcohol craving or the positive responses to the substances (see Chapter 23).

Psychiatric Disorders

When medical and substance-related disorders have been ruled-out, or adequately treated, the next task is to treat the psychiatric disorders that are causing or contributing to aggressive behaviors.

- *Intellectual disabilities.* There are no specific treatments for intellectual impairments or for the associated aggression. The AAs may be tried, with risperidone being a good first choice. If seizures are part of the clinical picture, then AED should be used first. The AED can also be used when the AAs are ineffective.
- *Autistic spectrum disorders* (ASD). Risperidone is approved for the treatment of irritability (and related aggression) in autistic disorder. If a seizure disorder is present (the prevalence of seizure disorders in autistic disorder is 20%-30%, and is correlated with intellectual level), then treatment should begin with AED. Risperidone may be used if seizures are well-controlled.
- *Speech-Language disorders.* Treatment is non-pharmacologic, and should be conducted by a qualified speech and language pathologist.
- *Disruptive behavior disorders.* The mainstay of treatment is a behavioral plan that consists of clearly defined, achievable goals and consistent consequences. If behavioral interventions are not working due to intense anger and aggressiveness, medications may have to be used. If other disorders are excluded or adequately treated, treatment with lithium may be initiated. Other options include alpha-2 agonists, AAs or even older antipsychotics, such as chlorpromazine.
- *Mood disorders.* For the aggression associated with depression, the first choice is fluoxetine, followed by another SSRI. In the event of SSRI failure, other types of antidepressants or lithium may be used. If bipolar depression is the cause of the aggressive behaviors, treatment choices are lithium, lamotrigine or quetiapine. If bipolar mania is the source of the aggression, agents to use are lithium, valproic acid, carbamazepine, or any AA approved for use in bipolar mania.
- *Anxiety disorders.* The agents of choice are the SSRI antidepressants. If they are ineffective, or if they worsen the aggression, then alternative choices are an alpha-2 agonist or buspirone.
- *Psychotic disorders.* One of the several available AA should effectively treat psychosis and its associated aggressive behaviors. In the event that the AA don't work, a first-generation antipsychotic (FGA), such as haloperidol, may be tried.
- *Tic disorders.* In the case of TS, medication selection is based on which symptom cluster- the tic disorder itself, ADHD, or anxiety- is most prominent and most likely to be driving the aggressive behaviors. A safe first-choice that may positively affect all three clusters is an alpha-2 agonist. For unresponsive tics AA or haloperidol can be used. Unresponsive ADHD may be addressed with atomoxetine or a cautious trial of a stimulant. For persistent anxiety, SSRI or buspirone are options.

Table 2: Recommended Pharmacotherapeutic Agents

Disorder*	Medications**		
	First choice	Second choice	Third choice
ADHD	Stimulant	2nd stimulant	Alpha-agonist or BB
Anxiety	SSRI	2nd SSRI or alpha-agonist	Buspirone
ASD ± MR	Risperidone	2nd AA	AED
Bipolar disorder:			
-Depressed	- Lithium or LTG	- LTG or lithium	- Quetiapine
-Manic	- Lithium	- VPA or CBZ	- 2nd AED or an AA
Conduct disorder	Lithium	AA	Alpha-agonist or chlorpromazine
Depression	Fluoxetine	2nd SSRI	Non-SSRI AD or lithium
DD:			
-FAS	- Lithium	- AED	- Risperidone or BB
-FXS	- AED	- Lithium	- AA or BB
-PWS	- SSRI or AED	- AED or SSRI	- Buspirone or AA
-TSC	- AED	- 2nd AED	- Stimulant
-SMS	- AED	- SSRI	- Stimulant or AA
Encephalitis	AED	2nd AED	3rd AED
IED	Lithium	AED	AA or SSRI
Psychosis	AA	2nd AA	3rd AA or FGA
TBI without seizures	Alpha-agonist or BB	AED or SSRI	SSRI or AED
TS; 1° symptoms:			
- tics	- Alpha-agonist	- AA	- Haloperidol
- ADHD	- Alpha-agonist	- Atomoxetine	- Stimulant
- anxiety	- Alpha-agonist	- SSRI	- Buspirone

* Abbreviations: ADHD = attention-deficit/hyperactivity disorder;
ASD = autistic-spectrum disorder; DD= developmental disorders; FAS= fetal alcohol syndrome;
FXS= fragile X syndrome; IED = intermittent explosive disorder; MR= mental retardation;
PWS= Prader-Willi syndrome; SMS= Smith-Magenis syndrome;
TBI = traumatic brain injury; TS= Tourette syndrome; TSC= tuberous sclerosis complex
** Abbreviations: AA = atypical antipsychotic; AD = antidepressant;
AED = antiepileptic drug; BB = beta-blocker;
CBZ = carbamazepine; FGA = first-generation antipsychotic; LTG= lamotrigine;
SSRI = selective serotonin reuptake inhibitor; VPA = valproic acid
Adapted, with permission, from Greydanus, et al. (see reference)

- *Intermittent explosive disorder* (IED). Lithium, followed by AED, and finally AA is my preferred medication sequence. The literature also reports good results with SSRI, but they should be avoided in patients with even minimal features of a cyclic mood disorder.

- *Personality disorders.* Patients with personality disorders can also suffer from other psychiatric conditions. However, pharmacotherapy will not alter the underlying pathologic character structure. Therefore, the treatment of personality disorders should be psychotherapeutic and should be carried out by a therapist experienced in working with younger people.

Table 2 summarizes the medication choices recommended for use in aggression associated with psychiatric disorders.

Conclusion

Aggressive behaviors that present in pediatric care settings are symptoms of underlying medical, substance-related and/or psychiatric disorders. This chapter has attempted to present a method of assessing the subjective and objective features of aggression, as well as a guide to rational pharmacotherapeutic interventions.

References

American Psychiatric Association. *Diagnostic and Statistical Manual of Mental Disorders,* Fourth Edition, Text Revision. Washington, DC, American Psychiatric Association; 2000.

Asendorpf JB, Denissen JJA, van Aken MAG. Inhibited and aggressive preschool children at 23 years of age: Personality and social transitions into adulthood. *Dev. Psychol.* 2008;44(4):997-1011.

Calles, JL. Psychopharmacology for the violent adolescent. *Prim. Care Clin. Office Pract.* 2006;33:531-544.

Campbell SB, Spieker S, Burchinal M, Poe MD, The NICHD Early Child Care Research Network. Trajectories of aggression from toddlerhood to age 9 predict academic and social functioning through age 12. *J. Child Psychol. Psychiatry* 2006;47(8):791-800.

Centers for Disease Control and Prevention. Youth Risk Behavior Surveillance- United States, 2007. Surveillance Summaries, June 6, 2008. *MMWR* 2008;57(No. SS-4).

Cohen R, Hsueh Y, Russell KM, Ray GE. Beyond the individual: A consideration of context for the development of aggression. *Aggression and Violent Behavior* 2006;11:341-351.

Elbers JM, Bitnun A, Richardson SE, et al. A 12-year prospective study of childhood Herpes simplex encephalitis: Is there a broader spectrum of disease? *Pediatrics* 2007;119;e399-e407.

Geraldina P, Mariarosaria L, Annarita A, Susanna G, Michela S, Alessandro D, Sandra S, Enrico C. Neuropsychiatric sequelae in TBI: a comparison across different age groups. *Brain Inj.* 2003 Oct;17(10):835-46.

Graves KN. Not always sugar and spice: Expanding theoretical and functional explanations for why females aggress. *Aggression and Violent Behavior* 2007:12(2):131-140.

Greydanus DE, Calles JL Jr, Patel DR. Disruptive behavior and aggressive disorders. In: Greydanus DE, Calles JL Jr, Patel DR. *Pediatric and Adolescent Psychopharmacology: A Practical Manual for Pediatricians.* Cambridge, UK: Cambridge University Press; 2008:117-131.

Gross A, Devinsky O, Westbrook LE, Wharton AH, Alper K. Psychotropic medication use in patients with epilepsy: effect on seizure frequency. *J. Neuropsychiatry Clin. Neurosci.* 2000;12(4):458-464.

Leschied AW, Cummings A, Van Brunschot M, Cunningham A, Saunders A. Female adolescent aggression: A review of the literature and the correlates of aggression, 2000-04. Public Works and Government Services Canada. Cat. No.: JS4-1/2000-2E.

Marsh L, Krauss GL. Aggression and violence in patients with epilepsy. *Epilepsy Behav.* 2000;1:160-168.

Roberts C, Hindley P. Practitioner review: The assessment and treatment of deaf children with psychiatric disorders. *J. Child Psychol. Psychiatry* 1999;40(2):151-165.

Stormshak EA, Bierman KL, McMahon RJ, Lengua LJ, Conduct Problems Prevention Research Group. Parenting practices and child disruptive behavior problems in early elementary school. *J. Clin. Child Psychol.* 2000;29(1):17-29.

Tremblay RE, Nagin DS, Seguin JR, et al. Physical aggression during early childhood: trajectories and predictors. *Pediatrics* 2004;114(1):43-50.

Weisbrot DM, Ettinger AB. Aggression and violence in mood disorders. *Child Adolesc. Psychiatric Clin. N. Am.* 2002 Jul;11(3):649-671.

Section IV. Mood Disorders

In: Behavioral Pediatrics, 3rd Edition
Editor: Donald E. Greydanus et al.

ISBN 978-1-60692-702-1
© 2009 Nova Science Publishers, Inc.

Chapter 14

Major Depressive and Dysthymic Disorders

Joseph L. Calles

Abstract

Depression is a fairly common psychiatric disorder in younger people, occurring in about 5% of children and adolescents. The disorder causes subjective distress and functional impairment. Pediatricians are often the first professionals to encounter depressed youth. It is important, therefore, that pediatric specialists learn to identify, fully assess, and appropriately treat depression in their patients. This chapter will address these issues.

Introduction

In human beings there has been described a continuum of low mood from ordinary *sadness*, to *dysphoria* (or depressed mood, the extreme end of normal sadness), to a *depressive syndrome* (a constellation of symptoms that we associate with depression, e.g. poor sleep and appetite), and finally to a *depressive disorder* (the requisite symptom cluster that also meets duration and impairment criteria). It is the depressive disorder that we refer to as the clinical state of depression. Our concepts of depression as a mental illness continue to evolve, as do the clinical criteria (the component symptoms and signs) which are currently incorporated into diagnostic systems such as the DSM-IV-TR.

Definitions

In this chapter only two depressive disorders will be discussed: Major depressive disorder (MDD) and Dysthymic disorder (DD) (see Chapter 14, "Bipolar Disorders," for information on Bipolar depression). The symptoms for the diagnosis of MDD in adults can be summarized in the well-known mnemonic "SIGECAPS" (Table 1).

Table 1. Criteria (SIGECAPS) for the diagnosis of MDD

At least five of the following symptoms during the same 2-week period*:
  Sleep disturbance, either insomnia or hypersomnia
  Interest in activities is diminished or absent**
  Guilt, or other thoughts of self-blame or low self-worth
  Energy is low and the person fatigues easily
  Concentration is poor, thinking and decision-making impaired**
  Appetite is poor and/or weight is lost (or not gained appropriately)
  Psychomotor retardation or agitation***
  Suicidal thoughts, plans, or attempts

* At least 1 symptom is either depressed mood or loss of interest/pleasure.
** Self-reported or observed by others *** Must be observed by others.

The symptoms of DD include similar disturbances of sleep, appetite, energy and concentration, with the additional symptoms low self-esteem and hopelessness. For MDD the symptoms must be present for at least 2 weeks.

The DSM-IV-TR does not specify unique diagnostic criteria for depression in children and adolescents. It has, however, modified the diagnostic criteria somewhat for younger patients, taking into consideration some developmental differences. For example, children or adolescents with either MDD or DD can have a mood that is irritable, rather than sad. Children with MDD may also not experience weight loss, but instead fail to make appropriate weight gains. For the diagnosis of DD in adults the duration of illness must be at least 2 years; for children and adolescents the duration is only 1 year.

Epidemiology

The reported incidence and prevalence data on child and adolescent depression has been highly variable, with several possible explanations for the differences. One factor is that different populations may have been studied, e.g. whether they were recruited from the community or from clinical settings. Another factor is the method of assessment; self-report questionnaires, general health surveys, and formal diagnostic interviews will elicit different types of psychological symptoms and yield different rates of depression.

In the 1990's a national survey of adolescent health, which used a standardized but non-clinical interview, found that 19% of adolescents reported mild depressive symptoms, while 9% endorsed symptoms of a moderate-to-severe degree. A more recent meta-analysis looked at rates of depression based on clinical samples, using standard diagnostic methodologies. Prevalence estimates for depressive disorder were 2.8% for those under 13-years of age and 5.7% for the 13-18-year-olds. The breakdown of the adolescent rates of depression by gender showed a female-to-male ratio of 5.9% to 4.6%, respectively. Those results were consistent with the post-pubertal predominance of female depression (although not at the usually cited 2:1, F:M ratio) and the increase in depression from childhood to adolescence. The rate of DD, although less frequently identified, is higher (about 8%) than that of MDD in adolescents.

Before puberty the rates of depression are equal between males and females. Hormonal changes during puberty seem to be a significant risk factor for the increase in depression in females, but there are likely other factors- including the environment- that also contribute to the increased risk. This is an especially important point to keep in mind, as external, non-biological issues (e.g. family dysfunction) need to be addressed for both prevention and treatment (see the section on "Treatment" below).

Clinical Features

The signs and symptoms of depression can present differently at different ages, with much of the variability being related to developmental factors.

Depression in Infants

An important feature of depression in this age group is *withdrawal*, the literal pulling away from the outside world. Depressed infants may stop responding to external stimuli, overreact to environmental stimulation, or display emotional distress with no apparent reason. They may also stop interacting with caregivers, e.g. avoiding eye contact or not reciprocating in social smiling. Attempts to console them by holding and cuddling may be met with indifference. The rhythms of normal biological functions- eating, sleeping, moving, etc. - become disturbed or never even get established. Appetite can decrease, and the infants will stop gaining weight, or actually lose weight. Sleep can be difficult to achieve or maintain, or can be excessive, but is always of poor quality. Motor activity is usually decreased, and the infant can appear listless or even catatonic. Previously acquired skills- such as crawling or speaking- may be lost.

Depressed infants may not necessarily display dramatic or obvious symptoms, especially early in the course of the illness. Vague or subtle changes may be missed or attributed to other reasons, which can delay diagnosis and treatment, placing the infant at risk for physical illness or even death.

Depression in Preschoolers

Children in this age group with clinical depression can meet the usual DSM-IV-TR criteria for MDD, with modifications to account for developmental differences from adults (e.g. changing the duration of symptoms to less than 2 weeks, which is a very long time in the life of a preschooler). Aggressive play- such as with dolls or action figures- could reflect underlying themes of destruction or suicide. Sad or irritable mood in these young people is considered a *sensitivity* symptom, as essentially all depressed patients will endorse it; by comparison, anhedonia (the lack of interest or pleasure in usually enjoyed activities/possessions) is a *specificity* symptom, helping to differentiate depression from other types of psychopathology. Contrary to a previously held belief in so-called "masked depression," somatic symptoms are not a significant feature of depression in young children, although they may be a marker for an increased risk of developing depression.

Depression in School-Age Children

As children get older their verbal skills increase. One would, therefore, expect that depressed children would articulate their distress to those around them. In fact, depressed school-age children do report high levels of depressive symptoms when asked on screening questionnaires or during psychiatric interviews. Unfortunately, those same children tend to not report depression spontaneously, nor will they necessarily endorse depressive symptoms when asked by parents, teachers, or other adults in their lives.

Parents and teachers will sometimes suspect that children in their charges are depressed. Teachers tend to have a higher level of suspicion (perhaps due to their experiences in working with large numbers of children) and are more likely than are parents to refer a depressed child for a formal evaluation. The school-age child who is depressed will often display similar signs of distress at home and at school. Social isolation and a preference to be alone manifest at home as staying in his/her room a lot, not eating with the family, etc; at school there can be sitting apart in the lunchroom or avoidance of group play. Even in the absence of ADHD, depressed children- boys and girls- can appear restless and inattentive, with negative effects on academic functioning. The combination of irritability and disobedience commonly results in temper tantrums- usually outside of school- in both boys and girls. School-related behavioral problems are different between boys and girls, with the former more likely to get into fights, steal, and be destructive, the latter to be truant. Depressed boys are more likely to be bullied at school than to display bullying behavior, although at home they can intimidate family members with their threatening behaviors. Somatic symptoms in this age-group may be more common than seen in depressed pre-schoolers, but it may be an artifact of the high degree of comorbidity between depression and anxiety (see "Diagnosis" below).

Depression in Adolescents

Although boys and girls in this age group who are depressed are more likely to present with an adult-like picture of depression, there can be some important differences. One notable variation is in the reporting of the mood state itself: depressed adolescents may not actually feel *sad*, but rather irritable or angry, frustrated, bored, or numb. Boys are more likely to experience a sense of restlessness, and tend to externalize their feelings, mostly with behaviors as verbal communication is diminished. They may attribute the cause of their suffering to people in the environment, especially parents. Girls are more likely to internalize their distress, feeling lonely, unattractive, and responsible for their misery.

Diagnosis

The presence of the previously described clinical features of depression should help the clinician to make the diagnosis of depression in a younger patient. There are, however, three issues that may jeopardize diagnostic accuracy: (1) medical conditions that may present as, or be comorbid with, depression; (2) substance use disorders that may cause or evolve from depression; and, (3) other psychiatric disorders that can mimic or coexist with depression.

Medical Disorders and Depression

Patients in both general and specialty pediatric settings present with a myriad of medical disorders. Depending on the medical condition being treated, its severity and its chronicity, it is not uncommon for pediatric patients to complain of disturbed sleep and appetite, low energy, and difficulty concentrating. They may look psychomotor slowed. They may express feelings of sadness, helplessness and hopelessness. They may even wonder if life is worth living or wish for an end to their physical distress. On the surface this all sounds like depression, and it is obviously important not to miss diagnosing- and treating- it if it's there. It is equally important, however, to distinguish the depressive signs and symptoms that are concomitants of the *medical* disorder from those that may be indicative of a comorbid *psychiatric* disorder. The former should improve as the child is reassured and medical treatment proceeds; the latter may persist in the face of response to medical treatments, or may even interfere with successful treatment of the medical disorders. Table 2 lists some medical disorders that may present with depression.

Table 2. Medical conditions that may present with depression

Infectious
   Mononucleosis (EBV or CMV)*
   Influenza
   Hepatitis
   Human immunodeficiency virus (HIV)
Neurologic
   Epilepsy
   Traumatic brain injury
   Demyelinating diseases
   Migraine headaches
Endocrine
   Diabetes mellitus (Types 1 and 2)
   Hypothyroidism
   Hypercortisolism
   Adrenal insufficiency
Exocrine
   Cystic fibrosis

Table 2. (Continued)

Hematologic
    Iron deficiency anemia
    Sickle cell anemia
Pulmonary
    Asthma
Cardiac
    Congenital anomalies
    Cardiomyopathy
    Post-transplantation
Renal
    Chronic renal failure
Rheumatologic
    Rheumatoid arthritis
    Systemic lupus erythematosus
Gastrointestinal
    Inflammatory bowel disease
Neoplastic
    Leukemia
    Lymphoma
Other
    Chronic fatigue syndrome
Fibromyalgia

* EBV= Epstein-Barr virus; CMV= Cytomegalovirus.

Substance Use Disorders (SUDS) and Depression

A second group of disorders that can precede or follow depression are the substance use disorders (see Table 3). The most common substances which have implications for effects on mood are:

Alcohol. At least one-third of young people with both depression and alcohol abuse/dependence develop their depression after the onset of the alcohol problem (this is not surprising given that alcohol is a CNS depressant). An especial concern is that alcohol overuse can also be a risk factor for suicide.

Cannabis. Another drug which can produce depression-like effects is cannabis, known more commonly as marijuana (MJ). Chronic users of MJ can develop what is known as an "amotivational syndrome." This is characterized by low energy and a lack of motivation, decreased concentration and memory, and a reduction or constriction of social relationships (associating mostly with other MJ users). At times the withdrawal from MJ can produce irritability, decreased appetite, and insomnia, which may be mistaken for depression.

Psychostimulants. The use of CNS stimulants (especially cocaine and the amphetamines-prescription or illicit) initially causes feelings of exhilaration and well-being. As their use continues and increasing amounts produce less and less of a "kick," the positive emotional effects are replaced by feelings of irritability or numbness, low energy and motivation, poor concentration, and even suicidality- a picture indistinguishable from a clinical depression (which is exacerbated during periods of withdrawal from the drug).

MDMA (3, 4-methylenedioxymethamphetamine). Known as "Ecstasy" on the street, this drug, which is a modified methamphetamine, produces many of the same effects as the parent drug, including a depressive state (usually transient) upon withdrawal.

Table 3. Substance use disorders that may present with depression

- Alcohol abuse or dependence
- Amphetamine withdrawal
- Cannabis abuse or dependence
- Cocaine withdrawal
- Hallucinogen abuse or dependence
- Inhalant abuse or dependence
- MDMA ("Ecstasy") withdrawal
- Opioid dependence
- Phencyclidine (PCP) abuse or dependence
- Sedative/hypnotic/anxiolytic intoxication

Other Psychiatric Disorders and Depression

Major depressive disorder in children and adolescents is highly comorbid with other psychiatric disorders, including the following:

- *Anxiety disorders.* These are the most common co-occurring conditions in child and adolescent depression, with up to three-fourths of depressed youth having at least one anxiety disorder. The anxiety disorder will also precede the onset of depression- sometimes by years- in about two-thirds of cases (the exception is panic disorder, which tends to develop after the depression). The combination of anxiety and depression is a risk factor for a more severe and longer lasting course of depression.
- *Dysthymic disorder.* At some point during the course of early onset DD (defined as starting before age 21 years) about 70%-80% of those who are suffering from it will also develop a MDD. Conversely, the presence of a MDD predisposes to the development of a DD, but at a lower rate (somewhere between 10% and 30%). Patients with this combination of "double depression" have more dysfunction, less competence, and a poorer prognosis than patients with either MDD or DD alone. The diagnosis of DD is likely to be missed due to a combination of its lower prevalence (vs. MDD) in the child population, less pronounced symptoms, and lower index of suspicion on the part of clinicians.
- *Disruptive behavior disorders.* Children and adolescents with conduct problems (i.e. Oppositional defiant disorder [ODD] and/or Conduct disorder [CD]) are at an increased risk for having a comorbid MDD, as are depressed youth at higher risk for

developing disruptive behaviors. In clinical samples at least one-third of youth with MDD also have conduct problems, and more than one-half with conduct problems also meet criteria for MDD. Both ODD and CD are much more likely to develop after the MDD than before it, which speaks to the need for early diagnosis and treatment of the depression. A more common disruptive behavior disorder, Attention-deficit/hyperactivity disorder (ADHD), also has high comorbidity with depression. It has been reported that 16%-26% of a school-aged, community sample with ADHD met criteria for a ''depressive syndrome.'' In well-designed prevalence studies rates of depression in the ADHD population were found to be between 9% and 38%, with the ADHD preceding the depression in the majority of cases.

- *Somatoform disorders*. Children and adolescents with recurrent or chronic abdominal pain (CAP) are commonly seen in pediatric practice. In the majority of those cases there is an absence of demonstrable physical illness. It has been known for some time that there is a correlation between functional abdominal pain and depression (but a question as to which one causes the other). One guide to the diagnosis of depression in CAP is the presence of other, non-gastrointestinal somatic symptoms. One study has suggested that the presence of 3 or more of the non-GI symptoms increases the sensitivity and specificity of identifying depression on more formal screening.

- *Developmental disorders*. The identification of depression in those with developmental disorders (DDs), and especially those with Mental retardation (MR), has been problematic. A more accurate diagnosis of depression in those with DDs and MR can be facilitated by relying less on subjective report (which is sometimes impossible to obtain in those populations) and more on objective observations- withdrawal, sleep and appetite change, irritability, etc.- by caregivers and clinicians. In some of the DDs (e.g. Down syndrome and Velocardiofacial syndrome) the risk of depression increases with age; in others (e.g. Fragile X syndrome) the degree of risk correlates with degree of impairment.

Treatment

There are three basic approaches to the treatment of depression in children and adolescents: (1) psychotherapy alone; (2) antidepressant (AD) medication alone; and, (3) the combination of medication and psychotherapy.

Psychotherapy

The indication for psychotherapy as the lone treatment for depression in younger patients is primarily based on the severity of the depression. In most cases of mild-to-moderate depression psychotherapy is a reasonable first step. The type of psychotherapy is crucial, as cognitive-behavioral therapy (CBT) has the best efficacy data behind it as a treatment for depression. Impediments to this approach are the lack of a qualified CBT therapist and/or inability to afford such therapy.

Medication

Although the prescribing of AD medication as the sole treatment for depression is common, it is usually not recommended, especially since its use may increase suicidal ideation in some patients (see "The 'black box' warning" below). Medication is also a poor substitute for psychotherapy, especially if psychological factors (such as low self-esteem or a pessimistic worldview) or environmental issues (such as a chaotic family life or poor peer relationships) are driving the depression. The use of AD medication would certainly be an important component in the treatment of depression that is more severe, is worsening, or is not responding to psychotherapy alone.

The "black box" warning. In late 2004, the U.S. Food and Drug Administration (FDA) issued an advisory recommending that manufacturers of AD medications place a "black box" (i.e. serious) warning in their prescribing information literature. The statement was to alert consumers and prescribers to the increased "risk of suicidal thinking and behavior (suicidality)" in younger patients treated with ADs for MDD (and "other psychiatric disorders"). Although the risks were small for both placebo and AD agents, the risk for the active agents were about two-times greater.

Subsequent to the original FDA recommendations, re-analyses of data and ongoing research studies have shown that the risk of depressed youth committing suicide is greater if they *are not treated with medication.* The best evidence to date comes from the federally-funded Treatment of Adolescents with Depression Study (TADS). This study determined that 4 children would need to be treated for 1 to show much/very much improvement; conversely, 25 children would need to be treated for 1 to display a harm-related event. This comparison yields a likelihood of helped-to-harmed ratio (LHH) of 7.

Combined Medication and Psychotherapy

The treatment of depression with both AD medication and CBT offers some advantages over either treatment approach alone. Firstly, the combination accelerates improvement, i.e. patients respond more quickly and achieve functional improvement earlier. Secondly, the combination treatment that successfully treats the depression also reduces suicidal ideation and suicidal events. The TADS also determined that when combining fluoxetine and CBT, 3 children would need to be treated for 1 to show much/very much improvement, whereas 50 children would need to be treated for 1 to display a harm-related event. This comparison yields an even better LHH (when compared to AD treatment alone) of 17.

This latter point should reassure parents about the use of ADs (see "How to use antidepressant medications" below). The clinician should remember that the positive results from combined treatment were achieved in studies that used fluoxetine, which at present is the only AD that is approved for the treatment of depression in younger patients. It is reasonable, however, to assume that other ADs also have the potential to achieve similar results in combination with CBT.

How to Use Antidepressant Medications

Once the decision is made to use AD medication, the next step is to choose a specific agent. As mentioned previously, fluoxetine is the only AD approved for the treatment of MDD in children and adolescents (those 8-years of age and older). Figure 1 shows one approach to the treatment of uncomplicated MDD in children and adolescents, and as can be seen fluoxetine is the medication of choice at Level I.

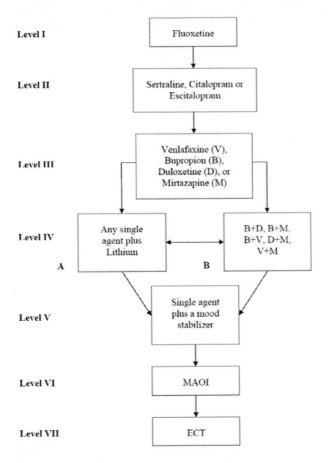

Figure 1. Treatment algorithm for uncomplicated MDD.

Fluoxetine- or any other SSRI (selective serotonin reuptake inhibitor)- would also be preferred for the treatment of depression that is comorbid with anxiety. For the depression associated with ADHD that is not improving with a stimulant, bupropion would be a reasonable first-choice.

There are no ADs approved for the treatment of DD at any age; however, the selection of fluoxetine as the first-line agent for DD as well seems reasonable. The dosing guidelines for the ADs can be seen in Table 4.

Whether dosing the AD by milligrams per day, or milligrams per kilogram per day, the amount used should begin at the lower end of the range. This is especially important in younger children, in those that are at a low weight for age, in those with hepatic impairment, and in those on multiple other medications that may have adverse interactions with the AD.

Fluoxetine may be given once daily, as may the extended-release forms of paroxetine, venlafaxine, and bupropion. The time of day chosen is usually the one that will best facilitate compliance, although mornings may be better in that an evening AD medication may disrupt sleep in some patients.

The SSRIs sertraline, citalopram, and escitalopram are typically prescribed in adults as once-daily medications. In children and adolescents, however, a split dosage may be better, as the higher hepatic metabolism and renal clearance in younger people makes it nearly impossible to maintain effective 24-hour blood levels with once-daily dosing.

As the risk for suicidality is highest early in the course of treatment with ADs, the FDA has suggested that patients be monitored face-to-face on a weekly basis during the first 4 weeks of treatment, then every other week for the next 4 weeks, then at 12 weeks, and as clinically indicated beyond that for the duration of treatment.

Table 4. Medications used for the treatment of depressive disorders

Class	Agent	Dosages (daily)
Antidepressants		
SSRIs	Fluoxetine	5-60 mg (0.25-1 mg/kg)
	Paroxetine	5-40 mg (0.25-1 mg/kg)
	Sertraline	12.5-200 mg (1.5-3 mg/kg)
	Citalopram	5-40 mg
	Escitalopram	5-20 mg
SNRIs	Venlafaxine	37.5-225 mg (1-3 mg/kg)
	Duloxetine	20-40 mg
Other	Trazodone	25-300 mg (2-5 mg/kg)
	Bupropion	75-300 mg (3-6 mg/kg)
	Mirtazapine	7.5-45 mg
MAOIs	Isocarboxazid	5-40 mg
	Phenelzine	7.5-45 mg
	Tranylcypromine	5-30 mg
	Selegiline (transdermal)	6, 9, or 12 mg*

* Each patch is effective for 24 hours.

The American Academy of Child and Adolescent Psychiatry has more reasonably suggested that monitoring be based on individual clinical needs and characteristics.

If the patient is not responding to the starting dose of medication, and if it is being tolerated, an increase in dose may be made after 1-2 weeks. Further dosage increases may be made every 2-4 weeks, depending on the degree of response and level of tolerance to the medication. If there is insufficient improvement in mood after 4-6 weeks at maximum dosage (or there are significant side effects at any dosage), the medication should be tapered off before starting another trial of AD medication.

If by Level III (Figure 1) there has been insufficient progress, if the depression is worsening, or if suicidality is emerging, a referral should be made to a child and adolescent psychiatrist. Most pediatricians would likely not feel comfortable initiating treatments beyond Level III, unless they have had additional training in, and experience with, those modalities. Other concerns beyond Level III are:

- The addition of Lithium in Level IV-A requires additional monitoring of hematologic, renal and thyroid parameters;
- Level IV-B increases the risk of med-med interactions;
- Level V may require additional monitoring of hematologic and hepatic parameters, depending on the mood stabilizer selected; and,
- Level VI requires close monitoring of diet and other medications used (including over-the-counter and herbal preparations) in order to avoid hypertensive crises.

Most depressed patients will fortunately respond to treatment well before Level VII. In those rare instances in which electroconvulsive therapy (ECT) is indicated, that particular treatment will need to be carried out in one of the few academic centers that are qualified and sanctioned to perform the procedure.

Conclusion

Given that the majority of depressed children and adolescents are seen first by their primary care physicians, it is hoped that the information contained in this chapter will prove useful in identifying and treating those patients. The clinician should be mindful of the variations in presentation of depression at different developmental stages, the conditions that can mimic or co-exist with depression, and the potential adverse effects of antidepressant medications.

References

American Psychiatric Association. *Diagnostic and Statistical Manual of Mental Disorders*, Fourth Edition, Text Revision. Washington, DC, American Psychiatric Association; 2000.

Angold A, Costello EJ. Puberty and depression. *Child Adolesc. Psychiatric. Clin. N Am.* 2006;15:919-937.

Avenevoli S, Stolar M, Li J, Dierker L, Ries Merikangas K. Comorbidity of depression in children and adolescents: models and evidence from a prospective high-risk family study. *Biol. Psychiatry* 2001;49(12):1071-1081.

Baker K. Treatment and management of depression in children. *Curr. Paediatrics* 2006;16:478-483.

Calles J. Depression in children and adolescents. *Prim. Care Clin. Office Pract.* 2007;34:243-258.

Costello EJ, Erkanli A, Angold A. Is there an epidemic of child or adolescent depression? *J. Child Psychol. Psychiatry* 2006;47(12):1263-1271.

Crowe M, Ward N, Dunnachie B, Roberts M. Characteristics of adolescent depression. *Int. J. Ment. Health Nursing* 2006;15:10-18.

Guedeney A. From early withdrawal reaction to infant depression: A baby alone does exist. *Infant Ment. Health J.* 1997;18(4):339-349.

Hughes CW, Emslie GJ, Crismon ML, Posner K, Birmaher B, Ryan N, et al. Texas Children's Medication Algorithm Project: Update from Texas Consensus Conference Panel on Medication Treatment of Childhood Major Depressive Disorder. *J. Am. Acad Child Adolesc. Psychiatry* 2007;46(6):667-686.

Keren M, Tyano S. Depression in infancy. *Child Adolesc Psychiatric Clin. N. Am.* 2006;15:883-897.

Little CA, Williams SE, Puzanovova M, Rudzinski ER, Walker LS. Multiple somatic symptoms linked to positive screen for depression in pediatric patients with chronic abdominal pain. *J. Pediatr. Gastroenterol. Nutr.* 2007 Jan;44(1):58-62.

Luby JL, Heffelfinger AK, Mrakotsky C, Brown KM, Hessler MJ, Wallis JM, Spitznagel EL. The clinical picture of depression in preschool children. *J. Am. Acad Child Adolesc. Psychiatry* 2003, 42(3):340-348.

Nobile M, Cataldo GM, Marino C, Molteni M. Diagnosis and treatment of dysthymia in children and adolescents. *CNS Drugs* 2003;17(13):927-946.

Puura K, Almqvist F, Tamminen T, et al. Children with symptoms of depression- What do the adults see? *J. Child Psychol. Psychiat* 1998;39(4):577-585.

Rey JM, Martin A. Selective serotonin reuptake inhibitors and suicidality in juveniles: review of the evidence and implications for clinical practice. *Child Adolesc. Psychiatric Clin. N Am.* 2006;15:221-237.

Rushton JL, Forcier M, Schectman RM. Epidemiology of depressive symptoms in the National Longitudinal Study of Adolescent Health. *J. Am. Acad Child Adolesc. Psychiatry* 2002;41(2):199-205.

Sheikh RM, Weller EB, Weller RA. Prepubertal depression: diagnostic and therapeutic dilemmas. *Curr. Psychiatry Rep.* 2006;8(2):121-6.

Wolff JC, Ollendick TH. The comorbidity of conduct problems and depression in childhood and adolescence. *Clin. Child Family Psychol. Rev.* 2006;9(3/4):201-220.

In: Behavioral Pediatrics, 3rd Edition
Editor: D. E. Greydanus et al.

ISBN 978-1-60692-702-1
© 2009 Nova Science Publishers, Inc.

Chapter 15

Pediatric Bipolar Disorder

Amy E. West and Mani N. Pavuluri

Abstract

The recent public awareness of pediatric bipolar disorder and the surge in the rate of its diagnosis has generated many questions and concerns about its validity as a distinct disorder. This chapter will review the issues relating to epidemiology, diagnosis and treatment of bipolar disorder in children and adolescents.

Introduction

It has become nearly impossible to avoid the topic of pediatric bipolar disorder (PBD). For the lay public, PBD is mentioned in magazines and newspapers, on television, and on internet websites (including some that specialize in helping people to identify PBD). For clinicians, increasing numbers of parents- and other caregivers- are bringing in children to be evaluated for PBD. Some will even come in with a presumed diagnosis in hand (thanks to those media sources), demanding that the children be placed on this-or-that medication, convinced that the "right treatment" will eliminate all of the problem behaviors that they're dealing with. The following information is intended to guide the pediatrician in the proper diagnosis and treatment of PBD.

Definition

Pediatric bipolar disorder (PBD) is a devastating illness that impairs children's emotional, cognitive, and social development. PBD causes severe mood instability, manifesting in chronic irritability, episodes of rage, tearfulness, distractibility, grandiosity or inflated self-esteem, hypersexual behavior, a decreased need for sleep, and behavioral activation coupled with poor judgment.

Epidemiology

There has been increasing recognition of PBD in the psychiatric literature during the past 15 years. Despite this, there are still no authoritative data on the prevalence of pediatric bipolar disorder and prevalence estimates depend on whether the disorder is defined as "narrow" or "broad" phenotypes. Children with the narrow phenotype fit symptom criteria for a bipolar diagnosis as defined by the DSM IV TR, while children with the broad phenotype experience serious mood dysregulation and associated symptoms, but may not meet symptom number, frequency, intensity, or duration criteria as defined by the narrow diagnosis. One community study evaluating rates of bipolar disorders in adolescents showed a lifetime prevalence of 1% in youths 14-18 years old using the Schedule for Affective Disorders and Schizophrenia for School-Aged Children (K-SADS). However, Brotman, et al., found the lifetime prevalence of severe mood dysregulation (SMD) to be 3.3% in children aged 9-19, indicating that a larger percent of the population may experience symptoms consistent with the broad phenotype of PBD. Retrospective studies of adults with bipolar disorder have reported that as many as 60% experienced symptoms before age 20 and 10-20% reported symptoms before 10 years of age. It remains unclear, however, how sub-threshold symptoms in childhood relate to adult onset of bipolar disorder, as well as whether there is continuity between the childhood-onset presentation and the more "classic" presentation of adult bipolar. Longitudinal studies will help clarify the progression of symptoms over the lifespan.

Despite a lack of knowledge on exact prevalence and the continuity/overlap between childhood-onset and adult-onset presentations, it is well-understood that the impact of symptoms of pediatric bipolar disorders (whether broad or narrow phenotype) on youth and their families is devastating. In one community study, it was reported that PBD was associated with substantial impairment in social (66%), family (56%) and school (83%) functioning. Geller, et al., found PBD was associated with behavioral problems in school, low grades, few or no friends, frequent teasing, poor social skills, poor sibling relationships, and parent-child relationships characterized by frequent hostility and conflict. In this study, parents also exhibited poor problem solving and poor agreement on parenting strategies. Clearly, the symptoms of PBD impact the child, peer, and family systems across a range of psychosocial and interpersonal domains.

Clinical Features

Research on PBD has been plagued by uncertainty in the past, primarily due to high overlap with symptoms of attention deficit hyperactivity disorder (ADHD), which causes confusion about whether PBD is a distinct disorder. However, recent research has led to a general recognition that PBD represents a discrete cluster of symptoms that can be validated by reliable assessment with stability over time. The NIMH Research Roundtable of prepubertal BD (2001) reached consensus that PBD can present as "narrow" or "broad" phenotypes. Children and adolescents with the "narrow" phenotype have recurrent periods of major depression and mania or hypomania fitting the classical definitions of BD type I or BD type II described in the DSM-IV. Based on these DSM-IV criteria, the symptoms of PBD may present clinically as follows:

- *Elated mood.* Patients are often excitable, silly, giddy, prone to uncontrolled laughter, feel invincible, and engage in excessive joking. They may describe feeling "overwhelmed" by their affect.
- *Irritable mood.* Patients present as easily irritated, aggressive, hostile, or acidic, with intense responses to affective stimuli, that are out of proportion to what would be expected, and after which they are inconsolable. These responses may comprise aggressive behavior such as throwing things, slamming doors, difficulty transitioning, screaming, and kicking. They may feel remorse after and apologize for their behavior, using explanations such as "I tried to say no to my brain, but I can't stop feeling angry." Parents often tell clinicians that they "feel like they are walking on eggshells." Children and adolescents with the "broad" phenotype have chronic, severe mood dysregulation and hyper-arousal that is episodic in nature, but episodes may not meet intensity or duration criteria for BD I or II as defined by the DSM-IV. These children have complicated mood symptoms with significant comorbidity and associated impairment. There is still some debate in the literature as to whether children with the "broad" phenotype of BD are best characterized as part of the bipolar spectrum (e.g. BP NOS) or as a distinct diagnostic category (e.g. Severe Mood Dysregulation or SMD).
- *Inflated self-esteem and grandiosity.* This is characterized by statements such as "I am the best baseball player in America," "I will teach the coach how to swim, he doesn't have a clue," "I am absolutely sure that I am going to be the President," 'I am going to make millions on E-trade," with no evidence to support these statements. As with adults, psychosis is often seen in the manic phase. Delusions of grandiosity are differentiated from bragging if the age-appropriate reality check is absent and the child acts on the delusions.
- *Decreased need for sleep.* Parents describe their children as playing, singing, or watching television into the early morning, refusing to go to bed, and still not feeling tired in the morning. Children may use the description "I feel like an Energizer Bunny."
- *Racing thoughts/Pressure to keep talking.* This state is often described by children as "My mind is going so fast, I can't stop it." Parents describe their children as constantly talking, never letting others have a say, being domineering, and constantly seeking attention by talking or "entertaining" excessively at home or school.
- *Constant goal-directed activity.* Patients are described as continually fiddling in everything and making a mess at home. When confronted by parents, children will become defensive or deny responsibility. Clinically, parents often report their children are "always lying." Children may describe "crazy maniacal spells." Parents

may also report constant goal–directed behavior such as feeding the dog, playing chess, going at, and fighting with siblings, all within a one-hour period.

- *Excessive pleasurable activities.* Children may engage in poor judgment and excessive risk-taking behavior. They may call sexually-oriented chat lines, dress inappropriately, masturbate excessively, hoard and carry around pornographic pictures, simulate sexual activity with animals, use their parents' credit cards to pay for mail-ordered sex items, or pressure parents to buy expensive clothes or other items. Sexual abuse is often considered a differential diagnosis of these sexually uninhibited children. In an ongoing phenomenological study, only 1.1% of the PBD sample had a history of sexual abuse or over-stimulation, while 43% exhibited hypersexuality, supporting this as a critical symptom for PBD (unpublished data).
- *Symptoms of depression.* These symptoms are often described in age-specific terms. Patients may feel crabby, excessively whine, cry for no reason, look unhappy, spend hours in a dark room, change moods rapidly from irritable to tearful, engage in skin-pinching and self-scratching at a young age, or complain of somatic symptoms. These children often experience intense rejection sensitivity after years of perceived rejection from others due to their mood dysregulation and associated unpredictable behavior. Even very young, prepubertal children may experience suicidal ideation and behavior, often stating a desire to stab or hang themselves. This likely represents a desperate attempt to regulate or escape from their intense mood swings. The rate of suicidal behavior in children with bipolar is reported to be high, with between one third and one half of children and adolescents with pediatric bipolar disorder (PBD) attempting suicide before they reach adulthood. In psychotic depressive episodes, mood-congruent delusions of doom, disaster, and nihilism are common.
- *Psychosis.* Patients can present with auditory or visual hallucinations, usually in addition to the mood-congruent delusions already described. Thought disorder can present as flight of ideas, becoming garbled if severe. Psychotic features vary according to the method of reporting and may be present in 17-60% of PBD patients.

Diagnosis

Bipolar I disorder is diagnosed if a child manifests abnormally elevated mood, grandiosity, or inflated self-esteem, extreme irritability, hypersexuality (not explained by a history of sexual abuse), decreased need for sleep, and behavioral activation (characterized by agitation and pressured speech) coupled with poor judgment. While there is persistent controversy as to which symptom is central to a Bipolar I diagnosis, irritability tends to be the most problematic and the symptom most responsible for treatment seeking. However, this does not necessarily mean that it is the central defining feature of the disorder. Elevated mood, grandiosity, and irritability are the core symptoms of mania. In our practice, we generally diagnose Bipolar I if a patient has at least two of these three central symptoms in addition to meeting DSM-IV-TR criteria. Sometimes, in children and adolescents, it can be difficult to differentiate between actual grandiosity and self-aggrandizement that can arise out of insecurity. In addition, it is critical to ask specifically about symptoms of psychosis and hypersexuality, as parents and children are not as likely to report these symptoms spontaneously. Several of the mania symptoms associated with Bipolar I may also present in unique ways depending on the child's developmental stage. For example, symptoms such as immodest attire or excessive spending may manifest as parents exert control over children's dress and spending. Symptom expressions such as inflated self-esteem and increased goal-directed activity are best judged in the context of the child's prior history, as behaviors may be misleading in isolation and must be considered in the context of the child's cognitive, biological, and social development. If several of the symptoms exist together, however, and present with substantial mood dysregulation associated with impairment in functioning, then PBD should be considered.

Bipolar disorder type II tends to present with major depressive episodes alternating with hypomanic episodes. In these patients, it is the depressive episodes that dominate the clinical picture and cause major dysfunction. It is often hard to characterize hypomania in youth, given developmentally appropriate excitability. Youth with Bipolar disorder not otherwise specified (NOS) have fewer symptoms or symptoms of shorter duration than necessary to meet the full DSM IV TR diagnosis. It is difficult to differentiate between bipolar disorder type I and bipolar disorder NOS if cycling and/or discrete episodes are not clearly established. It is important not to confuse between episodes and cycles. Rapid cycling as defined by the DSM IV TR should be differentiated from the rapid cycling variants of bipolar disorder as characterized by Geller and her colleagues. In DSM IV TR, rapid cycling is defined as having more than four episodes of either depression or mania or hypomania during a one year period. In phenomenological studies conducted by Geller and colleagues, parents often described mood dysregulation as rapid mood swings. Given the consistency of such parental report, they attempted to integrate this description into the phenomenology of PBD. For example, ultradian cycling is described as cycling within a day (or more than 365 cycles a year). This could be construed as mood or affect dysregulation. Ultra rapid cycles are those cycles occurring 5-365 times a year. Episodes clearly exist in some (discrete episodes of mania, mixed episode, hypomania and depression). Symptoms wax and wane with full respite; subsyndromal symptoms often remain in between episodes. The full extent of how much the symptoms subside in between recurrent episodes depends on severity of illness, availability of proper treatment, and the ability of the family to negotiate recovery with optimum treatment. However, PBD can often be non-episodic and chronic, especially if left untreated. Mixed episodes and comorbid attention deficit hyperactivity disorder (ADHD) and anxiety are very common in PBD. Chronic morbidity is common due to the presence of co-existing symptoms of other conditions, particularly ADHD. Oppositional defiant disorder (ODD) is reported to be present in up to 90% of youth with PBD, but cannot be diagnosed according to the strict criteria in the face of PBD. Such symptoms may represent reactive phenomena originating from the PBD.

It is critical to define the "signature of the illness." Symptoms, pattern of onset and offset of symptoms, and timeline will help the clinician establish the diagnosis. A comprehensive developmental history is important to understand the emergence of symptoms in a developmental context. For example, there is some evidence that PBD diagnosis may be preceded by a difficult temperament style in infancy and toddlerhood compared with children who do not develop PBD. Comorbid ADHD is diagnosed if symptoms precede the onset of

PBD symptoms or if the child has very early onset PBD with symptoms of ADHD unresolved after successful treatment of the PBD; however, it is possible that these symptoms represent residual symptoms of intrinsic over-activity and inattention observed in PBD. Family history of bipolar disorder, given the familial risk, adds value in considering the diagnosis. However, it is also important to underline that family history should not be considered as a diagnostic feature. Conversely, the absence of a family history does not rule out the diagnosis of PBD.

Screening measures can be used to preliminarily assess the presence of different types of mania symptoms. The Child Mania Rating Scale-Parent version (CMRS-P) is the first rating scale that was designed and tested specifically to screen for PBD. This measure has 21 developmentally specific items corresponding to DSM IV TR based symptoms. A score of 15 or above (out of potential total score of 63) indicates a 92% chance of having the diagnosis. This tool is a screening instrument with excellent psychometric properties. It is intended to help with the early identification of children with PBD with the hope of helping parents seek help for their child, but is not a diagnostic tool.

Once a formal diagnosis of PBD symptoms is made through comprehensive psychiatric evaluation, additional evaluation should include: (1) the level of distress of the patient and the family, (2) knowledge, skills and attitudes of parents, and (3) school functioning and neurocognitive problems, in order to address the systemic problems through psychosocial treatment that complements the medication management.

Treatment

Pharmacotherapy

In general, it appears that a combination of second generation antipsychotics and mood stabilizers is effective in the treatment of PBD, although further studies are needed. For example, the majority of these children need additional medications added to the primary mood stabilizer to treat concomitant symptoms such as attention-deficit, aggression, anxiety, psychosis, and sleep disturbance; however, results remain mixed in terms of the efficacy of additional medications to treat such co-occurring disorders. Pavuluri, et al. (2004), integrated much of the available data to develop and test an evidence-based pharmacotherapy algorithm. The basic principles of this algorithm model consist of (1) Prescription Hygiene, (2) Mood Stabilization, (3) Overcoming the obstacles in mood stabilization by addressing break-through symptoms, and (4) Problem Solving, for example, addressing treatment of comorbid conditions and/or adverse events of medications.

Prescription Hygiene

In establishing a pharmacotherapeutic plan for mood stabilization, four things are important to consider. First, a history should be obtained of which medications worsened the patient's clinical status in the past, which were ineffective, and which were transiently useful or helpful. Second, rapidly wean off all ineffective medications. Third, discontinue selective serotonin reuptake inhibitors (SSRIs). Despite compelling data in pediatric populations of SSRIs worsening the symptoms either by switching or worsening mania, several families bring children on substantial doses of SSRIs. PBD generally presents with mixed or dysphoric states, and many physicians tune into depressive symptoms at the cost of worsening the clinical state. Fourth, stimulants should be discontinued. Mood stabilization is the primary treatment objective and should be attained prior to controlling symptoms of ADHD. However, given the equivocal data and the negative influence of stimulants, if parents report that they have been singularly helpful and showed a pattern of response independent of affect dysregulation, the practitioner may elect to continue stimulants at the lowest possible doses and preferably in long acting form.

Table 1. Lithium and AED*: Rationale Behind the Sequence**

Name	Pros	Cons
Lithium (Geller et al, 1998; Kafantaris et al., 2003)	FDA approved in children for acute mania and maintenance; well studied in adults; works well in classic presentation.	Slow onset of action; poor response as monotherapy; frequent urination and hypothyroidism often cause concerns.
Divalproex sodium (Kowatch et al., 2000; Pavuluri et al., 2005)	Well studied in adult bipolar disorder; effective when coupled with stimulants for comorbid ADHD.	Poor response as monotherapy in children; poor tolerability secondary to excitability, GI side effects, weight gain, and sedation; potential adverse effects on the liver and thrombocytopenia require regular lab monitoring.
Carbamazepine (Kowatch et al, 2000)	Long standing efficacy in adults.	Efficacy in children not established; substantial side effect profile; large number of drug interactions; substantial lab monitoring required.
Oxcarbazepine	Anecdotal evidence suggesting that it may decrease aggression in PBD.	Efficacy not established.
Lamotrigine (Cheng et al, 2006)	Accruing evidence on maintenance for adult bipolar disorder; considered as a primary choice (along side lithium) for depression subtype; potentially useful in combination with SGA† or lithium for mixed or depressive episodes where depression is predominant.	Very slow titration over 6-8 weeks to avoid rash, although serious rash is uncommon; benign rash is treatable with prednisone and may limit ability to re-challenge.
Topiramate (DelBello et al, 2006)	May have some benefit in reducing weight.	Negative trial in adult bipolar disorder; cognitive dulling; equivocal evidence available in PBD, including that for neutralizing weight gain as an adjuvant; significant side effect profile.

*AED= anti-epileptic drugs **Janicak et al. (2003) offers comprehensive overview of the trials in adult bipolar disorder, currently being updated for fourth edition. †= second-generation antipsychotics.

Mood Stabilization

The first treatment of choice continues to be a mood stabilizer such as lithium or divalproex sodium due to an established track record of preventive properties (mainly based on studies of adult bipolar disorder). Lithium or divalproex sodium may not always be effective in PBD and/or slow in the onset of action. Consequently, second generation antipsychotics (SGA) are rapidly finding their place either as monotherapy (in emergency situations where stabilizing mania is a priority) or in combination with a mood stabilizer. The SGA alone may be effective when irritability is prominent and demands a faster response not possible with first-line mood stabilizers. Combination therapy of SGA plus lithium or divalproex is an effective strategy as first line for severe cases, especially those with psychotic features. This strategy has the advantage of needing lower doses of SGA compared to the doses potentially required for monotherapy, resulting in far less severe adverse events. While the practitioner excludes those medications that failed to be effective, he or she can choose the next best option in the list either as an alternative monotherapeutic agent or for the combination regimen (in severe cases or if monotherapy fails).

A sequence of medication choices in each group with some general rationale is provided in Tables 1 and 2. While these tables provide a basic guideline, the clinician needs to use his or her discretion in individual cases. In the development of this algorithm, levels of evidence dictated the order. General pros and cons of each medication are listed, as well as a rough estimate of relative efficacy. Some medications are better studied because of better funding based on the strategic plan of drug companies resulting in more and/or better data.

Table 2. SGAs: Rationale Behind the Sequence*

Name	Pros	Cons**
Risperidone (Frazier et al, 1999; Biederman et al, 2005)	Efficacy demonstrated in pediatric trials; has a predictable response profile; reduces aggressive behavior.	Weight gain is common; EPS and symptoms from prolactin elevation (e.g. menstrual disturbances) sometime affect tolerability.
Quetiapine (DelBello et al, 2002; 2006)	Efficacy demonstrated in pediatric trials; little/no EPS.	Sedation and weight gain are common.
Aripiprazole	Emerging data on adult bipolar disorder and pediatric disorders.	EPS; nausea and vomiting; response is not always predictable, with no knowledge about predictive factors.
Ziprasidone (Cheng-Shannon et al 2004)	Weight neutral in pediatric studies.	EPS; less evidence for efficacy; risk of prolonged QT interval requires cardiac monitoring.
Olanzapine (Frazier et al., 2001)	Good data in adult bipolar disorder and emerging data in PBD.	Severe weight gain limits tolerability and places children at risk for long-term sequelae.
Clozapine (Kowatch et al., 1995)	Potentially useful in treatment resistant cases.	Regulatory blood draws to check white blood count presents logistical challenges; significant side effect profile often limits tolerability in children and puts them at risk for long-term sequelae.

*Janicak et al. (2003) provides information on adult trials using SGA in bipolar disorder.
**With SGA use, one must consider the risk for metabolic syndrome (elevated lipids, high blood pressure and diabetes mellitus). Although the level of such risk in children and the life long consequences of their use are unknown, these parameters require close monitoring.

Other medications were considered as safe and effective based on studies in adult bipolar disorder. There is a paucity of head to head comparison trials that have been done in PBD. Furthermore, medications in these categories often take a long time to obtain pediatric indications. Therefore it is difficult to make broad statements about efficacy comparisons. Prescribing information of all the medications is beyond the scope of this article and is summarized in the "Handbook of Pharmacotherapy, A Life Span Approach."

Addressing Break-Through Symptoms

PBD presents a multitude of clinical challenges beyond acute mood stabilization that must be factored into both the acute and maintenance phases of treatment.

- *Depression.* If there are prominent symptoms of depression, lithium or lamotrigine are chosen as primary mood stabilizers either alone or as adjuvant to other partially effective agents. The second choice would be a combination of lithium plus lamotrigine. The third choice is a small dose of SSRI (in desperate circumstances of severe depression). Any SSRI in small doses of 2.5 to 5 mg in time limited manner and under close supervision and psychoeducation often is effective alongside a mood stabilizer. It is important to balance the risks versus benefits, given the black box warning associated with SSRI use in children.
- *Psychosis.* SGAs (if not on board already), must be added working down the list as indicated in Table 2.
- *Persistent aggression.* The tactic in this context is switching to SGA monotherapy if mild aggression is present. In moderate to severe presentations, combination of mood stabilizer and SGA is used, working down the list of choices (see Tables 1 and 2) after excluding ineffective medications and adequate trials of chosen medications. Clonidine can be used to subdue rage attacks when things are out of control. However, in our experience children can become disinhibited or become more aroused after persistent use, although this particular observation needs to be further examined.
- *Treatment resistance.* Chronic unremitting symptoms must be treated by using (1) alternative monotherapy, (2) at least two trials of combination regimens of mood stabilizers plus SGA, and then (3) moving on to triple therapy addressing comorbid conditions (for example, of additional stimulant for comorbid ADHD).
- *Sleep difficulties.* Primarily it is customary for the clinician to take advantage of increasing the PM dose of sedating mood stabilizers. Beyond that, melatonin 1-3 mg can be administered to establish sleep routine that is critical in PBD. While these compounds were not empirically supported by research in PBD youth for sleep in specific, these compounds were known to be sedative, safe in pediatric populations, and interfere minimally with REM sleep. In subjects with abuse potential, benzodiazepines may be misused and medications such as trazodone may be effective alternatives.

Problem Solving: Comorbid Diagnoses and Management

- *ADHD.* While ADHD is a distinct disorder separate from PBD, it is not understood if the ADHD-like symptoms in PBD warrant additional treatment beyond mood stabilization. In our study, several subjects continued to show symptoms of inattention post mood-stabilization that warranted stimulant medication. Cognitive difficulties such as shifting attention and executive function seen in both ADHD and PBD can potentially be addressed by stimulants. Stimulants are almost always given in long acting form unless an additional after-school dose is required to sustain the benefits. Among psychostimulants, long-acting methylphenidate or mixed amphetamine salts are equally effective. Atomoxetine is factored into the algorithm as an alternative treatment if stimulants have been ineffective or not tolerated. There are no data establishing the safety or efficacy of atomoxetine in treating youth with co-morbid ADHD and PBD. Atomoxetine is a selective norepinephrine reuptake inhibitor with potential antidepressant effects and could theoretically trigger or exacerbate symptoms of mania in patients with PBD. Atomoxetine should be used with great care in youth with PBD.
- *Anxiety.* Anxiety disorders, including generalized anxiety disorder and separation anxiety disorder, are relatively common, especially in BD type 1. Psychotherapeutic interventions, such as cognitive-behavioral therapy (CBT), remain the first choice of treatment in children and adolescents with comorbid PBD and anxiety disorder. Small dose of SSRIs such as escitalopram as adjuvant medication may be effective if mania is stabilized, though there are no controlled trials for anxiety comorbid with bipolar disorder. SSRIs are the only medications consistently shown to be effective in controlled trials for childhood anxiety disorders. This treatment intervention requires educating the family about the risk of a manic switch and close monitoring of the treatment response is necessary. Guanfacine may be considered if vigilance and autonomic hyperarousal are prominent. Benzodiazepines and buspirone follow as alternative choices. Risk for developing dependence needs to be considered for long-term use of benzodiazepines in adolescents. Buspirone may not be effective in all cases. Propranolol may be considered in cases of performance anxiety. Medication is often utilized in small doses, to reduce risks of exacerbating bipolar disorder and to enable patients to benefit from psychotherapeutic interventions.

Problem Solving: Management of Selected Common Side-Effects

Low doses and slow titration are two fundamental principles that one may utilize to minimize the occurrence of treatment-emergent side-effects. If problems still continue, switching to an alternative medication may be necessary. For persistent side-effects in the context of a child who has responded well to treatment, consideration should be given to trying a lower dose of the medication prior to switching medications or employing pharmacological management strategies, as many side-effects are dose-related. When a risk-benefit analysis indicates that the offending drug needs to be retained at the desirable dose, strategies must be implemented to manage them. Some of the common challenges that require specific attention are:

- *Weight gain.* Despite several antidotes for weight gain, the single most important intervention is diet and exercise. If possible, consultation with a dietician is helpful. In our experience, simple weight management programs (e.g. Weight Watchers®) have been successful when followed along with a parent, but should only be done after consultation with a knowledgeable health professional. Timely meals and wise food choices cut down excessive calories. Weight gain from atypical antipsychotics and some antiepileptic agents often results from an increased appetite secondary to some pharmacological properties of these medications. Counseling parents that this may occur may help them to limit access to high calorie foods that may exacerbate this problem. Weight gain from lithium may partially be due to increased consumption of high calorie soft drinks or juice to compensate for the increased thirst caused by this medication. Limiting fluid intake to low calorie drinks is an easy way to prevent unnecessary weight gain.
- *Extrapyramidal symptoms.* Benztropine 0.5-2 mg every other day to once a day is effective in combating extrapyramidal symptoms. Akathisia (a subjective sense of need to constantly move) in patients treated with SGA is often missed and often responds to low doses of propranolol.
- *Sedation.* Night-time dosing decreases problems with sedation. In the event of residual morning somnolence, the evening dose may be moved earlier in the evening.
- *Gastrointestinal (GI) symptoms.* GI upset from divalproex is dose related. Administering the medication with food and/or using a long acting preparation of divalproex sodium may decrease GI upset. Taking SGA with a small snack 30 minutes-one hour before bed may decrease GI upset. GI upset from lithium is dose related and management strategy depends on whether the intolerance is specific to the upper or lower GI. Upper GI effects from lithium tend to be associated with high doses that directly irritate the stomach mucosa as well as high peak serum levels. Switching to a sustained release formulation or dividing doses BID-TID and/or administering the medication with food will reduce GI upset. Lower GI effects such as diarrhea are correlated with high doses and high serum levels. This also may occur secondary to residual lithium left in the large intestine, which may create an osmotic effect, drawing excess water into the lower GI, resulting in diarrhea. Lower GI effects may be managed by reducing the overall dose, switching from sustained release formulations to immediate release tablets/capsules or liquid formulations. Dividing high QD doses of immediate release formulations to BID-TID may also help.
- *Lithium related high thyroid stimulating hormone (TSH).* Elevations in thyroid stimulating hormone (TSH) occur in approximately 15% of patients. This usually occurs within the first four weeks of therapy and may normalize after transient elevation. Usually new elevations are not evident after four years. In accordance with standard lithium monitoring guidelines, baseline monitoring of free T4 and TSH and then follow-up at one month, six months, then yearly until year four is recommended. Additional monitoring may be needed after substantial dose increases. If hypothyroidism occurs and lithium needs to be continued, this may be effectively treated with levothyroxine titrated based on levels of TSH on follow up.

Since the commencement of our algorithm project and the subsequent publication of our feasibility study we have continued to update our strategies and tactics based on new information. Aripiprazole is added to the list of SGAs. The role of lamotrigine has been elevated as specified in the scheme above. Atomoxetine was added as a second line medication after trying stimulants for comorbid ADHD. In our experience, clonidine has been shown to cause worsening of symptoms in a subgroup of patients with PBD despite excellent short-term response for autonomic arousal. We are closely monitoring this phenomenon. Consequently, we are currently choosing Guanfacine (given the longer half-life compared to clonidine) or propranolol as an alternative for extreme hyper-arousal that does not respond to mood stabilization. Given the recent review presenting equivocal evidence of trazodone's efficacy as sleep medication, it was placed lower on the list after medications such as melatonin that had better data to support its safety and efficacy in idiopathic insomnia, although not tested for sleep problems directly in PBD.

Psychosocial

Despite the obvious need for psychosocial interventions to address the complex presentation of symptoms in pediatric bipolar disorder and the impact of the disorder on peer, school, and family functioning, there are no proven psychosocial treatment methods for pediatric bipolar disorder. A few published preliminary studies exist. Fristad, et al., developed a multiple family group treatment (MFPG) for the parents and youths (8-12) with bipolar and depressive spectrum disorders focused primarily on psychoeducation about the disorders. The goals of MFPG include teaching parents and children about the child's illness and its treatment, symptom management, and improving problem-solving and communication skills; and providing support, both from other group members and professionals who understand the disorder. The initial randomized control trial of 35 children indicated that families accrued knowledge, skills, social support, and positive attitudes. A large randomized control trial of MFPG is nearing completion. In addition, that group developed an individual form of MFPG called IFP, incorporating similar concepts, but delivered across 16 child, parent, and family sessions. An initial randomized control trial of 20 children suggested that the intervention had a positive impact on children's' mood symptoms, family climate, and treatment utilization. They are currently conducting a pilot study of an expanded version (24 sessions) of IFP.

Miklowitz and Goldstein developed a manual-based family-focused therapy (FFT) for adults with bipolar disorder, and then adapted it for adolescents. FFT is based on the premise that patients with bipolar disorder will experience symptom relief as they acquire a greater awareness of how to cope with their disorder, decreased levels of expressed emotion from caregivers, and improvement in family problem-solving and communication skills. Randomized controlled trials of FFT in adult bipolar patients have shown lower relapse rates, lower hospitalization rates, better medication adherence, and reductions in mood symptoms for up to 15 months following the intervention. A year-long open trial of the adapted protocol for adolescents with bipolar disorder indicated that adolescents experienced symptomatic improvement in mania, depression, and behavioral problems. A multi-site RCT of FFT for adolescents is currently underway.

Finally, child and family-focused cognitive-behavioral therapy (CFF-CBT) was designed in our program to meet the specific developmental needs of children with pediatric bipolar disorder and their families. It offers a clear theoretical basis of amalgamating CBT principals and interpersonal psychology principles, with an intense focus on parent training and therapy along with child work to impact both symptom experience and psychosocial and interpersonal functioning. Diverse therapeutic techniques are employed across multiple domains, including individual, peer, family, and school to address the impact of PBD in the child's broader psychosocial context. CFF-CBT is a 12-session manual-based treatment program meant to be delivered weekly over the course of three months. It can be delivered in either individual or group format. For the individual psychotherapy format, each session is approximately one hour. The majority of sessions are for the parent and child together, but some the parent only, and some the child only. The group format consists of parallel parent and child groups that run for 1½ hours each week for 12 weeks. Although there is established content for each session and an ideal sequence to the delivery of this content, the treatment protocol can be implemented in a flexible manner as long as the essential elements are present. The acronym "RAINBOW" was formed to help parents and children remember the key components of CFF-CBT. The essential components of CFF-CBT "RAINBOW" covered throughout the treatment sessions are:

- *Routine.* Establishing a strict routine to allow stable circadian rhythm and sleep hygiene while cutting down room for negotiation towards distracting agendas.
- *Affect regulation/anger control.* Establishing techniques to self monitor mood using mood charts, educate about the disorder and the role of medications in controlling affect.
- *"I can do it."* Helping the child to conceptualize a positive self story, while the therapist generates positive statements to encourage and build self esteem
- *"No negative thoughts."* Restructuring negative thinking by guiding them to think of how to change unhelpful thoughts or experiences to helpful ones, helping parents to "live in the *now*."
- *Be a good friend/balanced life style.* Parents are encouraged to organize play dates and help children build positive ties as parents supervise them in real life settings. Parents are also advised to focus on obtaining a balanced life style in caring for themselves as they are in this for a long haul.
- *"Oh, how can 'we' solve it?"* This is a key point for CFF-CBT for PBD where families engage in collaborative problem solving with children after the rages pass through interpersonal and situational problem solving methods. Immediate consequences for undesirable behavior are not recommended in PBD and reward systems can get very intense. Teaching through "pep talks" is the key to influence children.
- *Ways to ask and get support.* Children are encouraged to draw a support tree and name all the people close to them in their lives, one on each branch. It is intended to crystallize in their minds that there is a supportive safety network or system around

them to nurture them when they are in need. They will be coached to reach out for support.

Preliminary studies suggest that CFF-CBT is feasible to deliver in a clinic-based setting and may improve symptomatic functioning. In addition, a study conducted in our program also found that a maintenance model of the child-and family-focused cognitive-behavioral therapy program (CFF-CBT), comprised of psychosocial booster sessions and optimized pharmacotherapy, indicated that participants were able to sustain improvements made during the acute phase treatment with the maintenance treatment program over a three-year follow-up. These findings suggest that maintenance treatment models may help facilitate the long-term management of symptoms and represent an important step in addressing the low recovery and high relapse rates associated with PBD.

Conclusion

PBD affects cognitive, behavioral and affective domains of a child's being. Affect dysregulation is the central feature of this disorder. It is not clear that the juvenile onset version of PBD is contiguous with the adult variant of bipolar disorder. The primary goal of pharmacotherapy is mood stabilization while including the problem solving approach to deal with complex comorbid, residual, breakthrough and/or associated symptoms. It is imperative that any medication management be coupled with a meaningful holistic therapeutic approach that is practical and tailored to the PBD. A comprehensive treatment approach includes evidence-based psychosocial intervention and ongoing parental and family support by linking them to community resources, including families affected by PBD.

References

American Psychiatric Association. *Diagnostic and Statistical Manual of Mental Disorders*, Fourth Edition. Washington, DC, American Psychiatric Association; 1994.

Biederman J, Mick E, Spencer T, Wilens TE, Faraone SV. Therapeutic dilemmas in the pharmacotherapy of bipolar depression in the young. *J. Child Adolesc. Psychopharmacol.* 2000;10:185-192.

Biederman J, Mick E, Wozniak J, Aleardi M, Spencer T, Faraone SV. Open label study of risperidone in children with bipolar disorder. *J. Child Adolesc. Psychopharmacol.* 2005;15:1-7.

Bowden CL. Lamotrigine in the treatment of bipolar disorder. *Expert Opin. Pharmacother.* 2002;3(10):1513-9. Review.

Brotman MA, Schmajuk M, Rich BA, et al. Prevalence, clinical correlates, and longitudinal course of severe mood dysregulation in children. *Biol. Psychiatry* 2006;60(9):991-7.

Calabrese JR, Suppes T, Bowden Cl, et al. A double-blind, placebo-controlled, prophylaxis study of lamotrigine in rapid-cycling bipolar disorder. Lamictal 614 Study Group. *J. Clin. Psychiatry* 2000;61(11):841-850.

Carlson GA, Kelly KL. Manic symptoms in psychiatrically hospitalized children-what do they mean? *J. Affect Disord*. 1998;51:123-135.

Carlson GA, Bromet EJ, Sievers S. Phenomenology and outcome of subjects with early- and adult-onset psychotic mania. *Am. J. Psychiatry* 2000;157:213-219.

Cheng-Shannon J, McGough JJ, Pataki C, McCracken. Second-generation antipsychotic medications in children and adolescents. *J. Child Adolesc. Psychopharmacol.* 2004;14:372-394.

DelBello M, Kowatch R, Adler C, et al. A double-blind randomized pilot study comparing quetiapine and divalproex for adolescent mania. *J. Am. Acad. Child Adolesc. Psychiatry* 2006;45:305-313.

DelBello MP, Schwiers ML, Rosenberg HL, Strakowski SM. A double-blind, randomized, placebo-controlled study of quetiapine adjunctive treatment for adolescent mania. *J. Am. Acad. Child Adolesc. Psychiatry* 2002;41:1216-1223.

DelBello MP, Soutullo CA, Hendricks W, Niemeier RT, McElroy SL, Strakowski. Prior stimulant treatment in adolescents with bipolar disorder: association with age at onset. *Bipolar Disord*. 2001;3:53-57.

Egeland JA, Hostetter AM, Pauls DL, Sussex JN. Prodromal symptoms before onset in manic-depressive disorder suggested by first hospital admission histories. *J. Am. Acad. Child Adolesc. Psychiatry* 2000;39:1245-1252.

Findling RL, McNamara NK, Gracious BL, et al. Combination lithium and divalproex sodium in pediatric bipolarity. *J. Am. Acad. Child Adolesc. Psychiatry* 2003;42(8):895-901.

Frazier JA, Biederman J, Tohen M, Feldman PD, Jacobs TG, Toma V. A prospective open-label treatment trial of olanzapine monotherapy in children and adolescents with bipolar disorder. *J. Child Adolesc. Psychopharmacol.* 2001;11:239-250.

Frazier JA, Meyer MC, Biederman J, Wozniak J, Wilens TE, Spencer TJ. Risperidone treatment for juvenile bipolar disorder: A retrospective chart review. *J. Am. Acad. Child Adolesc. Psychiatry* 1999;38:960-965.

Fristad MA, Goldberg-Arnold JS, Gavazzi SM. Multi-family psychoeducation groups (MFPG) for parents of children with bipolar disorder. *Bipolar Disord*. 2002;4:254-262.

Geller B, Craney JL, Bolhofner K, DelBello MP, Williams M, Zimerman B. One-year recovery and relapse rates of children with a prepubertal and early adolescent bipolar disorder phenotype. *Am. J. Psychiatry* 2001;158:303-305.

Geller B, Williams M, Zimerman B, Frazier J, Beringer L, Warner K. Prepubertal and early adolescent bipolarity differentiate from ADHD by manic symptoms, grandiose delusions, ultra-rapid or ultradian cycling. *J. Affect. Disord* 1998;51:81-91.

Geller B, Sun K, Zimerman B, Luby J, Frazier J, Williams M. Complex and rapid cycling in bipolar children and adolescents: a preliminary study. *J. Affect. Disord*. 1995;34:259-268.

Geller B, Tillman R, Craney JL, Bolhofner K. Four-year prospective outcome and natural history of mania in children with a prepubertal and early adolescent bipolar disorder phenotype. *Arch. Gen. Psychiatry* 2004;61(5):459-467.

Janicak PG, Davis JM, Preskorn SH, Ayd FJ Jr. *Principles and Practice of Psychopharmocotherapy.* Philadelphia: Lippincott Williams and Wilkins (3rd edition), 2001.

Kafantaris V, Coletti DJ, Dicker R, et al. Lithium treatment of acute mania in adolescents: a placebo controlled discontinuation study. *J. Am. Acad. Child Adolesc. Psychiatry* 2004;43:984-993.

Kowatch RA, Fristad M, Birmaher B, Wagner KD, Findling RL, Hellander M. Treatment guidelines for children and adolescents with bipolar disorder: Child psychiatric workgroup on bipolar disorder. *J. Am. Acad. Child Adolesc. Psychiatry* 2005;44:213-235.

Kowatch RA, Suppes T, Gilfillan SK, Fuentes RM, Grannemann BD, Emslie GJ. Clozapine treatment of children and adolescents with bipolar disorder and schizophrenia: a clinical case series. *J. Child Adolesc. Psychopharmacol.* 1995;5:241-253.

Leibenluft E, Charney DS, Towbin KE, Bhangoo RK, Pine DS. Defining clinical phenotypes of juvenile mania. *Am. J. Psychiatry* 2003;160:430-437.

Lofthouse N, Fristad M. Psychosocial interventions for children with early-onset bipolar spectrum disorder. *Clin. Child Fam Psychol Rev.* 2004;7(2):71-88.

Miklowitz DJ, Goldstein MJ. *Bipolar Disorder: A Family-focused Treatment Approach.* New York: Guilford Press. 1997.

Oravschel H, Puig-Antich J. Schedule for Affective Disorder and Schizophrenia for School-aged Children, *Epidemiologic*, 4th version. Ft. Lauderdale, FL: Nova University. 1987.

Pavuluri MN, Birmaher B, Naylor MW. Pediatric bipolar disorder: A review of the past 10 years. *J. Am. Acad. Child Adolesc. Psychiatry* 2005;44(9):846-871.

Pavuluri MN, Graczyk PA, Henry DB, Carbray JA, Heidenreich J, Miklowitz DJ. Child- and family-focused cognitive-behavioral therapy for pediatric bipolar disorder: development and preliminary results. *J. Am. Acad. Child Adolesc. Psychiatry* 2004;43:528-537.

Pavuluri M, Henry D, Carbray J, Sampson G, Naylor M, Janicak PG. Divalproex sodium in Pediatric Mixed Mania: a six month prospective trial. *Bipolar Disord.* 2005;7:266-73.

Pavuluri MN, Henry DB, Bhargavi D, Carbray JA, Birmaher B. Child Mania Rating Scale: Development, reliability and validity. *J. Am. Acad. Child Adolesc. Psychiatry* 2006;45(5):550-560.

Pavuluri MN, Henry DB, Devinini B, Carbray JA, Naylor MW, Janicak PG. A pharmacotherapy algorithm for stabilization and maintenance of pediatric bipolar disorder. *J. Am. Acad. Child Adolesc. Psychiatry* 2004;43:859-867.

Pavuluri MN, Henry D, Naylor M, Sampson G, Carbray J, Janicak PG. Open-label prospective trial of risperidone in combination with lithium or divalproex sodium in pediatric mania. *J. Affect. Disord.* 2004;82(Suppl 1):S103-11.

Pavuluri MN, Herbener ES, Sweeney AJ. Psychotic features in pediatric bipolar disorder. *J. Affect. Disorders* 2004;80:19-28.

Pavuluri MN, Janicak PG. *Handbook of Psychopharmocotherapy: Life Span Approach.* Philadelphia: Williams and Wilkins.2004.

Scheffer R, Kowatch R, Carmody T, Rush J. Randomized, placebo-controlled trial of mixed amphetamine salts for symptoms of comorbid ADHD in pediatric bipolar disorder after mood stabilization with divalproex sodium. *Am. J. Psychiatry* 2005;162(1):58-64.

Soutullo CA, DelBello MP, Ochsner JE, et al. Severity of bipolarity in hospitalized manic adolescents with history of stimulant or antidepressant treatment. *J. Affect. Disorders* 2002;70:323-327.

West AE, Schenkel LS, Pavuluri M. (in press). Early childhood temperament in pediatric bipolar disorder and attention deficit hyperactivity disorder. *J. Clin. Psychol.*

West AE, Pavuluri M. Maintenance model of integrated psychosocial treatment in pediatric bipolar disorder. *J. Am. Acad. Child Adolesc. Psychiatry* 2007;46(2):205-212.

Section V. Anxiety Disorders

In: Behavioral Pediatrics, 3rd Edition
Editor: D. E. Greydanus et al.

ISBN 978-1-60692-702-1
© 2009 Nova Science Publishers, Inc.

Chapter 16

Anxiety Disorders

Christopher K. Varley and Amy Henry

Abstract

Anxiety disorders are extremely common in youth and often present in primary care settings. Unfortunately, the affected youth often does not recognize their experience as a manifestation of anxiety, which complicates the assessment and treatment of their condition. This chapter will focus on reviewing several of the common anxiety disorders that can affect youth, the clinical presentation of these syndromes in children and adolescents and helpful strategies for evaluating, diagnosing and treating anxiety symptoms in this population.

Introduction

Anxiety is a normal part of human experience, but it can become maladaptive and functionally impairing if it is triggered inappropriately or if it is excessive in terms of intensity, frequency or duration. Anxiety disorders are the most frequent cluster of psychiatric illnesses diagnosed in youth. Naturally, anxiety symptoms are even more common. These symptoms regularly present to primary care providers, often in the context of confusing somatic concerns, behavioral outbursts or other functional impairments. As noted above, anxiety can be particularly difficult to diagnose, assess and treat in children and adolescents, since youth often do not have the ability to recognize their experience as related to an anxious mood.

Definitions

The anxiety disorders share some common features, can be comorbid with each other, and sometimes may be difficult to distinguish from each other. Following are descriptions of the DSM-IV-TR (American Psychiatric Association, 2000) anxiety disorders that may be seen in children and adolescents.

Separation Anxiety Disorder (SAD)

Separation anxiety is the only anxiety disorder in the DSM-IV that is included in the section devoted to disorders usually diagnosed in infancy, childhood or adolescence. By definition, the onset of this disorder is before age eighteen. This disorder includes an excessive amount of anxiety related to actual or impending separation from home and/or caregivers. Often, school refusal is a part of the presentation. Children may also present with significant somatic experiences of anxiety (e.g. stomachaches or headaches) in situations where separation is expected. The child's history of previous separation experiences often reveals great distress when they first entered daycare or preschool or when their parents first tried to leave them with babysitters. The child's level of distress is often very upsetting to their parents. Additionally, since separation anxiety often presents with somatic distress, many families may not recognize anxiety as the underlying concern. Since school is one of the most predictable separation expectations for most children, it is not surprising that this disorder commonly presents with increased symptomatology on Sunday evenings and Monday mornings, following a weekend without concern.

Returning to school after summer vacation or winter breaks can also exacerbate or reinitiate these symptoms. Separation anxiety should be recognized as distinct from school phobia, since separation anxiety involves distress separating from caregivers across contexts, whereas children with school phobia are able to separate easily for activities outside of school (e.g. sleepovers, camp, church, etc.).

Panic Disorder

Panic disorder occurs when a person experiences repeated panic attacks that interfere with their functioning, usually by prompting them to avoid situations where they feel panic is likely to occur or where it would be awkward to leave in the event of an attack. Panic attacks are very physical experiences. They can include heart palpitations, rapid breathing, dizziness, sensations of warmth, cold or choking, gastrointestinal upset and/or an extreme fear of dying or going crazy. They have an abrupt onset and escalate rapidly.

Typically they resolve over roughly twenty minutes. Given the various somatic experiences that can be associated with panic, it is understandable why many people initially pursue somatic causes for these symptoms. It should be noted that isolated panic attacks can occur in adolescents and do not always escalate to panic disorder. Panic disorder is often associated with agoraphobia, a fear of being in public ("fear of the marketplace"), which is thought to result from the fear of having a panic attack in public.

Generalized Anxiety Disorder (GAD)

Generalized anxiety disorder involves frequent worries about various day-to-day issues. These worries are maladaptive and extend beyond the intensity and frequency that would occur normally. This illness in youth was previously called overanxious disorder of childhood. Typical worries can center around competence, health, safety, novel situations, past mistakes and potential future pitfalls. Any of these worries in isolation might not seem unusual, but the overall level of distress is maladaptive in generalized anxiety disorder. Sometimes, children with generalized anxiety disorder can seem perfectionistic or appear to adhere very rigidly to rules in an effort to appease their anxiety. Alternatively, some children may present with defiance or more disruptive behaviors in reaction to their fear. Physical symptoms, such as insomnia, restlessness or headaches can also be associated with generalized anxiety disorder.

Social Phobia

Social phobia is sometimes referred to as social anxiety disorder. It reflects an intense and handicapping fear of evaluation in public situations. Commonly, sufferers will describe worries of being teased, humiliated or rejected. Physical symptoms are common with this disorder including blushing, shaking, gastrointestinal upset and sometimes panic attacks. Youth with this disorder may feel anxious participating in class, eating in public or engaging in social activities with their peers. The fear of these situations can be so intense that children may refuse expected activities and primarily present as oppositional. Selective mutism appears to be a specific example of this type of refusal as described below. Social anxiety disorder often starts in childhood or adolescence and can have a chronic course. Females are more commonly affected than males.

Selective Mutism

Selective mutism is currently formulated as an anxiety disorder similar to social phobia. It manifests as a refusal to speak in certain situations. The refusal to speak in a particular situation must be present for at least a month. Typically, children can speak normally at home but refuse to speak at school or around unfamiliar people. Selective mutism typically begins in early childhood. Extreme shyness is a common feature of the presentation.

Specific Phobias

A specific phobia is an extreme fear of a particular object or situation. The fear is maladaptive, functionally impairing and must persist for at least six months. Common triggers for specific phobias include spiders, snakes, heights, closed spaces, water or dogs. Youth who suffer from specific phobias may have had an unpleasant encounter with the object of their phobia and may avoid even reminders of their phobia. They can show prominent anticipatory anxiety when they believe there is some possibility of encountering the object of their fear. When actually faced with the feared stimulus, children show extreme distress and sometimes experience a panic attack.

Epidemiology

As noted previously, anxiety disorders are the most common category of psychiatric illness noted in youth. The point prevalence has been estimated between 3 and 13%. The prevalence varies somewhat across settings and upon the degree of impairment required to make a diagnosis. Higher rates have been noted in patients both in medical and mental health settings. Rates of anxiety disorders generally increase throughout childhood and adolescence, however there are some specific disorders that are more common in younger children (e.g. separation anxiety disorder and selective mutism). Anxiety disorders commonly co-occur with each other, with depressive disorders and with disruptive behavior disorders. In fact, up to one-half of youth who have an anxiety disorder will have a depressive disorder as well. The comorbidity of anxiety and depression is relevant for many reasons, but in particular, it should be noted that anxiety is a risk factor for completed suicides.

- *Separation Anxiety Disorder*. This is thought to be quite common, affecting 2 to 5% of children. The mean age of onset is just over seven years. Some studies suggest that low socioeconomic status may be associated with this illness. While separation anxiety disorder may resolve with a fairly benign course, it is oftentimes a harbinger of future mood problems such as depression and/or other anxiety problems.
- *Panic Disorder*. Actual panic attacks are thought to be rare in children, but quite common in adolescents. It should be noted, however, that while nearly two-thirds of adolescents have had the experience of a panic attack, less than 5% will have symptoms that evolve to meet criteria for panic disorder. Panic disorder is more common in females and tends to have a chronic course. Panic disorder appears to have a strong genetic component, based on twin studies and family histories. There also appear to be genetic links between panic disorder and other anxiety disorders. Panic disorder has also been linked to mitral valve prolapse. Specifically, up to half of the patients with panic disorder have been found to have mitral valve prolapse, whereas mitral valve prolapse is present in only 5% of the general population. Also of note, thyrotoxicosis has been associated with both panic disorder and mitral valve prolapse.

- *Generalized Anxiety Disorder*. This is estimated to have a prevalence of 3 to 5%. Compared to separation anxiety disorder, generalized anxiety disorder typically presents later in childhood. Additionally, older children with generalized anxiety disorder tend to have more symptoms than younger children with the disorder. Boys and girls appear to be equally affected by the illness in childhood but in adolescence it becomes more common in females. Twin studies show some genetic transmission of the disorder, however it appears to be inherited in a manner potentially distinct from panic disorder. Like most of the other anxiety disorders, it can have a chronic course, and it is commonly comorbid with mood disorders and other anxiety disorders.
- *Social Phobia.* This is thought to be present in roughly 1% of all youth. It is more common in adolescents. Because it is much more common in adults, it has been speculated that social phobia may be under-recognized in children and adolescents. As mentioned previously, social phobia often has a chronic course and it can have substantial negative effects on functioning over the lifespan.
- *Selective Mutism*. This is considered to be a rare condition, affecting less than 1% of children in mental health clinics and consequently an even smaller subset of children in the general population. It is thought to affect females somewhat more commonly than males. The onset of the illness is typically in preschool or the early school age years.
- *Specific Phobias*. These are estimated to affect roughly 2 to 3% of children. Girls are more commonly affected than boys.

Clinical Features

Primary care providers are often the first to see children and adolescents with issues related to anxiety. As described previously, these issues may initially appear completely unrelated to anxiety, such as tantrums, oppositionality or physical complaints. Consequently, these symptoms can be difficult to assess, diagnose and treat. When unrecognized, children can have prolonged medical evaluations that are intrusive, expensive and could potentially further fuel their anxiety and undermine their function unintentionally. As a result, it is helpful for primary care providers to be aware of the common manifestations of anxiety, to include these disorders early in the differential diagnosis and to have strategies to evaluate and treat anxiety disorders in their practice.

Anxiety is a normal human emotion. It serves an adaptive function and should not be considered pathologic in itself. It is the sense of fear or apprehension that accompanies threatened loss or perceived danger. Obviously this fear can be protective when an individual is faced with a threat that would require a quick and intense response, such as "flight or fight". Anxiety can be experienced in various forms, including cognitions, physiologic reactions and social behaviors. The cognitive experiences typically take the form of worries about anticipated loss, danger or failure. Again, these worries could be potentially adaptive if they are situationally appropriate and motivate the individual to take appropriate precautions (e.g. worry about failure can motivate studying for a test) and do not become overwhelming and inappropriate in terms of intensity or frequency. Similarly, the physiologic experiences of anxiety can be normal biologic features of human beings in response to threat. These physiologic manifestations of anxiety include activation of the autonomic nervous system with increased heart rate, shunting of blood to the muscles and periphery, increased rate of breathing, flushing, tremulousness, a sense of activation and gastrointestinal upset. With regard to the social behaviors that can be associated with anxiety, it can be helpful to think back to the concept of "fight or flight". When faced with perceived danger, it can be appropriate to either try to escape (avoid) the situation or react against the perceived threat. In youth, these social behaviors may present as clinging to caregivers, crying, arguing, tantrums, task refusal or as shy, withdrawn behaviors.

Again, any of the various manifestations of anxiety can be construed as potentially adaptive in appropriate situations but could be extremely functionally impairing if they were to manifest with inappropriate frequency, intensity or in response to non-threatening stimuli. This is one of the fundamental questions to be assessed when evaluating for possible anxiety disorders: are the symptoms functionally impairing, situationally and/or developmentally inappropriate or excessive in terms of frequency or intensity of presentation? When anxiety is pathologic in nature, it can lead to intense distress and suffering, both for the child and their family, it can hinder the normal developmental process and it can cause profound disturbances in adaptive function. School performance, family relationships and peer relationships are among the most common areas affected by inappropriate anxiety.

Perhaps one reason that anxiety disorders can be so complex to evaluate involves their combination of both categorical and dimensional elements. For example, there is some evidence for trying to define some anxiety disorders in categorical terms based on specific areas of brain pathology and some distinct patterns of inheritance (particularly regarding panic disorder and regarding obsessive compulsive disorder as noted in the subsequent chapter). In contrast, as described above, anxiety symptoms typically manifest as variations of normal anxiety experiences that are simply extreme in their presentation along a dimension of intensity, frequency or impairment. Studies of temperament support this notion of a range of inherent personality or behavioral styles including a dimension of variability loading for anxiety, around how prone an individual is to seek or avoid novelty. There have been longitudinal studies showing that children with temperaments prone to avoiding novelty are more vulnerable to anxiety disorders.

With regard to the manifestations of anxiety in youth, we have already discussed some examples. It should be emphasized that children often present with anxiety in a fashion very different from adults and often may not endorse a subjective sense of worry or awareness of anxiety. Instead, they may solely have awareness of the physical manifestations of the experience or they may present with severe behavioral problems such as tantrums as the only clue to their anxiety disorder. In order to distinguish between behavioral problems caused by anxiety compared to behavioral concerns related to other issues, it often requires a good understanding of the pattern and course of the problem. Children with anxiety are often compliant in general but then have outbursts that seem unexpected to their caregivers. Tantrums related to anxiety can appear extremely intense and can last for a prolonged period. The outbursts are often driven by an intense urge to avoid or terminate exposure to an event the child finds threatening. These tantrums driven by anxiety are often linked to specific situations (e.g. separation from parents).

Diagnosis

The first step in diagnosing anxiety disorders is including them in the differential diagnoses. Recurrent physical concerns, particularly those that drive avoidance of developmentally appropriate activities should trigger consideration of anxiety as the cause. Disruptive behaviors, including distractibility and restlessness in the classroom should also be a cue to consider anxiety in the differential.

Once anxiety has been raised as a consideration then the history around the presenting concern becomes essential. Gathering specific information about the onset of the symptoms, the course over time, the context of the concerns and the response to previous interventions can often help clarify what role anxiety might be playing in the situation. Eliciting any triggering events can be useful, since some anxiety disorders first appear following a frightening experience (e.g. a dog phobia after being chased by a big dog). Clarifying how the symptoms appear across settings can be helpful as well (e.g. is the child more compliant transitioning to a weekend with their grandparents compared to getting ready for school in the morning?). It is also crucial to assess how much the symptoms are compromising function. Concrete examples should be gathered whenever possible to help track symptoms over time.

Anxious children may have difficulty reporting about their symptoms, often directly as a result of their anxiety. Additionally, the notion of anxiety is a fairly abstract concept, so many children may not have the developmental abilities to communicate directly about this feeling state. They may not be able to link their emotional state to their thoughts, body sensations and actions without assistance. Additionally, children may not realize when or how their experiences are different from other children. Nevertheless, a child's report of their experience is invaluable in trying to assess the situation. Often, children will participate more openly when they can be reassured that you are trying to help and that you have helped other children with similar problems. Very young children may need concrete and non-verbal strategies to communicate. For example, preschoolers and young school age children can often indicate whether they feel something is a "big" problem or a "little" problem through hand/arm gestures or pictures. Similarly, cartoon pictures can be used to give children examples of feeling states to help them engage in the discussion. Older kids can be taught to use self-ratings (e.g. zero to ten scales) to describe their perceptions around the intensity of various experiences. These ratings can be adapted to make "feelings thermometers" to track emotional experiences across time. It is often helpful to first query a child's parents about the feeling words commonly used in the family and try to use a vocabulary similar to the family norms (i.e. worried, nervous, afraid, embarrassed, etc). Children should be asked about their typical worries and prompted to consider how their worries affect their daily life.

Additionally, the family history should be considered as part of the assessment since there is a substantial genetic component to anxiety disorders. It can be particularly helpful to learn whether anyone in the family has had a successful treatment of an anxiety disorder, since this may help guide future treatment decisions. Anxiety often has a socially contagious quality, so it is also essential to learn whether anyone in the environment is currently struggling with their own anxiety and to recognize when a child's symptoms may be triggering substantial anxiety in the family system. The family should also be asked about environmental stressors and typical parenting practices around anxiety and reassurance. Since there is substantial variability around acceptable emotional displays across cultures, it is often also very useful to understand the family's attitude about anxiety as well.

Since anxiety disorders are common, they should not be left as diagnoses of exclusion. Otherwise, children may be exposed to lengthy and unnecessary medical work-ups trying to exhaust all alternative explanations for their symptoms. If a child is generally healthy and their presentation is highly suggestive of an anxiety disorder, then aside from a routine physical examination, minimal medical testing is usually required, although thyroid testing may be warranted. Any additional medical evaluation should be guided by the child's personal medical history and the presentation of their symptoms. Since medications can sometimes cause anxiety symptoms, a child's medication list should be reviewed thoroughly. Common medications that can mimic or exacerbate anxiety disorders include asthma medications, steroids, stimulants and other sympathomimetic agents plus some naturopathic/herbal remedies such as ephedra and St. John's wort. Dietary caffeine can also induce or exacerbate anxiety. Recreational alcohol and/or illicit substance use can also be a cause of anxiety symptoms, and should be considered in older children and adolescents.

The diagnosis of anxiety disorders follows the criteria outlined in the DSM IV-TR. The American Academy of Child and Adolescent Psychiatry's Practice Parameter for the Assessment and Treatment of Children with Anxiety Disorders also provides a useful resource. Additionally, some rating scales and structured assessment tools can be useful in trying to evaluate concerns in this area, particularly since they offer a standard by which to compare symptoms across children of similar ages. The Diagnostic Interview Schedule for Children (DISC) is an example of a structured diagnostic interview. Semi-structured instruments include the Anxiety Disorders Interview of Children, the Schedule for Affective Disorders and Schizophrenia for School-Age Children (K-SADS) and the Diagnostic Interview for Children and Adolescents. Clinician rating scales like the Hamilton Anxiety Rating Scale (HAM-A) or the Screen for Child Anxiety Related Emotional Disorders (SCARED) can be very useful. Self-report measures are also available. Examples include the Multidimensional Anxiety Scale for Children (MASC) or the Revised Children's Manifest Anxiety Scale (RCMAS). A relatively new instrument, the Pediatric Anxiety Rating Scale (PARS), provides an index of anxiety across disorders. Some form of structured assessment tool can prove extremely helpful in both the initial evaluation of symptoms and in tracking symptoms over time.

Treatment

General Approach

Fortunately, anxiety disorders are treatable and substantial relief from symptoms can be achieved for many patients. In approaching the treatment of anxiety disorders in youth, a comprehensive treatment plan that is sensitive to the biopsychosocial circumstances is best. This approach could include any combination of various interventions, such as psychoeducation, environmental modifications, parent consultation, medication treatment and/or psychotherapy. Given the typical constraints of a primary care practice, it is common for primary care providers to develop skills in some first line treatment interventions for anxiety while providing the option of mental health referrals for those youth who do not appear to improve with these interventions or for those youth whose symptoms appear to extend beyond the scope of practice of a primary care setting. In this text, we will review some of the first-line treatment interventions that might be appropriate for a primary care setting.

There is evidence for the effectiveness of both psychotherapy and medication in the treatment of anxiety disorders. The literature specific to youth is smaller than what is known about treating anxiety disorders in adults. It should be noted that oftentimes, medication treatments offer relief to some anxiety symptoms but may not substantially affect psychosocial function, since they do not address maladaptive patterns of coping. Consequently, combined treatment is commonly recommended.

Education, Parent Consultation and Brief Psychotherapy

Once the symptoms have been assessed and found to be consistent with anxiety, it is important to gauge the severity of the problem. Children with mild, transient and developmentally appropriate anxieties often primarily need reassurance and brief consultation/education with their family.

For children with mild to moderate anxiety and minimal functional impairment, more in-depth education around anxiety will likely be necessary. This education could be offered by a primary care provider who has experience supporting youth with anxiety concerns and whose schedule allows for a series of repeated visits. Alternatively, the primary care provider may initiate the process by offering more focused counseling and then providing referrals to a community therapist. In this circumstance, the primary care provider may continue to support the process by reinforcing the therapist's work at future medical visits.

An example of cases that might be satisfactorily managed in a primary care office would include children who are early in a pattern of somatic concerns that have caused school avoidance. In this kind of circumstance, the child and family should be oriented to the basic anxiety cycle. Specifically, they should be reminded that while anxiety is a normal emotion, it can sometimes get triggered inappropriately or feel excessive to the situation. Examples of anxiety-provoking situations can be reviewed and the child and family can be encouraged to consider how fear responses can be triggered inappropriately (e.g. some kids feel like they are being chased by a tiger when they think about going to school). The child and family should be educated about the normal urge to avoid and escape anxiety-provoking triggers and the child and family's current pattern of coping with the anxiety should be reviewed. Typically, exposure to the triggering event (e.g. going to school) causes significant distress and anxiety which leads to an urge to resist or escape the trigger. In avoiding the trigger, the child often feels immediate, substantial relief, thereby reinforcing the decision to avoid the trigger. It is important to review with the family how much relief can come from avoidance behaviors and how quickly avoidance can become entrenched as a maladaptive pattern of behavior. Ultimately, this urge to escape can lead to functional impairments when it results in avoiding developmentally normal and healthy activities. While the avoidance initially feels good, over time, this feeds the sense of anxiety about the initial trigger and ultimately causes more distress and suffering over time (e.g. initially a child might only feel anxious about performing well at school during tests but over time if they avoid class due to anxiety, they inadvertently feed the feeling of anxiety about school while simultaneously falling behind in school and experience an increasing sense of inadequacy, making it even harder to return). Most families can relate to the concept of how avoiding things we fear tends to make the worry and fear stronger, whereas facing the fear will ultimately make it weaker. Once this basic anxiety cycle has been reviewed, the treatment starts to focus on GRADUALLY interrupting the pattern of avoidance. Effective treatment for anxiety depends upon gradual exposure to the anxiety. The family must be clearly informed that the goal is not to become free of anxiety, but rather to become able to tolerate feelings of anxiety while maintaining healthy function. Over time, the anxiety will decrease, but in the initial period, the anxiety is likely to escalate as the child is expected to gradually face the anxiety-provoking triggers. It is for this reason that exposure must be gradual, so that the child and family does not get overwhelmed and return to a pattern of avoidance. For example, if a child has already missed several days of school due to anxiety, they are not likely to be successful if they are expected to return for a full day immediately. Instead, it might be more realistic to start with a brief visit to the teacher before or after-school with the plan to resume a shortened work-day at first. Gradually the time at school can be expanded. It is important to recognize that this is a difficult task for an anxious child and their effort should be praised. Additionally, it is often very helpful to include motivators in the environment to support the child as they work on tolerating their anxiety (e.g. scheduling a favorite activity right after the school day). Younger children may need concrete and more immediate rewards to enhance their success (e.g. star charts or tokens that might later be exchanged for a privilege).

Parents should be advised that children will often protest engaging in exposure. This is very understandable, since they are clearly feeling overwhelmed by the anxiety-provoking trigger. Nevertheless, it can be very difficult for families to tolerate the increased tantrums and/or distress that can arise. Additionally, it should be noted that a child's anxiety can often elicit substantial anxiety and distress in a parent. Unfortunately, this can sometimes result in an escalating cycle of anxiety where everyone involved feels increasingly out of control. This underscores the need for gradual exposures. Parents should be encouraged to start with tasks that are manageable, so that the pattern of avoidance does not continue. It can be extremely helpful to negotiate some small tasks that could be considered first steps in the exposure process and then schedule a follow-up visit so that everyone knows they will have a chance to return and discuss the experience. This may also increase the likelihood that the family will proceed with the plan. Parents can also be reminded that intense anxiety in the face of a non-threatening trigger typically improves over twenty minutes, as this may help them persist in the face of their child's distress.

Children with more intense anxiety and more profound functional impairments should be referred for more structured psychotherapy to address these concerns. Appropriate referrals should include providers who have experience working with children and adolescents and who are familiar with evidence-based treatments for anxiety, such as exposure and response prevention or cognitive-behavioral psychotherapy. To date, nonspecific supportive psychotherapies or play therapy have not been shown to be as effective for treating anxiety.

Pharmacotherapy

Medication interventions often provide some relief to anxiety symptoms but may not be adequate to fully improve a child's functioning. Consequently, psychotherapeutic approaches should be combined with medication treatment to ensure an optimal effect.

Additionally, it is important to note that the medications used to address the types of anxiety disorders discussed in this chapter are not specifically approved for this purpose in children by the Food and Drug Administration. Consequently, their use in these circumstances is off-label. Several of the commonly used medications have been approved for use in children for other purposes, however.

Effective pharmacotherapy of anxiety requires collaboration with the family. The family should be clearly advised of the off-label use of medication and the potential benefits and risks. In particular, families should be advised that there are limitations in the knowledge base at this time around medication treatments for anxiety in children.

Generally, the first-line medication treatments for childhood anxiety disorders are the selective serotonin reuptake inhibitors (SSRIs). Medications in this family include fluoxetine (Prozac), sertraline (Zoloft), paroxetine (Paxil), fluvoxamine (Luvox), citalopram (Celexa) and escitalopram (Lexapro). There is a substantial evidence base regarding these medications in adults with anxiety disorders, and there are now some studies showing efficacy and safety in youth, including double-blind, placebo-controlled studies in children and adolescents showing positive results. There is no evidence that any particular medication in this class is more effective than another, so the selection of a medication may sometimes be driven by family history, tolerability of side effects, cost and/or formulary issues. For example, if a parent has a history of prominent anxiety symptoms and has gotten relief from one SSRI, but not another, it is appropriate to begin with the agent benefiting the parent. Typical benefits from medication treatment can include an overall decrease in anxiety, improvement in somatic concerns related to anxiety and an increased ability to tolerate distress. Relatively common side effects can include nausea, diarrhea, gastrointestinal upset, insomnia, sedation, agitation, headaches, decreased libido and sexual dysfunction. A less common, but potentially serious adverse effect is the possibility of inducing a manic episode. A family history of bipolar disorder should prompt providers to be more cautious about using these agents and to monitor more closely for signs of activation and/or mania. Additionally, there has recently been controversy about these agents increasing suicidal ideation in youth. As a result, these medications have a black-box warning, and families should be advised to monitor closely for any signs of suicidal thinking or behavior. This concern is not limited to the treatment of depression and appears to be relevant to SSRIs being used in the treatment of anxiety disorders as well. The current treatment guidelines suggest weekly contact for one month after initiating treatment with an SSRI to monitor for this symptom and then tapering down contact if no concerns about self-harm are noted.

An SSRI trial should generally be started at a low dose and gradually titrated up to an effective level in order to avoid inducing adverse effects. Anxious children can be particularly sensitive to somatic concerns and sometimes anxiety can be paradoxically increased when medications are increased too quickly. This cautious approach can also ultimately improve compliance since some children may refuse medications if they experience a side effect. Sample starting doses and target doses of the various SSRIs are provided in Table 1.

Table 1. SSRIs and typical daily dosing

Medication Name	Starting Dose	Target Doses
Fluoxetine	5 mg	10-40 mg
Sertraline	25 mg	50-200 mg
Paroxetine	5 mg	10-40 mg
Fluvoxamine	25 mg	100-300 mg divided b.i.d.
Citalopram	5 mg	10-40 mg
Escitalopram	5 mg	10-20 mg

It is safe to implement gradual dose increases every week as long as no side effects are reported. If a child has a positive response to a very low dose of an SSRI then the medication does not have to be pushed up to higher doses. The medication trial should be continued for at least a month at a therapeutic level to ensure adequate time for a response to emerge and oftentimes, continued benefits are noted over the course of eight to twelve weeks. The time of day of the medication administration can vary. Some children experience mild sedation with an SSRI and they tolerate their medication better at bedtime. Other children experience an increase in energy and alertness and find a morning dose to be preferable. If daytime sedation or a sleep disturbance emerges when using an SSRI, it is often helpful to try modifying the time of medication administration to see if the concern resolves.

With regard to duration of treatment, there are inadequate data to give a definite answer. In general, if a patient has found an SSRI to be substantially helpful and their symptoms have been stable for several months, then it may be appropriate to consider gradually tapering off the medication to clarify whether it is still necessary. It is often helpful to try to wait to taper down on medications until a time when the environment is relatively stable and limited stressors exist. There are some children and families who would prefer to continue medication treatment indefinitely due to an excellent response. In cases of chronic anxiety or strong family histories of anxiety, this may be a reasonable decision and can be discussed with the family. Some children may be candidates for chronic administration of medication, especially if they have experienced a relapse of symptoms during or after a discontinuation trail. The SSRIs vary significantly in terms of half-life and this can be relevant in deciding how rapidly to taper the medication. For example the half-life of fluoxetine is quite long in comparison to the other medications in the class, so it can self-taper. Abrupt discontinuation of agents with shorter half-lives can lead to muscle stiffness, runny nose and general malaise. Additionally, there is some evidence that children may metabolize these medications more rapidly than adults and consequently they may be more vulnerable to withdrawal symptoms.

Second-line agents for treating anxiety in youth include benzodiazepines. While these medications are known to be effective in adults with anxiety, they are inadequately studied in children. The scant evidence to date shows only mixed results in studies with children. The benzodiazepines have their effects by modulating the inhibitory neurotransmitter gamma aminobutryic acid (GABA). There are several different benzodiazepines and they largely vary according to duration of action. Among the most commonly prescribed agents are the long-lasting medication clonazepam (Klonopin), the intermediate acting lorazepam (Ativan) and the short-lasting alprazolam (Xanax). Benzodiazepines can appear to be a desirable intervention at times due to their potential for almost immediate relief. They can sometimes be used in conjunction with an SSRI in situations where severe symptoms are present, since they can provide some benefit in the early weeks of treatment while the antidepressant medication is still starting to take effect. Unfortunately, children are more likely to experience some adverse effects of benzodiazepines than adults, particularly disinhibition, paradoxical activation and agitation and parents should be cautioned that this could occur. Benzodiazepines can also impair memory and learning, making them less appealing to many families. As a result, when benzodiazepines are used, they should generally be considered cautiously as a short-term intervention and consultation with a child psychiatrist should be pursued if their use continues to appear necessary over the long-term. Dosing guidelines in children are not well studied. Starting at a low dose and advancing based on response are prudent. Some typical starting doses and target doses for youth are outlined in Table 2.

Insomnia can be a particularly problematic symptom for anxious children and their families. Long-term medication treatment is not recommended for sleeping problems in youth without consultation with a specialist, but for one to three days, a medication intervention may prove invaluable. Potential medication considerations could include benzodiazepines, zolpidem (Ambien), diphenhydramine (Benadryl), hydroxyzine (Vistaril) or melatonin. It should be noted, however that efficacy studies do not exist for these medications in youth, and they are not FDA approved for this indication for children.

Table 2. Benzodiazepines and typical daily dosing

Medication Name	Starting Dose	Target Doses
Clonazepam	0.25 mg, 1-2 times	0.25-1 mg, 2 times
Lorazepam	0.5 mg, 1-2 times	0.5-2 mg, 2-3 times
Alprazolam	0.25 mg, 1-2 times	0.25-1 mg, 3 times

Conclusion

Anxiety symptoms are common in youth and can be very challenging to assess. Children and families often present these symptoms to their primary care providers without realizing that anxiety is the underlying issue. Since anxiety disorders are treatable conditions it is important for family medical providers to be sensitive to possible anxiety disorders and to have strategies to follow-up on these concerns. An awareness of the definition and presentation of anxiety symptoms in children can help facilitate a timely diagnosis. Having a developmentally sensitive strategy to elicit the history from children and their parents is also essential. Environmental and genetic factors should be considered in the assessment process and structured assessment tools can prove very useful in confirming the diagnosis. Once anxiety has been recognized, a multimodal treatment approach should be employed which could include psychoeducation, environmental interventions, parent consultation, individual psychotherapy and/or medication treatment. Depending on the circumstances of the child and the severity of the problem, a primary care provider may be able to implement the treatment plan independently or they may initiate referrals for aspects of the care that are beyond the scope of their practice. Regardless, the primary care provider plays a crucial role in timely identification and treatment of anxiety.

References

American Academy of Child and Adolescent Psychiatry. Practice parameter for the assessment and treatment of children and adolescents with anxiety disorders. *J. Am. Acad. Child Adolesc Psychiatry* 2007;46(2):267-283.

American Psychiatric Association. *Diagnostic and Statistical Manual of Mental Disorders*, Fourth Edition, Text Revision. Washington, DC, American Psychiatric Association; 2000.

Beidel DC, Turner SM. *Shy Children, Phobic Adults: Nature and Treatment of Social Phobia.* Washington, DC: American Psychological Association; 1998.

Bernstein GA, Garfinkel BD, Borchardt CM. Comparative studies of pharmacotherapy for school refusal. *J. Am. Acad. Child Adolesc Psychiatry* 1990;29:773-781.

Bernstein GA, Borchardt CM, Perwien AR, et al. Imipramine plus cognitive-behavioral therapy in the treatment of school refusal. *J. Am. Acad. Child Adolesc. Psychiatry* 2000;39(3):276-283.

Birmaher B, Axelson DA, Monk K, et al. Fluoxetine for treatment of childhood anxiety disorders. *J. Am. Acad. Child Adolesc. Psychiatry* 2003;42:415-423.

Black B, Uhde TW, Tancer ME. Fluoxetine for the treatment of social phobia. *J. Am. Acad. Child Adolesc. Psychiatry* 1992;29:36-44.

Costello E, Angold A. Epidemiology. In: March J, ed. *Anxiety Disorders in Children and Adolescents.* New York: Guilford Press; 1995:109-124.

Fonagy P, Target M, Cottrell M, Phillips J, Kurtz Z. *What Works for Whom? A Critical Review of Treatments for Children and Adolescents.* New York: Guilford Press; 2002.

Kashani H, Orvashel H. A community study of anxiety in children and adolescents. *Am. J. Psychiatry* 1990;147:313-318.

Kendall P. Treating anxiety disorders in children: results of a randomized clinical trial. *J. Consult Clin. Psychol.* 1994;62(1):100-110.

Kendall PC, Flannery-Schroeder E, Panichelli-Mindel SM, et al. Therapy for youths with anxiety disorders: a second randomized clinical trial. *J. Consult Clin. Psychol.* 1997;65(3):366-380.

Rapee RM, Wignall AM, Hudson JL, Schniering CA. *Treating Anxious Children and Adolescents. An Evidence-Based Approach.* Oakland, CA: New Harbinger Publications, Inc; 2000.

Research Unit on Pediatric Psychopharmacology Anxiety Study Group (RUPP). Fluvoxamine for the treatment of anxiety disorders in children and adolescents. *N. Engl. J. Med.* 2000;344(17):1279-1285

Research Unit on Pediatric Psychopharmacology Anxiety Study Group (RUPP). Treatment of pediatric anxiety disorders: an open label extension of the research units on pediatric psychopharmacology anxiety study. *J. Child Adolesc. Psychopharmacol.* 2002;12(3):175-188.

Rynn MA, Siqueland L, Rickels K. Placebo-controlled trial of sertraline in the treatment of children with generalized anxiety disorder. *Am. J. Psychiatry* 2001;158(12):2008-20014.

Simeon JG, Ferguson HB, Knott V, et al. Clinical, cognitive and neurophysiological effects of alprazolam in children and adolescents with overanxious and avoidant disorders. *J. Am. Acad. Child Adolesc. Psychiatry* 1992;31:29-33.

Spence SH, Donovan C, Brechman-Toussaint M. The treatment of childhood social phobia: the effectiveness of a social skills training-based cognitive-behavioural interventions, with and without parental involvement. *J. Child Psychol. Psychiatry* 2000;41(6):713-726.

US Food and Drug Administration. Antidepressant use in children, adolescents, and adults. May 2, 2007. Available at: http://www.fda.gov/CDER/Drug/antidepressants/default.htm Accessed December 24, 2007.

Wagner KD, Berard R, Stein MB, et al. A multicenter, randomized, double-blind, placebo-controlled trial of paroxetine in children and adolescents with social anxiety disorder. *Arch. Gen. Psychiatry* 2004;61(11):1153-1162.

In: Behavioral Pediatrics, 3rd Edition
Editor: D. E. Greydanus et al.

ISBN 978-1-60692-702-1
© 2009 Nova Science Publishers, Inc.

Chapter 17

Obsessive Compulsive Disorder

Amy Henry and Christopher K. Varley

Abstract

Obsessive Compulsive Disorder (OCD) can be a chronic condition that results in substantial functional impairments. It often initially presents in childhood or adolescence, but it can be difficult to detect. Many patients suffer for years with their symptoms before their illness is diagnosed. Consequently, primary care providers are often the first to realize that a youth is experiencing problems but may not know how to proceed in offering either further evaluation or treatment. Fortunately, OCD is a treatable illness. This chapter will provide a review of obsessive compulsive disorder (OCD) in youth. In particular, we will review the typical presentation of OCD in this population, the epidemiology of this illness, common clinical features, assessment and treatment strategies.

OCD is discussed separately from other anxiety disorders in this text because it has been studied as a distinct disorder, and there is a unique body of literature around the course and treatment of this illness.

Introduction

While comprehensive treatment of OCD is likely beyond the scope of most primary care settings, it is very likely that youth with OCD may initially present to their primary care provider. Oftentimes, however, it can be extremely challenging to accurately diagnose OCD in youth, since the presenting concerns often overlap with other illnesses that are more common. Additionally, youth with OCD often do not recognize that their obsessive and compulsive behaviors are problematic. Alternatively, some affected individuals may recognize their symptoms as inappropriate and try to conceal them from others. Consequently, youth may present to their primary care provider with typical symptoms of OCD or other complaints such as explosive outbursts, tantrums or dramatic functional impairments (e.g. school failure) that do not immediately trigger consideration of obsessive compulsive disorder as the cause. Since OCD is a treatable illness with the potential to become both chronic and disabling, it is important for primary care providers to be able to identify and initiate treatment as soon as possible.

Definition

Obsessive compulsive disorder (OCD) is a distinct illness in the category of anxiety disorders. The disorder consists of the presence of either obsessions, compulsions or both, which cause either substantial distress or functional impairment. Obsessions are persistent, automatic, undesirable thoughts, images or impulses that cause anxiety or distress. Classically, the affected person recognizes that the obsessive thought is excessive, maladaptive and/or inappropriate. However, in children and adolescents this level of insight is not typical. Compulsions are repetitive actions (including mental actions such as counting) driven by obsessions. The compulsions are intended to decrease the anxiety and distress induced by the obsessive worry. However, the compulsive behaviors are illogical and excessive responses to the anxious obsession and the relief that they produce is generally short-lived so the compulsions must be repeated. OCD can evolve into a chronic illness and frequently first appears in childhood or adolescence.

Epidemiology

Obsessive compulsive disorder can present at various ages. Roughly one-third of cases present before fifteen years of age. Current epidemiologic data suggest the point prevalence of OCD in youth is roughly 1%, with up to 2 to 3% of children having experienced obsessive compulsive disorder at some time by the end of adolescence. There are inadequate prospective data regarding this illness, however retrospective studies suggest that it is common for the illness to persist through adolescence and into adulthood. Adolescent males and females appear to be equally affected, but the onset of the illness is generally earlier in males. The onset of OCD can be either insidious or abrupt. Studies suggest the illness can be present for an average of six or seven years before reaching medical attention, with males generally suffering longer than females. Eighty percent of patients experience a combination of both obsessions and compulsions.

While there are clearly environmental factors that can influence the presentation of OCD (see discussions of Pediatric Autoimmune Neuropsychiatric Disorders Associated with Streptococcal Infection [PANDAS] below), family and twin studies suggest a genetically inherited vulnerability to the disorder. Neuroimaging techniques suggest that variations in the functioning of the corticostriatothalamic circuit are likely involved in the presentation of OCD.

Clinical Features

Obsessive compulsive disorder in children often manifests with fears regarding safety, health and/or contamination. Ritualized actions typically present related to eating, dressing, grooming, checking, symmetry and/or reassurance-seeking. It is common for the intensity of the symptoms to fluctuate over the affected individual's lifetime. Similarly, the focus of the obsessions and compulsive behaviors frequently changes over time as well.

As noted previously, while the hallmark symptoms of OCD are obsessions and compulsions, youth rarely present complaining of these symptoms. Instead, children and their families typically present due to the associated functional impairments that stem from these symptoms. Younger children commonly present with severe tantrums that are unusually intense and prolonged. These children may be compliant and well-behaved in general but become extremely dysregulated in the circumstances when their obsessive worries are triggered or their compulsions are challenged (e.g. around grooming or bath time). The precipitating event for these tantrums may seem unusual compared to other children. Youth frequently do not recognize their fears as excessive or unusual, and younger children generally can not articulate the source of their fear initially. Nevertheless, their parents can often describe the pattern of avoidance and rituals that is associated with the illness.

It is common for families to accommodate to OCD to the point that everyone in the home may play a role in the extensive rituals and avoidance behaviors driven by the illness. Parents will often report that the level of their child's distress is so overwhelming in particular situations that they have either consciously or unconsciously joined in avoiding the circumstances that might trigger their child's OCD. Since OCD can exist for years before coming to clinical attention, this often means that the entire family may have lost sight of how the symptoms have come to interfere in activities of daily living.

Obsessive compulsive disorder can be an associated feature of other illnesses. Tourette's syndrome, for example, commonly presents with a triad of not only tics, but also attention-deficit hyperactivity disorder and obsessive-compulsive disorder. Similarly, a subset of cases of OCD has been associated with Pediatric Autoimmune Neuropsychiatric Disorders Associated with Streptococcal Infection (PANDAS). PANDAS are currently conceptualized as autoimmune responses to group A beta hemolytic streptococcal infections. It should be noted however that the PANDAS syndrome is currently only poorly understood and somewhat controversial. The principle symptoms of PANDAS include obsessions and compulsions in combination with abnormal movements such as tics. In PANDAS, the onset of the OCD symptoms is typically quite abrupt.

Diagnosis

Establishing an accurate diagnosis of OCD can be extremely challenging for many reasons. Youth and families often do not have an accurate appreciation of the range and limitation of normal behaviors of their peers; affected children often do not recognize their symptoms as maladaptive; sufferers may conceal their symptoms out of embarrassment; families may accommodate slowly to the symptoms over time; and children with OCD frequently present with concerns that appear unrelated to the underlying illness. As noted in the previous chapter on other anxiety disorders, the first step in diagnosing OCD is to include it in the differential diagnosis.

It should be noted, however, that subclinical symptoms of obsessions and/or compulsions are common in youth, particularly in younger children but these should not be mistaken for OCD. In fact, self-report measures in community samples reveal that a majority of children may experience transient preoccupations with particular worries (e.g. fear of the dark, monsters, guilt about lying or superstitious fears). Similarly, it is extremely common for children, particularly younger children, to engage in some rituals that are not functionally impairing (e.g. minor bedtime rituals).

Consequently, when clinicians are trying to evaluate for possible OCD, they want to both elicit the history of any potential symptoms while also assessing the frequency and intensity of these concerns, and their associated functional impairment. Providers should pursue descriptions of both past and present symptomatology. As discussed previously, obsessions in children often focus on worries about contamination (e.g. germs, pollution, dirt, etc.), safety issues (e.g. burglars, natural disasters, safety of caregivers, etc.) and/or health issues (e.g. fear of developing cancer or becoming infected with HIV). Compulsions commonly manifest around eating, dressing/grooming, symmetry, checking and/or reassurance-seeking. Perfectionism can be another manifestation of this illness. Primary care providers may need to ask about possible symptoms in various domains and provide examples. Questions such as, "Has your child ever had any unusual behaviors related to food or eating?" can be helpful and can be adapted to various aspects of functioning. Particular examples can be illustrative, for example, extreme food avoidance driven by contamination or health fears (e.g. young children avoiding meat due to contamination fears when this is not a family value), insisting that food must come pre-packaged or be prepared in a highly particular fashion (e.g. cut into a certain number of pieces or arranged in a set fashion on the plate). Examples of bathing and grooming compulsions can include engaging in extremely long bathing or grooming rituals (e.g. insisting on repeated hand or body washing, using multiple hair or body hygiene products) or insisting on a certain sequence at bath time or when dressing. Similar examples can be provided for checking (e.g. repeatedly checking the locks or stove in the house), symmetry (e.g. lining up objects or tapping items in a symmetric fashion), perfectionism (e.g. erasing and re-writing homework repeatedly) or reassurance-seeking (e.g. persistently questioning parents that an adverse outcome will not occur without actually feeling reassured).

If the screening questions for OCD arouse suspicion, then a more comprehensive inventory of potential symptoms and their sequelae should be pursued. The Yale-Brown Obsessive Compulsive Scale (Y-BOCS) can be helpful in this regard, since it offers a comprehensive list of OCD symptoms. This tool can also help track symptoms over time.

In youth who present with an acute onset of OCD symptoms in the context of a sore throat or recent upper respiratory infection, then suspicion for PANDAS should arise and a throat culture should be obtained to screen for group A beta hemolytic streptococcal infections.

Treatment

Youth with obsessive compulsive disorder generally require specialty care by a mental health provider trained in the treatment of OCD in children and adolescents. Evidence-based treatments for OCD exist and can be quite helpful in addressing the symptoms of this potentially disabling illness. The optimal treatment for OCD is a combination of both psychotherapy and pharmacotherapy. Medication treatment alone does not appear to be as effective as combined treatment with psychotherapy. Unfortunately, nonspecific supportive psychotherapy is usually not effective, and it may be difficult to find providers who are familiar with the psychotherapeutic strategies proven to be helpful for OCD. The Obsessive Compulsive Foundation website (www.ocfoundation.org) can be a helpful resource in identifying providers with expertise in treating this illness.

Since the psychotherapy treatment of obsessive compulsive disorder is generally beyond the scope of a routine primary care practice, only a brief review will be offered here. The initial stages of a cognitive-behavioral treatment for OCD usually focus on engaging the youth and their family in treatment through reassurance, rapport-building, psychoeducation and storytelling techniques developed to allow children to conceptualize recovery from their symptoms. Thereafter, the child and/or family work to describe the range of symptoms they experience and the level of distress they would face if they were to challenge their symptoms. Once the patient and/or family seems to understand the importance of learning to tolerate anxiety without succumbing to maladaptive compulsive behaviors, then the process of gradually exposing the patient to triggers for their symptoms can begin. This process typically results in increased anxiety initially, so the importance of psychoeducation, rapport-building and gradual exposure cannot be overemphasized. If exposure proceeds too quickly or before the child and/or family recognize the importance of tolerating anxiety, then the exposure may simply result in the child and family is becoming overwhelmed and either withdrawing from treatment or resuming maladaptive compulsions. Since the task of exposure-based treatment is so challenging, children may find external motivators in the environment to be helpful (e.g. scheduling pleasant activities after exposure practice or planning celebration ceremonies as they accomplish new exposures).

With regard to medical and medication treatment, if a case of PANDAS is diagnosed, a full antibiotic course should be completed for active infections. Antibody titers for streptococcal infections should also be obtained at the time of initial presentation and one month later. When new upper respiratory infections present, follow-up cultures should be obtained. Similarly, when close contacts have known streptococcal infections, there should be a low threshold for offering antibiotic treatment and/or obtaining cultures. The intensity of symptoms can be tracked and correlated to the antibody titers and culture results. Referrals to neurologists and/or immunologists with expertise in PANDAS may also be helpful.

The most extensive evidence for medication efficacy in child and adolescent anxiety disorders exists for OCD. While the first controlled trial demonstrating medication efficacy in OCD was with clomipramine, the first-line agents for treating OCD are the selective serotonin reuptake inhibitors (SSRIs) due to their superior risk and safety profiles. Clomipramine and three SSRIs have been FDA approved for the treatment of OCD in youth: fluoxetine (Prozac), fluvoxamine (Luvox) and sertraline (Zoloft). Other medications in the family of SSRIs include paroxetine (Paxil), citalopram (Celexa) and escitalopram (Lexapro), however they do not have FDA approval for treating OCD in youth. There is no evidence currently to suggest that any particular SSRI is superior in the treatment of OCD. The SSRIs have been well studied in adults, and there are now also several studies showing the safety and efficacy of these medications in children and adolescents with OCD.

The effective treatment of OCD frequently requires higher doses of SSRIs compared to the dosages commonly used to treat depression or other anxiety disorders. Similar to the treatment of other anxiety disorders, however, it is often necessary to start with low doses and proceed slowly in advancing the dose in order to avoid adverse side effects. It is safe to increase the dose weekly so long as no side effects are reported, however it may be necessary to advance more slowly in children who are sensitive to adverse effects. Table 1 below offers some guidelines for starting doses and target doses of various SSRIs. As described in the previous chapter on anxiety disorders, typical SSRI side effects include gastrointestinal upset, diarrhea, headaches, sexual dysfunction, insomnia, sedation and/or agitation. Manic episodes can also be induced in those individuals predisposed to bipolar disorder. Additionally, an increased risk of suicidal ideation and behavior has been noted in youth taking antidepressants and has resulted in black-box warnings for these medications whether prescribed for depression or anxiety.

Once a medication is at a therapeutic dose, the medication trial for OCD should typically be continued for at least eight weeks and preferably twelve to sixteen weeks. Some studies have even suggested that continued benefits may accrue for months beyond this initial period, so patience should be encouraged. It should be emphasized that pharmacologic treatments for OCD are generally only partially effective. Typically, the goal of treatment is focused on symptom reduction and improved functioning. Once a medication has shown some benefit in addressing OCD symptoms, it can be difficult to decide how long to continue treatment. Many individuals with OCD experience their illness as a chronic condition and find medication treatment to be helpful indefinitely. Since this illness often presents in childhood, however, it is natural that youth and their families would want to reassess the necessity of the medication periodically. At least a year of treatment is generally necessary. In general, it is best to continue medication treatments until the symptoms are under good control and remain in good control for several months before considering a careful tapering. Additionally, relapse-prevention and psychotherapeutic techniques for symptom management should be emphasized prior to medication discontinuation.

It is often helpful to consider a very slow taper off medication (i.e. over a period of several months) rather than a more rapid discontinuation so that re-emerging symptoms can be recognized before the medication is completely discontinued.

Clomipramine (Anafranil) can be considered as a second-line agent for the treatment of OCD. It is usually only considered after a patient has failed adequate trials of at least two SSRIs. Clomipramine is a tricyclic antidepressant with serotonergic reuptake inhibition effects. It has been FDA approved for the treatment of OCD in youth, but it is generally reserved for cases that have not responded to alternative medication interventions due to the risk of serious adverse effects. The majority of clomipramine's side effects are relatively benign, such as dry mouth, sedation, dizziness, constipation and urinary hesitancy. More serious adverse effects can occur, however, such as tachycardia and cardiac conduction problems. Clomipramine, like other tricyclic antidepressants, can be lethal in overdose and the therapeutic window is relatively narrow. Other toxic effects in overdose include seizures and coma. Consequently, ECGs must be checked before and during the course of a tricyclic antidepressant trial, with special attention to evidence of QTc prolongation, which may be a precursor to ventricular tachyarrthymias. Serum drug levels also must be monitored so as not to exceed 400ng/ml. As a result, clomipramine is typically only prescribed after consultation with a psychiatrist.

Atypical antipsychotics are another class of medications that are sometimes used to augment treatment for severe and treatment-resistant OCD. Medications in this class include risperidone (Risperdal), olanzapine (Zyprexa), quetiapine (Seroquel), ziprasidone (Geodon), aripiprazole (Abilify) and paliperidone (Invega). None of these medications has been FDA approved for this indication in youth. Atypical antipsychotics have several potentially serious adverse effects including the risk of substantial weight gain, hyperlipidemia, diabetes, tardive dyskinesias and neuroleptic malignant syndrome. Consequently, consultation with a child psychiatrist is generally warranted before starting one of these agents.

Table 1. SSRIs and typical daily dosing

Medication Name	Starting Dose	Target Doses
Fluoxetine	5-10 mg	10-60 mg
Sertraline	25-50 mg	50-200 mg
Paroxetine	5-10 mg	10-60 mg
Fluvoxamine	25-50 mg	100-300 mg divided b.i.d.
Citalopram	5-10 mg	10-60 mg
Escitalopram	5-10 mg	10-30 mg

Conclusion

Obsessive compulsive disorder is a specific anxiety disorder that typically presents in early life and often evolves into a chronic condition. While it can be very challenging to diagnose, there are evidence-based treatments available for children with OCD, so the timely identification of this illness can improve the quality of life of these youth and their families. Optimal treatment typically involves a combination of psychotherapeutic and pharmacologic treatment. Consequently, collaboration with specialty providers is usually required.

References

American Academy of Child and Adolescent Psychiatry. Practice parameters for the assessment and treatment of children and adolescents with obsessive-compulsive disorder. *J. Am. Acad. Child Adolesc. Psychiatry* 1998;37(suppl 10):27-45.

Franklin ME, Abramowitz JS, Kozak MJ, Levitt JT, Foa EB. Effectiveness of exposure and ritual prevention for obsessive-compulsive disorder: randomized compared with nonrandomized samples. *J. Consult Clin. Psychol.* 2000;68:594-602.

Geller D, Biederman J, Faraone SV, et al. Clinical correlates of obsessive compulsive disorder in children and adolescents referred to specialized and nonspecialized clinical settings. *Depress Anxiety 2000*;11:163-168.

Geller DA, Biederman J, Stewart SE, et al. Which SSRI? A meta-analysis of pharmacotherapy trials in pediatric obsessive-compulsive disorder. *Am. J. Psychiatry* 2003;160:1919-1928.

Geller DA, Hoog SL, Heiligentein JH, et al. Fluoxetine treatment for obsessive-compulsive disorder in children and adolescents: a placebo-controlled clinical trial. *J. Am. Acad. Child Adolesc. Psychiatry* 2001;40:773-779.

March JS, Biederman J, Wolkow R, et al. Sertraline in children and adolescents with obsessive-compulsive disorder: a multicenter randomized controlled trial. *J. Am. Med. Assoc.* 1998;280:1752-1756.

March J, Frances A, Kahn D, Carpenter D. Expert Consensus Guidelines: Treatment of Obsessive-Compulsive Disorder. *J. Clin. Psychiatry* 1997;58(suppl 4):1-72.

March J, Mulle K. *OCD in Children and Adolescents: A Cognitive-Behavioral Treatment Manual.* New York, NY: Guilford Press;1998.

The Pediatric OCD Treatment Study (POTS) Team. Cognitive-behavior therapy, sertraline, and their combination for children and adolescents with obsessive-compulsive disorder. The Pediatric OCD Treatment Study (POTS) Randomized Controlled Trial. *J. Am. Med. Assoc.* 2004;292:1969-1976.

Riddle MA, Reeve EA, Yaryura-Tobia JA, et al. Fluvoxamine for children and adolescents with obsessive-compulsive disorder: a randomized, controlled, multicenter trial. *J. Am. Acad. Child Adolesc Psychiatry* 2001;40: 222-229.

Scahill L, Riddle MA, McSwiggin-Hardin M, et al. Children's Yale-Brown Obsessive-Compulsive Scale: reliability and validity. *J. Am. Acad. Child Adolesc. Psychiatry* 1997;36:844-852.

Section VI. Sexuality

In: Behavioral Pediatrics, 3rd Edition
Editor: D. E. Greydanus et al.

ISBN 978-1-60692-702-1
© 2009 Nova Science Publishers, Inc.

Chapter 18

Childhood and Adolescent Sexuality

Donald E. Greydanus, Artemis K. Tsitsika,
Lyubov A. Matytsina and Antonio C. Sison

Abstract

Human sexuality is a complex phenomenon involving the interaction of one's biologic sex, core gender identity, and gender role behavior. Successful completion of normal stages of sexuality development is important for children and adolescents to allow for optimal life as an adult. Controversies arise for clinicians as they work with their pediatric patients regarding health care sexuality issues. It is important that clinicians help these patients in an unbiased and neutral manner. As adults, these children and adolescents will function in a number of sexuality roles, whether heterosexual, homosexual, or bisexual. This chapter reviews many of these complex and critical issues that involve the fascinating development of human sexuality in pediatric patients.

Introduction

Sexuality education is the knowledge that we are all sexual human beings, that our sexuality is part of our lives and can be an enhancement or enrichment of our total personality.
Mary Calderone MD

Sexuality is a complex phenomenon involving interaction between one's a) *biologic sex*; b) *core gender identity* (sense of maleness and femaleness); c) *gender role behavior* (nonsexual as well as sexual) (Tables 1 and 2). Sexuality is also a basic yet profound recognition that humans need other humans and that this human capacity to give and receive love represents a continuum from birth to death. Human sexuality involves the process of the individual at any age interacting with others and how one learns to get others to interact with oneself. As sexuality develops, the success or failure experienced by the child and teenager has much to do with eventual success or failure as an adult. Childhood sexuality is often viewed in terms of how concepts of human sexuality progress throughout stages of childhood - *infancy, toddlerhood, preschool period, school age period,* and *adolescence* (Appendix A). A key component to the healthy development of the teenager is how he/she proceeds with the stages of adolescent sexuality. *Adolescence* is the critical period of physical, psychosocial, as well as cognitive growth, leading from childhood to maturation and adult life. *Puberty* is the word used to describe the physical-somatic changes of adolescence. During the adolescent years, the individual must develop a healthy self-esteem and also sexual comfort---learning to deal with those in his/her "sexual" universe.

Table 1. Components of sexuality

Biologic Sex	The biologic sex (XX or XY) is determined at conception, but postnatal sex hormones also have influence on the developing fetus. Between the sixth and twelfth fetal week, androgens program the XY fetus to develop biologically, and to some extent, behaviorally into a male. The presence of female hormones along with the absence of a critical level of fetal androgens allows the XX fetus to develop into a normal female. Rare situations involving an excess or deficiency of sex hormones can alter the normal male or female outcome; likewise, chromosomal abnormality can cause intersex conditions. However, in nearly all cases, the XX or XY fetus is normally programmed in a poorly understood manner; and the biologic sex is clearly assigned at birth.
Core Gender Identity	During early childhood, individuals learn various behaviors associated with masculinity or femininity and then establish what can be called non-sexual gender role behavior. Thus, girls play with dolls and wear dresses; boys do not and normally will not even consider such activities.
Gender Role Behavior	Gender role behavior from a sexual viewpoint refers to behavior influenced or precipitated by a personal desire for some type of sexual pleasure. This desire for physical sex resulting in orgasm is mainly explored during adolescence and frequently modified during adulthood. However, many experts emphasize that the sexual orientation (heterosexual or homosexual) of an individual develops in childhood by ages 6 – 8, and not in adolescence.

Table 2. Definitions of terms in sexuality

Genetic sex - Chromosomally determined sex (XX, XY, XXY, XYY, XO, others).

Anatomic sex - Phenotypic appearance (male, female, intersex, includes variations such as congenital adrenal hyperplasia (adrenogenital syndrome) and incomplete masculinization syndrome).

Sexual dimorphism - The structural, physiologic, and behavioral differences between the sexes.

Core gender identity - Self-identification as either male or female, typically occurs by age 3 years.

Gender role identity - The summation of actions that indicate to self and society the degree to which one is male, female, or ambivalent. It is influenced by familial, cultural, and social role expectations, and includes but is not limited to sexual arousal and response. It may also be referred to as one's "sex role".

Transsexualism - The expression or belief that one's gender identity does not match one's anatomic sex ("woman trapped in a man's body, or the reverse").

Sexual (erotic) orientation - Defined by one's prevailing, unrepressed sexual longings and fantasies.

Heterosexuality - An erotic preference, including fantasies and experiences, for persons of the opposite sex, with minimal erotic interest in the same sex.

Bisexuality - The capacity to respond to both sexes to a significant but not necessarily equal degree.

Homosexuality - An erotic preference, including fantasies and experiences, for persons of the same sex, with minimal erotic interest in the opposite sex.

Homophobia - The condition in which those whose love and lust are attached to others of the same sex are dreaded or feared.

Anti-homosexualism - The pervasive and often institutionalized attitudes denigrating homosexuality. Experienced as self-negating and precipitating significant insecurity, ambivalence, and self-loathing toward persons who are homosexually oriented.

Hyposexuality - The paucity of erotic response or motivation.

Asexuality - The absence of erotic response or motivation

Transvestism - Dressing in clothing of the opposite sex, predominantly by males, for the purpose of erotic stimulation.

Cross dressing - Dressing in clothing of the opposite sex with the intention of expressing identification with or caricaturing the opposite sex role identity; does not generally involve erotic stimulation.

*Reprinted with permission: Behavioral Pediatrics, 2nd Edition. Eds: DE Greydanus, DR Patel, HD Pratt. NY: iUniverse, pages 331-333, 2006.

Psychosexual Development

Sexuality begins at birth or even at conception. At age 8-10 months, infants become aware of their genitalia (penis or vagina) and by the age of three, they usually have developed a fixed gender identify. By the time of their fourth birthday, they perceive themselves as being either boys or girls for life. The psychoanalytic view of adolescent sexual development by Freud offers health care professionals a framework for assessing adolescent sexuality. Freud contended that adults develop as sexual beings from birth through adulthood (Table 3). Though various scholars disagree on the exact meaning of these stages, there is agreement that by the time a child enters puberty, he/she should have developed a good self-image, a sense of security, a willingness to trust others, and a conscience with a normal sense of right versus wrong. It is the parents that must first accept their children's gender, and, then, communicate to them that they are intact, beautiful, and well-formed. If this is not the case, major problems in adolescence and adulthood are likely to unfold.

Table 3. Freud's psychosexual stages of development

Oral Stage	Feeding; pleasure derived through the mouth; ages birth-1½ years; security and optimism develop, while conflicts at this stage may lead to distrust of one's environment and a sense of generalized hostility.
Anal Stage	Toilet training and control over self and environment through elimination functions; ages 1-6 years.
Phallic Stage	Discovery of genitals, pleasure derived through the genitals. Boys experience *castration anxiety*, fearing genital damage or loss. *Oedipus Complex* in males as a result of competitive feelings with the father is resolved when the boy develops normal identification with the father. Girls develop *penis envy*—similar concept for girls is called *Electra Complex*. This stage is considered ended when temporary resolution of the Complex occurs; ages 3-6 years.
	NOTE: Freud's controversial theories of psychosocial development provide a framework for understanding human psychopathology as a failure to resolve the *Oedipus* or *Electra Complex*.
Latency Stage	Child expands intellectual and social skills while repressing childhood sexuality development. End of this stage signaled by the onset of puberty; ages 6 to 9 years.
Genital Stage	*Oedipus* or *Electra Complex* is once again raised; the development of normal sexual health dictates successful resolution of this complex. Healthy adult sexuality begins to occur with puberty; ages 6-15 years.

A review of normal childhood behavior reveals that physiologic components to sexuality are evident at an early age (Tables 1 and 2) (Appendix A). During the first year of life (*infancy*), exploration is through mouthing and sucking while trust in the caretaker (especially the mother) develops; aggression may develop in the form of biting. Infants learn to be sexual by touching and being touched; how they are held, soothed, and nurtured impacts their emerging sexuality and sets the stage for their sexuality throughout life. Sexual exploration may involve the skin as an erotic organ and some genital touching. Male erections are noted even *in utero*; orgasm as a neurophysiological phenomenon can occur as early as the fourth month of life and is common in males 6 to 8 years of age. Female newborns often have leukorrhea or vaginal discharge as a result of maternal hormones.

During the *toddler* period (ages 2-3 years) children develop mobility and language skills; the process of autonomy is noted and parents learn to deal with the word "no!" The toddler also learns what boys and girls do, how sex roles are different, and the names of body parts. Masturbation or self-genital manipulation for pleasure is very common between ages 2 – 6 years. Children during the pre-school period (ages 3-5 years) continue with an interest in masturbation, but also learn more of the differences in males versus females; a curiosity develops about sex play experimentation and exhibitionism. Table 4 provides guidelines for distinguishing between experimentation and sexual exploitation. The reaction of parents to their child's growing interest in sexuality sets the tone for the incorporation of human sexuality into the child's sense of self esteem.

Table 4. Distinguishing sexual exploitation from experimentation

1.   What is the age difference between the participants?
If the children are not peers in terms of age or cognitive level, exploitation is likely.

2.   Is the activity consistent with the developmental level of the participants?

Pre-pubertal exploratory behavior typically involves mutual genital display, touching, and fondling; intercourse or attempted intercourse is atypical among preschoolers and is rare in the young school aged child (6-9 years).

3.   What is the motivation of the participants?

Young children are motivated to exploratory behavior by curiosity about differences and similarities in anatomy and pleasurable feelings associated with masturbation. The older child adds interest in sexual roles and sexual identity to the curiosity and pleasure motivations. Participants who are not mutually motivated by these factors may be involved in exploitative sexual contact.

4.   Is the activity consensual or coercive?
Mutual consent is typical of exploratory behaviors. Abusive behavior often involves elements of pressure, misrepresentation, force, threat, secrecy, or other forms of coercion. Although some of the threat or coercion is obvious and violent, the evaluator must take care to recognize subtle emotional pressure or the use of implied authority by an older child or adolescent in some cases.

5.   Is there an outside influence involved?
Two children or adolescents may be involved in age-appropriate exploratory behavior, but if the contact has been arranged for the pleasure of another older individual, it is exploitative.

6.   What is the response of the child to the contact?
Mutual exploratory behavior may engender some guilt feelings in children; however, feelings of anger, fear, sadness, or other strongly negative responses are unusual. Exploitation is more often viewed in negative terms by the child; however, some abused children will appear to have a neutral or positive emotional response to abuse. The victim's denial may mask the negative responses in some cases, or the child's emotional needs for positive aspects of the relationship may outweigh the negative aspects of the sexual abuse.

Reprinted with permission: *Behavioral Pediatrics, 2nd Edition*. Eds: DE Greydanus, DR Patel, HD Pratt. NY: iUniverse, page 299-301, 2006. (Adapted from De Jong, 1989).

Children first learn about their personal boundaries from their parents (e.g., that not all exploratory behaviors are appropriate in every place and time); thus, trusting relationships and open communication between them are very significant. Parents should also communicate the rights for privacy and hygiene, and the necessity to share fears and concerns with trusted adults (e.g., nobody is to touch their body inappropriately or have them keep secrets from either parent). The establishment of core gender identity develops as the child enters the *school-age period* (5 years of age to the beginning of puberty). The latency age child has same-sex friends and sexuality is often expressed with an intense interest in prurient or salacious stories, jokes, riddles, and songs; interest in masturbation may recede until puberty develops. However, latency stage children are naturally curious about the anatomy of the opposite sex.

These are normal developmental phenomena, and parental attitudes are a major influence on attitudes that children develop about sexual behavior and feelings. As noted by Mary Calderone:

Whatever happens, it is clear that by the time the child arrives at school, it has already received, for good or ill, the most profound as well as the most unchangeable sex education it will ever receive in the child's life.

If a parent finds a 4 year old masturbating and aggressively reacts to inform the child it is "unclean" and not "respectable", the child clearly learns to associate normal sexuality with negativism – a lesson carried throughout his/her life. If the natural curiosity of the latency age child is totally repressed, the child receives the wrong message about human sexuality.

Misinformation on the part of parents and failure to teach the child normal sexual concepts result in numerous psychosexual difficulties in adolescence and adulthood. It is curious to see 5 year olds who can name the most common body parts but not their own genitals. It is even more curious to see health care professionals contribute to this by not exploring such ideas with parents and by not even including the genitals as part of the normal physical examination. Health care professionals should teach normal concepts of human sexuality and encourage parents to do so also. Proper naming of their infant's genitalia (e.g., vagina or penis) is a step towards this goal. Other groups, such as religious and educational institutions, profoundly affect children and must actively join parents in the area of sex education of children and adolescents.

As the grade school child transitions into adolescence, their interests and actions regarding their sexuality expands. The manner in which the adolescent deals with his/her sexuality is far more influenced by what he/she experienced as a child at home, viewing and interacting with parents, than from what they may learn during adolescence. Unfortunately, the negative mixed messages they receive about human sexuality contributes to the many sexuality-related problems seen in many youth and adults: a) depression, b) serious rebellion against society, c) sexually transmitted diseases, d) unwanted pregnancy, e) incest, f) runaway behavior, g) adolescent prostitution, h) marital dysfunction, and i) sexual dysfunction. It is important to remember that sexuality is simply a very important, normal, and crucial part of life and that failure to deal with normal concepts results in major problems in adolescence and adulthood.

Attitudes and Sexuality: Masturbation

An excellent example of the potential detrimental effect that negative societal attitudes can have on sexuality is offered by looking at historical views on masturbation. For centuries, this persistent aspect of sexuality was condemned as sinful and/or harmful to human health. Some incorrectly attributed this conclusion to *Genesis 38:9* when Onan was condemned for not impregnating his brother's wife after the brother died. This was actually part of the *Levirate Marriage Concept* which was intended to assure survival of human civilization at a time of very high infant mortality rates and relatively short human life spans. Onan performed *coitus interruptus*, but his action was incorrectly called masturbation or *Onanism* by later generations. Galen (180 A.D.), the famous Roman physician, wrote that masturbation was a very harmful habit and when encountering a male who engaged in this practice, Galen warned:

> *Watch carefully over this young man, leave him alone neither day nor night; at least sleep in his chamber. When he has contracted this fatal habit (masturbation), the most fatal to which a young man can be subject, he will carry its painful effects to the tomb – his mind and body will always be enervated.*

In 1716, Bekker wrote a book call *Onania, The Heinous Sin of Self Pollution*, which strongly advocated the view that masturbation was immoral and caused many health problems. In 1760, an influential Swiss physician, Tissot (1728-1787), wrote what was to become a well-known book called A Treatise on the *Disorders Produced by Onanism*. His book offered this same thesis and such a conclusion became the dominant medical view for the next 150 years or more; it was taught in medical schools that most of human medical and mental illnesses were the result of masturbation.

Various treatments were devised to stop masturbation including prayer, diverse dermatological agents, opium, diet, genital cautery, electrodesiccation of rectum or genitals, devices to prevent penile tumescence (including the spermatorrhea ring with spikes in its middle), circumcision, clitorectomy, castration and others. From 1890 to 1925 there was an American group of surgeons (called the Orificial Surgery Society) who taught and practiced genital surgery as treatment measures for masturbation. The roots of such ideas are deeply imbedded in religious dogma and fear that masturbation injures spermatozoa – thus possibly interfering with the survival of civilization.

A gradual change in such attitudes was observed in the past century. During the early part of the 20th Century, authors stressed that masturbation as such may not be harmful, but guilt over such worry certainly can be injurious to mental health. By the middle of the 20th century, many physicians accepted this concept and numerous researchers began to study masturbation as a very common aspect of normal human sexuality. It was noticed that genital self-stimulation for pleasure is practiced by most adults in some manner or other without deleterious effects on human physiology.

Pediatricians now teach that "excessive" masturbation in infants may result from such problems as pinworm infestation, diaper dermatitis, tight clothes, non-specific genital pruritus, phimosis and other medical conditions. Freud's view that masturbation drained energy (psychic energy or libido) from children is not accepted now. However, it is known that certain masturbation variations can be harmful; an example is the adolescent *sexual asphyxia syndrome* – in which the young person attempts to partially hang himself/herself by the neck ("partial hanging") while masturbating in order to achieve an orgasm.

Current teaching among academic medical or psychological groups is that masturbation is not harmful by itself and can be useful as part of a therapeutic approach to correct various sexual dysfunctions. Some youth, encouraged by their "peer" journals, are encouraged to masturbate in order to relieve sexual tension. However, there still exists considerable worry by parents about the "perceived" effects of masturbation on their children. Thus, anxiety about masturbation and other important aspects of human sexuality remains today, especially because comprehensive sexuality education is rarely granted to children and youth in the United States. Young children reflect this ignorance and uneasiness about their own sexuality with resultant negative effects. As parents have the greatest influence on sexual decision making of youth, a partial solution for this complex issue is to encourage them to acquire a broad knowledge of human sexuality, which is consistent with their own moral philosophy and culture, and then to share this with their offspring. Health care professionals can assist in this goal as well, as they interact with children and youth.

The Role of Central Nervous System Maturation

Brain cells consist of neurons and glia; the glia support, nourish, and clean the neurons. After the billions of central nervous system (CNS) cells are developed by late fetal life, CNS *pruning* and *differentiation* occurs in an aggressive fashion in the young child and young adolescent. Approximately three-fourths of the brain growth in weight occurs by age 2, while CNS maturation continues throughout childhood and adolescence; this includes axon myelination, a process increasing the efficiency and speed of nerve conduction. The ability of CNS cells to adapt to challenges is called *plasticity*; another process is the *pruning* or *sculpting* of these cells starting in late fetal life and accelerating in the young child and young adolescent.

The excessive number of CNS cells that develops in fetal life is reduced by the process of *apoptosis* (programmed cell death) in which cells are destroyed; as the hormones of *puberty* are increasing, apoptosis accelerates, leading to massive death of neurons and the removal of half of the cortical synaptic connections. Puberty is a very significant neurobiological event that has profound effects on the growth and development of the adolescent.

Puberty

The hallmark of adolescence is the process of *puberty* (Table 5), a profound neurobiological/psychological event in the life of each child that prepares the way for eventual adulthood. The exact trigger for puberty is not yet clear, but it involves central nervous system (CNS) maturation with reduced hypothalamic sensitivity to gonadal steroids by changes in the GnRH pulse generator; there is also adrenal gland maturation (Biro, 2007).

The progression (Table 6) through puberty is predictable, but there is considerable variation in its onset, timing, tempo, and magnitude of changes (Table 7). There are 5 stages of pubertal development due to hypothalamic-pituitary-gonadal maturation, called *Sexual Maturity Ratings* (SMR) or *Tanner Stages* (Tables 8 and 9).

Table 5. Major physical changes of puberty

Major increase in genital system (primary and secondary sex characteristics)
Gaining of 25% of final height (distal growth, e.g., of feet, may precede that of proximal parts, e.g., the tibia, by 3 to 4 months)
Doubling of lean and nonlean body mass (gaining by 50% of the ideal body weight)
Doubling of the weight of the major organs
Central nervous system maturation (without increase in size)
Maturation of facial bones
Marked decrease in lymphoid tissue

Table 6. The sequential changes of puberty [a]

Adolescent Female	Adolescent Male
Breast bud (thelarche)	Early testicular growth
Pubic hair development (pubarche)	Pubarche
Height velocity peak	Testicular and penile growth
Menarche (onset of menstruation)	Nocturnal emissions
Axillary hair	Height velocity peak
Final pubertal changes, e.g., full breast, pubic hair, and completed height development	Marked voice changes
	Facial hair growth and final pubertal changes, e.g., full genital, height, and muscle development

[a] Normally over two to four years.
Reprinted with permission: *Behavioral Pediatrics, 2nd Edition.* Eds: DE Greydanus, DR Patel, HD Pratt. NY: iUniverse, pages 331-333, 2006.

Table 7. Variations in pubertal changes

Pubertal Changes	Age Range of Appearance (yrs)
Thelarche	8-14.8
Pubarche	9-14
Menarche	10-17
Testicular Enlargement	9-14.8
Peak Height Velocity (Male)	10-16.6
Peak Height Velocity (Female)	10-14
Adult Breast Stage (V)	12-19
Adult Genitalia (Male V)	13-18

Table 8. Sexual maturity rating or Tanner staging in females

Stage	Breasts	Pubic Hair	Range
I	None	None	Birth to 15 yr
II	Breast bud (thelarche): areolar hyperplasia with small amount of breast tissue	Long downy pubic hair near the labia; may occur with breast budding or several weeks to months later (pubarche)	8 ½ to 15 yr (some use 8.0 yr)
III[b]	Further enlargement of breast tissue and areola	Increase in amount of hair with more pigmentation	10 to 15 yr
IV[c]	Double contour form: areola and nipple form secondary mound on top of breast tissue	Adult type but not distribution	10 to 17 yr
V[d]	Larger breast with single contour form	Adult distribution	12 ½ to 18 yr

[b] 25% develop menarche in late III.

[c] Most develop menarche in stage IV 1 to 3 yr after thelarche.

[d] 10% develop menarche in stage V.

Reprinted with permission: *Behavioral Pediatrics*, 2nd Edition. Eds: DE Greydanus, DR Patel, HD Pratt. NY: iUniverse, page 306, 2006.

Table 9. Sexual maturity rating or Tanner staging in males

Stage	Testes	Penis	Pubic Hair	Range
I	No change, testes 2.5 cm or less	Prepubertal	None	Birth to 15 yr
II	Enlargement of testes, increased stippling and pigmentation of scrotal sac	Minimal or no enlargement	Long downy hair often occurring several months after testicular growth; variable pattern noted with pubarche	10 to 15 yr
III[a]	Further enlargement	Significant penile enlargement, especially in length	Increase in amount, now curling	10 ½ to 16 ½ yr
IV[b]	Further enlargement	Further enlargement, especially in diameter	Adult type but not distribution	Variable; 12 to 17 yr
V[c]	Adult size	Adult size	Adult distribution (medial aspects of thighs, linea alba)	13 to 18 yr

[a] Peak height spurt usually between III and IV.

[b] Axillary hair develops, as well as some facial hair.

[c] 20% have peak height velocity now. Body hair and increase in musculature, etc., continues for several months to years.

Reprinted with permission: *Behavioral Pediatrics, 2nd Edition*. Eds: DE Greydanus, DR Patel, HD Pratt. NY: iUniverse, page 307, 2006.

Eventually there is a rise in gonadotropins (Follicle Stimulating Hormone [FSH], Luteinizing Hormone [LH]), sex hormones (i.e., estrogen, testosterone), adrenal gland steroids, growth hormone, insulin-like growth factors (IGFs or somatomedins) and other hormones. *Thelarche* (breast budding or SMR 2) is the first clinical evidence of puberty in females, developing between 6 and 14 years of age, typically between 11 and 12 years of age; *menarche* (onset of menstruation) usually follows in 1 to 3 years in SMR 4, often between 12 and 13 years of age (range of 10 -17 years). The first clinical event of puberty (SMR 2) in the male is enlarged testicles (over 3 mL or 2.5 cm in diameter) and scrotal thinning; ejaculation is seen at SMR 3 and fertility at SMR 4.

The growth spurt results in the final 25% of the adult height and is an *early* pubertal event in females (SMR 2) often at age 11.5 years and a *late* pubertal event in males (SMR-4), typically at age 13.5 years of age; the average growth spurt lasts 24 to 36 months. Those who have early (precocious) or late (delayed) puberty can have considerable psychosocial consequences. For example, the female and male who develops much earlier than peers, may be subjected to sexual behavior (including abuse) much earlier than peers who develop puberty at a normal chronological period.

Puberty stimulates more interest in sexuality in the growing and rapidly changing adolescent. Young teen males may be concerned about spontaneous erections, nocturnal emissions, and same-sex sexual experimentations. Males may also be concerned about the development of *gynecomastia*, or the usually transient development of breasts noted in as many as two-thirds of SMR 2-3 males. Though usually resolved in 12 to 18 months, gynecomastia may cause confusion about male identity and intense anxiety while undressing in front of peers in physical education *classes*. Reassurance from the trusted clinician about the benign nature of this phenomenon is very helpful to the male, though temporary release from situations of being undressed in front of peers may be necessary; surgery is also necessary in some situations of persistent gynecomastia, large breasts, or severe psychosocial stress. Education about puberty is an important and needed task for primary care clinicians.

Females may be worried about vaginal discharge (estrogen-stimulated "physiologic leukorrhea"), nocturnal sexually-oriented dreams, homosexual interests (including sexual experimentation), and pressure from peers and society to be sexually active (also seen in the male as well!), Both males and females may be concerned with the effects of acne vulgaris, body odor, seborrheic dermatitis, and other dermatologic effects of puberty. Crushes on non-parent figures is common in both sexes, and includes interest in teachers, youth leaders, coaches, and others. If adults misinterpret these "crushes", sexual abuse results with severe negative consequences for this adolescent. The influence of parents' reactions to these changes and that of the family's religious teaching have profound effects on how adolescents deal with these emerging concepts of human sexuality.

Normal Adolescent Sexuality Stages

Adolescent psychosocial and cognitive development is typically divided in three classic periods: *Early, Middle, and Late Adolescence* (Table 10). The *young* adolescent resumes previously acquired interest in the development of interpersonal relationships. Typically, the youth approaches this from a narcissistic viewpoint in which the individual's interest comes first and concerns of others are not considered. This "selfish" attitude starts with those of the same sex and extends to those of the opposite sex during mid-adolescence. First, there is exploration of one's own body linked with concerns of normality; then comes the comparison with peers of the same gender. Interest towards the opposite sex finally occurs; it is basically platonic for early adolescents and it is gradually expressed through sexual experimentation during middle adolescence.

Considerable energy is spent acquiring social skills and friendships with same-sex individuals. Thus, boys tend to develop "gangs" of males who engage in various behaviors, as each member tests the others in diverse aspects of adolescence. Definitions of masculinity are tested and confirmed within such groups. Homosexual experimentation and considerable false braggadocio about sexuality are quite common.

Girls tend to associate with a few very close girlfriends and then, to a lesser extent, deal with a larger group of females.

Table 10. Adolescent psychosocial development

COGNITIVE THINKING	Early adolescence (11-14 yr)	Middle adolescence (15-17 yr)	Late adolescence (18-25 yr)
	Concrete thinking: here and now. Appreciate immediate reactions to behavior but no sense of later consequences	Early abstract thinking: Inductive/deductive reasoning. Able to connect separate events, understand later consequences. Very self-absorbed, introspective, lots of daydreaming and rich fantasies	Abstract thinking: Adult ability to think abstractly. Philosophical. Intense idealism about love, religion, social problems
TASK AREAS	Early adolescence (11-14 yr)	Middle adolescence (15-17 yr)	Late adolescence (18-25 yr)
Family – Independence	• Transition from obedient to rebellious • Rejection of parental guidelines • Ambivalence about wishes (dependence/independence) • Underlying need to please adults • Hero worship ("crushes")	• Insistence on independence, privacy • May have overt rebellion or sulky withdrawal • Much testing of limits • Role playing of adult roles (but not felt to be "real" – easily abandoned)	• Emancipation (leave home) • Reestablishment of family ties • Assume true adult roles with commitment

Table 10.- Continued

Peers – Social/sexual	▪ Same-sex "best friend" ▪ "Am I normal?" concerns ▪ Giggling boy-girl fantasies ▪ Sexual experimentation not normal at this age: Done to ▪ Obtain "friends" ▪ Humiliate parents	▪ Dating, intense interest in "boys" ▪ Sexual experimentation begins ▪ Risk-taking actions ▪ Unrealistic concept of partner's role ▪ Need to please significant peers (of either sex)	▪ Partner selection ▪ Realistic concept of partner's role ▪ Mature friendships ▪ True intimacy possible only after own identity is established ▪ Need to please self too ("enlightened self-interest")
School – Vocation	▪ Still in a structured school setting ▪ Goals unrealistic, changing ▪ Want to copy favorite role models	▪ More class choices in school setting ▪ Beginning to identify skills, interests ▪ Start part-time jobs ▪ Begin to react to system's expectations: may decide to beat the establishment at its own game (super achievers) or to reject the game (dropouts)	▪ Full-time work or college ▪ Identify realistic career goals ▪ Watch for apathy (no future plans) or alienation, since lack of goal-orientation is correlated with unplanned pregnancy, juvenile crime, etc.
Self-perception	▪ Incapable of self-awareness while still concrete thinkers	▪ Confusion about self-image	▪ Realistic, positive self-image

Reproduced with permission from Dr. Roberta K. Beach, MD, Director Emeritus of Adolescent Ambulatory Services, Denver Department of Health and Hospitals, Denver, CO. Reprinted with permission: Behavioral Pediatrics, 2nd Edition. Eds: DE Greydanus, DR Patel, HD Pratt. NY: iUniverse, page 308-310, 2006.

The extent of female masturbation and homosexual experiences is unknown, but is probably less than that reported in males. This early adolescent phase of development is often referred to as the homosexual phase and is considered normal. Also, classic Freudian theory teaches that early adolescence is the time for re emergence of the Oedipus Complex and, if normal sexual health is to occur, it must be finally resolved (Table 3).

Middle adolescence is typically called the *heterosexual* stage, as youth acquire diverse experiences with the opposite sex; these experiences can be quite short (even one or two days) and intensive (Table 10). This mainly occurs during this "selfish" period, because of partner idealization, followed by disappointment and moving on to the next partner (e.g., serial monogamy phenomenon). During middle adolescence, depending on the youth's self-image, opportunity, and parental influence, there is a normal sequencing of this heterosexual development. It begins with interest in the opposite gender, and is followed by group dating, individual dating, and eventually sexual intimacy. Such intimacy runs an individual course including hand-holding, superficial versus "serious" kissing, petting, oral sex, anal sex, and/or vaginal coitus. This relationship is also described as narcissistic (generated from self-interest) and deeply embedded in resolution of the Oedipus or Electra Complex (Table 3). Late adolescence is normally the time to begin consideration of available adult lifestyles. The ability of having functional non-selfish relationships finally develops (Table 10).

Adolescent Coital Experience

Kinsey, 1948, reported that 20% of females aged 16 – 20 were coitally experienced. Sorensen, 1973, surveyed 400 American youth and reported coital experience in 44% of males versus 30% of females aged 13 – 15; this contrasted with 72% of males and 57% of females aged 16 – 19. Kantner and Zelnik published several well known survey reports from the 1970s; they noted that 30% of females 15-19 years were coitally experienced in 1971, 43% in 1976, and 50% in 1979; males aged 17-21 years were at 70%. The average age of sexarche was 16.2 years for females and 15.7 for males. The average age of sexual "debut" / first sexual intercourse is approximately the same (16 years) in Canada and Western (United Kingdom, France) and Eastern Europe (Ukraine, Russia). Early age at first intercourse can depend on many factors, such as personal or family income or level of education.

In the mid-1990s, 66% of females and 70% of males had coitus before their 18th birthday; 9% of 12 year olds and 38% of 14 year olds were sexually active—this increased to 47% by age 16 and 68% by age 18. This data also noted that 13% of those 14-17 years of age and 41% of those 18-21 years of age had 4 or more sexual partners; 79% of African-Americans were sexually active vs. 48% of Caucasians, and 56% of Hispanic students.

The 1999 Centers for Disease Control (CDC) Youth Risk Behavior Survey (YRBS) noted that 49.9% of high school students (12-18 years of age) were coitally experienced; this was broken down as 45.1% for Caucasians, 54.1% for Hispanics, and 71.2% for African-Americans. Also, 8% were coitally active before age 13 (12.2% for males, 4.4% for females) and 16% had 4 or more partners (19.3% in males and 13.1% in females). Adolescents are noted to practice *serial monogamy*, having one partner at a time, though often for a short time. Studies noted that 31% of sexually active female adolescents reported two to three sex partners, 9% had four or five partners, and 10% claimed over five sex partners.

Data from the 2002 National Survey of Family Growth notes that 47% of never-married female youth (ages 15-19 years of age-4.6 million) have had coitus and 46% of never – married male youth (ages 15-19 years-4.7 million) ever had coitus. For the males, this was a significant decline from 55% in 1995. Among sexually active females in the 2002 survey, 83% said they used contraception the last time having sex, in contrast with 71% in 1995. The 2007 YRBS noted that 47.8% of 15 to 19 year old adolescents are sexually experienced and 61.5% used a condom during the last intercourse, in contrast to 46.2% condom use in 1991.

Factors that Impede
Normal Sexuality Development

In the 21st century, pediatric sexuality develops in a society characterized by a rapidly changing environment, intense migration, and expanding opportunities to communicate with others in a modern global network that has become a widely-used resource for sexual health information among adolescents around the world. Major problems for childhood and adolescent sexuality that are emerging in today's global society include a change in the concept that heterosexual relationship is the norm, the development of casual relationships, and changes in what is termed the *love ideology.*

There is a noticeable cultural difference in the acceptance of and breadth of casual sexual relationships in youth. Examples of visible changes in the love ideology among young people throughout the world include the increase in the number of sexual partners, a rise in casual sex episodes, more openness to group sex relationships, and open discussion among youth as well as popularity of such relationships as a sex buddy (f*** buddy or FB), friends with benefits (FWB), and sexualized friendships (Table 11).

Table 11. Definitions of terms in adolescent causal relationships

Casual Relationship	Physical and emotional relationship between two people who may have a sexual relationship or a near-sexual relationship without necessarily demanding or expecting a more formal relationship as a goal. It is different from a one-night stand or more than just casual sex.
Friends With Benefits (FWB)	Two friends with a very casual dating relationship. The benefits can be really good, long, flirty conversations, make-out sessions, and sex with no other commitments.
Sex Buddy (F…buddy; FB)	Sexual partner (male or female) with whom there is no danger of attachment, commitment or other complications. A person with whom you have sexual relations, on the mutual understanding that you both want sex and nothing more.

There is enormous influence from the mass media on adolescents around the world in which sex is often presented as a casual pastime that is normative behaviour without negative consequences. The media (television, movies) and the internet present the message that "everyone is doing it and having fun." Some youth view oral sex as not "real sex" and use it to maintain a state of "technical" virginity, not realizing that sexually transmitted diseases are acquired with this form of sexual behavior including gonorrhea, syphilis, herpes, human papillovirus infection, and HIV. One study of 9th graders in San Francisco noted that nearly 30% were engaged in oral sex and 13.5% intended to have oral sex in the next six months (Halpern-Fisher, 2005); another study of 10th graders in New England noted that nearly 48% of the males and 42% of the girls reported experience with oral sex (Prinstein, 2003).

Adolescent Pregnancy and Sexually Transmitted Diseases

Since young people often lack comprehensive information about human sexuality, it is not surprising to note that these millions of sexually active youth produce approximately 800,000 pregnancies and several million sexually transmitted disease (STDs) cases each year in the United States. Such behavior also results in 31,000 pregnancies in females 15 years of age or under and in approximately 400,000 annual abortions in females under 20 years of age. Adolescent females account for 13% of all U.S. births (4,158,212 in 1992) and 26% of all abortions. The birth rate was 48.5/1000 in 2000, 45.9 in 2001, 43 in 2002, 40.5 in 2005, and 41.9 in 2006. The negative psychosocial risks to the adolescent mother and offspring are well described in the literature. Marriage is often not seen as a consequence of adolescent pregnancy in contemporary American society; 11% of teens are married before age 18 and percentage of teen births taking place out of marriage has risen from 15% in 1960 to 80% in 1999. The divorce rate among adults is 50% and 70% among teens.

Hypersexuality

The term, *hypersexuality*, has been used in various ways to refer to adolescent sexual behaviour. However, it should be used to refer to inappropriate or ill-regulated behavior and can be a cause of disruption among children and adolescents who are hospitalized for psychiatric disorders. It refers to "inappropriate" sexual behavior that involves sexual fantasies that increase abruptly in frequency and become of sufficient severity to disrupt expected or usual functioning. Though not a common cause of hypersexuality, virilization should be considered in its differential diagnosis.

Sexual Abuse

Although most data on sexual abuse is focused on females, recent research is acknowledging that males are also sexually abused. Surveys of adults note 27% of adult females were sexually abused, with a peak at 16-19 years of age; 25% of college females report sexual assault at some point in their lives. The child and adolescent must survive in a world with many dangers of unwanted sexual and physical abuse (chapter 26). There are 3 million reported annual cases of abuse in those under 18 years in the US; these are classified as *neglect* (53%), *physical abuse* (26%), *sexual abuse* (14%), and *emotional abuse* (5%). The abuse may be from the father, step-father, uncle, teachers, boyfriend, or in 10% to 33% of the cases, strangers. Finkehor noted that 5 of every 1000 college female reported being victims of incest from their fathers. Pregnancy and STDs may be signs of sexual abuse in young teens.

Between 50,000 and 70,000 cases of rape are reported each year, while the estimated number of actual cases exceeds 400,000 to 700,000 each year. Adolescents have the highest rates of rape and other sexual assaults. The United States Department of Justice notes there are 3.5 assaults per 1000 ages 12-15 years, 5.0 for 16-19 years, 4.6 for those 20-24, and 1.7 for those 24-29; half of these rapes and other sexual assaults are to those under age 25 and the female-male ratio is 13.5 to 1.

Sexual abuse is reported in 13% of females aged 13-14 in the United States; forced coital behavior occurs in over 70% of sexually active females under 14 years of age and 60% in sexually active females under age 15. Forced sex among sexually active teens occurs in 74% at 13 years of age, 60% at 14 years of age, 40% at 15 years of age, and 15% at 19 years of age. In the 1999 YRBS, sexual assault was noted in 12.5% of high school females and 5.2%

of males. The 2001 Youth Risk Behavior Survey reports 10% of high school girls with forced coitus in contrast to 5% of the males. There were 272,350 victims of sexual assaults (including rapes and attempted rapes) reported in 2006 (versus 191,670 in 2005) with over 40% being under age 18 years and an estimated one-sixth being under age 12. Factors increasing chances of being sexually assaulted include hitchhiking, living on the streets, and prior assault. Unwanted sexual overtures and harassment can even occur over the internet.

Dating Violence

Up to 87% of high school students receive unwanted sexual comments or actions at school-lewd comments, jokes, being touched or grabbed by others. Studies suggest that the majority of female youth eventually become victims of some violence while dating. This may be *physical, verbal* and/or *sexual* in nature. As many as 60% of adolescents experience dating violence and this involves youth from all ethnic groups and socioeconomic strata. Studies with college students note dating violence in 36% of the males and 59% of the females. Acquaintance or date rape may be the cause in 60-70% of adolescent assaults.

Adolescents need to learn potential signs that their dating partner may be too aggressive and may resort to violent means to control the relationship. Concerns in this regard should be raised if the partner is too controlling (Greydanus, 2003). Youth and their parents need to be educated that these are warning signs and to avoid dating or stop dating such individuals. Adolescents should also know that violent dating partners become violent spouses.

Table 12. Psychosexual development problems in youth with chronic illness/deformities

Concerns about ability to reproduce and parent
Difficulties finding peer friends
Doubts about future self-sufficiency
Increased risk for abuse (physical and sexual)
Increased risk for bullying and harassment
Limited social skills
Poor body image
Reduced self-esteem

Adolescent Sexual Offenders

Adolescents can also be involved in being sexual perpetrators (chapter 27). Teens under age 18 account for 20% of arrests for all sexual offenses (not including prostitution), 20-30% of rape cases, 14% of aggravated sexual assault offenses, and 27% of child sexual homicides. Adolescent sexual offenders represent a serious problem in the American society. These offenders commit multiple offenses, usually have more than one victim, and may not limit their offenses to one type of victim. These adolescents represent all races, social classes, and regions throughout the United States. This supports the need for comprehensive service delivery and the importance of having a continuum of treatment services that are available in all communities for this disorder. Within the context of anticipatory guidance, child health clinicians can incorporate office screening questions regarding sexually deviant behaviors to detect aberrant or deviant sexual behavior, allowing for early referral and intervention (Table 4). They can play an important role in the education of parents about the importance of appropriate professional help for deviant sexual behavior in children and adolescents.

Chronic Illness and Physical Disability

Adolescents with chronic illnesses and deformities (i.e., cerebral palsy, spina bifida, others) are also invested in the development of their sexuality, even if society and parents are not focused on these issues (Greydanus, 2008). Growing youth worry over their changing bodies, and disabled adolescents need to learn to accept actual abnormalities and tolerate deviations from an idealized body image. Table 12 lists potential complications in the psychosexual development of youth with chronic deformities/illness. For example, youth with colostomies become anxious about being accepted because of odor, while those with arthritis become concerned about problems with pain as well as limitations. Some chronically ill teens are stimulated to coital activity to prove normalcy, while others are slow to develop healthy sexuality; the clinician can be of considerable help to both groups to encourage normal sexual development. Parents and clinicians should seek to help adolescent females develop a positive self-esteem and body image despite impaired fertility noted with various genetic and endocrine disorders.

Other Consequences Related to Sexuality

There are an estimated one million runaway youths, and an estimated one million adolescent prostitutes (male and female) who exist in the United States. Some youth run away from home while others are thrown out by parents or guardians ("throwaways"), leading to a harsh life on the street as homeless youth. Many will turn to prostitution, using survivor sex as a way to remain alive. Children and adolescents living on the streets of the *world* are the product of war, poverty, domestic violence, and abuse (physical, sexual, mental). Homeless youth are subject to many dangers of the street—as physical/sexual abuse, substance abuse, sexually transmitted diseases, various medical disorders and others. Their main medical treatment is usually through the hospital emergency department, if they receive any care at all. Estimates of the number of children and adolescents who live on the *world's* streets range from 30 million to 170 million. Children and youth are sold into slavery and prostitution in various parts of the world. There are an estimated 1 million children abducted or coerced into the global sex trade industry each year. Estimates suggest there are 300,000 child soldiers around the world—some as young as 10 years of age. Their duties are varied, from becoming overt soldiers to providing sexual services for the adult soldiers.

Responsible Female and Male Sexuality

Researchers and educators in sexuality often note considerable differences in how both sexes view sexuality. The male development of sexuality is termed presocial versus females who learn their early concepts of sexuality in the context of social relationships. American society conditions males early in their development to define masculinity as synonymous with such destructive concepts as dominance, competition, performance, and achievement.

The American media is often indicted in this regard for teaching males that masculinity implies that one is aggressive, has a "duty" to perform (whether scoring in basketball or coitus), and has an out-of-control sex drive that can only be controlled by one's partner. This same philosophy implies that if a girl gets pregnant (by not saying "no" or not using contraceptives), it is her fault, not his. Males are taught that "shared contraceptive" responsibility is not an important concept which applies to them. Even the media censors often remove the topic of contraception when coitus is demonstrated or implied. Insurance plans in the United States often cover prescriptions for erection dysfunction medications but not oral contraceptives!

Males lacking extended contact with their fathers for appropriate role model patterns are especially vulnerable to such misogynic cues from the media. Males are taught from early life and throughout life to be more distrustful and insecure than females. Males are taught to control their sexual thoughts in regard to males and to use homophobia as a guiding principle. Males are more likely to carry negative attitudes about their bodies from their childhood throughout adolescence and adulthood. Though males tend to masturbate earlier than females, they are more likely to avoid group masturbation due to societal homophobic attitudes.

The adolescent male is generally exposed to very limited sexuality education and receives little contraceptive information/services. Sexuality educations programs are often geared toward females, and birth control clinics often provide inadequate services to males or exclude males altogether. A common reason given by males for not using contraception is their limited knowledge base, and studies also suggest that the male exerts more influence than the female regarding the use (or non-use) of contraception.

Others conclude that the changes in sexual values in America over this past century have allowed males to be raised with much conflict and confusion in regard to their sexuality and in methods of sexual expression. This confusion and lack of control contribute to the high morbidity and mortality, currently described in adolescent males. The current adolescent male is exposed to a hostile environment that promotes violence (suicide and homicide), homophobia, limited sexuality education, limited exposure to medical services, and limited knowledge of disease prevention (such as use of condoms or self testicular examinations). This dangerous risky environment continues throughout adulthood. Health care professionals should be trained in techniques helping to talk with males and females about their specific concerns and needs. While females are expected to control their sexuality, males are not by society. Males use the Internet more for sexual purposes, though both sexes also use the Internet for social contact. Certainly more open communication between sex partners is important to increase effective contraceptive use for improved responsible sexual decision-making.

Clinicians as Counselors

Limited sex education can be invoked as a partial explanation for current adolescent sexuality statistics. Youth are naturally curious about sexuality and often experiment widely, especially starting during mid-adolescence. Today's society stresses the enjoyment of human sexuality but often, paradoxically, ignores the responsibility and potentially negative consequences of unwise sexual experimentation. Part of this is the "normal" narcissistic stage of adolescent sexuality, while part of it results from a society which exposes young people to sexual advertisements and promiscuous lifestyles that do not show the consequences of irresponsibility. As note, the modern media (cable T.V., videos, etc) has a profound effect on America's youth, without parents really being aware of what is being taught. Porno websites are also used by adolescents (especially males) for sexual education needs. Sex is presented on these websites in a non-realistic way, in order to please the experienced and not by any means educate the non-experienced.

As previously noted, most youth begin to overcome their narcissistic heterosexual experimentation in late adolescence; at this stage youth begin to prepare for adulthood by serious consideration of a job investment as well as an adult lifestyle. Relationships in late adolescence should switch from "selfish" concerns to overt caring about the other individual, which should be the goal of adult sexual relationships. Unfortunately, the high rate of divorce and sexual dysfunction reported in current adult populations indicates that this is not always the case.

The result of fewer teens being sexually active and more of the sexually-active teens using contraception has resulted in a decline in adolescent pregnancy from the early 1990s to the early part of the 21st century. However, despite access to effective contraception and use of condoms, pregnancy rates in the United States, Western Europe, Eastern Europe, and Russia remain high.

Primary care clinicians can encourage those who are abstinent to continue with this choice until they really feel mature and ready to become involved in a sexual relationship. Abstinence is the best way to prevent unwanted pregnancy and sexually transmitted diseases (STDs). Primary care clinicians should be prepared to ask basic questions about their teenage patients' sexuality, including if they are sexually active, what type of sex are they doing, when was the last time, how many partners, are they using condoms, and are they interested in using contraception?

Clinicians should be aware of factors that place youth at increased risk for early coital activity, such as poor school attendance, early menarche, behavioral problems, drug use (including tobacco, marijuana, alcohol, methamphetamine, heroin, cocaine, others), absence of religious ties, limited training in refusal of unwanted sex, survival sex, and others. Those who choose to be sexually active should have appropriate information about contraception and STD protection. Role plays on refusal of unwanted sex or convincing one's partner to use effective contraceptive methods if sexually active is about to take place, are very helpful in this education.

Sexuality education is important for all adolescents and should be offered as well as encouraged by various segments of society, including parents, clinicians, and schools. One survey of adults in the United States (N of 1,096) looked at three types of sex education in schools: abstinence-only, comprehensive sexuality education, and condom instruction; abstinence-only programs received the lowest public support at 36% and the highest level of opposition by the surveyed public at 50%. Research has noted the failure of abstinence-only programs to provide sufficient information about sexuality to allow adolescents to reduce unwanted pregnancy and sexually transmitted diseases.

Advice about sexuality should be provided in a friendly, confidential, and safe manner. The attitudes and beliefs of clinicians can influence their ability and willingness to provide counsel for teens regarding sexual orientation, pregnancy, abortion, contraception, and STDs. Clinicians can introduce the subject of sexuality into the doctor-patient communication on a regular basis and set the youth at ease while talking about sexuality. Youth may have a hidden agenda regarding various aspects of sexuality, and clinicians should be attuned to this agenda. A number of factors can compromise sexual health and careful screening will often uncover these issues. Sexuality involves various family, legal, ethical, moral, and religious issues and clinicians need training to be able to help these youth as these various factors influence the youth.

Anticipatory guidance by clinicians is important to promote healthy sexuality development in children as well as adolescents and prevent complications (as unwanted pregnancy, STDs, abuse). Youth involved in abusive relationships need the guidance of trusted clinicians to steer them toward healthy adulthood. Counselling can encourage the growth of various resiliency factors that promote healthy sexuality and healthy living, enabling these youth to deal with adversities and lead a productive adolescent as well as adult life. These factors include a sense of belonging with other peers, acquiring a healthy value system, receiving appropriate education (including sexuality education), and learning to enjoy the fascinating phenomenon of life itself. Youth need an adviser and a guide in life, one who can provide support and accurate education in important facets of life, such as human sexuality. One should follow local laws for confidentiality and provision of reproductive rights.

Conclusion

Primary care clinicians should understand and appreciate the importance of sexuality in the lives of the children and adolescents they care for in their practices. Normal sexuality is a critical part of normal growth and development. Children and adolescents need knowledgeable health care professionals who can supplement the parents' teaching about human sexuality in a confidential and sensitive manner. Clinicians can also learn of potential problems with sexuality development, including unwanted pregnancy, sexually transmitted diseases, sexual assault, dating violence, homosexuality and others. Adolescents who are not sexually active, can be encouraged to continue in this lifestyle. Those who choose to be sexually active, need information about STDs/STIs (safe sex) and pregnancy prevention (i.e., contraception). Counselling about fertility, sexual dysfunction, and other aspects of sexuality is an important role for clinicians caring for adolescent (See Appendix A).

Acknowledgement

This chapter is adapted with permission from:

Greydanus DE, Fonseca H, Pratt HD: "Childhood and Adolescent Sexuality" In: *Behavioral Pediatrics, 2nd Ed.* Eds: DE Greydanus, DR Patel, HD Pratt. NY and Lincoln, NE: iUniverse Publishers, ch. 12: 295-330, 2006.

Greydanus DE, Sison AC: "Homosexual Attraction and Adolescent Sexuality" In: *Behavioral Pediatrics, 2nd Ed.* Eds: DE Greydanus, DR Patel, HD Pratt. NY and Lincoln, NE: iUniverse Publishers, ch. 13: 331-352, 2006.

Greydanus DE, Tsitsika AK, Matytsina LA, Sison AC: Pediatric and Adolescent Sexuality. In: *Pediatric and Adolescent Sexuality and Gynecology.* Eds; HA Omar, DE Greydanus, A Tsitsika, L Matytsina, DR Patel, J Merrick. NY: Nova Science Publishers, Inc. Ch. 2, 2009.

Appendix A. Anticipatory Guidance: Sex Education

Age	Child's needs or interests	Anticipatory guidance
Newborn	▪ Cuddling, sucking, loving touch (foundations for security, trust and later ability to give physical affection are established now)	▪ Teach parents the importance of touch, of warm, loving cuddling ▪ Encourage breastfeeding, front packs, rocking chairs ▪ "You can't spoil a baby at this age – it's okay to pick her up when she cries" ▪ Observe parents' interactions with newborn – demonstrate behaviors if parents seem uncomfortable ▪ Comment on role expectations – by choosing "pink or blue" we are already sending sex role messages to the infant
6 months	▪ Infant discovers body ▪ Self-stimulation and touching of genitals	▪ Tell parents to expect this behavior and that it's normal ▪ Ask parents about their own attitudes toward infant self-stimulation ▪ Remind them, "Don't slap his hands", as this sets up negative messages (i.e., that part of your body is "bad") ▪ Show the parents the parts of genitalia – teach them the vocabulary to use ▪ Encourage questions – let them know sexually related topics are appropriate to discuss during health care visits
1 year	▪ Curiosity as to what daddy and mommy look like without clothes on	▪ Guidelines for household nudity. Explore parents' own attitudes – what's best is what they are comfortable with ▪ Children begin to establish gender identity by observing differences in male and female bodies ▪ Use picture books if nudity is uncomfortable ▪ Parents should avoid messages that convey nudity as "dirty" or "pornographic"

Appendix A. (Continued)

Age	Child's needs or interests	Anticipatory guidance
$1^{1/2}$ – 3 years	• Self-respect and self-esteem develop. Feelings form about being a boy or a girl • Effectiveness of toddler discipline at this age determines later ability to handle frustration and have self-control • Exploration of body parts is common • Bathroom activities are of great interest (toilet training) • Sense of privacy develops	• Teach parents how self-esteem is developed. Need for lots of positive feedback ("catch them being good"). Give praise and positive messages about being either a girl or a boy. Let children seek own preferences for sex role behavior (okay for boys to play with dolls or girls to play with trucks) • Discuss plans for discipline. Teach parents methods (e.g., time out). Emphasize how to give positive reinforcement ("I like it when you__") • Encourage parents to help children learn correct words for genitals and body functions (penis, vulva, BM) • Discuss toilet training – using rewards and reinforcing positive attitudes about genitals
3 - 5 years	• Child needs answers to "sexual questions" appropriate to cognitive level of development • Grasping genitals is clearly pleasurable, may occur when child is upset • Children become very seductive toward opposite sex parent • Role-modeling (assimilation of characteristics of same-sex role model) takes place • Children begin learning what is socially acceptable, what behaviors are public or private, and how to show respect for others	• Tell parents to expect sexual questions ("where do babies come from") and give examples of how to answer them • Give techniques for determining level of understanding ("where do you *think* they come from") • Child needs to learn it's okay to talk about sex • Give booklets or suggest additional educational materials • Prepare parent for child's seductive behavior • Encourage parents to support each other and put their needs as a couple first (bad time to get divorced) • Remind them to role model the kind of male-female relationship they want their children to imitate (because the kids will!) • This is the time to begin demonstrating that women have rights and men are equally responsible for outcomes
5 – 7 years	• "Playing doctor" is universal • Kids have learned parents' discomforts, starting with "keeping secrets" about sex • Peer discussions provide many ideas about sex – dirty jokes among playmates common • Four-letter words (for exhibitionist behavior) used for shock value • Starting school – so stranger awareness is important	• Let parents know that childhood genital exploration is typical – it satisfies curiosity about opposite sex • Ask parents about their own childhood experiences "playing doctor" • Discuss ways to handle the situation ("It's normal to be curious – we consider other people's bodies private – I'd like you to get dressed and play other games") • Same with four-letter words ("be cool") • Encourage parents to bring up sexual questions, rather than waiting to be asked, utilize "teachable moments" to reinforce that it's okay to talk about sex. Need ample family discussion to balance what is learned from playmates • Discuss sexual molestation as a risk – discuss prevention techniques to teach children

Appendix A. (Continued)

Age	Child/Teen's needs or interests	Anticipatory guidance
7 – 9 years	■ Child needs answers to more advanced sexual questions (often scientific) e.g., "How does the baby get into the womb" ■ Needs preview of changes in sexual development that will be associated with puberty ■ Values are instilled now that will last a lifetime (e.g., self-responsibility, kindness)	■ Ask if parents have been getting any sexual questions (if not, child may feel it's not okay to ask). Dispel myth that information leads to sexual experimentation or that child is "too innocent" to hear about sex ■ Encourage them to use experiences such as TV shows, mating animals, new babies in neighborhood, as opportunities to bring up questions ■ Assure parents it's okay not to know all the answers. Guide them to resources (books) for information ■ Give parents an understanding of wide range of pubertal development (e.g., breast budding at age 8-9 is normal) ■ Encourage parents to teach difference between facts and opinions, e.g., that nearly all young men masturbate is a fact; that masturbation is bad (or good) is an opinion (with which others may not agree) ■ Important to teach child the family values and beliefs, as well as facts
10 – 12 years	■ Pubertal changes are of great importance – hormone levels rise ■ Both sexes need to know about body changes, menarche, wet dreams, and sexual fantasies ■ Sex behavior "rehearsal" is common (looking through *Playboy*, spin-the-bottle games) ■ Questions about homosexuality arise ■ Need for privacy intensifies ■ Self-esteem is very fragile	■ *By now, caregivers should start giving anticipatory guidance directly to young teens as well as to parents* ■ Parents need to understand the normalcy of preadolescent sexual concerns and be willing to discuss them in a nonjudgmental way (last chance to be an important source of information – later it will be peers) ■ Empathize with parental discomfort ("sometimes we feel uneasy talking about sex, but-") ■ ■ Model nonjudgmental ways of asking questions ("some parents don't mind their children looking at *Playboy*, and some parents disapprove. What are your feelings about that?") ■ Parents must set aside time to talk with children about puberty and sexual changes ■ School and community groups (Scouts, Church) should be encouraged to provide sex education for young adolescents ■ Build self-esteem – preteens need lots of positive feedback

Appendix A. (Continued)

Age	Teen's needs or interests	Anticipatory guidance
11 – 15 years (early adolescence)	▪ Obsessive concern with body and appearances (breast size, penile erections, acne, etc.) ▪ Pubertal changes are completed – need for a solid understanding of reproductive physiology ▪ Sexual behaviors emerge (masturbation, homosexual encounters, sex dreams) ▪ "First dates" start – questions about "what is love" ▪ Peer pressure becomes significant ▪ Need for assertiveness skills, right to say "NO" ▪ Boys need to know they are equally responsible for consequences of sexual activity ▪ Both sexes need to be prepared to use contraception when the time comes ▪ Education about STDs, AIDs prevention is a priority ▪ Self-esteem still low	▪ At puberty, parents will reap the results of their past efforts ▪ Parents need to learn how to "let go with love" and let the teen take responsibility for choices ▪ Reflective *listening* is far more important than talking ▪ Affirm wholesomeness of sexual feelings ("it's natural to want to have sex") while conveying own opinions ("it would be wiser to wait until you're sure") ▪ Parent should be sure teens have access to educational resources (e.g., *books*) that will answer questions in detail ▪ Many heterosexual young teens have some experimental homosexual encounters prior to dating. They may need reassurance and information ▪ ▪ Parents need to prepare teens to use contraception – discuss realities, give permission, explain about resources. Dispel parental myths (e.g., that access to family planning promotes promiscuity) ▪ Message should be "wait until you're sure you're ready, then use reliable birth control each and every time" ▪ Do not give messages that "good girls" don't have sex – guilt induction leads to denial and inability to accept responsibilities for choices (e.g., unprotected sex) ▪ Risks of STDs and AIDs should be discussed openly. Help teen realistically plan for self-protection (abstinence, monogamy, condoms) ▪ Continue to discuss personal values (continue to separate facts from opinions) ▪ Continue to reinforce positive self-esteem *Caregivers:* The same anticipatory guidance should be given directly to teen in the office setting.

Appendix A. (Continued)

Age	Teen's needs or interests	Anticipatory guidance
15 – 17 years (middle adolescence)	▪ Sexual activity begins ▪ Services for sexual issues (family planning, STD, pregnancy tests) are essential ▪ Meaning of relationships is explored ("Does he really love me") ▪ Life planning becomes serious (high-risk low-income teens needs to see options beyond pregnancy) ▪ Increased independence can lead to risks (date-rape, sexual assault) ▪ Sexual preference becomes apparent to self – homosexual teens may feel much confusion and self-doubt	▪ *Ask parent*, "What have you done to prepare your teen to use contraception when the time comes?" "How much have you discussed STD or AIDS with your teen?" ▪ Encourage parents to give teens permission to obtain contraception, and acquaint them with resources and means ▪ Allow confidentiality and independence for teens seeking health care ▪ Parents can continue to raise questions ("What did you think of that TV scene that showed __?") and give teens a chance to look at choices and consequences. But be prepared for either unwillingness to talk or challenges to parental viewpoints ▪ Most teens do not want to discuss their personal sexual activities with their parents ▪ Suggest to parents that they discuss teen's plans for the future, and then ask how plans would be affected by pregnancy, or marriage, etc. ▪ Teens need to know family, society *expect* them to prevent unplanned pregnancy, STDs if they choose to have sex ▪ Discuss prevention techniques for sexual assault ▪ Sexual orientation should be asked about (rather than presumed) ▪ Referral to support resources may be helpful to gay teens or their parents if emotional or societal stress is present

Reproduced with permission from Dr. Roberta K. Beach, MD, Director Emeritus of Adolescent Ambulatory Services, Denver Department of Health and Hospitals, Denver, CO. Reprinted with permission: Behavioral Pediatrics, 2nd Edition. Eds: DE Greydanus, DR Patel, HD Pratt. NY: iUniverse, page 326--330, 2006.

References

Abma JC, Martinez GM, Mosher WD, Dawson BS: Teenagers in the United States: Sexual activity, contraceptive use, and childbearing: 2002. National Center for Health Statistics. *Vital Health Stat* 23(24):1-2, 2004.

Adams JA: Sexual abuse and the adolescent patient. In: *Essential Adolescent Medicine*. Eds: DE Greydanus, Patel DR, Pratt HD. NY: McGraw-Hill Medical Publishers, 333-340, 2006.

Alan Guttmacher Institute: Into a New World: Young Women's Sexual and Reproductive Lives. 1-56 pages, New York: The Alan Guttmacher Institute, (120 Wall Street, NY, NY USA 10005), 1998. (www.agi-usa.org).

American Academy of Pediatrics. Care of the adolescent sexual assault victim. Committee on Adolescence. *Pediatrics* 2001; 107:1476-79.

American Academy of Pediatrics. Sexuality education for children and adolescents. Committee on Psychosocial Aspects of Child and Family Health and Committee on Adolescence. *Pediatrics* 108:498-502, 2001.

American Academy of Pediatrics. Sexuality, contraception and the media. Committee on Public Education. *Pediatrics* 2001; 107:191-194.

Auslander, S. Rosenthal, J. Fortenberry, et al: Predictors of sexual satisfaction in an Adolescent and College Population. *J. Pediatr. Adolesc. Gynecol.* 2007; 20:25-28.

Bell DL, Ginsburg KR: Connecting the adolescent male with health care. Adolesc Med 2003; 14:555-564.

Biro FM: Puberty. *Adol. Med: State of the Art Reviews* 2007; 18: 425-434.

Bleakley A, Hennessy M, Fishbein M: Public opinion on sex education in US schools. Arch *Pediatr. Adolesc Med.* 2006; 160: 1151-1156.

Bourguignon JP: Control of the onset of puberty. In: *Pediatric Endocrinology: Mechanisms, Manifestations, and Management.* Eds: OH Pescovitz, EA Eugster. Philadlephia, PA: Lippincott Williams and Wilkins. Ch. 19: 285-299, 2004.

Brown JD, Strasburger VC: From Calvin Klein to Paris Hilton and MySpace: Adolescents, Sex, and the media. *Adol Med: State of the Art Rev.* 2007; 18(3):484-507.

Centers for Disease Control and Prevention Surveillance Summaries. *Morb. Mort. Week Rep.* 2008; 57 (SS-4): 1-36.).

Centers for Disease Control and Prevention. Youth Risk Behavior Surveillance- United States, 2001. MMRW Surveillance Summaries, 2002; 51:1-64. Available at: http://www.cdc.gov/mmwr/preview/mmwrhtml/ss5104a.htm.

Covington SN, Martinex PE, Popat V et al: The psychology of antecedents to adult reproductive disorders in adolescent girls. *Ann. NY Acad. Sci.* 2008; 113: 155-62.

Crime Victimization, 2006. US Department of Justice. Bureau of Justice Statistics, Washington, DC. NCJ 219413, December, 2007.

De Jong AR: Sexual interactions among siblings and cousins: Experimentation or exploitation? *Child Abuse and Neglect* 1989;13:271-279.

Dixon SD: Gender and sexuality: normal development to problems and concerns. In: Nelson *Textbook of Pediatrics.* 17th ed. Eds: RE Behrman, RM Kliegman, HB Jenson. W.B. Saunders Co., ch. 5.6.10: 470-476, 2004.

El-Gabalawi F, Johnson RA: *Hypersexuality in inpatient children and adolescents:recognition, differential diagnosis, and evaluation.* CNS Spectrum 2007; 12:821-7.

English A: Sexual and reproductive health care for adolescents: Legal rights and policy challenges. *Adol. Med: State of the Art Reviews* 2007; 18(3): 571-581.

Farrow JA, Deisher W, Brown R et al: Health and health needs of homeless and runaway youth: A position paper of the Society for Adolescent Medicine. *J. Adolesc. Health* 1992; 13:717-726.

Felitti VJ, Anda RF, Nordenberg D et al: Relationship of childhood abuse and household dysfunction to many leading causes of death in adults: The Adverse Childhood Experience (ACE) Study. *Am. J. Prev. Med.* 1998; 14: 245-257.

Finkelhor D, Hotaling G and Sedlak A: Missing, Abducted, Runaway and Throwaway Children in America. *First Report: Numbers and Characteristics.* Washington, DC: US Department of Justice, Office of Juvenile Justice and Delinquency Prevention, May, 1990.

Finkelhor D: *Child Sexual Abuse: New Theory and Research.* NY: Free Press, 1984.

Finkelhor V, Dziuba-Leatherman J: Children as victims of violence. *Pediatrics* 94:413-420, 1994.

Finkelhor V, Hotaling G, Lewis I: Sexual abuse in a national survey of adult men and women: Prevalence, characteristics and risk factors. *Child Abuse Negl.* 1990; 14:9-11.

Fonseca F, Greydanus DE: Sexuality in the child, teen, and young adult: Concepts for the clinician. *Prim. Care Clin. Off Pract.* 2007; 34 (2): 275-292.

Ford C, English A, Sigman G: Confidential health care for adolescents: Position paper of the Society for Adolescent Medicine. *J. Adolesc. Health* 2004; 35:160-7.

Forsberg M. *Adolescent sexuality in Sweden - A research review*, 2005, p 13-20.

Freud S: *Three Essays on the Theory of Sexuality.* Vol 7. London: Hogarth Press, 125-243, 1953.

Friedrich WN, Grambsch P, Broughton D et al: Normative sexual behavior in children. *Pediatrics* 88:456-464, 1991.

Greydanus DE, Geller B: *Masturbation: Historic perspective.* N Y State J Med 1980; 80:1892-96.

Greydanus DE: "Adolescent sexuality: An overview and perspective for the 1980's." *Pediatric Annals* 1982; 11:714-726.

Greydanus DE, Shearin R: Incest and sexual assault. In: *Adolescent Sexuality and Gynecology.* Philadlephia, PA: Lea and Feibiger, 244-261, 1990.

Greydanus DE, Patel DR: Consent and confidentiality in adolescent health care. *Pediatr. Ann.* 1991; 20:34-40.

Greydanus DE, Pratt HD and Dannison LL: Sexuality education programs for youth: Current state of affairs and strategies for the future. *J. Sex Education and Therapy* 1995; 21(4): 238-254.

Greydanus DE, Pratt HD and Baxter T: Sexual dysfunction and the primary care physician. *State of the Art Reviews: Adolescent Medicine* 1996; 7: 9-26.

Greydanus DE, Senanayake P and Gains MJ: Reproductive Health: International Perspectives. *Indian J. Pediatrics* 1999; 66(3):339-348.

Greydanus DE, Patel DR and Rimsza ME: Contraception in the Adolescent: An Update. *Pediatrics* 2001; 107 (3): 562-573.

Greydanus DE, Patel DR, Pratt HD, Bhave SY (eds): *Course Manual for Adolescent Health.* Indian Academy of Pediatrics. Delhi, India: Cambridge Press, 528 pages, 2002.

Greydanus DE, Patel DR: The female athlete: Before and beyond puberty. *Pediatric. Clin. No Am.* 2002; 49: 553-580.

Greydanus DE, Rimsza ME and Newhouse PA: Adolescent sexuality and disability. *Adolescent Medicine* 2002; 13(2): 223-247.

Greydanus DE (Ed): Caring for Your Adolescent. 2nd Edition. Elk Grove Village, IL: *American Academy of Pediatrics*, 606 pages, 2003.

Greydanus DE, Pratt HD and Patel DR: The First Three Years of Life and the Early Adolescent: Comparisons and Differences—Lessons for Child Rearing. *International Pediatrics* 2004;19:68-80.

Greydanus DE, Rimsza ME, Matytsina LA: Contraception for College Students. *Pediatr. Clin. No Am.* 2005; 52: 135-161.

Greydanus DE, Sison AC: Homosexual Attraction and Adolescent Sexuality In: *Behavioral Pediatrics*, 2nd Ed. Eds: DE Greydanus, DR Patel, HD Pratt. NY and Lincoln, NE: iUniverse Publishers, ch. 13: 331-352, 2006.

Greydanus DE, Patel DR: Adolescent health. In: *Adolescent Rheumatology*. Eds: JE McDonagh, P White. NY/London: Infomma Healthcare. ch 13:291-310, 2008.

Greydanus DE, Patel DR, Pratt HD (editors): Developmental disabilities. Parts I & II. *Pediatric Clin North America*. 2008; 55(5): 1071-1257; 55 (6): 1259-1425.

Greydanus DE, Omar H, Tsitsika A, Patel DR: Menstrual disorders in adolescent females: current concepts. Disease-A-Month 2009; 55(2); 39-114.

Guttmacher Institute. US Teenage Pregnancy Statistics. National and State Trends and trends by race and ethnicity. Available online:http://www.guttmacher.org/pubs/2006/09/12/USTPstats.pdf.

Haffner D: Facing facts: Sexual health for American adolescents. *J. Adolesc. Health* 22:453-459, 1998.

Halpern CT, Martin SL, Oslak SG et al: Partner violence among adolescents in opposite-sex romantic relationships: Findings from the National Longitudinal Study of Adolescent Health. *Am. J. Publ Health* 2001; 91:1679-85.

Halpern-Fischer BL, Cornell JL, Kropp RY et al: Oral sex versus vaginal sex among adolescents: perceptions, attitudes, and behavior. *Pediatrics* 2005; 115: 845-851.

Hatim HA, Merrick J: School sex education. In: *Adolescent Behavior Research: International Perspectives*. Eds: J Merrick, HA Omar. NY: Nova Science Publishers, Inc. ch. 11: 101-108, 2007.

Hibbard RA, Desch LW, Committee on Child Abuse and Neglect and Council on Children with Disabilities. *Pediatrics* 2007;119 (5): 1018-1021.

Hofmann AD, Greydanus DE: *Adolescent Medicine*, 3rd Edition. Stamford, CT: Appleton-Lange, 913 pages, 1997.

Johnston MV, Nishimura A, Harum K et al: Sculpting the Brain. *Advances in Pediatrics* 2001; 48:1-38.

Kann L, Kinchen SA, Williams JG et al: Youth Risk Behavior Surveillance-United States, 1999. *Morb. Mort Week Rep*. 49 (No. SS-5): 1-94, 2000.

Kanuga M, Rosenfeld WD: Adolescent sexuality and the internet: the good, the bad, and the URL. *J. Pediatr. Adolesc. Gynecol*. 2004; 17:117-124.

Leung AKC, Robson WLM: Childhood masturbation. *Clin. Pediatr*. 4:238-241, 1999.

Lin AJ, Raymond M, Catallozzi M et al: Relationship of violence in adolescence. *Adol. Med.*: *State of the Art Reviews* 2007; 18(3): 530-543.

Lyren A, Silber TJ: Consent, confidentiality, and other related issues in the care of adolescents: medical, legal ethical, and practical considerations.In: *Essentials Adolescent*

Medicine. Eds: DE Greydanus, DR Patel, HD Pratt. NY: McGraw-Hill Medical Publishers, ch. 3: 444-454, 2006.

MacKay AP, Duran C: *Adolescent Health in the United States*, 2007. National Center for Health Statistics. DHHS Publication no. 2008-1034, 2007.

Marcell AV, Monasterio EB: Providing anticipatory guidance and counseling to the adolescent male. *Adolesc. Med.* 2003; 14:565-582.

Matytsina L A, Greydanus D E: Contraception in high school environment. *Woman's Health*. 2006; 3 (27):115-120.

Matytsina LA, Greydanus DE, Danisson LL, Pratt HD: Strategies of Youth Reproductive Health and Sex Educational Programs. *Woman's Health.* 2004; 4(20):126-135.

Mitchell KJ, Finkelhor D and Wolak J: Risk factors for and impact of online sexual solicitation of youth. *JAMA* 2001; 285:3011-3014.

Montagu A: Touching: The Human Significance of the Skin. New York: Columbia University Press, 1971.

Muram D: Sexual Assault. In: *The 5-Minute Obstetrics and Gynecology Consult*. Ed: PJA Hillard. Philadelphia, PA: Wolters Kluwer/Lippincott Williams and Wilkins, pages 602-3, 2008.

Murphy N, Young PC: Sexuality in children and adolescents with disabilities. *Develop. Med.* 2005; 47:640-644.

Murphy NA, Elias ER, Council on Children with Disabilities. *Pediatrics* 2006; 118: 398-403.

Omar HA, Merrick J: Adolescents and Puberty. *Adolescent Behavior Research: International Perspectives.* Eds: Merrick J. and Omar HA. NY: Nova Science Publishers, Inc. ch 12: 109-114, 2007.

Ott MA, Santelli JS: Approaches to adolescent sexuality education. *Adol. Med.: State of the Art Rev 2007*; 18(3): 558-570.

Ott MA, Santelli JS: Approaches to sexuality education. *Adolesc. Med.* 2008; 18: 558-570.

Paul C, Fitzjohn J, Herbison P et al: The determinants of sexual intercourse before age 16. *J. Adolesc. Health* 27:136-147, 2002.

Pratt HD, Greydanus DE: Adolescent violence: Concepts for a new millennium. *Adolesc. Med.* 2000; 11:103-125.

Pratt HD, Patel DR, Greydanus DE et al: Adolescent sexual offenders. *International Pediatrics* 2001; 16:73-80.

Pratt HD: Homeless adolescents in the United States. *Internal. Pediatr.* 2002; 17:70-76.

Pratt HD: Office counselling for the adolescent. Prim Care Clin Off Pract 2007; 33:349-390.

Prinstein MJ, Meade CS, Cohen GL: Adolescent oral sex, peer popularity, and perceptions of best friends' sexual behaviour. *J. Pediatr. Psychol.* 2003; 28:243-249.

Rakic P: Genesis of neocortex in human and nonhuman primates. In: *Child and Adolescent Psychiatry.* A Comprehensive Textbook, 3rd Edition. Ed: M. Lewis, Philadelphia: Lippincott Williams and Wilkins, ch 3: 25-42, 2002.

Regushevskaya E, Dubikaytis T, Nikula M et al: The socioeconomic characteristics of risky behaviour among reproductive-age women in St. Petersburg. *Scand J. Public Health* 2008; 36:143-52.

Rennison CM: Criminal Victimization 1998: Changes 1997-1998 With Trends 1993 to 1998. Washington DC: Bureau of Justice Statistics, 1997. Available at http://www.ojp.usdoj.gov/bjs/abstract/cv98.htm.

Resnick MD: Protective factors, resiliency, and healthy youth development. *Adolesc. Med.* 2000; 11:157-164.

Rew L: Sexual health of adolescents with chronic health conditions. *Adol. Med.: State of the Arts Review* 2007; 18(3): 519-529.

Rome ES: "Adolescent sexuality." In: *Essential Adolescent Medicine.* Eds: DE Greydanus, DR Patel, HD Pratt. NY: McGraw-Hill Medical Publishers, ch. 22: 481-496, 2006.

Rosen DS, Rich M: The adolescent male. Adolesc Med 2003; 14: 525-737.

Rosenthal SL, Blythe MJ: Adolescent sexuality. *Adol. Med: State of the Art Reviews* 2007; 18: 425-587.

Santelli J, Ott MA, Lyon M et al: Position paper. Abstinence-only education policies and programs: A position paper of the Society for Adolescent Medicine. *J. Adolesc. Health* 2006; 83-87.

Shafii T, Burstein GR: An overview of sexually transmitted diseases among adolescents. *Adolesc. Med.* 2004; 15:201-214.

Siegel EJ: Adolescent growth and development. In: *Essentials of Adolescent Medicine.* Eds: DE Greydanus, DR Patel, HD Pratt. NY: McGraw-Hill Medical Publishers, ch. 1:1-16, 2006.

Silverman A, Reinherz H and Giaconia F: The long-term sequela of childhood and adolescent abuse: A longitudinal community study. *Child Abuse and Neglect* 20:709-723, 1996.

Sionean S, DIClemente RJ, Wingoode GM et al: Psychosocial and behavioral corrclates of refusing unwanted sex among African-American adolescent females. *J. Adolesc. Health* 30:55-63, 2002.

Sonenstein FL: What teenagers are doing right: Changes in sexual behavior over the past decade. *J. Adolesc.* 2004; 35:77-78.

Sorenson RC: *Adolescent Sexuality in Contemporary America.* NY: World Publishing, 1983.

Stewart DC, Hofmann AD: Adolescent sexuality. In: *Adolescent Medicine*, 3rd Edition. Eds: Ad Hofmann and DE Greydanus. Stamford, CT: Appleton and Lange, ch. 21: 457-472, 1997.

Strasburger VC, Greydanus DE: At-risk adolescents: An update for the new century. *Adolesc. Med.* 2000; 1-210.

Strasburger VC, Greydanus DE: The at-risk adolescent. *Adolesc. Med.* 1990; 1:1-198.

Swahn MH, Bossarete RM, Sullivent EE: Age of alcohol use initiation, suicidal behavior, and peer dating violence victimization and perpetration among high-risk, seventh-grade adolescents. *Pediatrics* 2008; 121 (2): 297-305.

Tanner JM: *Growth at Adolescence.* 2nd Edition. Oxford, Blackwell Scientific, 1962.

Tissot SA: *Onanism or a treatice upon the disorders produced by masturbation; or the dangerous effects of secret and excessive venery.* Translated by A. Hume. London, England: M. Chapins and Company, 1776.

U.S. General Accounting Office: Homeless Children and Youths. Washington, DC: US Government Accounting Office, June, 1989.

United States Department of Health and Human Services, National Center on Child Abuse and Neglect. Child Maltreatment, 1994: Report from States to the National Center for Child Abuse and Neglect. Washington, DC: U.S. Government Printing Office, 1996.

Werry JS, Zametkin A, Ernst M: Brain and behavior. In: Child and Adolescent Psychiatry. *A Comprehensive Textbook,* 3rd Edition. Ed: M. Lewis, Philadelphia: Lippincott Williams and Wilkins, ch 8: 120-125, 2002.

Wikipedia, the free encyclopedia http://en.wikipedia.org/wiki.

Wilson M, Joffe A: Adolescent medicine. *JAMA* 1995; 273:1657-1659.

Zelnik M, Kantner JF, Ford K: *Sex and Pregnancy in Adolescence*. Beverly Hills, CA: Sage Publishing, 133 pages, 1981.

Zilka NY, Matytsina LA, Gorbenko AC: Contraception and holistic approach of sexual health. *Reproductive Woman's Health* 2005; 2 (22): 153-156.

In: Behavioral Pediatrics, 3rd Edition
Editor: D. E. Greydanus et al.

ISBN 978-1-60692-702-1
© 2009 Nova Science Publishers, Inc.

Chapter 19

Homosexual Attraction and Sexual Behavior in Adolescents

Donald E. Greydanus, Antonio C. Sison and Kristin W. Guilonard

Abstract

Adolescence is characterized by rapid biological, psychological, and social changes. As puberty progresses, attraction to and sexual experimentation with the opposite sex is a classic feature of youth. Also, during early puberty, transient attraction *to* and sexual experimentation *with* members of the same sex may occur. Some adolescents go through a phase of homosexual behavior and proceed toward a heterosexual behavior pattern; other adolescents proceed toward a homosexual life pattern. This chapter reviews the definitional perspectives, evaluation, and management of issues related to adolescent homosexual attraction and sexual behaviors.

Introduction

Clinicians may not only care for heterosexual adolescents, but also gay, lesbian, bisexual, transgender, or questioning (*GLBTQ*) youth. Sexual behavior, whether heterosexual or homosexual, places adolescents at risk for sexually transmitted diseases or infections (STDs or STIs). However, adolescents with persistent homosexual attraction and sexual behavior additionally have to cope with social pressures associated with homosexuality that may place them at risk for various psychosocial problems as well as diverse medical complications.

Definitions

Table 1 provides definitions of terms used in this chapter and others related to the discussion of sexual orientation in general (see chapter 18).

Table 1. Definitions of Terms in Sexuality

Term	Definition
Anatomic sex	Phenotypic appearance (male, female, intersex) (includes variations such as the adrenogenital syndrome and the incomplete masculinization syndrome).
Antihomosexualism	The pervasive and often institutionalized attitudes denigrating homosexuality. Experienced as self-negating and precipitating significant insecurity, ambivalence, and self-loathing toward persons who are homosexually oriented.
Asexuality	The absence of erotic response or motivation.
Bisexuality	The capacity to respond to both sexes to a significant but not necessarily equal degree.
Core gender identity	Self-identification as either male or female, typically occurs by age 3 years.
Cross dressing	Dressing in clothing of the opposite sex with the intention of expressing identification with or caricaturing the opposite sex role identity; does not generally involve erotic stimulation.
Gender role identity	The summation of actions that indicate to self and society the degree to which one is male, female, or ambivalent. It is influenced by familial, cultural, and social role expectations, and includes but is not limited to sexual arousal and response. It may also be referred to as one's "sex role".
Genetic sex	Chromosomally determined sex (XX, XY, XXY, XYY, others).
Heterosexuality	An erotic preference, including fantasies and experiences, for persons of the opposite sex, with minimal erotic interest in the same sex.
Homophobia	The conditions in which those whose love and lust are attached to others of the same sex are dreaded or feared.
Homosexuality	An erotic preference, including fantasies and experiences, for persons of the same sex, with minimal erotic interest in the opposite sex.
Hyposexuality	The paucity of erotic response or motivation.
Sexual dimorphism	The structural, physiologic, and behavioral differences between the sexes.
Transsexualism	The expression or belief that one's gender identity does not match one's anatomic sex ("woman trapped in a man's body", or the reverse).
Transvestism	Dressing in clothing of the opposite sex, predominantly by males, for the purpose of erotic stimulation.

From Rowlett J and Greydanus DE: "Gender Identity" chapter 3 in *Behavioral Pediatrics*. DE Greydanus and M Wolraich (eds), NY: Springer-Verlag, 40-65, 1991.

Homosexual attraction and various aspects of sexuality in adolescents are better understood and defined with appropriate considerations of biological, psychological, diagnostic, and sociocultural perspectives.

Biological Perspectives

Though there has been considerable research about the etiology of homosexuality, controversy remains and further research is needed. Some maintain that homosexuality results from *in utero* sex hormone-controlled "programming" of the brain (hypothalamus) in combination with complex social learning factors in childhood. It has been observed that if a female (XX) fetus is exposed to excessive male hormones (as noted with some forms of congenital adrenal hyperplasia), the resultant female child may exhibit some "masculine" traits (such as seeking male aggressive play or ignoring doll playing).

Several genetic studies noted a higher incidence of homosexual concordance among monozygotic twins than among dizygotic twins. Although these results suggest a genetic predisposition to homosexuality, chromosome studies have been unable to differentiate homosexual persons from heterosexual persons. No consistent difference has been found in hormone levels between homosexual individuals and heterosexual individuals, although some data suggest that homosexuals respond differently to certain hormone injections vs. heterosexuals. Some researchers point out differences in hypothalamic size and structure or anterior commissure size, while others look for a potential genetic marker for homosexuality. However, there is no agreement on biologic differences at this time.

Psychological Perspectives

Psychological studies and theories abound regarding homosexuality, but so do the disagreements. Freud wrote that individuals began human life with bipotentiality; they could become homosexual or heterosexual, and in his view, usually the heterosexual aspect dominated. Freud did not consider homosexuality a mental illness, as noted by his famous 1935 response to an American mother of a homosexual:

> *"Homosexuality assuredly is no advantage, but nothing to be ashamed of, no vice, no degradation; it cannot be classified as an illness; we consider it to be a variation of sexual functioning produced by a certain arrest of sexual development."*

Diagnostic Perspectives

It was in 1973 when homosexuality as a diagnostic category was eliminated by the American Psychiatric Association. Seven years later in 1980, it was removed from its *Diagnostic and Statistical Manual (DSM-III)*; it is not present in the DSM-IV-TR edition. The American Psychological Association officially accepted this same concept in 1975. The 10th revision of the *International Statistical Classification of Diseases and Related Health*

Problems (ICD-10) states "Sexual orientation alone is not to be regarded as a disorder." This view reflects a change in the perception of homosexuality of most researchers from a pathological disorder to a variant of human sexuality. However, profound concerns still continue toward such declarations.

Same-sex Identity Acquisition Perspectives

The process of acceptance of a homosexual identity has been described by different researchers. Green (1974) identifies three stages in this process: a) first, feeling "different", b) then, developing a crush on a same sex person, and finally, c) becoming aware of his/her homosexual orientation. There may be a subsequent "coming out" phase in which the teenager seeks to reveal this "secret" to others, as family, peers or a health care professional. Troiden (1979) has outlined 4 stages in the development of a gay identity (Table 2). While this model may be a good guide from which to start, it may be too linear, and many experts contend that widespread disclosure should not be the only measure of integrated identity. Other factors, like geography, ethnicity/culture, family situation, support system, and legal and economic realities help determine the extent to which disclosure is possible.

Table 2. Troiden's Stages of Gay Identity Development

Stage	Name	Description
1	Sensitization	Before puberty, children feel "different" from peers, based on behaviors that are gender-neutral or atypical gender role choices. Few see themselves as different before puberty.
2	Identity Confusion	After puberty, awareness of same-sex thoughts and feelings. Lack of accurate information, socialization with other gay/lesbian youth, and/or positive role models increases isolation and confusion. Coping behaviors are developed, sexual identity is hidden, or identity of bisexuality may occur. When heterosexual peers are learning skills to form intimate relationships, lesbian and gay youth are learning how to hide their identity.
3	Identity assumption	Self identification and "coming out" occurs to other homosexuals. Positive experiences among gay/lesbian peers help strengthen identity. Strategies are developed to help manage stigmatized identity.
4	Commitment	Sexual identity is incorporated into one's life. Identity is shared with non-gay friends and family. Not all reach this step; integration depends on experiences with discrimination, personal strengths and weaknesses, and support and access to role models.

Ethnic and Cultural Minority Perspectives

For members of ethnic minority groups, culture, ethnicity and race form core components of identity. A sense of self is framed by these components as well as gender and sex roles. Primary identity is well established by the time an adolescent becomes aware of same sex feelings or attractions; also, in a society that discriminates on the basis of race and ethnicity, connections within the minority group are essential for survival. Within many ethnic groups, homosexuality is considered a "western" or "white" phenomenon, and being lesbian or gay is a rejection of one's ethnic heritage. Openly identifying as being homosexual may jeopardize support within an already marginalized group, and hence, many lesbian and gay ethnic minorities continue to stay closeted.

Parental Perspectives

The process of "coming out" for a homosexual youth can be very difficult, not just for the teenager, but also for the parents, who may feel they cannot talk to others and feel isolated. Parents may say it is "just a phase my child is going through" and may not take seriously the young person's exploration. They may feel that their adolescent's sexual orientation can be changed, or blame themselves for having a gay or lesbian teen. One can also see some parents who become so angry and threatened by this declaration that they physically abuse their teenager or throw them out of the house ("throwaway teens"), forbid them from talking about this to anybody, and/or forbid them from contact with other siblings in the family. Parents may also worry about increased risks of violence their children may face and fear that their teen may not become a happy, adjusted adult. They mourn the loss of never becoming traditional grandparents and never having their child married in a heterosexual relationship having children.

Social Perspectives

Past societal attitudes generally have been intolerant of same sex orientation, especially for males; various religions have often condemned homosexuality as being immoral. Homophobia (Table 1) is a negative attitude toward or fear of homosexuality or homosexuals, while heterosexism is the belief that a heterosexual relationship is preferable to all others; it implies discrimination against those practicing such forms of sexuality. Some adults prefer to identify sexual orientation by using terms like "lesbians" and "gay men" rather than *homosexual* which may imply pathology.

Epidemiology

A variety of sexual orientations have been described since the ground-breaking work of Kinsey et al, who surveyed over 5,000 adult males and 6,000 adult females in the 1930s and

1940s in the United States. This research concluded that 4% of adult males and 2% of adult females are exclusively homosexual in their sexual fantasy and sexual behavior; in addition, 50% of these adult males had a homosexual experience before puberty, 37% had at least one such experience leading to orgasm, and 10% were homosexual for at least 3 years after puberty.

Other studies have shown adult homosexual behavior and self identification to range from 1-8% in males and 3-7% in females. Among middle and high school youth, one study noted that over 10% were unaware of their sexual identity, and approximately 1% were self identified as bisexual. Same sex attraction statistics are higher, with up to 21 % of men and 18 % of women reporting some same-sex attraction.

Evaluation

Approach by the Clinician

The clinician should introduce himself or herself to the adolescent and explain that a complete medical evaluation includes both an interview and a physical examination. The clinician should also reassure the adolescent patient that whatever is discussed in the interview remains confidential except in situations in which the safety of the patient may be compromised, as with the youth having suicidal or homicidal thoughts or intentions. While evaluating an adolescent, the practitioner should not make assumptions about the youth's sexual orientation; for example, questions such as "do you have a girlfriend" to a male, while seeming innocuous can actually hinder communication.

Those who have same-sex relationships do not necessarily self identify as gay or lesbian, especially among ethnic and cultural minorities. It is essential, therefore, to be careful and clear in discussions about sexual relationships and orientation. In adults, a common sexual history question is, "Do you have sex with men, women, or both?" However, this can be perceived as being too aggressive and ambiguous by adolescents, since many teens do not define sex in the same terms as health care providers. A gentler question is: "Do you have a crush on someone?" This opens the discussion, is gender neutral, and does not broach sexual behavior at all. Another good follow-up question is: "Are you in a relationship with anyone?" Once the discussion on relationships is begun, more forthright questions can be asked regarding specific sexual attitudes and behaviors, such as "have you determined your sexual orientation?"

Self Evaluation of the Clinician

Part of the process of being a competent clinician is being aware of personal issues that may influence clinical evaluation and management. The clinician should be familiar with four interrelated psychosexual factors (Table 3) and review past experiences and personal feelings regarding these issues. This is important so as to minimize the risk for unconscious negative biases against the GLBTQ adolescent.

Table 3. Psychosexual Factors

Sexual Identity	This refers to one being genetically male (XY) or genetically female (XX). The clinician should conduct a thorough physical examination, including gross examination of the genitalia and determine the development of secondary characteristics or sexually maturity ratings.
Gender Identity	This refers to one's sense of *masculinity* and *femininity*. The clinician should observe the degree of masculinity and femininity of the adolescent and ask questions regarding their sense of being "male" or "female", history of cross-dressing (wearing clothes of the opposite sex [*transvestism*]), whether they would like to be a member of the opposite sex and whether they feel uncomfortable with their genitalia (*transsexualism*).
Sexual Orientation	This refers to the sexual attraction to the opposite sex (*heterosexual*), same sex (*homosexual*) or both sexes (*bisexual*). The clinician should ask questions regarding sexual attraction to the opposite sex, same sex or both sexes.
Sexual Behavior	This refers to the range of sexual activity. The clinician should ask specific questions on sexual activities, the number of sexual partners, use of prophylactics, use of sex toys, pornography, and use of alcohol as well as substances (as club drugs) prior to or during sexual activity.

The primary care practitioner ideally is comfortable in eliciting information regarding sexual fantasies, sexual history, and sexual behaviors when obtaining a comprehensive sexual history in adolescent and young adult patients. Though GLBTQ youth often wish their clinician would ask them about their sexual orientation and provide information in this regard, most primary care clinicians fail, tending to ignore this important aspect of their patients' lives. Clinicians must understand that homosexual youth have increased risks for depression, suicide attempts/completions, eating disorders, alcohol and drug abuse (including club or date-rape drugs), eating disorders, sexually transmitted diseases (including HIV), violence-related injuries (including homicides), becoming pregnant or getting someone pregnant, homelessness, and other psychological as well as medical problems. Clinicians must also understand that GLBTQ youth often have limited access to health care, and utilize health care less than their heterosexual counterparts.

General Evaluation of Sexuality

Sexuality is influenced by four interrelated psychosexual factors: sexual identity, gender identity, sexual orientation and sexual behavior (Table 3). The clinician should evaluate sexuality in all adolescents, asking questions in these different domains; these factors affect personality growth, development, and functioning.

In evaluating the *sexual identity* of the adolescent, a general examination can help in addressing this concept. Table 7 provides a checklist for clinicians when evaluating concepts of sexuality in their adolescent patients. Should there be any genital anomaly (*ambiguous genitalia*), the adolescent should be further evaluated by the appropriate specialist whether by an endocrinologist, urologist or gynecologist. In evaluating the *gender identity* of the adolescent, clinicians should determine any history of cross-dressing (*transvestism*) or the sense of feeling "trapped in the body of the opposite sex" (*transsexualism*). These symptoms should be further evaluated by a psychiatrist or other appropriate mental health professional to determine the possibility of *transvestic fetishism* or *gender identity disorder* (Table 1).

Sexual orientation is a very complex but poorly understood phenomenon which is established by middle childhood (ages 7-9). In evaluating for sexual orientation, the clinician should identify whether the sexual attraction of the adolescent is directed towards the opposite sex, the same sex, or both sexes. Adolescents who have homosexual attraction and sexual behavior can be advised to wait until late adolescence or early adulthood before concluding they are homosexual or lesbian; by that time most are aware of their real sexual orientation - and usually this is heterosexual. Early and mid-adolescence stimulate various stages of experimentation while late adolescence may allow some resolution in the area of acceptance of one's sexual orientation.

Some youth enter adulthood committed to a homosexual lifestyle; they state that their sexual orientation as well as commitment began even in early adolescence. Variations on such timing certainly do occur. Part of the management of adolescents with homosexual attraction and sexual behavior includes evaluation of their knowledge and misconceptions regarding homosexuality. Also, the perceived need for secrecy and their often limited sexuality education result in various potential psychological and physiological difficulties. In this regard, the Internet can be a dangerous place for youth seeking information about sexuality, including homosexuality; the result may be sexual abuse instead of appropriate sexuality information.

Medical Evaluation

Table 4 lists various reasons why GLBTQ youth may seek advice or an evaluation by the primary care clinician. However, the vast majority of interactions that primary care providers will have with these youth are through general appointments, such as well "child" visits, sports physicals, and visits for illnesses. The interactions among GLBTQ youth should cover the same basic issues as with heterosexual youth, but some issues need increased vigilance; these include support systems, risk for depression, suicide, violence, and substance use because of the increased risks of these issues noted with GLBTQ youth. Table 5 provides an outline to the medical evaluation of this patient and is followed by Table 6 which lists sexually transmitted diseases in homosexual and bisexual adolescents. Table 8 provides a sexuality checklist for clinicians.

After viral upper respiratory infections, STDs are the second most commonly diagnosed infectious disease in adolescents. Nearly two-thirds of STDs occur in persons younger than 25 years old, while nearly half of all U.S. high school youth report having had sexual intercourse and one-third report current sexual activity.

In evaluating for sexual behavior, the clinician should ask about the different aspects of the adolescent's sexual behavior and risk factors (chapter 18.

Table 4. Reasons that GLBTQ Youth Seek Medical Attention

Information	Information about homosexuality or other aspects of human sexuality
Medical	• Sexually transmitted disease(s), including fears of STDs and information • Infection with human immunodeficiency virus (HIV) or concerns about HIV or acquired immunodeficiency syndrome (AIDS) • Other medical disorders
Psychological	• Personal problems • Depression and Suicide • Substance use or abuse
Familial	• Familial conflict • Abuse
Social	• Sexual relationships • Peer pressure • Bullying
Religious	Difficulties reconciling religious beliefs with homosexual attraction
Legal	• Prostitution • Hate crime • Rape

Table 5. Medical Evaluation of GLBTQ Adolescents

History	• Social • School • Family • Employment • Substance use • Assessment of psychosocial problems, including suicidal ideations • Review of systems • Sexual history
Physical Examination	• General • Close inspection for sexually transmitted diseases or infections (STDs/STIs) • Other procedures as indicated (pelvic examination, anoscopy)
Laboratory	Laboratory evaluation as warranted: • *Neisseria gonorrhoeae* • *Chlamydia trachomatis* • *Treponema pallidum* • Human immunodeficiency virus (HIV) • Others (herpes simplex virus [HSV], human papillomavirus [HPV], etc) • Hepatitis B immunization, Human Papillomavirus (HPV) immunization, Tdap, meningococcal vaccine and others as they become available
Treatment	• Appropriate treatment of STDs (including partners) and any medical problems • Discussion of risk reduction, abstinence, contraception, condoms • Referral to support groups as necessary • Follow-up visit(s) with primary care physician (including family)

Table 6. Sexually Transmitted Diseases in Homosexual/Bisexual Adolescents

Urethritis	*Neisseria gonorrhoeae*
	Chlamydia trachomatis
	Mycoplasma hominis
	Ureaplasma urealyticum
Ulcerative lesions	Syphilis (*Treponema pallidum*)
	Herpes simplex virus (HSV)
	Chancroid (*Haemophilus ducreyi*)
	Lymphogranuloma venereum (*Chlamydia trachomatis*)
	Granuloma inguinale (*Calymmatobacterium granulomatis*)
Enteritis/proctocolitis	*Giardia lamblia*
	Salmonella *species*
	Entamoeba histolytica
	Cryptosporidium species
	Campylobacter species
	Shigella species
Genital warts	Human Papillomavirus (HPV)
Parasites	Ectoparasites
	Lice
HIV	Acquired immunodeficiency syndrome or AIDS (persons with HIV infection may acquire various other opportunistic infections not listed)
Other Viral Infections	Hepatitis A, B, C, D, and/or E virus
	Cytomegalovirus (CMV)
	Epstein-Barr virus (EBV)

Table 7. Sexuality Evaluation Checklist for Clinicians

Factor	Evaluation	Issues	Recommendations
Sexual Identity	Complete physical examination	Ambiguous genitalia Genital abnormalities	Genetic testing Gynecological evaluation Urological evaluation
Gender Identity	Observation of gender behaviors Interview	History of persistent cross-dressing Persistent feelings of being "trapped in the body of the opposite sex" Persistent desire to be the opposite sex Persistent repulsion towards genitals Persistent gender behaviors of the opposite sex	Psychiatric evaluation

Sexual Orientation	Interview	Predominant sexual fantasy and attraction towards the: Opposite sex Same sex Both sexes Knowledge and awareness of variations of sexual orientations Psychological adjustment Depression Suicidal ideation and plan Substance abuse Familial knowledge and support Family unaware Family unsupportive Social knowledge and support School Friends Sexual relationships Religious conflicts Legal problems Prostitution Special problems Bullying Violence	Reassurance Advise on Gay and Lesbian resources (See Resources) Referral to Mental Health Professional
Sexual Behavior	Interview	Pattern of Sexual relationships Sexual Behaviors Masturbation Oral sex Sexual intercourse Anal sex Related behaviors Drugs Sex toys Pornography	Advise on options for safe sex and condom use Advise on family planning Advise on risk for STDs/STIs Hepatitis B immunization Medical testing (See Tables 5 and 6)

Research on adults shows that between 75-80% of lesbians have been sexually active with men, frequently without contraception or STD prophylaxis. While risk for STDs is substantially lower among lesbians who have sex only with women, STDs can be transmitted between women. A female who self reports as a lesbian may be overlooked by a health care provider for STDs and gynecological screening if she is assumed to only have sex with women; also, lesbian women underutilize health care services and present later for health care compared to heterosexual women, especially regarding such issues as contraception and reproduction.

Statistics among young homosexual males have shown that STDs are highest in the youngest age group. Young homosexual males often report that having sex is a way they learn about being homosexual, and not unexpectedly, unprotected sex puts them at high risk for STDs, including urethritis from *Neisseria gonorrhoeae* or *Chlamydia trachomatis*. Other sexually transmitted diseases include dermatologic conditions (scabies, pediculosis), warts (HPV: penile, anal and rectal), and oropharyngeal conditions (most commonly gonorrhea, but also syphilis, herpes, and venereal warts [HPV]) (Table 6).

Unprotected sex also places homosexual males at risk for gastrointestinal diseases (Table 6), including proctitis, proctocolitis, and enteritis as a result of anal intercourse with anal contact; these diseases are more likely to masquerade as non-STDs. Proctitis can be due to gonorrhea, chlamydia, herpes simplex, syphilis, or HPV. Proctocolitis can be due to agents noted with gastrointestinal infections such as bacteria (shigella, salmonella) while enteritis can be due to intestinal parasites (*Giardia lamblia, Entamoeba histolytica*.) Hepatitis A and B are also transmitted sexually, and although Hepatitis C can be transmitted sexually, research has shown it to be more likely transmitted via blood contact.

Young adolescents may only find same-sex contact at public places where problems with sexually transmitted diseases (including HIV infection) often exist. About 25% of those with HIV/AIDS in the United States contracted their infection by the age of 21. For those in their twenties with HIV, many, if not most of them, were infected while they were still teenagers or in their early twenties. Even if the adolescent engages in same-sex behavior for economic reasons and not because of being homosexual, risks for STDs remain.

Advice regarding testing for sexually transmitted diseases includes explaining possible risk factors and treatment options; such discussions should also present issues of confidentiality as well.

Advice regarding options for self protection includes safe sex awareness and practice, including sexual abstinence and use of latex condoms. In addition, the adolescent can be taught techniques to handle peer pressure regarding sexual behavior. Part of the evaluation of sexual behavior includes inquiry about the use of alcohol or substances before or during sexual activity.

Violence is a serious reality for many gay and lesbian youth in America and the clinician should provide anticipatory guidance on what can be done if violence has become a threat to the life and well-being of this young individual; this violence can include assaults, homicides and even suicides. Also, as noted with heterosexual youth, adolescents involved in gay or lesbian relationships may experience dating violence.

The Centers for Disease and Prevention (CDC) now recommends that HIV screening be routinely performed in most care settings on *all* adolescents and adults unless they specifically "opt out" of such testing. HIV testing should be done twice yearly in high risk situations, such as MSM (men having sex with men) and especially those youth engaging in unprotected sex with men known or likely to be infected with HIV. Males and females who have low risk behaviors can be asked at the annual exam if they elect to be tested.

Psychological Evaluation

Depression and Suicide

Part of the evaluation of adolescents with homosexual attraction and sexual behavior includes evaluation of risks for depression and suicide. Data suggest that homosexual youth account for approximately 30% of completed suicides in adolescents, while 30% of a surveyed group of homosexual and bisexual males have attempted suicide at least once. One study of 137 gay and bisexual males (ages 14-21 years) noted nearly 30% had a suicide attempt, and almost half of this group had multiple suicide attempts. (Table 4) The clinician can help those with overt depression and suicide risks by referral to an appropriate mental health professional.

Substance Abuse

Substance abuse and use is a concern for all adolescents, not just those who are GLBTQ. In addition, substance abuse increases risk for sexually transmitted diseases (STDs). Many adolescents report using alcohol before having intercourse which obviously impairs judgment and increases high risk behaviors. Lesbian, gay, and bisexual youth report more current alcohol use and binge drinking than their heterosexual counterparts; there is also more cigarette smoking and other substance use.

Family and Social Evaluation

Part of the evaluation of adolescents with homosexual attraction and sexual behavior includes evaluation of family and social support. Youth who are going through various stages of homosexual identity (Table 3) need as much support as possible. Guidance should be given about when and how to "come-out" to parents, friends, and others. Disclosure should be done very carefully because of the risk of rejection, discrimination, and violence. Rejection can be so severe as to precipitate homelessness. Adolescents should be encouraged to consider the repercussions for coming out and to take time in sharing information that can have many consequences (Table 4).

The clinician can provide information regarding gay-straight alliances at some schools for all adolescents receiving support from others who are interested in their emotional and physical health. The growth of organizations like Parents and Friends of Lesbians and Gays (*PFLAG*) has been very important in helping both parents and teenagers understand these issues. The clinician can address the lack of information by providing resources available on the Internet or through libraries (See Resources section).

Management

Evaluating adolescents with homosexual or bisexual attraction and sexual behavior includes assessing self-esteem and social integration. Reaction to Troiden's Stage Two (Table 2) may include denial, despair, avoidance of social as well as sexual relationships, and perhaps, eventual acceptance or rejection of having a homosexual or bisexual orientation. They may develop poor social skills and suffer due to a lack of appropriate adult role models.

It is not surprising that many such youth struggle intensely to develop an acceptable self-identity. Health care professionals can help such individuals by

a) providing non-prejudicial counseling (or referring to someone who can provide this!),
b) teaching improved social skills,
c) arranging family counseling if necessary, and
d) reminding youth to keep their sexual orientation options open while being safe.

If the individual does seem disturbed by a homosexual orientation, referral to appropriate mental health or counseling facilities may be helpful. However, there is no scientific evidence to support the process of "reparative therapy" ("conversion therapy") or trying to force sexual orientation change on a youth who seems content with his/her gay or lesbian lifestyle. In fact, The American Academy of Pediatrics, The American Psychiatric Association and the National Association of Social Workers are all opposed to this sort of "therapy." The 1980 DSM-III contained the term, "ego dystonic homosexuality" in reference to those who were homosexual but in conflict with this orientation or wished to change their orientation; the 1987 revision of the DSM-III deleted this term, noting that most individuals who are homosexual normally go through a phase of conflict over this orientation in current society.

The clinician should be able to summarize findings with the adolescent and discuss options that do not emotionally threaten this youth. It is critical to establish a trusting relationship based on respect and honesty using a professional demeanor. Explanation for laboratory work-up should be provided and issues regarding confidentiality clearly addressed. Additionally, information on how the clinician or others may be reached in case of crisis should be provided. Advice about caring for children whose parents are gay is provided by Perrin.

Conclusion

Clinicians should be aware of personal issues regarding sexuality and homosexuality which may affect their clinical evaluation of these adolescents. Clinicians should be comfortable in asking questions regarding the different aspects of sexuality. The primary care doctor should evaluate the different dimensions of sexuality for all adolescents and also be sensitive to unique issues of adolescents with homosexual attraction and sexual behavior. Additionally, the clinician should also appreciate the possible need for other medical specialties, school and community resources, and internet sites that may be helpful for the adolescent with sexuality concerns (See Resources). The GLBTQ youth lives in a very difficult and potentially dangerous environment and the clinician may serve as an important lifeline in stabilizing this youth allowing successful transitioning from adolescence to healthy adulthood.

References

Abadalian SE, Remafedi G. Sexually transmitted diseases in young homosexual men. *Sem. Pedistr Infect Dis*. 4:122, 1993.

Alexander E: Working with youth with special needs. *Prim Care: Clinics in Office Practice* 2006; 33:20-28.

Allen L, Gorski R: Sexual orientation and the size of the anterior commissure in the human brain. *Proc. Natl. Acad. Sci.* 1992; 89:7199.

Allen LB, Glicken AD, Beach RK et al: Adolescent health care experience of gay, lesbian, and bisexual young adults. *J. Adol. Health* 1998; 23: 212-220.

Allen LB, Glicken AD: Depression and suicide in gay and lesbian adolescents. *Phys. Assist* 1996; 20:44-60.

American Academy of Pediatrics. Homosexuality and Adolescence. Committee on Adolescence. *Pediatrics* 1993; 92: 631-634.

American Medical Association. Council on Scientific Affairs. Health care needs of gay men and lesbians in the United States. *JAMA* 1996; 275(17): 1354-59.

American Psychiatric Association. *Diagnostic and Statistical Manual of Mental Disorders*, DSM-IV, 4th ed., (text revision) (DSM-IV-TR). Washington, DC: American Psychiatric Association, 2000.

Bell A, Weinberg M: *Homosexuality: A Study of Diversity among Men and Women*. NY: Simon and Schuster, 1978.

Branson BM, Handsfield HH, Lampe MA et al: Revised recommendations for HIV testing of adults, adolescents, and pregnant women in health care settings. MMWR 2006; 55 (RR 14): 1-17.

Byrne W and Parsons B: Human sexual orientation: The biologic theories reappraised. *Arch. Gen. Psychiatry* 1993; 50:228.

Catallozzi M, Rudy BJ: Lesbian, gay, bisexual, transgendered, and questioning youth: the importance of a sensitive and confidential sexual history in identifying the risk and implementing treatment for sexually transmitted infections. *Adolesc. Med.* 2004; 15:353-367.

Chan CS: Issues of identity development among Asian-American lesbians and gay men. *J. Counsel. Dev.* 68: 16, 1989.

Chen-Hayes SF: Counseling and advocacy with transgendered and gender-variant persons in schools and families. *J. Humanistic Counseling, Education, and Development* 1998; 40:34-48,

Dalton R: "Homosexuality" In: *Nelson Textbook of Pediatrics*, 17th Ed. Eds: RE Behrman, RM Kliegman, HB Jenson. Philadelphia: WB Saunders Co., ch. 26.2: 91-92, 2004.

Deneberg R. Report on lesbian health. *Womens Health Issues*. 1995;5:81.

Diamond M: Homosexuality and bisexuality in different populations. *Arch. Sex Behav.* 1993; 22:291-310.

Dundas S: Family therapy in gay and lesbian-parented families. *J. Gay Les Med. Assoc.* 1997; 1(2): 111-7.

East JA, El Rayess F: Pediatricians' approach to the health care of lesbian, gay, and bisexual youth. *J. Adolesc. Health* 1998; 23:191-193.

Eaton DK, Kann L, Kinchen S. *Youth risk behavior surveillance – United States*, 2005. MMWR Surveill Summ 2006; 55:1

Espin OM. Issues of identity in the psychology of Latina Lesbians. In Garnets L, Kimmel D (eds). *Psychological perspectives on Lesbian and Gay Male Experiences*. New York, Columia University Press, 1993.

Fassinger RE. The hidden minority: Issues and challenges in working with lesbian women and gay men. *The Counseling Psychologist* 19:157, 1991.

Fonseca H, Greydanus DE: Sexuality in the child, teen, and young adult: Current concepts for the clinician. *Prim. Care: Clin. Off Pract*. 2007; 34:275-292.

Ford C, English A, Sigman G: Confidential health care for adolescents: Position paper of the Society for Adolescent Medicine. *J. Adolesc. Health* 2004; 35: 160-167.

Frankowski BL: Committee on Adolescence. American Academy of Pediatrics. Sexual orientation and adolescents. *Pediatrics* 2004; 113:1827-1832.

Friedman RC, Downey JI: Homosexuality. *N. Engl. J. Med*. 1994; 331(14): 923-930.

Garofalo R, Harper GW: Not all adolescents are the same: addressing the unique needs of gay and bisexual male youth. *Adolesc. Med*. 2003; 14:595-611.

Garofalo R, Katz E: Health care issues of gay and lesbian youth. *Curr. Opin. Pediatr*. 2001; 13:298-302.

Garofalo R, Wolf C, Wissow LS et al: Sexual orientation and risk of suicide attempts among a representative sample of youth. *Arch. Pediatr. Adolesc. Med*. 1999; 153:487-493.

Garofalo R, Wolf R, Kessel S, Palfrey J, Durant R. The Association Between Health Risk Behaviors and Sexual Orientation Among a School-based sample of Adolescents, *Pediatrics*. 101:895-902, 1998.

Green R (ed.): *Sexual Identity Conflict in Children and Adults*: New York: Basic Books, 1974.

Greene B: Ethnic Minority lesbian and gay men: Mental health treatment issues. *J. Consult. Clin. Psychol*. 62:243, 1994.

Greydanus DE, Calles JL: Suicide in children and adolescents. Prim Care: Clin Off Pract 2007; 34:259-274.

Grunbaum JA, Kann L, Kinchen S, et al. Youth risk behavior surveillance – United States, 2003. MMWR Surveill Summ 2004; 53:1.

Halcon L, Blum RW: Adolescent health in the Caribbean: A regional portrait. *Amer. J. Publ. Health* 2003; 93:1851-1857.

Halpern CT, Young ML, Waller MW et al: Prevalence of partner violence in same-sex romantic and sexual relationships in a national sample of adolescents. *J. Adolesc. Health* 2004; 35:124-131.

Harrison AE, Silenzio VMB: Comprehensive care of lesbian and gay patients and their families. *Prim. Care* 1996; 23(1): 31-45.

Hershberger SL, Pilkington NW, D'Augelli AR: Predictors of suicide attempts among gay, lesbian, and bisexual youth. *J. Adolesc. Res*. 1997; 12:477-497.

Hunter J: Violence against lesbian and gay male youths. *J. Interpersonal Violence* 1990; 5:295-300.

Icard L. Black gay men and conflicting social identities: Sexual identity vs racial identity. *J. Soc. Work and Human Sexuality* 4:83, 1986.

International Classification of Diseases and Related Health Problems, 10th Revision. (ICD-10), 2004.

Kinsey A, Pomeroy W, Martin C, Gebbard P. *Sexual Behavior in the Human Female.* Philadelphia: W.B. Saunders, 1953.

Kinsey A, Pomeroy W, Martin C. *Sexual Behavior in the Human Male.* W.B Philadelphia: W.B. Saunders, 1948.

Knight D: Health care screening for men who have sex with men. *Amer. Fam. Phys.* 2004; 69:2149-56.

Lemp GF, Jones M, Kellog TA, Nieri GN. HIV seroprevalence and risk factors among lesbians and bisexual women in San Fransisco and Berkeley, California. *Am. J. Public Health* 1995; 85:1549.

Levay, Simon: *Queer Science: The Use and Abuse of Research into Homosexuality.* Cambridge, MA: MIT Press, 364 pages, 1997.

Marazzo JM, Stine K. Reproductive health history of lesbians: Implications for care. *Am. J. Obstet Gynecol.* 2004;190:1298.

Marmor J, Green R: Homosexual behavior. In: Money J, Musaph H (Eds): *Handbook of Sexuality.* Amsterdam: Elsevier/North Holland Biomedical Press, 1051-68, 1977.

McConaghy N, Armstrong B, Birrell P et al: The incidence of bisexual feelings and opposite sex behavior in medical students. *J. Nerv. Ment. Dis.* 1979; 167:685-8.

National Institute of Allergy and Infectious Diseases: Workshop Summary: Scientific Evidence on Condom Effectiveness for Sexually Transmitted Diseases (STD) Prevention. http://www.niaid.nih.gov/dmid/stds/condomreport.pdf, 2001.

Nicholas J, Howard J: Better dead than gay: depression, suicide ideation, and attempt among a sample of gay and straight-identified males 18 to 24. *Youth Stud. Aust.* 1998; 17:28-33.

O'Hanlon KA, Cabaj RP, Schatz B et al: A review of the medical consequences of homophobia with suggestions for resolution. *J. Gay Les Med. Assoc.* 1997; 1(1): 25-39.

Paroski PA: Health care delivery and the concerns of gay and lesbian adolescents. *J. Adolesc. Health Care* 1986; 7:1-7.

Perrin EC and Kulkin H: Pediatric care for children whose parents are gay or lesbian. *Pediatrics* 1996; 97:629-635.

Perrin EC: *Sexual Orientation in Child and Adolescent Health Care.* NY: Kluwer Academic/Plenum Publishers, 182 pages, 2002.

Pillard RC, Bailey JM: A biologic perspective on sexual orientation. *Psychiatr. Clin. North Am.* 1995; 18:71-84.

Remafedi G: Fundamental issues in the care of homosexual youth. *Med. Clin. No Amer.* 1990; 74(5): 1169-1176.

Remafedi G, Farrow JA and Deisher RW: Risk factors for attempted suicide in gay and lesbian youth. *Pediatrics* 1991; 87(6): 869-75.

Remafedi G, Resnick M, Blum R et al: Demography of sexual orientation in adolescents. *Pediatrics* 1992; 89:714-721.

Remafedi G: Sexually transmitted diseases in young homosexual men. *Sem. Ped. Infect Dis.* 4:122, 1993.

Remafedi G: Sexual orientation and youth suicide. *JAMA* 1999; 282:1291-2.

Remafedi G, French S, Story M et al: The relationship between suicide risk and sexual orientation: results of a population-based study. *Am. J. Publ. Health* 1998; 88:57-60.

Remafedi G: "Adolescent homosexuality" In: *Nelson Textbook of Pediatrics*, 18th Edition. Eds: RM Kliegman, RE Behrman, HB Jenson, BF Stanton. Philadelphia, PA: Saunders Elsevier, chapter 13.3: 68-70, 2007.

Rome ES: "Adolescent sexuality." In: *Essential Adolescent Medicine*. Eds: DE Greydanus, DR Patel, HD Pratt. NY: McGraw-Hill Medical Publishers, ch. 22: 481-496, 2006.

Rowlett J and Greydanus DE: "*Gender Identity*" In Behavioral Pediatrics. DE Greydanus and M Wolraich (eds), NY: Springer-Verlag, ch 3: 40-65, 1991.

Rowlett JD and Greydanus DE: Homosexuality in adolescence. *Adolescent Medicine*. 994; 5(3):509-526.

Ryan CR, Futterman D(eds): Gay and lesbian youth. *Adolescent Medicine* 1997; 8(2): 199-397.24.

Ryan C and Futterman D: *Lesbian and Gay Youth: Care and Counseling*. NY: Columbia University Press, 175 pages, 1998.

Sadock, Benjamin James and Sadock, Virginia Alcott. *Kaplan and Sadock's Synopsis of Psychiatry*. 10th Edition Lippincott Williams and Wilkins, 2007.

Santelli J, Ott MA, Lyon M et al: Position paper. Abstinence-only education policies and programs: A position paper of the Society for Adolescent Medicine. *J. Adolesc. Health* 2006; 83-87.

Seidman SN, Rieder RO: A review of sexual behavior in the United States. *Am. J. Psychiatr*. 1994; 151:330-341.

Sell RL, Wells JA, Wyrij D: The prevalence of homosexual behavior and attraction in the United States, the United Kingdom, and France: results of national population-based samples. *Arch. Sex Behav*. 1995; 24:235-48.

Sexually transmitted diseases treatment guidelines 2006. Centers for Disease Control and Prevention. *MMWR Recomm. Rep*. 2006; 55 (RR-11): 1-94.

Shaffer D, Fisher P, Hicks RH, et al: Sexual orientation in adolescents who commit suicide. *Suicide Life Threat Behav*. 1995; 25 (Suppl):64-71.

Sison AC, Greydanus DE: Deconstructing adolescent same-sex attraction and sexual behavior in the twenty-first century: Perspectives for the clinician. *Prim. Care: Clin. Off Pract*. 2007; 34:293-304.

Troiden R: Homosexual identify development. *J. Adoles. Health Care* 1989; 9:105.

Troiden RT: Becoming homosexual: A model of gay identity acquisition. *Psychiatry* 1979; 42:362-373.

White JC, Levinson W: Lesbian health care: What a primary care physician needs to know. *West J. Med*. 1995; 162:463-466.

Zea MC, Reisen CA, Poppen PJ: Psychological well-being among Latino lesbians and gay men. *Cultural Diversity and Ethnic Minority Psychology* 1999; 5(4):371-379.

Resources

National Federation of Parents and Friends of Lesbians and Gays (PFLAG)
1726 M Street NW-Suite 400
Washington, DC 20036

Phone: 202-467-8180
www.pflag.org

Gay and Lesbian Medical Association
459 Fulton Street, Suite 107
San Francisco, CA 94102
Phone: 415-255-4547
FAX: 415-225-4784
www.glma.org

National Youth Advocacy Coalition
1638 R Street., NW, Suite 300
Washington, DC 20009
Phone: 202-319-7596
FAX: 202-319-7365
E-mail: nyac@nyacyouth.org
http://www.nyacyouth.org
(Referral information for youth-serving agencies and services)

Section VII. Special Issues

In: Behavioral Pediatrics, 3rd Edition   ISBN 978-1-60692-702-1
Editor: D. E. Greydanus et al.   © 2009 Nova Science Publishers, Inc.

Chapter 20

Suicidal Behavior in Children and Adolescents

Kimberly K. McClanahan and Hatim A. Omar

Abstract

This chapter addresses a variety of issues related to suicidality in prepubertal children and adolescents. Risk factors, including personal/individual characteristics, family characteristics/psychopathology, and negative life stressors/environmental influences, are reviewed. Methods of suicide utilized by children and adolescents, and considerations regarding suicidal behavior in children and adolescents in different cultures are discussed. Identification of the at-risk child and adolescent, prevention, treatment, and postvention issues are considered. Finally, legal issues surrounding the care of suicidal children and adolescents are mentioned.

Introduction

Suicide is the 11th leading cause of death across the lifespan in the United States (US) and is not uncommon among prepubertal children and adolescents. It is the 4th leading cause of death in 1-19 year olds and was the 6th leading cause of death in 5–14-year-olds, but has recently moved to 5th place. Suicide is the 3rd leading cause of death in 15-24-year-olds.

While suicide completion in prepubertal children is relatively rare, there is consistent evidence for the association between prepubertal suicidal behavior and later adolescent suicide attempts. The Surgeon General's 1999 Call to Action to Prevent Suicide [9] reported a 100% increase in suicide among 10-14-year-olds between the years of 1980 and 1996, and youth suicide has been estimated to reach its peak between the ages of 18 and 24. Suicide across the pediatric age span is a serious public health concern that warrants continued clinical and research attention.

Suicidal Behavior in Prepubertal Children

Much study has been given to adult and adolescent suicide while suicide in prepubertal children has only recently become a significant focus for researchers and clinicians, even though it is the 5th leading cause of death within the 10-14-year-old age group. While suicide among prepubertal children and young adolescents (ages 5–14) involved only 292 deaths in 2004, the lowest age-specific mortality rate for suicide (0.7 per 100,000) for all ages, the rise in suicide in the last several decades among young children is a matter of significant concern.

Given the significant increase in rates of suicide in adolescence, with a peak in the mid-to-late adolescent years, studies have begun to look at precursors in prepubertal children. Childhood behaviors, attitudes, experiences, and risk factors are associated with suicidal behavior in adolescents and young adults. By studying and understanding the developmental processes of suicidal behavior and thinking, important information can be gleaned which will inform suicide prevention and intervention efforts. As Cynthia Pfeffer, one of the leading researchers in prepubertal suicidal behavior, has stated, "Suicidal behavior is a developmental process that begins at an earlier phase of the life cycle than when this behavior manifests (p. 560)."

In the US, ascertaining exact numbers for suicide in prepubertal children is impossible. First, there is no central reporting agency for suicide, making accurate numbers difficult to obtain. Second, the categorization of national statistics, with an age range of 5-14, includes numbers from early adolescence, i.e., 13-14 years of age, and most completed suicides within the 10-14-year-old group are 12-14 years old, indicating that reported numbers of suicide in prepubertal children are inflated by the upsurge of suicide in adolescence. Third, death in 1–4 year olds is never attributed to suicide, although there have been documented cases of suicidal children as young as three years of age. In 2003, the number one reported cause of death in 1-4-year-olds was unintentional injury, which may mask some deaths with intention. In older prepubertal children, death may be more likely attributed to an accident rather than suicide, possibly because parents and authorities refuse to admit that young children kill themselves.

Risk Factors for Suicide in Children

Risk factors for suicidal thinking and behavior in prepubertal children span the range from individual to environmental influences and stressors, and there is consistent evidence for the association between prepubertal suicidal ideation and later adolescent suicide attempts.

Personal/Individual Characteristics

Psychiatric Co-Morbidity

Psychopathology is a common finding with regard to risk factors for suicide in prepubertal children, with mood disorders, especially depression, being the most significant.

In both inpatient and outpatient samples, depression has been significantly associated with suicidal ideation and behavior in prepubertal children.

In a follow-up study of prepubertal children 6–8 years after initial hospitalization, Pfeffer *et al* found that prepubertal suicide attempters were six times more likely and prepubertal suicidal ideators were three times more likely than nonpatients to attempt suicide during the follow-up period. The strongest factor for recurrence of a suicide attempt was impairment in social adjustment immediately prior to the attempt. Children who reported an attempt in the follow-up period were four times more likely to have poor social adjustment and 3.5 times more likely to have a mood disorder than non-attempters.

Gould *et al*, [21] using a probability sample of 9–17-year-olds, found that mood and anxiety disorders were significant independent correlates of suicide attempts in participants 12 years or younger and that disruptive behavior disorders independently increased the risk of suicidal ideation in that age group. In a prospective study using a prepubertal, nonclinical sample, O'Leary *et al* measured suicidal ideation and found that 14.5% of the 131 children reported suicidal ideation associated with depressive symptoms.

In a longitudinal study, self-report of depressed mood in urban first graders predicted later suicidal ideation. In a follow-up study of 6-15-year-olds diagnosed with major depression, depressed children were five times more likely to have attempted suicide than their nondepressed peers 10 years later, and 7% committed suicide in later life. Kovacs *et al*, in a longitudinal investigation, found that depression in prepubertal children gave a four to five times higher likelihood for a suicide attempt than for children without depression.

Jackson and Nuttall, in an outpatient mental health sample of 5–12 year olds, asked children to self-report suicidal behavior and found that 42% had one or more suicidal behaviors. Depression was the most frequent diagnosis, but no specific diagnosis was significantly associated with suicidality, suggesting that factors other than diagnosis be considered in determining suicidality. This is consistent with findings by Nock and Kazdin who studied 6-13-year-old inpatients. They found that depression was significantly associated with suicidal ideation, the presence of a current suicide attempt, and suicidal intent. However, they also found that when depression was statistically controlled, negative automatic thoughts, hopelessness, and anhedonia, i.e., lack of pleasure in activities and play, remained significantly associated with the presence of a current suicide attempt. Hopelessness also remained significantly associated with suicidal intent, suggesting that these three variables provide unique information about suicidal behavior beyond a diagnosis of depression. Of particular note is the finding that those children who had a current suicide attempt were distinguished from all other children by higher scores on a measure of anhedonia and by a higher number of past suicide attempts. Luby *et al*, in a study of depression in preschool children, found anhedonia to be a highly specific symptom of depression, suggesting that a preschool child presenting with anhedonia is extremely likely to be clinically depressed. Thus, the presence of anhedonia at an early age may be a predictor of suicidal behavior in prepubertal children.

While depression is the most common disorder associated with suicidality in prepubertal children, other disorders have also been linked to it. Studies of community and psychiatric samples suggest that dysthymia, disruptive behavior disorders, including attention deficit hyperactivity disorder, oppositional defiant disorder, and conduct disorder, schizophrenia, and developmental disorders are correlated highly with childhood suicidal tendencies. Additionally, prepubertal psychiatrically hospitalized children with psychotic symptoms are at risk for suicidal behavior.

Prior Suicide Attempts

The axiom that past behavior predicts future behavior appears to hold true with suicide. Previous suicide attempts predict the higher probability of future suicide attempts. Nock and Kazdin, in their sample of 6-13 year-old inpatients, found that those who had a current suicide attempt reported a higher number of suicide attempts in the past year than those who had no current suicide attempt. This is consistent with work demonstrating that past attempts predict additional attempts in adolescents, and it appears to hold true with children as well.

Gender

In prepubertal children, no difference in suicidal behavior between males and females has been found, although Pfeffer *et al* noted that prepubertal girls were more likely than boys to make multiple suicide attempts as they became adolescents. Nock and Kazdin found, as children near early adolescence, girls become more likely to make a suicide attempt than boys, and as adolescence progresses, girls are twice as likely as boys to attempt suicide; adolescent boys are much more likely to complete suicide than are girls, with an approximate ratio of 5.5:1 in 15-24-year-olds.

Risk factors for suicide vary by gender. Reinherz *et al,* in assessing children at ages 5, 9, 15, and 18, found that psychosocial risk factors from as early as age 5 proved a significant risk for suicidal ideation in midadolescence, but the risk factors varied by gender. For males, the risk factors were early health problems, childhood behavior and emotional problems, and the early onset of psychiatric disorder. For females, the risk factors were family issues, early behavior and emotional problems, poor self-perceptions, and early onset of psychiatric disorder. Early gender-specific risks for suicidal ideation in adolescence included emotional and behavioral problems contrary to gender expectations. Specifically, young girls with aggression and hyperactivity and young boys with anxiety and dependence were more likely to have suicidal ideation in adolescence than those children who exhibited more traditional gender roles in early childhood.

Genetics

Evidence suggests a genetic component to suicidal behavior. Family studies, including first-degree relatives, and twin studies, show genetic vulnerability to suicide. Agerbo *et al* found youth suicide to be nearly five times more likely in children of mothers who had completed suicide and twice as common in children of fathers who completed suicide. Additional evidence for the heritability of suicidality is found in a meta-analysis of twin data. This showed that first-degree relatives of people who completed suicide have more than twice the risk of suicide than the general population, with relative risk increasing among identical co-twins of a completed suicide to about 11 times that of the general population [30].

Cognitive Development

The variability of children's cognitive maturity through prepuberty has implications for their understanding of the seriousness and finality of suicide. Although the 6–12-year-old age group may include children at a number of Piagetian stages, i.e., preoperations, concrete operations, formal operations, most will have predominantly concrete operational levels of cognitive development. As such, they tend to think concretely, utilize a present orientation, and view choices as black or white. They have limited ability to project into the future and may not perceive the long-range implications of current decisions. Thus, prepubertal children may not appreciate the finality of a suicidal act,[5] although they will usually have some concept of death.

Young children's understanding of death may be akin to death in fairy tales or cartoons, where the protagonist is ultimately revived; two-thirds of children, by age 6-7, understand that everyone dies, but some studies suggest that only by age 9 or 10 do children begin to understand death as final and permanent. Also, by age 10, most children know what suicide means. Regardless of prepubertal children's level of cognitive maturity, young children are capable of implementing a suicide plan successfully, with younger children using less complex and more easily available methods.

Family Characteristics/Psychopathology

Family factors increase risk for suicidal behavior in prepubertal children. Family discord, lack of family cohesion and poor family behavioral control, parental loss due to separation or divorce and/or death, especially death of a parent before the child reaches the age of 12, are all associated with an increased risk of suicidal behavior in prepubertal children.

Parental psychopathology is also a risk factor. In a follow-up study of prepubertal children 6–8 years after initial hospitalization, Pfeffer, Normandin, and Tatsuyuki assessed their relatives. Suicidal behavior in children was associated with suicidal behavior in their families, notably mothers; 50% of mothers of suicide attempters reported a history of suicide attempts. Additionally, more first-degree relatives of child suicide attempters, mostly fathers, compared to first-degree relatives of control children, had antisocial personality disorder, assaultive behavior, and substance abuse. Pfeffer, Normandin, and Tatsuyuki, in further assessment of the cohort of children referenced above, found that family discord, suicide attempts by mother, and substance abuse of mothers and fathers were significantly more prevalent among adolescents with a lifetime history of a suicide attempt. Klimes-Dougan *et al* found that young children of unipolar depressed mothers were more likely to report suicidal thoughts or behaviors than children of well mothers.

Negative Life Stressors/Environmental Influences

Brown *et al*, in a study beginning when children were five years of age through adulthood, looked at the effects of childhood neglect, physical abuse, and sexual abuse. They found that adolescents and young adults with a history of childhood maltreatment were three times more likely to become depressed or suicidal when compared to individuals with no maltreatment history. Both childhood physical and sexual abuse were associated with later depression and suicidality, with sexual abuse carrying the greatest risk for suicide. Pfeffer *et al* found that prepubertal children with poor social adjustment have a four times greater risk for a suicide attempt in adolescence than children with good social adjustment. Exposure to violence and distress in response to witnessing violence are also associated with suicidal ideation in prepubertal children.

Suicidal Behavior in Adolescents

Suicide in youth has increased significantly over the past 50 years with 4.0 suicides per 100,000 in 15-24-year-olds in 1957 to a peak of 13.3 per 100,000 in this age group in 1977. From 1950 to 2000, suicide rates in youth increased with each passing decade, even with national goals set for decreasing youth suicide. *Healthy People 2010* reestablished goals for suicide reduction, with a specific objective to decrease rates of suicide attempts in adolescents.

Since 2000, suicide rates have decreased in youth, perhaps due to increased prevention efforts in the past decade. In 2003, the rate for recorded suicides for young people between the ages of 15 and 24 was 9.7 per 100,000, [40] a slight decrease from 2000, at which time there were 10.4 suicides per 100,000.

Across time, 15-19-year-olds had fewer suicides than 20-24-year-olds. In 2003, for 15-19-year-olds, there were 7.3 suicides per 100,000, a slight decrease from 2002 of 7.4 per 100,000 while the suicide rate for 20-24-year-olds was 12.1 per 100,000, also a slight decrease from 2002 of 12.4 suicides per 100,000. In 1999, in the US, almost 60% of youth suicide deaths occurred among those 20 to 24, indicating that what is often described as "youth suicide" is actually suicide in young adults.

Recent data from the 2005 Youth Risk Behavior Survey, a national self-report measure completed by ninth – twelfth graders, indicated that nationwide, 16.9% of high school students had seriously considered attempting suicide during the 12 months preceding the survey; 13.0% of students nationwide had made a plan about how they would attempt suicide, and 8.4% had actually attempted suicide. Of those who had attempted suicide, 10.8% were female, 6.0% were male, and 2.3% made a suicide attempt that resulted in an injury, poisoning, or overdose that had to be treated medically.

Older youth, those aged 18 to 24, represent both college- and noncollege-attending youth. Studies have shown differing statistics regarding whether noncollege or college student youth are more likely to commit suicide. Some authors have reported that the average level of suicidal ideation experienced by college students is higher than that experienced by same-age young adults in the community. College student surveys have shown that as many as 50% admit to past year suicidal thinking with 8-15% acting on those thoughts. Suicide has been estimated to be the second leading cause of death among college students.

Other studies challenge the claim of a higher suicide rate among college students compared to noncollege peers when reported figures are scrutinized statistically. In a comprehensive attempt to compare the incidence of suicide among college students to a matched national sample of noncollege peers, Silverman *et al* found that for the 10-year period studied, college students had one-half the suicides of the noncollege sample, i.e., 7.5 vs. 15 suicides per 100,000, respectively. They concluded that their findings supported those of others who found a lower overall suicide rate in college students vs. the general population [49, 50].

An underrepresented group of youth suicides, however, includes those who drop out of college and are not counted as college suicides. Haas *et al* [51] noted that an elevated rate of suicide among college drop-outs has long been known. For example, a longitudinal study of 50,000 students [52, 53] found failure to graduate college associated with a 50% greater risk of suicide, and later analysis of these data [54] showed evidence that students drop out of college before committing suicide. These uncounted college-related suicides artificially lower the rate relative to the general population, [51] indicating that rates of college and noncollege young adult suicides may be comparable.

Risk Factors for Suicide in Adolescents

Risk factors for suicidal thinking and behavior in adolescents are often present in earlier childhood and may be exacerbated as adolescent development occurs. Disruption in one or more developmental domains, i.e., physical, cognitive, emotional, or social, during adolescence can bring great challenges and may increase risk for suicidal behavior.

Developmental Issues

Developmental Tasks of Early Adolescence

Early adolescence is characterized by major physical changes with the onset of puberty. Cognitive changes occur as young adolescents begin the transition from concrete to formal operational thought (i.e., abstract thinking), [55-57] including a limited ability to think hypothetically and to take multiple perspectives [32, 58, 59]. They begin to think abstractly at times, and can have an orientation toward the future, perceive implications of actions, and look at things from the perspective of others. However, these capacities fluctuate and do not consolidate fully until late adolescence.

Early adolescence also elicits changes in the social and emotional domains. Social roles are largely defined by external sources, and social relationships are centered in the peer group with group values tending to govern individual behavior. The emotional domain finds the early adolescent strongly identified with a peer group and dependent upon it for emotional stability, support, and molding of emerging identity. Acceptance by peers is critical to self-esteem. Hormonal changes tend to increase early adolescents' emotional lability, and they may show exaggerated affect and frequent mood swings.

Developmental Tasks of Middle and Late Adolescence

Middle and late adolescence bring continued developmental changes. In middle adolescence, physical maturation continues, and cognitive development progresses with advancement toward full formal operational thinking, thus allowing an adolescent to think abstractly more consistently. By the time an adolescent reaches late adolescence, most physical and cognitive changes have occurred, but social and emotional changes continue. As late adolescence is reached, social values are more likely to become individualized and internalized after careful consideration and independent thought. Friends are more often selected on personal characteristics and mutual interests rather than some external criterion (e.g., popularity). Having a large peer group usually declines in importance, individual friendships are strengthened, and more youth "date" in one-on-one relationships [32]. The emotional domain finds the older adolescent with a more individualized identity, a sense of self that is separate from family and peer group, and self-esteem more influenced by the ability to live up to internalized standards for behavior rather than acceptance or rejection by others. Self-assessment and introspection are common, and full operational thought will likely be achieved by the end of late adolescence, thus allowing the youth to consistently have future orientation, view the implications of decisions and circumstances, and place oneself in someone else's position.

Potential Disruptions in Developmental Domains

Adolescence has been described as a period of "storm and stress" in which children question and contradict their parents, have disruptions in mood, and show a propensity to rebelliousness and risk-taking behaviors [60]. Recent empirical data show that adolescence is indeed a difficult period of time, [61] and storm and stress are a part of this period of life for the majority of adolescents.

In the early adolescent years, disruptions in development may occur in any domain. While progress has been made toward formal operational thought, this is not finalized, and early adolescents might still presume that suicide is not really final. In the social and emotional domains, peer group is extremely important, and rejection by the peer group can lead to suicidal thinking and behavior. Additionally, the mood lability of early adolescence may lend itself to impulsive behavior that is irreversible. Another area of potential stress is young adolescents' satisfaction or dissatisfaction with their physical appearance.

Whether older adolescents are college students or members of the general population, this developmental stage of life presents multiple challenges, including the need to accomplish independence and individuation while maintaining connectedness to family, the development of intimate relationships, and the pursuit of personal and career goals.[62] These tasks may provide a level of stress that will precipitate suicidal thinking and behavior. Additional stressful tasks for college students include the pressure of academic endeavors, and their noncollege peers must establish a work ethic upon which to build their lives. Also, the development of formal operational thinking may lead older youth to more fully contemplate the questions of life and death because these issues have become real to them. How the issues of life and death are dealt with depends upon the ability of the older adolescent to successfully negotiate the challenges of this development phase of life.

Personal/Individual Characteristics

Psychiatric Co-Morbidity

Psychiatric disorders have been shown to play a major role in adolescent suicidal behavior, [42] and up to 90% of adolescent who complete suicide have at least one disorder at the time of death [63, 64]. Further, those with multiple or co-morbid mental disorders have an elevated risk of suicidal behavior compared to those with no disorder [64] Beautrais [65] estimated that young people with a single disorder were 8 times and those with two or more disorders 15 times more likely than those with no disorder to attempt suicide. Mood, substance abuse, and conduct disorders tend be the most prevalent diagnoses in reports of completed and attempted suicide among adolescents [39].

Schaffer *et al* [64] found that the odds of suicide were more than 10 times greater among adolescents with a mood disorder in comparison to those without mood disorders. Mood disorders have been shown to produce significantly elevated risks of suicidal behavior in college students, [66, 67] and depression is the most common diagnosis among youth who have attempted or completed suicide [68].

Alcohol and drug abuse have also been associated with suicidal behavior in adolescents[5] and have often been found among suicide completers [69, 70] and among lethal and sublethal attempters [71]. Studies have found evidence of alcohol/drug abuse in 38 to 54% of youth suicide completers [72] Abel and Zeidenberg [73] found that 35% of their sample of 15-24-year-old suicide completers had medical records indicating significant blood alcohol levels at the time of death. Other studies have found substance abuse histories in 15 to 33% of adolescent suicide completers [74, 75].

In studies of adolescent substance abusers, suicide attempts have been found to occur at three times the rate of that of control subjects, with suicidal thinking increasing dramatically after the onset of substance use [76]. Substance use at the time of suicidal behavior has been found to be related to the lethality of the method used [77] Further, risk of suicide appears to increase when heavy substance use is 1) co-morbid, especially with depression, 2) active and frequent, 3) accompanied by loss or anticipated loss of a significant relationship, 4) deteriorated social status or school performance, and 5) co-occurring with chronic social isolation [39].

Externalizing disorders, i.e., conduct disorder, oppositional defiant disorder, antisocial personality disorder, have significant correlations with suicidal behavior in adolescents. Shaffer *et al* [64] found that those with conduct disorder had three times the probability of suicide than those without such disorder. Shafii *et al* [78] found that 70% of their psychological autopsy subjects had exhibited antisocial behavior whereas only 24% of control subjects had done so. The role of conduct disorder in adolescence may be even greater than that of depression [39]. In a study by Apter *et al* [79] higher scale scores on suicidality were found for conduct-disordered adolescents than for depressed adolescents, even though those with conduct disorder were less depressed.

Anxiety disorders have also been shown to have a small, but significant association with suicidal behavior in youth, [42] and those with psychotic disorders are at high-risk for suicidal behaviors. However, since these disorders affect relatively few young people, they make a small contribution to overall rates of suicidal behavior in this population [42].

A number of studies have looked at personality characteristics associated with suicidality in adolescents and young adults. Among the characteristics found to be associated are dependency and self-criticism, [80] high scores on measures of neuroticism [81] and hopelessness, [64] and positive attitudes toward suicide [82, 83] Borderline personality disorder is also related to suicidality in adolescents and is often associated with sublethal self-harm behaviors [84].

Prior Suicide Attempts

Previous suicide attempts predict higher probability of future suicide attempts [5, 6] Stoelb and Chiriboga [85] reported that a high school student who has made one suicide attempt is 18 times more likely to make another in 12 months. Estimates have ranged from 18-50% for completed suicides with a past attempt, [86] indicating wide variability in studies regarding numbers of attempters completing. Rudd *et al*, [86] in an effort to bring clarity to the issue of which attempters become completers, divided their sample into ideators, attempters, and multiple attempters. These authors found that multiple attempters showed more severe symptoms and elevated suicide risk relative to both ideators and attempters. A more recent study [87] looked at four different samples differing in age, clinical severity, and gender, and found that past to current suicidality was direct and not accounted for by covariates, indicating that past suicidiality may be a causal factor in future suicidality.

Gender

In adolescence, being male places one at much higher risk for a completed suicide. While females attempt suicide much more frequently than males, [5] with estimated ratios ranging from 2:1 to 3:1 [88, 89] among 15-19-year-olds, the ratio of male to female completed suicide is 4.7:1, [90] and among 20-24-year-olds, the ratio is greater than 6:1. [40]. Method of suicide also varies between genders, with ingestions accounting for approximately 16% of 15-24-year-old female suicides, but for only 2% of male suicides; males are much more likely to use firearms [5]. In 2003, the male to female ratio of firearm use for suicide was 11.4 to 1.2 per 100,000, respectively [40].

Genetics

As noted earlier, a strong predictor of suicidal behavior in young people is the presence of a family history of suicidal behavior, [91] suggesting a genetic component to suicide. Brent *et al*, [92] in their controlled family study of adolescent suicide victims, showed that propensities toward suicidal behaviors may be familially transmitted as a trait independent of diagnosable mental disorders in terms of suicidal attempts and completions. Twin studies have shown moderate levels of heritability in which up to 45% of variance in suicidal behavior may be genetic [93]. Much research is ongoing regarding abnormalities of serotonin function in suicidal individuals, [6] some of which has been completed with suicidal adolescents [94]. There is speculation that this research will determine a genetic link regarding suicidality in relatives, but to date, results have been inconsistent [6].

Sexual Orientation

Research has shown that young people who identify as gay, lesbian, or bisexual (GLB) are twice as likely to have a history of suicidal behavior as their heterosexual peers [95]. However, to date, no empirical data has clearly linked completed suicide to homosexual orientation [39]. Stressors associated with suicidal behavior in this population include interpersonal turmoil associated with publicly acknowledging one's sexual identity, especially to parents, [96] and discrimination and victimization related to sexual orientation [97]. A recent study showed that primarily heterosexual college students did not respond empathically to GLB's suicidal behavior following a negative response from parents to "coming out," in contrast to their empathic response to suicidal behavior in someone informed about an incurable illness [98]. These results suggest that young heterosexual adults may not be accepting of gay lifestyles.

Family Characteristics/Psychopathology

Compared to normal adolescents, suicidal adolescents report poorer familial relationships and more interpersonal conflict with parents with less affection [69, 99]. Further, they describe time with parents as less enjoyable and hold more negative views of their parents [100]. A family history of suicide, current or past family or parental psychopathology, depression, and substance abuse [12, 101, 102] all contribute as risk factors for adolescent suicide. Parental or family discord and/or parental separation or divorce [103] has an impact as well.

Negative Life Stressors/Environmental Influences

Negative life events have been shown to be related to suicidality in youth [104]. A history of physical and/or sexual abuse during childhood [35, 105] has also been associated, with sexual abuse being more significant. Brown et al [35] estimated that between 16.5 and 19.5% of suicide attempts in youth may be due to child sexual abuse. Other forms of childhood maltreatment have also been shown as risk factors [106]. Environmental factors that influence suicidality in youth include media-generated contagion. Media coverage of suicide or the fictional representation of suicide in the media is associated with suicide in vulnerable teenagers [5]. Schmidtke and Hafner [107] and Hawton et al (1999) [108] found an increase in suicides and an increase in the depicted method of suicide following suicides shown on television. Adolescents and young adults appear to be most easily affected by media contagion with only minimal effects after age 24 [6].

Methods of Suicide in Children and Adolescents

In the US, firearms have been the leading method used to commit suicide across all age groups, including prepubertal children, [109] although this has recently changed in the 10-14-year-old age group. Beginning in 1997, among children ages 10-14, suffocation surpassed firearms as the most common suicide method [110] Suffocation suicides began occurring with increasing frequency in the 1990s and by 2001, a total of 1.8 suffocation suicides occurred for every firearm suicide among 10-14-year-olds, with poisoning as the third most common suicide method in that age group [110].

Although suicidal death by firearms has decreased in the 10-14-year-old age group, firearms remain a significant means of violent death among US children 5–14 years old, and from the period of 1988–1997, 1,588 firearm suicides were documented [111]. Children were seven times more likely to die from a firearm suicide if they lived in a state with high vs. low gun levels. The relationship between guns and violent death remained statistically significant even after controlling for state-level poverty, education, and urbanization, [111] suggesting that access to guns is a serious risk variable in child suicide. Other methods for suicide attempts in the 6-12 year age group include severe self-hitting and head banging, [7] jumping from heights, drowning, running into traffic, ingesting poison, hanging, stabbing, and burning [5, 28].

In 2000, the overwhelming methods of choice for suicide among 15-24-year-olds were firearms and explosives, accounting for 57% of all completed suicides in that age group [90]. Firearms are the modal method used by adolescent males to complete suicide, and contrary to popular belief, firearms are also the modal method used by adolescent females to complete suicide [39]. In 2000, 15-19-year-old females showed a 14% increase in the use of firearms to complete suicide, accounting for 39% of all female suicides in that age range, and a 69% decline in deaths by poisoning, accounting for only 15% of deaths in that age group [90]. It has been estimated that eliminating access to guns would prevent as much as 32% of completed suicides among minors [112]. Of other methods to commit suicide, hanging has been more frequent among males, with ingestions predominating in females [39].

Cross-Cultural Aspects of Suicide in Children and Adolescents

Worldwide, hanging is the most frequently used method of suicide, and in agrarian economies, the use of pesticides is the most common method [39]. However, in the US, firearms remain the most commonly used method of suicide overall [109]. In a comparison of the US with 26 other industrialized countries between the years of 1990-1995, US children ages 1-14 had a suicide rate twice that of other countries combined (0.55 vs. 0.27), and suicide by firearm in the US was almost 11 times the rate for other countries combined (0.32 vs. 0.03).

In 5-14 year olds, nonfirearm-related suicides were the same among children in the US and other countries (0.35 vs. 0.35), but firearm-related suicide rates were 10 times greater for US children (0.49 vs. 0.05) [2, 113]. The high rate of suicide by firearms in the US appears to be a cultural phenomenon reflecting the high degree of access US children have to guns [111]. A cross-cultural study of rates of suicide by firearm between 1990 and 1995 among 15-24-year-olds in 34 countries [114] found that they ranged from 0 per 100,000 in Mauritius, Hong Kong, and Kuwait to 11.4 per 100,000 in Finland. The US ranked second among these countries in rates of firearm suicide yet had the highest proportion of suicides by firearm relative to all other methods. Male suicide rates in the 15-24 age range exceed those of females in all countries except in some areas of China [39]. Moreover, in some countries the ratio of male to female suicide rates in this age group is as high as 10:1.

Pritchard and Hansen, [115] utilizing World Health Organization data from 1974-1999, found cross-cultural differences in rates of suicide in children aged 5-14. In general, they found that child suicide rates were statistically low, and Canadian male children had the highest rate of suicide at 15 per million, followed by the US and the Netherlands at 12 and 8 per million, respectively. Lowest rates of child suicide in males were reported for England and Wales, Italy, and Spain, at 1, 2, and 3 per million, respectively. For females in the same age group, rates were small across countries, with a range of 1 to 4 per million. Pritchard and Hansen [115] also utilized the data pool described above to look at cross-cultural differences in rates of suicide in adolescents aged 15-24. Rates increased as children reached adolescence. In this age group, Australian males had the highest suicide rate at 260 per million followed by Canada and Japan at 226 and 149 per million, respectively. Lowest rates of adolescent and youth suicide in males were reported for Italy, Spain, and England and Wales, at 76, 77, and 95 per million, respectively. As with males, suicide completions increased substantially for females in the 15-24-year-old age group. Japan had the highest rate at 67 per million, followed by Australia and Canada at 60 and 47 per million, respectively. Lowest rates of female suicide in this age group were found in Italy, Spain, and England and Wales at 18, 20, and 22 per million respectively. Across cultures, suicide rates differ and are intimately tied to the mores and customs of a given country or region of the world. Religious beliefs, taboos against or acceptance of suicide, laws, access to means, poverty, and level of industrialization are just a few of the cultural considerations that impact suicide rates in different countries [116].

Identification of Suicidal Children and Adolescents

Assessment of suicide risk in children and adolescents is not only key in protecting them from self-harm, accurate assessment is also necessary for treatment planning and management. Assessment of suicidality is an ongoing process, and the assessment may be generated from several different sources. One source of assessment is the clinical interview and ongoing clinical inquiry across time. Quantitative and qualitative assessments are also often used. Distinguishing between risk factors and warning signs of suicidality can also inform the practitioner regarding level of risk and likelihood of imminent danger. Finally, for those who are practitioners who come into contact with children and adolescents but are not schooled in suicidology, there are brief screenings available as well.

Methods of Assessment

Clinical Interviews

Suicide risk assessment involves active inquiry of suicidal youth on the part of the practitioner and covers a number of areas, as shown in Table 1.

Table 1. Assessment of Suicidality through Clinical Interview Areas of Inquiry

Predisposing vulnerabilities
–   Triggers or precipitating events
–   Mental status: affective, cognitive, and behavioral states
–   Contraindications: coping skills and resources versus failed protections
–   Suicidal intent, reasons for suicide, and lethality
–   Compliance

Adapted from: Berman, A. L., Jobes, D. A., and Silverman, M. M. (2006): *Adolescent suicide: Assessment and intervention.* Washington, DC: American Psychological Association; 124.

Table 2. Points for Assessment and Documentation of Suicidality

–   At intake for all new patients
–   At mention, observation, or report of suicidal ideation or past suicidal behavior
–   When there are signs of change in mental status
–   During increased environmental stressor-worsening symptoms
–   When there is a predisposition to be suicidal
–   Immediately after self-harm behavior
–   At times of management transition (e.g., rotation of psychiatric residents, therapist vacations of changes) when there is a history or signs of emotional reactivity and behavioral instability

Adapted from: Berman, A. L., Jobes, D. A., and Silverman, M. M. (2006): *Adolescent suicide: Assessment and intervention.* Washington, DC: American Psychological Association; 120.

The practitioner must assess predisposing vulnerabilities to commit suicide, determine if there are current triggers that raise the risk of suicidal behavior, evaluate mental status and assess whether it has changed from a previous level of functioning, and seek out protective factors such as coping skills and gage those protective factors relative importance and weight in relation to the risk factors. Additionally, the practitioner must inquire about degree of intent, reasons for wishing to die, and level of lethality for suicide as well as form an opinion as to whether the patient will be compliant with treatment. As shown in Table 2, suicide risk cannot be assessed only once, but must be reassessed at critical points in treatment. Additionally, each assessment should be thoroughly documented [39].

Clearly, adequate initial clinical interview and ongoing clinical assessment of suicidal patients are necessary for adequate and competent care to be given, for only then can a comprehensive treatment plan be formulated and implemented.

Quantitative Assessment

Quantitative assessment procedures are also often used in conjunction with clinical interview in the assessment of risk of suicidal behavior in children and adolescents. Goldston [117] reviewed more than 60 instruments that have been used to evaluate suicidal behaviors in children and adolescents. He reviewed instruments that assessed the presence of suicidal behaviors, risk or propensity for suicidal behaviors, intentionality and medical lethality of suicidal behaviors, and various others. He noted that all of the instruments had strengths and weaknesses, and stated that very few instruments demonstrated the ability to predict attempted suicide. Goldston stated that when claims are made regarding an instrument's ability to predict future suicidal behavior, those claims are false because the empirical data do not support them. Based upon his review of available instruments, Goldston recommended two instruments for use: Beck's Scale for Suicidal Ideation[118] and Linehan's Reasons for Living (RFL) Inventory [119]. These scales are primarily geared toward adolescents, although there are also screening tools available to assess suicidal ideation and intent in young children [120].

Given the inadequacy of psychometric scales to predict future suicidal behavior and given ongoing issues with high rates of false positives and false negatives in using them, it appears reasonable to suggest that such scales be a part of a comprehensive evaluation of suicide risk that includes both testing and in-depth clinical interview [39].

Qualitative Assessment

There has been a recent increase in interest in the utilization of qualitative measures for suicidal assessment, i.e., obtaining and assessing patients' experiences by having them write their perceptions of their own suicidality in response to different stimulus prompts. In a recent study, Jobes *et al* [121] conducted an exploratory investigation into suicidal patients' qualitative written responses to five open-ended prompts from the Suicide Status Form. The authors found that two-thirds of the written responses could be reliably categorized under four major headings: relational, role responsibility, self, and unpleasant internal states, thus giving the clinician a view of how suicidal patients describe their own experience. While recognizing the possible superiority of quantitative methods of assessment over qualitative ones, these authors argue that both quantitative and qualitative assessment methods are important and may prove additive, thereby providing a more comprehensive assessment of suicidality, leading to more effective interventions.

Risk Factors vs. Warning Signs as Assessment

Rudd *et al* [122] have offered another way to look at risk for suicide and suggest that differentiating risk factors from warning signs can help establish a level of imminent danger in the suicidal patient. Table 3 shows the difference between risk factors and warning signs.

Risk factors are static and enduring (e.g., life-time psychiatric diagnoses) whereas warning signs (e.g., thoughts of suicide, behaviors preparing for suicide) are episodic and variable. Risk factors generally are well-defined constructs, such as DSM-IV diagnoses, whereas warning signs may be poorly defined as a construct (e.g., behaviors such as buying a weapon). Risk factors are often not much help in intervention because they are defined and static; they don't usually change (e.g., age, gender, family history).

Warning signs demand a specific and immediate intervention because they indicate the presence of an active suicidal crisis. Risk factors are more objective (diagnosis, family history, history of suicidal behavior) and warning signs may be more subjective (e.g., threats, talking, writing about suicide), but ultimately, it is warning signs that provide the best information about imminent danger.

Table 3. Risk Factors vs. Warning Signs of Suicide

Risk Factors	Warning Signs
Distal	Proximal
Implies enduring or longer -term risk	Implies imminent risk
Static nature	Episodic or transient nature
Defined constructs	Poorly defined constructs
Limited implications for	Specific intervention
Intervention	demanded

Adapted from Rudd, M. D., Berman, A. L., Joiner, T. E., Nock, M. K., Silverman, M. M., Mandrusiak, M., Van Orden, K., and Witte, T. (2006): Warning signs for suicide: theory, research, and clinical applications. *Suicide and Life-Threatening Behavior*, 36; 257.

Brief Screening for Suicidality in Children and Adolescents

Unless involved in the mental health field, few people have in-depth knowledge about suicide, even though suicide touches many people's lives. In an effort to provide suicide assessment skills to people who are not mental health practitioners, gatekeeper training is often utilized. Gatekeeper is a term used to define the role of people who are taught basic suicide prevention and intervention steps [123, 124]. The term "gatekeeping" describes the protective functions gatekeepers use in the process of recognizing, responding to, and referring a suicidal person to the appropriate resources. Gatekeepers often use brief methods of suicide assessment that are easily remembered because they are acronyms. One regularly used acronym is S.L.A.P. (Native Hawaiian Youth suicide prevention project and the Gatekeeper training, 2004) which stands for Specificity, Lethality, Availability, and Proximity. S.L.A.P. can be used by any practitioner who comes into contact with children and adolescents to perform a brief suicide assessment [123, 124].

Greater specificity of plan for suicide increases the risk of suicide completion, although children and adolescents sometimes may be impulsive and act without a plan. More lethal means increases the risk of suicide completion. In general, a firearm is going to be the most lethal means because it is usually irreversible. Also, because children and adolescents may not conceive of death as final, they may choose more lethal means than they intend. The higher the availability of the means chosen for suicide, the greater the risk that suicide will occur. If children or adolescents have access to the means by which they are choosing to die, they are more likely to carry out the attempt. Finally, proximity is an important consideration because the greater the distance from rescue, the higher the risk of a completed suicide. Proximity is measured in physical, geographical, and emotion terms [123, 124].

Additional Considerations in Identifying at-Risk Prepubertal Children

Identification of young children at-risk for suicide may be increased by considering the risk factors identified as associated with potential suicidal behavior. These include psychiatric disorders, most notably depression, past suicide attempts, family history of first-degree relatives having attempted suicide, especially mothers, parental substance abuse, child abuse, family discord, parental loss, and other negative life experiences. However, many young children have some or all of these risk factors and do not become suicidal, so it is important to consider characteristics that have been found to be predictive of suicidality independent of the above-mentioned risk factors.

Nock and Kazdin's [3] finding that the presence of anhedonia, negative automatic thoughts, and hopelessness predicted suicidal thinking and behavior independent of depression has implications for assessment of suicidality in prepubertal children. The presence of anhedonia, in particular, was highly associated with children's current suicide attempts, and given that anhedonia has also been found to be a highly specific symptom of depression in preschool children [25] it seems reasonable to consider anhedonia as a potential "red flag" for suicidal thinking in at-risk prepubertal children.

Prevention

Prevention programs to reduce suicide include primary, secondary, and tertiary approaches [39] and range from federal and public health initiatives, [9, 38] state [125] and local Stop Youth Suicide campaigns, [126] crisis intervention and telephone hotline services, and school- and college-based prevention programs [39].

Studies indicate that the best way to prevent suicide is through early detection and treatment of depression and other psychiatric illnesses that increase suicide risk. Beautrais *et al* [105] found evidence that the elimination of mood disorders would result in reductions, up to 80%, in risk of a serious suicide attempt. Other data support that claim as well [127]. This is not to imply that factors other than mood disorders are unimportant in suicidal risk, but adequate recognition and treatment of mental disorders are good first steps toward suicide prevention [127].

Most youth prevention programs for suicidality are focused on adolescents, [6, 16] but that may be too late for the at-risk child. Mishara [33] suggests that school-based primary prevention programs may have significant beneficial effects and could be used to prevent suicidal behavior in prepubertal children. Further, he suggests that these programs should be implemented at an early age, prior to the onset of suicidal thinking, if possible [33].

For college students, campus mental health services must be enhanced and adequately staffed to ensure the best outcome for those with mental health problems. Past-year prevalence of mental illness is highest (39%) for youth ages 15-21, suggesting that college students have a high level of psychological distress that may lead to suicide [62]. Post-attempt interventions are also necessary and may include cognitive therapy, dialectical behavior therapy, and pharmacological approaches [127].

Prevention of suicide may often depend upon front-line practitioners who see suicidal youth. These practitioners will likely not be mental health practitioners, but are more likely to be primary care physicians and pediatricians who have substantial contact with youth. They need to be aware of and screen for suicidal ideation; such assessment needs to occur before a suicide attempt as well as after an unsuccessful one. However, when surveyed, fewer than half of pediatric and primary care physicians reported that they routinely screen their adolescent patients for suicide risk [128]. A number of studies show that deliberate self-harm patients who presented to emergency rooms and left without a psychosocial and/or psychiatric assessment were more likely to engage in subsequent self-harm [129, 130]. Thus, prevention of suicide must include intervention regarding the precursors of the ideation, intention, and behavior as well as continued assessment and treatment subsequent to a suicide attempt.

Prepubertal children are even less likely than adolescents to be referred to a mental health practitioner for suicide assessment. Primary care and pediatric physicians are also more likely to see these children, and suicidality will rarely be assessed. Jellinek [131] suggests that pediatricians feel overwhelmed and are unlikely to use mental health screening tools because they will not be reimbursed. Furthermore, he states that many primary care physicians and pediatricians are not trained to interview school-age children about suicidal ideation.

Pediatricians and primary care physicians, as front-line practitioners dealing with young children, should be given training in mental health issues in general, and suicidality, in particular. Voelker [132] found that 72% of 600 family physicians and pediatricians in his study had prescribed a Selective Serotonin Reuptake Inhibitor (SSRI) for a child or adolescent patient, but only 8% said they had received adequate training in the treatment of childhood depression, and only 16% reported that they felt comfortable treating children for depression. In addition to medical practitioners, Jackson and Nuttall[7] suggest that teachers, parents, and school counselors should also be trained to screen for suicidality in children.

There is little empirical evidence that suggests which suicide prevention strategies work best with children and adolescents. However, there is evidence from adolescent suicide prevention studies regarding what does not work. Unhelpful strategies include scare tactics and health-awareness programs that focus solely on suicide prevention [133]. There is also no evidence to suggest that exposure to suicide prevention programs increases suicidal behavior [134].

Treatment

Shaffer *et al* [5] outline appropriate treatment options for suicidal prepubertal children and adolescents. If actively suicidal, they should be hospitalized until the acute crisis has passed; hospitalization may be followed by partial hospitalization, if deemed necessary. Outpatient treatments are appropriate if the child or adolescent is not actively suicidal and there are sufficient supports at home. Different methods of treatment have been found to be useful and include cognitive-behavioral therapy (CBT) which seeks to change the way the child or adolescent thinks, interpersonal therapy which addresses interpersonal problems, and dialectical-behavioral therapy which involves problem-oriented strategies to increase distress tolerance, emotion regulation, interpersonal effectiveness, and the use of both rational and emotional input to make balanced decisions [135]. Although individual therapy is the usual treatment of choice for treating suicidal youth, family therapy may sometimes be the treatment of choice [39]. When family discord, poor communication, lack of cohesion, parental conflict, and parental psychopathology are contributors to suicidality in a child or adolescent, family treatment is likely to be the best treatment format because the primary system of support is targeted for intervention.

No formal studies of psychopharmacological interventions have been completed with regard to prepubertal children. However, there has been at least one randomized, controlled trial addressing this issue in adolescents between the ages of 12 and 17. The Treatment for Adolescents with Depression Study (TADS) followed a volunteer sample of 439 patients with a primary diagnosis of Major Depressive Disorder. The study sought to determine the effectiveness of each of four treatment groups over a course of twelve weeks: 1) fluoxetine alone, 2) CBT alone, 3) fluoxetine and CBT, and 4) placebo. It was found, compared with placebo, that the combination of fluoxetine and CBT was statistically significant on the Children's Depression Rating Scaled-Revised. Compared with fluoxetine alone and CBT alone, treatment of fluoxetine with CBT was superior, whereas fluoxetine was superior to CBT alone. While clinically significant suicidal thinking, found in 29% of the sample, significantly decreased in all four treatment groups, the greatest decrease was in the fluoxetine with CBT group [136].

Recent controversy about the possible increase of suicidality in children and adolescents treated with SSRIs led the US Food and Drug Administration to direct pharmaceutical companies to place "black box warnings" on package inserts of all antidepressant drugs. This warning alerts health care providers to an increased risk of suicidality, i.e., suicidal thinking and behavior, in children and adolescents and states that patients should be provided with a patient medication guide advising them of risks and precautions [137]. Currently, only fluoxetine is approved for the treatment of depression in pediatric youth; any other anti-depressant used for youth under the age of 18 is considered "off label" use, i.e, used in a way other than that for which it was approved by the FDA.

Postvention:
Caring for the Survivors of Suicide

Surviving the suicide of a loved one leaves survivors with a profound sense of grief, loss, anger, questions regarding motivation, and sometimes a sense of overwhelming guilt, perhaps due to thoughts that the survivor was not good enough to have made the suicide victim value life enough to stay alive or thoughts of having done something to make the suicide victim want to complete suicide [138]. When the suicide victim is a child or adolescent, those reactions may be even more profound. Over the past thirty years, suicide survivorship and healing work has emerged as a major area of attention within the field of suicidology [138]. Survivors of suicide often have special treatment and support needs that may be met through various settings, modalities, and activities. Four main areas for postvention include: 1) group and systems postvention, 2) clinical response, e.g., therapy, 3) support groups, and 4) training of first responders [138]. While a full discussion of the area of postvention is beyond the scope of this chapter, it is an important component of current suicidology. For a more complete description of postvention see *Adolescent suicide: Assessment and intervention*, chapter 9, pp. 335-364 [138].

Standards of Clinical Care for the Suicidal Patient

Survivors of suicide often seek legal representation in order to allege malpractice on the part of the clinical care practitioner. One recent survey found that the majority of family survivors of a suicide victim in treatment at the time of death considered contacting an attorney; 25% did so [139]. Litman [140] estimated that 1 in 3 suicides by inpatients results in a lawsuit, and over the past 20 years, there has been a substantial increase in lawsuits against outpatient practitioners [39]. Psychologists have more than a 1 in 5, and psychiatrists have a 1 in 2 chance of having one or more patients complete suicide over the course of their career [39]. It is, therefore, incredibly important to provide a level of care that will discourage litigation in the unfortunate circumstance of a patient suicide.

Practitioners have both a duty and a standard of care for their patients. Duty of care is a legal term, and with at-risk patients it carries with it responsibilities to act affirmatively to protect them from their own violent acts. Depending upon the nature of the relationship between practitioner and patient, the scope of the duty may vary. With regard to mental health practitioners, the duty of care is clear. The court expects the practitioner to attempt to prevent the suicide of patients. If the court finds that this duty was breached through negligence, either by acts of omission or commission, relative to the accepted standard of care, negligence or malpractice may result. It is, however, the responsibility of the plaintiff, usually the suicide victim's family, to establish negligence through proving that there was a dereliction of duty by the practitioner that directly caused the damages [39].

A practitioner also has a standard of care to uphold; the standard of care specifies that services will be provided with the degree of skill and care customarily used in similar circumstances by similar practitioners [141]. Two factors related to standard of care usually determine liability in death by suicide: foreseeability and reasonable care. Foreseeability regards the assessment of risk. If a practitioner fails to assess suicide risk, the standard of care has not been met and an egregious clinical error has been made.

Reasonable care refers to the ongoing treatment of suicidal patients. Treatment plans should be developed consistent with patients' diagnoses and assessed suicide risk and should include appropriate precautions as dictated by evaluated risk. If those things are not carried out in a dependable fashion, the standard of care is not met; thus, negligent practice has occurred and malpractice may be determined.

Conclusion

Clearly, the responsibility of the practitioner treating a suicidal child or adolescent is a daunting proposition fraught with peril for both the suicidal patient and practitioner. Working with suicidal patients has consistently been found to be the most stressful of all clinical endeavors, [142] and practitioners should be aware of their abilities in the area of suicidality and act accordingly. It is unfortunate that mental health professionals receive so little training in the area of suicidology and often are not prepared for dealing the suicidal [39].

If a practitioner does not have the ability to provide a recognized standard of care to a suicidal patient, that patient should be referred to a practitioner with the requisite skills and resources to provide a standard of care to decrease the likelihood of a successful suicide completion because every life has worth and should be protected. The lives of children and adolescents, as the future generation, must also be protected, and as practitioners working with the pediatric population, it is our duty to do so.

In the words of Dr. Forest Witcraft [143]:

One hundred years from now it will not matter what your bank account was, the sort of house you lived in, or the kind of car you drove...but the world may be different because you were important in the life of a child.

References

[1]   Hoyert DL, Matthews TJ, Menacker F, et al. Annual summary of vital statistics. *Pediatrics*. 2006;117:168-193.

[2]   Prevention CfDCa. Rates of homicide, suicide, and firearm-related death among children--26 industrialized countries. *Morbidity and Mortality Weekly Report* 1997;46:101-105.

[3]   Nock MK, Kazdin AE. Examination of affective, cognitive, and behavioral factors and suicide-related outcomes in children and young adolescents. *Journal of Clinical Child and Adolescent Psychology*. 2002;31:48-58.

[4]   Minino AM, Heron MP, Smith BL. Deaths: Preliminary data for 2004. In Report NVS, (Ed): National Center for Health Statistics 2006.

[5]   Shaffer D, Pfeffer CR, Bernet W, et al. Practice parameters for the assessment and treatment of children and adolescents with suicidal behavior. *Journal of the American Academy of Child and Adolescent Psychiatry*. 2001;40:24S-51S.

[6]   Gould MS, Greenberg T, Velting DM, et al. Youth suicide risk and preventive interventions: A review of the past 10 years. *Journal of the American Academy of Child and Adolescent Psychiatry*. 2003;42:386-405.

[7]   Jackson H, Nuttall RL. Risk for preadolescent suicial behavior: An ecological model. *Child and Adolescent Social Work Journal*. 2001;18:189-203.

[8]   Pfeffer CR, Klerman GL, Hurt SW, et al. Suicidal children grow up: Rates and psychosocial risk factors for suicide attempts during follow-up. *Journal of the American Academy of Child and Adolescent Psychiatry*. 1993;32:106-113.

[9]   Service USPH. The Surgeon General's Call to Action to Prevent Suicide. Washington, D. C. 1999.

[10]   Organization WH. Figures and Facts about Suicide. Geneva, Switzerland: Department of Mental Health, World Health Organization 1999.

[11]   Greene DB. Childhood suicide and myths surrounding it. *Social Work*. 1994;39:230-232.

[12]   Pfeffer CR, Normandin L, Tatsuyuki K. Suicidal children grow up: Relations between family psychopathology and adolescents' lifetime suicidal behavior. *Journal of Nervous and Mental Disease*. 1998;136:269-275.

[13] Pfeffer CR, Normandin L, Tatsuyuki K. Suicidal children grow up: Suicidal behavior and psychiatric disorder among relatives. *Journal of the American Academy of Child and Adolescent Psychiatry*. 1994;33:1087-1097.

[14] Reinherz HZ, Giaconia RM, Silverman AB, et al. Early psychosocial risks for adolescent suicidal ideation and attempts. *Journal of the American Academy of Child and Adolescent Psychiatry*. 1995;34:599-611.

[15] Pfeffer CR. Childhood suicidal behavior: A developmental perspective. *Psychiatric Clinics of North America*. 1997;20:552-562.

[16] Moskos MA, Achilles J, Gray D. Adolescent suicide myths in the United States. *Crisis*. 2004;25:176-182.

[17] Prevention CfDCa, (Ed). Web-based Injury Statistics Query and Reporting System (WISQARS). Atlanta, GA: US Department of Health and Human Services, CDC, National Center for Injury Prevention and Control 2003.

[18] Patros P, Shamoo R. Depression and suicide in chidlren and adolescents: Prevention, intervention, and postvention. Needham Heights, MA: Simon and Schuster 1989.

[19] Workman CG, Prior M. Depression and suicide in young children. *Issues in Comprehensive Pediatric Nursing*. 1997;20:125-132.

[20] O'Leary CC, Frank DA, Grant-Knight W, et al. Suicidal ideation among urban nine and ten year olds. *Developmental and Behavioral Pediatrics*. 2006;27:33-39.

[21] Gould MS, King R, Greenwald S, et al. Psychopathology associated with suicidal ideation and attempts among children and adolescents. *Journal of the American Academy of Child and Adolescent Psychiatry*. 1998;37:915-923.

[22] Kovacs M, Goldston D, Gatsonis C. Suicidal behaviors and childhood-onset depressive disorders: A longitudinal investigation. *Journal of the American Academy of Child and Adolescent Psychiatry*. 1993;32:8-20.

[23] Ialongo NS, Edelson G, Kellam SG. A further look at the prognostic power of young children's reports of depressed mood. *Child Development*. 2001;72:736-747.

[24] Weissman MM, Wolk S, Goldstein RB, et al. Depressed adolescents grow up. *Journal of the American Medical Association*. 1999;281:1707-1713.

[25] Luby JL, Heffelfinger AK, Mrakotsky C, et al. The clinical picture of depression in preschool children. *Journal of the American Academy of Child and Adolescent Psychiatry*. 2003;42:340-348.

[26] Livingston RL, Bracha HS. Psychotic symptoms and suicidal behavior in hospitalized children. *American Journal of Psychiatry*. 1992;149:1585-1586.

[27] Cohen-Sandler R, Berman AL, King RA. A follow-up study of hospitalized suicidal children. *Journal of the American Academy of Child Psychiatry*. 1982;21:398-403.

[28] Pfeffer CR, Plutchik R, Mizruchi MS, et al. Suicidal behavior in child psychiatric inpatients and outpatients and in nonpatients. *American Journal of Psychiatry*. 1986;143:733-738.

[29] Agerbo E, Nordentoft M, Mortensen PB. Familial, psychiatric, and socioeconomic risk factors for suicide in young people: Nested case control study. *British Medical Journal*. 2002;325:74-78.

[30] McGuffi P, Marusic A, Farmer A. What can psychiatric genetics offer suicidology. *Crisis*. 2001;22:61-65.

[31] Jacobsen LK, Rabinowitz I, Popper MS, et al. Interviewing prepubertal children aboub suicidal ideation and behavior. *Journal of the American Academy of Child and Adolescent Psychiatry* 1994;33:439-452.

[32] Monasterio E. Fundamental skills for case managers: A self-study guide. UNIT 3: Stages of development--Adolescents and their children. Oakland, CA: Center for Health Training 2003.

[33] Mishara BL. How the media influences children's conceptions of suicide. *Crisis.* 2003;24:128-130.

[34] Klimes-Dougan B, Free K, Ronsaville D, et al. Suicidal ideation and attempts: A longitudinal investigation of children of depressed and well mothers. *Journal of the American Academy of Child and Adolescent Psychiatry.* 1999;38:651-659.

[35] Brown J, Cohen P, Johnson JG, et al. Childhood abuse and neglect: Specificity of effects on adolescent and young adult depression and suicidality. *Journal of the American Academy of Child and Adolescent Psychiatry.* 1999;38:1490-1496.

[36] Berman AL, Jobes DA. Adolescent suicide: Assessment and intervention. Washington, DC: American Psychological Association 1991.

[37] Rosenberg ML, Smith JC, Davidson LE, et al. The emergence of youth suicide: An epidemiologic analysis and public health perspective. *Annual Review of Public Health.* 1987;8:417-440.

[38] Services USDoHaH. Healthy people 2010: With understanding and improving health objectives for improving health Washington, DC: U. S. Government Printing Office 2000.

[39] Berman AL, Jobes DA, Silverman MM. Adolescent suicide: Assessment and intervention. Washington, DC: American Psychological Association 2006.

[40] Prevention) NCfHSCfDCa. Death rates for 113 selected causes, by 5-year age groups, race, and sex: United States, 1999-2003. 2006:373-376.

[41] Statistics NCfH. DHHS, Mortality statistics branch. Annual summary. Hyattsville, MD: U. S. Public Health Service 2002.

[42] Beautrais AL. Life course factors associated with suicidal behaviors in young people. *American Behavioral Scientist.* 2003;46:1137-1156.

[43] Prevention CfDCa. Youth risk behavior surveillance--United States, 2005. *Morbidity and Mortality Weekly Report.* 2006;55(SS-5).

[44] Reynolds WM. Psychometric characteristics of the adult suicidal ideation questionnaire in college students. *Journal of Personality Assessment.* 1991;56:289-307.

[45] Brener ND, Hassan SS, Barrios LC. Suicidal ideation among college students in the U.S. *Journal of Consulting and Clinical Psychology.* 1999;67:1004-1008.

[46] Barrios LC, Everett SA, Simon TR, et al. Suicidal ideation among U. S. college students: Association with other injury risk behaviors. *Journal of American College Health.* 2000;48:229-233.

[47] Lipschitz A. College Suicide: A Review Monograph. New York: American Suicide Foundation 1990.

[48] Silverman MM, Meyer PM, Sloane F, et al. The Big Ten student suicide study: A 10-year study of suicide on Midwestern university campuses. *Suicide and Life-Threatening Behavior.* 1997;27:285-303.

[49] Schwartz AJ. The epidemiology of suicide among students at colleges and universities in the United States. *Journal of College Student Psychotherapy*. 1990;4:25-44.

[50] Schwartz AJ, Whitaker LC. Suicide among college students: Assessment, treatment and intervention. In Blumenthal SJ, Kupfer DJ, (Eds). Suicide over the Life Cycle: Risk Factors, Assessment, and Treatment of Suicidal Patients. Washington, D. C.: American Psychiatric Press 1990:303-340.

[51] Haas AP, Hendin H, Mann JJ. Suicide in college students. *American Behavioral Scientist*. 2003;46:1224-1240.

[52] Paffenbarger RS, Asnes DP. Chronic disease in former college students, III. Precursors of suicide in early and middle life. *American Journal of Public Health*. 1966;56:1026-1036.

[53] Paffenbarger RS, King SH, Wing AL. Chronic disease in former college students, IX. Characteristics in youth that predispose to suicide and accidental death in later life. *American Journal of Public Health*. 1969;59:900-908.

[54] Arnstein RL. The place of college health in the prevention of suicide and affective disorders. In Klerman GL, (Ed). Youth in Despair: Preventive Aspects of Suicide and Depression among Adolescents and Young Adults. Washington, D. C.: American Psychiatric Press 1986:337-361.

[55] Piaget J. The psychology of the child. New York: Basic Books 1972.

[56] Piaget J. The child's conception of the world. New York: Littlefield Adams 1990.

[57] The essential Piaget (100th anniversary edition). In Piaget J, Gruber H, Voneche JJ, (Eds). New York: Jason Aronson 1995.

[58] Program PCWT. The effects of abuse and neglect on child development.

[59] Transition NCoY. Developmental milestones: University of South Florida 2005.

[60] Hall GS. Adolescence: Its psychology and its relation to physiology, anthropology, sociology, sex, crime, religion, and education. Englewood Cliffs, NJ: Prentice-Hall 1904.

[61] Buchannan CM, Eccles JS, Flanagan C, et al. Parents' and teachers' beliefs about adolescents: Effects of sex and experience. *Journal of Youth and Adolescence*. 1990;19:363-394.

[62] Mowbray CT, Megivern D, Mandiberg JM, et al. Campus mental health services: Recommendations for change. *American Journal of Orthopsychiatry*. 2006;76:226-237.

[63] Houston K, Hawton K, Sheppard R. Suicide in young people 15-24: A psychological autopsy study. *Jounral of Affective Disorders*. 2001;63:159-170.

[64] Shaffer D, Gould MS, Fisher P, et al. Psychiatric diagnosis in child and adolescent suicide. *Archives of General Psychiatry*. 1996;53:339-348.

[65] Beautrais AL. Serious Suicide Attempts in Young People: a Case Control Study. Dunedin, New Zealand: University of Otago 1996.

[66] Dean PJ, Range LM. The escape theory of suicide and perfectionism in college students. *Death Studies*. 1996;20:41-424.

[67] Lester D. Locus of control and suicidality. *Perceptual and Motor Skills*. 1999;89:1042.

[68] Langhinrichsen-Rohling J, Arata C, Bowers D, et al. Suicidal behavior, negative affect, and self-reported delinquency in college students. *Suicide and Life-Threatening Behavior*. 2004;34:255-266.

[69]   Brent DA, Perper J, Moritz G, et al. Stressful life events, psychopathology, and adolescent suicide: A case-control study. *Suicide and Life-Threatening Behavior.* 1993;23:179-187.

[70]   Brent DA, Perper JA, Moritz G, et al. Suicide in affectively ill adolescents: A case control study. *Journal of Affective Disorders.* 1994;31:193-202.

[71]   Overholser J, Freheit SR, DiFilippo JM. Emotional distress and substance abuse as risk factors for suicide attempts. *Canadian Journal of Psychiatry.* 1997;42:402-408.

[72]   Miller AL, Glinski J. Youth suicidal behavior: Assessment and intervention. *Journal of Clinical Psychology.* 2000;56:1131-1152.

[73]   Abel EL, Zeidenberg P. Age, alcohol, and violent death. *Journal of the Study of Alcohol.* 1985;46:228-231.

[74]   Hoberman HM, Garfinkel BD. Completed suicide in youth. *Canadian Journal of Psychiatry.* 1988;33:494-502.

[75]   Poteet DJ. Adolescent suicide: A review of 87 cases of completed suicide in Shelby County, TN. *American Journal of Forensic Medicine and Pathology.* 1987;8:12-17.

[76]   Berman AL, Schwartz R. Suicide attempts among adolescent drug users. *American Journal of Diseases of Children.* 1990;144:310-314.

[77]   Brent DA, Perper JA, Allman CJ. Alcohol, firearms and suicide among youth: Temporal trends in Allegheny County, Pennsylvania, 1960-1983. *Journal of the American Medical Association.* 1987;257:3369-3372.

[78]   Shafii M, Carrigan S, Whittinghill JR, et al. Psychological autopsy of completed suicide in children and adolescents. *American Journal of Psychiatry.* 1985;142:1061-1064.

[79]   Apter A, Bleich A, Plutchick R, et al. Suicidal behavior, depression, and conduct disorder in hopitalized adolescents. *Journal of the American Academy of Child and Adolescent Psychiatry.* 1988;27:696-699.

[80]   Fazaa N, Page S. Dependency and self-criticism as predictors of suicidal behavior. *Suicide and Life-Threatening Behavior.* 2003;33:172-185.

[81]   Chioqueta AP, Stiles TC. Personality traits and the development of depression, hopelessness, and suicide ideation. *Personality and Individual Differences.* 2005;38:1283-1291.

[82]   Gibb bE, Andover MS, Beach SRH. Suicidal behavior and attitudes toward suicide. *Suicide and Life-Threatening Behavior.* 2006;36:12-18.

[83]   McAuliffe C, Corcoran P, Keeley HS, et al. Risk of suicide ideation associated with problem-solving ability and attitudes toward suicidal behavior in university students. *Crisis.* 2003;24:160-167.

[84]   Crumley FE. Adolescent suicide attempts. *Journal of the American Medical Association.* 1979;241:2404-2407.

[85]   Stoelb M, Chiriboga J. A process model for assessing adolescent risk for suicide. *Journal of Adolescence.* 1998;21:359-370.

[86]   Rudd MD, Joiner TE, Rajab MH. Relationships among suicide ideators, attempters, and multiple attempters in a young-adult sample. *Jounral of Abnormal Psychology.* 1996;105:541-550.

[87] Joiner TE, Conwell Y, Fitzpatrick KK, et al. Four studies of how past and current suicidality relate even when "everything but the kitchen sink" is covaried. *Journal of Abnormal Psychology*. 2005;114:291-303.

[88] Prevention CfDCa. Surveillance summaries. *Morbidity and Mortality Weekly Report*. 2002b;51(4).

[89] Oregon State Health Division CfHS. Oregon vital statistics report. Portland, OR: Oregon State Health Division, Center for Health Statistics 2000.

[90] Control NCfIPa. WISQARS fatal injuries: Mortality reports Abailable: http://webapp.cdc.gov/sasweb/ncipc/mortrate.html.

[91] Mann JJ, Brent DA, Arango V. The neurobiology and genetics of suicide and attempted suicide: A focus on the serotonergic system. *Neuropsychopharmacology*. 2001;24:467-477.

[92] Brent DA, Bridge J, Johnson BA, et al. Suicidal behavior runs in familes. *Archives of General Psychiatry*. 1996;53:1145-1152.

[93] Statham DJ, Heath AC, Madden PAF, et al. Suicide behavior: An epidemiological and genetic study. *Psychological Medicine*. 1998;28:839-855.

[94] Bennett PJ, McMahon WM, Watabe J, et al. Tryptophan hydrolase polymorphiasms in suicide victims. *Psychiatric Genetics*. 2000;10:13-17.

[95] Russell ST, Joyner K. Adolescent sexual orientation and suicide risk: Evidence from a national study. *American Journal of Public Health*. 2001;91:1276-1281.

[96] D'Augelli AR, Hershberger SL, Pilkington NW. Suicidality patterns and sexual orientation-related factors among lesbian, gay, and bisexual youths. *Suicide and Life-Threatening Behavior*. 2001;31:250-264.

[97] Cochran SD. Emerging issues in research on lesbians' and gay men's mental health: Does sexual orientation matter? *American Psychologist*. 2001;56:931-947.

[98] Cato Je, Canetto SS. Young adults' reactions to gay and lesbian peers who became suicidal following "coming out" to their parents. *Suicide and Life-Threatening Behavior*. 2003;33:201-210.

[99] Wagner BM, Cole RE, Schwartzman P. Psychosocial correlates of suicide attempts among junio and senior high school youth. *Suicide and Life-Threatening Behavior*. 1995;25:358-372.

[100] McHenry PC, Tishler CL, Kelly C. The role of drugs in adolescent suicide attempts. *Suicide and Life-Threatening Behavior*. 1983;13:166-175.

[101] Gould MS, Fisher P, Parides M, et al. Psychosocial risk factos of child and adolescent completed suicide. *Archives of General Psychiatry*. 1996;53:1155-1162.

[102] Gould MS, Kramer RA. Youth suicide prevention. *Suicide and Life-Threatening Behavior*. 2001;31 (Suppl.):6-31.

[103] Fergusson DM, Woodward LJ, Horwood LJ. Risk factors and life processes associated with the onset of suicidal behavior during adolescence and young adulthood. *Psychological Medicine*. 2000;30:23-29.

[104] Joiner TE, Rudd MD. Intensity and duration of suicidal crises vary as a function of previous suicide attempts and negative life events. *Journal of Consulting and Clinical Psychology*. 2000;68:909-916.

[105] Beautrais AL, Joyce PR, Mulder RT, et al. Prevalence and comorbidity of mental disorders in persons in serious suicide attempts: A case-control study. *American Journal of Psychiatry*. 1996;153:1009-1014.

[106] Gratz KL. Risk factors for deliberate self-harm among female college students: The role and interaction of childhood maltreatment, emotional inexpressivity, and affect intensity/reactivity. *American Journal of Orthopsychiatry*. 2006;76:238-250.

[107] Schmidtke A, Hafner J. The Werther effect after television films: New evidence for an old hypothesis. *Psychological Medicine*. 1988;18:665-676.

[108] Hawton K, Simkin S, Deeks JJ, et al. Effects of a drug overdose in a television drama on presentations to hospital for self poisoning: Time series and questionnaire study. *British Medical Journal*. 1999;318:972-977.

[109] Roche AM, Giner L, Zalsman G. Suicide among prepubertal children. In Merrick J, Zalsman G, (Eds). Suicidal Behavior in Adolescents: An International Perspective. London: Freund Publishing House Limited 2005:33-37.

[110] Prevention CfDCa. Methods of suicide among persons 10-19 years-United States, 1992-2001. *Morbidity and Mortality Weekly Report* 2004;53:471-474.

[111] Miller M, Azrael D, Hemenway D. Firearm availability and unintentional firearm deaths, suicides, and homicide among 5-15 year olds. *Journal of Trauma*. 2002;52:267-275.

[112] Shenassa ED, Catlin SN, Buka SL. Lethality of firearms relative to other suicide methods: A population based study. *Jounral of Epidemiology and Community Health*. 2003;57:120-124.

[113] Justice UDo. Kids and Guns. Washington, D.C.: Office of Juvenile Justice and Delinquency 2000.

[114] Johnson GR, Krug E, Potter LB. Suicide among adolescents and young adults: a cross-national comparison of 34 countries. *Suicide and Life-Threatening Behavior*. 2000;30:74-82.

[115] Pritchard C, Hansen L. Child, adolescent and youth suicide or undetermined deaths in england and Wales compared with Australia, Canada, France, Germany, Italy, Japan, and the USA. In Merrick J, Zalsman G, (Eds). *Suicidal Behavior in Adolescence*: An International Perspective. London: Freund Publishing House Limited 2005:201-217.

[116] Maharajh HD, Abdool PS. Culture and suicide. In Merrick J, Zalsman G, (Eds). Suicidal Behavior in Adolescence: An International Perspective. London: Freund Publishing House Limited 2005:19-32.

[117] Goldston D. Measuring suicidal behaviors and risk among children and adolescents. Washington, DC: American Psychological Association 2003.

[118] Beck AT, Steer R. Manual for the Beck Scale for Suicide Ideation. San Antonio, TX: Psychological Corporation 1991.

[119] Linehan MM, Goodstein JL, Nielsoen SL, et al. Reasons for staying alive when you are thinking of killing yourself: Reasons for living inventory. *Journal of Consulting and Clinical Psychology*. 1983;51:276-286.

[120] Pfeffer CR, Jiang H, Kakuma T. Child-adolescent suicidal potential index (CASPI): a screen for risk for early onset suicial behavior. *Psychological Assessment*. 2000;12:304-318.

[121] Jobes DA, Nelson KN, Peterson EM, et al. Describing suicidality: An investigation of qualitative SSF responses. *Suicide and Life-Threatening Behavior*. 2004;34:99-112.

[122] Rudd MD, Berman AL, Joiner TE, et al. Warning signs for suicide: Theory, research, and clinical applications *Suicide and Life-Threatening Behavior*. 2006;36(3):255-262.

[123] Yuen N, Yahata D, Nahulu A. Native Hawaiian youth suicide prevention project: A manual for gatekeeper trainers. HI: Injury Prevention and Control Program 1999.

[124] Coleman L, O'Halloran S. Preventing youth suicide through gatekeeper training: a resource book for gatekeepers. Augusta, ME: Medical Care Development, Inc. 2004.

[125] Bloodworth R. The Oregon plan for youth suicide prevention: A call to action: Oregon Department of Human Services: Injury Prevention and Epidemiology Program 2000.

[126] Omar HA. A model program for youth suicide prevention *International Journal of Adolescent Medicine and Health*. 2005;17(3):275-278.

[127] Goldney RD. Suicide prevention: A pragmatic review of recent studies. *Crisis*. 2005;26:128-140.

[128] Frankenfield DL, Keyl PM, Gielen A, et al. Adolescent patients: Healthy or hurting? Missed opportunities to screen for suicide risk in the primary care setting. *Archives of Pediatric and Adolescent Medicine*. 2000;154:162-168.

[129] Hickey I, Hawton K, Fagg J, et al. Deliberate self-harm patients who leave the accident and emergency department without a psychiatric assessment: A neglected population at risk of suicide. *Journal of Psychosomatic Research*. 2001;50:87-93.

[130] Kapur N, House A, Dodgson K, et al. Effect of general hospital management on repeat episodes of deliberate self-poisoning: Cohort study. *British Medical Journal*. 2002;325:866-867.

[131] Jellinek J. Suicidal ideation in prepubertal children: What does it mean? What to do? *Developmental and Behavioral Pediatrics*. 2006;27:40-41.

[132] Voelker R. SSRI use common in children. *Journal of the American Medical Association*. 1999;281:1882.

[133] Shaffer D, Garland A, Vieland V, et al. The impact of a curriculum-based suicide prevention program for teenagers. *Journal of the American Academy of Child and Adolescent Psychiatry*. 1991;27:675-687.

[134] Prevention CfDCa. Suicide among children, adolescents, and young adults. *Morbidity and Mortality Weekly Report*. 1995b;44:289-291.

[135] Linehan MM. Skills training manual for treaating borderline personality disorder. New York: Guilford Press 1993b.

[136] Team T. Fluoxetine, cognitive-behavioral therapy, and their combination for adolescents with depression. Treatment for Adolescents with Depression Study (TADS) randomized controlled trial. *Journal of the American Medical Association*. 2004;292:807-820.

[137] Administration USFaD. Antidepressant use in children, adolescents, and adults Abailable: http://www.fda.gov/cder/drug/antidepressants/ http://www.fda.gov/bbs/topics/news/2004/NEW01124.html. Accessed June 29,2007.

[138] Berman AL, Jobes DA, Silverman MM. Survivors of suicide and postvention. Adolescent suicide: Assessment and intervention. Washington, DC: American Psychological Association 2006:335-364.

[139] Peterson EM, Luoma JB, Dunne E. Suicide survivors' perceptions of the treating clinician. *Suicide and Life-Threatening Behavior*. 2002;32:158-166.

[140] Litman RE. Hospital suicides: Lawsuits and standards. *Suicide and Life-Threatening Behavior*. 1982;12:212-220.

[141] Simon RI. Assessing and managing suicide risk: Guidelines for clinically based risk management. Washington, DC: American Psychiatric Publishing, Inc. 2004.

[142] Deutsch CJ. Self-report sources of stress among psychotherapists. *Professional Psychology: Research and practice*. 1984;15:833-845.

[143] Witcraft FE. Within my power. Scouting 1950:2.

In: Behavioral Pediatrics, 3rd Edition
Editor: D. E. Greydanus et al.

ISBN 978-1-60692-702-1
© 2009 Nova Science Publishers, Inc.

Chapter 21

Schizophrenia in Childhood and Adolescence

Gretchen R. Gudmundsen and Jon M. McClellan

Abstract

Schizophrenia is disabling neuropsychiatric disorder characterized by disturbances in perception, thought, emotion, affect, and social relatedness. Schizophrenia in youth presents with distinct developmental, social and contextual challenges. This chapter reviews current research findings on the etiology, epidemiology, clinical features, diagnosis, and treatment of early onset schizophrenia in children and adolescents.

Introduction

Schizophrenia is disabling neuropsychiatric disorder characterized by disturbances in perception, thought, emotion, affect, and social relatedness. Early onset schizophrenia (EOS) is defined as onset prior to age 18, with childhood onset (COS) referring to onset prior to age 13 years. EOS is considered to be continuous with the adult onset form. However, schizophrenia in youth presents with distinct developmental, social and contextual challenges. EOS is often associated with elevated rates of premorbid neurodevelopmental abnormalities, significant long-term morbidity and poor outcome. This chapter reviews current research findings on the etiology, epidemiology, clinical features, diagnosis, and treatment of early onset schizophrenia in children and adolescents.

Definition

The DSM-IV-TR (American Psychiatric Association, 2000) diagnosis of schizophrenia requires the presence of two or more of the following symptoms to be substantially present during a 1-month period: a) delusions, b) hallucinations, c) disorganized speech, d) grossly disorganized or catatonic behavior and e) negative symptoms (including flat affect, poverty of speech, or diminished initiative). The diagnosis may also be made in cases evidencing any one of the following symptoms: a) bizarre delusions, b) auditory hallucinations consisting of either a voice maintaining a running commentary on an individual's behavior or thoughts, or c) auditory hallucinations consisting of two or more voices conversing with each other. In addition to the one month of active psychotic symptoms, an individual must experience significant functional impairment for at least six months. If the duration criterion of six months is not met, a diagnosis of schizophreniform disorder is made. Further, the following conditions should also be ruled out: 1) schizoaffective disorder, 2) mood disorders with psychotic features, 3) substance use or a general medical condition, or a 4) pervasive developmental disorder, unless hallucinations or delusions are evident.

These diagnostic criteria apply to individuals of all ages. However, the interpretation of symptoms in youth requires some familiarity with developmental psychopathology in order to avoid misdiagnosis of more commonplace childhood disorders.

Epidemiology

In the general adult population, the prevalence of schizophrenia is approximately 1%. There are few systematic epidemiological studies examining schizophrenia in pediatric populations; however, prevalence rates are estimated at 14 per 100,000 in children less than 15 years of age. While there are case reports of schizophrenia diagnoses in children younger than 6 years of age, the diagnostic validity of schizophrenia in preschoolers has not been established. The rate of onset sharply increases during adolescence, with the peak age of onset ranging from 15 to 30 years of age.

EOS is more prevalent among males. With age, the gender difference decreases, reaching approximately 1.4:1 in adult populations (male: female). The average age of onset in males is approximately 5 to 6 years earlier than that in females. This may explain the male predominance in EOS. Additionally, males also tend to have fewer affective symptoms, more structural brain anomalies, and worse prognosis than females.

In addition to gender differences, rates of schizophrenia are higher in urban areas, lower socioeconomic classes and certain categories of migrant status.

Etiology

Schizophrenia is viewed as a heterogeneous disorder with multiple etiologies. Presently, no single set of causes of the disorder has been identified. Current evidence suggests that the development of schizophrenia is best explained by a multifactorial neurodevelopmental model, whereby the disorder results from an interaction of underlying genetic vulnerabilities and environmental risk factors.

Neurobiologic Deficits

Adult studies demonstrate evidence of early neurobiologic origins including minor physical anomalies, neurologic soft signs, and structural abnormalities on brain imaging.

Variable differences in brain regions have been reported in schizophrenia at frst diagnosis regardless of age. Reductions in hippocampus, thalamus and frontal lobe volumes, and increased volumes of lateral ventricles have been consistently noted. Recent studies suggest cortical thickness differences in prefrontal temporal and parietal regions using newer imaging technologies in individuals experiencing the initial onset of schizophrenia.

Data from pediatric populations are consistent with findings in adults with schizophrenia. A National Institute of Mental Health (NIMH) study of COS demonstrated significant grey matter volumetric reductions compared to children in the control condition. Additionally, longitudinal studies demonstrate that compared to matched controls (1-2%), children with EOS show a more rapid progressive loss of grey matter (3-4% per year). Follow-up longitudinal studies show that cortical thinning in EOS may plateau in early adulthood when it becomes similar to the adult regional pattern.

The volumetric reductions in gray matter found in EOS are theorized to be due to the disruption of specific neurodevelopmental processes that occur during adolescence, such as synaptic pruning. The presence of structural brain anomalies in first episode patients suggests that these abnormalities predate the onset of the disorder. These neuroimaging findings are less likely to be the result of antipsychotic medications or environmental insults secondary to schizophrenia, such as substance abuse or recurrent institutionalization.

Genetic Factors

Family, twin and adoption studies all support a strong genetic component for schizophrenia. The lifetime risk of developing the illness is 5 to 20 times higher in first-degree relatives of affected persons compared to the general population. The rate of concordance among monozygotic twins is approximately 40-60%, whereas the rate of concordance in dizygotic twins and other siblings is 5-15%. In comparison to adult onset schizophrenia, the variant of early onset schizophrenia appears to be even more strongly influenced by genetic factors.

Most current genetic schizophrenia research hypothesizes that the schizophrenia is the sum result of different susceptibility genes, with each genetic risk variant only contributing a small degree of risk. This is the common-disease common-variant model, which underlies most approaches for gene finding in psychiatric research. In this model, the combination of shared risk variants and/or exposures to environmental risk factors ultimately leads to the illness.

An exhaustive review of linkage and candidate gene findings associated with schizophrenia is beyond the scope of this chapter. The best supported regions supported by linkage findings include 6p22-24, 1q21-22, and 13q32-34. Other regions supported by linkage findings include 1q42, 5q21–33, 6q21–25, 8p21–22, 10p15–11, and 22q11–12. Promising candidate genes within these regions include dysbindin, neuregulin, DAOA/G30, catechol-O-methyl transferase, RGS4 and DISC1.

For COS, positive association studies have been found for candidate genes implicated within the adult literature, including dysbindin, neuregulin, DAOA/G30, GAD1, Prodh2/DGCR6 and DISC1.

However, definitive causal relationships with the disorder have been generally lacking and the effects of disease-associated variants are for the most part small. Limitations with this literature include variability in findings, lack of replication of associations of putative risk-increasing alleles with the disorder, limited understanding of the functional effects of disease-associated haplotypes, and limited power given that very large sample sizes are needed to detect individual alleles conferring modest risks. Furthermore, recent studies using genome-wide association strategies have not replicated putative candidate genes or genomic regions previously thought to play a role in with schizophrenia.

In contrast, several studies have now replicated the role of rare structural mutations in schizophrenia. Patients with schizophrenia harbor significantly more rare deletions and duplications that impact genes than healthy controls. In these reports, most affected individuals harbor a different mutation. Individuals with sporadic schizophrenia, i.e., no family history of the disorder, have an 8-fold risk of harboring a *de novo* structural mutation. Genes disrupted by structural mutations in affected individuals are more likely to be involved with neuronal signaling, including glutamate and neuregulin pathways.

The risk for harboring a rare structural mutation is higher for patients that have an earlier onset of illness. Consistent with these findings is the observation that youth with COS appear to have a higher rate of cytogenetic abnormalities than reported in affected adults, including 22q11 deletion syndrome. Across studies that have examined for rare, potentially large effect mutations, most affected individuals have a different mutation that impacts different genes.

The rare allele model suggests that many cases of schizophrenia arise from individually rare, large effect mutations. In this model, the illness may arise from many different mutations that arise in any of a large number of genes involved with brain function and development. Many disease-risk mutations are suspected to be of recent origin, some *de novo* in the present generation. The recent findings suggest that many individuals with schizophrenia have a unique genetic cause. If so, most current gene-finding strategies based on the common disease – common allele model will predictably struggle to detect genes important to the illness.

Environmental Factors

Environmental exposures may mediate disease risk through a number of different mechanisms, including direct neurological damage, gene-environment interactions, epigenetic effects and/or *de novo* mutations. Such environmental exposures have been hypothesized to contribute to the development of schizophrenia. The best replicated risk exposures are maternal famine and paternal age. Other putative risk factors include prenatal infection, parental history of Type 2 diabetes, and place and time of birth.

Clinical Features

Schizophrenia is comprised of positive and negative symptoms. Positive symptoms include hallucinations, delusions, and disordered thinking and speech; and are historically considered to be characteristic of the illness. Negative symptoms refer to flat affect, anhedonia, anergia, and paucity of thought and speech and demonstrate more overlap with other psychiatric disorders.

While EOS is considered to developmentally continuous with the adult-onset form, the range and quality of symptom presentation demonstrates some differences. In EOS, loose associations, illogical thinking, impaired discourse skills, hallucinations, and negative symptoms have all been consistently reported, while delusions, catatonic symptoms and thought disorder symptoms of incoherence and alogia seem to be less frequent . EOS is also characterized by a higher rate of insidious onset, severe negative symptoms and greater cognitive impairments when compared to the adult-onset form of the disorder. Thus, EOS appears to represent a more severe variant of the illness.

The majority of youth with EOS have histories of premorbid problems, including cognitive delays, learning problems, behavioral difficulties and social withdrawal or oddities. Comorbid psychiatric disorders are common in this population, including ADHD, disruptive behavior disorders, anxiety and mood disorders, and, in adolescents, substance abuse. Treatment planning needs to account for these conditions, although effective treatment for psychosis may lead to improvement in these other areas as well.

Approximately ten to twenty percent of EOS youth have intellectual deficits, with borderline mental retardation or worse. Neuropsychological studies suggest that children with schizophrenia have global impairments across tasks that require greater capacity for information processing, rather than deficits isolated to specific functions or areas of the brain. However, it is important to recognize that there is no specific neuropsychological profile diagnostic for schizophrenia. Children with EOS who have identified genetic disorders, such as velocardiofacial syndrome (VCFS) may demonstrate greater neuroanotomical and neuropsychological abnormalities.

Course of Illness

The course of schizophrenia is characterized by prodromal, acute, recovery, and residual phases. As a result of the fluctuation of symptoms across phases, accurate assessment must account for these variations in clinical presentation.

- Premorbid Functioning/Prodromal Phase. The prodromal phase represents a significant decline from baseline functioning or a worsening of premorbid personality/behavioral characteristics. Presentations can include the development of odd or idiosyncratic beliefs, unusual or disruptive behaviors, worsening school performance, social isolation and withdrawal, dysphoria, speech and language problems, and/or worsening hygiene. The duration of the prodromal phase can vary from an acute change (days to weeks) to chronic impairment (months to years). COS appears more often associated with an insidious onset , whereas the onset in adolescents can be more variable. In general, an insidious onset predicts a more severe course of illness. Given the high rate of premorbid abnormalities associated with EOS, it can be difficult to distinguish between premorbid personality/cognitive problems and the onset of the disorder. One group found that greater premorbid global impairment, social withdrawal and schizoid/schizotypal personality types differentiated children with EOS from those diagnosed with bipolar disorder or atypical psychosis. Another study showed that impaired premorbid social functioning differentiated children with EOS from children with other psychotic disorders.

- Acute Phase. The acute phase is marked by a predominance of positive symptoms (i.e., hallucinations, delusions, disorganized speech and behavior), as well as a significant deterioration in functioning. During this phase patients may be grossly disorganized, confused and potentially dangerous to themselves or others. This phase generally lasts up to six months or longer depending in part on the response to treatment. Most children with EOS will have subsequent acute episodes. Over time, individuals tend to evidence a shift from positive to negative symptoms. Most youth do not have a complete recovery.

- Recuperative/Recovery Phase. Following the acute phase, with the remission of the acute psychosis, there is generally a several month period where the patient continues to experience significant impairment. This is primarily due to negative symptoms (flat affect, anergia, social withdrawal), although some positive symptoms may persist. In addition, some patients may develop a post-schizophrenic depression characterized by dysphoria and flat affect.

- Residual Phase. Youth with EOS may have prolonged periods (several months or more) between acute phases during which they do not experience significant positive symptoms. However; most patients will continue to demonstrate negative symptoms, including social isolation, residual disordered thinking (i.e. tangentiality, circumferentiality), peculiar behaviors (e.g. food hoarding, poor hygiene, and inappropriate affect), poverty of speech, odd beliefs and/or anergia.

Longitudinal Outcome

Most youth with schizophrenia demonstrate some degree of lifelong . Predictors of a worse prognosis include poor premorbid functioning, insidious onset, diagnosis prior to adolescence, low intellectual functioning, and severe symptoms during acute phases. When followed into adulthood, children with EOS demonstrated greater social deficits, lower levels of employment, and were less likely to live independently, relative to those with other childhood onset psychotic disorders. Individuals with EOS also have a high risk of eventual suicide. The risk of suicide or accidental death directly due to behaviors caused by psychotic thinking appears to be at least 5%. In adults with schizophrenia, there is an increased risk for medical illnesses and mortality, including a suicide rate of approximately 10 %.

Diagnosis

Misdiagnosis at the time of onset of schizophrenia is common. Many psychiatric disorders manifest symptoms that either overlap or are easily mistaken for the primary symptoms of schizophrenia. Discriminating among these various disorders can be difficult. A thorough diagnostic evaluation, including a thorough understanding of a child's symptomatic and psychosocial history, along with regular monitoring are necessary to rule out all possible disorders that may mimic schizophrenia.

Differential Diagnosis

- *Psychotic Mood Disorders.* Youth with psychotic mood disorders often present with a variety of affective and psychotic symptoms that can be easily confused with schizophrenia. Mania in adolescents is often associated with psychotic symptoms. Compared to youth with schizophrenia, bipolar youth typically evidence more mood congruent delusions, fewer hallucinations, less loosening of associations, and fewer negative symptoms. In addition, youth with bipolar disorder are less likely to have negative symptoms. Depressive symptoms are less specific, since schizophrenia also tends to be associated with dysphoria and anhedonia. Longitudinal assessment and retrospective evaluation of temporal overlap of mood episodes and psychotic symptoms is critical for an accurate diagnosis. Schizoaffective disorder is diagnosed when both mood disorder and schizophrenia are met and mood symptoms are present for a significant portion of the psychotic illness.
- *Atypical reports of psychotic symptoms.* Most children reporting psychotic-like symptoms are not truly psychotic. Many children report symptoms suggestive of hallucinations and delusions, yet do not present with overt evidence of psychosis. Overactive imaginations can be normal and characteristic of prepubertal children and developmentally disabled individuals. Youth with traumatic histories, including physical, sexual, or emotional abuse, especially those with posttraumatic stress disorder, may report symptoms suggestive of auditory or visual hallucinations or paranoid delusions. These symptom reports tend to be atypical in nature and the child generally lacks other hallmark symptoms associated with a diagnosis of schizophrenia. These atypical symptom reports may be reinforced in the context of a chaotic environment, or by well meaning clinicians and caretakers.

  Of course, a history of trauma or abuse does not preclude a primary psychotic illness. The proper assessment of psychosis in youth requires the gauging of potential symptom reports in the context of normal development. Characteristics that help distinguish true psychotic symptoms include the presence or absence of disorganized thought and behavior, the qualitative nature of reported symptoms, and the context within which symptoms are reported.
- *Substance-induced psychosis.* Psychotic symptoms can arise secondary to substance intoxication or delirium. Adolescents with substance-induced psychosis typically experience an acute onset of symptoms that are temporally related to the intake of

the drug. Hallucinogens can cause dramatic or vivid hallucinations and delusions, while psychostimulants are associated with disorientation and paranoid delusions. Substance intoxication and/or withdrawal can also induce delirium which is associated with fluctuating mental status, varied levels of consciousness, and altered short-term memory. Substance-induced psychosis usually clears within hours to days. Thus, psychotic symptoms that persist for longer than a week following complete detoxification from the substance(s) are generally attributed to a psychotic disorder that may have been precipitated or exacerbated by the substance use. However, there are reports of more persistent psychotic states occurring secondary to methamphetamine abuse. In addition, cannabis use in adolescents appears to be associated with a higher risk of eventually developing psychosis. Since comorbid substance abuse is common in adolescents with schizophrenia, discerning whether the substance was causal, contributory or simply complicating the psychotic illness can be a challenge.

- *Pervasive Developmental Disorders.* Autism and pervasive developmental disorders (PDD) share common symptomatology with schizophrenia, including behavioral oddities, interpersonal deficits, restricted or bizarre range of interests, and deviant language patterns. Most children with autism or PDD will not experience acute psychosis or will experience symptoms only transiently, thereby differentiating these disorders from early onset schizophrenia. In cases where diagnostic criteria are met for autism or other pervasive developmental disorders, symptoms of active psychosis (e.g., overt hallucinations and/or delusions) must be present for at least one month and other explanations for these symptoms should be ruled out (e.g., belief in fantasy vs. delusions or hallucinations, a lack of interest in social relationships vs. negative symptoms).

Assessment

A diagnosis of early onset schizophrenia is made when DSM-IV-TR criteria are met and other relevant diagnoses are ruled out. A thorough history and medical evaluation are necessary to provide an accurate assessment of psychosis in children and adolescents. Standard psychiatric diagnostic guidelines should be followed including an interview with the child, the family, and a thorough review of the patient's psychiatric history and medical records. It may also be necessary to obtain a history from other available sources including caregivers, past treatment providers, teachers, case workers or probation officers.

The psychiatric history should review the child's current and previous psychiatric symptomatology, the longitudinal course of symptom development, psychosocial functioning (including current and past academic and interpersonal functioning; current and past abuse history), family psychiatric history, an any exacerbating or comorbid conditions including substance use, developmental problems, or mood disorders. A clinician must carefully establish the pattern of symptoms development and course of the illness while also assessing the type, number, duration, and combination of symptoms necessary for a diagnosis of schizophrenia.

A comprehensive physical examination is necessary to rule out any organic causes of psychotic symptoms. Potential medical causes of psychosis include delirium, seizure disorders, central nervous system infections or lesions, tumors, bacterial or viral infections, neurodegenerative disorders, metabolic disorders, immune, or neurological disorders (e.g. lipid storage diseases, endocrinopathies, Wilson's disease, or HIV), developmental disorders, infectious diseases, and drug or alcohol intoxication. A complete neuropsychological assessment may be indicated if there is evidence of a developmental delay or cognitive deficit that affects the presentation of psychotic symptoms.

The reliability of a diagnosis can be improved by the use of structured interviews, symptom scales, and diagnostic decision trees. Laboratory tests, neuroimaging studies, and neuropsychological assessments are indicated to rule out other disorders or to clarity intellectual functioning. These tests, however, are not be used to confirm the diagnosis of schizophrenia since to date there are no biomarkers, neuroanatomical or functional imaging findings or neuropsychological profiles that are specifically diagnostic for schizophrenia.

Treatment

Most individuals with EOS will require long-term treatment comprised of both pharmacotherapy and psychosocial interventions. Individualized treatment planning must consider an individual's developmental stage, the needs of the family, as well as the current phase of the disorder.

Pharmacotherapy

The short term efficacy of antipsychotic agents for adults with schizophrenia is well established. These medications reduce psychotic symptoms, help prevent relapse, and improve general functioning. Second generation ("atypical") antipsychotic medications, with the exception of clozapine, are generally considered first line treatments.

However, the CATIE study (Clinical Antipsychotic Trials of Intervention Effectiveness) raises questions about the utility and safety of antipsychotic medications for schizophrenia in adults. CATIE examined four second generation agents, olanzapine, quetiapine, risperidone and ziprasidone, and one traditional neuroleptic, perphenazine, in 1493 adults with chronic schizophrenia, across 57 U.S. sites. Overall, 74% of patients discontinued their study medication before completing 18 months of treatment. The time to discontinuation was significantly longer for olanzapine compared to risperidone and quetiapine, but not compared to perphenazine or ziprasidone. Olanzapine was more often discontinued due to weight gain and metabolic concerns. Perphenazine was more often discontinued secondary to extrapyramidal side effects. Thus, most patients could not maintain treatment long-term with any one treatment. Furthermore, the superiority of atypical agents was not demonstrated in CATIE.

Antipsychotic agents are also considered the first line treatment for schizophrenia spectrum disorders in youth, with second generation agents typically preferred in community settings. There are controlled trials supporting the effectiveness of first generation agents loxapine and haloperidol. More recently, for adolescents with EOS, randomized placebo-controlled trials found benefit for risperidone and aripiprazole in adolescents with EOS. In contrast, a large placebo-controlled trial found olanzapine superior to placebo on symptom ratings, but not on rate of treatment response.

Clozapine is the best studied antipsychotic agent in youth, with demonstrated superiority over haloperidol and olanzapine for treatment refractory EOS. Yet given the side effect profile, clozapine is reserved for treatment refractory cases.

The recently completed Treatment of Early Onset Schizophrenia Spectrum Disorders Study (TEOSS) compared olanzapine, risperidone and molindone for youth with early onset schizophrenia spectrum disorders. Fifty percent or fewer participants (n = 119) responded in each treatment arm over 8 weeks. There were no significant differences found between the treatment groups in response rates or the magnitude of symptom reduction. Patients receiving olanzapine gained significantly more weight, and had more metabolic side effects, than participants in the other two treatment arms.

At this time, aripiprazole and risperidone are currently the only second generation antipsychotic agents that have received FDA approval for the acute treatment of EOS. Both atypical and traditional agents, with the exception of clozapine, can be considered primary treatment options given the findings of CATIE and TEOSS. Individual responses to different antipsychotics are variable, and if insufficient effects are evident after a 6-week trial using adequate dosages, a different antipsychotic agent should be tried. Clozapine should be considered for treatment resistant cases. When using clozapine, systematic monitoring of side effects, including following established protocols for blood count monitoring, is required.

Depot antipsychotics have not been studied in pediatric age groups and have inherent risks with long-term exposure to neuroleptic side effects. Therefore, they should only be considered in schizophrenic adolescents with documented chronic psychotic symptoms and a history of poor medication compliance.

Safety Monitoring

Youth may develop the same spectrum of side effects noted in adults taking antipsychotic agents, including weight gain, metabolic syndrome, extrapyramidal symptoms, sedation, tardive dyskinesia, and neuroleptic malignant syndrome. The risk for weight gain and adverse metabolic side effects with second generation agents appears to be more problematic in youth populations.

Prior to initiating treatment, a thorough medical assessment is needed in order to correctly monitor and measure any symptoms or behaviors that are consequences of the medication(s). When using second-generation antipsychotic agents, monitoring for weight gain and other metabolic problems (e.g. type 2 diabetes, hyperlidemia) is critical. Baseline and follow up assessments include body mass index (BMI), blood pressure, fasting glucose, and a fasting lipid panel. Some agents have additional monitoring requirements (e.g. white blood cell counts with clozapine, cardiac monitoring with ziprasidone). Extrapyramidal side effects, including tardive dyskinesia, also need to be monitored.

Psychosocial Interventions

While pharmacotherapy is the mainstay of treatment for schizophrenia, growing evidence indicates that additional benefits are associated with adjunctive psychosocial interventions. When used in conjunction with pharmacotherapy, the following interventions have demonstrated utility including psychoeducation, behaviorally based family therapy, cognitive-behavioral therapy (CBT), and integrated psychological therapy. Treatment goals include a reduction in symptoms and relapse, as well as improved social and occupational functioning. Many interventions are effective with targeted skills, but perhaps less beneficial for general functioning. A review of the literature suggests that family therapy may yield more benefit than individually delivered therapy.

Psychoeducation should address education about the illness, treatment options, social skills training, relapse prevention, basic life skills training, and problem solving strategies. It is critical for family members and other care providers to receive education about a child's illness, treatment options, short- and long-term prognosis, as well as customized support with behavior modification planning.

CBT strategies focus on challenging and testing key beliefs associated with hallucinations and delusions, teaching problem solving skills, enhancing coping strategies, and increasing medication adherence. Many types of CBT interventions have demonstrated effectiveness in adults, with some interventions integrating psychosocial rehabilitation showing quite promising effects. There are no published studies examining CBT for EOS and developmentally-based therapies are likely needed for this age group.

Youth with EOS will have specific developmental needs requiring specialized intervention or resources. Educational programs and/or vocational training may be indicated to address the cognitive and functional deficits associated with the disorder. Behavioral interventions for weight management may also be indicated for youth with medication side effects. Comprehensive treatment needs to address comorbid conditions, such as substance abuse. Some children will require more intensive community support services including day programs and/or community caseworkers.

Conclusion

Schizophrenia is disabling neuropsychiatric disorder characterized by disturbances in perception, thought, emotion, affect, and social relatedness. These diagnostic criteria apply to individuals of all ages. However, the interpretation of symptoms in youth requires some familiarity with developmental psychopathology in order to avoid misdiagnosis of more commonplace childhood disorders Schizophrenia in youth presents with distinct developmental, social and contextual challenges. Most individuals with EOS will require long-term treatment comprised of both pharmacotherapy and psychosocial interventions. Individualized treatment planning must consider an individual's developmental stage, the needs of the family, as well as the current phase of the disorder. Therefore, treatment of schizophrenia in youth will require specialized intervention or resources.

References

Addington AM, Gornick M, Duckworth J, et al. GAD1 (2q31.1), which encodes glutamic acid decarboxylase (GAD67), is associated with childhood-onset schizophrenia and cortical gray matter volume loss. *Mol. Psychiatry* 2005;10:581-8.

Addington AM, Gornick MC, Shaw P, et al. Neuregulin 1 (8p12) and childhood-onset schizophrenia: Susceptibility haplotypes for diagnosis and brain developmental trajectories. *Mol. Psychiatry* 2007;12:195-205.

Addington AM, Gornick M, Sporn AL, et al. Polymorphisms in the 13q33.2 gene G72/G30 are associated with childhood-onset schizophrenia and psychosis not otherwise specified. *Biol. Psychiatry* 2004;55(10):976-80.

Aleman A, Kahn RS, Selten JP. Sex differences in the risk of schizophrenia: evidence from meta-analysis. *Arch. Gen. Psychiatry* 2003;60(6):565-71.

American Academy of Child and Adolescent Psychiatry. Practice Parameter for the Assessment and Treatment of Children and Adolescents with Schizophrenia, Revised. *J. Am. Acad Child Adol. Psychiatry* 2001;40(7 Suppl):4S-23S.

American Academy of Child and Adolescent Psychiatry. Practice Parameter for the Assessment and Treatment of Children and Adolescents with Bipolar Disorder. *J. Am. Acad. Child Adol. Psychiatry* 2007;46(1):107-25.

American Psychiatric Association. *Diagnostic and Statistical Manual of Mental Disorders, 4th edition, Text-Revised (DSM-IV-TR)*. Washington, DC: American Psychiatric Association. 2000.

Asarnow JR, Ben-Meir S. Children with schizophrenia spectrum and depressive disorders: A comparative study of premorbid adjustment. *J. Child Psychol. Psychiatry* 1988;29:477-488.

Asarnow JR, Tompson MC, Goldstein MJ. Childhood-onset schizophrenia: a followup study. *Schizophr. Bull* 1994;20(4):599-617.

Asarnow RF. Neurocognitive impairments in schizophrenia: a piece of the epigenetic puzzle. *Eur. Child Adolesc. Psychiatry* 1999;8 Suppl 1:I5-8.

Asarnow RF, Nuechterlein KH, Fogelson D, et al. Schizophrenia and schizophrenia-spectrum personality disorders in the first-degree relatives in children with schizophrenia, *Arch. Gen. Psychiatry* 2001;58:581-588.

Barr AM, Panenka WJ, MacEwan GW, et al. The need for speed: an update on methamphetamine addiction. *J. Psychiatry Neurosci.* 2006;31(5):301-13.

Beitchman JH. Childhood schizophrenia: A review and comparison with adult-onset schizophrenia. *Psychiatr. Clin. North Am.* 1985;8:793-814.

Benes, FM. Altered glutamanergic and GABAergic mechanism in the cingulated cortex of the schizophrenic brain. *Archives of General Psychiatry* 1995;52:1015-1018.

Bettes BA, Walker E. Positive and negative symptoms in psychotic and other psychiatrically disturbed children. *J. Child Psychol. Psychiatry* 1987;28:555-568.

Biederman J, Petty C, Faraone SV, Seidman L. Phenomenology of childhood psychosis: findings from a large sample of psychiatrically referred youth. *J. Nerv. Ment. Dis.* 2004;192(9):607-14.

Blouin JL, Dombroski BA, Nath SK, et al. Schizophrenia susceptibility loci on chromosomes 13q32 and 8p21. *Nat. Genet* 1998;20(1):70-3.

Bradbury TN, Miller GA. Season of birth in schizophrenia: A review of evidence, methodology, and etiology. *Psychol. Bull* 1985;98:569-594.

Brenner HD, Roder V, Hodel B, Kienzle N, Reed D, Liberman RP. *Integrated Psychological Therapy for Schizophrenic Patients*. Seattle, Washington: Hogrefe and Huber. 1994.

Breslau N. Inquiring about the bizarre: False positives in Diagnostic Interview Schedule for Children (DISC), ascertainment of obsessions, compulsions and psychotic symptoms. *J. Am. Acad Child Adolesc*. *Psychiatry* 1987;26:639-655.

Brown AS. Prenatal infection as a risk factor for schizophrenia. *Schizophr. Bull.* 2006;32(2):200-2.

Brown AS, Begg MD, Gravenstein S, et al. Serologic evidence of prenatal influenza in the etiology of schizophrenia. *Arch. Gen. Psychiatry* 2004;61(8):774-80.

Brzustowicz LM, Hodgkinson KA, Chow EW, Honer WG, Bassett AS. Location of a major susceptibility locus for familial schizophrenia on chromosome 1q21-q22. *Science* 2000;288(5466):678-82.

Buchanan RW, Heinrichs DW. The Neurological Evaluation Scale (NES): A structured instrument for the assessment of neurological signs in schizophrenia. *Psychiatr. Res.* 1989;27(3): 335-50.

Cantor-Graae E, Selten JP. Schizophrenia and migration: a meta-analysis and review. *Am. J. Psychiatry* 2005;162(1):12-24.

Caplan R. Thought disorder in childhood. *J. Am. Acad. Child Adolesc. Psychiatry* 1994;33(5):605-15.

Caplan R, Guthrie D, Fish B, Tanguay PE, David-Lando G. The Kiddie Formal Thought Disorder Rating Scale: clinical assessment, reliability, and validity. *J. Am. Acad. Child Adolesc. Psychiatry* 1989;28(3):408-16.

Caplan R, Guthrie D, Tang B, Komo S, Asarnow RF. Thought disorder in childhood schizophrenia: replication and update of concept. *J. Am. Acad. Child Adolesc. Psychiatry* 2000;39(6):771-8.

Cardno AG, Gottesman II. Twin studies of schizophrenia: from bow-and-arrow concordances to star wars Mx and functional genomics. *Am. J. Med. Genet.* 2000;97(1):12-7.

Carlson GA. Child and adolescent mania--diagnostic considerations. *J. Child Psychol. Psychiatry* 1990;31(3):331-41.

Cornblatt B, Obuchowski M, Roberts S, Pollack S, Erlenmeyer-Kimling L. Cognitive and behavioral precursors of schizophrenia. *Dev. Psychopathol.* 1999;11(3):487-508.

Davies G, Welham J, Chant D, Torrey EF, McGrath J. A systematic review and meta-analysis of Northern Hemisphere season of birth studies in schizophrenia. *Schizophr. Bull.* 2003;29(3):587-93.

Dickerson FB, Lehman AF. Evidence-based psychotherapy for schizophrenia. *J. Nerv. Ment. Dis.* 2006;194(1):3-9.

Eggers C. Course and prognosis of childhood schizophrenia. *J. Autism Child Schizophr.* 1978;8:21-36.

Eggers C. Schizo affective psychosis in childhood: A follow-up study. *J. Autism Dev. Disord.* 1989;19:327-334.

Eggers C, Bunk D. The long-term course of childhood-onset schizophrenia: a 42-year follow-up. *Schizophr. Bull.* 1997;23:105-117.

Faloon IRH, Boyd JL, McGill CW. Family management in the prevention of exacerbation of schizophrenia: A controlled study. *N. Engl. J. Med.* 1982;306:1437-1440.

Fernandez-Egea E, Miller B, Bernardo M, Donner T, Kirkpatrick B. Parental history of type 2 diabetes in patients with nonaffective psychosis. *Schizophr. Res.* 2008;98(1-3):302-6.

Findling R, Robb A, Nyilas M, et al. Tolerability of aripiprazole in the treatment of adolescents with schizophrenia. *Paper presented at: 160th Annual Meeting of the American Psychiatric Association*, May 2007; San Diego, Calif.

Frazier JA, Giedd JN, Hamburger SD, Albus KE, Kaysen D, Vaituzis AC. Brain anatomic magnetic resonance imaging in childhood-onset schizophrenia. *Arch. Gen. Psychiatry* 1996;53:617-624.

Frazier JA, Hodge SM, Breeze JL, et al. Diagnostic and sex effects on limbic volumes in early-onset bipolar disorder and schizophrenia. *Schizophr. Bull.* 2007;34(1):37-46.

Garralda ME. Hallucinations in children with conduct and emotional disorders: II. The follow-up study. *Psychol. Med.* 1984;14(3):597-604.

Gogtay N, Giedd JN, Lusk L, et al. Dynamic mapping of human cortical development during childhood through early adulthood. *Proc. Natl. Acad. Sci. USA* 2004;101(21):8174-9.

Goldstein MJ, Miklowitz DJ. The effectiveness of psychoeducational family therapy in the treatment of schizophrenic disorders. *J. Marital Fam. Ther.* 1995;21(4):361-376.

Gornick MC, Addington AM, Sporn A, et al. Dysbindin (DTNBP1, 6p22.3) is associated with childhood-onset psychosis and endophenotypes measured by the Premorbid Adjustment Scale (PAS). *J. Autism Dev. Disord.* 2005;35(6):831-8.

Gothelf D, Feinstein C, Thompson T, et al. Risk factors for the emergence of psychotic disorders in adolescents with 22q11.2 deletion syndrome. *Am. J. Psychiatry* 2007;164(4):663-9.

Gourion D, Goldberger C., Bourdel MC, Bayle FJ, Loo H, Krebs MO. Minor physical anomalies in patients with schizophrenia and their parents: Prevalence and pattern of craniofacial abnormalities. *Psychiatr. Res.* 2004;125:21-28.

Green WH, Padron-Gayol M. Schizophrenic disorder in childhood: its relationship to DSM-III criteria. In *Biological Psychiatry*, Shagass C, Ed. Amsterdam: Elsevier, pp 1484-1486. 1986.

Green WH, Padron-Gayol M, Hardesty AS, Bassiri M. Schizophrenia with childhood onset: a phenomenological study of 38 cases. *J. Am. Acad. Child Adolesc. Psychiatry* 1992;31(5):968-76.

Greenstein D, Lerch J, Shaw P, et al. Childhood onset schizophrenia: cortical brain abnormalities as young adults. *J. Child Psychol. Psychiatry* 2006;47(10):1003-12.

Gupta S, Andreasen NC, Arndt S, et al. Neurological soft signs in neuroleptic-naive and neuroleptic-treated schizophrenic patients and in normal comparison subjects. *Am. J. Psychiatry* 1995;152(2):191-6.

Haas M, Unis A, Copenhaver M, Quiroz S, Kushner S, Kusumakar V. Efficacy and safety of risperidone in adolescents with schizophrenia. *Paper presented at: 160th Annual Meeting of the American Psychiatric Association*, May 2007; San Diego, CA.

Häfner H, Nowotny B. Epidemiology of early-onset schizophrenia. *Eur. Arch. Psychiatry Clin. Neurosci.* 1995;245(2):80-92.

Hata K, Iida J, Iwasaka H, Negoro HI, Ueda F, Kishimoto T. Minor physical anomalies in childhood and adolescent onset schizophrenia. *Psychiatry Clin. Neurosci.* 2003;57:17-21.

Hlastala SA, McClellan J. Phenomenology and diagnostic stability of youths with atypical psychotic symptoms. *J. Child Adolesc. Psychopharmacol.* 2005;15:497-509.

Ho BC, Black DW, Andreasen NC. *Schizophrenia and other psychotic disorders*. In: Hales RE, Yudofsky SC (eds). *Textbook of Clinical Psychiatry* (4th ed). Washington, DC: American Psychiatric Publishing; 2003.

Hollis C. Adult outcomes of child- and adolescent-onset schizophrenia: Diagnostic stability and predictive validity. *Am. J. Psychiatry* 2000;157:1652-1659.

Hollis C. Developmental precursors of child- and adolescent-onset schizophrenia and affective psychoses: Diagnostic specificity and continuity with symptom dimensions. *Br. J. Psychiatry* 2003;182:37-44.

Hsiao R, McClellan JM. Substance abuse in early onset psychotic disorders. *J. Dual Diagn.* 2007;4:87-99.

Huxley NA, Rendall M, Sederer L. Psychosocial treatments in schizophrenia: A review of the past 20 years. *J. Nerv. Men. Dis.* 2000;188(4):187-201.

Huttunen MO, Machon RA, Mednick SA. Prenatal factors in the pathogenesis of schizophrenia. *Br. J. Psychiatry* 1994;164(Suppl. 23):15-19.

International Schizophrenia Consortium. Rare chromosomal deletions and duplications increase risk of schizophrenia. *Nature* 2008;epub Jul 30.

Ismail B, Cantor-Graae E, McNeil TF. Minor physical anomalies in schizophrenic patients and their siblings. *Am. J. Psychiatry* 1998;155:1695-1702.

Jarbin H, Ott Y, von Knorring, AL. Adult outcome of social functioning in adolescent-onset schizophrenia and affective psychosis. *J. Am. Acad. Child Adolesc. Psychiatry* 2003;42:176-183.

John JP, Arunachalam V, Ratnam B, Isaac MK. Expanding the schizophrenia phenotype: a composite evaluation of neurodevelopmental markers. *Compr. Psychiatry* 2008;49:78–86.

Johnstone EC, Owens DG, Bydder GM, Colter N, Crow TJ, Frith CD. The spectrum of structural brain changes in schizophrenia: age of onset as a predictor of cognitive and clinical impairments and their cerebral correlates. *Psychol. Med.* 1989;19(1):91-103.

Joyce, PR. Age of onset in bipolar affective disorder and misdiagnosis as schizophrenia. *Psychol. Med.* 1984;14(1):145-9.

Kendler KS. "A gene for...": the nature of gene action in psychiatric disorders. *Am. J. Psychiatry* 2005;162(7):1243-52.

Kirov G, O'Donovan MC Owen MJ. Finding schizophrenia genes. *J. Clin. Invest.* 2005;115(6):1440-8.

Kolvin I. Studies in the childhood psychoses. *Br. J. Psychiatry* 1971;6:209-234.

Kumra S, Ashtari M, McMeniman M, et al. Reduced frontal white matter integrity in early-onset schizophrenia: a preliminary study. *Biol. Psychiatry* 2004;55(12):1138-45.

Kumra S, Frazier JA, Jacobsen LK, et al. Childhood-onset schizophrenia. A double-blind clozapine-haloperidol comparison. *Arch. Gen. Psychiatry* 1996;53(12):1090-7.

Kumra S, Kranzler H, Gerbino-Rosen G, et al. Clozapine and "high-dose" olanzapine in refractory early-onset schizophrenia: a 12-week randomized and double-blind comparison. *Biol. Psychiatry* 2008;63(5):524-9.

Kumra S, Oberstar JV, Sickich L, et al. Efficacy and tolerability of second-generation antipsychotics in children and adolescents with schizophrenia. *Schizophr. Bull.* 2008;34(1):60-71.

Kumra S, Schulz SC. Editorial: Research progress in early-onset schizophrenia. *Schizophr. Bull* 2007;34(1):15-7.

Kumra S, Wiggs E, Bedwell J, et al. Neuropsychological deficits in pediatric patients with childhood-onset schizophrenia and psychotic disorder not otherwise specified. *Schizophr. Res.* 2000;42:135-144.

Lawrie SM, Abukmeail SS. Brain abnormality in schizophrenia. A systematic and quantitative review of volumetric magnetic resonance imaging studies. *Br. J. Psychiatry* 1998;172:1110-1120.

Lewandowski KE, Shashi V, Berry PM, Kwapil TR. Schizophrenic-like neurocognitive deficits in children and adolescents with 22q11 deletion syndrome. *Am. J. Med. Genet. B Neuropsychiatr. Genet.* 2007;144(1):27-36.

Lieberman JA, Stroup TS, McEvoy JP, et al. Effectiveness of antipsychotic drugs in patients with chronic schizophrenia. *N. Engl. J. Med.* 2005;353(12):1209-1223.

Lim KO, Harris D, Beal M, et al. Gray matter deficits in young onset schizophrenia are independent of age of onset. *Biol. Psychiatry* 1996;40(1):4-13.

Lipska BK, Peters T, Hyde TM, et al. Expression of DISC1 binding partners is reduced in schizophrenia and associated with DISC1 SNPs. *Hum. Mol. Genet.* 2006;15(8):1245-58.

Liu H, Abecasis GR, Heath SC, et al. Genetic variation in the 22q11 locus and susceptibility to schizophrenia. *Proc. Natl. Acad. Sci. USA* 2002;99(26):16859-64.

Loranger AW. Sex difference in age at onset of schizophrenia. *Arch. Gen. Psychiatry* 1984;41(2):157-61.

Lyon M, Barr CE, Cannon TD, Mednick SA, Shore D. Fetal neural development and schizophrenia. *Schizophr. Bull.* 1989;15(1):149-61.

Malaspina D, Harlap S, Fennig S, et al. Advancing paternal age and the risk of schizophrenia. *Arch. Gen. Psychiatry* 2001;58(4):361-7.

Marcelis M, Navarro-Mateu F, Murray R, Selten JP, Van Os J. Urbanization and psychosis: a study of 1942-1978 birth cohorts in The Netherlands. *Psychol. Med.* 1998;28(4):871-9.

Maynard TM, Haskell GT, Peters AZ, Sikich L, Lieberman JA, LaMantia AS. A comprehensive analysis of 22q11 gene expression in the developing and adult brain. *Proc. Natl. Acad. Sci. USA* 2003;100(24):14433-8.

Maziade M, Bouchard S, Gingras N, et al. Long-term stability of diagnosis and symptom dimensions in a systematic sample of patients with onset of schizophrenia in childhood and early adolescence. II: Postnegative distinction and childhood predictors of adult outcome. *Br. J. Psychiatry* 1996;169(3):371-8.

Maziade M, Gingras N, Rodrigue C, et al. Long-term stability of diagnosis and symptom dimensions in a systematic sample of patients with onset of schizophrenia in childhood and early adolescence. I: nosology, sex and age of onset. *Br. J. Psychiatry* 1996;169(3):361-70.

McClellan J, Breiger D, McCurry C, Hlastala SA. Premorbid functioning in early-onset psychotic disorders. *J. Am. Acad. Child Adolesc. Psychiatry* 2003;42(6):666-72.

McClellan J, McCurry C. Neurocognitive pathways in the development of schizophrenia. *Sem. Clin. Neuropsychiatry* 1998;3:320-322.

McClellan J, McCurry C, Speltz ML, Jones K. Symptom factors in early-onset psychotic disorders. *J. Am. Acad. Child Adolesc. Psychiatry* 2002;41(7):791-8.

McClellan J, Prezbindowski A, Breiger D, McCurry C. Neuropsychological functioning in early onset psychotic disorders. *Schizophr. Res.* 2004;68:21-26.

McClellan JM, Susser E, King MC. Schizophrenia: a common disease caused by multiple rare alleles. *Br. J. Psychiatry* 2007;190:194-9.

McClellan, JM, Susser E, King MC. Maternal famine, de novo mutations, and schizophrenia. *JAMA* 2006;296(5): 582-4.

McClellan JM, Werry JS, Ham M. A follow-up study of early onset psychosis: comparison between outcome diagnoses of schizophrenia, mood disorders and personality disorders. *J. Autism Dev. Disord.* 1993;23:243-262.

McGrath JJ. The suprisingly rich contours of schizophrenia epidemiology. *Arch. Gen. Psychiatry* 2007;64:14-16.

McGrath J, Saha S, Welham J, El Saadi O, MacCauley C, Chant D. A systematic review of the incidence of schizophrenia: the distribution of rates and the influence of sex, urbanicity, migrant status and methodology. *BMC Med.* 2004;28;2:13.

McGrath J, El-Saadi O, Grim V, et al. Minor physical anomalies and quantitative measures of the head and face in patients with psychosis. *Arch. Gen. Psychiatry* 2002;59:458-464.

Mehler C, Warnke A. Structural brain abnormalities specific to childhood-onset schizophrenia identified by neuroimaging techniques. *J. Neural. Transm.* 2002;109(2):219-34.

Moore TH, Zammit S, Lingford-Hughes A, et al. Cannabis use and risk of psychotic or affective mental health outcomes: a systematic review. *Lancet* 2007;370(9584):319-28.

Mortensen PB, Pedersen CB, Westergaard T, et al. Effects of family history and place and season of birth on the risk of schizophrenia. *N. Engl. J. Med.* 1999;340(8):603-8.

Narr KL, Toga AW, Szesko P, et al. Cortical thinning in cingulated and occipital cortices in first episode schizophrenia. *Biol. Psychiatry* 2005;58(1):32-40.

Narr KL, Bilder RM, Toga AW, et al. Mapping cortical thickness and gray matter concentration in first episode schizophrenia. *Cereb. Cortex* 2005;15(6):708-19.

Neale BM, Sham PC. The future of association studies: gene-based analysis and replication. *Am. J. Hum. Genet.* 2004;75(3):353-62.

Nicolson R, Brookner FB, Lenane M, et al. Parental schizophrenia spectrum disorders in childhood-onset and adult-onset schizophrenia. *Am. J. Psychiatry* 2003;160(3):490-5.

Nicolson R, Lenane M, Hamburger SD, Fernandez T, Bedwell J, Rapoport JL. Lessons from childhood-onset schizophrenia. *Brain Res. Brain Res. Rev.* 2000;31(2-3):147-56.

Norton N, Williams HJ, Owen, MJ. An update on the genetics of schizophrenia. *Curr. Opin. Psychiatry* 2006;19(2):158-64.

Owen MJ, O'Donovan M, Gottesman II. *Psychiatric genetics and genomics.* Oxford: Oxford University Press, pp 247-266. 2003.

Pavuluri MN, Herbener ES, Sweeney JA. Psychotic symptoms in pediatric bipolar disorder. *J. Affect Disord.* 2004;80(1):19-28.

Pedersen CB, Mortensen PB. Family history, place and season of birth as risk factors for schizophrenia in Denmark: a replication and reanalysis. *Br. J. Psychiatry* 2001;179:46-52.

Pool D, Bloom W, Mielke DH, Roniger JJ Jr, Gallant DM. A controlled evaluation of loxitane in seventy-five adolescent schizophrenic patients. *Curr. Ther. Res. Clin. Exp.* 1976;19(1):99-104.

Quitkin, F, Rifkin, A, Klein, DF. Neurologic soft signs in schizophrenia and character disorders. Organicity in schizophrenia with premorbid asociality and emotionally unstable character disorders. *Arc. Gen. Psychiatry* 1976;33(7):845-53.

Rapoport JL, Addington A, Frangou S. The neurodevelopmental model of schizophrenia: what can very early onset cases tell us? *Curr. Psychiatry Rep.* 2005;7(2):81-2.

Rapoport JL, Giedd JN, Kumra S, et al. Childhood-onset schizophrenia. Progressive ventricular change during adolescence. *Arch. Gen. Psychiatry* 1997;54(10):897-903.

Rapoport JL, Inoff-Germain G. Update on childhood-onset schizophrenia. *Curr. Psychiatry Rep.* 2000;2(5):410-5.

Rector NA, Beck AT. Cognitive behavioral therapy for schizophrenia: An empirical review. *J. Nerv. Ment. Dis.* 2001;189:278-287.

Remschmidt H, Martin M, Schulz E, Gutenbrunner C, Fleischhaker C. The concept of positive and negative schizophrenia in child and adolescent psychiatry. In A. Marneros, N.C. Andreasen, M.T. Tsuang (Eds.), *Positive Versus Negative Schizophrenia* (pp. 219-242). Berlin: Springer-Verlag Berlin. 1991.

Roder V, Mueller DR, Mueser KT, Brenner HD. Integrated psychological therapy (IPT) for schizophrenia: is it effective? *Schizophr. Bull.* 2006;32 Suppl 1:S81-93.

Ropcke B, Eggers C. Early-onset schizophrenia: A 15-year follow-up. *Eur. Child Adolesc. Psychiatry* 2005;14:341-350.

Ross RG, Heinlein S, Tregellas H. High rates of comorbidity are found in childhood-onset schizophrenia. *Schizophr. Res.* 2006;88(1-3):90-5.

Rund BR, Moe L, Sollien T, Fjell A. The psychosis project: Outcome and cost-effectiveness of a psychoeducational treatment programme for schizophrenic adolescents. *Acta Psychiatr. Scand.* 1994;89:211-218.

Russell AT, Bott L, Sammons C. The phenomenology of schizophrenia occurring in childhood. *J. Am. Acad. Child Adolesc. Psychiatry* 1989;28(3):399-407.

Sanders AR, Duan J, Levinson DF, et al. No significant association of 14 candidate genes with schizophrenia in a large European ancestry sample: implications for psychiatric genetics. *Am. J. Psychiatry* 2008;165:497-506.

Sullivan PF, Lin D, Tzeng JY, et al. Genomewide association for schizophrenia in the CATIE study: results of stage 1. *Mol. Psychiatry* 2008;13:570-84.

Satcher D. Mental health: A report of the surgeon general. Available: http://www.surgeongeneral.gov/library/mentalhealth/home.html.

Shaw P, Sporn A, Gogtay N, et al. Childhood-onset schizophrenia: A double-blind, randomized clozapine-olanzapine comparison. *Arch. Gen. Psychiatry* 2006;63(7):721-30.

Sikich L, Frazier JA, McClellan J, et al. Double-blind comparison of antipsychotics in early onset schizophrenia and schizoaffective disorder. In press, *American Journal of Psychiatry.*

Sipos A, Rasmussen F, Harrison G, et al. Paternal age and schizophrenia: a population based cohort study. *BMJ* 2004;329(7474):1070.

Spencer EK, Kafantaris V, Padron-Gayol MV, Rosenberg CR, Campbell M. Haloperidol in schizophrenic children: early findings from a study in progress. *Psychopharmacol. Bull.* 1992;28(2):183-6.

Sporn A, Addington A, Reiss AL, et al. 22q11 deletion syndrome in childhood onset schizophrenia: an update. *Mol. Psychiatry* 2004;9(3):225-6.

Sporn AL, Greenstein DK, Gogtay N, et al. Progressive brain volume loss during adolescence in childhood-onset schizophrenia. *Am. J. Psychiatry* 2003;160(12):2181-9.

St Clair D, Xu M, Wang P, et al. Rates of adult schizophrenia following prenatal exposure to the Chinese famine of 1959-1961. *JAMA* 2005;294(5):557-62.

Stefansson H, Rujescu D, Cichon S, et al. Large recurrent microdeletions associated with schizophrenia. *Nature* 2008; epub Jul 30.

Straub RE, MacLean CJ, O'Neill FA, et al. A potential vulnerability locus for schizophrenia on chromosome 6p24-22: evidence for genetic heterogeneity. *Nat. Genet.* 1995;11(3):287-93.

Susser E, Lin SP. Schizophrenia after prenatal famine. Further evidence. *Arch. Gen. Psychiatry* 1996;53(1):25-31.

Thompson PM, Vidal C, Giedd JN, et al. Mapping adolescent brain change reveals dynamic wave of accelerated gray matter loss in very early-onset schizophrenia. *Proc. Natl. Acad. Sci. USA* 2001;98(20):11650-5.

Toga AW, Thompson PM, Sowell ER. Mapping brain maturation. *Trends Neurosci.* 2006;29(3):148-59.

Tohen M, Kryzhanovskaya L, Carlson G, et al. Olanzapine versus placebo in the treatment of adolescents with bipolar mania. *Am. J. Psychiatry* 2007;164(10):1547-56.

Turkington D, Kingdon D, Weiden PJ. Cognitive behavior therapy for schizophrenia. *Am. J. Psychiatry* 2006;163(3):365-73.

Usiskin SI, Nicolson R, Krasnewich DM, et al. Velocardiofacial syndrome in childhood-onset schizophrenia. *J. Am. Acad. Child Adolesc. Psychiatry* 1999;38(12):1536-43.

Volkmar FR, Cohen DJ, Hoshino Y, Rende RD, Paul R. Phenomenology and classification of the childhood psychoses. *Psychol. Med.* 1988;18(1):191-201.

Walsh T, McClellan JM, McCarthy SE, et al. Rare structural variants disrupt multiple genes in neurodevelopmental pathways in schizophrenia. *Science* 2008;320:539-43.

Weiser M, Werbeloff N, Vishna T, et al. Elaboration on immigration and risk for schizophrenia. *Psychol. Med.* 2007;8:1-7.

Werner S, Malaspina D, Rabinowitz J. Socioeconomic status at birth is associated with risk of schizophrenia: population-based multilevel study. *Schizophr. Bull.* 2007;33(6):1373-8.

Werry JS, McClellan J, Chard L. Early-onset schizophrenia, bipolar and schizoaffective disorders: a clinical follow-up study. *J. Am. Acad. Child Adolesc. Psychiatry* 1991;30:457-465.

Wright IC, Rabe-Hesketh S, Woodruff PW, David AS, Murray RM, Bullmore ET. Meta-analysis of regional brain volumes in schizophrenia. *Am. J. Psychiatry* 2000;157:16-25.

Xu B, Roos JL, Levy S, van Rensburg EJ, Gogos JA, Karayiorgou M. Strong association of de novo copy number mutations with sporadic schizophrenia. *Nat. Genet.* 2008;40:880-885.

In: Behavioral Pediatrics, 3rd Edition
Editor: D. E. Greydanus et al.

ISBN 978-1-60692-702-1
© 2009 Nova Science Publishers, Inc.

Chapter 22

Personality Disorders and Adolescents: A Developmental Perspective

Helen D. Pratt

Abstract

Children and Adolescents who manifest devastating symptoms of personality disorders often live in the wake of very aversive events and consequences. Personality disorders (PD) are representative of personality traits that are enduring, stable, maladaptive, and seriously affect at least two areas of function: a) cognition; b) affectivity; c) interpersonal functioning, or impulse control. Personality disorders are most often diagnosed in the adult population; although rare, children and adolescents sometimes exhibit symptoms of these disorders. Caution must be taken when diagnosing children and adolescents. Current research indicates there are three major treatment modalities: Cognitive Therapy, Dialectical Behavior Therapy, and Pharmacotherapy.

Introduction

Personality traits can be observed in infants, small children and adolescents and endure throughout adulthood. Infants are sometimes labeled easy to sooth, irritable, happy, or whiney. These descriptors often follow these youth to adulthood. Individuals, who are considered mentally healthy, are able to adapt to conditions and situations in their environment with enough flexibility in their manner of perceiving, relating to and thinking about the environment such that they can make healthy adjustments. These mentally and socially successful adults exhibit healthy functioning in a wide range of social and personal contexts (See Table 1). Individuals with personality disorders never learn to make these adjustments; they develop personality traits that are inflexible and maladaptive and cause significant functional impairment or subjective distress; this constitutes personality disorders.

Children and Adolescents who exhibit devastating the symptoms of personality disorders (PD) often live in the wake of very aversive events and consequences.

Table 1. Cognitive and Psychosocial Growth of Adolescents Who Are Typically Developing

EARLY ADOLESCENCE

- Cognitive Development
    - Concrete level of cognitive functioning ("here and now basis, "black and white")
    - Formal Operational Stage of cognitive development beginning
    - Beginning of abstract thinking, analytical abilities, problem solving skills, improved inductive and deductive reasoning, and transitional skills, comprehension of and memory for complex strategies, prepositional logic (think about thinking itself), understand the basic theories and concepts
    - Difficulty extrapolating general rules of an activity, event, or setting from one situation to another
    - Awakening sense of morality and altruism
    - Future time perspective not fully developed
    - Selective attention
    - Memory is more mature
    - Growth in cognitive aspects of ability to understand the semantics of language
    - Ability to use language to convey the variety and quality of information.
    - Can use symbols, signs and coded words to understand activities and actions
    - Preoccupation with physical (bodily) concerns
    - Emotionally sensitive may respond to minor injuries or comments from others may exhibit disproportionate reactions
    - Engages in finding differences or similarities between self and peers
    - Moving towards independence and emancipation
- Psychosocial development
    - Peer acceptance is important but the approval and support from family are still *significant* guiding forces
    - Able to enjoy and take pride in increasingly complex accomplishments
    - Can begin to improve their self-image.
    - Past experiences contribute to positive or negative self image
    - Exposure to bullying and teasing begins to increase at this developmental stage
    - Unable to depersonalize criticism, and may even believe parents, teachers, siblings, peers or other hates them
    - Limited life experiences make reactions to rejection, emotional pain or fears erratic may result in engaging in or very risky behavior

MIDDLE ADOLESCENCE

- Cognitive Development
- Formal Operational Stage of cognitive development continues to develop
    - More sophisticated abstract thinking, analytical abilities, problem solving skills, inductive and deductive reasoning, and transitional skills, comprehension of and

memory for complex strategies, prepositional logic,
- Is better able to extrapolate general and specifics about values, mores, family teachings, rules of society
  o Improved sense of morality and altruism
  o Future time perspective continuing to develop
  o Attending skills well developed
  o Memory continuing to mature
  o All language skills improving
  o Preoccupation with physical (bodily) concerns continues and heightens
  o Better able to handle and regulate emotional issues
  o Better ability to accept self
  o Continuing to move towards independence and emancipation
- Psychosocial development
  o Peer acceptance is important but the approval
  o Less reliance on from family but it remains and important guiding forces
  o Able judge own value and accept compliments and criticism from others
  o Past experiences continue to contribute to positive or negative self image
  o Exposure to bullying and teasing peaks at this developmental stage
  o Better able to depersonalize criticism, and may be able to understand the reactions of others to own actions
  o Limited life experiences make reactions to rejection, emotional pain or fears erratic - may result in engaging in or very risky behavior
  o Increased levels of independence from parents and authority figures
  o Capable of multiple relationships
  o Increased family and authority figure conflict may occur and the teen asserts him or self in words and decision making

LATE ADOLESCENCE
- Final pubertal changes have been completed
- Cognitive Development
  o Able to set realistic goals about one's abilities
  o Setting or thinking about the future and career plans
  o Cognitive skills fully developed and will become more mature with transition to early adulthood
  o Decision making becomes future oriented
  o Personal values are now clearer and well defined.
  o Fully capable of competitive activities and situations; they have the ability to specialize
- Psychosocial development
  o most issues of emancipation should be essentially resolved
  o Interpersonal relationships may include dating
  o Now better able to deal with pressures from parents, peers and society, as well as handle personal failures
  o If mentally and physically healthy, the adolescent has developed a secure, acceptable body image and gender role

Although personality disorders are most often diagnosed in the adult population, children and adolescents may exhibit symptoms of these severe and enduring disorders. Individuals diagnosed with PDs manifest enduring and stable patterns of maladaptive behaviors across a wide array of situations and environments; these patterns are inflexible and pervasive. Such patters of behavior begin in childhood, adolescence or early adulthood. Clinicians who understand and recognize the characteristics of PDs may be better able to help their adolescent patients and their families manage these disorders.

Definition

A personality disorder is identified by a pervasive pattern of abnormal experience and behavior with respect to any two of the following: thinking, mood, personal relations, and the control of impulses. Youth who show symptoms of PDs may be described as having bizarre thinking, being suspicious, paranoid, may prefer to be alone, and may often get angry at others for reasons not congruent with the facts. These youth may seem strange, be described as manipulative, self centered, grandiose, etc. This mixture of descriptors does not represent any one specific disorder.

Epidemiology

The DSM-IV-TR 4th ed. states the estimated prevalence rate for any personality disorder (in the general adult population in the United States) is 9.1 percent. The prevalence rate in general population for Cluster A disorders is estimated to be 5.7%, that of Cluster B disorders to be 1.5%, and Cluster C disorders to be 6%. Research studies offer that the estimated prevalence rate for borderline personality disorder is 1.4 - 2.0%, antisocial personality disorder is 0.6%. Researchers also offer that borderline personality disorder is diagnosed more often than schizophrenia or bipolar disorder (manic-depressive illness), mostly PD traits tend to decline steadily in prevalence during adolescence and early adulthood, however, the prevalence rates of PDs in adolescents is unknown.

Clinical Features

Individuals who present with symptoms of PD must have exhibited those symptoms for a long enough time to establish that their behavior represents a enduring, stable, pervasive pattern; these symptoms must seriously affect at least two areas of function: a) cognition; b) affectivity; c) interpersonal functioning, or impulse control. The reader is referred to the *Diagnostic and Statistical Manual, fourth edition – Text Revision* [*DSM-IV-TR*] for specific diagnostic criteria.

The personality disorders are divided into three categories label as Clusters A – C to designate their general presentations which represent ten very serious mental illnesses [See Table 2]. General or basic criteria for PDs are summarized below:

- The behavioral manifestations of the disorder causes severe distress and impaired function in the following areas: Personal, familial, and interpersonal relationships; social; occupational; other important areas of function.
- Those impairments are present across a broad range of personal and social situations.
- Some symptoms are present in some disorders as early as ages 9 or 10 years old.
- The symptoms are not be due to other disorders on Axis I, substance abuse, or medical problem.
- Symptoms must be distinguishable from characteristics that emerge in response to specific situational stresses or more acute mental states (such as those diagnosed on Axis I).
- If a PD is diagnosed in children or adolescents under age 18 years, the symptoms must be present at least 1 year; except in the case of anti-social personality disorder which can be diagnosed prior to age 18.

Table 2. Personality Disorders: Characteristics as listed in the DSM-IV-TR (2000)

Cluster	Characteristics	Subtypes
A	Odd and eccentric	Paranoid Schizoid Schizotypical
B	Dramatic, emotional, erratic	Antisocial Borderline Histrionic Narcissistic
C	Anxious and Fearful	Avoidant Dependent Obsessive-compulsive personality disorder not otherwise specified

Subcategories

Detailed criteria for the ten subcategories are not offered in this chapter but a comparison table for functional characteristics is presented in Tables 3, 4 and 5. Based on the general descriptors applicable to all subtypes of personality disorders, the personality traits are inflexible, maladaptive, persistent, and cause significant functional impairments or subjective distress in the individual who has a personality disorder.

Associated Symptoms

The available literature on PDs contends severe emotional and behavioral disturbances during childhood are associated with both adolescent maladaptive personality functioning. However, most personality disorder traits that appear in childhood will not persist into adolescence. But the presences of several symptoms or disorders during childhood serve as independent predictors of PD:

- Conduct problems serve as an independent predictor of personality disorders in all three clusters.
- Depressive symptoms serve as an independent predictor of cluster A personality disorders in boys.
- Immaturity as an independent predictor of cluster B personality disorders in girls.

Table 3. Personality Disorders Comparison: Cluster A Odd and Eccentric Adapted from *DSM-IV-TR, 4th ed.*, 2000, p. 690-701

Subtype of Disorder	Paranoid Personality Disorder	Schizoid Personality Disorder	Schizotypical Personality Disorder
Prevalence Rates	0.5% – 2.5%	• Uncommon in clinical settings; onset must be prior to diagnosis of schizophrenia	3%
Cognition	• Extremely suspicious of others • Misinterprets	• Indifferent to feedback from others • Misinterprets	• Perceptual and cognitive distortions • Ideas of reference (no delusions) • Believes may have special powers and control over others
Affectivity	• Do not trust others • Private • Holds grudges	• Emotional coldness • Detached or flattened affect • Restricted range of affect • Not interested in sex • Usually does not engage in sexual behavior • Indifferent to praise	• Eccentricities of behavior • Inappropriate or constricted affect • Superstitious or preoccupied with paranormal
Interpersonal	• Believes other's intent is malevolent exploitive, harmful or deceptive in the face of a lack of evidence • Difficult to get along with • Problems with close relationships	• Solitary • Little or no interest in sexual experiences with another person • Few activities viewed as pleasurable	• Interpersonal deficits acute discomfort with and reduced capacity for close relationships • No close friends except parents or siblings • Excessive social anxiety
Impulse Control	• Poor	• Poor	• Poor
Differential Diagnosis	• Pervasive developmental disorder • Schizophrenia • Mood disorders with psychotic features • Psychotic disorders • Direct physiological effects of neurological or other general medical condition • Medication side effects		

Table 4. Personality Disorders Comparison: Cluster B Dramatic, Emotional, Erratic Adapted from *DSM-IV-TR*, 4th ed., 2000, p. 701 -718

Subtype of Disorder	Antisocial Personality Disorder	Borderline Personality Disorder	Histrionic Personality Disorder	Narcissistic Personality Disorder
Prevalence Rates	3% in Males 1% Females	2%	2% - 3%	< 1%
Cognition	• Disregard for violation of rights of others • Rationalizes hurting others or stealing for personal profit • Exploits	• Instability in close personal relationships • Poor self image • Idealization to devaluation • Identity Disturbances • Unstable self image • Paranoid Disassociates	• Suggestible • Easily influenced by others • Believes relationships are more intimate than they are	• Exaggeration of sense of self • Fantasies • Sees self as special • Requires excessive admiration • Sense of entitlement • May have some perfectionist qualities • May believe he or she has already achieved perfection
Affectivity	• Lack of remorse	• Intense anger • Unstable • Marked reactivity • Episodic dysphoria • Irritable • Anxious • Chronically feels empty	• Excessive emotionality	• Grandiosity • Excessive need for admiration • Lack of empathy • Occasionally suspicious • Lacks empathy
Interpersonal	• Deceitful • Aggressive • Indulges self • Not generous to others • Fails to conform to social norms or ideals • Irresponsible	• Transient • Frantic effort to avoid abandonment, • Unstable intense experiences	• Must be the center of attention or is uncomfortable • Inappropriate sexually; seductive, provocative • Rapid shifts/shallow emotions • Uses physical appearance to draw attention to self • Speech lacks detail • Dramatic	• Indulges self but is not generous to others • Exploitive • Envious • Arrogant • May alienate self or withdraw socially to prevent others from discovering personal flaws or deficits

Table 4. (Continued)

Subtype of Disorder	Antisocial Personality Disorder	Borderline Personality Disorder	Histrionic Personality Disorder	Narcissistic Personality Disorder
Impulse Control	• Impulsive	• Marked impulsivity • Very high risk for self-mutilation & suicidal behavior sex and substance abuse, bingeing, and drinking	• Marked impulsivity	
Course	• Enduring, usually begins before age 15, but not diagnosed until after age 18 • May become less evident as person grows older or remit, most often diagnosed in males			
Differential Diagnosis	• Rule out schizophrenia and manic episode	• Absence of pervasive suspiciousness, may become less evident or remit as the person ages • Most often diagnosed in females	• Personality change due to a general medical condition • Symptoms that develop in association with chronic substance abuse	• Schizoptypal personality disorder • Paranoid personality disorder
Co-morbidity	• Having 5 or more symptoms of CD, dysthymia, alcohol use disorder, or generalized anxiety disorder was significantly associated with developing modified APD			

Table 5. Personality Disorders Comparison: Cluster C Anxious and Fearful Characteristics Adapted from *DSM-IV-TR*, 4th ed., 2000, p. 718 -729

Subtype of Disorder	Avoidant Personality Disorder	Dependent Personality Disorder Most frequently (Diagnosed in Mental Health)	Obsessive-Compulsive Personality Disorder	Personality Disorder Not Otherwise Specified
Prevalence Rates	0.5% – 1.0%	Most frequent in mental health clinics	1.0 % community samples	
Cognition	• Sees self as inept, unappealing	• Difficulty initiating anything • Submissive • Difficulty making decisions • Always attempts to get others to assume responsibility	• Preoccupations with orderliness, perfectionism, control • Perfectionist • Over conscientious, scrupulous • Rigid • Stubborn • Self-critical • Life is governed by details, rules • Devoted • Can't discard useless or worthless items • Miserly	
Affectivity	• Very shy, fear of embarrassment, negative self evaluations	• Strong feelings of helplessness	• May experience discomfort with emotions	
Interpersonal	• Avoids activities that have significant interpersonal contact, requires guarantee of being liked, fear of shame • Social inhibition, inadequacy, hypersensitivity to negative criticism	• Fears abandonment, afraid to disagree with others • Excessive and urgent need for care • Goes to excessive lengths to gain nurturing and support • Clingy	• Not generous • Inflexible in morals and ethics for the behavior of others • May be socially detached • May exhibit excessive devotion to work	

Table 5. (Continued)

Subtype of Disorder	Avoidant Personality Disorder	Dependent Personality Disorder Most frequently (Diagnosed in Mental Health)	Obsessive-Compulsive Personality Disorder	Personality Disorder Not Otherwise Specified
Impulse Control			<ul><li>Life is governed by details, rules</li><li>Devoted</li><li>Can't discard useless or worthless items, miserly</li></ul>	
Differential Diagnosis	<ul><li>Rule out social phobia</li><li>Caution in diagnosing in children and adolescents whom shy and avoidant behavior may be developmentally appropriate</li><li>May be result of problems with acculturation following immigration.</li></ul>	<ul><li>Most often diagnosed in females</li><li>Mood disorders</li><li>Panic disorders</li><li>Personality disorders</li><li>Agoraphobia</li><li>General medical condition</li><li>Caution in diagnosing in children and adolescents</li></ul>	<ul><li>Rule out substance abuse, especially substances that impact the central nervous system</li><li>OCD</li><li>Personality disorder due to a general medical condition</li><li>Narcissistic, antisocial and schizoid personality disorders</li></ul>	
Co-morbidity	<ul><li>May share features with social phobia</li></ul>	<ul><li>Mood disorders</li><li>Panic disorders</li><li>Agoraphobia</li><li>Result of general medical conditions</li></ul>	<ul><li>Other personality disorders</li></ul>	

Diagnosis

It is essential that clinicians carefully examine the data they use to diagnose personality disorders in children and adolescents:

(1) Clinicians must consider subculture norms for the child or adolescent and his or her family.

(2) They must remember that parents who are not college educated or sophisticated may present data using language that paints a harsher picture of the child's or adolescent's behavior than may be warranted; for example, "I whooped his butt," versus "I spanked him as a last resort when nothing else worked," versus I put him in timeout [but the parent forgot or withheld that she whipped the child after he came out of timeout several times]. The language used to describe a child's or adolescent's behavior will impact the clinician's perception and representation of the presenting problems.

(3) Africa-Americans, Hispanics, and gays, may be diagnosed more often with certain personality disorders if they do not meet the norms of Euro-American citizens who are not culturally competent. For example, Afro-Caribbean's often are diagnosed: antisocial, schiozotypal, avoidant and narcissistic; while Hispanics may be seen as histrionic because they tend to offer somatic complaints versus state their mental health problems; e) female and gays are more likely to be diagnosed with borderline personality disorders; f) males are more often diagnosed with antisocial personality disorders than females; g) females and effeminate or gay males are more often diagnosed with borderline, histrionic and dependent personality disorders than other males. Each of the listed items results because of the cultural biases of the diagnosing clinician.

Co-Morbidity

There is an association between mental disorders in childhood and adolescence and adult personality disorders. However, for youth who show symptoms of APD, one should be aware that with that those symptoms tend to gradually dissipate as the youth matures. Those who develop this disorder become increasing shy during adolescence and early adulthood. Disruptive disorder, substance abuse disorder, conduct disorders, juvenile delinquency, severe aggression or violence have all been identified as being co-morbid with PDs. The likelihood of being diagnosed with PD increases if a person has already been diagnosed with other mental disorders (especially major depressive disorder) or has multiple diagnoses. The presence of PD symptoms during adolescence is associated with an increase risk for violent behavior that persists into early adulthood. When compared to teens not diagnosed with a PD, adolescents with PD are more likely to engage in heavy alcohol consumption, cigarette smoking, s and reported a heavy alcohol consumption; adolescents diagnosed with APD are also more likely to use illicit drugs.

Treatment

There is minimal research on treatment of PDs with any population but especially with adolescents. Researchers contend that effective therapy must address two major issues: Emotional regulation and changing core beliefs. Two treatment modalities that offer evidence based data on their potential effectiveness in treating some PDs are: dialectical behavior therapy (DBT) which was developed specifically to treat BPD. Cognitive Behavior Therapy is the other promising treatment strategy; this treatment has been used to treat individuals with BPD and ASPD. Both therapies address teaching individuals to control, modulate and manage their emotions. Secondly, they help teach strategies to address distortions in thinking, perceptions and impulse control.

Pharmacological treatments are not designed to treat the personality disorders but had been the most often employed treatment strategy. Medication can be very useful in controlling or minimized symptoms of depression, anger and psychosis. Antidepressant drugs and mood stabilizers may be helpful for depressed and/or labile mood. Antipsychotic drugs may also be used when there are distortions in thinking.

Clinicians must remember that the focus of care should be on controlling the aversive outcomes of disturbances in emotional regulation and core beliefs. Impulse control and faulty thinking can result in the manifestation of maladaptive and sometimes dangerous behaviors that may be symptomatic of personality disorders.

Conclusion

Children and Adolescents who manifest devastating the symptoms of personality disorders often live in the wake of very aversive events and consequences. Personality disorders (PD) are representative of personality traits that are enduring, stable, maladaptive, and seriously affect at least two areas of function: a) cognition; b) affectivity; c) interpersonal functioning, or impulse control. Personality disorders are most often diagnosed in the adult population, although rare, children and adolescents sometimes exhibit symptoms of these disorders. Youth who manifest symptoms of PDs may be responding to abuse, trauma, chaotic environments or may simply be a product of their specific sub group's cultural norms. Therefore, caution must be taken when diagnosis children and adolescents with these "rare" disorders because they are not in control of their lives or environments.

Treatment is challenging, current research indicates that those who receive Cognitive Therapy or Dialectical Behavior Therapy have responded well to interventions that teach emotional regulation and how to change core beliefs. Pharmacotherapy does not treat PD, but can be used to address states of depression, anger, anxiety, psychosis and other affective states. A diagnosis of PD indicates a) there is no cure for these disorders; b) the affected person has an enduring, pervasive, and stable set of personality traits and c) will present with the associated accompanying social and emotional deficits. Individuals can still be helped to manage potential negative outcomes through learning emotional regulation, and how to change distorted cognition. Although the diagnosis of a personality disorder means that the person can not change the associated deficits, he or she can be helped to manage potential negative outcomes.

References

Abe JA, Izard CE. A Longitudinal Study of Emotion Expression and Personality Relations in Early Development. *Journal of Personality and Social Psychology*, 1999; 77(3):566-577.

Bernstein DP, Cohen P, Skodol A, Bezirganian S, Brook JS. Childhood antecedents of adolescent personality disorders. *Am. J. Psychiatry.*, 1996;153:907-913. http://ajp.psychiatryonline.org/cgi/content/abstract/153/7/907 Accessed 8/15/08.

Dingfelder SF. Personality Disorders Treatment for the 'untreatable.' *Monitor on Psychology,* 2004; 35(3):46.

Elkind D: *The Hurried Child: Growing Up Too Fast, Too Soon.* Reading, MA, 1988, Addison-Wesley.

Erickson, E. *Childhood and Society,* New York: W.W. Norton and Co., Inc., 1963.

Erickson, E. *Identity, Youth and Crisis,* New York: W.W. Norton and Co., Inc., 1968

Gemelli R: *Normal Child and Adolescent Development.* American Psychiatric Press, Washington, DC, 1996.

Gesell A, Ilg FL, Ames LB: *The Child from Five to Ten.* Harper and Row Publishers, New York. 1946.

Illingworth RS: *The Development of the Infant and Young Child.* Churchill Livingstone, London, 7th ed, 1980.

Johnson JG, Cohen P, Kasen S, Skodol AE, Hamagami F, Brook JS. Age-Related Change in Personality Disorder Trait Levels Between Early Adolescence And Adulthood: A Community-Based Longitudinal Investigation. *Acta Psychiatr. Scand.,* 2000;102:265-275.

Johnson JG, Cohen P, Smailes E, Kasen S, Oldham JM, Skodol AE, Brook JS. Adolescent Personality Disorders Associated With Violence and Criminal Behavior During Adolescence and Early Adulthood, *Am. J. Psychiatry, 2000157:1406-1412.*

Lenzenweger MF, Lane MC, Loranger AW, Kessler RC. DSM-IV personality disorders in the National Comorbidity Survey Replication. *Biol. Psychiatry,* 2007; 62(6):553-64.

National Institute of Mental Health, U.S. Department of Health and Human Services. *Borderline Personality Disorder.* Author, October 18, 2007. Reviewed: June 26, 2008

http://www.nimh.nih.gov/health/publications/borderline-personality-disorder.shtml Assessed August 3, 2008.

Murrie DC, Cornell DG. The Millon Adolescent Clinical Inventory and Psychopathy. *Journal of Personality Assessment,* 2000; 75(1), 110–125.

Ramklint M, von Knorring A-L, von Knorring L, Ekselius L. Child And Adolescent Psychiatricdisorders Predicting Adult Personality Disorder: A Follow-Up Study. *Nord. J. Psychiatry,* 2003; 57:23–28.

Serman, N, Johnson J.Geller, P. Personality Disorders associated with substance use among American and Greek Adolescents. *Adolescence*, 2002; 37(148):841-854.

Washburn JJ, Romero EG, Welty LJ, Abram KM, Teplin LA, McClelland GM, Paskar LD. Development of Antisocial Personality Disorder in Detained Youths: The Predictive Value of Mental Disorders. *Journal of Consulting and Clinical Psychology,* 2007; 75(2): 221-231.

Westen D, Nakash O, Thomas C, and Bradley R. Clinical Assessment Of Attachment Patterns And Personality Disorders In Adolescent And Adults. *Journal of Consulting and Clinical Psychology*, 2006; 74(6):1065-1085.

In: Behavioral Pediatrics, 3rd Edition
Editor: D. E. Greydanus et al.

ISBN 978-1-60692-702-1
© 2009 Nova Science Publishers, Inc.

Chapter 23

Anorexia Nervosa and Bulimia Nervosa

Vinay N. Reddy and Lesley A. Reid

Abstract

The prevalence of anorexia nervosa is estimated to be 0.5-2% and that of bulimia nervosa 1-3%, both reported predominantly in young females. The etiology is multifactorial and includes societal, familial, socioeconomic, and genetic risk factors. Both disorders can lead to a wide range of clinical manifestations and complications, often life threatening. The management requires a coordinated multiple disciplinary approach. This chapter reviews the history, definitions, epidemiology, clinical presentation, diagnosis, and treatment of anorexia and bulimia nervosa.

Introduction

The term *anorexia nervosa* (Greek: "nervous loss of appetite") was first used in 1873 to describe formally women with self-restriction of food intake, increased physical activity, psychologic disturbance including distorted self-perception of appearance, severe weight loss, and amenorrhea. However, descriptions of women, and some men, with these classic features and clinical course date back to the sixteenth century. In the fourth century, Blessila, sister of a protégé of St. Jerome who followed his advice to be "pale and thin with fasting" and died of the regimen, may have been the first recorded case of death due to anorexia. *Bulimia nervosa* (Greek: "nervous ox hunger") "an irresistible urge to overeat, followed by self-induced vomiting or purging" was first described by Russell in 1979, but overeating has been mentioned as far back as Greek mythology and purging has often been associated with overeating.

Definitions

Anorexia nervosa was described in DSM-III and -III-R, as was bulimia nervosa. The diagnostic criteria were made more specific in DSM-IV, with subtyping of anorexia nervosa patients into "restrictors" and "purgers", and more stringent criteria for "binge eating" were introduced as part of the definition of bulimia. DSM-IV also includes a category of "eating disorders not otherwise specified" (acronym: EDNOS).

Table 1. DSM-IV TR diagnostic criteria for anorexia nervosa

Diagnostic criteria for anorexia nervosa

- Refusal to maintain body weight at or above a minimally normal weight for age and height (less than 85% of expected weight for age and height, or a body mass index (weight in kg divided by height in meters squared) of 17.5 or less).
- Intense fear of gaining weight or becoming fat, even though underweight.
- Distorted perception of one's own body weight or shape, undue influence of body weight or shape on self-evaluation, or denial of the seriousness of currently low body weight.
- In postmenarcheal females, amenorrhea (absence of at least three consecutive menstrual periods; a woman is considered amenorrheic if her periods occur only following hormone administration.)

Restricting type: The patient has not regularly engaged in binge-eating or purging behavior (self-induced vomiting or misuse of laxatives, diuretics, or enemas). during the current episode of AN.

Binge-eating/Purging type: The patient has regularly engaged in binge-eating or purging behavior during the current episode of AN.

This category includes patients with "binge eating disorder", a term used to describe marked binge eating or overeating with significant associated distress, but not followed by purging or other compensation for excessive food intake. However, the EDNOS category also includes patients who restrict and purge without binging (and are therefore not considered bulimic), and patients who are not yet 15% below expected weight or have not yet missed enough menstrual periods to meet the strict definition of anorexia. Binge eating disorder is defined as a disorder for further study in DSM-IV. Although many patients with binge eating disorder are overweight, excessive weight is not a required criterion for the diagnosis of binge eating disorder.

DSM-IV criteria for the diagnosis of anorexia nervosa are listed in Table 1.

DSM-IV criteria for diagnosis of bulimia nervosa are listed in Table 2.

Table 2. Diagnostic criteria for bulimia nervosa

- Recurrent episodes of binge eating, characterized by both of the following:
  - o Eating, in a given period of time (e.g. within any 2-hour period), an amount of food definitely larger than most people would eat during a similar period of time and under similar circumstances.
  - o A sense of loss of control over eating during the episode (e.g. a feeling that one cannot stop eating or control what or how much one is eating)
- Recurrent inappropriate compensatory behavior to prevent weight gain, such as
  - o Self-induced vomiting
  - o Misuse of laxatives, diuretics, enemas, or other medications
  - o Fasting, or
  - o Excessive exercise.
- Binges and inappropriate compensatory behavior both occur, on average, at least twice a week for 3 months.
- Self-evaluation is unduly influenced by body shape and weight.
- The disturbance does not occur exclusively during episodes of anorexia nervosa.

Purging type: the patient has regularly engaged in self-induced vomiting or the misuse of medications (laxatives, diuretics, or enemas) during the current episode of BN.
Nonpurging type: the patient has used other inappropriate compensatory behaviors, such as fasting or excessive exercise, but has not regularly engaged in self-induced vomiting or the misuse of medications during the current episode of BN.

Epidemiology

It is estimated that about 0.5 - 2 % of women will meet all of the criteria for diagnosis of anorexia nervosa during their lifetimes. Some studies suggest that the incidence of anorexia is increasing, while others do not show a change. However, patients are frequently found to have only some of the clinical features of anorexia while still being sufficiently ill to require medical treatment for its complications. Bulimia nervosa is much more common than anorexia: lifetime prevalence of bulimia is about 1-3%, as opposed to the 0.5 - 2% incidence of anorexia.

Both anorexia nervosa and bulimia nervosa predominantly affect women. Men are also seen with both disorders: the ratio of affected women to affected men is about 10-20:1 for anorexia and about 10:1 for bulimia but the incidence of eating disorders, especially among adolescent males, has been increasing. The higher incidence of eating disorders in women may be related to societal and cultural pressures regarding appearance; this is discussed further below.

Risk Factors

Societal

Eating disorders are by their nature biologic, psychologic, social, and developmental. They are diseases of affluence, in that they occur in societies where food is plentiful and yet in which "thinness" is valued over "fatness". In such societies people, especially the young, constantly receive both overt and covert messages that fat is bad and "the thinner is the winner" (a phrase that appears on many so-called "pro-ana" or pro-anorexic Web sites) (Table 3). Many eating disorder patients can trace their desire to lose weight to specific stimuli of this type. Often a patient starts to lose weight to improve her physical appearance after hearing critical remarks about her weight or appearance from family, teachers (especially physical education or health teachers), peers, or romantic interests, or after disorders related to excess weight are diagnosed in family or friends. Family discord and high parental demands are also possible risk factors for development of anorexia nervosa. Western societies in particular tend to emphasize thinness as a goal, and the prevalence of eating disorders in formerly isolated, primitive societies has been seen to increase sharply with exposure to Western culture and values.

Table 3. A list of "safe foods" developed by an anorexic patient (ravenrockcandy.org, 2004)

- Diet soda
- Sugar free Jello®
- Skim milk
- Rice ("in moderation")
- Lettuce
- Pickles
- Egg white
- Broth ("only 5 cals per cube")
- I Can't Believe It's Not Butter® Spray (0 calories)
- Saltine crackers ~ light ~ (40 calories per 5 crackers)
- Apples (90)
- Oranges (65)
- Tomatoes (24)
- Cucumbers (16)
- Water (0)
- Coffee (0)
- Watermelon ("50 Cals Per Half Cup")
- Lemon (10)
- Salsa (24)
- Strawberries (45 Per Cup)
- Campbell's® chicken noodle soup ("only 150 cals per can")

Familial

The family can influence the development of eating disorders in many ways. There is evidence for genetic inheritance -- if not of the eating disorder itself, then of a predisposition to develop an eating disorder. Psychiatric disorders in other family members, especially parents, have been associated with an increased risk of developing eating disorders.

Socioeconomic Status, Gender, and Ethnicity

Possibly because of correlation between ethnic background and socioeconomic status, the majority of anorexic patients in North America are Caucasian adolescent and young adult women. Patients from other ethnic backgrounds are being seen more frequently, and about 5-10% of anorexic patients in previous studies are male, although the proportion of males with eating disorders has risen in recent years. It has been observed that a disproportionate number of male anorexics are homosexual; studies on whether lesbians are at higher or lower risk for eating disorders than heterosexual women have shown conflicting results. Similarly, male homosexuality has been mentioned as a risk factor for bulimia.

Sport Participation

Athletic participation also seems to be a risk factor for eating disorders, although the effect is related to the specific sport involved. Participants in sports that emphasize thinness, especially performance sports such as ballet and other forms of dance, cheerleading, swimming, water polo, and aerobic instruction, have been shown to have a significantly higher incidence of eating disorders. Dancers, in particular, tend to see themselves as heavier than they actually are and tend to prefer weighing less than they currently weigh. Gymnasts show the same risk statistically in some studies, but not in others. "Elite" athletes appear to be at higher risk for eating disorders than nonathletes.

Genetics

There is evidence for a genetic component to eating disorders. Female relatives of an anorexic or bulimic patient are 7 to 12 times more likely to develop anorexia or bulimia themselves, and an increased risk among monozygotic twins of eating disorder patients has also been shown. Most studies of candidate genes have shown no significant association with eating disorders, but many of these studies were small and the study populations were heterogeneous.

Concomitant Psychologic Disorders and History of Abuse

The formal definitions of personality disorders exclude diagnosis of such disorders in patients under 18 years of age. This restriction notwithstanding, there are strong associations between the eating disorders and certain personality disorders. In particular, the cluster C personality disorders (avoidant, dependent, and obsessive-compulsive) are much more common in patients with the restricting subtype of anorexia nervosa than in the general population. The cluster B disorders are more prevalent in the binge/purge subtype of anorexia nervosa and in bulimia nervosa, especially borderline personality disorder, whose DSM-IV diagnostic criteria are met by 20-42% of bulimic patients.

There are also strong associations between a history of sexual abuse and the development of eating disorders. A 1999 survey of American women found that the lifetime prevalence of completed forcible rape among women with bulimia nervosa was 26.6%, versus 11.5% for women with binge eating disorder and 13.3% for females with no history of either disorder. A history of aggravated assault was also significantly more frequent in females with bulimia nervosa, as was a history of post-traumatic stress disorder. A meta-analysis showed a small but significant positive relationship between a history of childhood sexual abuse and a subsequent history of eating disorders (anorexia nervosa, bulimia nervosa, or binge eating disorder); bulimia nervosa was the sole or primary focus of most of the included studies, while a more recent survey showed a 2.5-fold to 4.9-fold increase in incidence of bulimia nervosa among women who were sexually abused as children, with the higher increase seen in women who were abused on more than one occasion. Purging behaviors, especially self-induced vomiting, may be related to feelings of disgust after sexual assault and in particular after forced fellatio. Restriction and weight loss may be an attempt by the patient to make herself less attractive or even "invisible" to men, as well as a way to soothe her own anxiety. Physical child abuse may also be a risk factor, but a recent retrospective study showed no significant association between a history of physical abuse and later development of an eating disorder.

Clinical Features

Anorexia Nervosa

Eating disorder patients, especially anorexics, tend to be perfectionist even without overt signs of obsessive-compulsive disorder (OCD). As an example, it is common for anorexics to be straight-A+ student and many will try to achieve performance levels far beyond all of their peers in everything they do. OCD is frequently found in conjunction with eating disorders and particularly with anorexia nervosa, although it is possible to confuse the obsessive and compulsive tendencies related to eating in anorexics with those of frank OCD. Obsessive-compulsive behaviors of such patients that are not related to eating indicate that a primary obsessive-compulsive disorder also exists. OCD also appears to be familial, and it has been suggested that the two disorders may be inherited together, although the coupling of inheritance does not appear to be strong.

Most often, anorexia develops during adolescence or young adulthood; occasionally children develop anorexia before puberty, and anorexia can present before menarche -- sometimes as early as ages 7-9 years -- as short stature or growth retardation, inadequate weight gain before onset of weight loss and an associated decrease in appetite which may appear before growth retardation is noted. Puberty may be a risk factor on its own: changes in hormone levels, especially that of estrogen, have been shown to affect appetite in animal models, and it has been postulated that some patients' sensitivity to these hormone changes appears as disordering of eating behavior. There is also evidence that altered brain serotonin contributes to impulse control, dysregulation of appetite, and mood changes in both anorexia nervosa and bulimia nervosa. Disturbance of serotonin levels and serotonin modulation may start before the onset of anorexia nervosa, contributing to such symptoms as dysphoric mood. Also, patients with anorexia nervosa may find initially that decreased food intake itself may help improve dysporic mood, since decreased protein intake reduces plasma tryptophan levels, thus reducing serotonin levels and decreasing anxiety. However, decreased weight also produces changes in neuropeptide and monoamine levels which may worsen anxiety and dysphoria.

Anorexics usually lose weight mainly by restricting food intake. Initially, an anorexic patient's dietary changes may seem innocuous or even desirable, such as elimination of desserts or a progressive turn toward vegetarianism. As the disease progresses, the patient systematically eliminates any food with any fat content: a common behavior among anorexics is to read nutrition labels, choosing foods for their labeled (lack of) fat or calorie content. Health and nutrition classes in school are often identified by anorexic patients as the point at which they decided to eliminate "unhealthy foods" (i.e. fat) from their diets. Eventually patients develop their own shrinking lists of "safe" foods: one such list, found on a "pro-ana" Web site and shown in Table 3, demonstrates the lengths to which anorexic patients can go to avoid fat intake. Anorexics eat more slowly than do normal people, and take in fewer calories per meal and per day than others. It is not uncommon to find that an anorexic sufficiently malnourished to require hospitalization at diagnosis is taking 500-700 kcal/day at presentation.

As patients continue to lose weight, they become more and more focused on achieving thinness. They may weigh themselves several times a day; they will feel satisfaction briefly with a decrease in weight, but will then set their goal even lower. Any weight gain, no matter how little is cause for self-punishment and increased efforts to lose weight, whether by even more severe intake restriction, purging (by emesis or by laxative use), or increased exercise. Their eating behaviors and exercise regimens become increasingly severe, ritualistic, and inflexible.

Excessive exercise as part of weight loss is a common feature -- some call it a hallmark -- of anorexia. It may take the form of excessive participation in athletic activities, especially running or "power walking" or long series of repetitive calisthenics such as sit-ups or jumping jacks. Running 15-20 miles/day or doing sets of up to 500 abdominal "crunches" at night is not uncommon, and increased exercise may precede other behavioral signs of anorexia. Anorexic patients are significantly more active than persons without eating disorders both during the acute phase of their disorder and for up to one year before its onset: thus increased exercise may in some cases be an early warning sign of anorexia nervosa. Frequently patients in advanced stages of anorexia will conceal the extent of their exercise from their families, friends, and caregivers, resorting to calisthenics in the middle of the night or leaving the house to run at 3:00 am in order to keep their families from learning the true extent of their regimens.

In the early stages of the disease family and friends may ignore or even encourage diet changes and increased exercise, especially if a patient is overweight or obese. Only after cachexia becomes apparent does the patient's family begin to worry. Overt attention to a patient's weight or attempts at intervention may lead her to conceal the extent of her behaviors from her family, friends, and medical caregivers. Anorexics often wear baggy clothes to conceal signs of cachexia such as prominent ribs and vertebrae, and will "water-load" (sometimes drinking several liters of water) before examination or conceal weights under their clothing to mislead their physicians. Although physicians experienced in eating disorder management take precautions against such manipulation, including measuring urine specific gravity and serum electrolyte levels, many primary caregivers can be fooled by these tactics.

As the disease progresses, anorexics begin to avoid situations in which they might be observed not eating. They will stop eating meals with their families, saying that "I just ate" or "I'll eat later". If they are made to eat with their families they will argue over the food they are served, cut food into minute pieces and spread it around their plates, or will hide food in their napkins or pockets for later disposal. They may resort to purging after meals; even though they do not binge in the clinically accepted sense, they feel like they have eaten excessively and purge to compensate. They may try to take over family grocery shopping and meal preparation so that they can control their own intake; in this way they can also exert some measure of control over their families' meals and at the same time distract family members from their own lack of intake by pushing others to eat. Eventually they may withdraw from all activities except exercise, work or school, and the rituals they have associated with eating.

An anorexic's behavior problems may be exacerbated by acquaintances who are themselves anorexic: anorexics have been known to compete to see who can lose the most weight, but will also trade techniques and tips for weight loss and for concealing intake restriction. "Pro-ana" Web sites have exacerbated this problem in recent years by making information on such techniques available to anyone with Internet access and by extolling anorexia and bulimia as "lifestyle choices" rather than life-threatening diseases. These Web sites often focus on themes of self-control, restriction and over-exercising as paths to success, and reaching for perfection through control of their own weight. They often include collections of "thinspirational" photographs of thin, if not cachectic, women depicted as being of ideal appearance and/or of obese women whose obesity will inspire the viewer to seek thinness even more avidly.

Bulimia Nervosa

Bulimia and anorexia have many risk factors in common. Abnormally low body weight excludes the diagnosis of bulimia, but all bulimics are excessively concerned with body image and weight, as many as 30% of bulimics have a prior history of anorexia, and bulimia, like anorexia, tends to run in families. However, there are important differences in associated factors between bulimia and anorexia: childhood and parental obesity are more common in bulimics than in the general population or in patients with non-eating-disorder-related psychiatric problems, in contrast to anorexics, and criticism by family and friends regarding diet and habitus are more common in bulimics. Anxiety, mood, and personality disorders and substance abuse are also more common in bulimics than in other groups; in particular, up to 75% of bulimics also have or have had an affective disorder and up to 41% meet criteria for borderline disorder. Many studies indicate that a history of abuse, particularly sexual abuse, in childhood is associated with the later development of eating disorders, particularly bulimia, and many theories have been advanced as to the mechanisms, including development of a disassociative coping style, poor self-esteem and self-hatred, and attempts to reexert control over the patient's own life. Bulimics also seem to have a higher incidence of novelty-seeking behavior and impulsivity, and an increased incidence of self-injurious behavior including self-mutilation, substance abuse, and suicidal behavior. This may be due to the relation between bulimia nervosa and borderline personality disorder noted above, since self-injurious behaviors are often seen in the borderline patient due to their inability to modulate impulsive behaviors.

Bulimia appears to develop in early adulthood or late adolescence, in contrast to the association with puberty seen in anorexia. Disordered eating in bulimics typically begins during or after a period of dieting, when a patient learns that it is possible to cut caloric and nutritional absorption by purging after eating, but a significant number of patients begin to binge before making other diet changes. Emetics such as ipecac are sometimes used to purge, but more often patients learn to induce vomiting with the fingers or with objects such as toothbrush handles. Others use laxatives or enemas in an attempt to increase stool output, reduce weight, and decrease absorption of nutrients, or take diuretics to lose weight acutely, not understanding that these measures simply redistribute fluid. Bulimic (and anorexic) diabetics have been known to stop their own insulin to cause hyperglycemia leading to hyperglucosuria and osmotic diuresis, and some bulimics and anorexics have resorted to abuse of stimulants or thyroid hormone to induce weight loss.

As bulimia develops, the initial feeling of control over weight and the satisfaction of eating large amounts of food without gaining weight decreases. Hunger after purging leads to "compensatory" bingeing, and a vicious cycle develops, made worse by other provocations to binge such as anxiety, depressed mood, boredom, and use of alcohol and other substances that reduce inhibition. Certain "forbidden" foods may also trigger binges. Binges tend to occur while alone, and patients may hoard food for later bingeing in privacy; as with anorexia, bulimic patients will go to great lengths to conceal their disordered eating behavior from family and friends. The amount of food ingested may be massive (>10,000 kcal in a single binge), but may also be no larger than a normal meal and distinguished from normal eating only by the patient's perceived loss of control during the meal.

Diagnosis

The high prevalence of eating disorders in adolescents makes screening patients for signs and symptoms imperative. This is especially true for bulimics: although the reported mortality rates for anorexics exceeds that for bulimics, a bulimic patient may appear relatively normal physically with no outward signs of potentially lethal metabolic derangements. Patients in the early stages of anorexia may not yet show the stigmata of chronic malnutrition, and anorexics will go to great lengths to conceal their physical state in order to avoid intervention by family and caregivers.

A potential obstacle to diagnosis is the patient's desire to maintain her current weight and diet. Because of their distorted view of themselves, these patients will often see nothing wrong with their current state. However, they will go to great lengths to conceal their true physical condition from their family, friends, and caregivers. These measures may range from wearing baggy clothes to fluid loading before physician visits and concealing weights in their clothing while being weighed at examination. Physicians experienced in eating disorder management will weigh patients according to a set protocol, usually including weighing the patient clad only in underwear and an exam gown, after voiding, positioning her with her back to the scale dial, and sharing the weight with her and her family only in certain circumstances, as well as checking urine specific gravity to detect water loading. A similar procedure is used for inpatients, but they are weighed on awakening and after their first void ("basal" weight). Initial screening questions useful in assessment are listed in Table 4. Follow up questions are listed in Table 5.

Table 4. Initial screening questions for disordered eating

For the patient:
- Are you now on a diet?
- Have you been on a diet in the past? If so, when and how often?
- How do you feel about your weight and appearance?
- What do you see when you look in the mirror? Is there anything you see that you want to change?
- Do you think about food and food choices often? Do you wish you could think about it less?
- Do you do things to control your weight that you wish you did not have to do?
- Do you feel that you control the way you eat?

For the parents:
- Have your child's eating patterns changed?
- Does your child worry too much about her weight or the foods she eats?
- Have you seen your child avoiding certain foods, exercising excessively, or frequently weighing herself?
- Does your child avoid eating meals with the family more often than in the past?
- Does your child eat very slowly or play with her food rather than eating it?

Table 5. Follow up Questions

If an eating disorder is suspected in a patient, follow-up questions should include:
- What did you have for (the most recent meal -- usually breakfast or lunch)?
- What did you have for (the two previous meals)?
- Did you eat any snacks in between meals?
  - Meal information should include portion sizes as well as specific foods and beverages.
    - Are you taking any medicines to lose weight?
  - These may include over-the counter diet pills, prescription stimulants such as amphetamines, emetics, laxatives, or diuretics. Patients should also be questioned specifically regarding their use of herbal remedies and other alternative treatments, as these are frequently used by patients with eating disorders for weight control and for purposes beside weight control and since many users of these agents have little or no knowledge of their primary effects, side effects, and interactions with other medications.
- Are you exercising to lose weight?

o   If so, types, durations, and frequencies of exercise should be assessed.
• What made you decide that you needed to lose weight?
o   Inquiries like this regarding triggers need to be open-ended because of the many
     different known psychosocial triggers. Specific questions regarding family and friends
     and their attitude towards the patient and her appearance are often useful, including:
   – How do other people feel about your appearance?
   – Has anyone criticized your appearance in your hearing?
   – How did you feel/what did you think when you heard these criticisms?

The findings to look for on physical examination are listed in Table 6, and laboratory findings in anorexia nervosa and in bulimia nervosa are listed in Table 7.

Table 6. Physical findings commonly seen in eating disorder patients

- General: impaired linear growth.
- Skin: sallow appearance, carotenemia, dry skin, brittle hair and nails, appearance of lanugo hair.
- Eyes: subconjunctival hemorrhages (appear after retching and vomiting).
- Mouth and throat: dry mucosa (from dehydration), palatal and pharyngeal lacerations (from fingers or other objects used to induce vomiting), erosion of the posterior surfaces of teeth.
- Chest: prominent ribs.
- Lungs: rales from pulmonary edema due to hypoproteinemia (rare).
- Heart: bradycardia, hypotension, orthostatic hypotension and tachycardia, heart rate lability even at rest; gallop rhythms.
- Abdomen: scaphoid with wasting of abdominal wall musculature, hypoactive bowel sounds; palpable stool in descending colon.
- Back: prominent vertebrae, lanugo; sacral edema.
- Extremities: muscle wasting and prominent joints, lacerations on dorsal knuckles (Russell sign); dependent edema
- Neurologic: slow mentation, cognitive dysfunction, poor short-term memory.

Table 7. Laboratory findings in anorexia nervosa and bulimia nervosa

- Signs of bone marrow suppression, including leukopenia and neutropenia.
- Anemia.
- Thrombocytopenia.
- Decrease in complement levels, especially C_3 and alternative pathway components.
- Deficiency of vitamin-K dependent clotting factors.
- Hypokalemia (especially in bulimics)
- Elevated blood urea nitrogen
- Hypoglycemia
- Hypocalcemia
- Hypomagnesemia
- Hypophosphatemia

- Hypozincemia
- Hypoproteinemia
- Hypoalbuminemia and low prealbumin (prealbumin falls before albumin and often rises before albumin normalizes since it reflects a shorter time frame)
- Decreased antidiuretic hormone
- Hypochloremic metabolic alkalosis with vomiting
- Metabolic acidosis (especially with laxative abuse)
- Elevated amylase with normal lipase

Treatment

There are many aspects in common in the treatment of patients with anorexia nervosa or with bulimia nervosa. The psychologic aspects of treatment are especially similar. Unfortunately, although there is some evidence to support the use of certain forms of therapy for adults with eating disorders, there have been few published studies on the effectiveness of particular therapies for adolescents with eating disorders, especially anorexia. For a patient with anorexia nervosa to maintain a healthy body weight, she must develop some insight into the nature of her disease so that she is motivated to make healthy choices. She cannot be rushed or forced to gain weight, although a severely ill patient may require emergent treatment of critical biochemical abnormalities such as electrolyte disturbances: the concept of "a work in progress" should be emphasized, rather than fixed goals which may be frightening to the patient.

Treatment Team

Whether an outpatient or an inpatient, the patient with an eating disorder is treated most effectively by a team. The multifactorial nature of eating disorders makes it unlikely that any one person will have all the therapeutic and medical skills a patient needs to be treated effectively, and the patient will need a great deal of support from several team members to overcome her fears of weight gain.

The core of a typical treatment team includes a physician, a psychotherapist, and a nutritionist. Other members such as a social worker or a recreational therapist can also contribute greatly to the patient's care. Especially in inpatient, residential, and day-treatment programs, other staff working with the patient -- such as nurses, patient care assistants, and perhaps resident physicians and medical students -- are also important members of the team.

The physician is responsible for the patient's medical supervision, including overall regulation of nutrition and medication, monitoring of symptoms, physical findings, and laboratory studies, and treatment of complications of malnutrition, refeeding, and purging. Often a pediatrician or internist works in partnership with a psychiatrist, since the latter is more familiar with psychotropic agents and their uses and side effects. Subspecialists in adolescent medicine and pediatric hospitalists are often well-versed in eating-disorder management. Continuity of care is important in both the inpatient and outpatient settings both for optimal care and to prevent "splitting" of the treatment team. "Splitting" in this context refers to the patient's attempts to play members of the team off against each other to achieve her own goals rather than those of treatment. This is different from the use of the term "splitting" to describe the patient with a borderline personality disorder who views everyone she interacts with, including therapists, in black-and-white terms. However, the black-and-white outlook may well be related to the patient's seeking out the team members who will give her what she wants.

The therapist concerns himself with the psychologic and social aspects of the patient's eating disorder, as well as concurrent and contributing problems such as obsessive-compulsive disorder or prior abuse. A clinical psychologist or a psychiatric social worker experienced in working with adolescents with eating disorders and their families is ideal. Family therapy and parent coaching are also important in treating adolescents with eating disorders, since adolescents live in the context of their families. Some therapists can provide both individual and family therapy, or collateral therapy in which the patient is seen separately from the parents by the same provider, but in other situations separate individual and family therapists may be required. Cognitive-behavioral therapy (CBT) is the approach most commonly used and most studied for treatment of patients with eating disorders, and has been shown in controlled trials to be the most effective approach for patients with bulimia nervosa. Dialectical-behavioral therapy, an adaptation of CBT which includes concepts such as "mindfulness" taken from Zen Buddhism and was originally developed for treatment of patients with borderline personality disorder, has also been used with some success in treating patients with bulimia. No treatment modality has yet been shown to be superior in the treatment of anorexia nervosa, but no large trials have yet been reported and analyzed.

Although the medical aspects of refeeding need close medical supervision, a dietitian is also an essential part of the team. Her role includes not only helping to determine patients' nutritional needs, but educating patients and their families on the role of specific nutrients, assisting in planning menus, and addressing the patient's beliefs, attitudes, and misconceptions about various foods. As with other members of the team, a dietitian who has experience working with adolescents with eating disorders is desirable, but dietitians without such experience can be helpful in communication with other, more experienced professionals on the patient's team.

A social worker can contribute to treatment in ways other than providing direct therapy to the patient and family. He can assist in resolving conflicts between the patient and family, and can help identify patient/family needs and locate resources. A recreational therapist or child-life specialist can be very valuable in helping patients with improving their social interactions and with learning relaxation techniques.

Nursing staff and patient care assistants are also important members of an inpatient team. They often have closer contact with the patient than do the specialists and therapists. In particular, they may have to provide mealtime and postprandial observation for ED patients. This requires training in techniques these patients use to avoid receiving nutrition, even if parenteral: ED patients on total parenteral nutrition have been known to turn off their infusion pumps or disconnect their lines and let the TPN solution flow into the garbage. Since these team members may gain the most practical experience in patient observation, they are also in an excellent position to help family members learn what to watch for when the patient returns home and the family needs to observe. Equally important, they can help the patient immensely with food-related anxiety by talking with them during meals and postprandial observation, and model this type of assistance for family members.

Inpatient versus Outpatient Treatment

The majority of ED patients, and in particular most bulimics, can be managed as outpatients. Anorexics are hospitalized more often than bulimics in part because of physiologic changes that accompany chronic malnutrition. Indications for inpatient treatment are listed in Table 8.

Table 8. Indications for admission

- Body weight that is dangerously low or has dropped rapidly
- Electrolyte disturbances, including hypokalemia and hypophosphatemia
- Symptomatic bradycardia or orthostatic hypotension, or signs of heart failure
- Risk of self-injury (suicide, or ED behaviors that have potential for physical injury)
- Concomitant medical or psychiatric conditions requiring hospitalization
- Failure of outpatient treatment to arrest the progress of the disease

Nutrition and Weight Goals

Eating-disorder patients and the people who treat them have a common goal: they all want the patient to "eat healthy". The difference between patients and therapists is in the definition of "healthy eating": one feature of eating disorders is distortion of the patient's view of what healthy eating really involves. The modern Western world values thinness, and we are continuously bombarded with messages extolling thinness and denigrating fat. As a result, many ED patients learn to fear fat and to avoid fat intake at all costs, not realizing that fatty acids are essential to many physiological functions, from hormone production to nerve-fiber myelination.

The general aims of providing nutrition to an ED patient are listed in Table 9.

Table 9. General Nutritional Goals

- Returning the patient to a state of adequate nutrition
- Repleting nutritional deficiencies
- Restoring energy
- Restoring nutrient reserves
- Avoiding pathologic conditions resulting from chronic malnutrition
- Avoiding refeeding complications
- Maintain a healthy weight
- Avoid food-related anxiety

Chronic malnutrition, especially of long standing, usually results in depletion of critical nutrients, including potassium, phosphorus, and calcium. Some of these, particularly potassium and phosphorus, are also in high demand once refeeding is started. Total-body potassium depletion is also worsened by self-induced vomiting in bulimics. As caloric intake increases, glucose becomes more available and insulin production increases; since potassium is co-transported into cells with glucose, this can result in an additional and sometimes precipitous drop in extracellular potassium which can evoke arrhythmias and even asystole as well as delirium. Depletion of phosphorus stores makes nucleotide phosphorylation infeasible, resulting in insufficient supply of ATP at the cellular level with impairment of cell -- especially muscle cell -- function. The refeeding syndrome initially manifests as drops in serum phosphorus which are seen during the first 3-4 days of refeeding, or 7-10 days after refeeding is started when the body's metabolic rate increases. If these drops are not corrected by supplementation, arrhythmias and heart failure can be seen. Dependent edema, especially pretibial and sacral, is also common in early refeeding due to increased fluid intake and hypoproteinemia. This may be a sign of impending heart failure, but a syndrome of refeeding edema, whose exact mechanism is unclear, has also been described. Strategies to prevent refeeding syndrome are summarized in Table 10.

Table 10. Strategies to Prevent Refeeding Syndrome

- Beginning refeeding at a low caloric intake, preferably slightly higher than that the patient was taking before beginning treatment. It is usually but not always safe to start at 1000 to 1200 kcal/day. Determining the patient's intake prior to the start of treatment may be problematic, since she may overstate her actual intake in order to minimize her medical condition.
- Increasing caloric intake gradually until the patient is on a consistent weight-gain trend (usually by 200 kcal/day; occasionally we will increase by 300 kcal/day for 1-3 days initially).
- Measuring calcium, phosphorus, and potassium frequently over the first few days (in some cases every 8-12 hours), and again when heart rate, metabolic rate, and weight gain begin to pick up.
- Giving phosphorus, potassium, and calcium supplements when needed, keeping in mind that a slight initial fall in, for example, phosphorus can be followed very quickly by a further and precipitous drop.

Weight gain of 0.1-0.3 kg/day during inpatient treatment is desirable. In the first few days of hospitalization it is common to see an initial rise, typically associated with rehydration since many anorexics are moderately to markedly dehydrated on admission, followed by constant or slowly falling weight until the patient is receiving sufficient calories to replete catabolized tissue and begin gaining weight. This is feasible in inpatients, since we can enforce a reduced level of activity. Once a patient is discharged we expect little or no weight gain for the first 1-2 weeks, as her activity increases and she and her team make adjustments in exercise, other activity, and nutrition. After the first 1-2 weeks, we expect weight gain of 0.3-0.5 kg/week until she reaches her goal range. If her weight gain exceeds this rate, we will make appropriate changes in her diet plan. If her weight gain falls below 0.3 kg/week, or if she loses weight, we may start with increasing her diet or adding a liquid supplement. We warn her in advance that falling weight or persistent inadequate weight gain is an indication for hospitalization for acute treatment and may be a sign that more intensive treatment in a residential program is needed.

The ultimate goal is for the patient to reach and maintain good health in a healthy weight *range*. The concept of a range must be emphasized, since the patient will focus on a particular number as a goal and feel that she has failed if her weight exceeds that number. The healthy range, or goal range, is that in which she has normal physical, endocrine, metabolic, and reproductive function. The latter is one factor used in choosing a healthy weight range for a patient. A weight at least 90% of ideal body weight for height, gender, and age is necessary for resumption of menses, but some patients require a higher weight or a longer duration in the target weight range to reestablish menses. It is common to choose a goal weight range corresponding to 10-15 percentiles below the patient's height percentile, based on National Center for Health Statistics standard growth charts.

Medical Complications

Even before admission, cardiac dysrhythmias due to electrolyte imbalance are the most concerning complication of anorexia and bulimia. Electrolyte imbalances are most often due to purging, whether by vomiting (which results in both potassium loss and hypochloremic metabolic alkalosis), laxative abuse (leading to metabolic acidosis because of bicarbonate loss in stools), or excessive use of diuretics (also leading to metabolic alkalosis). Prolonged QT intervals are also often seen in ED patients: the mechanism for this is unclear but may be related to deficiency of magnesium and/or potassium. Prolonged QT intervals may also be a contraindication to many medications that might otherwise be useful in these patients. Abuse of ipecac for purging may result in skeletal and cardiac myopathy due to toxic effects of emetine. Excessive vomiting, regardless of how it is induced, may cause upper gastrointestinal trauma ranging from a Mallory-Weiss tear to rupture of the esophagus or stomach. Recurrent vomiting for a long period of time (at least six months) may result in erosion of dental surfaces, usually on the lingual aspects of the teeth. Patients who induce vomiting with fingers or objects inserted into the posterior pharynx may have palatal lacerations, and those who induce vomiting with their fingers may have scars or calluses on the dorsal knuckles. The latter finding is known as the Russell sign.

Osteopenia is a common long-term effect of eating disorders. The combination of small habitus, inadequate calcium intake, excessive exercise, and low estrogen with amenorrhea results in a high incidence of osteoporosis in female ED patients, as well as increased risk of fracture. Some authors suggest that even 6 months of amenorrhea may be enough to result in bone mineral loss; dual-energy X-ray absorptiometry (DEXA) is recommended for any patient who has been amenorrheic for 6-12 months or more. Since restoring bone mass once it is lost is difficult, it is best to prevent osteopenia, and this is best done by restoring and maintaining good nutrition.

Infrequent bowel movements are common in anorexics during initial refeeding, because of metabolic changes and their effect on gastrointestinal motility and also because motility will be low for some time after adequate oral intake is restored. In addition, patients will often have a subjective feeling of constipation due to their altered perception of food and digestion. Laxatives are not indicated in this situation since post-refeeding constipation resolves once adequate nutrition is established and maintained. Occasionally one or two doses of a fiber-based laxative or of milk of magnesia may be helpful, but in general the best treatment for constipation is to increase fiber (as fruits, vegetables, and cereals), dietary fat, and fluid intake. Motility-enhancing agents such as metoclopramide are occasionally used to promote gastric emptying, but other laxatives such as senna are best avoided.

Structural abnormalities have been found in the brains of adolescents with anorexia nervosa and chronic starvation. These changes seem to occur early in the course of the disorder, when weight is low but before treatment is begun, and include decreased volumes of both gray and white matter with increased cerebrospinal fluid volume. It is not yet clear if or when these changes reverse with restored nutrition.

Counseling and Therapy

Since eating disorders are biopsychosocial in nature, individual and family therapy are essential to recovery and to preventing relapse. This is true for inpatients and outpatients, and therapy for the two groups is largely similar.

Severely malnourished patients pose an additional problem for the treatment team. Their malnutrition results in slowed mentation, including impairments of cognitive function, attention, concentration, and memory, which make in-depth therapy very difficult. Some patients, at the end of a 3-4 week hospitalization for acute malnutrition, do not recall much of the events or therapeutic conversations of the first week after admission. Because of this, some psychiatrists and physicians who treat anorexic patients prefer to treat acute malnutrition first, sometimes with nasogastric or orogastric enteral feeding or even with parenteral nutrition, before beginning therapy aimed at the eating disorder, and not to begin meals until late in the hospitalization and after acute refeeding issues have been addressed. Other eating disorder specialists prefer to begin giving meals to the patient at admission, even though the portions may be small at first, and to avoid tube or parenteral feeding except in cases of extreme malnutrition and to couple parenteral nutrition with scheduled meals and snacks. This approach has the advantage of allowing the patient to become reaccustomed gradually to eating an appropriate diet.

Of course, many patients attempt to continue their intake restriction even after admission, by stretching out meal times and by concealing food. One protocol is to require that a patient complete each meal and snack in a pre-set amount of time; any food left at the end of the time limit is taken from the patient and replaced with a liquid nutritional supplement approximately equal in calorie content to the remaining food. A time limit is also given for drinking the supplement, and supplement remaining at the end of this second time limit is fed to the patient by nasogastric tube. It is important to emphasize to patients that nasogastric feeding is *not* a punitive measure, but a necessary medical therapy to help them overcome their disease. Whether patients themselves regard the nasogastric tube as punitive or therapeutic is unclear, but rarely does a patient require nasogastric tube feeding more than once in a given hospital stay.

Psychotherapy, including individual, family, and group therapy, should begin as soon as possible after diagnosis, and is generally started or restarted almost immediately after inpatient medical admission; it is, of course, the mainstay of residential therapy for eating disorder patients. In the case of patients hospitalized for severe malnutrition, initial therapy may consist of little more than supportive counseling, coupled with simple explanations of the disease and its effect on the patient that can be repeated and varied as necessary. An analogy helpful in explaining nutritional needs to ED patients in the early stages of inpatient treatment is the "cabin in the Arctic".

Imagine that your body is a cabin in the Arctic in winter. Like other cabins up there, it is built of wood. It has a fireplace inside to keep you warm, and a woodpile outside the door to fuel the fire, and wooden furniture for you to sit and sleep on. Normally you gather enough firewood each day (eating) to keep the fire burning and keep you warm. Your body is the cabin (skeletal and other structural tissue, and critical muscle including cardiac muscle) and furniture (muscles), and the woodpile is your body's natural energy reserve (body fat). You have to keep the fire burning, though: even if you have no wood in the woodpile you have to throw whatever you have around that will burn on the fire to stay warm (this represents catabolism of muscle and other tissue in the absence of nutritional intake).

Right now (at the beginning of inpatient treatment) you have burned the woodpile, you have burned most of the furniture, and you're working on burning the walls...

This analogy is simple enough for many severely malnourished patients to grasp. It can also be extended as a patient's mentation improves: for example, the need for different nutrients can be discussed in terms of different kinds of wood for rebuilding different parts of the cabin and furniture.

Cognitive-behavioral therapy (CBT) has been shown in randomized controlled trials to be effective in the treatment of bulimia nervosa, and is felt by some to be the psychotherapy of choice in those patients, whether conducted on an individual or a group basis. Guided self-help programs, based on the principles of CBT but using books on bulimia nervosa written for lay people in conjunction with a limited number of therapy sessions aimed at encouraging patients to follow treatment programs described in the books, appear to be as effective a form of intensive outpatient therapy as formal CBT.

Very few studies have been reported on the effectiveness of therapeutic modalities for anorexia nervosa in adolescents. The general goals of treatment include persuading patients that anorexia nervosa is a serious disease and not a lifestyle, and addressing in therapy their body image disturbance, diet choices, and general psychosocial function, as well as psychological comorbidities such as obsessive-compulsive disorder which are often found to be easier to address but which often underlie the anorexia. Both family and individual therapy appear to be effective for anorexia, but one form of family therapy -- behavioral family-systems therapy -- seems to produce faster return to health than individual therapy and family therapy appears to have long-term benefits apparent even after completion of therapy. Group therapy, for patients or for patients and their families together, is commonly used in treatment of bulimia but has not been studied as well in anorexic patients. CBT is used in the treatment of anorexic adults but has not been studied as yet in anorexic adolescents.

Psychotropic Medications

Psychotropic medications have also been used to treat patients with eating disorders. There is good evidence supporting the use of selective serotonin reuptake inhibitor (SSRI) antidepressants in the treatment of bulimia: such treatment improves the patient's mood and quickly reduces the frequency of bingeing and purging, and also seems to be of use in the treatment of binge-eating disorder. Higher doses are required to reduce bingeing and purging (40-60 mg fluoxetine per day) than are need to treat depression (20-40 mg fluoxetine per day) However, the salutary effect of SSRIs in these patients is not as great, or as long-lasting, as that of CBT, and it appears that the most effective treatment for bulimia is the combined use of CBT and an SSRI.

SSRIs have also been used in the treatment of anorexia, but their efficacy has not been as well studied as with bulimia. The evidence so far shows that SSRIs have little or no effect in the acute treatment of anorexia, but that there is a slight decrease in relapse rate when SSRIs are given by way of maintenance therapy. SSRIs are often used to treat anorexics with concomitant depressive disorders and may be helpful when the anorexia is secondary to depression. However, since tryptophan is required for the synthesis of serotonin, a severely malnourished patient may be deficient in serotonin, making inhibition of serotonin reuptake futile, and a recent randomized controlled trial of fluoxetine in anorexic patients after some weight restoration (to a body mass index of 19) showed no benefit with fluoxetine compared with placebo. There may be some benefit to SSRIs in patients with concomitant disorders such as depression, however. Psychiatrists will often wait until some weight gain has been achieved before beginning SSRI therapy, and will begin treatment at low doses with gradual increases as patients gain weight. Also, weight gain is a listed side effect of some SSRIs. The effect is not sufficiently dependable to be useful for medical management, but many anorexics are aware of SSRI-associated weight gain and may refuse to take a prescribed SSRI for fear of gaining weight. As with any other patient, it is best to discuss the indications and effects of an SSRI with a patient prior to starting therapy: it may be wise to discuss, but deemphasize, the effect of the agent to be used on weight. Antipsychotic agents have been used as well in the treatment of anorexic patients, but have not been well studied. They seem to have a beneficial effect in some cases, particularly in those patients in whom anorexia is associated with obsessive-compulsive behavior (OCD) since these agents do appear to be effective in the treatment of primary OCD.

Cyproheptadine, an agent similar to phenothiazine, is a first-generation (sedating) histamine H_1-receptor antagonist that is also known to block serotonin receptors. It is not widely used at present as an antihistamine, in part because of its sedating properties. However, its reported side effects include weight gain and increased growth in children. Cyproheptadine has been used as an appetite enhancing agent in patients with anorexia due to other diseases, and in particular has been shown to increase weight gain in patients with cystic fibrosis and patients with attention-deficit hyperactivity who are being treated with psychostimulants but not consistently in patients with advanced malignancies. Although large trials have not been conducted, cyproheptadine has not been consistently shown to improve weight gain directly in patients with anorexia nervosa. Even so, many physicians experienced in eating-disorder management use cyproheptadine routinely, in part for the possible effect on weight gain but also for its sedating effect which appears to reduce anxiety associated with refeeding.

Conclusion

Anorexia nervosa and bulimia nervosa have both been observed to be potentially chronic illnesses. As with many other aspects of eating-disorder management, it has been difficult to assess prognosis rigorously, but it is clear that anorexia nervosa has the highest mortality rate of *any* psychiatric disorder.

To date, the most comprehensive study of prognosis for patients of all ages with anorexia nervosa is the meta-analysis of Steinhausen, based on studies published over a 50-year period. He found that overall mortality in anorexic patients was 5%, with recovery from all clinical symptoms of anorexia in 47% of survivors and chronic illness in 21%. However, wide variability in the definitions of full and partial recovery, inconsistency in the use of mortality figures, and methodological differences between the source studies make it difficult to predict prognosis for a specific patient. A more rigorous, prospective study by Strober et al gives a more optimistic outlook for adolescent patients with anorexia: nearly 76% of study patients met criteria for full recovery, although the time to recovery ranged from 57 to 79 months from the time of initial admission.

Similar problems arise in predicting prognosis of bulimic patients. Two meta-analyses show that about 50% of bulimic patients have a "good outcome", but the percentage of patients with "good outcomes" ranged from 24 to 74% and some studies included in the analyses defined "good outcome" with less rigorous criteria than others. Again, the published data is not sufficient to predict outcomes for specific patients.

Acknowledgements

Many thanks to Kathleen A. Mammel, M.D., Division of Adolescent Pediatrics, William Beaumont Hospital, Royal Oak, Michigan, and to Dilip Patel, M.D., Department of Pediatrics, Michigan State University, Kalamazoo Center for Medical Studies, Kalamazoo, Michigan, for their numerous helpful suggestions regarding this chapter.

References

American Psychiatric *Association. Diagnostic and Statistical Manual of Mental Disorders, Fourth Edition, Text Revision*. Washington, D.C.: American Psychiatric Association; 2000.

Chen EY, Matthews L, Allen C, Kuo JR, Linehan MM. Dialectical behavior therapy for clients with binge-eating disorder or bulimia nervosa and borderline personality disorder. *International Journal of Eating Disorders* 2008;41(6):505-512.

Dare C, Eisler I, Russell G, Treasure J, Dodge L. Psychological therapies for adults with anorexia nervosa. *Br. J. Psychiat.* 2001;178:216-221.

D'Arrigo T. Dropping insulin to drop pounds: the practice of withholding insulin as a way to lose weight is a serious eating disorder with devastating consequences. *Diabetes Forecast* 2008;61(7):42-44.

Davis C, Blackmore E, Katzman D, Foz J. Female adolescents with anorexia nervosa and their parents: a case-control study of exercise attitudes and behaviours. *Psychol. Med.* 2005;35(3):377-386.

Dennis AB, Sansone RA. Treating the Bulimic Patient with Borderline Personality Disorder. In: *Advances in Eating Disorders*: JAI Press; 1989. p. 237-265.

Dresser LP, Massey EW, Johnson EE, Bossen E. Ipecac myopathy and cardiomyopathy. *J. Neurol. Neurosurg. Psychiatry* 1992;56(5):560-562.

Ehrlich S, Querfeld U, Pfeiffer E. Refeeding oedema: an important complication in the treatment of anorexia nervosa. *Eur. Child Adolesc. Psychiatry* 2006;15(4):241-243.

Eisler I, Dare C, Russell G, Szmukler G, LeGrange D, Dodge E. Family and Individual Therapy in Anorexia Nervosa: A 5-Year Follow-up. *Arch. Gen. Psychiatry* 1997;54:1025-1030.

Fairburn C, Doll H, Welch S, Hay P, Davies B, O'Connor M. Risk Factors for Binge-Eating Disorder: A Community-Based Case-Control Study. *Arch. Gen. Psychiatry* 1998;55:425-432.

Fairburn C, Welch S, Doll H, Davies B, O'Connor M. Risk Factors for Bulimia Nervosa: A Community-Based Case-Control Study. *Arch. Gen. Psychiatry* 1997;54:509-517.

French S, Story M, Remafedi G, Resnick M, Blum R. Sexual orientation and prevalence of body dissatisfaction and eating disordered behaviors. Int J Eat Disord 1996;19:119-126.

Gill W. Anorexia nervosa (apepsia hysterica, anorexia hysterica). *Trans Clin. Soc. London* 1874;7:22-28.

Golden N, Jacobson M, Schebendach J, Solanto M, Hertz S, Seigel W. Resumption of menses in anorexia nervosa. *Arch. Pediatr. Adolesc. Med.* 1997;151(1):16-21.

Gowers S, Bryant-Waugh R. Management of child and adolescent eating disorders: the current evidence base and future directions. *J. Child Psychol. Psychiatry* 2004;45(1):63-83.

Handa M, Nukina H, Hosoi M, Kubo C. Childhood physical abuse in outpatients with psychosomatic symptoms. *Biopsychosoc. Med.* 2008;2:8.

Homnick D, Homnick B, Reeves A, Marks J, Pimentel R, Bonnema S. Cyproheptadine is an Effective Appetite Stimulant in Cystic Fibrosis. *Pediatr. Pulmonol.* 2004;38:129-134.

Jones B, Duncan C, Brouwers P, Mirsky A. Cognition in Eating Disorders. *J. Clin. Exp. Neuropsychol.* 1991;13(5):711-728.

Joy E, Wilson C, Varechok S. The multidisciplinary team approach to the outpatient treatment of disordered eating. *Curr. Sports Med. Rep.* 2003;2(6):331-336.

Katzman D, Christensen B, Young A, Zipursky R. Starving the brain: structural abnormalities and cognitive impairment in adolescents with anorexia nervosa. *Semin. Clin. Neuropsychiatry* 2001;6(2):146-152.

Katzman D. Medical complications in adolescents with anorexia nervosa: a review of the literature. *Int. J. Eat Disord.* 2005;37(Suppl):S52-59, discussion S87-89.

Kaye W. Neurobiology of anorexia and bulimia nervosa. *Physiol. and Behavior* 2008;94(1):121-135.

Keel P, Mitchell J. Outcome in Bulimia Nervosa. *Am. J. Psychiatry* 1997;154(3):313-321.

Klein D, Walsh B. Eating disorders: clinical features and pathophysiology. *Physiol. and Behavior* 2004;81:359-374.

Norris M, Boydell K, Pinhas L, Katzman D. Ana and the Internet: a review of pro-anorexia websites. *Int. J. Eat Disord.* 2006;39(6):443-447.

Rayworth B, Wise L, Harlow B. Childhood Abuse and Risk of Eating Disorders in Women. *Epidemiology* 2004;15:271-278.

Robb N, Smith B, Geidrys-Leeper E. The distribution or erosion in the dentitions of patients with eating disorders. *Br. Dent. J.* 1995;178(5):171-175.

Robin A, Siegel P, Moye A, Gilroy M, Baker-Dennis A, Sikand A. A Controlled Comparison of Family Versus Individual Therapy for Adolescents With Anorexia Nervosa. *J. Am. Acad. Child Adolesc. Psychiatry* 1999;38(12):1482-1489.

Rome E, Ammerman S, Rosen D, Keller R, Lock J, Mammel K, et al. Children and Adolescents With Eating Disorders: The State of the Art. Pediatrics 2003;111:e98-e108.

Russell G. Bulimia nervosa: an ominous variant of anorexia nervosa. *Psychol. Med.* 1979;9(3):429-448.

Sigman G. Eating disorders in children and adolescents. *Ped. Clin. N Am.* 2003;50:1139-1177.

Strober M, Freeman R, Morrell W. The long-term course of severe anorexia nervosa in adolescents: survival analysis of recovery, relapse, and outcome predictors over 10-15 years in a prospective study. *Int. J. Eat Disord.* 1997;22(4):339-360.

Tey H, Lim S, Snodgrass A. Refeeding oedema in anorexia nervosa. *Singapore Med. J.* 2005;46(6):308-310.

Walsh B, Wilson G, Loeb K, Devlin M, Pike K, Roose S, et al. Medication and psychotherapy in the treatment of bulimia nervosa. *Am. J. Psychiatry* 1997;154(4):523-531.

Walsh BT, Kaplan AS, Attia E, Olmsted M, Parides M, Carter JC, et al. Fluoxetine After Weight Restoration in Anorexia Nervosa: A Randomized Controlled Trial. *JAMA* 2006;295(22):2605-2612.

Winchester E, Collier D. Genetic Aetiology of Eating Disorders and Obesity. In: Treasure J, Schmidt U, van Furth E, editors. *Handbook of Eating Disorders*. 2nd ed. Chichester: John Wiley and Sons; 2003.

In: Behavioral Pediatrics, 3rd Edition

Editor: D. E. Greydanus et al.

ISBN 978-1-60692-702-1

© 2009 Nova Science Publishers, Inc.

Chapter 24

Obesity

Vinay N. Reddy

Abstract

Obesity in children and adolescents has reached epidemic proportions in the United States. Multiple factors have been looked at by researchers to explain the high and rising prevalence of obesity in children including societal, familial, media, lifestyle, and genetics. Childhood onset obesity has life-long adverse medical and psychosocial consequences. Management of obese children and adolescents requires participation of the family and caregivers and a team comprised of multiple disciplines. There needs to be appropriate public policy to address this public health problem. This chapter reviews definitions, epidemiology, complications, and management of childhood obesity.

Introduction

The epidemiology and management of obesity in children and adolescents can be better understood with a basic understanding of multiple risk factors that are believed to contribute to obesity. Many health-care professionals, and many lay people, assume that increases in children's caloric intake, coupled with decreases in their physical activity, are responsible for much of the increased prevalence of obesity. Published data shows that caloric intake among children over the last three decades remained relatively constant from the 1970s until the late 1980s. From then until 2000, caloric intake increased among adolescent females, especially white and black females, with larger increases toward the end of this period. Similarly, United States Department of Agriculture data shows decreased average caloric intake for the general US population from the mid-1960s to 1991, followed by an increase in the mid-1990s. These trends do not explain the steady and accelerating increase in prevalence of obesity over the past thirty years, nor do they fit the observed increases in prevalence among ethnic groups, especially Hispanics.

It is also felt by many that decreased physical activity and the resulting fall in caloric consumption have contributed to the increase in obesity. This has been attributed, first to the rapid increase in television watching dating back to the 1960s, and more recently to the (even more rapid) increase in children's use of the Internet, both of which are physically sedentary activities. Many studies of risk factors for obesity in adolescents and particularly of the relationship between obesity and television watching have shown significant associations between the two, although some studies were not able to support this. There is specific evidence that increased television watching is associated with increased BMI, increased food consumption, and decreased fruit and vegetable consumption.

Other contributing factors for children in urban areas may include use of automobiles or mass transportation rather than walking and inability to play safely outdoors due to neighborhood crime; the latter appears also to be associated with low socioeconomic status. Significantly decreased physical activity has been observed among female college freshmen within 5 months after starting college: although accompanied by a significant decrease in caloric intake, body-weight parameters also increased significantly, suggesting that decreased activity was a major contributor to weight gain. Unfortunately, there is little data available on how children's physical activity and caloric consumption have changed over the years, and there is evidence that decreased physical activity occurs after obesity develops, rather than before.

Changes in dietary carbohydrate and fat intake have also been considered as possible causes of increased obesity. Excessive fat intake by some persons, especially those predisposed to obesity, certainly seems to lead to obesity. However, although fat-laden foods -- especially fast foods -- have been strongly linked to the development of obesity in the media, fat consumption by children has decreased over the last 30-35 years. Carbohydrate consumption, on the other hand, has increased over the same time period, and seems to be related to the emphasis seen in recent years on decreasing dietary fat intake: fat calories have been largely replaced by simple carbohydrate calories. This has had other effects, including a decrease in calcium intake due to the substitution of soft drinks and non-citrus fruit juices for milk, which is perceived to be a source of fat. Carbohydrate composition of foods is commonly classified using the glycemic index, which is in general higher for simple sugars and starches (e.g. potatoes, refined grains), lower for whole grains and legumes, and lowest for nonstarchy fruits and vegetables. High glycemic-index diets have been associated with obesity and type II diabetes mellitus in adults: it is reasonable to think that those associations exist in children and adolescents, but there have not yet been studies to confirm or disprove this. Also, postprandial hyperinsulinemia seems to be associated with weight gain, and low glycemic-index diets appear to decrease postprandial hyperinsulinemia, while also being associated with weight loss in obese patients.

Unfortunately, foods high in fat and/or in refined carbohydrates taste good, especially to children. They are also much less expensive, and much more convenient, than more nutritionally valuable foods, especially in the Western world: this likely explains why economically disadvantaged children in the United States are more prone to obesity. Attempts to replace high-fat, high-carbohydrate foods in school lunch programs have been met with protests from children served by those programs, who would much rather eat nachos and pizza.

There is an inherited component to obesity as well. Many genetic syndromes are well-known for their association with obesity (some common syndromes are listed in Table 1), as well as endocrine disorders such as Cushing's disease and hypothyroidism. Hypothyroidism does not appear to be a primary cause of massive obesity, although modest weight loss is seen with treatment. However, much of the familial component of obesity seems to be environmental. Obesity in children and adolescents has been associated with both maternal and paternal obesity. Although this may be partly genetic and, in the case of maternal obesity partly due to gestational influences, socioeconomic factors shared by parents and children are certainly responsible as well: examples include lack of physical activity and indulgence in fast foods and other high-fat, high-carbohydrate food.

In some countries, although not in Western countries, adolescents have been found to underestimate their body weight significantly, especially when they are overweight or obese. This is in contrast to the overestimation seen in anorexia nervosa and bulimia nervosa, but appears to be related to cultural norms and their effect on self-image.

Obesity has also been associated with social factors, including low family income and lower cognitive stimulation at home. This may explain in part racial and ethnic differences in the prevalence of obesity, although some of these differences persist when corrected. A history of neglect and/or abuse, especially sexual abuse, is also associated with obesity.

Table 1. Genetic syndromes associated with obesity. Mode of inheritance is indicated in parentheses, except for duplication and deletion syndromes where the genotype is given (AR: autosomal recessive; AD: autosomal dominant; XL: X-linked)

- Achondroplasia (AD)
- Alstrom syndrome (AR)
- Angelman syndrome with obesity (AD; partial deletion of maternal 15q)
- Bardet-Biedl syndrome (formerly Lawrence-Moon-Biedl syndrome) (AR)
- Carpenter syndrome (AR)
- Cohen syndrome (AR)
- Down's syndrome (Trisomy 21)
- Fragile X with Prader-Willi-like phenotype (X)
- Fanconi-Bickel syndrome (AR)
- Inherited insulin resistance syndromes (AD)
- Isolated growth hormone deficiency (AR)
- Kabuki syndrome (S)
- Klinefelter's syndrome (XXY)
- McKusick metaphyseal dysplasia (AR)
- Prader-Willi syndrome (AD; partial deletion of paternal 15q)
- Psuedohypoparathyroidism (Albright hereditary osteodystrophy) (AD)
- Thyroid hormone resistance syndrome (AD)
- Trisomy 4p
- Turner's syndrome (XO)

Epidemiology

In recent years, the prevalence of obesity has increased steadily in the United States, and the rate of increase has itself increased, especially over the last 25 years, to the point where it is common in both the medical and lay literature to refer to an obesity epidemic. Although it might seem at first glance that obesity would be more prevalent among people of higher socioeconomic status, since they might be expected to have better nutritional access, the converse has proven to be true: the prevalence of obesity in the United States increases with poverty.

Minorities are bearing the brunt of the problem: obesity is much more prevalent among American Hispanics (21.8%) and African-Americans (21.5%) than among Caucasians (12.3%), and among teenage and preteen African-American females the prevalence is 26.6%. As a result, obesity-related illnesses such as type II diabetes mellitus, previously seen only in later adulthood, are being seen more often in adolescence and sometimes in the preteen years.

Definition

Obesity can be defined based on the body mass index (BMI) [BMI = Wt (kg) ÷ (Ht (m)^2 Or BMI = Wt (lbs) × 704.7 ÷ (Ht (in)^2]. It is a standard and widely-used indicator for obesity as it is for anorexia. Here we are concerned with high BMI: an expert panel convened by the United States Department of Health and Human Services has recommended that "obesity" be defined for diagnostic purposes as a BMI greater than the 95th percentile for age and sex, while being "overweight" -- BMI greater then the 85th percentile for age and sex or a large or rapid increase in BMI -- should prompt close observation for possible complications.

Direct measurement of body fat has been suggested as a more precise marker of overweight and obesity: for example, muscular people such as football players tend to have high BMIs but relatively little fat. Measurement of skinfold thickness over the triceps is used for many studies of obesity, and skinfold thickness over several sites is helpful as an indicator of fat distribution. Waist circumference and waist-circumference-to-hip-circumference ratios can yield useful indirect information on abdominal fat, and are associated with cardiovascular and metabolic disease in obese children, but only limited reference values for children have been published. Other methods of measuring body fat, including bioelectric impedance, hydrodensitometry, and dual-energy X-ray absorption, are at present limited to research use.

Clinical Features

In the past, obese children have not generally suffered direct medical consequences until they have reached adulthood. However, the rising prevalence of obesity has made medical sequelae much more common even in pediatric practice.

There is a strong association between obesity and type 2 (non-insulin-dependent) diabetes mellitus in adolescence, consistent with the observed rise in prevalence of type 2 diabetes; there are strong family histories of obesity, type 2 diabetes, and insulin resistance in these patients as well. Impaired glucose tolerance has been shown to occur in 20-25% of obese children and adolescents. Insulin resistance is seen often in obese adolescents; acanthosis nigricans -- hyperpigmentation and thickening of the skin, most often seen on the neck and in the axillae and groin -- which is a common early sign of insulin resistance, is being seen more frequently in obese adolescents as well. (Acanthosis nigricans is sometimes familial, and is also seen, among others, in association with excessive corticosteroids and Prader-Willi syndrome, both of which can cause obesity.) These patients and their families share lifestyles featuring high fat intake and little or no regular physical activity; in addition, some of these patients meet some or all of the diagnostic criteria for binge-eating disorder.

Hypertension associated with obesity in children is also increasing in prevalence. Obese children are at a risk for hypertension 3 times that of non-obese children; pathophysiologic mechanisms being studied include insulin resistance, autonomic dysfunction, and vascular structural changes and dysfunction. Many cardiovascular changes related to obesity, previously thought to occur only in adults, have also been seen in children and adolescence, including increased heart weight and the presence of fatty streaks and fibrous plaques in aorta and coronary artery intima. Fatty streaks and/or fibrous plaques were associated with elevated BMI, blood pressure (both systolic and diastolic), and levels of total and low-density-lipoprotein (LDL) cholesterol, and inversely associated with levels of high-density-lipoprotein (HDL) cholesterol. Several studies suggest that weight loss results in a decrease in blood pressure. National Heart, Lung, and Blood Institute recommendations regarding treatment of hypertension in children and adolescents state that "weight reduction is the primary therapy for obesity-related hypertension" and that "regular physical activity and restriction of sedentary activity will improve efforts at weight management and may prevent an excess increase in (blood pressure) over time", and that pharmacologic therapy should be used only when lifestyle changes are ineffective, hypertension is secondary to other disorders or accompanied by symptoms, diabetes is seen, or hypertensive damage to target organs is seen. Another obesity-related endocrine problem is polycystic ovary syndrome, which is closely related to insulin resistance. The syndrome can affect adolescent females psychologically through changes in appearance from hyperandrogenism-related acne and hirsutism, and the associated insulin resistance and increased risk of atherosclerosis bodes poorly for long-term health.

Obesity can also lead to respiratory compromise in the form of obstructive sleep apnea. This can manifest as learning and school-performance problems including apparent lack of attention (from falling asleep in school) and impairment in memory and learning, and often leading to referrals for evaluation of possible attention-deficit disorder. Although treatment for obstructive sleep apnea must sometimes be surgical, weight loss can be beneficial in cases related to obesity.

The mechanical stress of excess weight leads to orthopedic problems as well. Slipped capital femoral epiphysis is sometimes seen in children of normal weight, but is more common in obese adolescents. Blount's disease, or tibia vara, a rare pathology of the medial tibial growth plate at the knee resulting in pathologic bowleggedness, has also been associated with obesity.

Perhaps more important in childhood and adolescence are the psychosocial consequences of obesity. There is a significant association between overweight and negative body image, and between negative body image and psychiatric diagnoses and morbidity in overweight female adolescents. Many studies have shown that obesity is associated with decreased self-esteem a finding that may vary with gender and age and may be related to negative body image but there are some studies in which no such association was found and studies that report the association also show that self-esteem in the obese, once corrected for poorer body image perception, is not significantly decreased. Low self-esteem in obese adolescents is also associated with weight-based teasing from peers, as are poor body image, depressive symptoms, and even suicidal ideation and attempts. There may be less negative effect among lower socioeconomic groups and minorities, but gender differences are important here as well: for example, African-American girls report fewer weight-related concerns than white girls, but African-American boys report more such concerns than white boys. Depression and adult obesity have been associated, especially among women; depressed adolescents appear to be at higher risk for becoming obese as adolescents and remaining obese into adulthood, although obesity does not predict later development of depression. Even young children often describe overweight people as lazy, stupid, dirty, sloppy, ugly, lying, and cheating: obese children are viewed by peers as the least desirable candidates for friendship and social stratification, both subjective and socioeconomic, are associated with overweight.

Diagnosis

A major potential pitfall in caring for the obese patient is the physician's own attitude toward the obese. The negative reaction to obese people seen in their peers is, consciously or not, shared by many of us, and to treat these patients effectively the physician must set these reactions aside. Also, as with other eating disorders, treatment of obesity is often a lengthy and drawn-out process, complicated by socioeconomic factors affecting both patients and their families and that may make it difficult for them to improve their diet and exercise. Simply helping the patient to maintain a stable weight may be more feasible than trying to achieve actual weight loss.

Initial assessment of overweight or obesity, as with any other disease, begins with a complete history and physical examination. The history should include assessment of diet and exercise, both for the patient and for the family. Dietary history is important for the information it yields on the patient's and family's eating and snacking habits, but only an accurate and comprehensive diet diary can be used to determine caloric intake, and many patients and families are unable or unwilling to keep such a document. Levels of activity for each member of the family, not just the patient, are also important. The family history will also indicate parental attitudes toward nutrition, exercise, and obesity which may complicate treatment: parents who spend most of their free time in front of the TV are less likely than others to understand the need for their children to exercise regularly. Review of systems, and physical examination, should emphasize symptoms and signs of obesity-related medical conditions (Table 2). Laboratory testing, including glucose, cholesterol, and triglyceride levels, may be helpful in detecting medical complications of obesity or confirming suspicions of underlying genetic or endocrine abnormalities, but abnormal laboratory findings are unlikely to scare a young patient into weight loss.

Table 2. Symptoms and physical signs associated with obesity

Abnormality	Symptoms	Signs
Blount's disease	Gait abnormality	Tibial bowing
Diabetes mellitus, type 2	Polyuria, nocturia, polydipsia, fatigue	Acanthosis nigricans
Gallstones	Abdominal pain or vomiting with fatty foods, recent rapid weight loss	
Hypercortisolism (Cushing's disease)		Short stature, hypertension, truncal obesity, acne, hyperpigmentation
Hypothyroidism	Constipation, mental sluggishness, cold intolerance	Short stature, diminished or delayed deep tendon reflexes
Polycystic ovary syndrome	Amenorrhea	Acanthosis nigricans, hirsutism, increased muscle mass
Pseudotumor cerebri	Recurrent headaches, especially with associated vomiting	Papilledema
Sleep apnea	Daytime somnolence, loud snoring, changes in breathing pattern while asleep	Tonsillar enlargement, small airway
Slipped capital femoral epiphysis	Hip or knee pain, gait abnormality	Limp, reduced internal or external rotation of hip

Treatment

A cursory examination of the lay media reveals multitudes of weight-loss programs, diets, and medical treatments for obesity. Some of them may actually work, at least for a while, at least in adults, and at least until deleterious effects or lack of long-term relief are seen (remember fenfluramine…). Obese children and adolescents are more difficult to treat: social and economic considerations, and especially familial issues, must be addressed, and the entire family must make the necessary changes in lifestyle. The goals of treatment must also be realistic. Many patients look for results similar to the before-and-after advertisements for weight-loss programs, but weight loss of that extent is usually not possible without medication and/or surgery. However, moderate weight loss -- 5-10% of weight at presentation -- can produce significant improvement in blood pressure, glucose, and lipids. It may be most practical, and beneficial especially to the growing youngster, to maintain weight at a particular range rather than to seek actual weight loss. Also, early treatment is of benefit even in young children, both to avoid childhood (e.g. sleep apnea, orthopedic disease) and adult (e.g. type 2 diabetes, coronary vascular disease) complications and to avoid or ameliorate the psychosocial consequences of obesity.

The cornerstones of therapy for obesity are dietary modification and increased and regular physical activity. These interventions work best when they take place simultaneously. Diet changes should be made by the entire family and emphasize healthy food choices and relative avoidance of high-fat, high-simple-carbohydrate foods. One program, the "Traffic Light Diet" uses simple categories (avoid vs. approach-with-caution vs. eat-all-you-want) to subdivide foods in each of the major groups (grains, fruits/vegetables, dairy, and meat, with a fifth miscellaneous category) in order to teach families to make healthy food choices; used in combination with exercise and behavioral modification this diet has produced long-term weight loss in children. Severely obese patients may need more restricted diets, such as those high in protein and very low in calories, but these may be dangerous and must be used under close monitoring by the physician and by a nutritionist.

Exercise is important, but cannot by itself reduce weight. Since ability to exercise decreases with increased BMI, regular exercise must begin before morbid obesity renders the patient immobile. There are many approaches possible to increasing children's physical activity and reducing their sedentary, including increased activity at school during lunch and recess, walking or bicycling to school, enrollment in summer schools or summer camps, and reducing television viewing. Psychotherapy may also be helpful in selected cases, and inpatient treatment may be especially useful when family support for treatment is lacking: a combination of dietary changes, organized and supervised exercise, and cognitive-behavioral therapy in a 10-month (one school year) inpatient program resulted in weight loss at discharge that was sustained 14 months after discharge.

If diet modification and increased exercise do not yield weight stabilization or weight loss, further investigation should address the extent and severity of comorbidities. Pharmacologic treatment may be considered at this stage as an adjunct to continued diet and exercise. Available pharmacologic agents for weight loss fall into four categories: stimulants to increase energy expenditure, anorectics to decrease caloric intake, drugs that limit nutrient absorption, and drugs that modulate insulin production or effect. Stimulant treatment for weight loss have a long and not very honorable history: they have for the most part been abandoned due to severe complications ranging from cardiac dysfunction to drug dependence, and even such apparently benign agents as caffeine have shown adverse effects. Sibutramine, a non-selective serotonin/norepinephrine/dopamine reuptake inhibitor, is the only anorectic agent currently approved for treating obese adolescents and is not approved for use below age 16 years; there is a high incidence of side effects and potential interactions with other drugs including selective serotonin reuptake inhibitors (e.g. fluoxetine) or dextromethorphan (a common over-the-counter cough suppressant), and most observed weight loss occurs in the first few months of treatment. Leptin may be helpful in those patients with genetic leptin deficiency. Orlistat, a pancreatic lipase inhibitor, results in increased fecal loss of triglyceride; in adults orlistat administration results in decreased body weight, decreased total and low-density lipoprotein cholesterol, and decreased risk of type 2 diabetes mellitus in the presence of impaired glucose tolerance. It is approved for use above age 12 years in the United States. Loss of fat-soluble vitamins may occur with orlistat despite supplementation, and orlistat use requires a low-fat diet to avoid diarrhea and flatulence. Metformin, an insulin-uptake stimulator, is usually used to treat type 2 diabetes in adults; its use has resulted in weight loss in randomized controlled trials in adolescents, but it is not currently approved for treatment of childhood obesity. Octreotide inhibits glucose-dependent insulin secretion in pancreatic beta cells; it has been shown to produce weight loss in adolescents with obesity following hypothalamic injury, but its side effects include cholelithiasis, cardiac dysfunction, and GH and TSH suppression.

Bariatric surgery has been investigated for the treatment of obese adolescents. The two most common procedures are gastric banding and Roux-en-Y gastric bypass. Complication rates are fairly high. As with adults, only extremely obese adolescents with serious complications should be considered for such procedures.

Conclusion

Obesity in children and adolescents is a public health problem of great enormity. The health care problems and costs will be significant for years to come. On an individual level these children face many medical and psychosocial challenges. Multiple factors increase the risk or predispose the child to develop obesity and include many environmental factors in the setting of underlying genetic risk. The management of children and adolescents who have obesity is best accomplished by a coordinated effort of a team comprised of multiple disciplines and on a larger scale by development and implementation of appropriate public health policies.

References

Barlow S, Dietz W. Obesity evaluation and treatment: expert committee recommendations, The Maternal and Child Health Bureau, Health Resources and Services Administration and the Department of Health and Human Services. *Pediatrics* 1998;102:E29.

Berenson G, Srinivasan S, Bao W, Newman III W, Tracy R, Wattigney W. Association Between Multiple Cardiovascular Risk Factors and Atherosclerosis in Children and Young Adults. *N. Engl. J. Med.* 1998;338(23):1650-1656.

Boynton-Jarrett R, Thomas T, Peterson K, Wiecha J, Sobol A, Gortmaker S. Impact of Television Viewing Patterns on Fruit and Vegetable Consumption Among Adolescents. *Pediatrics* 2003;112:1321-1326.

Braet C, Tanghe A, Decaluwe V, Moens E, Rosseel Y. Inpatient Treatment for Children With Obesity: Weight Loss, Psychological Well-being, and Eating Behavior. *J. Pediatr. Psychol.* 2004;29(7):519-529.

Buddeberg-Fischer B, Klaghofer R, Reed V. Associations between Body Weight, Psychiatric Disorders, and Body Image in Female Adolescents. *Psychother. Psychosom.* 1999;68:325-332.

Dietz W, Gortmaker S. Do we fatten our children at the TV set? Obesity and television in children and adolescents. *Pediatrics* 1985;75:807-812.

Eisenberg ME, Neumark-Sztainer D, Story M. Associations of Weight-Based Teasing and Emotional Well-Being among Adolescents. *Arch. Pediatr. Adolesc. Med.* 2003;157:733-738.

Eliakim A, Kaven G, Berger I, Friedland O, Wolach B, Nemet D. The effect of a combined intervention on body mass index and fitness in obese children and adolescents - a clinical experience. *Eur. J. Pediatr*. 2002;161:449-454.

Erler T, Paditz E. Obstructive sleep apnea syndrome in children: a state-of-the-art review. *Treat Respir. Med.* 2004;3(2):107-122.

Homburg R, Lambalk C. Polycystic ovary syndrome in adolescents - a therapeutic conundrum. *Human Reproduction* 2004;19(5):1039-1042.

Inge T, Zeller M, Garcia V, Daniels S. Surgical approach to adolescent obesity. *Adolesc. Med. Clin*. 2004;15(3):429-453.

Jago R, Baranowski T. Non-curricular approaches for increasing physical activity in youth: a review. *Preventive Medicine* 2004;39(1):157-163.

Kennedy E, Bowman S, Powell R. Dietary fat intake in the US population. *J. Am. Coll. Nutr*. 1999;18:207-212.

Maffeis C, Pietrobelli A, Grezzani A, Provera S, Tato L. Waist Circumference and Cardiovascular Risk Factors in Prepubertal Children. *Obes. Res*. 2001;9(3):179-187.

McDuffie JR, Calis KA, Uwaifo GI, Sebring NG, Fallon EM, Hubbard VS, et al. Three-Month Tolerability of Orlistat in Adolescents with Obesity-Related Comorbid Conditions. *Obes. Res.* 2002;10(7):642-650.

National High Blood Pressure Education Program Working Group on High Blood Pressure in Children and Adolescents. The Fourth Report on the Diagnosis, Evaluation, and Treatment of High Blood Pressure in Children and Adolescents. *Pediatrics* 2004;114(2S):555-576.

Neumark-Sztainer D, Croll J, Story M, Hannan PJ, French SA, Perry C. Ethnic/racial differences in weight-related concerns and behaviors among adolescent girls and boys: Findings from Project EAT. *Journal of Psychosomatic Research* 2002;53(5):963-974.

Pesa JA, Syre TR, Jones E. Psychosocial differences associated with body weight among female adolescents: the importance of body image. *Journal of Adolescent Health* 2000;26(5):330-337.

Renman C, Engstrom I, Silfverdal S, Aman J. Mental health and psychosocial characteristics in adolescent obesity: a population-based case-control study. *Acta Paediatr*. 1999;88(9):998-1003.

Robinson TN. Reducing Children's Television Viewing to Prevent Obesity: A Randomized Controlled Trial. *JAMA* 1999;282(16):1561-1567.

Rocchini A, Katch V, Anderson J, Hinderliter J, Becque D, Martin M, et al. Blood pressure in obese adolescents: effect of weight loss. *Pediatrics* 1988;82:16-23.

Rocchini A. Childhood Obesity and a Diabetes Epidemic. *N. Engl. J. Med.* 2002;346(11):854-855.

Slyper A. The Pediatric Obesity Epidemic: Causes and Controversies. *J. Clin. Endocrinol.* Metab 2004;89:2540-2547.

Speiser PW, Rudolf MCJ, Anhalt H, Camacho-Hubner C, Chiarelli F, Eliakim A, et al. CONSENSUS DEVELOPMENT: CHILDHOOD OBESITY. *J. Clin. Endocrinol. Metab.* 2004:jc.2004-1389.

St. Jeor ST, Howard BV, Prewitt TE, Bovee V, Bazzarre T, Eckel RH. Dietary Protein and Weight Reduction: A Statement for Healthcare Professionals From the Nutrition

Committee of the Council on Nutrition, Physical Activity, and Metabolism of the American Heart Association. *Circulation* 2001;104(15):1869-1874.

Stradmeijer M, Bosch J, Koops W, Seidell J. Family Functioning and Psychosocial Adjustment in Overweight Youngsters. *Int. J. Eat Disord.* 2000;27(1):110-114.

Strauss R. Childhood Obesity. *Ped. Clin. North Am.* 2002;49(1):175-201.

Sugerman HJ, Sugerman EL, DeMaria EJ, Kellum JM, Kennedy C, Mowery Y, et al. Bariatric Surgery for Severely Obese Adolescents. *Journal of Gastrointestinal Surgery* 2003;7(1):102-

Troiano R, Briefel R, Carroll M, Bialostosky K. Energy and fat intakes of children and adolescents in the United States: data from the National Health and Nutrition Examination surveys. *Am. J. Clin. Nutr.* 2000;725(5 Suppl):1343S-1353S.

Tucker L. The relationship of television viewing to physical fitness and obesity. *Adolescence* 1986;21:797-806.

US Centers for Disease Control and Prevention. Waist circumference in centimeters for persons 2-19 years - number of examined persons, mean, standard error of the mean, and selected percentiles, by sex and age: United States, 1988-1994.

Zametkin AJMD, Zoon CKBS, Klein HWBS, Munson SBA. Psychiatric Aspects of Child and Adolescent Obesity: A Review of the Past 10 Years. *J. Am. Acad. Child Adolesc. Psychiatry* 2004;43(2):134-150.

In: Behavioral Pediatrics, 3rd Edition
Editor: D. E. Greydanus et al.

ISBN 978-1-60692-702-1
© 2009 Nova Science Publishers, Inc.

Chapter 25

Substance Use and Abuse in Adolescents

Donald E. Greydanus and William J. Reed

Abstract

Substance use and abuse remains a major public health issue of adolescents throughout the world, including the United States. Encouragement by the media, peers, and many adults along with easy access to drugs of all types continues to lure countless millions of youth into use and abuse of many drugs. In spite of a 19% decline in the use of illicit drugs between 2001-2005 based on a sample of 49,000 8th, 10th, and 12th graders, there is significant abuse of prescription medications including stimulants, synthetic narcotics, and "recreational" cough syrups. This chapter considers various drugs, including tobacco, alcohol, marijuana, cocaine, heroin, hallucinogens and inhalants (Table 1).

Introduction

It is important that clinicians caring for adolescents be directly involved in teaching their patients how to prevent the use and abuse of drugs; clinicians can also remain active in the management of substance abuse disorder, if it develops in their patient. Screening for substance abuse is critical because the neuro-psychiatric changes caused by some drugs (i.e. *Ecstasy*) may be irreversible and there have been reports of acute psychosis following marijuana and phencyclidine (PCP). One should also consider the likelihood of co-morbid conditions (Table 2) in any adolescent or young adult with a history of continuing or repeated substance abuse; these conditions include ADHD, especially when associated with or secondary to a learning disorder where treatment is protective. Risk factors for drug abuse are reviewed in Table 3, while Table 4 considers non-specific indicators of drug abuse and Table 5 outlines protective factors for drug abuse. Screening tests may be helpful, such as the

CRAFFT questions for alcohol use. Straightforward talk with teens about drug use is important in the screening process, though the teenager's estimates are often lower than the actual use. The clinician can work with the community in supporting community-based drug abuse prevention programs.

Table 1. Drugs of Abuse

- Tobacco
- Marijuana
- Alcohol
- Cocaine
- Heroin
- Amphetamine
- Methamphetamine
- MDMA [*Ecstasy*]
- flunitrazepam [Rohypnol]
- Gamma-hydroxybutyrate [*GHB*]
- Ketamine [Ketalar]
- LSD {*lysergic acid diethylamide*}
- *PCP {phencyclidine}*
- *Tryptamines*
- Barbiturates
- *Sports Doping and Performance Enhancing Drugs*

Table 2. Co-Morbid Disorders of Substance Abuse Disorder

- ADHD
- Oppositional Defiant Disorder
- Conduct Disorder
- Mood Disorders
- Anxiety Disorders
- Evolving Psychosis
- Post-traumatic Stress Disorder

Table 3. Risk Factors for Substance Abuse in Adolescents*

Genetics	Alcoholism among 1st or 2nd degree relatives
	Male gender
Self/Individual/Personal	Abuse
	Early onset of drug use
	Early sexual activity
	Attention deficit disorders
	Antisocial behavior
	Aggressive temperament
	Depression
	Poor self image
	Learning disorders
	Parental rejection
	Lack of self control
	Low self-esteem
	Euphoric/mood altering effects of drugs
	Body modification(as cutting)
Family	Dysfunctional family dynamics
	Permissiveness
	Authoritarianism
	Parental conflict, divorce, separation
	Poor supervision, lack of supervision
	Poor parental role modeling
Community/Environmental/ Societal	Easy availability of drugs and alcohol
	Acceptance of drug use behavior
	Poor general quality of life in the neighborhood
	Media influence
	Criminal activities in neighborhood
	Cultural and religious sanction
	Low religiosity
	Employment
	Increased use of drugs and alcohol in certain ethnic groups
Peer Group Influence	Drug using peers
	Rebellion
	Rites of passage of puberty
	Risk-taking behavior
	Curiosity
	Desire to belong
	Independence
	Early tobacco use
School/Academic	Poor school performance
	Poor school environment
	Truancy

*Modified with permission: Patel DR and Greydanus DE: Substance abuse: a pediatric concern. *Indian J. Pediatrics* 66:557-567, 1999.

Table 4. Non-Specific Indicators of Substance Abuse*

Physical indicators	Academic indicators	Behavioral and psychological indicators
Unexplained weight loss	Deterioration of short-term	Risk taking behavior
Hypertension	memory	Mood swings
Red eyes	Poor judgement	Depression, withdrawal
Nasal irritation	Falling grades	Panic reaction
Frequent "colds" or	Frequent absence	Acute psychosis
"allergies"	Truancy	Paranoia
Hoarseness	Conflicts with teachers	Lying
Chronic cough	Suspension	Stealing
Hemoptysis	Expulsion	Promiscuity
Chest pain		Conflict with authorities and family
Wheezing		members
Frequent unexplained		Runaway behavior
injuries		Altered sleep pattern
Needle tracks		Altered appetite
Blank stares into space		Poor hygiene
Scratch marks		Loss of interest in extracurricular
Tattoos		activities
Excessive acne		Drug using peers
Testicular atrophy		Preferences for dress, music, movies,
Malaise		identifying with drug using culture
		Drug paraphernalia

*Used with permission: Patel DR and Greydanus DE: Substance abuse: a pediatric concern. Indian J Pediatrics 66:557-567, 1999.

Table 5. Factors Protective of Substance Abuse in Adolescents*

- Nurturing home environment
- Good communication within family
- Supportive parents, intact family, appropriate adult supervision
- Positive self-esteem
- Assertiveness
- Social competence
- Academic success
- Good schools
- Good general health
- High intelligence
- Positive adult role models
- Peer group with positive personal attributes
- Religious involvement
- A personal sense of morality

*Used with permission: Patel DR and Greydanus DE: Substance abuse: a pediatric concern. Indian J Pediatrics 66: 557-567, 1999.

Adolescents generally progress from initial drug use to more serious drug use behavior in a pattern that is recognizable (Table 6). At first, there is curiosity about drugs, though no drug use may be occurring; a need for acceptance by some peer group along with a low self esteem may lead to experimentation with some drugs—often the "gateway" drugs--- tobacco, alcohol and/or marijuana.

Table 6. MacDonald's Stages of Substance Abuse*

Stage	1. Learning the mood swing	2. Seeking the mood swing	3. Preoccupation with the mood swing	4. Using drugs to feel normal
Mood Alteration	Euphoria Normal	Euphoria Normal Some pain	Euphoria Normal Definite pain	Euphoria Normal Marked pain
Feelings	Feels good; few consequences	Excitement; early guilt	Euphoric highs; doubts, including severe shame and guilt; depression, suicidal thoughts	Chronic guilt; shame, remorse, depression
Drugs	Tobacco Marijuana Alcohol	All of the above plus inhalants, hashish, depressants, methamphetamine, prescription drugs	All listed plus psilocybin, PCP, LSD, cocaine	Whatever is available
Sources	Peers	Buying	Selling	Any way possible
Behavior	Little detectable change; moderate after-the-fact lying	Dropping extracurricular activities and hobbies; mixed friends (straight and drug users); dress changing; erratic school performance and truancy; unpredictable mood and attitude swings; manipulative behavior	"Cool" appearance; straight friends dropped; family fights (verbal or physical); stealing (police incidents); pathological lying; school failure; truancy, expulsion, jobs lost	Physical deterioration (weight loss, chronic cough); severe mental deterioration (memory loss and flashbacks); paranoia, volcanic anger; school dropout; frequent overdosing
Frequency	Progress to weekend use	Weekend use progressing to four to five times per week; some solo use	Daily; frequent solo use	All day every day

PCP = phencyclidine; LSD = lysersic acid diethylamide.
*Used with permission: Patel DR and Greydanus DE: Substance abuse: a pediatric concern. Indian J Pediatrics 66:557-567, 1999.

At some point the euphoria some drugs deliver is felt by the adolescent, typically at weekend parties. In some youth, there develops a state of actively seeking out the euphoria of drug use with widening of the types of drugs used (ie, cocaine, Ecstasy, heroin, others), using personal drug paraphernalia, buying and/or stealing drugs on a regular basis, and becoming more dependent on one or more drugs. There is often a drop in grades, change of clothes, switching of peer group, and a strong denial of using/abusing any drugs. Seeking the euphoric state becomes the center piece of the individual's life and life becomes out of control and the menu of drugs tried increases in scope. There may also be evidence of depression, worsening mood swings, acting out behaviors, suicide, violence, malaise, and lethargy. At this stage, the abuser seeks the euphoric state to feel "normal." This progression from experimenting with drugs to abuse and burnout can be seen over months to years.

Tobacco

Tobacco remains a widely used and abused drug that enjoys a high level of acceptance by society, including governments that allow it to be grown for profit. In a 1999 national survey conducted by the Centers for Disease Control, one in every eight middle-school students reported using some form of tobacco (*cigarettes*, *cigars*, *bidis*, or *kreteks*) in the past month. Bidis (or beedies) are brown, hand-rolled, flavored tobacco while Kreteks (clove cigarettes) contain a mixture of tobacco and cloves; both are imported from Indonesia.

High school seniors report a 58% lifetime prevalence for smoking cigarettes that includes a 37% use over the past survey month, and 22% on a daily basis. While these numbers are down from 1993, tobacco remains the drug most frequently used by young people on a daily basis. While 57% of teen smokers state they have tried to quit tobacco, approximately 3000 teens start smoking tobacco every day in the United States; nine out of ten adults who smoke started this addiction during the teen years. Tobacco use remains common among college students as well. Nearly one in ten experiment with smokeless tobacco, and cigar smoking is gaining popularity among adolescents. The overall rate of cigar use during the previous 30 days was 17.7% among high school students; current use among males was 25.4%, while females reported 9.9%. Another survey prepared by the U.S. Surgeon's Office, found that 8.8% of African-American middle-school students smoked cigars, versus 4.9% of their Caucasian peers. In the past, cigar smoking was low in the African-American community; however, it has recently increased, possibly due to influence of star athletes who advocate this addiction to indicate success in one's life.

The smoke of cigars is more alkaline than that of cigarettes, dissolves more easily in saliva, and achieves the desired dose of nicotine without the need to inhale smoke into the lungs. Cigars are capable of providing high levels of nicotine at a rate fast enough to produce clear dependence, even if the smoke is not inhaled. The risk of lung cancer for cigar affecionados (well-known to cigarette smokers), is much higher than once thought. This rate increases more for cigar smokers if they were previous cigarette smokers. A class of carcinogenic compounds known as tobacco-specific, N-nitrosamines (TSNA) is present in cigar smoke at significantly higher levels than in cigarette smoke. Examination on a "per gram of tobacco smoke" basis reveals that tar, carbon monoxide, and ammonia are produced at greater quantities by cigars. When equal doses are applied, the tar produced by cigars exerts a greater tumor-producing activity in mice because of higher concentrations of carcinogenic polycyclic aromatic hydrocarbons.

Nicotine, an important component in tobacco, is highly addictive. Current research shows that adolescents experience symptoms of nicotine dependence long before they become everyday smokers. Early and continued intervention, including the clinical use of such instruments as the HONC (Hooked On Nicotine Checklist), is required because initiation of smoking during adolescence is related to drunkenness-oriented alcohol use and an increased risk for future substance abuse. The most powerful predictor of drunk driving in this research is regular smoking at age 14.

Nicotine is absorbed over various sites: lungs, buccal mucosa, skin, and gastrointestinal tract. Approximately 10 mg of nicotine is found in one cigarette; when smoked, 1.0 to 3.0 mg of nicotine is absorbed by the user. Nicotine is rapidly taken up by the brain's nicotinic acetylcholine receptors that are found in numerous non-cholinergic presynaptic and postsynaptic areas. The tobacco addict has chronic exposure to many dangerous chemicals, including nicotine, tar, carbon monoxide, arsenous oxide, radioactive polonium, benzopyrene, others. The addicted cigarette abuser becomes an adult with significant risks for the many well-known complications of this drug—lung cancer, emphysema, laryngeal carcinoma, other cancers, heart disease, and many other disorders. Lung cancer in female adult smokers is now more common than breast cancer.

A common condition noted in smokers and reverse smokers is keratosis of the mucosal palate posterior to the rugae. This was originally described in 1926 and is caused by the concentrated hot steam of smoke and chemicals producing a nicotine or "smoker's patch". Reverse smoking has been associated with dysplastic and malignant changes over time. Recent research also notes negative effects which occur from smoking during pregnancy, including lower birth weight and attention deficit hyperactivity disorder. Nicotine staining of the teeth, crows feet from the occlusion of micro-arterioles near the eyes, bad breath, cough, and dyspnea are also well-recognized and widespread stigmata of smoking. Passive smoking is also known to be dangerous to those exposed to the smoking of others. Oral cancer is a serious consequence of using chewing tobacco.

It is important for clinicians caring for adolescents to join the struggle to limit the use of tobacco by adolescents. For example, advertising to youth must be prevented, and efforts to reduce the acceptance of tobacco by society strengthened. The prevention and reduction of adolescent tobacco use and abuse must be encouraged on a national and statewide level. On a local level, a broad range program is recommended that targets the family, community, and schools.

Pharmacologic Management

Nicotine Therapies (NTs)

Table 7 reviews current pharmacologic management options for tobacco addicts who are motivated to quit using tobacco products. Clinicians should take every opportunity to remind tobacco-addicted teens that their habit is very dangerous and help is available when they are ready to stop. Psychosocial issues in the lives of teen smokers and underlying cues to smoking should be reviewed with the adolescent. Special situations may arise, such as the pregnant adolescent who also smokes. A variety of nicotine replacement (NT) products are produced, as reviewed in Table 7 and 8; the rate of quitting smoking is doubled by use of these products for the motivated smoker (i.e., 30%), in contrast to those seeking to stop smoking without pharmacologic agents (i.e., 15%). The choice of NT product is patient-driven; teens should not smoke while on NT products, though no overt negative sequelae have been reported in such cases.

Table 7. Pharmacologic Products Available in the USA to Treat Tobacco Addiction*

Nicotine Medications	
Nicotine gum	– Nicorette OTC
	– Nicorette DS OTC
Nicotine patch	– Nicoderm CQ(SmithKline Beecham) OTC
	– Nicotrol Patch (McNeil) OTC
Nicotine inhaler	– Habitrol (Novartis)
Nasal spray	– Prostep (Lederle)
	– Nicotrol Inhaler (McNeil)
	– Nicotrol Nasal Spray (McNeil)
Non-Nicotine Medications	Zyban SR (Glaxo Wellcome)
Bupropion	sustained-release tablets

*Reprinted with permission from: Patel DR and Greydanus DE: Office interventions for adolescent smokers. State of the Art Reviews: Adolescent Medicine 11 (3): 1-11, 2000.

Table 8. Nicotine Patch Regimens*

Brand	Duration	Dosage
Nicoderm CQ and	4 weeks	21 mg/24 hours
Habitrol	then 2 weeks	14 mg/24 hours
	then 2 weeks	7 mg/24 hours
Prostep	4 weeks	22 mg/24 hours
	then 4 weeks	11 mg/24 hours
Nicotrol	8 weeks	15 mg/24 hours

*Reprinted with Permission from: Patel DR and Greydanus DE: Office interventions for adolescents smokers. State of the Art Reviews: Adolescent Medicine 11 (3): 1-11, 2000.

The *NT patch* is prescribed for 2 months (changed each morning), using a high strength patch for one month, and then the lower dose for one more month (Table 8). The patch is not placed over a site with hair. Up to half will develop local dermatitis, usually improved with local hydrocortisone application. The patch is applied only while awake if patch-induced secondary vivid dreams or insomnia develop. The NT gum (nicotine polacrilex) has a bitter taste that many teens do not like; some youth feel embarrassed while choosing the nicotine gum. If the tobacco addict smokes over 25 cigarettes a day, prescribe the 4 mg gum; eventually lower the patient to the 2 mg gum. Since acidic liquids reduce nicotine absorption, they should not be used for 15 minutes before gum use and while chewing. Instructions to give patients who chew this gum are provided in Table 9. Adverse effects of this gum, though temporary, include dyspepsia, mouth soreness, jaw ache and hiccups.

Table 9. Recommendations for Use of Nicotine Gum

Chew a piece each hour for 6 weeks.

Then, chew a piece every 2 hours for 3 weeks.

Finally, chew a piece every 4 hours for 3 weeks.

Maximum limit is 30 pieces per day for the 2 mg gum and 20 pieces per day for the 4 mg gum.

Chewing instructions:

- Chew slowly until a peppery taste appears (often after 15 chews)
- Then put the gum between the cheek and buccal mucosa until the peppery taste has disappeared (often one minute)
- Start chewing again and repeat the above cycle
- Get rid of the gum when the peppery taste is gone (often 30 minutes).

The nicotine inhaler is designed to mimic the hand-to-mouth movement of the smoker; 4 mg of nicotine are delivered from the cartridge which contains about 10 mg overall (Table 7). Low nicotine levels are produced and the user inhales 6-16 cartridges daily. Adequate nicotine absorption is accomplished with 80 inhalations over 20 minutes; absorption is through the oral mucosa. It is prescribed for 3 months and then slowly tapered off over 3 months. Adverse effects that often improve over time include coughing, dyspepsia, irritation of the mouth and throat, and nasal irritation.

The nicotine nasal spray is provided as one to two doses (1 to 2 mg of nicotine) per hour over 3 months; there is a rapid rise in nicotine serum levels (Table 7). It is prescribed as a minimum of 8 doses per day, not over 40 per day or over 5 inhalations per hour. Bronchospasm may occur and the nasal spray is not used for nicotine addicts with asthma. Other adverse effects include cough, rhinitis, nasal irritation, sneezing, and water eyes.

Non-Nicotine Therapy

The use of bupropion (Table 7) in the nicotine addict who is motivated to quit smoking is helpful in up to 40%; its relative success is attributed to the drug's ability to lower the classic nicotine craving while improving the nicotine-withdrawal problems of weight gain and depression. It was found to be twice as effective as placebo. It is prescribed as Zyban in a sustained-release form that is provided as 150 mg a day for three days; if tolerated, it is increased to 150 mg twice daily. The dose should not be over 300 mg a day and it should not be given less than 8 hours apart, to reduce the incidence of a seizure. Though NT replacement therapies should not officially be started while the adolescent is still smoking, it is acceptable to start the teen smoker on bupropion while still using nicotine; a date of stopping the tobacco should still be negotiated while providing the bupropion. Bupropion is contraindicated in youth who have overt seizures and those with factors that increase the risk for seizures; the latter includes those with a history of epilepsy, an eating disorder, central nervous system tumor, and any medications that may lower the seizure threshold. Bupropion is contraindicated in those on MAO inhibitors. Bupropion adverse effects include insomnia, skin reactions, tremors, headaches and dry mouth.

Clonidine and nortriptyline may be useful to some adult smokers to help them quit. Various medications have been studied but not shown to help improve the craving for nicotine; these include buspirone, mecamylamine, naltrexone, doxepin, and oral dextrose. The latest product on the market for smoking cessation is varenicline tartrate (Chantrix®, Pfizer), an alpha-4 beta-2- nicotinic acetylcholine receptor partial agonist that binds to central nervous system receptors with a greater affinity than nicotine. It is FDA approved for adults with nicotine addiction and may be more effective than bupropion. Abstinence rates were 22% verses 16% for bupropion and 8% for placebo. In the short term, 44% of study patients quit smoking v. 30% using Zyban. Starting dose is 0.5 mg per day for three days, twice a day for 4-7 days, then 1 mg twice daily. Chantrix® decreases the pleasure of nicotine use and lessens the withdrawal craving. The major side effect is nausea, but weight gain is not a problem. There are reports of suicidality, agitation, hostility, and agitation (Varenicline, 2008; Greydanus, 2008). A novel nicotine antibody being developed in Switzerland by Cytos/Novartis is in phase II trials and seems promising following even a single dose.

Marijuana

Marijuana remains a popular euphoric and hallucinogenic drug for millions of youth and adults; it has many names, including "pot", "hash", "weed",. "doobs", "BC Bud", "Ganja", "grass", "smoke", and others. It is the most widely used illicit drug in the United States, accounting for up to 85% of the illicit drug trade. In 2003, 46.1% of high school seniors in the United States had a lifetime use of this drug; this included 34.9% over the past year of the survey and 21.2% over the past survey month. Lifetime use in the 2007 CDC YRBS ranged from 35.5 to 40.7%. Marijuana has been prohibited in the U.S. since the Marijuana Tax Act of 1937. United Nations estimates that 12.2% "use" it more than 300 days a year. The White House Office of National Drug Control Policy estimates that there are 141 million regular users of "pot" in the U.S. This controversial drug is derived from Cannabis sativa (hemp plant) and the active euphoric chemical is delta-9-tetrahydrocannabinol or THC. It is present in the dried leaves, stems, seeds, flowers (sensimilla) and oil. This major lipophilic drug works on the cannibinoid receptors (ECS) in the mesocortical and limbic systems. The marijuana of the 1960s and 1970s' hippie generation contained only 2% THC, while the Hawaiian sensimilla product was about 3% THC. Today's street pot can vary from 3 to 7% THC content, while cultivated sensimilla can contain 7 to 9%. The Potency Monitoring Project which evaluates seized samples of marijuana since 1976, recently recorded the highest THC ever at 8.5%. A popular brand of pot is BC Bud, a product imported by the ton from Canada at $3000- 10,000 dollars per pound; it is grown in British Columbia and may contain up to 15% THC content. Many growers, commercial exporter consortiums (Canada), a significant fraction of the public and their elected officials, as well as active pot users are actively advocating for the legalization of marijuana.

Though usually smoked, marijuana can also be eaten in such homemade concoctions as cookies, brownies, and spaghetti. Dronabinol (C III) is a synthesized gelatin capsule previously used experimentally for the treatment of chemotherapy-induced vomiting and also to decrease intraocular pressure in some patients with glaucoma. The marijuana cigarette (joint) usually contains approximately 20 mg of THC obtained from about a gram of leaves and buds; however, much variation can be noted. The "blunt" is another popular way to smoke pot and consists of a cigarette with marijuana added to a hollowed cigarette. "Pot" is often combined with other drugs, such as phencyclidine, though glutethimide and methaqualone were also popular in the past as additives. PCP (phencyclidine) is frequently dissolved in an organic solvent, such as formaldehyde, in which a joint or hand-rolled cigarette is first dipped, dried, and then smoked. This preparation is variously referred to as "wet"" "water", or "Sherms"; the latter term refers to the well-known tobacconist Nat Sherman.

Marijuana use results in potent sensations of euphoria that is noted within minutes of its use, and which can last for hours. The user develops psychological addiction and a withdrawal syndrome often compared to that seen with heroin addicts. Heavy marijuana use can also result in psychological dependency and tolerance. A flu-like reaction can be seen 24 to 60 hours after stopping this drug, and lasting up to 2 weeks. A persistent insomnia may develop as well, somewhat similar to that noted when discontinuing benzodiazepines; trazodone may be beneficial in this situation. Frequent users of marijuana may develop reduced processing speed, reduced reflexes, impaired memory spans, altered perceptions of time, confusion, and impairment of cognition. This can lead to serious problems in being successful in important environments of the adolescent, such as school, work, and others. Daily tasks become difficult for many, and driving becomes very dangerous, especially if high while driving.

The *amotivational* syndrome has been classically described in some chronic pot users who become very lethargic, losing interest in social obligations, work, and school. A variety of psychological reactions may be seen in pot users, including fear, violent behavior, anxiety, depression, and overt hallucinations. In the teenager with a previously diagnosed or undiagnosed behavioral or psychiatric disorder (ie, ADHD, dysthymia, evolving bipolar disorder), the use of marijuana may trigger clinical depression, mood shift or an atypical psychosis. It is implicated in panic episodes and obstructive sleep apnea. Medical sequelae include chronic cough, bronchitis, and bronchospasm. Some drugs (as alcohol or diazepam) potentiate the sedative effects of marijuana, while other drugs (as cocaine or amphetamines) worsen the stimulatory effects of marijuana.

Research has implicated marijuana with the development of amenorrhea, immunologic dysfunction, reduction in sperm, and interference with DNA functioning. Marijuana remains for up to one month after even a single episode of use. The combination of pot and alcohol leads to thousands of motor-vehicle accidents and deaths each year. Pot shares the risks of second hand-tobacco smoke with the developing fetus and growing child. It has negative effects on the fetus if the pregnant mother uses it. Though marijuana is noted by research to be a generally benign drug compared to many others, its classic euphoric effects have led to its widespread acceptance by many elements of society ignorant of its potential dangers. It is important for clinicians caring for adolescents to dispel the many positive myths of marijuana.

Alcohol

Alcohol continues to be among the most used and abused illicit drugs (29% youth choice # 1) that enjoys a wide range of societal acceptance (Figure 2). Alcohol is the leading cause of substance use morbidity and mortality contributing to 8,000 deaths each year. High school seniors have a lifetime prevalence of over 80%, with over 50% noting alcohol use during the previous survey month, and 4% admitting to daily use. Drinking in American society begins early, with over 14% of 8th graders admitting to having 5 or more drinks in a row once or twice a weekend; this alarming figure increases to over 24% in the 10th grade and 32% in the 12th grade. The average age that alcohol is first misused is age 12. Males abuse alcohol more often than females, and African American youth have lower rates of use than do Hispanic or Caucasian youth. Approximately 13% of adolescents report driving a vehicle after drinking alcohol, while 31% have ridden in a car whose driver had been drinking. About half of adolescents who are victims of a motor vehicle accident or suicide were drinking before their death. The most common pattern of alcoholic consumption is binge drinking, as defined by 5 drinks in a row in males, and four in females. Blacking out spells are frequently a result of binge drinking behavior. Binge drinking is directly related to drunk driving, increased sexual activity, smoking, dating violence, attempted suicide and other substance abuse. It is important to ask youth if they drink and if so, what their drinking pattern is; repeated use of alcohol or other substances is not part of normal adolescent defiant behavior. The CRAFFT screening test for adolescent substance abuse is an easy to use instrument for screening drug use.

Alcohol is a central nervous system depressant that also induces euphoria in the user; tolerance and psychological dependence may develop, in addition to physiologic dependence in alcoholics. Alcohol drinks vary in their amount of this drug, ranging from 3% to 6% in beer, 12% in wine, and 50% in various liquors. Legal intoxication is usually 0.08 to 0.10 g/dl, though judgment may be impaired at a blood alcohol concentration (BAC) of 0.01 g/dl or lower. Central effects occur at 20-30 ng/dl. Acute intoxication may lead to respiratory depression, coma, and death. Adolescents should be carefully educated about the dangers of alcohol consumption, including the deadly mixture of driving and drinking that kills "innocent" as well as alcohol-consuming victims.

Alcoholism is a serious disease in adults, and youth may be involved in this disorder as well. The abuse of alcohol depletes a number of so-called "comfort" hormones (opioid peptides, serotonin, gamma aminobutryic acid, dopamine) in addition to inducing stress hormone release (ie, corticotropin releasing factor). Many adolescents do not stop at the social drinking or experimental stage and quick progression can develop through the later stages of drug abuse. Youth who abuse alcohol tend to come from families where problem drinking occurs and where there is no drinking.

Medical complications of problem drinking include intoxication, pancreatitis, gastritis, worsening of co-morbid medical disorders (ie, diabetes mellitus, epilepsy), and toxic psychosis. The alcohol withdrawal syndrome presents with such symptoms as tremors, seizures, hallucinations and even overt delirium tremens. Youth who abuse alcohol may develop anemia, macrocytosis, and elevation in alkaline phosphatase, bilirubin, uric acid, glutamic-oxaloacetic, gamma glutamyl transpeptidase, or pyruvic transaminases. The diagnosis of alcohol abuse disorder is made mainly on a history of excessive alcohol use, and not on the basis of a positive serum or drug screening test. The fetal alcohol syndrome and the effect of alcohol on neuronal migration and pruning (apoptosis) in the unborn fetus exposed to intrauterine alcohol are well recognized consequences of alcohol comsumption during pregnancy. The mortality risk to the fetus is 5%, while the accidental risk of harm to family members of alcohol users is increased considerably.

Management of Alcohol Abuse

Acute alcohol ingestion is treated with gastric emptying, intravenous fluids, glucose, respiratory support, and sometimes, dialysis. The possibility of additional drug use is suggested by respiratory depression greater than that suggested by the available BAC; head injury may also have occurred in this situation. Medications used in the management of alcohol withdrawal syndrome include clorazepate, lorazepam, chlordiazepoxide, diazepam and various antipsychotics. Medications approved for the management of adults with alcohol dependence include acamprosate, calcium carbimide, naltrexone, tiapride, and disulfiram. Various medications have been used, but have not been approved for use in adults with alcohol dependence; these include buspirone, carbamazepine, nalmefene, selective serotonin reuptake inhibitors and tricyclic antidepressants (Greydanus, 2008). *Mothers Against Drunk Drivers (MADD)* and self-help groups (*Alcohol Anonymous [AA]* and *Alateen*) are important programs found in many communities that help with the wide-spread program of alcohol use and abuse in adolescents and adults.

Amphetamines

Amphetamine (*chalk, meth, speed*) is a classic central nervous system stimulant which leads to a variety of complications, as listed in Table 10. Amphetamines can be taken to develop euphoria, lessen fatigue, improve attention, lose weight, and/or allow continued sports performance. In 2003, high school seniors reported a lifetime use of 14.4%, 9.9% over the past year, and 5.0% over the past 30 days of the survey. Amphetamine can be abused in various forms—oral, subcutaneous, or intravenous.

An infected needle may lead to HIV/AIDS, endocarditis, hepatitis, and other infections. An abstinence or withdrawal syndrome is described in amphetamine abusers, with the development of severe apathy, depression, and hypersomnia. Amphetamine abusers develop tolerance and an overdose can lead to hyperthermia, hypertension, cardiac arrhythmias, seizures, and death. Table 11 outlines basic medical support for an amphetamine overdose; avoid the use of phenothiazines, since rapid decrease in blood pressure and increased seizures activity may result.

Table 10. Amphetamine Adverse Reactions

- Anorexia
- Anxiety
- Exhaustion
- Hyperactivity
- Hyperhidrosis
- Hypertension
- Insomnia
- Mydriasis
- Personality changes
- Psychotic experiences
- Tachycardia
- Tolerance
- Weight loss
- Withdrawal syndrome

Table 11. Management of Amphetamine Overdose

Cooling blanket for hyperthermia
Medical control of hypertension and arrhythmias
Haloperidol or droperidol for agitation or delusions
Lorazepam (Ativan®) or diazepam (Valium®) for agitation

Clinicians using stimulant medications to manage adolescents with attention deficit hyperactivity disorder (ADHD) should appreciate the potential for abuse of short acting Adderall® and Ritalin® (methylphenidate). In a survey of 545 patients with ADHD (ages12-25), 18.2% reported abusing their prescription. Almost 80% abused short acting preparations, 17% long acting, and 2% both; also, 130/499 abused cocaine or methamphetamine. Ritalin is also called "the smart drug" and "vitamin R" by abusers, who crush the methylphenidate tablets and snort this chemical to obtain an intense euphoria; large doses can lead to seizure activity, stroke, and psychosis. Published guidelines should be followed carefully when providing stimulant medications to adolescents. This should include the use of the long-acting preparations, such as Concerta®, which have formulations that reduce the risk for dispersion and the quick "buzz". A recent stimulant addition with diminished abuse potential is lisdexamfetamine (Vyvanse®) a prodrug formulation The long-acting preparations used for the treatment of ADHD do not produce tachyphylaxis, nor do they lead to addiction.

Methamphetamine

This illicit drug (*meth, ice, crystal, fire, glass, chalk, crank*) is an N-methyl homolog of amphetamine and has become the stimulant favored by most adolescents, due to its potent stimulant effect on the central nervous system. It is a highly addictive drug prepared by illicit drug laboratories using relatively inexpensive chemicals and sold on the streets and using drug networks. The term "ice" or "crystal" comes from its production as clear, chunky *crystals* that look like *ice;* it can also be bought as an odorless, bitter-tasting, white powder that easily dissolves in liquids. In the 2000 Monitoring the Future Study, 2.5% of 8th graders tried *meth* versus 4.0% of 10th graders and 4.3% if 12th graders; the lifetime use in the 2007 YRBS ranged from 3.7 to 5.3%. Methamphetamine is now responsible for one-quarter of illicit stimulant use.

This drug can be taken as a pill or its powder can be snorted, leading to a "high" or euphoria; when inhaled via smoking or taken intravenously, methamphetamine hydrochloride induces an immediate, potent euphoria that is described as a "flash" or "rush" lasting a few minutes. It is this intense feeling that abusers seek leading to rapid addiction with increased dosage and frequency of use. This is not the case with the long acting amphetamine salts medication (Adderall [XR]) that is used to manage patients with ADHD.

Users of this drug note that there is increased wakefulness, less need for sleep, and increased physical activity; anorexia, sometimes extreme, may develop along with weight loss. The temperature, respirations, pulse, and blood pressure are increased; there may be excited speech. Methamphetamine releases much dopamine and thus can affect body movements and mood in these addicts. Central nervous system cells that contain dopamine and serotonin are damaged, eventually leading to low levels of dopamine, thinking dysfunction, and a depressed mood (called "blue Tuesdays"). A Parkinsonian-like movement disorder can also be seen.

Methamphetamine releases high levels of dopamine that affects mood and body movements. Central nervous system cells containing dopamine and serotonin are damaged; eventually dopamine levels are reduced with the development of slowed thinking and a depressed mood ("Blue Tuesdays").

Table 12. Adverse Effects of Methamphetamine

- Irritability
- Anxiety
- Confusion
- Memory loss
- Insomnia
- Tremors
- Convulsions
- Hypertension
- Cardiac damage
- Paranoia and psychotic behavior
- Increased aggressiveness with violent behavior
- Cardiovascular collapse and death

A motor impairment or Parkinsonian-like movement disorder can develop. Adverse reactions are many and some are listed in Table 12. As with other illicit drugs that are taken intravenously, this drug can lead to various infectious diseases, including sexually transmitted diseases, such as hepatitis B and HIV/AIDS. Management of this severe drug addiction is difficult and current research is seeking a medication to block the euphoric effects of methamphetamine to allow the addict to get off the drug, if there is motivation. This antibody-type medication research is part of other addiction research studies seeking to neutralize the euphoric effects of drugs, such as cocaine, heroin, and others.

Cocaine

This central nervous system stimulant is an alkaloid made from leaves of the South American plant, *Erythroxylon coca*. There are a number of ways to take this drug: intranasal, intravenous, inhalation, smoking, chewed (coca leaves), or swallowed. Previously, this drug was produced as a crystalline powder that is water soluble and developed from an alkaloidal paste of the plant's leaves. "Free base" and "crack" ("rock") are popular cocaine products used for smoking. Free-base cocaine is vaporized in a water piper (bong) or even a soda can with a hole in it. Crack is named on the street for cocaine bicarbonate pellets that are pea-sized and produced with ammonia or sodium bicarbonate (baking soda); heating this concoction to remove its hydrochloride component produces a "crackling" sound. Crack may be crushed, tobacco added, and then this "cigarette" is smoked; other chemicals often added include mannitol, quinine, or marijuana. Over half of the cocaine used on the streets is now crack cocaine.

Crack cocaine has become relatively inexpensive and very popular with adolescents. The 1999 Youth Risk Behavior Survey (YRBS) of the Center for Disease Control reported that 9.5% of high school seniors had tried cocaine (freebase, powder, or crack) at least once; 4.0% had tried cocaine at least once over the previous 30 days of the survey. The 2003 Monitor the Future survey reported that high school seniors had a lifetime use of 7.7% (versus 7.1% in 1997) that included 4.8% over the past survey year and 2.1% over the past survey month. The range of lifetime cocaine use in the 2007 YRBS was 6.2 to 8.2% Approximately 25% of Americans report they have experience with cocaine before turning 30. This drug interferes with neuronal catecholamine reuptake and dopamine reabsorption. The popularity of cocaine is based on its ready availability and the potent euphoric feeling it produces; this high lasts 5 to 10 minutes if cocaine is smoked, in contrast to 10 to 30 minutes if taken intravenously. Once the euphoria is gone, irritability and fatigue set in. Addicts of this powerfully addicting drug develop severe psychological and physiological addiction along with tolerance. A partial list of the side effects of cocaine is listed in Table 13. Increased pregnancy complications are listed in Table 13.

Table 13. Adverse Effects of Cocaine

- Anxiety
- Irritability and restlessness
- Confusion
- Peripheral blood vessel constriction
- Pupillary dilation
- Hyperpyexia, tachycardia, and hypertension
- Cardiac complications
- Angina pectoris
- Myocardial infarction
- Ventricular arrhythmia
- Sudden death
- Seizures
- Nasal septum infection and perforation
- Fontal lobe infarction
- Intravenous needle complications (including hepatitis B, HIV/AIDS, endocarditis)
- Increased premature delivery
- Abruption (bleeding between placenta and uterine wall)
- Adverse neurodevelopmental sequelae in infant
- Vascular spasm-induced limb reduction anomalies and strokes

As with other drugs, addicts look to mix various drugs together to intensify the pleasant or euphoric feeling of their drug of choice. When alcohol is mixed with cocaine, *cocaethylene* is produced in the liver; this chemical heightens the cocaine euphoria (ie, more potent and lasts longer), blunts some of the stimulant adverse cocaine effects, and increases the sudden death risk. The term, *speedballing*, refers to the mixture of cocaine and heroin or morphine and this combination also increases the sudden death risk.

The method of using cocaine leads to various complications, as nasal perforation/infection with snorting and the infectious sequelae from intravenous use. The high abuse rate of cocaine is associated with increased risk of sexually transmitted diseases among adolescents and young adults; this includes HIV/AIDS, lymphogranuloma venereum, and chancroid. Smoking crack may lead to the development of a very aggressive paranoia. Sudden death occurs and is a constant risk, whether it is the first time or the user is very experienced with this drug; such death is probably due to a terminal ventricular arrhythmia.

Management of Cocaine Addiction

Cocaine addiction is a difficult central nervous system disorder to manage. If tachycardia and hypertension develop while on cocaine, short acting beta-blockers and short-acting direct vasodilators (as esmolol) may be helpful; clinicians should avoid long-acting vasodilators, since cocaine intoxication is typically a short, self-limited phenomenon and use of these other drugs (as morphine, propranolol, thorazine) may lead to severe hypotension. Though naloxone is helpful for opioid addiction, it does not help with cocaine addiction.

Cocaine addicts with ADHD may observe that methylphenidate calms them down along with improving their concentration abilities; a reduction in cocaine use has been observed in some cocaine addicts who have ADHD and use methylphenidate.

Current addiction research seeks to find a way to stop the potent euphoric effects of cocaine and enable the motivated abuser to stop this drug. Dependence on cocaine involves various pathways (ie, noradrenergic and dopaminergic) in the primitive midbrain reward center. Multiple CNS sites are involved with the addiction and thus any drug used to help the addict must work over many areas. Table 14 lists potential drug mechanisms that are being researched to potentially manage cocaine addiction by blocking this drug's many effects.

Table 14. Potential Mechanism to Manage Cocaine Addiction

- Bind to cocaine molecules and prevent movement into the CNS via the blood-brain barrier
- Change cocaine molecules into harmless (inactive) particles
- Remove the cocaine molecule as a vaccine using an antibody-type response
- "Catalytic" antibodies changing cocaine into inactive fragments

For example, research is looking at drugs called "peripheral blockers", such as Dopamine D3 Receptor Agonists (D3 agonists), to prevent cocaine-induced CNS stimulation by neutralizing this drug in the blood; such drugs may help with addiction as well as with overdose and cocaine-induced seizures. If the addict uses other drugs, treatment of dependence on those other drugs may help. For example, naltrexone or disulfiram may help with alcohol abuse and be of benefit to the addict who uses both cocaine and alcohol.

Opioids

A number of opiate narcotics are abused by adolescents and adults, as reviewed in Table 15. Prescribed narcotics have been popular for many years, and are available in many ways, as stealing them from home medicine supplies, obtained from emergency room or office clinicians by faking (exaggerating) injuries or illnesses (migraine headaches, dysmenorrhea), or simply buying the opiate of choice on the street.

Table 15. Narcotic Opiates

- Codeine
- Fentanyl
- Heroin
- Meperidine
- Methadone
- Morphine
- Oxycodone
- Pentazocine
- Propoxyphene
- Others

Clinicians may forget or not be aware of the addictive potential of such classic analgesics as Darvocet®, Dilaudid®, Percocet®, Stadol®, Vicodin®, or Ultram®. News media have covered the recent increased popularity of Oxycodone (OxyContin®), a narcotic that is abused by some in place of heroin; a variety of ways of abuse are noted, including chewing an oxycodone tablet, crushing the pill and either snorting the contents or intravenous use after boiling the powder. Its acceptance by addicts is reflected in the many street names it has acquired, including *OXY, OC, oxycotton and killers*. Fentanyl is a prescribed narcotic that is ten times more potent than heroin and there are a number of reported overdoses from this drug.

Heroin

Inexpensive and potent heroin (diacetyl morphine hydrochloride) is available and comes from Mexico, Columbia, Afghanistan, and Pakistan. Heroin (*junk, smack, Mexican brown, China white*) can be abused in a snuff form, intravenously, or subcutaneously (skin-popping). Speedballing, as noted, refers to the combination of heroin or morphine with cocaine in an effort to block the sedative effect of heroin. The mean age of using heroin dropped from 27 years of age in 1988 to 19 years of age in 1995. There was a doubling of high school seniors who used this drug from 1990 to 1996 at a time when the price of heroin was dropping along with a 40% increase in drug purity. The 1999 YRBS noted that 2.4% of high school students had tried heroin on at least one occasion; this was broken down to 3.5% males and 1.3% females. The 2003 Monitor the Future Study recorded that 1.5% of high school seniors had a lifetime use of heroin, 0.8% over the past year and 0.4% over the past survey month. The lifetime heroin use for these seniors was 1.5% in the 2007 YRBS. Unfortunately, this use increases as these seniors leave school and also increases in those who drop out of school before graduation.

The typical situation is an adolescent who begins to snort this drug, develops an intense craving for the resultant euphoria, and progresses to smoking or intravenous use (mainlining). An all-consuming addiction with tolerance develops, as noted by the saying: "*once is too much, 1000 times not enough*;" also classic is the development of physical addiction, psychological dependence, and a narcotic withdrawal syndrome. Approximately 30% of adolescents who smoke heroin become mainlining adults. Those who smoke or snort this drug often mistakenly feel they are bypassing the dangerous effects of heroin by smoking. However, this is not true, and the younger the addiction starts, the greater is the risk for post-cessation relapse.

Table 16 lists some of the medical complications of heroin abuse, including an overdose that leads to death from respiratory depression and pulmonary edema. Clinicians should observe for the use of tattoos to obscure puncture wounds or needle-tract marks made by the heroin intravenous abuse; such mainlining and tattooing phenomena increase the infectious complications of needle use. A newborn withdrawal syndrome is described in newborns whose mothers abuse narcotics; heroin withdrawal in utero can lead to meconium aspiration, bile pneumonitis, and severe respiratory distress.

Table 16. Medical Complications of Heroin Abuse

- Amenorrhea
- Endocarditis (from *Staphylococcus aureus*)
- False-positive VDRL
- Fat necrosis
- HIV/AIDS
- Hepatitis (B and C)
- Lipodystrophy
- Osteomyelitis
- Peptic ulcer disease
- Pulmonary edema and pneumonia
- Respiratory arrest
- Skin infections
- Tetanus
- Others

Management of Opioid Addiction

Addiction research of the last part of the 20th century led to the conclusion that opioid dependence is a neurobiological central nervous system disorder that involves brain receptors. This science looks at *reward circuits* controlling such processes as hunger, thirst, reproduction, and even drug addiction. Drug-induced alterations in CNS opiate receptors leads to drug dependence and tolerance phenomena. Opiate addiction induces significant social dysfunction with complex biological and psychological components that are not corrected by incarceration. Unfortunately, the majority of such addicts are not in treatment designed to treat their brain disorder. These patients often need acute detoxification measures followed by residential and/or outpatient management of sufficient nature to blunt their often overwhelming need to find the narcotic euphoria. Community programs as the 12-Step groups (ie, Narcotics Anonymous) can be very helpful to these individuals to stay off the drug (s).

The opioid addict may benefit from the judicious use of various medications that are available as part of the overall management program (Table 17) (Greydanus, 2008). Naltrexone (*ReVia®, Depade®*) is an opiate antagonist that can help many with opiate addiction, including addicts with additional alcohol dependence.

Methadone may block classic narcotic effects without giving the user the classic opiate euphoria; it can also remove withdrawal symptomatology and help with on-going desires for additional drugs. Clinicians have used this drug as a substitute agonist for opiate dependence since the 1960s. Pharmacogenetics allows once a day dosing and the patient officially must be at least 18 years of age or older. Daily doses may range from 40 mg to 400 mg and successful patients, while on methadone, are then able to maintain a more normal life, in contrast to the addict's chaotic life of only seeking money for another high.

In search of longer-acting alternatives to methadone, addiction specialists have turned to levomethadyl acetate and buprenorphine, both of which are medications that are effective with narcotic addicts Clinicians can also use the sublingual combination of buprenorphine/naloxone that provides benefit at least equal to that of methadone. The naloxone part of this dual treatment is used to stop diversion of the buprenorphine to intravenous administration. There have been some reports of ventricular tachycardia with prolonged QT intervals (*Torsade de pointes*) after taking LAAM and more research is needed to see if this drug is safe enough to be used.

Table 17. Medications Available for Opioid Addiction

– Naltrexone
– Methadone hydrochloride
– LAAM (levo-alpha-acetyl methadol or levomethadyl acetate)
– Buprenorphine
– Anti-depressant drugs (as selective serotonin reuptake inhibitors)
– Anti-stress medications (as buspirone)

Hallucinogenic Drugs

Both the hallucinogens and dissociative drugs may alter a youth's state of mind and mood. Hallucinogens include Psilocybin, Psilocyn (mushrooms), LSD, and mescaline (peyote); these drugs can cause auditory, visual, and tactile hallucinations. Dissociative drugs, such as Ketamine or PCP, alter a persons' state of mind and mood, causing a "feeling of detachment" or "dissociate reaction," but do not cause hallucinations.

PCP (*phencyclidine* and LSD (*lysergic acid diethylamide*) are taken as pills to induce a potent reality distortion with synesthesias or alterations of sensory perception (involving sight and sound) and emotions (involving euphoria and intense fears), in addition to time and place. Tolerance is described in these individuals as are cases of psychosis and the well-known flashback that can be induced by antihistamines or marijuana. Overdosing can induce respiratory depression with coma and death.

Phencyclidine (PCP)

This drug has many street names, including *peace, pill, sternly, peace pill, angel dust, hog,* and *sheets*. PCP is an arylcyclohexalamine that can be made in illict laboratories; it causes adrenergic potentiation by inhibition of neuronal catecholamines. PCP can be taken as tablets, liquid, or in a powder form, sometimes sprinkled on marijuana or cigarettes (*joints*) to augment pot's potency.

Management of a PCP-induced "trip" (bad reaction) involves keeping the patient in a dark, padded room with the provision of diazepam (10-20 mg orally or 10 mg intramuscularly every four hours) or haloperidol if severe agitation develops. Death may be caused by PCP because of the development of hypothermia, seizures, trauma, severe hypertension or hypotension, and/or psychotic delirium. Psychosis may be helped with D3 agonists and research seeks chemicals to act as "antibodies" to neutralize PCP molecules.

Lysergic Acid Diethylamine (LSD)

LSD is the most powerful hallucinogen and has earned many street names, including *acid, "L", sugar, dots, cubes, big "D",* and *blotters.* LSD is found in morning glory seeds and rye fungus (*Ergot*). It is easy to produce by amateur chemists and easy to hide since it is odorless, tasteless, and colorless; because of this, it has become popular at marathon dances ("raves") where it can be given to unsuspecting victims. A dose as low as 20 mcg (placed on small objects as a sugar cube, paper blotter, or postage stamps) can lead to its classic euphoric or hallucinogen effects by increasing serotonin; sympathetic activity is potentiated, with resultant tachycardia, fever, mydriasis, and hypertension. Most youth with a bad trip or unpleasant flashback respond to a reassurance and calm interaction with the clinician; if necessary, haloperidol has been given for major reactions, including prolonged seizure activity.

Tryptamines

Tryptamines include a number of naturally occurring Schedule I hallucinogenic substances obtained from "magic mushrooms" indigenous to South America, Mexico, and the United States. They can be synthetically produced and include Psilocybin (0-phosphoryl-4-hydroxy-N, N-dimethyltryptamine) and Psilocyn (4-hydroxy-n, n-dimethyltryptamine). These chemicals produce muscle relaxation, mydriasis, vivid auditory and visual distortions, as well as emotional liability. These drug effects are not well predictable and vary by the specific mushrooms used as well as the manner in which they are dried, brewed, and consumed. Users of tryptamines often experience a multitude of effects that include hallucinations, euphoria, dilated pupils, empathy, emotional distress, "feelings of love," and visual-auditory disturbances or distortions. Some experience gastrointestinal effects, as nausea, emesis, and diarrhea. Dimethyltryptamine (DMT) occurs naturally in a variety of wild plants and seeds. It is usually smoked, sniffed, or injected. DMT is inactivated orally and rapidly metabolized. The drug experience is called a "businessman's trip" because its effects are for only one hour. Diethyltryptamine (DET) is an analogue of DMT and produces the same pharmacologic effects, but is less potent than DMT. Alpha-ethyltryptamine (AET) is another tryptamine class hallucinogen added to the list of Schedule I hallucinogens in 1994.

N,N-Diisopropyl-5-methoxytryptamine (referred as "Foxy-Methoxy") is an orally active tryptamine recently encountered in the United States. Alpha-methyltryptamine (AMT), known as "spirals", was designated a Schedule I drug in 2003. Tryptamines, like "Foxy" and AMT, are very dose dependent, which means that the doubling of a moderate dose could result in effects similar to LSD. The duration of effects from 20 mg of AMT usually last between 12 and 24 hours, while the effects from 6 to 10 mg of Foxy reportedly last from 3 to

6 hours. 5-methoxy-alpha-methyltryptamine (*5-MeO-AMT*) is also a tryptamine. Other common names for 5-MeO-AMT are "alpha-O", "alpha" and "O-DMS."

Bufotenine (bufagin, 5-hydroxy-N-N-dimethyltryptamine) is a Schedule I substance found in certain mushrooms, seeds, and most notably, the skin glands of the green and red Cane Toad (*Bufo marinus*). In the 1960s-70s, the "toads milks" in northern Florida were obtained by daring to lick ("suck the toad") which lead to accidental handling of the toads. Historically, these toads were killed and their skin boiled to produce a bitter tasting broth. In Australia, the milk is dried into a powder and smoked. In South America, this substance is used as snuff. A mild, though frightening "trip" occurs as this 3-indoleamine works on serotonergic sites in the amygdale and ventral lateral geniculate. The toad can continuously replace the supply and, in general, most bufotenine preparations from natural sources can be extremely toxic.

MDMA (Ecstasy)

Phenethylamines are a family of over 100 chemicals that are hallucinogenic. MDMA (3,4 methylenedioxymethamphetamine) is a phenethylamine that resembles both a stimulant (methamphetamine) and a hallucinogen (mescaline). The U.S. Food and Drug Administration classified MDMA as a Schedule I drug in 1985. MDEA (3,4-methylenedioxy-N-ethyl-amphetamine) or *Eve* is a close congener of MDMA. There is also a designer version of the banned decongestant and "diet" drug, phenylpropanolamine; it is referred to as *U4ia* and is similar in action to MDMA with both stimulant and hallucinogenic effects.

MDMA was developed in 1912 by German scientists and synthesized as an appetite suppressant; it was utilized in the 1970s and 1980s in an attempt to improve psychotherapy. Concern over this drug developed as its severe side-effects became evident. The 2000 Monitor the Future Study noted that 8.2% of high school students had experience with this drug in constrast to 5.6% in 1999. The 2003 MTF study reported that 8.3% of high school seniors had lifetime use of MDMA; this included 4.5% over the past year and 1.3% over the past survey month. The lifetime use for these seniors in the 2007 YRBS was 6.1%.

MDMA produces an intense euphoria and energizing effect in users and thus is popular at dance or club halls (called "raves, trances, or dance parties that last all night); it is also popular with college students. It is a designer drug that abusers feel is safe at 1-2 mg/kg and produces prolonged effects; because of this, its availability and use is more common than cocaine at teenage raves. Its effect is normally 3 to 6 hours, though it may be several days. Its purest form is as a white crystalline powder and if red or brown MDMA is found, this suggests impurities are present. MDMA has many street names, such as *ecstasy, XTC, X,hug drug, lover's speed, diamonds, clarity, dex, essence, roll, bean, M, E, and Adam.*

MDMA has mescaline like effects, probably due to interaction with and destruction of serotoninergic neurons in the central nervous system that are involved with thought and memory. This may result from the formation of quinones which can combine with glutathione and other thiols. MDMA produces an anxious state of "well-being," changes in perception, moderate derealization and depersonalization without producing psychomotor agitation.

MDMA abuse may lead to cognitive dysfunction, memory impairment, and behavioral problems. If taken during pregnancy, the risk for congenital anomalies is increased.

Users take MDMA to enhance sensual awareness and augmented psychic or emotional energy. A number of side effects are noted, as listed in Table 18.

Table 18. Side Effects of MDMA

- Hypertension and increased pulse
- Dehydration and possible heat stroke
- Fatigue
- Sleep dysfunction
- Muscle spasms
- Sweating
- Organ dysfunction: renal, liver, CNS, muscular
- Intracerebral hemorrhage
- Irreversible CNS damage with memory loss in chronic abuse
- Confusion and paranoia
- Psychosis
- Depression
- Anxiety, including panic attacks

It can hide thirst and eventual death that may be due to dehydration (which is not uncommon and hence its association with water bottles at raves), hyperthermia, hyponatremia, or cerebral edema. High doses can lead to muscle breakdown, breakdown of muscles, malignant hyperthermia, renal failure, and cardiovascular failure at the raves. MDMA and some of the other "designer" drugs have been associated with intracerebral hemorrhage in adolescents and young adults who have undiagnosed vascular malformations. Also, anxiety (including paranoia and panic attacks) may last for weeks after drug cessation. MDMA is a popular date-rape drug (see below).

MDMA users may mix this drug with alcohol, marijuana, LSD, dextromethorphan, and other drugs. Preparations with camphor, menthol, and ephedrine are applied to the nasal mucosa or chest to enhance the desired MDMA effects. MDMA can also be taken in increasing doses in a "stacked" schedule similar to that used with anabolic steroids. The drug user may also take chemicals that are ecstasy-like in appearance, such as ketamine ("special K"), alpha-methyl fentanyl ("synthetic heroin", "china white") and ephedrine tablets ("herbal ecstasy", "Chinese ephedra", "Ma Huang"); large amounts of these chemicals may lead to hypertension, cardiac arrhythmias, myocardial infarction, cerebrovascular accidents, and death. The ephedrine found in Herbal ecstasy products as found in "health" food stores has only recently been banned.

"Date Rape" Drugs

Novel and more creative uses for previously legitimate pharmaceuticals and "nutriceuticals" continue to emerge "on the street", including familiar drugs as marijuana (ie, increased THC content), phencyclidine (PCP), crack cocaine (or opium) with Viagra, variations on MDMA described previously, short acting benzodiazepines, and those compounds readily made using recipes available on the internet and concocted by amateur chemists. A variety of chemicals have been used to lower external and internal inhibitions and/or consciousness, helping to facilitate sexual assault. These so-called "date rape" drugs are named for their strong sedative and hypnotic effects that are enhanced with alcohol. They continue to be popular at all night dance parties or "raves", and thus, have also been called Club Drugs or Party Drugs. Some are sold in "nutrition" stores or via magazine ads as sleep aids, muscle builders, and even as "party drugs". A variety of drugs have been used, as partially listed in Table 19; this list includes MDMA-methylenedioxy-methamphetamine (*Ecstasy*) previously discussed.

Flunitrazepam (Rohypnol®)

This is a potent benzodiazepine with sedative, anxiolytic, and anticonvulsant effects. It belongs to the same group as Halcion, Ambien, Xanax, Klonipin, Sonata, Versed, and Valium. Flunitrazepam is a central nervous system depressant produced commercially in Switzerland that reduces inhibition and results in memory loss (blackouts) with short term anterograde amnesia for activity that takes place while under the influence of the drug.

Table 19. Club Drugs

– Methylenedioxymethamphetamine (*Ecstasy*, MDMA)
– Rohypnol (Flunitrazepam; *Roofies, The Date Rape Drug, Roches,*
– *Rope*)
– Gamma-hydroxybutyrate (*GHB, Liquid Ecstasy*)
– Gamma-butryl lactone (*GBL, Blue nitro, Renewtrient*)
– Butanediol (*BD, soap, Revitalize plus*)
– Methamphetamine (*meth, ice, crystal, fire, glass, chalk, crank*)
– LSD (*acid, "L", sugar, dots, cubes, big "D", and blotters*)
– Ketamine (Ketalar; *Special K, Cat Valiums*)

It can also lead to such adverse effects as urinary retention, drowsiness, confusion, dizziness, gastrointestinal dysfunction, visual disturbances, hypotension and others. It is available by prescription in Europe (not the United States) and used as a sedative for management of insomnia and also as a pre-surgery anesthetic.

Flunitrazepam is a tasteless, odorless, and colorless chemical that can be taken as a pill or dissolved in a beverage; anecdotal reports of snorting are noted as well. One milligram can be secretly placed in a liquid to sedate a victim for 8 to 12 hours with unfortunate amnesia for the sexual assault that may follow the ingestion. The victim is seen voluntarily leaving with the rapist, recalls little if anything of the events, and is unable to testify in any later prosecution. It has become a popular and classic date rape drug used by gang members and even high school or college students operating at local parties. Its many street names include *forget-me pills, Rope, Roche, Mexican valium,* and *roofies.* It is also an addictive drug used voluntarily by youth as an alternative or adjunctive drug to marijuana or LSD, as well as the self-treatment of anxiety. Its effects are enhanced with alcohol. If used on a regular basis, increasingly higher doses are needed for the desired euphoric effect. Its use has increased 50% over the past several years. In South Texas, along the United-States-Mexico border, it is frequently replaced by the more readily available Klonipin or Xanax, both of which are associated with blacking-out spells and seizures, especially when abused with alcohol and marijuana.

Gamma-Hydroxybutyrate (GHB)

This is a CNS depressant that induces euphoria and lowered inhibition. It has many street names, including: *Liquid X, Liquid E, Liquid XTC, Liquid Ecstasy, Natural Sleep-500, Organic Quaalude, G Caps, Gamma Hydrate, Georgia Home Boy, Growth Hormone Booster, Cherry Meth, Sodium oxybutyrate, Somatomax PM, Grievous Bodily Harm, G-Riffick, Oxy-Sleep, Scoop, Fantasy, Easy Lay, Soap, Salty Water, Vita G, Gamma OH, Somsanit, GHB; Liquid Ecstasy; G; Georgia home boy, caps, organic qualude,* and *goop.*

Like Rohypnol, GHB and its analogs are used as "date rape" drugs. It has a soapy or salty taste, and hence the name *salt* is used until it is mixed with any liquid, including water. Because it is colorless, tasteless, and odorless, it is easily and quietly slipped into an unattended party drink to induce sedation and amnesia. Effects develop in 10-20 minutes, peak in 1 to 2 hours, and last for 4 hours. GHB is rapidly cleared from the body and is undetected in subsequent rape investigations. The clinician providing care in an emergency situation must request that the laboratory specifically look for GHB. Adolescent females need to be warned about the danger of leaving drinks unattended.

It is used by bodybuilders and athletes because of beliefs that GHB will augment endogenous HGH release while sleeping. GHB is available in single doses that augment or mimic effects of alcohol; increasingly higher doses are needed for desired effects. The risk of seizures and death caused by GHB-induced respiratory depression is raised when mixing this with other drugs, such as alcohol, heroin, LSD and psilocybin. The CNS depression occurs because of increasing CNS dopamine and GABA; the endogenous opioid system is also activated. It became a Schedule I substance in March of 2000 and in July, 2002, GHB was approved by an FDA advisory committee for study in the treatment of cataplexy. Most of the GHB used in the United States is illegally manufactured in the US. Law enforcement in every region of the United States report that GHB has surpassed Rohypnol as the most common substance used in drug-facilitated sexual assaults.

Gamma-Butyro-Lactone (GBL)

Because the DEA is cracking down on GHB use, some are using GHB precursors, such as GBL as well as BD (1-4 butanediol), an industrial solvent; both are promoted to enhance sexual ability and pleasure. Street names for GHB are many, including *Renewtrient, Revivarant, Reivivarant G, Blue Nitro, Blue Nitro Vitality, GH Revitalizer, Gamma G, Remforce, and Soap*; it is found in paint thinners and floor stripper products. BD leads to bradypnea and can induce emesis, aspiration, and coma. GBL and BD are both easily changed to GHB *in vivo*, and *in vitro* by adding water. Some producers are substituting BD for GHB, even though the FDA has identified BD as a potentially life-threatening drug. It is sold as a dietary supplement in a number of sleep aid and muscle enhancing products; names include *SomatoPro, NR63, Thunder Nectar, Enliven, GHRE, Weight Belt Cleaner, Revitalize Plus,* and *Serenity*. The FDA asked that products with GBL be recalled in January, 1999; some states, such as California, have told manufactures that it is illegal to sell these products or market them as a supplement or nutritional substance. GBL-related products have been associated with reports of at least 55 adverse health effects, including one death. In 19 of these cases, the consumers became unconscious or comatose, several requiring intubation for assisted breathing.

Ketamine

This drug has been approved since 1970 in the role of an injectable airway preserving veterinary anesthetic; it is taken orally to induce dissociative states, described as dream-like and hallucinatory. Street names include *K, Cat Valium, Special K, and Vitamin K.* It can be obtained as a white powder that can be added to tobacco or marijuana or the powder can be snorted; intramuscular abuse is also described.

The effects of ketamine last one half to two hours producing an "out of body" distortion of time and space. Ketamine in low doses can lead to dysfunction of learning ability, memory, and attention span; in high doses, it can lead to myalgia, paranoia, elevated blood pressure, delirium, motor function impairment, amnesia, long term flashbacks, and respiratory depression-induced death. There is no urine metabolite.

Inhalants

Inhalant drugs (Table 20) are depressants of the central nervous system typically abused by young (ages 6-8, peaks at 14), often male, and homeless adolescents to induce temporary euphoria and excitement. These inhaled chemical vapors are viewed as easily available, inexpensive substitutes or precursors to other drugs, such as alcohol or marijuana. Delivery is by "sniffing, huffing, or bagging".

Table 20. Types of Inhalant Drugs*

Solvents	Gases	Nitrites (Aliphatic nitrites)

Industrial or household solvents or solvent-containing products	Gases used in household or commercial products
	    Butane lighters
	    Propane tanks
		Cyclohexyl nitrite (available to general public)

Paint thinners or solvents	Whipping cream aerosols or dispensers (whippets)	Amyl nitrite (available only with prescription)
Degreasers (dry-cleaning fluids)	Refrigerant gases	
Gasoline		Butyl nitrite
Glues	Household aerosol propellant and associated solvents	(Illegal substance)
Art or office supply solvents	Found in spray paints Found in hair or deodorant sprays	
Correction fluids	Found in fabric protector sprays	
Felt-tip-maker fluid		

Electronic contact cleaners	Medical anesthetic gases
	    Ether
	    Chloroform
	    Halothane
	    Nitrous oxide	

* Greydanus DE, Patel DR: Substance abuse in adolescents: A complex conundrum for the clinician. Pediatric Clin No Amer 59(5): 1179-1223, 2003. (with permission).

In 1995 the lifetime use was 21.6% for 8th graders versus 19.7% in 1999, 17.3% in 2004. Approximately 5% of adolescent girls (age 12-17) used the following including the illicit used of nitrous oxide vials (19.3%): glue sniffing (34.9%), correction fluid (23.4%), hair spray (23%), and inhalation of paints or sprays (6-16%) (MTF 2006). The main ingredient in airplane glue and some rubber cements is toluene. Another popular inhalant is gasoline, noted especially in rural areas of the United States and with Native American adolescents. Amyl nitrite, butyl nitrite, and other volatile nitrates are found in room deodorizers and are used by older adolescents to induce "aphrodisiac" effects.

Inhalation occurs after these substances are placed in a plastic bag or wrap to induce the intoxicating (psychoactive) effects lasting from a few minutes to several hours. After a mild stimulatory effect, an inhibition reduction occurs, followed by unconsciousness. Table 21 lists various complications known to occur with various inhalants. Most abusers of inhalants discontinue these drugs by stopping substance abuse in general or moving onto other drugs. Management of those who become chronic inhalant abusers is difficult, often being hindered by their many, varied behavioral and social problems.

Table 21. Effects of Inhalants*

Hearing loss
    Toluene (paint sprays, glues, dewaxers)
    Trichloroethylene (cleaning fluids, correction fluids)
Peripheral neuropathies or Limb spasms
    Hexane (glues, gasoline)
    Nitrous oxide (whipping cream, gas cylinders)
CNS or Brain Damage: toluene
Bone Marrow Damage: benzene (gasoline)
Liver and Kidney Damage
    Toluene-containing substances
    Chlorinated hydrocarbons
        Correction fluids
        Dry-cleaning fluids
Blood Oxygen Depletion
    Organic nitrites ("*poppers*," "amyl", "*bold*" and "*rush*")
    Methylene chloride
        Varnish removers
        Paint thinners
Loss of the sense of smell (nitrites)
Thermal burn injury with nebulized alcohol/Robitussin® ("RoboFires")
Death
Kaposi's sarcoma

*Greydanus DE, Patel DR: Substance abuse in adolescents: A complex conundrum for the clinician. Pediatric Clin No Amer 59(5): 1179-1223, 2003. (with permission).

Barbiturates

These are CNS depressants that are classified as sedative-hypnotic drugs. They act on the CNS by enhancing the neuroinhibitory action of gamma-aminobutyric acid (GABA) and producing relief from anxiety and sedation. They are classified as ultra-short acting (thiopental), short acting (pentobarbital [*yellow jackets*], secobarbital [*reds*]), and long acting (phenobarbital). The short acting barbiturates have a higher potential for abuse and are more lipid soluble than the long acting formulations.

They can become very addicting in 1 to 2 months and are deadly in high doses or when combined with opioids or alcohol. Abuse of these drugs leads to physical addiction, abstinence, and discontinuation syndrome, similar to that noted with alcohol abuse. Barbiturates are detoxified in the liver and/or excreted unchanged in the urine. Symptoms of acute use and overdose are similar to those of alcohol and include euphoria, slurred speech, lethargy, miosis, and ataxia. Overdosing leads to low blood pressure, bullous dermatological lesions, respiratory depression, coma, and death. It is not commonly abused at current times and involves less than 3% of high school students. This reduced abuse probably reflects infrequent clinician prescription of these drugs, reduced availability on the streets, and the availability of many other illicit drugs. Barbiturates should usually not be prescribed to adolescents and only do so with extreme caution.

Conclusion

Substance abuse continues to be a wide-spread and very serious phenomenon for our adolescents and young adults in the United States and around the globe. Many factors draw our youth into these deadly drugs, leading to many acute and chronic sequelae, ranging from addiction to death. Youth must be clearly taught that drug use and abuse comes with considerable complications for their current and future life. Clinicians must join with other members of society to educate our patients to the many deadly and dangerous drugs of abuse that are available and to work with society (including governments) to reduce the availability of drugs. The human instinct for pleasure at any cost must be tempered with education and direction from clinicians. Management of those addicted to drugs is a complex, often discouraging process. Psychosocial and behavioral therapies are important that involve a variety of health specialists. Group, family, and individual therapy all have a place in management and many need intensive treatment in drug abuse programs. Medications are being developed to render certain drugs "harmless" to the user.

References

American Academy of Pediatrics Policy Statement: Tobacco, alcohol, and other drugs: the role of the pediatrician in prevention and management of substance abuse. *Pediatrics* 101:125, 1998.

Anton RF: Naltrexone for the management of alcohol dependence. *N Engl J Med* 2008; 359: 715-721.

Doyon S: The many faces of ecstasy. *Curr. Opinion Pediatr*. 13: 170-176, 2001.

Baker F, Ainsworth SR, Dye JT, et al: Health risks associated with cigar smoking. *JAMA* 284 (6): 735-740, 2000.

Bauer UE, Johnson TM, Hopkins RS, et al: Changes in youth cigarette use and intentions following implementation of a tobacco control program. Findings from the Florida Youth Tobacco Survey, 1998-2000. *JAMA* 284 (6):723-728, 2000.

Belcher HME, Shinitzky HE: Substance abuse in children: Prediction, protection and prevention. *Arch. Pediatr. Adolesc. Med*. 152:952-960, 1998.

Biederman J, Wilens T, Mick E, Spencer T, Faraone SV: Pharmacotherapy of attention-deficit/hyperactivity disorder reduces risk for substance use disorder. *Pediatrics* 104:e20, 1999.

Burd L, Wilson H: Fetal, Infant, and child mortality in a context of alcohol use. Am J Med Genet 15;127C(1):51-8. 2004.

Cami J, Farre M, Mas M, et.al: Human pharmacology of 3-4-demethylenedioxymethamphetamine ("Ecstasy", MDMA), psychomotor performance and subjective effects. *J. Clin. Psychopharm* 19:241-251, 1998.

Cami J, Farre M: Drug addiction. *N Engl J Med* 2003; 349:975-986.

Centers for Disease Control and Prevention: Tobacco use among middle and high school students. United States, 1999. MMWR 49(3):49. 2000.

Cigars - Health Effects and Trends. Tobacco Control Monograph No. 9. National Cancer Institute, US Dept of Health and Human Services, 1998.

Clinical Practice Guideline. Treating Tobacco Use and Dependence. 2008 Update. US Dept Health and Human Services. http://www.ahrg.gov/path/tobacco.htm. Accessed: 1/16/09.

Comerci GB, Schwebel R: Substance abuse: *Adolesc. Med.* 11(1): 79-101, 2000.

Coupey SM: Barbiturates. *Pediatr. Rev.* 18: 260-265, 1997.

Covey LS, Sullivan MA, Johnston JA, et al: Advances in non-nicotine pharmacotherapy for smoking cessation. *Drugs* 59(1):17, 2000.

Crowley TJ MacDonald MJ Whitmore EA, et al: Cannabis dependence, withdrawal, and reinforcing effects among adolescents with conduct symptoms and substance use disorders. *Drug Alcohol. Depend* 50:27-37, 1998.

DiFranza JR, Savageau JA, Fletcher K, et al: Measuring the loss of autonomy over nicotine dependence in youth (DANDY Study). *Arch. Ped. Adolesc. Med.* 156: 397-403, 2002.

Duffy A Milin R Case study: withdrawal syndrome in adolescent chronic cannabis users. *J. Am. Acad. Child Adolesc. Psychiatry* 35: 1618-162, 1996.

Fahey, RT Brown, LL Gabel (eds.): *Primary Care: Clinics in Office Practice: Adolescent Medicine.* Philadelphia: WB Saunders, 1998.

Fiore MC, Jaén CR, Baker TB et al: *Treating Tobacco Use and Dependence. Clinical Practice Guideline.* U.S. Department of Health and Human Services, 2008.
Available at: www.surgeongeneral.gov/tobacco/treating_tobacco_use08.pdgf

Fisher LB, Miles IW, Austin SB et al: Predictors of initiation of alcohol use among US adolescents. *Arch Pediatr Adolesc Med* 2007; 161: 959-966.

Friedman RA: The changing face of teenage drug abuse—the trend toward prescription drugs. *N Engl J Med* 2006; 354:1448-50.

Goldenring JM, Rosen D: Getting into adolescent heads: an essential update. *Contemp. Peds* 21: 64, 2004.

Greydanus DE (Editor): *Caring for your Adolescent. Second Edition*, American Academy of Pediatrics and Bantam Books (NY), 2003. (Guide for parents of adolescents).

Greydanus DE, Patel DR: Sports doping in the adolescent athlete. *Asian Journal of Paediatric Practice* 4(1): 9-14, 2000.

Greydanus DE, Patel DR: Sports doping in the adolescent: The hope, the hype and the hyperbole. *Pediatr. Clin. No Amer* 49(4): 829-855, 2002.

Greydanus DE: Substance Abuse in Adolescents: Basic chemistry lessons gone awry. *International Pediatrics* 17(1): 3-4 2002.

Greydanus DE, Patel DR: Substance abuse in adolescents: A complex conundrum for the clinician. *Pediatric. Clin. No Amer.* 59(5): 1179-1223, 2003.

Greydanus DE, Patel DR: Adolescents *and Drug Abuse. In: Essentials of Adolescent Medicine*, NY: McGraw-Hill Medical Publishers, ch. 36, 2006.

Greydanus DE, Patel DR: *Substance abuse in adolescents: current concepts.* Disease-a-Month 2005; 51 (7): 392-431.

Greydanus DE, Calles JL, Jr., Patel DR: *Pediatric and Adolescent Psychopharmacology: A Practical Manual for Pediatricians*. Cambridge, England: Cambridge University Press, ch 13: 241-277, 2008.

Grunbaum JA, Kann, L Kinchen S, et.al: YRBSS-U.S. 2003 in Surveillance Summaries May 21, 2004, *MMWR* 53: 1-96 2004.

Heischober BS, Hofmann AF: "Substance abuse" IN: *Adolescent Medicine*, Third Edition Eds: AD Hofmann and DE Greydanus. Norwalk, Conn: Appleton and Lange, ch. 32:703-739, 1997.

Heyman RB: Tobacco and the 21st Century. *Adoles. Med.* 11(1):69-78, 2000.

Hogan MJ: Diagnosis and treatment of teen drug use. *Med. Clin. No Amer.* 84 (4): 927-966, 2000.

Hughes JR, Goldstein MG, Hurt RD, Shiffman S: Recent advances in the pharmacotherapy of smoking. *JAMA* 281:72. 1999.

Jenkins RR, Adger H: "Substance abuse" IN: *Nelson Textbook of Pediatrics*, 17th Edition, Eds: RM Kliegman, RE Behrman, HB Jenson, Stanton BF. Philadelphia: Saunders/Elsevier, ch.113:824-834, 2007.

Johnston LD, O'Malley PM, Bachman JG: The Monitoring the Future Study: National Survey Results on Adolescent Drug Use. *Overview of Key Findings*, 1999. University of Michigan Institute for Social Research.

Johnston L: *National Survey Results on Drug Use from the Monitoring the Future Study*, 2003.

Kaul P, Coupey SM: Clinical evaluation of substance abuse. *Pediatrics in review* 23: 85-94, 2002.

Knight J, Sherrit L, Shrier L: Validity of the CRAFFT substance abuse screening test among adolescent clinic patients. *Arch. Pediatr. Adol. Med.* 156: 607, 2002.

King C, Siegel M, Celebucki C, et al: Adolescent exposure to cigarette advertising in magazines. *JAMA* 279(7):499-520, 1998.

Lancaster T, Stead LF: *Individual behavioral counseling for smoking cessation: Cochrane review.* In The Cochrane Library, Issue 2, 2000. Oxford: Update Software Ltd, England.

Lancaster T, Stead LF: Self-help interventions for smoking cessation: Cochrane review. In The Cochrane Library, Issue 2, 2000. Update Software Ltd, Oxford, England.

Landry DW: Immunotherapy for cocaine addiction. *Scientific American* 276 (2): 42-5, 1997.

Leshner AL: Club drugs. NIDA Community Drug Alert Bulletin. *National Institute on Drug Abuse.* U.S. Department of Heath and Human Services, National Institutes of Health. Bethesda, MD. 1-4, December, 1999.

Liepman MR, Keller DM, Botelho RJ, et al: Understanding and preventing substance abuse by adolescents. *Prim. Care* 25:137-162, 1998.

Liepman MR, Keller DM, Botelho R, Monroe AD, Sloane MA: Preventing substance abuse by adolescents: A guide for primary care clinicians. In PJ Lillington GA, Leonard CT, *Sachs DPL: Smoking cessation: Techniques and benefits. Clinics in Chest Medicine.* 21(1):199. 2000.

LoVecchio F, Curry SC, Bagnasco T: Butyrolactone-induced central nervous system depression after ingestion of RenewTrient, a "dietary supplement" {Letter}. *N. Engl. J. Med.* 339:847-8, 1998.

Lyttle, T, Goldstein D, Gartz J: Bufo toads and bufotenine: Fact and fiction surrounding an alleged psychedelic. *Journal of Psychoactive Drugs* 28 (3): 267-90. 1996. Abstract.

McCance-Katz EF, Kosten, TR: New Treatments for Chemical Addictions. *Review of Psychiatry Series,* Volume 17, Washington, DC: American Psychiatric Press, 211 pages, 1998.

McEvoy AW, Kitchen ND: Thomas DG: Intracrebral haemorrhage and drug abuse in young adults. *Br. J. Neurosurg.* 14: 449-454, 2000.

Marsh LA, Bickel WK, Badger GJ et al: Comparison of pharmacological treatments for opioid-dependent adolescents. *Arch Gen Psychiatry* 2005; 62:1157-64.

Milroy CM, Clark JC, Forrest ARW: Pathology of deaths associated with "Ecstasy" and "Eve" misuse. *J. Clin. Pathol.* 49: 149-153, 1996.

Moniter the Future, 2008. Released: 12/11/08; www.monitorthefuture.org

Montero JA, Larissa L, Zaulyanov MS*: Infect.Med.* 19:4; 174-178 2002.

Morgan MJ: Ecstasy (MDMA): A review of its possible persistent psychological effects. *Psychopharm* 152: 230-248, 2000.

National Consensus Development Panel on Effictive Medical Treatment of Opiate Addiction. Effective Medical Treatment of Opiate Addiction. *JAMA* 280(2): 1936-43, 1998.

National Drug Threat Assessment, NDIC/USDOJ 2002.

National Institute on Drug Abuse. National Institutes of Health: Cigarettes and other nicotine products. www.nida.nih.gov.

National Institute on Drug Abuse; United States Department of Health and Human Services. NIH Publication No. 00-4690, 2000.

O'Connor PG: Treating opioid dependence—New data and new opportunities. *N. Engl. J. Med.* 343 (18): 193-195, 2000.

Palmer RB: γ-Butyrolactone and 1,4-Butanediol: Abused analogues of γ-hydoxybutyrate *Toxocol. Rev.* 23: 1, 21-31, 2004.

Patel DR: Smoking and children. *Ind. J. Pediatr.* 66:817-824, 1999.

Patel DR, Greydanus DE: Substance abuse: A pediatric concern. *Indian J. Pediatr.* 1999.

Patel DR, Greydanus DE, Rowlett JD: Romance with the automobile in the 20th Century: Implications for adolescents in a new millennium. *Adolesc. Med.* 11(1): 127-139, 2000.

Patel DR, Greydanus DE: Office interventions for adolescent smokers. *Adolesc. Med.* 11 (3): 1-11, 2000.

Pierce JP, Gilpin EA, Choi WS: Sharing the blame: smoking experimentation and future smoking-attributable mortality due to Joe Camel and Marlboro advertising and promotions. *Tobacco Control,* 8:37. 1999.

Poikolainen K: Ecstasy and the antecedents of illicit drug use. *BMJ* 2006; 332: 803-4.

Public health and injection drug use. Morb Mort Week Report 50:377- 399, 2001 (May 18). *Report of the Scientific Committee on Tobacco and Health*, Department of Health, 1998.

Riala K, Hakko H, Isohanni M, et al: Teenage smoking and substance use as predictors of severe alcohol problems in late adolescence and young adulthood. *J. Adol. Health* 35: 245-254, 2004.

Rigotti NA, Lee JE, Wechsler H: US college students' use of tobacco products: Results of a national survey. *JAMA* 284 (6): 699-705, 2000.

Ricaurte GA, McCan UD: Recognition and management of complications of new recreational drug use. *Lancet* 2005; 365: 2137-45.

Schwartz RH, Miller NS: MDMA (Ecstasy) and the Rave: A review. *Pediatrics* 100(4): 705-708, 1997.

Schwartz RH: Adolescent heroin use: A review. *Pediatrics* 102(6): 1461-66, 1998.

Schydlower M (ed): *Substance Abuse: A Guide for Health Professionals*. American Academy of Pediatrics. Elk Grove Village, IL, 2000.

Schydlower M, Arredondo RM: Substance abuse among adolescents. Adolesc Med Clinics 2006; 17 (2): 259-504.

Shiffman S, Johnston JA, Khayrallah M, et al: The effect of bupropion on nicotine craving and withdrawal. *Psychopharmacology* 148:33, 2000.

Shulgin AT: The background and chemistry of MDMA. *J. Psychoactive Drugs* 18: 291-304, 1986.

Spoth RL, Clair S, Shin C et al: Long-term effects of universal interventions on methamphetamine use among adolescents. *Arch Pediatr Adoelsc Med* 2006; 160: 876-82

Steele TD, Mc Cann UD, Ricaurte GA: 3-4-methylenedioxymethamphetamine (MDMA, "Ecstasy") pharmacology and toxicology in animals and humans. *Addiction* 89: 539-551 1994.

Stevens LM, Lynm C, Glass RM: Cocaine addiction. *JAMA* 287:146, 2002.

Swift RM: Drug therapy for alcohol dependence. *N. Engl. J. Med.* 340(19): 1482- 1490, 1999.

Teter CJ, Guthrie SK: A comprehensive review of MDMA and GHB: Two common club drugs. *Pharmacotherapy* 21;12: 1486-1513 2001.

Tobacco and alcohol act synergistically multiplying the risk of oral and pharyngeal cancers. *Report of the Scientific Committee on Tobacco and Health*, Department of Health, 1998.

United States Conference of Mayors: No place to hide: Substance abuse in mid-size cities. *Drug Enforcement Administration and National Institute on Drug Abuse*. 1-41, January, 2000.

Varenicline (Chantix) Warnings: Risk versus benefit. *Med Lett Dr Ther* 2008; 50: 53.

Wheeler KC, Fletcher KE, Wellman RJ, DiFranza JR: Screening adolescents for nicotine dependence: The Hooked on Nicotine Checklist. *J. Adolesc. Health* 35: 225-230, 2004.

Wilens TE, Biederman J, Mick E, Faraone SV, Spencer T: Attention deficit hyperactivity disorder (ADHD) is associated with early onset substance use disorders. *J. Nerv. Ment. Dis.* 185:475-482, 1997.

Wilens TE: ADHD and the substance use disorder: the nature of the relation, subtypes at risk, and treatment issues. *Psychiatr. Clin. North Am.* 27; 283 2004.

WHO: *The World Health Report 1999: Combating the tobacco epidemic*. Geneva, WHO. 2000.

Internet:

National Institute on Drug Abuse: www.nida.gov/NIDAHome.html.

National Clearinghouse on Alcohol and Drug Information: www.health.org.

National Institute on Alcohol Abuse and Alcoholism: www.niaaa.nih.gov.

http://www.MonitoringTheFuture.org

In: Behavioral Pediatrics, 3rd Edition
Editor: D. E. Greydanus et al.

ISBN 978-1-60692-702-1
© 2009 Nova Science Publishers, Inc.

Chapter 26

Abuse in the Child and Adolescent

Vincent J. Palusci and Margaret T. McHugh

Abstract

This chapter serves as a primer for professionals who, regardless of their individual fields of expertise, will treat abused children and adolescents in a variety of medical settings. It provides an overview of the types of maltreatment, the medical assessment, treatment, and preventive community services that can be provided to help children and families. The experience of the past fifty years has established a solid foundation for the work that child health clinicians need to address in the field of child abuse and neglect.

Introduction

The victimization of children through abuse and neglect remains an all-too common occurrence. With three million reports and over 900,000 substantiated victims of child maltreatment annually, the United States child abuse and neglect reporting system continues to document the effects of maltreatment and violence on children. Injuries overall place a heavy burden on children and inflicted injuries affect far too many as well. Health care costs for inflicted injures are difficult to estimate, but estimates place the total costs associated with abuse as over $9 billion annually in the U.S. Maltreated children suffer from a variety of behavior problems, mental injuries, and physical maladies. The Adverse Childhood Experiences study has noted the powerful relationship between adverse childhood experiences and several conditions of adulthood including risk for suicide, alcoholism, depression, illicit drug use and other lifestyle changes which have direct and indirect costs. While the exact pathways are still being explored, childhood abuse is thought to adversely affect adult health by increased risk for depression and post-traumatic stress disorders, participation in harmful activities, difficulty in forming and sustaining healthy relationships, and negative beliefs and attitudes towards others.

In the past forty-seven years since the publication of Dr. C. Henry Kempe's landmark article, "The Battered Child Syndrome," the subject of child maltreatment has become a universal topic, not restricted to one community or to one type of provider. As the field has grown, professionals have had to broaden their intellectual and personal perspectives to not only identify maltreatment but also to provide interventions to prevent further abuse. An important goal for professionals dedicated to this field is primary prevention: to ensure that child abuse, like many infectious diseases of the past century, will be eradicated.

Definitions

Using a disease model, child maltreatment can be thought of as the second most common chronic disease of childhood, following asthma and allergies, based on incidence and prevalence in the pediatric population. Child maltreatment has been subdivided in several ways, but most systems separately identify physical abuse, sexual abuse, neglect, and psychological maltreatment (Table 1). A variety of codes are available for medical and mental health diagnosis and counseling in the ninth revision of the International Classification of Diseases; the Diagnostic and Statistical Manual of mental health disorders uses similar coding (Table 2). External injury (E Codes) allow for the assignment of the alleged offender based on relationship to the child (E967), but use of these codes has been less than complete, particularly with reference to child abuse fatalities.

Table 1. World Health Organization Definitions*

Child Abuse	Child abuse or maltreatment constitutes all forms of physical and/or emotional ill-treatment, sexual abuse, neglect or negligent treatment and commercial or other exploitation, resulting in actual or potential harm to the child's health, survival, development, or dignity in the context of a relationship of responsibility, trust or power.
Physical Abuse	Physical abuse of a child is that which results in actual or potential physical harm from an interaction or lack of an interaction, which is reasonably within the control of a parent or person in a position of responsibility, power or trust. There may be single or repeated incidents.
Emotional Abuse	Emotional abuse includes the failure to provide a developmentally appropriate, supportive environment, including the availability of a primary attachment figure, so that the child can establish a stable and full range of emotional and social competencies commensurate with her or his personal potentials and in the context of the society in which the child dwells. There may also be acts towards the child that cause or have a high probability of causing harm to the child's health or physical, mental, spiritual, moral or social development. These acts must be reasonably within the control of a parent or person in a position of responsibility, power or trust. Acts include restriction of movement, patterns of belittling, denigrating, scapegoating, threatening, scaring, discriminating, ridiculing or other non-physical forms of hostile or rejecting treatment.

Neglect and negligent treatment	Neglect is the failure to provide for the development of the child in all spheres: health, education, emotional development, nutrition, shelter and safe living conditions, in the context of resources reasonably available to the family or caretakers and causes or has a high probability of causing harm to the child's health or physical, mental, spiritual, moral or social development. This includes the failure to properly supervise and protect children from harm as much as is feasible.
Sexual abuse	Child sexual abuse is the involvement of a child in sexual activity that he or she does not fully comprehend or is unable to give informed consent to, or that violates the laws or social taboos of society. Child sexual abuse is evidenced by this activity between a child and an adult or another child who by age or development is in a relationship of responsibility, trust or power, the activity being intended to gratify or satisfy the needs of the other person. This may include but is not limited to: – The inducement or coercion of a child to engage in any unlawful activity – The exploitative use of a child in prostitution or other unlawful sexual practices – The exploitative use of children in pornographic performances and materials
Exploitation	Commercial or other exploitation of a child refers to the use of the child in work or other activities for the benefit of others. This includes, but is not limited to, child labour and child prostitution. These activities are to the detriment of the child's physical or mental health, education, or spiritual, moral or social-emotional development.

*World Health Organization (WHO). (1999). *Report of the consultation on child abuse prevention.* Geneva, Switzerland: Author.

Table 2. International Classification of Disease Codes Applicable to Child Abuse (ICD-9)*

Condition Codes	995
	
	Certain adverse effects not elsewhere classified
		995.5	Child maltreatment syndrome
			Use additional code(s), if applicable, to identify any associated injuries
			Use additional E code to identify:
			   nature of abuse (E960-E968)
			   perpetrator (E967.0-E967.9)

		995.50	Child abuse, unspecified
		995.51	Child emotional/psychological abuse
		995.52	Child neglect (nutritional) Use additional code to identify intent of neglect (E904.0,E968.4)
		995.53	Child sexual abuse
		995.54	Child physical abuse Battered baby or child syndrome *Excludes: Shaken infant syndrome (995.55)*

Table 2. (Continued)

		995.55	Shaken infant syndrome Use additional code(s) to identify any associated injuries
		995.59	Other child abuse and neglect Multiple forms of abuse Use additional code to identify intent of neglect (E904.0,E968.4)
Counseling Codes	V61.2 Parent-child problems	V61.20	Counseling for parent-child problem, unspecified Concern about behavior of child Parent-child conflict Parent-child relationship problem
		V61.21	Counseling for victim of child abuse Child battering Child neglect *Excludes: current injuries due to abuse (995.50-995.59)*
		V61.22	Counseling for perpetrator of parental child abuse *Excludes: counseling for non-parental abuser (V62.83)*
		V61.29	Other Problem concerning adopted or foster child
E Codes	E960-969 Homicide and injury purposely inflicted by other persons	E967	Perpetrator of child and adult abuse Note: selection of the correct perpetrator code is based on the relationship between the perpetrator and the victim.
		E967.0	By father, stepfather, or boyfriend Male partner of child's parent or guardian
		E967.1	By other specified person
		E967.2	By mother, stepmother, or girlfriend Female partner of child's parent or guardian
		E967.3	By spouse or partner Abuse of spouse or partner by ex-spouse or ex-partner
		E967.4	By child
		E967.5	By sibling
		E967.6	By grandparent
		E967.7	By other relative
		E967.8	By non-related caregiver
		E967.9	By unspecified person

*U.S. Department of Health and Human Services, Centers for Disease Control and Prevention, & National Center for Health Statistics, 1998.

Epidemiology

National incidence studies and the National Child Abuse and Neglect Data System (NCANDS) report contain over three million children reported for abuse and neglect annually, with more than fourteen hundred deaths. Other than documentation of fatalities and risks, however, information regarding the physical injuries and health effects of child abuse has only recently been systematically collected on a national basis. Given that child abuse and neglect affect one to two percent of children per year, this translates into two to four patients per month per pediatrician who will present for medical care because of victimization.

Physical abuse leads to hospitalization or death in 5-10 per 1,000 live births, with increased risk noted in families with teen parents, low parental education, substance abuse, and poverty. While overall pediatric traumatic brain injury (TBI) has been estimated at 60-80 per 100,000 children, inflicted TBI has been found in 27 per 100,000 children under age two years. We are beginning to use methods derived from economics to understand the medical and nonmedical costs of victimization.

Although the focus of concern about maltreatment is usually younger children, statistics show that 30 to 50% of all reported cases involve adolescents. In New York State in 1985, for example, there were 84,119 child maltreatment reports with substantiation rate of 35%. Within the adolescent reports, 19% were for physical abuse, 42.4% for sexual abuse, and the remainder for neglect. In 2002, there were 153,603 reports of child maltreatment in New York with a substantiation rate of 31.1%. Of those, children from ages 10-17 years accounted for 47.9 % (21,727 children) of the cases. Almost half (47%) of children entering foster care were over 10 years of age and approximately 75% remained in care for longer than one year. Based on other sources of information regarding adolescent behaviors, maltreatment is given as a comorbid factor in a spectrum of adolescent problems, such as substance abuse, truancy, runaways, and psychiatric disorders. Often there has been no disclosure of maltreatment prior to entry into such treatment programs, a fact that reflects the under-identification of cases in this age group.

The risk factors for child victimization are only now emerging. Despite the fact that the National Child Abuse and Neglect Data System (NCANDS) has over ten years of information from the states and there have been three independent national incidence studies, a complete epidemiologic picture of child abuse and neglect in the United States remains in its infancy. Race, for example, has been implicated to explain disparities in some outcomes and reporting. Several studies have assessed risk factors in specific populations for certain types of abuse, but a true longitudinal approach to understanding and preventing injuries from child victimization awaits the results of LONGSCAN, a longitudinal, multi-site study of maltreatment incidence and risk factors, originally sponsored by the National Center on Child Abuse and Neglect. Risk factors for infant deaths and abusive head trauma are being assessed in retrospective studies, but prospective incidence studies of inflicted traumatic brain injury have only recently been undertaken. Neglect continues to affect more than 50% of those children reported to child protective services. The parents of young neglected children were less likely to have completed high school, had more preschool children, and had less parenting skills and social support. Disability also doubles the risk of subsequent maltreatment.

While there are varying schools of thought on the origins of maltreatment, most theories of child maltreatment recognize that the root causes can be divided into four principal systems: (1) the child, (2) the family, (3) the community, and (4) society. While children are certainly not responsible for the abuse inflicted upon them, there are certain characteristics that have been found to increase the risk for maltreatment. Children with disabilities or mental retardation, for example, are significantly more likely to be abused. Evidence also suggests that age and gender are predictive of maltreatment risk. Younger children are more likely to be neglected, while the risk for sexual abuse increases with age. Female children and adolescents are significantly more likely than males to suffer sexual abuse.

Important characteristics of the family are linked with child maltreatment. Families in which there is a history of abuse of the parents or substance abuse are more likely to experience abuse or are at a higher risk of abuse. Recent studies have established a link between having a history of childhood abuse and becoming a victimizer later in life; childhood sexual abuse increased the risk of perpetrating physical abuse on children as adults. Domestic violence and lack of parenting or communication skills also increase the risks of maltreatment to children.

Community and social factors also play a role in child maltreatment. Poverty, for example, has been linked with maltreatment, particularly neglect, in each of the national incidence studies, and has been associated with child neglect, a strong predictor of substantiated child maltreatment. The following factors have been linked to child maltreatment: fewer friends in their social support networks, less contact with friends, and lower ratings of quality support received from friends. Violence and unemployment are other community-level variables that have been found to be associated with child maltreatment. Perhaps the least understood and studied level of child maltreatment is that of societal factors. Ecological theories postulate that factors such as the narrow legal definitions of child maltreatment, the social acceptance of violence (as evidenced by video games, television and films, and music lyrics), and political or religious views that value noninterference in families above all may be associated with child maltreatment.

Researchers have continued to explore why certain children with risk factors become victims and other children with the same factors do not become victims. What are the *protective* factors within children and families that appear to protect children from the risks of maltreatment? Child factors that may protect children include good health, above-average intelligence, hobbies or interests, good peer relationships, an easy temperament, a positive disposition, an active coping style, positive self-esteem, good social skills, an internal locus of control, and a balance between seeking help and autonomy. Parent and family protective factors that may protect children include secure attachment with children, parental reconciliation with their own childhood history of abuse, supportive family environment, household rules and monitoring of the child, extended family support, stable relationship with parents, family expectations of pro-social behavior, and high parental education. Social and environmental risk factors that may protect children include middle to high socioeconomic status, access to health care and social services, consistent parental employment, adequate housing, family participation in a religious faith, good schools, and supportive adults outside the family who serve as role models or mentors. Families with two married parents have more stable home environments, fewer years in poverty, and diminished material hardship.

Clinical Features

Several health effects of child maltreatment have been identified (Table 3). While there is considerable overlap, specific health effects and injuries are often related to a major subtype of child abuse.

Table 3. Physical Health Effects of Child Abuse and Neglect

Neurologic Handicap and Disability
    Mental retardation
    Cerebral palsy
    Hydrocephalus
    Seizures
    Developmental delays in language, cognition, learning
    Attention-Deficit Disorders with and without hyperactivity
    Blindness
    Deafness
    Inability to swallow, eat
    Weakness or loss of sensation
    Loss of posture, balance, or ambulation

Abdominal organ dysfunction
    Intestinal perforation, malabsorption, hemorrhage
    Jaundice from liver injury
    Toxemia from kidney failure
    Peritonitis
    Difficulties with defecation, soiling, encopresis, eneuresis

Other
    Skin infection, disfigurement, and scarring from lacerations and burns
    Loss of function, growth abnormalities, and disfigurement from bony fracture
    Infertility and genitourinary infections from trauma and sexually transmitted infections
    Premature Death

Physical Abuse

Physicians have intermittently noted specific injuries as stemming from abuse and neglect through the years, with early identification of maltreatment as a disease in the medical literature by John Caffey. In the 1950s, Woolley and Evans in Detroit noted the presence of significant injuries that were inconsistent with parental explanations. Discussions of diagnoses in the medical literature began to remark upon the types of injuries from physical abuse, with Silverman's identification of fractures and Henry Kempe's landmark article naming the "Battered Child Syndrome" prominent among them. Since that time, articles in the medical literature on maltreatment, escalating steadily in number, have concentrated on physical abuse in the 1960s and 1970s, sexual abuse and domestic violence in the late 1970s and 1980s, and neglect in the 1990s.

The leading cause of abusive mortality and morbidity is inflicted traumatic brain injury. With mortality rates of 10-20% and more than 90% of survivors having significant handicap, physical abuse to the head has been noted to have patterns of injuries that are distinct from accidental or medical causes. The evaluation of abusive head trauma and other injuries has been greatly enhanced by the development of specialized imaging and diagnostic techniques. This technology has allowed the medical community to better understand the wide range of injuries from child abuse and neglect (Table 3); New diagnostic technologies developed in the last century, from the x-ray to sophisticated computer-assisted imaging techniques such as CT or "CAT" scans and medical resonance imaging (MRI), have proved invaluable in visualizing internal bleeding and injury. Abdominal injuries compromise less than 10% of child abuse fatalities and are much more difficult to assess because of their occult nature, relative lack of bruising, and potential for significant delay in symptoms.

The most common physical injury from abuse is bruising. Key concepts in assessing bruising include comprehensive documentation regarding location, pattern, depth, and color. The aging of bruises in children has received considerable attention, and current guidelines are limited in their ability to precisely "date" when an injury occurred. Similar assessments of burns and other electrical and radiation injuries have also been identified for the detection of abuse. Specific patterns of fracture have been associated with physical abuse, and growing knowledge of abdominal and chest inflicted trauma has been sought to differentiate these often 'silent' injuries with potentially devastating consequences. Physicians have increasingly honed their skills in medical photography and imaging to better depict injuries and provide more precise clinical documentation of those injuries for use by the child welfare and legal systems.

Sexual Abuse

Sexual abuse has been defined as sexual contact or exploitation of children by adults, which cannot be consented to by the child and which violate social laws or taboos. *Sexual assault* is a comprehensive term encompassing several types of forced sexual activity, while the term *molestation* means non-coital sexual activity between a child and an adolescent or adult. *Rape* is defined as forced sexual intercourse with vaginal, oral or anal penetration by the offender. *A*cquaintance or *date rape* apply when the assailant and victim know each other. *Statutory rape* involves sexual penetration of a minor by an adult as defined in state law, regardless of assent.

The prime injury of sexual abuse is emotional. While most young children with proven sexual abuse have few physical injuries, patterns of anogenital injury and sexually transmitted diseases have been identified. Several large case series have been published, highlighting the normalcy of most examinations and the effects of healing. Assessing sexual abuse requires detailed knowledge of anogenital anatomy and STDs in children, both of which have important differences from adults, and specialized skills and examination techniques have had to be developed. It has become apparent that most physicians have little knowledge about prepubertal genital anatomy and cannot identify key landmarks. When confronted with concerns of potential sexual abuse, the pediatrician should obtain key elements of the history, such as type, frequency and timing of contact and physically assess the child for gross injuries or infection. Definitive assessment and treatment is increasingly handled by referral to pediatricians with specialized experience in testing, interpretation and documentation of anogenital findings. The development of a subspecialty of pediatrics called "Child Abuse Pediatrics" has added additional expertise in areas of clinical diagnostics, such as the performance of forensic interviewing, colposcopy and videocolposcopy.

The issues surrounding sexual abuse are compounded during adolescence. In surveys of high school students, over 25% reported that they have experienced unwanted sexual contact; in clinical populations, the rates are even higher. Repeated sexual contact and pregnancy places teenagers at increased risk for several health harms. Repeated sexual contact has been associated with younger ages of sexual initiation, higher rates of depression, anxiety, substance abuse and delinquency. Most adolescent rape and sexual assault is perpetrated by an acquaintance or relative of the adolescent, with younger adolescents having assailants more likely from the extended family. Increased rates of sexual assault are seen in adolescents with disabilities, alcohol use and other family dysfunction. Males are less likely to report sexual assault, less likely to receive treatment, and more likely to become perpetrators themselves after being victimized than are female adolescents.

Psychological Maltreatment

Psychological maltreatment (PM) is commonly associated with other forms of abuse but may also occur in isolation in a small number of cases. By definition, PM is a repeated pattern of interaction between a parent and child that harms the child's emotional well-being. Spurning, belittling, degrading, ridiculing, or shaming a child is considered harming a child's self-worth. Terrorizing and otherwise exploiting the child increases the harm further. The shear denial of emotional closeness leads to physical and developmental delays in young children and failure to thrive in infants. Rejection, isolation, and inconsistent parenting styles lead children to feel insecure in their home and relationships. An emerging form of PM occurs when a child witnesses violence in the home, including spousal violence, community violence, or even violence on television or movies.

Increasingly, behavioral problems, depression, post-traumatic stress and other problems are being identified after PM. The true prevalence is not known, but less than 10% of reports in the United States detail PM. Its impact may lead to juvenile delinquency, depression or mental illness in adolescence or be more severe during adulthood. Parental factors contributing to PM include poor parenting skills, inappropriate expectations, substance abuse, psychological problems, poor social skills, lack of empathy, social stress, domestic violence and other family dysfunction. Children at increased risk are those in families with divorce or separation, with an unwanted pregnancy, with behavior problems, or with physical or emotional delays, or who are socially isolated or emotionally handicapped. Psychological neglect has been significantly associated with behavior problems and poor cognitive development, even while controlling for poverty.

Neglect

Child neglect is the most common form of child maltreatment, affecting 50% or more of children reported annually to Child Protective Services. Dr. Ray Helfer reminded pediatricians about the significant harms caused by the 'litany of smoldering neglect' and the de-emphasis of neglect that has caused mandated reporters to have second thoughts about reporting neglect because little, if anything, could supposedly be done by overwhelmed, understaffed child protective services agencies. Neglect is the omission or lack of a minimal level of care by the parents or caretakers that results in actual or potential harm to the child. Neglect is often associated with poverty, but poor families are not necessarily neglectful. Many subtypes of neglect often occur concurrently, but our understanding of its outcome is often aided by identifying subtypes that can direct potential interventions. Physical neglect is the lack of food, clothing or shelter; emotional neglect is a form of psychological maltreatment, and educational neglect refers to the lack of proper educational resources. Pediatricians are most likely to identify and treat medical care neglect and failure to thrive resulting in illness.

The morbidity and mortality associated with neglect are substantial. Although poorly identified on death certificates, child death review teams consistently identify supervisional and other forms of neglect as causing as many or more deaths from physical abuse. Physical conditions caused by neglect include injuries, ingestions, inadequately treated illnesses, dental problems, malnutrition, and neurological and developmental deficits. Manifestations in neglectful families include noncompliance or non-adherence to medical recommendations, delay or failure in seeking appropriate health care, hunger, failure to thrive and unmanaged morbid obesity, poor hygiene and physical and medical conditions contributing to poor cognitive and educational achievement. Poor supervision is less defined but has been broken down into broad categories, consisting of not watching the child closely enough, inadequate substitute child care, failure to protect from third parties, knowingly allowing the child to participate in harmful activities, and driving recklessly or while intoxicated. A comprehensive response requires that the pediatrician address the actual or potential harms that have occurred to the child and to make appropriate referrals to a myriad of community services to address a variety of social and economic issues in the family.

Special Issues for Adolescents

Pediatricians should be knowledgeable about legal definitions and reporting requirements; they also should provide preventive counseling and screen adolescents for a history of assault and potential emotional effects. They should be knowledgeable about the physical findings associated with sexual assault and testing for STDs and pregnancy and be able to provide these services or refer the adolescent to other providers in the community. There has been considerable growth in treatments available for victims of child abuse and neglect, but adolescents face the additional burdens of developing risk-taking behaviors, paraphilias or becoming perpetrators as the result of their victimization, if not appropriately treated. Sexual abuse, in particular, appears to be a strong risk factor for subsequent perpetration, influencing adolescents and young adults to develop an orientation that is abusive to other children. An adolescent's exposure to a pervasive atmosphere of violence in the home is a key risk factor of future perpetration and suggests the need to address the specific behaviors and risks in the child as well as the overall environment.

There is a proper focus on the need to confront offending behavior while taking into account the developing cognitive and social abilities of the adolescent. Sex offenders report more histories of maltreatment, both physical and sexual, compared to generally conduct-disordered young people. Thus, any treatments must take into account the adolescent's victimization as well as their developing patterns of perpetration and their environment. When young people are identified as being responsible for committing abusive acts against others, it is essential to assess and intervene in their own victimization experiences to prevent post-traumatic stress and other emotional effects. Pediatricians need to be sensitive to the psychological needs of the adolescent and provide initial psychological support after sexual assault while making referrals to appropriate mental health professionals and community resources for longer-term assessment and counseling.

Diagnosis

At a minimum, the clinician caring for children should be able to recognize and report potential child maltreatment using standard methods of obtaining history, physical examination and selected laboratory and imaging tests. This clinician must also be cognizant that multiple forms of maltreatment may co-exist, understand the importance of certain risk factors, assist in choosing the appropriate location and timing of evaluation, and appropriately refer children and families to specialized medical and social services. In health care, a clinical assessment of child victimization begins with a medical encounter that usually follows information-gathering, physical assessment, testing, and clinical diagnosis followed by treatment and referral (Table 4).

Medical history, a cornerstone of medical diagnosis, plays the most important part in the diagnosis of child abuse and neglect. It is the history, taken with the physical examination findings and imaging studies, that offers a sound basis for diagnosis and treatment recommendations for the child and family. First, the main reason for the medical encounter or "chief complaint" is recorded from the child or family, followed by delineation of appropriate elements of the medical history. Inquiring and recording the specific complaints and disclosures of maltreatment by the child and parent, if any, in their own words is vitally important to the ultimate protection of the child. Behavioral and emotional issues are important in this assessment. Certain non-specific behaviors, developmental delays, and history of abuse should be recorded as part of the medical history; this history aids in assessing harm and planning for appropriate treatment. A simple set of screening questions for use during the general pediatric encounter has been developed but has yet to be widely implemented.

Table 4. Medical Diagnostic Evaluation in Child Victimization Emphasizing Identification of Cause and Sequelae of Physical Injury

History	Questions asked by healthcare professionals of the child and caretakers during medical encounter
Chief Complaint	Why are you here today?
History of Present Illness	– Circumstances surrounding injury – Physical symptoms such as pain, bleeding, sensory problems – Events leading to seeking medical care – Timing
Past History	– Prior medical treatments, surgery, medications, hospitalizations, mental health services – Prior evaluations for victimization – Chronic medical conditions, particularly bleeding, neurologic, metabolic, growth disorders, fractures – Immunizations received – Known allergies – Psychosocial history (caretakers, school attendance, housing, income, family structure)
Physical Examination	– Done by the physician, nurse, or other practitioner based on history – Vital signs (pulse, respiration rate, height, weight, head circumference, Glasgow Coma Scale, pain scale) – Skin (bruising, burns, pattern marks, contusions, tenderness) – Head (presence of skin swelling, bruising, skull deformity, fontanels) – Eyes (pupillary response, sclera, retina, periorbital tissues) – Ears (earlobes, canals, tympanic membranes) – Nose (bleeding, nares, deformity) – Mouth, throat (condition of teeth, tonsils, pharynx, frenula) – Neck (flexibility, lymph glands, thyroid) – Chest (rib deformities, air movement and congestion, tenderness) – Heart (heart sounds, rhythm) – Abdomen (tenderness, organ swelling, bowel sounds) – Genitals (penis, scrotum, testes, urethra in males; labia, hymen, urethra, vagina in females) – Anorectal (perineum, internal and external anal sphincters, ruggal folds, tone) – Extremities (movement, tenderness, swelling, joint involvement, pulses, ambulation) – Neurological (alertness, reflexes, muscular strength and tone, cranial nerves, sensation)

Laboratory	– Tests performed as indicated by history and physical findings – Complete blood count (white and red blood cells, hematocrit, platelet counts) – Coagulation studies (prothrombin, partial thromboplastin times, fibrinogen, platelet function) – Blood chemistries, liver function tests – X-rays of affected areas or skeletal survey of all bones for children less than two years – Computer-assisted tomography (CT) scan of brain or other affected part – Magnetic Resonance Imaging (MRI) of head or other affected part – Specialized metabolic tests (collagen, organic and amino acids, others) – Microbiologic cultures and tests for sexually transmitted infections – Collection of forensic trace specimens (less than 72-96 hours after contact) – Pregnancy testing (depending on sexual development and potential contact)
Diagnosis and Treatment	– Identification of disease or sequelae of trauma – Hospitalization for further diagnostic assessment or treatment (based on severity of illness/injury and/or need for surgical or supportive care) – Reassurance and emotional support – Referral for ongoing medical and mental health treatment – CPS reporting and provision for immediate safety needs and protection

The health care professional then examines the child using a variety of techniques and procedures that, while gleaned from adult medicine, have been specifically adapted to meet the special needs of children. In cases of child victimization, the content and methods used to obtain the patient's history and the techniques used for physical examination are further specialized to concentrate on areas of increased risk and the types of suspected maltreatment.

The examining practitioner then arrives at an assessment or diagnosis, usually utilizing schema of diagnostic categories, such as the International Classification of Disease or a specialized diagnostic scheme for certain types of abuse. This presumptive diagnosis leads the practitioner to request diagnostic tests for the child, such as x-rays, blood work, or microbiologic cultures, if such tests are indicated. The presumptive diagnosis also leads the practitioner at the time of the encounter to begin treatment of any acute injury, prevent disease, ensure protection of the child from further harm, and arrange referrals to appropriate physical or mental health specialists for further evaluation and treatment. Unique to child maltreatment diagnosis is a consideration of certainty. A low level of certainty is required to meet general standards of a 'reasonable cause to suspect' that maltreatment has occurred for mandated reporting.

Treatment

Pediatricians have historically had an important role in the assessment and reporting of suspected child abuse and neglect, while mental health professionals, community, and government services have been responsible for treatment and prevention activities. Medical professionals have had a long history of evaluating children and participating as team members in the interdisciplinary assessment of child maltreatment. Abraham Jacobi, a forefather of modern pediatric medicine, joined the Committee for the Prevention of Cruelty to Children in New York City in 1878. These early child welfare advocacy efforts in the United States highlighted the physical and emotional effects of abuse, which resulted in the creation of multidisciplinary committees to address this multidimensional problem. These committees consisted of social workers, physicians, nurses, and other child advocates. A key element of pediatric involvement is the pediatrician's understanding of child development, how injuries occur accidentally and non-accidentally, basic concepts of good parenting, and other family violence, such as intimate partner violence and elder abuse. In a recent survey, two-thirds of pediatricians reported treating injuries from child abuse, two-thirds had treated injuries from other community violence, and [one-half] treated injuries related to domestic violence. Pediatricians assist the community response to child abuse and neglect by collaborating with community agencies (such as child advocacy centers and social services agencies) and governmental entities (such as police and child protective services) that have the resources, responsibility, and authority to protect and improve the lives of child victims. Nurses have been increasingly called upon to perform more than routine nursing services in the evaluation of suspected abuse. For example, "Sexual Assault Nurse Examiners" or "SANE" nurses have provided medical examinations for the collection of forensic evidence of suspected sexual and physical assault; in addition, some nurses also visit homes of new parents to help reduce the risk of child maltreatment.

Reporting

The practice of health care professionals is regulated by a series of laws in the states' public health statutes and through licensing requirements specific to individual disciplines. Pediatricians have legal responsibilities to report their concerns of child abuse and neglect to appropriate state agencies in all fifty states in the United States. Although the forms of the legislation vary from state to state, these "child protection laws" stipulate that certain professionals must report their concerns of child abuse and neglect to appropriate governmental agencies. The reporting requirements of these laws supersede the confidentiality of medical records and the patient-provider relationship. The "mandated reporters" generally include physicians, nurses, and other professionals working in hospitals, in addition to a variety of other licensed professionals who include teachers, counselors, law enforcement officers, and mental health professionals. Specific protections are usually given for reports made "in good faith," and certain penalties are listed for the failure to report when child maltreatment would "reasonably" have been suspected.

It is important to note that child abuse reporting is one of the few instances in which health care professionals are required to contact a governmental agency in the routine course of their practice. While disease reporting has traditionally existed within public health (particularly when a contagious infection may pose a hazard to the community's health), reporting actions that are deemed to be "crimes" has historically been less accepted by the medical community. Less clear statutory requirements have been enacted in the United States for the reporting of victimization of elderly, vulnerable adults and of domestic violence. Physicians have historically underreported suspected maltreatment. Several reasons have been identified for this failure, such as fear of losing patients, distaste for the legal system and liability concerns. Penalties for not reporting range from fines in some states to criminal charges in others, but also include civil penalties so that the child and/or the child's family may litigate to redress financial losses sustained because maltreatment was not reported. Recent federal legislation in the United States specifically allows child abuse reporting and exempts such state reporting laws from HIPAA requirements.

Reporting child victimization to governmental agencies begins an investigation to identify the presence or absence of "evidence" to support or "substantiate" the suspicions. Requirements vary from state to state and no national criteria exist for determining whether to report suspected abuse or neglect. General guidelines have been suggested that include the patient meeting the definition of being a child, the act or omission having been committed by the parent or caretaker, the history is inconsistent with the injury, or the features of an episode fulfill other criteria for abuse or neglect in the medical record. Multiple missed medical appointments, unreasonable delay in seeking medical treatment, abandonment, illnesses that could be prevented by routine medical care, and inadequate care have been identified as potential minimal criteria for a neglect report. Fractures, soft tissue injuries of normally protected body parts, inflicted traumatic brain injury and witnessed physical injury caused by the caretaker indicate cause to suspect physical abuse. Statements made by the child or parent disclosing potential sexual contact with a caretaker or contrary to state law, certain anogenital injuries, and sexually-transmitted infection are generally a basis for diagnosing suspected sexual abuse.

Physical Abuse

Several physical findings have been noted in child abuse and neglect (Table 3). Recognition and documentation of bruises, burns and other skin lesions requires complete undressing of the child and comprehensive physical examination. Skin lesions should describe location, size, color, depth, and integrity of the epidermis and may be documented using notes, hand-drawn diagrams or photographs; law enforcement and child protection workers often have resources to assure high quality photodocumentation. Even if photographs are taken, the pediatrician should also contemporaneously document skin injuries identified. Additionally, specific statements by the family and child should also be copied verbatim in the medical chart for potential use later in the legal system. In the case of bruising, standard coagulation tests should be ordered to objectively assess to platelet count and function as well as coagulation factors. Suspicion of internal injury requires medical imaging, with computerized tomography generally used for abdomen, chest and acute head trauma, and magnetic resonance imaging indicated for less acute or chronic head and soft tissue imaging. Plain radiographs continue to be important to better document skull and body fractures and should be ordered with head CT or MRI when skull or extracranial injury is suspected. In the presence of skin injury, a survey of several bones is indicated to identify additional 'silent' trauma. Protocols have been developed to direct the physician and radiologist as to the number, type, and repetition of dedicated x-ray images required for such child abuse skeletal surveys. Abnormalities in serologic tests for liver function have been correlated with inflicted abdominal trauma, and new serologic markers are being identified for TBI.

Sexual Abuse

Clinicians caring for sexual abuse victims should be trained in the procedures required for documentation and collection of evidence and the steps to minimize the child from further victimization. They should inquire about psychological traits and behaviors; also, there should be specific inquiry about the types and timing of reported sexual contact. The examination begins with a comprehensive general examination followed by detailed visualization of the genitals, anus and oral cavity. New procedures such as colposcopy and videocolposcopy offer a way to better document and record trauma, to allow the child to be more relaxed and cooperative during examination, and to begin the process of emotional healing. While it is beyond the scope of this chapter to detail all of the findings associated with sexual abuse, recent research suggests that only limited findings have high specificity, such as lacerations and transections of the hymen and bruising or other injury to the anus and genitals. Several findings which were once thought to indicate trauma are now considered non-specific, accidentally acquired, or congenital variations.

While all STIs should raise the suspicion of possible sexual contact, infections with *Neisseria gonorrhea* and *Treponema pallidum* are most specific for mucosal sexual contact and must generally be reported. The presence of STIs needs to be evaluated on a case-by-case basis, and the possibility of non-sexual or vertical transmission ruled out. Other infections to be considered include *Chlamydia trachomatis*, Trichomonas species, herpes simplex virus, human papilloma virus, human immunodeficiency virus and hepatitis B virus. The clinician should be knowledgeable about the potential sources of infection, body sites, types of contact and testing strategies before treatment eradicates microbiologic evidence, the need to collect forensic trace evidence (especially within 24-72 hours after contact), and to carefully consider the types and timing of any prophylaxis for STI or pregnancy based on the age and development of the child, the type and timing of contact, and the risk factors for disease in the alleged perpetrator.

Neglect and Non-Organic Failure to Thrive

Management of neglect first centers on properly identifying the sources contributing to neglect. For example, while malnutrition is medically addressed through proper provision of fluids, calories, and protein as dictated by commonly accepted parameters, the pediatrician must also assess the lack of appropriate food, the provision of that food to the child, and the explanation, if any, as to why it was not provided. Important screening questions that can elicit further avenues of intervention include inquiring about the family's access to food, their access to appropriate medical and dental services and medicines, substance abuse during and after pregnancy, homelessness, housing and environmental safety, depression, domestic violence, and degree of supervision.

Failure to thrive, otherwise known as the lack of normal physiological development, is associated with malnutrition in infancy, and has historically been grouped into organic, non-organic (NOFTT), and mixed varieties. NOFTT is more realistically called malnutrition due to neglect. To the extent that many cases fall into the mixed category, it is important to sort out the contribution of neglect in a particular case. While a full discussion of the evaluation of NOFTT is beyond the scope of this chapter, it is important to emphasize that the findings on a comprehensive history and physical examination should guide management and initial laboratory testing. In the face of normal basic metabolic requirements, a careful observation of parental feeding practices and the child's intake and output is often illuminating. Height and weight need to be precisely measured over multiple visits and compared to currently accepted norms, some of which are modified by race, prematurity or other medical conditions. With acceptable weight gain under direct observation and lack of significant medical cause for malnutrition, a presumptive diagnosis of NOFTT can be made and community services put in place.

Psychological Effects

The psychological effects of maltreatment may be very difficult to recognize in the medical office. Sometimes the poor parent-child relationship is seen and the verbal stigmata of PM exposed, but often there are little or no physical findings demonstrating the emotional harm, other than weight loss or excessive weight gain. The quiet, depressed child is not often identified as a victim of neglect as readily as is the hyperactive, aggressive child. The pediatrician needs to evaluate the harm or potential harm to the child's mental health, while realizing that it many take several years for such harm to become apparent, and that the effects are often confounded with exposure to other violence. Documentation must be objective, with appropriate use of psychological tests and mental health referrals in the evaluation. Behavioral changes in the child are early but non-specific events, and assessment should include multiple domains, including function at home, school and at play. The psychological effects of malnutrition are further modified by the intensity, type, frequency, and severity of exposure as well as the developmental stage and resiliency of the child.

Medical-Legal Certainty and Predictive Values

Medical diagnosis of child abuse and neglect follows commonly-accepted practices for other medical diagnosis. Pediatricians should consult current Clinical Procedural Terminology for coding for encounters and International Classification of Disease codes for diagnosis. While the use of such coding does not guarantee reimbursement, it highlights the standard approach to maltreatment as a concern of the health care system and allows collection of population data from hospital discharge and emergency department databases.

One key difference of child abuse diagnosis is the concept of medical certainty. Given the medical-legal nature of these cases, a clinician's documentation must also support the 'reasonable degree of medical certainty' under which the diagnosis is made to support treatment recommendations. As clinicians make medical diagnoses based on history and physical examination findings in non-abuse cases, they should use similar but perhaps more detailed documentation to support the diagnosis of abuse or neglect. One method for sexual abuse assessment, for example, uses the concepts of definitive evidence, probable, possible or no evidence for sexual abuse. The clinician should also be aware of the specificity and predictive value of key elements of the history and physical examination. While a discussion of Bayesian analysis is beyond the scope of this chapter, child care clinicians should familiarize themselves with the basic concepts of epidemiology to better understand the predictive factors of case characteristics in children presenting for maltreatment assessment.

The ultimate and perhaps most important action to protect a child from further victimization is going to court. Physicians and other health care providers are routinely called to provide information regarding their medical evaluation of children, particularly with regard to statements made by the child, the medical history obtained, and any findings of physical examination. While giving testimony in court, physicians and other health care professionals are often asked their opinion, "within a reasonable degree of medical certainty," concerning the diagnosis of child abuse and neglect or victimization. Significant differences exist between standards for medical diagnosis and those for civil or criminal adjudication. Medical diagnosis is defined as "the act of distinguishing one disease from another" or "the determination of the nature of a case of disease." A constellation of the patient's history, physical examination, and laboratory findings may result in multiple diagnoses, which may lead the practitioner to a treatment plan without 100 percent or even probable certainty after diagnosis. These criteria differ significantly from legal standards, by which a level of certainty must be carefully crafted to include "credible" evidence, a "preponderance" of evidence, "clear and convincing" evidence, or evidence "beyond a reasonable doubt." These standards of evidence in the legal system are defined by a state's case law and/or statute and are distinct from those in medical practice, where the certainty of medical diagnosis may be "possible," "probable," or "definitive." Differences in interpretation of certainty lead to difficulty in communication between legal and medical practitioners.

Court appearance and testimony, while inconvenient, is vital to provide the evidence and opinion for the state to take action to protect children. Recently, testimony provided by physicians has been considered part of medical practice, and providing "irresponsible testimony" may have negative repercussions for a physician's practice. Despite the legal system's need for health care professionals to provide evidence in maltreatment cases, it is relatively uncommon for health care professionals to be required to attend court hearings, even if they specialize in caring for maltreated children.

Other Steps to Protect Children

Several strategies have been reported for primary care provider assessment of child abuse in the outpatient setting. Primary care physicians often have first contact with children who are maltreatment victims and have the greatest opportunities to identify, treat, and report child abuse and neglect and to prevent further maltreatment. The average pediatrician, for example, may see thirty to forty children per day, four to six days a week, resulting in 3,000 to 5,000 patient visits per year. Primary care providers have the added advantage of having extended or longitudinal contact with families and have the opportunity to understand the more global medical and mental health needs of the adults as well as the children in a family. Children who do not have an identified primary care provider are more likely to be identified as victims of maltreatment.

Beyond the traditional medical model, multidisciplinary teams have been formed in many institutions to address the issues of assessment, training, education, and research at specialized institutions such as children's hospitals and universities. The first such "child protection teams" were formed in the 1950s in San Diego and Colorado, and many children's hospitals and university settings now utilize some form of a child protection team to coordinate and provide services for children, both within the hospital; early research suggests such teams decrease needless referrals to CPS.

Communities have several mechanisms by which health care professionals can intervene in response to child victimization. Once children have been identified as being victims, several community organizations can utilize the experiences of health care practitioners in their assessment. Child Protective Services, with the ultimate responsibility for the protection of victims of child abuse and neglect, can employ the services of medical practitioners through direct contact or by way of community participation, as in multidisciplinary team reviews. These reviews, which are usually protected by statute for family privacy and confidentiality of team discussions, enable the health care professional to provide a unique perspective on the child's medical conditions. Health care professionals can also provide expert knowledge to aid in the assessment of actual or potential harm to the child. Various strategies have been devised to provide medical services to child protective services agencies.

Many such services occur in what are now called "child advocacy centers." Child advocacy centers (or CACs) began in the 1980s to provide specialized services for children, usually for concerns of sexual abuse. The CAC model utilizes professionals from a variety of disciplines, including police, child protective services agencies, social services, counselors, physicians, and nurses to provide "a coordinated response" to child abuse in a community. CACs generally have a law enforcement or Child Protective Services focus in their investigations, but have increasingly involved medical professionals and medical services. These centers have developed both within and separate from hospitals, and there is early evidence suggesting that CACs increase the number of children receiving medical evaluations and improve legal outcomes.

Training and Education

Health care professionals have a unique role in the training of child welfare professionals, law enforcement and child protection services workers and all professionals who manage the day-to-day care of children. To fulfill their mandatory roles in reporting child abuse and neglect, teachers, child development specialists, mental health workers and others who provide daycare, education, and counseling services need to understand the medical manifestations of child victimization. They also need to identify the physical as well as emotional signs of abuse and neglect so that they can provide the optimal outcome for children in their care. Professionals from a variety of health care disciplines provide specialized training at a national level for medical and nonmedical providers through multidisciplinary organizations such as the American Professional Society on the Abuse of Children (APSAC) or medical organizations such as the American Academy of Pediatrics (AAP). Additionally, various child protective service agencies and university programs render services to nonmedical providers and offer information about medical issues related to child victimization. National conferences sponsored by the International Society for the Prevention of Child Abuse and Neglect and APSAC also offer nonmedical providers training in recognizing and confronting medical manifestations of child abuse. Statewide conferences such as those sponsored by the San Diego Children's Hospital, the Children's Advocacy Centers in Huntsville, Alabama, the Midwest Child Advocacy Center in Minneapolis, and universities frequently provide specialized training in medical topics for nonmedical professionals. Such training and licensure requirements have also been used as a means to improve reporting by mandated professionals.

Prevention

The prevention of child abuse and neglect ultimately rests with the family, but pediatricians and the community can still play important roles preventing abuse from occurring. Local county councils for the prevention of child abuse and neglect sponsor programs; social service agencies provide childcare or foster care, and state departments of social services have the legal authority to investigate suspected child maltreatment. Community approaches, such as home visitation, parenting classes, certain cognitive behavioral therapies for children, and parent-child interaction therapy, have been shown to be effective in changing parents' behavior, and reducing social isolation and stress, particularly in families at risk for maltreatment. Society and our global community have realized the international effects of child maltreatment and have further articulated basic standards and prevention strategies. Clinicians play an important role in identifying risk factors and potential maltreatment and linking families with these services.

Sexual assault and rape prevention strategies begin with the child and family being able to identify and avoid high-risk situations and immediately reporting potential sexual contact. Pediatricians and others can provide screening for victims of domestic violence during routine medical history and can provide guidance and strategies to prevent or minimize abuse (such as avoiding late night use of alcohol or drugs or seeking immediate medical care after assault). School-based information programs have shown some promise in preventing and reporting sexual abuse, but are more effective for elementary students. Pediatricians have the ability to explain child development and the special health needs of children, particularly those with chronic medical conditions, to the community and to provide the scientific background and structure for the implementation and evaluation of community programs such as nursery head trauma programs. Prenatal clinics and other services for high-risk adolescents need to provide primary care interventions to prevent future maltreatment.

Clinicians should also screen for maltreatment during regular health maintenance visits and provide anticipatory guidance regarding violence prevention. They can provide children and families with tools to prevent abuse and neglect from happening in the first place and to stop revictimization after maltreatment has already occurred. Clinicians can provide developmentally appropriate anticipatory guidance about the dangers of psychological aggression by modeling healthy parenting approaches in the office. They can provide educational brochures with age-appropriate materials regarding discipline, body safety, and parenting skills. They can teach parents that children need consistent love, acceptance and attention, and community support. Finally, they can offer referrals to services that have been shown to improve long-term outcomes, such as cognitive behavioral, group, and parent-child interaction therapies.

Pediatricians may also participate in multidisciplinary reviews after the abuse or death of a child. The "child death review" movement (CDR) began in 1978 as a response to the serious and significant misidentification of child abuse deaths in vital statistics records. The state of Missouri recognized that most or many child abuse fatalities were not properly labeled as such and began a movement to identify the cause of child abuse fatality correctly and to prevent additional deaths through child death review.

Conclusion

Pediatricians and other child care clinicians play a vital role in the assessment, care, and treatment of victims of child abuse and neglect. Physicians, nurses, and other health professionals have historically identified the physical injuries of victimization and have developed increasingly sophisticated techniques for diagnosing and documenting physical abuse, abusive head trauma, Shaken Baby Syndrome, fractures, anogenital trauma, and sexually transmitted infections. They have integrated such diagnostic findings with referral to specialized services. They are using diagnostic methods to provide information for the community to take additional steps to protect children. They are important members of the crew of the 'lifeboat' needed to save children in the sometimes turbulent 'ocean of life.'

While C. Henry Kempe first taught us about the battered child in 1962 and Ray E. Helfer showed the importance of understanding a child's perspective in 1984, we still have a long way to go in solving the problems of child neglect and victimization in our communities. Many segments of our population do not understand the impact of higher rates of poverty, unique health concerns, and other special circumstances of children. Our response to the needs of abused and neglected children requires earnest dedication by all medical professionals in clinical care, training, research, and advocacy to identify, treat, and prevent the devastating physical and emotional consequences of child victimization.

An emerging area of research involves designing and evaluating health services for victimized children. Such "health services research" offers the opportunity to study the types of such services, their accessibility, costs, and ability to provide specialized care for child victims and children in foster care. This type of research can examine and evaluate the effectiveness of certain types of services and compare different settings such as inpatient hospitalization, emergency departments, offices, and child advocacy centers. For example, little is known about the recurrence of abuse after hospitalization and recent studies are just beginning to explore the factors associated with reabuse after medical intervention. What services are most effective in decreasing the risk of future maltreatment and improving developmental and emotional outcomes? Are diagnosis and treatment best provided by primary care physicians or by specialists? Do child abuse pediatricians, for example, truly offer better care as compared to generalists, or is there really no difference in outcome for the child? Does reporting suspected abuse and providing prevention services reduce further victimization and other harm? While various programs have been designed to integrate medical services in the child welfare system, what is their effectiveness? Few prospective studies have reported outcomes after child welfare interventions such as foster care and mandated child abuse reporting systems through child protective services agencies. The opportunity exists for medical professionals to make important contributions in this non-traditional area of medical research that can improve the lives of children and adolescents.

References

Aberle, N., Ratkovic-Blazevic, V., Mitrovic-Dittrich, D., Coha, R., Stoic, A., Bublic, J., et al. (2007). Emotional and physical abuse in family: survey among high school adolescents. *Croatian. Medical Journal, 48*(2), 240-248.

Adams, J. A. (1997). Sexual abuse and adolescents. *Pediatric Annals, 26*, 299-304.

Adams, J. A., Harper, K., Knudson, S., and Revilla, J. (1994). Examination findings in legally-confirmed child sexual abuse: It's normal to be normal. *Pediatrics, 94*, 310-317.

Adams, J. A., Kaplan, R. A., Starling, S. P., Mehta, N. H., Finkel, M. A., Botash, A. S., et al. (2007). Guidelines for medical care of children who may have been sexually abused. *Journal of Pediatric and Adolescent Gynecology, 20*, 163-172.

American Academy of Pediatrics. (1966). Maltreatment of children: The physically abused child. *Pediatrics, 37*, 377-381.

American Academy of Pediatrics. (1993). Shaken baby syndrome: Inflicted cerebral trauma. *Pediatrics, 92*, 872-875.

American Academy of Pediatrics. (1996). Adolescent assault victim needs: A review of issues in a model protocol. *Pediatrics, 98*, 991-1001.

American Academy of Pediatrics. (1998a). Gonorrhea in prepubertal children. *Pediatrics, 101*, 134-135.

American Academy of Pediatrics. (1998b). The role of home visitation programs in improving health outcomes for children and families. *Pediatrics, 101*, 486-489.

American Academy of Pediatrics. (1998c). The role of the pediatrician in recognizing and intervening on behalf of abused women. *Pediatrics, 101*, 1091-1092.

American Academy of Pediatrics. (2001a). American pediatrics: Milestones at the millennium. *Pediatrics, 107*, 1482-1491.

American Academy of Pediatrics. (2001b). Care of the adolescent sexual assault victim. *Pediatrics, 107*, 1476-1479.

American Academy of Pediatrics. (2001c). Shaken Baby Syndrome: Rotational Cranial InjuriesTechnical Report. *Pediatrics, 108*, 206-210.

American Academy of Pediatrics. (2002). When skin injuries constitute child abuse. *Pediatrics, 110*, 644-645.

American Academy of Pediatrics, Section on Radiology. (1991). Diagnostic imaging of child abuse. *Pediatrics, 87*, 262-264.

American Academy of Pediatrics, Task Force on Violence. (1999). The role of the pediatrician in youth violence prevention in clinical practice and at the community level. *Pediatrics, 103*, 173-181.

American Medical Association. (1985). AMA diagnostic and treatment guidelines concerning child abuse and neglect. *Journal of the American Medical Association, 254*, 796-800.

American Psychiatric Association. (2000). *Diagnostic and Statistical Manual of Mental Disorders (DSM-IV-TR®)* (4th ed.). Arlington, VA: American Psychiatric Publishing Inc.

Ammerman, R. T., Hersen, M., and Hasselt, V. (1989). Abuse and neglect in psychiatrically hospitalized, multihandicapped children. *Child Abuse and Neglect, 13*, 335-343.

Anne E. Casey Foundation. (2001). *Kids Count Data Book: State Profiles of Child Well-being, 2000*. Baltimore, MD: Anne E. Casey Foundation.

Ards, S., and Harrell, A. (1993). Reporting of child maltreatment: A secondary analysis of the national incidence surveys. *Child Abuse and Neglect, 17*, 337-344.

Arizona Child Fatality Review Team. (2001). Annual Report [Electronic Version]. Retrieved September 14, 2001.

Barnes, P. M., Norton, C. M., Dunstan, F. D., Kemp, A. M., Yates, D. W., and Sibert, J. R. (2005). Abdominal injury due to child abuse. *Lancet, 366*, 234-235.

Bays, J., and Chadwick, D. (1993). Medical diagnosis of the sexually abused child. *Child Abuse and Neglect, 17*, 91-110.

Bechtel, K., and Podrazik, M. (1999). Evaluation of the adolescent rape victim. *Pediatric Clinics of North America, 46*, 809-823.

Bennett, M. D., Jr., Hall, J., Frazier, L., Jr., Patel, N., Barker, L., and Shaw, K. (2006). Homicide of children aged 0-4 years, 2003-04: results from the National Violent Death Reporting System. *Injury Prevention, 12 Suppl 2*, ii39-ii43.

Bentovin, A. (2002). Preventing sexually abused young people from becoming abusers, and treating the victimization experiences of young people who offend sexually. *Child Abuse and Neglect, 26*, 661-678.

Berger, R. P., Hymel, K., and Gao, W. (2006). The Use of Biomarkers After Inflicted Traumatic Brain Injury: Insight into Etiology, Pathophysiology, and Biochemistry. *Clinical Pediatric Emergency Medicine, 7*, 186-193.

Berger, R. P., Kochanek, P. M., and Pierce, M. C. (2004). Biochemical markers of brain injury: Could they be used as diagnostic adjuncts in cases of inflicted traumatic brain injury? *Child Abuse and Neglect, 28*(7), 739-754.

Black, D. A., Heyman, R. E., and Smith, A. M. (2001). Risk factors for child physical abuse. *Aggression and Violent Behavior, 6*, 121-188.

Black, M. M., Dubowitz, H., Casey, P. H., Cutts, D., Drewett, R. F., Drotar, D., et al. (2006). Failure to thrive as distinct from child neglect. *Pediatrics, 117*(4), 1456-1458; author reply 1458-1459.

Block, R. W., and Krebs, N. F. (2005). Failure to thrive as a manifestation of child neglect. *Pediatrics, 116*(5), 1234-1237.

Blythe, M. J., and Orr, D. P. (1995). Childhood sexual abuse: Guidelines for evaluation. *Indiana Medicine, 88*, 11-18.

Brayden, R. M., Altemeier, W. A., Tucker, D. D., Dietrich, M. S., and Vietze, P. (1992). Antecedents of child neglect in the first two years of life. *Journal of Pediatrics, 120*, 426-429.

Brewster, A. L., Nelson, J. P., Hymel, K. P., Colby, D. R., Lucas, D. R., McCanne, T. R., et al. (1998). Victim, perpetrator, family and incident characteristics of 32 infant maltreatment deaths in the United States Air Force. *Child Abuse and Neglect, 22*, 91-101.

Briere, J., Berliner, L., Bulkley, J. A., Jenny, C., and Reid, T. (Eds.). (1996). *The APSAC Handbook on Child Maltreatment*. Thousand Oaks, California: Sage.

Bross, D. C., Krugman, R. D., Lenherr, M. R., Rosenburg, D. A., and Schmitt, B. D. (Eds.). (1988). *The New Child Protection Team Handbook*. New York, NY: Garland Publishing.

Brown, J., Cohen, P., Johnson, J. G., and Salzinger, S. (1998). A longitudinal analysis of risk factors for child maltreatment: Findings of a 17-year prospective study of officially recorded and self-reported child abuse and neglect. *Child Abuse and Neglect, 22*, 1065-1078.

Burke, E. C. (1998). Abraham Jacobi: The man and his legacy. *Pediatrics, 101*, 309-312.

Caffey, J. (1946). Multiple fractures of the long bones of infants suffering from chronic subdural hematoma. *American Journal of Roentgenology, 56*, 163-173.

Caffey, J. (1972). On the theory and practice of shaking infants. Its potential residual effects of permanent brain damage and mental retardation. *American Journal of Diseases in Children, 124*, 161-169.

Caffey, J. (1974). The Whiplash Shaken Baby Syndrome: A manual shaking by the extremities with whiplash-induced intracranial and intraocular bleeding, linked with residual permanent brain damage and mental retardation. *Pediatrics, 54*, 396-403.

Cahill, L. T., Kaminer, R. K., and Johnson, P. G. (1999). Developmental, cognitive and behavioral sequelae of child abuse. *Child and Adolescent Psychiatric Clinics of North America, 8*, 827-843.

Centers for Disease Control and Prevention. (2002). Sexually transmitted diseases treatment guidelines. *Morbidity and Mortality Weekly Report, 51*(RR-6), 1-80.

Centers for Disease Control and Prevention. (2003). First reports evaluating the effectiveness of strategies for preventing violence: early childhood home visitation and firearms laws. Findings from the Task Force on Community Preventive Services. *Morbidity and Mortality Weekly Report, 52* (RR-14), 1-9.

Chadwick, D., and Krous, H. F. (1997). Irresponsible medical testimony by medical experts in cases involving the physical abuse and neglect of children. *Child Maltreatment, 2*(4), 313-321.

Chartier, M. J., Walker, J. R., and Naimark, B. (2007). Childhood abuse, adult health, and health care utilization: results from a representative community sample. *American Journal of Epidemiology, 165*(9), 1031-1038.

Christian, C. W., Lavelle, J. M., De Jong, A. R., Loiselle, J., Brenner, L., and Joffe, M. (2000). Forensic evidence findings in prepubertal victims of sexual assault. *Pediatrics, 106*, 100-104.

Cohen, J., Mannarino, R., Zhitova, A., and Capone, M. (2003). Treating child abuse-related posttraumatic stress and comorbid abuse in adolescents. *Child Abuse and Neglect, 27*, 1345-1365.

Coohey, C. (2003). Defining and classifying supervisory neglect. *Child Maltreatment, 8*, 145-156.

Council of the American Academy of Child and Adolescent Psychiatry. (1997). Statement: Practice parameters for the forensic evaluation of children and adolescents who may have been physically or sexually abused. *Journal of the American Academy of Child and Adolescent Psychiatry, 36*, 423-442.

Cross, T. P., Jones, L. M., Walsh, W. A., Simone, M., and Kolko, D. (2007). Child forensic interviewing in Children's Advocacy Centers: Empirical data on a practice model. *Child Abuse and Neglect, 31*(10), 1031-1052.

Crosse, S., Kaye, E., and Ratnofsky, A. (1993). *A Report on the Maltreatment of Children with Disabilities*. Washington, DC: National Clearinghouse on Child Abuse and Neglect Information.

Crume, T. L., DiGuiseppi, C., Byers, T., Sirotnak, A. P., and Garrett, C. J. (2002). Underascertainment of child maltreatment fatalities by death certificates, 1990-1998. *Pediatrics, 110*(2 Pt 1), e18.

Cupoli, J. M., and Sewell, P. M. (1988). One thousand fifty-nine children with a chief complaint of sexual abuse. *Child Abuse and Neglect, 12*, 151-162.

Dias, M. S., Smith, K., DeGuehery, K., Mazur, P., Li, V., and Shaffer, M. L. (2005). Preventing abusive head trauma among infants and young children: a hospital-based, parent education program. *Pediatrics, 115*(4), e470-477.

Dorland. (1974). In *Dorland's Illustrated Medical Dictionary* (25 ed., pp. 435). Philadelphia, PA: WB Saunders and Co.

Dube, S. R., Anda, R. F., Felitti, V. J., Chapman, D. P., Williamson, D. F., and Giles, W. H. (2001). Childhood Abuse, Household Dysfunction and the Risk of Attempted Suicide throughout the Lifespan: Findings from the Adverse Childhood Experiences Study. *Journal of the American Medical Association, 286*, 3089-3096.

Dube, S. R., Felitti, V. J., Dong, M., Giles, W. H., and Anda, R. F. (2003). The impact of adverse childhood experiences on health problems: evidence from four birth cohorts dating back to 1900. *Preventive Medicine., 37*(3), 268-277.

Dubowitz, H. (2000). Child neglect: Guidance for pediatricians. *Pediatrics in Review, 21*, 111-116.

Dubowitz, H., Black, M., and Harrington, D. (1992). The diagnosis of child sexual abuse. *American Journal of Diseases of Children, 146*, 688-693.

Dubowitz, H., Papas, M. A., Black, M. M., and Starr, R. H. (2002). Child neglect: Outcomes in high-risk urban preschoolers. *Pediatrics, 109*, 1100-1107.

Duhaime, A. C., Alario, A. J., and Lewander, M. D. (1992). Head injury in very young children: mechanisms, injury types, and ophthalmologic findings in 100 hospitalized patients younger than 2 years of age. *Pediatrics, 90*, 179-185.

DuMont, K. A., Widom, C. S., and Czaja, S. J. (2007). Predictors of resilience in abused and neglected children grown-up: the role of individual and neighborhood characteristics. *Child Abuse and Neglect, 31*(3), 255-274.

Durfee, M., Durfee, D. T., and West, M. P. (2002). Child fatality review: An international movement. *Child Abuse and Neglect, 26*, 619-636.

Ettaro, L., Berger, R. P., and Songer, T. (2004). Abusive head trauma in young children: characteristics and medical charges in a hospitalized population. *Child Abuse and Neglect, 28*(10), 1099-1111.

Ewigman, B., Kivlahan, C., and Land, G. (1993). The Missouri child fatality study: Under-reporting of maltreatment fatalities among children younger than 5 years of age, 1983 through 1986. *Pediatrics, 91*, 330-337.

Ewing-Cobbs, L., Kramer, L., Prasad, M., Canales, D. N., Louis, P. T., Fletcher, J. M., et al. (1998). Neuroimaging, physical and developmental findings after inflicted and non-inflicted brain injury in young children. *Pediatrics, 102*, 300-307.

Falcone, R. A., Jr., Brown, R. L., and Garcia, V. F. (2007a). Disparities in child abuse mortality are not explained by injury severity. *Journal of Pediatric Surgery, 42*(6), 1031-1036; discussion 1036-1037.

Falcone, R. A., Jr., Brown, R. L., and Garcia, V. F. (2007b). The epidemiology of infant injuries and alarming health disparities. *Journal of Pediatric Surgery, 42*(1), 172-176; discussion 176-177.

Faller, K. C., and Palusci, V. J. (2007). Children's advocacy centers: Do they lead to positive case outcomes? *Child Abuse and Neglect, 31*(10), 1021-1029.

Ferguson, D., Horwood, L. J., and Lynskey, M. (1997). Childhood sexual abuse, adolescent sexual behaviors and sexual revictimization. *Child Abuse and Neglect, 21*, 789-803.

Fingerhut, L. A. (1989). *Trends and Current Status in Childhood Mortality, U.S. 1900-85.* Washington, DC: U.S. Department of Health and Human Services.

Finkelhor, D. (1979). *Sexually Victimized Children.* New York, NY: The Free Press.

Finkelhor, D. (2007). Prevention of sexual abuse through educational programs directed toward children. *Pediatrics, 120*(3), 640-645.

Fischer, G. (2006). Anogenital warts in children. *Pediatric Dermatology, 23*(3), 291-293.

Flaherty, E. G., Sege, R., Price, L. L., Christoffel, K. K., Norton, D. P., and O'Connor, K. G. (2006). Pediatrician characteristics associated with child abuse identification and reporting: results from a national survey of pediatricians. *Child Maltreatment, 11*(4), 361-369.

Fluke, J. D., Yuan, Y. Y., and Edwards, M. (1999). Recurrence of maltreatment: an application of the National Child Abuse and Neglect Data System (NCANDS). *Child Abuse and Neglect, 23*(7), 633-650.

Fontana, V. J. (1989). Child abuse: The physician's responsibility. *New York State Journal of Medicine, 89*, 152-155.

Gallmeier, T. M., and Bonner, B. L. (1992). University-based interdisciplinary training in child abuse and neglect. *Child Abuse and Neglect, 16*, 513-521.

Gessner, B. D., Moore, M., Hamilton, B., and Muth, P. T. (2004). The incidence of physical abuse in Alaska. *Child Abuse and Neglect, 28*, 9-23.

Giedinghagen, D. H., Hoff, G. L., and Biery, R. M. (1992). Gonorrhea in children: Epidemiologic unit analysis. *Pediatric Infectious Disease Journal, 11*, 973-974.

Gordon, M., and Palusci, V. J. (1991). Physician training in the recognition and reporting of child abuse, maltreatment, and neglect. *New York State Journal of Medicine, 91*(1), 1-2.

Gushurst, C. A. (2003). Child abuse: behavioral aspects and other associated problems. *Pediatric Clinics of North America, 50*(4), 919-938.

Hammerschlag, M. R. (1998). The transmissibility of sexually transmitted diseases in sexually abused children. *Child Abuse and Neglect, 22*, 623-635.

Heger, A., Emans, S. J., and Muram, D. (Eds.). (2000). *Evaluation of the Sexually Abused Child* (2 ed.). Oxford, England:: Oxford University Press.

Heger, A., Ticson, L., Velasquez, O., and Bernier, R. (2002). Children referred for possible sexual abuse: medical findings in 2384 children. *Child Abuse and Neglect, 26*, 645-659.

Helfer, M. E., Kemp, R. S., and Krugman, R. D. (Eds.). (1997). *The Battered Child* (5 ed.). Chicago, IL: University of Chicago Press.

Helfer, R. E. (1990). The neglect of our children. *Pediatric Clinics of North America, 37*, 923-942.

Hennes, H., Kini, N., and Palusci, V. J. (2001). The epidemiology, clinical characteristics and public health implications of Shaken Baby Syndrome. *Journal of Aggression, Maltreatment and Trauma 5*(1), 19-40.

Herman-Giddens, M. E., Brown, G., Verbiest, S., Carlson, P. J., Hooten, E. G., Howell, E., and Butts, J. D. (1999). Underascertainment of child abuse mortality in the United States. *Journal of the American Medical Association, 282*, 463-467.

Herr, S., and Fallat, M. E. (2006). Abusive Abdominal and Thoracic Trauma. *Clinical Pediatric Emergency Medicine, 7*, 149-152.

Hobbs, C. J., and Osman, J. (2007). Genital injuries in boys and abuse. *Archives of Diseases in Childhood, 92*(4), 328-331.

Hobbs, C. J., and Wynne, J. M. (1996). *Physical Signs of Child Abuse: A Colour Atlas*. London: W.B. Saunders Co., Ltd.

Hornor, G. (2006). Ano-genital herpes in children. *Journal of Pediatric Health Care, 20*(2), 106-114.

Hudson, M., and Kaplan, R. (2006). Clinical response to child abuse. *Pediatric Clinics of North America, 53*(1), 27-39.

Hymel, K. P. (2006). Distinguishing sudden infant death syndrome from child abuse fatalities. *Pediatrics, 118*(1), 421-427.

Hymel, K. P., and American Academy of Pediatrics. (2006). When Is lack of supervision neglect? *Pediatrics, 118*, 1296-1298.

Hymel, K. P., Makoroff, K. L., Laskey, A. L., Conaway, M. R., and Blackman, J. A. (2007). Mechanisms, clinical presentations, injuries, and outcomes from inflicted versus noninflicted head trauma during infancy: results of a prospective, multicentered, comparative study. *Pediatrics, 119*(5), 922-929.

Ingram, D. L., Everett, V. D., Flick, L. A. R., Russell, T. A., and White-Sims, S. T. (1997). Vaginal gonococcal cultures in sexual abuse evaluations: Evaluation of selective criteria for preteenaged girls. *Pediatrics, 99*, e8.

Ingram, D. L., Everett, V. D., Lyna, P. R., White, S. W., and Rockwell, L. A. (1992). Epidemiology of adult sexually transmitted disease agents in children being evaluated for sexual abuse. *Pediatric Infectious Disease Journal, 11*, 945-950.

Jason, J. (1983). Fatal child abuse in Georgia: The epidemiology of severe physical child abuse. *Child Abuse and Neglect, 7*, 1-9.

Jason, J., Gilliland, J. C., and Tyler, C. W. (1983). Homicide as a cause of pediatric mortality in the United States. *Pediatrics, 72*, 191-197.

Jenny, C. (1999). *Application to the American Board of Pediatrics from the American Academy of Pediatrics Section on Child Abuse and Neglect for establishment of subspecialty boards in child abuse and forensic pediatrics*. Chicago, IL: American Academy of Pediatrics.

Jenny, C., and American Academy of Pediatrics. (2006). Evaluating Infants and Young Children With Multiple Fractures. *Pediatrics, 118*, 1299-1303.

Jenny, C., and American Academy of Pediatrics. (2007). Recognizing and responding to medical neglect. *Pediatrics, 120*(6), 1385-1389.

Johnson, C. F. (1993). Physicians and medical neglect: Variables that affect reporting. *Child Abuse and Neglect, 17*, 605-615.

Johnson, C. F. (1999). Medical evaluation of child abuse. *Children's Health Care, 28*, 91-108.

Johnson, T. C. (1988). Child perpetrators--Children who molest other children: Preliminary Findings. *Child Abuse and Neglect, 12*, 219-229.

Jones, L. M., Cross, T. P., Walsh, W. A., and Simone, M. (2007). Do Children's Advocacy Centers improve families' experiences of child sexual abuse investigations? *Child Abuse and Neglect, 31*(10), 1069-1085.

Kairys, S. W., Johnson, C. F., and American Academy of Pediatrics. (2002). The psychological maltreatment of children - Technical report. *Pediatrics, 104*, e68.

Kaplan, S. J., Labruna, V., Pelcovitz, D., Salzinger, S., Mandel, F., and Weiner, M. (1999). Physically abused adolescents: Behavior problems, functional impairment, and comparison of informants' reports. *Pediatrics, 104*, 43-49.

Keenan, H. T., Runyan, D. K., Marshall, S. W., Nocera, M. A., and Merten, D. F. (2004). A population-based comparison of clinical and outcome characteristics of young children with serious inflicted and noninflicted traumatic brain injury. *Pediatrics, 114*(3), 633-639.

Keenan, H. T., Runyan, D. K., Marshall, S. W., Nocera, M. A., Merten, D. F., and Sinal, S. H. (2003). A population-based study of inflicted traumatic brain injury in young children. *Journal of the American Medical Association, 290*, 621-626.

Kellogg, N., and American Academy of Pediatrics. (2005). The evaluation of sexual abuse in children. *Pediatrics, 116*, 506-512.

Kelly, P., and Koh, J. (2006). Sexually transmitted infections in alleged sexual abuse of children and adolescents. *Journal of Paediatric Child Health, 42*(7-8), 434-440.

Kempe, C. H., Silverman, F. N., Steele, B. F., Droegemueller, W., and Silver, H. K. (1962). The battered child syndrome. *Journal of the American Medical Association, 181*, 17-24.

Kendall-Tackett, K. (2002). The health effects of childhood abuse: Four pathways by which abuse can influence health. *Child Abuse and Neglect, 26*, 715-729.

Kleinman, P. K. (1989). Radiologic contributions to the investigation and prosecution of cases of fatal infant abuse. *New England Journal of Medicine, 320*, 507-511.

Kleinman, P. K. (1998). *Diagnostic Imaging of Child Abuse* (2 ed.). St. Louis, MO: Mosby.

Knight, L. D., and Collins, K. A. (2005). A 25-year retrospective review of deaths due to pediatric neglect. *American Journal of Forensic Medicine and . Pathology, 26*(3), 221-228.

Kolbo, J. R., and Strong, E. (1997). Multidisciplinary team approaches to the investigation and resolution of child abuse and neglect: A national survey. *Child Maltreatment, 2*, 61-72.

Kotch, J. B., Browne, C. B., Dufort, V., Winsor, J., and Catellier, D. (1999). Predicting child maltreatment in the first 4 years of life from characteristics assessed in the neonatal period. *Child Abuse and Neglect, 23*, 22-32.

Krugman, R. D. (1984). The multidisciplinary treatment of abusive and neglectful families. *Pediatric Annals, 13*, 761-764.

Krugman, S. D., Lane, W. G., and Walsh, C. M. (2007). Update on child abuse prevention. *Current Opinion in Pediatrics, 19*(6), 711-718.

Kydd, J. W. (2004). Preventing child maltreatment: An integrated, multisectoral approach. *Health and Human Rights, an International Journal, 6*, 34-63.

Ladson, S., Johnson, C. F., and Doty, R. E. (1997). Do physicians recognize sexual abuse? *American Journal of Diseases of Children, 144*, 411-415.

Lamb, M. E. (1994). The investigation of child sexual abuse: An interdisciplinary consensus statement. *Child Abuse and Neglect, 18*, 1021-1028.

Lazoritz, S. (1990). Whatever happened to Mary Ellen? *Child Abuse and Neglect, 14*, 143-150.

Lee, C., Barr, R. G., Catherine, N., and Wicks, A. (2007). Age-related incidence of publicly reported shaken baby syndrome cases: is crying a trigger for shaking? *Journal Of Developmental and Behavioral Pediatrics, 28*(4), 288-293.

Leventhal, J. M., Larson, I. A., Abdoo, D., Singaracharlu, S., Takizawa, C., Miller, C., et al. (2007). Are abusive fractures in young children becoming less common? Changes over 24 years. *Child Abuse and Neglect, 31*(3), 311-322.

Leventhal, J. M., Pugh, M. C., Berg, A. T., and Garber, R. B. (1996). The use of health services by children who are identified during the postpartum period as being at high risk of child abuse and neglect. *Pediatrics, 97*, 331-335.

Little, K. (2001). *Sexual assault nurse examiner (SANE) programs: Improving the community response to sexual assault victims* (No. NCJ 186366). Washington, DC: U.S. Department of Justice, Office of Justice Programs.

Liu, J., Raine, A., Venables, P. H., Dalais, C., and Mednick, S. A. (2003). Malnutrition at age 3 years and lower cognitive ability at age 11 years. *Archives of Pediatric and Adolescent Medicine, 157*, 593-600.

Loder, R. T., and Feinberg, J. R. (2007). Orthopaedic injuries in children with nonaccidental trauma: demographics and incidence from the 2000 kids' inpatient database. *Journal of Pediatric Orthopedics, 27*(4), 421-426.

Maas, C., Herrenkohl, T. I., and Sousa, C. (2008). Review of Research On Child Maltreatment and Violence in Youth. *Trauma, Violence, and Abuse, 9*(1), 56-67.

Maguire, S., Mann, M. K., Sibert, J., and Kemp, A. (2005). Are there patterns of bruising in childhood which are diagnostic or suggestive of abuse? A systematic review. *Archives of Diseases of Childhood, 90*(2), 182-186.

Makoroff, K. L., Brauley, J. L., Brandner, A. M., Myers, P. A., and Shapiro, R. A. (2002). Genital examinations for alleged sexual abuse of prepubertal girls: Findngs by pediatric emergency medicine physicians compared with child abuse trained physicians. *Child Abuse and Neglect, 26*(12), 1235-1242.

Mathews, B., and Kenny, M. C. (2008). Mandatory reporting legislation in the United States, Canada, and Australia: a cross-jurisdictional review of key features, differences, and issues. *Child Maltreatment, 13*(1), 50-63.

McCann, J., Miyamoto, S., Boyle, C., and Rogers, K. (2007a). Healing of hymenal injuries in prepubertal and adolescent girls: a descriptive study. *Pediatrics, 119*(5), e1094-1106.

McCann, J., Miyamoto, S., Boyle, C., and Rogers, K. (2007b). Healing of nonhymenal genital injuries in prepubertal and adolescent girls: a descriptive study. *Pediatrics, 120*(5), 1000-1011.

McClain, P. W., Sacks, J. J., Froehlke, R. G., and Ewigman, B. G. (1993). Estimates of fatal child abuse and neglect, United States, 1979 through 1988. *Pediatrics, 91*, 338-343.

McHugh, M. T. (1991). *Suspected Child Abuse and Neglect: Protocol for Identification, Reporting and Treatment*. New York: New York City Health and Hospitals Corporation.

Michigan Child Death State Advisory Team. (2001). *Child Deaths in Michigan: Second Annual Report*. Okemos, MI: Michigan Public Health Institute.

Migley, G., Wiese, D., and Salmon-Cox, S. (1996). *World Perspectives on Child Abuse: The Second International Resource Book.* . Chicago, IL: International Society for Prevention of Child Abuse and Neglect.

Morris, J. L., Johnson, C. F., and Clasen, M. (1985). To report or not to report: Physicians' attitudes toward discipline and child abuse. *American Journal of Diseases of Children, 139*, 194-197.

Muram, D., and Jones, C. E. (1993). The use of videocolposcopy in the gynecologic examination of infants, children and young adolescents. *Adolescent and Pediatric Gynecology, 6*, 154-156.

Myers, J. E. B. (2002). Keep the lifeboat afloat. *Child Abuse and Neglect, 26*, 561-567.

National Committee to Prevent Child Abuse. (1998). *Child abuse and neglect statistics*. Chicago, IL: National Committee to Prevent Child Abuse.

National Research Council. (1993a). Consequences of child abuse and neglect. In *Understanding Child Abuse and Neglect* (Vol. 40, pp. 208-252). Washington, DC: National Academy of Sciences Press.

National Research Council. (1993b). Interventions and treatment. In *Understanding Child Abuse and Neglect* (Vol. 40, pp. 253-291). Washington, DC: National Academy of Sciences Press.

New York State, Office of Child and Family Services. (2003). *1998-2002 Monitoring and Analysis Profiles*. Albany, NY: New York State Office of Children and Family Services.

Ojo, P., Palmer, J., Garvey, R., Atweh, N., and Fidler, P. (2007). Pattern of burns in child abuse. *Annals of Surgery, 73*(3), 253-255.

Olds, D. L. (1992). Home visitation for pregnant women and parents of young children. *American Journal of Diseases in Children, 146*, 704-708.

Olshen, E., Hsu, K., Woods, E. R., Harper, M., Harnisch, B., and Samples, C. L. (2006). Use of human immunodeficiency virus postexposure prophylaxis in adolescent sexual assault victims. *Archives of Pediatric and Adolescent Medicine, 160*(7), 674-680.

Ommaya, A. K., Fass, F., and Yarnell, P. (1968). Whiplash injury and brain damage: An experimental study. *Journal of the American Medical Association, 204*, 285-289.

Overpeck, M., Brenner, R., Trumple, A., Trifiletti, L., and Berendes, H. (1998). Risk factors for infant homicide in the United States. *New England Journal of Medicine, 339*, 1211-1216.

Palusci, V. J. (2003). The Role of the Health Care Professional in Response to Victimization. In J. L. Mullings, Marquart, J.W., Hartley, D.J. (Ed.), *The Victimization of Children: Emerging Issues* (pp. 133-171). Binghamton, NY: The Haworth Maltreatment and Trauma Press.

Palusci, V. J., Bliss, R., and Crum, P. (2007). Outcomes for groups for children exposed to violence with behavior problems. *Trauma and Loss, 7*(1), 27-38.

Palusci, V. J., Cox, E. O., Cyrus, T. A., Heartwell, S. W., Vandervort, F. E., and Pott, E. S. (1999). Medical assessment and legal outcome in child sexual abuse. *Archives of Pediatric and Adolescent Medicine, 153*(4), 388-392.

Palusci, V. J., Cox, E. O., Shatz, E. M., and Schultze, J. M. (2006). Urgent medical assessment after child sexual abuse. *Child Abuse and Neglect, 30*(4), 367-380.

Palusci, V. J., and Cyrus, T. A. (2001). Reaction to videocolposcopy in the assessment of child sexual abuse. *Child Abuse and Neglect, 25*(11), 1535-1546.

Palusci, V. J., Hicks, R. A., and Vandervort, F. E. (2001). "You are hereby commanded to appear": Pediatrician subpoena and court appearance in child maltreatment. *Pediatrics, 107*(6), 1427-1430.

Palusci, V. J., and Marshall, J. (2003). An open letter to Michigan physicians. *Michigan Medicine, 102*(2), 6.

Palusci, V. J., and McHugh, M. T. (1995). Interdisciplinary training in the evaluation of child sexual abuse. *Child Abuse and Neglect, 19*(9), 1031-1038.

Palusci, V. J., and Palusci, J. V. (2006). Screening tools for child sexual abuse. *Journal Of Pediatrics (Rio), 82*(6), 409-410.

Palusci, V. J., and Reeves, M. J. (2003). Testing for genital gonorrhea infections in prepubertal girls with suspected sexual abuse. *Pediatric Infectious Disease Journal, 22*(7), 618-623.

Palusci, V. J., Smith, E. G., and Paneth, N. (2005). Predicting recurrence of child maltreatment in young children using NCANDS. *Children and Youth Services Review, 27*(6), 667-682.

Paradise, J. E., Bass, J., Forman, S. D., Berkowitz, J., Greenberg, D. B., and Mehta, K. (1995). Minimum criteria for reporting child abuse from health care settings. *Pediatric Emergency Care, 11*, 335-339.

Powers, J. L., and Eckenrode, J. (1988). The maltreatment of adolescents. *Child Abuse and Neglect, 12*, 189-200.

Pratt, H. D., and Greydanus, D. E. (2003). Violence: concepts of its impact on children and youth. *Pediatric Clinics of North America, 50*, 963-1003.

Pratt, H. D., Patel, D. R., Greydanus, D. E., Dannison, L., Walcott, D., and Sloane, M. A. (2001). Adolescent sexual offenders: Issues for pediatricians. *International Pediatrics, 16*, 1-8.

Reading, R., and Rannan-Eliya, Y. (2007). Evidence for sexual transmission of genital herpes in children. *Archives of Diseases of Childhood, 92*(7), 608-613.

Reid, S. R., Roesler, J. S., Gaichas, A. M., and Tsai, A. K. (2001). The epidemiology of pediatric traumatic brain injury in Minnesota. *Archives of Pediatric and Adolescent Medicine, 155*, 784-789.

Reiniger, A., Robison, E., and McHugh, M. T. (1995). Mandated training of professionals: A means for improving reporting of suspected child abuse. *Child Abuse and Neglect, 19*, 63-69.

Ricci, L. R. (1988). Medical forensic photography of the sexually abused child. *Child Abuse and Neglect, 12*, 305-310.

Ricci, L. R. (2001). Photodocumentation of the abused child. In R. M. L. Reese, S. (Ed.), *Child Abuse Medical Diagnosis and Management* (2 ed., pp. 385-404). Philadelphia, PA: Lipincott, Williams and Wilkins.

Rimsza, M. E., and Niggermann, E. H. (1982). Medical evaluation of sexually abused children: A review of 311 cases. *Pediatrics, 69*, 8-14.

Robinson, A. J., Watkeys, J. E., and Ridgway, G. L. (1998). Sexually transmitted organisms in sexually abused children. *Archives of Diseases in Childhood, 79*, 356-358.

Rovi, S., Chen, P. H., and Johnson, M. S. (2004). The economic burden of hospitalizations associated with child abuse and neglect. *American Journal of Public Health, 94*(4), 586-590.

Runyan, D. K. (2001). Formation of the Ray E. Helfer Society (letter). *Child Abuse and Neglect, 25*, 199-201.

Sacco, K. A., Head, C. A., Vessicchio, J. C., Easton, C. J., Prigerson, H. G., and George, T. P. (2007). Adverse childhood experiences, smoking and mental illness in adulthood: a preliminary study. *Annals of Clinical Psychiatry, 19*(2), 89-97.

Sackett, D. L., Haynes, R. B., Guyyatt, G. H., and Tugwell, P. (1991). *Clinical Epidemiology: A Basic Science for Clinical Medicine* (2 ed.). Boston, MA: Little Brown and Company.

Salvagni, E. P., and Wagner, M. B. (2006). Development of a questionnaire for the assessment of sexual abuse in children and estimation of its discriminant validity: a case-control study. *Journal of Pediatrics (Rio), 82*(6), 431-436.

Schnitzer, P. G., Covington, T. M., Wirtz, S. J., Verhoeck-Oftedahl, W., and Palusci, V. J. (2008). Public Health Surveillance of Fatal Child Maltreatment: Analysis of 3 State Programs. *American Journal of Public Health*, 98(2), 296-303.

Sedlak, A. J., and Broadhurst, D. D. (1996). *The Third National Incidence Study of Child Abuse and Neglect (NIS-3)*. Washington, DC: US Department of Health and Human Services.

Shapiro, R. A., and Makoroff, K. L. (2006). Sexually transmitted diseases in sexually abused girls and adolescents. *Current Opinion Obstetrics and Gynecology, 18*(5), 492-497.

Shapiro, R. A., Schubert, C. J., and Siegel, R. M. (1999). Neisseria gonorrhea infections in girls younger than 12 years of age evaluated for vaginitis. *Pediatrics, 104*, e72.

Showers, J. (1992). Don't shake the baby: Effectiveness of a prevention program. *Child Abuse and Neglect, 16*, 11-18.

Sicoli, R. A., Losek, J. D., Hudlett, J. M., and Smith, D. (1995). Indications for Neisseria gonorrhoeae cultures in children with suspected sexual abuse. *Archives of Pediatric and Adolescent Medicine, 149*, 86-89.

Siegel, R. M., Schubert, C. J., Myers, P. A., and Shapiro, R. A. (1995). The prevalence of sexually transmitted diseases in children and adolescents evaluated for sexual abuse in Cincinnati: Rationale for limited STD testing in prepubertal girls. *Pediatrics, 96*, 1090-1094.

Silverman, F. M. (1953). The roentgen manifestations of unrecognized skeletal trauma in infants. *American Journal of Radiology, 69*, 413-426.

Silverman, F. M. (1972). Unrecognized trauma in infants, the battered child syndrome, and the syndrome of Ambroise Tardieu. *Radiology, 104*, 347-353.

Socolar, R. R. S., Fredrickson, D. D., Block, R., Moore, J. K., Tropez-Sims, S., and Whitworth, J. M. (2001). State programs for a medical diagnosis of child abuse and neglect: Case studies of five established or fledgling programs. *Child Abuse and Neglect, 25*, 441-455.

Spady, D. W., Saunder, D. L., Schopflocher, D. P., and Svenson, L. W. (2004). Patterns of injury in children: A population-based approach. *Pediatrics, 113*, 522-529.

Springer, K. W., Sheridan, J., Kuo, D., and Carnes, M. (2007). Long-term physical and mental health consequences of childhood physical abuse: results from a large population-based sample of men and women. *Child Abuse and Neglect, 31*(5), 517-530.

medicine fellowship curriculum statement. *Child Maltreatment, 5*, 58-62.

Stockwell, M. S., Brown, J., Chen, S., and Irigoyen, M. (2007). Is there a relationship between lacking a primary care provider and child abuse? *Ambulatory Pediatrics, 7*(6), 439-444.

Swerdlin, A., Berkowitz, C., and Craft, N. (2007). Cutaneous signs of child abuse. *Journal Of the American Academy of Dermatology, 57*(3), 371-392.

Thomas, D. E., Leventhal, J. M., and Friedlander, E. (2001). Referrals to a hospital-based child abuse committee: A comparison of the 1960's and 1990's. *Child Abuse and Neglect, 25*, 203-213.

U.S. Department of Health and Human Services, Centers for Disease Control and Prevention, and National Center for Health Statistics. (1998). *ICD-10: International statistical classification of diseases and related health problems, tenth revision.* Washington, DC: U.S. Government Printing Office.

U.S. Department of Health and Human Services, Administration for Children, Youth and Families. (1992). *Child abuse and neglect: A shared community concern.* Washington, DC: U.S. Department of Health and Human Services (ACF).

U.S. Department of Health and Human Services, Administration on Children, Youth and Families, Children's Bureau. (2006). *Child Maltreatment 2004: Reports from the states to the national child abuse and neglect data system.* Washington, DC: US Government Printing Office.

U.S. Department of Health and Human Services, Administration on Children, Youth and Families, Children's Bureau. (2004). *Child Maltreatment 2001: Reports from the states to the national child abuse and neglect data system*. Washington, DC: US Government Printing Office.

United States Advisory Board on Child Abuse and Neglect. (1995). *A Nation's Shame: Fatal child abuse and neglect in the United States*. Washington, DC: U.S. Government Printing Office.

Wallace, G. H., Makoroff, K. L., Malott, H. A., and Shapiro, R. A. (2007). Hospital-based multidisciplinary teams can prevent unnecessary child abuse reports and out-of-home placements. *Child Abuse and Neglect, 31*(6), 623-629.

Walsh, W. A., Cross, T. P., Jones, L. M., Simone, M., and Kolko, D. J. (2007). Which sexual abuse victims receive a forensic medical examination? The impact of Children's Advocacy Centers. *Child Abuse and Neglect, 31*(10), 1053-1068.

Warner, J. E., and Hansen, D. J. (1994). The identification and reporting of physical abuse by physicians: A review and implications for research. *Child Abuse and Neglect, 18*, 11-25.

Williams, L. M., and Herrera, V. M. (2007). Child maltreatment and adolescent violence: understanding complex connections. *Child Maltreatment, 12*(3), 203-207.

Woodling, B. A., and Heger, A. (1986). The use of the colposcope in the diagnosis of sexual abuse in the pediatric age group. *Child Abuse and Neglect, 10*, 111-114.

Woolley, P. V., and Evans, W. A. (1955). Significance of skeletal lesions in infants resembling those of traumatic origin. *Journal of the American Medical Association, 158*, 539-547.

Wright, C. M. Identification and management of failure to thrive: a community perspective. *Archives Of Diseases of Childhood,2000; 82*(1), 5-9.

Young, K. J., Jones, J. G., Worthington, T., Simpson, P., and Casey, P. H. (2006). Forensic laboratory evidence in sexually abused children and adolescents. *Archives of Pediatrics and Adolescent Medicine, 160*, 585-588.

Zimmerman, S., Makoroff, K., Care, M., Thomas, A., and Shapiro, R. (2005). Utility of follow-up skeletal surveys in suspected child physical abuse evaluations. *Child Abuse and Neglect, 29*(10), 1075-1083.

In: Behavioral Pediatrics, 3rd Edition
Editor: D. E. Greydanus et al.

ISBN 978-1-60692-702-1
© 2009 Nova Science Publishers, Inc.

Chapter 27

Sexual Offenders

Helen D. Pratt, Dilip R. Patel and Donald E. Greydanus

Abstract

Children and adolescents under the age of 18 years account for one-fifth of arrests for all sexual offenses (excluding prostitution). These young perpetrators can be found among all socio-economic groups and live in all regions of the United States. They often come to the attention of primary care clinicians when their parents bring them in for protection from the authorities and help with addressing their maladaptive behavior. Clinician collected information may get used as a part of criminal investigations or to facilitate initial evaluation and coordination of services. Frequently, parents will bring their child or teen when the parents have caught then engaging in some form of sexual activity. Their concern is whether or not this is normal or abnormal behavior. Physicians who are aware of adolescent sexual offending can increase their ability to detect adolescents who have aberrant or deviant sexual behavior patterns allowing for *early* referral and comprehensive intervention.

Introduction

Most of the sexual abuse literature focuses on adult perpetrators or child/teen victims. In the past five years, 15 new articles have been published discussing adolescent sexual offenders. Most of those articles were case studies with one to three cases being reported. Otherwise the literature has not changed since the original article we published on adolescent sexual offending. There is still a paucity of data available in the literature on adolescent sexual offenders, who are involved in sexual abuse of younger children. Primary care clinicians must be prepared to act in a manner that does not contaminate forensic evidence or alter the testimony of either the perpetrator or victims in a legal trial. Clinicians may encounter these youth in their practices under several circumstances: adolescent revelation, parental report, or at the request of legal representatives.

What we know about sexual offenders in general is based only on those individuals who are caught or prosecuted. Even youth who are caught; arrested, and convicted, frequently receive minimal punishments (i.e., probation, community service). The costs to society for the crimes of juvenile sex offenders are considerable, not only those inflicted on crime victims and society as a whole, but also those imposed on offenders and their families. The rehabilitation focus of interventions for those youth referred to treatment programs is considered to be controversial because the interventions are not evidenced based for the adolescent sexual offender population. Most adjudicated adolescents live and are treated in community settings and often reoffend. Unfortunately, there remains little empirical evidence of the long-term effects of different intervention with adolescent sexual offenders.

Definition

Adolescent sex offenders are defined as youth between the ages of 13 to 17 years who commit illegal sexual behavior as defined by the sex crimes statues of the legal jurisdictions in which they reside. Legal meanings of sexual offenses vary from state to state. However, statutes typically define sexual offenses in terms of: a) penetration offenses, which include penetration of virtually any body orifice for a sexual purpose, and are felonies; and b) crimes not involving physical contact (e.g., voyeurism, exhibitionism, obscene phone calls). Such offenses progress from privacy issues at the misdemeanor level to the felony level, depending on the specific circumstances of each case. The addition of physical force or coercion will almost always result in a felony life offense.

Epidemiology

The incidence of sexual victimization of children by adolescents has become a serious problem in our society. The percentages of adolescents arrested for sexual offending in 2004 are as follows: 28% of youth ages 12–14 years, 37% ages 15-17 years, and 42% ages 18-20 years; about 6% of all statutory rapes and 12% of forcible rapes were cleared by the arrest of the juvenile. In 2003 law enforcement agencies reported 2.2 million arrests of person under 18 for criminal acts. Of all arrests 15% of them were male and 20% were females under 18; of the sexual offenses (excluding forcible rape and prostitution) were 20% committed by males and 22% females. Approximately one-third of sexual offenses against children are committed by teenagers. Sexual offenses against young children are typically committed by boys between the ages of 12 to 15 years old.

Clinical Features

Researchers generally agree that there are *multiple* factors (psychological, biological and sociological) that interact in complex and poorly understood ways; these factors include the adolescent's temperament, cognitive abilities, impulse control, family variables, and socioeconomic factors as well as access to potential victims and opportunities to offend. A history of prior physical or sexual abuse, impaired family functioning, alcohol and substance abuse, exposure to erotica, neurobiological factors, and psychiatric co-morbidity have been found to be associated with a higher prevalence of adolescent sexual offending. However, we do not know specific and direct causation.

Presentation in the Office

The serious psychosocial and legal implications for the offender and his or her family often prevent parents from seeking help. More often the offender will be brought to their physician by an appropriate agency in the course of a child abuse investigation for a) assistance with medical and psychological evaluation, b) to facilitate further expert evaluation, c) specialized referral, or d) to co-ordinate on-going care.

Sometimes parents may bring their teen in with concerns about his or her social development and provide indirect or non-specific indicators of an adolescent being involved in the sexual abuse of younger children. The parent may express concern about their teen's sexual activities with a younger child (sibling, other relative, or acquaintance); they may also ask if such activities are "normal." Also, the parents of the victim may report fear of the offender or incidences of sex play between their young child with an older teen to the offender's parents; then the offender's parents presents that information to the physician. The goal of the parent is for the physician to tell them how to help their offending teen.

Most offenses are committed by a small number of adolescents who repeatedly reoffend and account for the molestation and sexual abuse of half of the male victims and one quarter of the female victims. Juveniles who have committed sex offenses are males who represent a heterogencous mix, commit multiple offenses, usually have more than one victim, and usually offend against females; if they violate very young children, then their victims are usually male; unfortunately, they may have several types of victims. The juvenile offenders differ according to victim and offense characteristics and a wide range of other variables, including types of offending behaviors, histories of child maltreatment, sexual knowledge and experiences, academic and cognitive functioning, and mental health issues. They usually have not been victims of childhood sexual abuse. Also, very little data are available on female sexual offenders.

Adolescent sex offenders rarely have previous convictions for sexual assault, but are likely to have committed nonsexual offenses. Those who have been physically abused were 7.6 times more likely to rape or sodomize other children when compared to adolescents who were sexually abused or neglected. One in two adult sex offenders began their sexually abusive behavior as a juvenile. Adolescents who commit incest offenses do so in the victim's home and often when providing child care services. Adolescent rapists, on the other hand, tend to victimize strangers. As the age of the victim increases, sexual intercourse becomes a part of the offense.

The families of adolescent sexual offenders tend to be two parent families, have at least one sibling living with them, and more closely resemble those of youth with severe emotional or behavioral problems. Their parents often deny sexual tensions and exhibit a paucity of sexual knowledge or education; also, one quarter of their parents have known sexual pathology. Adolescent sexual offenders who had committed sexual homicides experienced exaggerated personal and family dysfunction.

Diagnosis

A significant percentage of reported criminal sexual acts against children are various types of paraphilias. The *paraphilias* represent a diagnostic category in the 2000 *Diagnostic and Statistical Manual of Mental Disorders; Fourth Edition (DSM-IV-TR)*. and consists of the following subcategories: exhibitionism, fetishism, frotteurism, sexual masochism, sexual sadism, transvestic fetishism, voyeurism, and pedophilia. The victimization is by perpetrators who have intense sexually arousing urges, fantasies, or behaviors; also, a number of other issues are involved in adult perpetrators, though this discussion involves children and adolescents. The reader is referred to the *DSM-IV-TR* for further details in this regard. A psychiatric diagnosis is made if the behaviors have occurred for at least six months and caused distress or impairment that impedes social, occupational, or other important areas of functioning. Pedophilia is the diagnosis of our focus and involves sexual activity with a prepubescent child or children (generally ages 13 years or younger). A 5 years age difference is required between perpetrator and victim.

Sexual Exploitation Versus Normal Sexual Play

When a parent presents with a teen who was accused or caught engaging in sexual play with a younger child or a developmentally younger child, the physician may be asked to tell the parent if this is normal or not. The physician who understands the differences between sexual *exploration* and *exploitation* will be better prepared to make that distinction when faced with a report of adolescent sexual behavior. "Normal" or *Developmentally Sexual Curiosity* and exploration are a normal part of the developmental play and should meet the criteria listed:

1. The two involved individuals who are age and developmental peers.
2. Children and pre-pubertal adolescents may engage in exploratory behaviors.
   - The play or exploration usually involves only mutual genital display, touching, and fondling.
   - Curiosity about the differences and similarities in anatomy is normal.
   - Exploratory sexual play is not coercive.
   - Mutual consent is typical of exploratory behaviors.
   - Does not include multiple participants.
   - Observers or additional participants are not acceptable.
   - Manifestations of anger, fear, sadness, or other strongly negative responses are not present.

Exploitation involves the absence of the factors listed above and the inclusion of the following:

- If one of the individuals is cognitively impaired, then a peer relationship does not exist.
- Attempted intercourse is atypical among preschoolers and is rare in the young school-aged child (6-9 years).
- Abusive behavior often involves elements of pressure, misrepresentation, force, threat, secrecy, or other forms of coercion. Although some of the threat or coercion is obvious and violent, the evaluator must take care to recognize subtle emotional pressure or the use of implied authority by an older child or adolescent in some cases.
- If the sexual contact has been arranged for the pleasure of another older individual, it is exploitative.
- One of the participants manifests feelings anger, fear, sadness, or other strongly negative responses.
- The victim views the experience in negative terms; however, some abused children will appear to have a neutral or positive emotional response to this abuse.

Regardless of whether or not the sexual play is normal or abnormal, parents and adult caregivers need to be vigilant and give children other healthy outlets. Parents should be encouraged to always keep young children under surveillance, especially when older individuals are around.

If the "sex play" is determined to be experimental or exploratory, the physician should discuss normal childhood and adolescent sexual behavior with parents and outline measures to minimize inappropriate sexual stimulation in the home. Parents should be advised to provide closer supervision of the adolescent. Older adolescents can be instructed to stay away from compromising situations with younger children.

In the event that the physician determines that sexual abuse has occurred, he or she should follow the guidelines from the governing Child Protective Services Organizations, medical oversight organizations and with medical examination and documentation performed as required by state child abuse laws. The family should be referred to the appropriate agency for further evaluation. If the adolescent has access to other children, especially very young ones, the physician should assess the level of risk posed to those children.

When it is determined that the child or adolescent is at high risk of sexually offending, then the physician should inform the family and the appropriate persons. Furthermore, the family should be advised to stop all baby-sitting and childcare activities to limit the adolescent offender's opportunity to re-offend. A more definitive treatment may not be within the purview of all clinicians and generally, the adolescent offender will be referred to professionals and programs specializing in such treatment.

Co-Morbid Disorders

Adolescent sexual offender can have concurrent diagnoses of psychopathology. They rarely exhibit behavior problems; they are more likely to be shy, and more comfortable with younger children. The most common psychiatric diagnoses, respectively, are conduct disorder, substance abuse disorders, adjustment disorders, attention-deficit/hyperactivity disorder, specific phobia, and mood disorder. They frequently engage in distorted thinking to make their offenses more socially acceptable to themselves and others, much like other delinquents, their distorted thinking allows them to excuse their offenses. Male offenders are more often diagnosed with paraphilias and antisocial behavior. Female offenders are more likely to be diagnosed with mood disorders and engage in self mutilation.

Intervention

In most states adolescent sexual offenders can be adjudicated for criminal behavior as young at 6 years old. However, most states set 10 years as the lowest age of criminal responsibility. Victim consent is not always considered important. Once there is sufficient evidence to identify an offender, a decision regarding prosecution is often made at the juvenile court level. If the child or adolescent goes to trial, the setting in the juvenile justice system is usually less formal and hearings are often conducted in private without the use of a jury. Juveniles in this system are more likely to receive efforts at rehabilitation and less likely to be held fully accountable for their actions, than if they were adjudicated in the adult courts. However, in the case of rape, sodomy or sexual homicide, most states have moved to address adolescent offending in the adult criminal justice system, which can impose harsher punishments.

Local statutes usually govern physician-patient privileges (i.e., the right to respect the confidentiality of all communications). Thus, the development of such privileges in each state is subject to *local* interpretation and state-by-state case law developments. Physicians should explain, at the outset, to all adolescents and their families the limits of confidentiality. If the adolescent's behavior must be reported to the authorities or potential victims warned, the physician should inform the patient and the family.

Professionals, who deal with children, have an *enforceable* mandate to report *suspected* child abuse. All fifty states have "mandated reporting" laws which require professionals to report "reasonable suspicions" that abuse or neglect has occurred. Professional obligations pertaining to confidentiality may be seriously challenged by the requirements of the law and the local community, particularly when it involves sexual conduct. It is helpful to explain the parents and the patient that reporting any crime changes the status of the act from private to criminal; however, is required as part of mandatory reporting laws.

No clinician should consider serving as a witness or expert witness in sexual abuse cases involving adolescent offenders without *specific* training in this area.

Conclusion

Children and adolescents under the age of 18 years account for one-fifth of arrests for all sexual offenses (excluding prostitution). They commit multiple offenses, usually have more than one victim, and may not limit their offenses to one type of victim. These young perpetrators can be found among all socio-economic groups and live in all regions of the United States. They often come to the attention of primary care clinicians when their parents bring them in for protection for the authorities and help with addressing their maladaptive behavior. Because most offenders are not detected, and those who are discovered are not often adjudicated, the physician can help to prevent and minimize the occurrence of sexual offending by educating parents about the importance of close supervision and seeking appropriate professional help for deviant sexual behavior in children and adolescents.

References

American Psychiatric Association: *Diagnostic and Statistical Manual of Mental Disorders; Fourth Edition (DSM-IV-TR)*. Washington, DC: American Psychiatric Association 2000.

Awad G, Saunders E, Levere J. A clinical study of male adolescent sexual offenders. *Internat J. Offender Ther. and Compar Criminol*. 1984;28:105-116.

Becker JV, Stein RM. Is sexual erotica associated with sexual deviance in adolescent males? *Internat J Law Psychiatr*. 1991;14:85-95.

Berlin FS, Meinecke CF. Treatment of sex offenders with antiandrogenic medication: conceptualization, review of treatment modalities, and preliminary findings. *Am. J. Psychiatr*. 1981;138:601-7.

Berlin FS. "Chemical castration" for sex offenders. *N. Engl. J. Med*. 1997;336(14):103035.

Blaske DM, Bourduin CM, Henggeler SW, Mann BJ. Individual, family, and peer characteristics of adolescent sex offenders and assaultive offenders. *Develop. Psychol*. 1989;25:846-855.

Bischof GP, Stith SM, Whitley ML. Family environments of adolescent sex offenders and other juvenile offenders. *Adolesc*. 1995;30:157-170.

Chaffin M, Bonner B, Pierce K: What Research Shows About Adolescent Sex Offenders. National Center on Sexual Behavior of Youth at the Center on Child Abuse and Neglect Alexandria, VA American Prosecutors Research Institute, 2002, Online. Accessed 9/5/08. *http://www.ndaa.org/publications/newsletters/in_re_volume_5_number_2_2002. html*

Borduin CM, Henggeler SW, Blaske DM, Stein RJ. Multisystemic treatment of adolescent sexual offenders. *Internat J. Offend Ther. Compar Criminol*. 1990;34:105-113.

Cooper AJ. Review of the role of two antilibidinal drugs in the treatment of sex offenders with mental retardation. *Men. Retard*. 1995;33:42-48.

De Jong AR. Sexual interactions among siblings and cousins: Experimentation or exploitation? *Child Abuse and Neglect*. 1989;13:271-279.

Elliott M, ed. *Female Sexual Abuse of Children*. New York, NY: Guilford Press; 1993.

Freeman-Longo RE, Burotn D, Levins J, Fiske JA. *Nationwide survey of treatment programs and models Brandon VT*. The Safer Society Foundation, INC 1998.

Greenfeld LA. *Child victimizers: Violent Offenders and their victims*. Bureau of Justice Statistics U.S. Department of Justice Office of Justice programs and Office of Juvenile Justice and Delinquency Prevention. Washington DC. 1996; NCJ-153258.

Haapasalo J, Kankkonen M. Self-reported childhood abuse among sex and violent offenders. *Arch. Sex Behav.* 1997; 26:421-431.

Kaplan MS, Morales M, Becker JV. The impact of verbal satiation of adolescent sex offenders: A preliminary report. *J. Child Abuse.* 1993;2:81-88.

Kole SM. *Statute protecting minors in a specified age range from rape o other sexual activity as applicable to defendant minor within protected age groups*. American Law Reports (ALR5th) Annotations and Cases 18 ALR 5th: 856-890; 1994.

Lab SP, Shielf G, Schondel C. Research note: An evaluation of juvenile sexual offender treatment. *Crime and Delinq.* 1993;39:543-553.

Matthews R, Hunter JA, Vuz J. Juvenile female sexual offenders: Clinical characteristics and treatment issues. *Sex Abuse: J. Res. Treat.* 1997;9:187-199.

McConaghy N. Assessment and treatment of sex offenders: The Prince of Whales Programme. *Aust. NZ J. Psychiatr.* 1990;24:175-181.22. Carnes PJ. Addiction or compulsion: Politics or illness? *Sex Addict Compul.* 1996;3:127-150.

Myers WC, Burgess AW, Nelson JA. Criminal and behavioral aspects of juvenile sexual homicide. *J Forensic Sci.* 1998;43:340-347.

National Council of Juvenile and Family Court Judges: The Revised Report from the National Task Force on Juvenile Sexual Offending, The National Adolescent Perpetrator Network. *Juv Fam Court J.* 1993; 44(4):5-100.

Pratt HD, Patel DR, Greydanus DE, Dannison L, Walcott D, Sloane MA: Adolescent Sexual Offenders: Issues for Family Physicians. *International Pediatrics,* 2001; 16(2).

Prentky RA, Knight RA, Lee AFS. *Child Sexual Molestation: Research Issues National Institute of Juvenile Research Report*. June NCJ 163390; 1997.

Righthand S, Welch C. *Juveniles Who Have Sexually Offended: A Review of the Professional Literature: Report*. Washington, DC: U.S. Department of Justice, Office of Justice Programs, Office of Juvenile Justice and Delinquency Prevention; 2001 NCJ 184739.

Ryan G, Lane S. *Theories on etiology*. In Ryan G, Lane S, eds. *Juvenile Sexual Offending: Causes, Consequences, and Correction.* 1997; 267- 321.

Ryan G, Lane S. Theories on etiology. In Ryan G, Lane S, eds. *Juvenile Sexual Offending: Causes, Consequences, and Correction.* 1997; 267- 321.

Ryan G, Miyoshi T, Metzner J, Krugman R, et al. Trends in a National Sample of Sexually Abusive Youths. *J. Am. Acad Child Adolesc. Psychiatr.* 1996;35:17-25.

Sermabeikian P, Martinez D: Treatment of adolescent sexual offenders: Theory-based practice. *Child Abuse and Neglect,* 1994; 18:969-976.

Sipe R, Jensen EL, Everett RS. Adolescent sexual offenders grown up: Recidivism in young adulthood. *Crim. Just. Behav.* 1998;25:109-124.

Snyder HN: *Juvenile Arrests 2004.* Washington, DC:U.S. Department of Justice, Office of Justice Programs, Office of Juvenile Justice and Delinquency Preventio, 2006 NCJ 214562 www.ojp.usdoj.gov/ojjdp.

Valliant PMA, Bergeron T. Personality and criminal profile of adolescent sexual offenders, general offenders in comparison to nonoffenders. *Psychol. Rep.* 1997;81:483-48.

Widom CS. *Victims of childhood sexual abuse-later criminal consequences National Institute of Justice Research in Brief.* March 1995. US Department of Justice Office of Justice Programs National Institute of Justice Washington DC 1995.

In: Behavioral Pediatrics, 3rd Edition
Editor: D. E. Greydanus et al.

ISBN 978-1-60692-702-1
© 2009 Nova Science Publishers, Inc.

Chapter 28

Behavioral Aspects of Chronic Illness

Dilip R. Patel, Kristin Guilonard and Helen D. Pratt

Abstract

Chronic disease is common in children and adolescents. Most children with chronic conditions survive into adulthood. Provision of health care to children and adolescent who have chronic disease requires participation of multiple disciplines in a coordinated manner. Youth who have chronic disease and their families face enormous challenges negotiating the complexities of health care system. This chapter provides an overview of behavioral aspects of chronic illness in children and adolescents.

Introduction

In the past, many children with various chronic conditions died young, but medical advances in detection, diagnosis, and management mean that in general over 90% survive into young adulthood. The difficulties faced by these children and their families can be especially cumbersome. Parents of children with chronic diseases or disabilities have described mourning the loss of the idealized healthy child image they had. Financial burdens, even with health insurance can be overwhelming. These burdens are partly influenced by extra child care, out-of-pocket health expenses, adaptations to the home, and costs of transportation. Other family members get less attention because of the demands of the ill child, stressing the family further.

Definition

Chronic disease in childhood generally refers to an illness that exists or is expected to exist for at least three months. Examples of chronic diseases include asthma, epilepsy, and diabetes, whereas examples of physical disability include cerebral palsy and visual impairment. A child can also have a chronic condition, even without meeting the time frame of several months, if the condition is known to have permanence such as in sickle cell anemia or Crohn's disease.

Prior to 1990, the Social Security Administration considered children disabled only if they had certain defined diagnoses. However, a landmark US Supreme Court case in 1990 (Sullivan vs. Zebley) required the administration to develop a method to determine function in each of the following five areas: cognition, communication, motor abilities, social abilities, and patterns of interaction, regardless of the specific diagnosis. This policy change thus heralded the recognition that the impact on the child should also be included in determining disability.

Experts now agree that in order to be considered chronic or disabling, a condition must influence a child's life in two ways. First, there is limitation in what would be considered normal activity for a healthy child, be it in school, play, or recreational activities. Second, there is need for increased medical attention which can include recurrent hospitalizations or physician visits, need for nursing care, or use of medications.

Epidemiology

Demographic studies vary widely in prevalence rates of chronic conditions, depending on the definition used, from as low as 3.5 % to as high as 35 %. But evidence does suggest that prevalence of chronic conditions is increasing over the past several decades, likely due to medical advances in detection, diagnosis, and management. In the 2006 National Health Interview Survey, 14 % of US children have ever been diagnosed with asthma, the most frequently diagnosed chronic disease, up from < 4 % prior to 1980. In the 2007 National Health Interview Survey, 6.3 % of children under 12 years had limitation in usual activity due to one or more chronic condition, and 8.8 % of children aged 12-17 had limitation. This compares with only 2% of all children in 1962.

Clinical Features

The risk for psychological and behavioral problems is increased in children and adolescents with chronic illness, with approximately twice the likelihood compared to healthy controls. Children who have chronic illness or disability may face prejudice and discrimination. Adjustment disorders like anxiety and depression are the most commonly diagnosed psychological problem, but certain family factors can be protective. Reduced family conflict, increased family cohesion, and increased expressiveness among family members are associated with better adjustment of the child.

Coping strategies can also influence adjustment of the child with chronic disease or disability. Coping can take the form of two general types: emotion focused, where the person regulates the feelings toward the stressor, and problem-focused, where the person tries to alter or regulate the stressor itself. With chronic illness, many stressors cannot be dealt with in a problem-focused manner, as the child has little control over the stressor itself: e.g. need for lab tests, dietary changes, and medication. However, when coping strategies are too restricted or avoidance is used almost exclusively, psychological adjustment suffers. This is especially important the first year after diagnosis, when coping skills and adjustment are at their worst. Interventions that have been implemented to promote use of problem-focused coping have shown positive results.

Psychologically, internalizing difficulties, such as depression, anxiety, and social withdrawal are increased in children with chronic illness, when compared to those who are healthy or have acute illness. Externalizing problems like aggression and noncompliance with treatment regimen are also increased in children with chronic disease. Internalizing behaviors can simmer at subclinical levels and not be addressed by parents until they represent serious problems. In order to detect these problems at early stages, the health care provider must specifically screen for depression, anxiety, etc. Externalizing behaviors are easier to diagnose and less common than internalizing behaviors. Both internalizing and externalizing problems can hinder interactions among peers and potentially exacerbate an already tenuous social situation for the child who already may suffer with chronic absenteeism, physical differences, and low self esteem.

Youth with chronic disease and disability are more likely to miss a substantial amount of school, be it from hospitalizations, treatments, illnesses, and/or appointments, ranging from 13 % for those with orthopedic problems to 35 % for those with cancer. In addition to health related absences, ill children are more likely to skip school and miss because of parental misperceptions of vulnerability.

Academic performance has been shown to vary among illness types. Children and adolescents who have asthma have shown similar school performance compared to otherwise healthy children, despite significantly higher missed school days, whereas children with spina bifida and sickle cell disease have shown to have academic difficulty, even when intellect is within the normal range.

Long term, when youth, with chronic illness reach adulthood, they are no more likely than healthy youth to experience psychiatric disorders. However, social and functional outcomes are more likely to be impaired. Educational level, employment, and social maturity have all been demonstrated to be lower among children and adolescents with chronic disease and disability.

Family Impact

The family whose child has a chronic condition faces numerous stressors. The demands of caring for child increases dependence on family, and can cause significant economic, emotional, and social costs. With increased burden of care, comes increased risk of psychological problems for parents and siblings and discord within the family (Table 1). Research findings have been mixed, with some showing no difference in family functioning, whereas others demonstrating lower family cohesiveness. As is to be expected, positive parental psychological adjustment and adaptive relationships are related to positive adjustment of the child with the chronic disease and vice versa.

Mothers tend to be the traditional caregivers of children with chronic illness and are more likely to not work outside the home so that they can take care of the child. Mothers have been shown to have increased risk of depression, whereas fathers have reported increased levels of stress, especially when the child is an adolescent. When fathers are more involved in disease management, marital, maternal, and family functioning are improved. Siblings of youth with chronic disease have increased psychological and behavioral problems, reported at over 50%.

Table 1. Major Reactions of Parents and Families of Children/Adolescents with Chronic Illness

- Disappointment, shame, guilt
- Resentment or anger over the burden of caring for the child
- Anxiety leading to over protectiveness, over-restrictiveness, over-indulgent care
- Excessive attention to child with chronic illness at the expense of attending to other children or family members
- Fatigue, depression, family impoverishment
- Distortion of family life with respect to where to live and what to do
- Sibling resentment of the child who had chronic illness as the recipient of special attention
- Shame caused by having "abnormal" sibling
- Sibling vulnerability with respect to parental transference or over protectiveness
- If child is no expected to live long, grief, depression in anticipation of the outcome

Treatment

As treatment regimens with chronic disease and disability can be complex, it is essential to determine the extent of adherence so as to not alter therapeutic course based on misperception. Adherence not only involves taking medication appropriately, but also attendance at appointments, and following recommended dietary and lifestyle changes. Many modalities exist to assess adherence, from devices that measure how often a medication bottle is opened, to written logs used by the family to keep track of therapies. Of most importance, however, is to assess honestly; it is near impossible for anyone to adhere 100%, and an open dialogue between the physician and family will promote trust and appropriate management. Families and patients should be encouraged to give input into care regimens to the degree that is feasible to improve adherence and to facilitate ownership of treatment plans.

Medical Home

Children and adolescents with chronic disease and disability need to receive the recommended preventive care and supervision. In addition, screening for behavioral and developmental problems should be an integral part of their health maintenance. Families should be assessed for coping ability, distress, discord, and adjustment. The child/adolesent and family need to be educated about the illness and care should be coordinated as much as possible among all providers involved. Although most children with chronic illness are psychologically healthy and do not have developmental problems, it is essential that the provider assess and offer support and referral if the need arises, especially because children with chronic disease routinely do not receive mental health services at higher rates than those without disabilities. Similarly, referral to appropriate mental health services for parents and or siblings should also be made available if signs of maladjustment become evident.

Probably the most important role a physician can play in working with children and adolescents with chronic disease and disability is to provide a medical home, a place where care is coordinated among the providers involved in the child's/adolescent's care, families are linked to social and educational resources, and where the physician serves as a gatekeeper for referrals to ancillary and subspecialty care. Family members should be allowed, if they are willing and able to be a primary partner in care coordination, as it is linked to improved health outcomes. When families and providers do not work together, care can become disorganized and fragmented, satisfaction can decrease, and costs can increase.

Conclusion

Chronic diseases are common in children and adolescents with an estimated prevalence of approximately 20-30%. The severity of clinical manifestations, functional impairment, impact on social functioning, and long-term outcomes vary depending up on multiple factors including the nature of the condition, access to medical care, and family adjustment and coping abilities. Practitioners who provide care to children and adolescents who have chronic conditions play a pivotal role in specific medical treatment of the child as well as in providing overall care coordination and supervision. Most children and adolescents who have chronic illness now survive into adulthood and with appropriated support systems can be expected to lead productive and independent lives.

References

Edwards M, Davis Hilton. *Counselling Parents of Children with Chronic Illness or Disability.* Wiley-Blackwell, 1993.

Goldson E. Behavioral issues in the care of children with special health care needs. In Greydanus DE, Patel DR, Pratt HD, ed. *Behavioral Pediatrics*, 2nd edition, New York:iUniverse, 2006:182-205.

Hilton D. *Counselling Children with Chronic Illness or Disability.* Wiley-Blackwell, 1997.

LeBlanc LA, Goldsmith T, Patel DR. Behavioral aspects of chronic illness in children and adolescents. *Pediatr. Clin. North Am.* 2003;50:859-878.

Lewis M, Vitulano LA. Biopsychosocial issues and risk factors in the family when the child has a chronic illness. *Child Adolesc. Clin. North Am.* 2003;12(3):389-399.

Wallander JL, Thompson RJ Jr, Alriksson-Schmidt A. Psychosocial adjustment of children with chronic physical conditions, In Roberts MC, ed. *Handbook of Pediatric Psychology*, 3rd edition. New York: Guilford Press, 2003:141-158.

In: Behavioral Pediatrics, 3rd Edition
Editor: D. E. Greydanus et al.

ISBN 978-1-60692-702-1
© 2009 Nova Science Publishers, Inc.

Behavioral Pediatrics
Third Edition, 2009
Contributors

Nova Science Publishing, New York

Editors

Donald E. Greydanus MD

Professor, Department of Pediatrics and Human Development
Michigan State University College of Human Medicine, East Lansing, Michigan
Pediatrics Program Director, Kalamazoo Center for Medical Studies
Kalamazoo, Michigan

Dilip R. Patel MD

Professor, Department of Pediatrics and Human Development
Michigan State University College of Human Medicine, East Lansing, Michigan
Divisions of Developmental-Behavioral Pediatrics and Neurodevelopmental Disabilities
Pediatrics Residency Program, Kalamazoo Center for Medical Studies
Kalamazoo, Michigan

Helen D. Pratt PhD

Professor, Department of Pediatrics and Human Development
Michigan State University College of Human Medicine, East Lansing, Michigan
Director, Behavioral-Developmental Pediatrics,
Pediatric Residency Program, Kalamazoo Center for Medical Studies
Kalamazoo, Michigan

Joseph L. Calles Jr., MD

Associate Professor, Department of Psychiatry
Michigan State University College of Human Medicine, East Lansing, Michigan
Director, Child and Adolescent Psychiatry

Psychiatry Residency Program, Kalamazoo Center for Medical Studies
Kalamazoo, Michigan

Contributors

Ben Atchison PhD, OTR, FAOTA
Professor, Department of Occupational Therapy
Western Michigan University
Kalamazoo, Michigan

Joseph L. Calles Jr., MD
Associate Professor, Department of Psychiatry
Michigan State University College of Human Medicine, East Lansing, Michigan
Director, Child and Adolescent Psychiatry
Psychiatry Residency Training Program
Michigan State University Kalamazoo Center for Medical Studies
Kalamazoo, Michigan

Arthur N Feinberg, MD
Professor, Department of Pediatrics and Human Development
Michigan State University College of Human Medicine, East Lansing, Michigan
Michigan State University Kalamazoo Center for Medical Studies
Kalamazoo, Michigan

Cynthia Feucht, Pharm D, BCPS
Assistant Professor of Pharmacy Practice
Ferris State University College of Pharmacy
Michigan State University Kalamazoo Center for Medical Studies
Kalamazoo, Michigan

Donald E. Greydanus MD
Professor, Department of Pediatrics and Human Development
Michigan State University College of Human Medicine, East Lansing, Michigan
Director, Pediatrics Residency Program
Michigan State University Kalamazoo Center for Medical Studies
Kalamazoo, Michigan

Gretchen R. Gudmundsen PhD
Seattle Children's Hospital Research Institute
Division of Child and Adolescent Psychiatry
Department of Psychiatry and Behavioral Science
Seattle, Washington

Kristin W. Guilonard, DO
    Pediatric Primary Care Research Fellow
    Department of Pediatrics
    Medical College of Wisconsin, Milwaukee, Wisconsin

Amy Henry MD
    Seattle Children's Hospital
    Division of Child and Adolescent Psychiatry
    Department of Psychiatry and Behavioral Sciences
    University of Washington School of Medicine
    Seattle, Washington

Heather K. Koole, MA, CCC-SLP
    Doctoral Student, PhD Program in Interdisciplinary Health Sciences
    Western Michigan University, Kalamazoo, Michigan

Margo A. Larsen, Ph D
    Pediatric Psychologist
    Center for Health Promotion and Prevention Research
    University of North Dakota School of Medicine and Health Sciences
    Grand Forks, North Dakota

Lyubov A. Matytsina, MD, PhD
    Professor of the Postgraduate Chair
    Obstetrics, Gynecology, Perinatology, and Pediatric and Adolescent Gynecology
    Donetsk Medical University, Donetsk, Ukraine
    Visiting Academic, Peninsula Medical School
    Plymouth, United Kingdom

Kimberly K. McClanahan PhD
    Associate Professor, Division of Adolescent Medicine
    Department of Pediatrics, University of Kentucky
    Lexington, Kentucky

Jon M. McClellan MD
    Associate Professor
    Seattle Children's Hospital Research Institute
    Division of Child and Adolescent Psychiatry
    Department of Psychiatry and Behavioral Sciences
    University of Washington School of Medicine
    Seattle, Washington

Margaret T. McHugh MD MPH
    Loeb Child Protection and Development Center
    Bellevue Hospital Center

Department of Pediatrics
New York University School of Medicine
New York, New York

Joav Merrick, MD, MMedSci, DMSc
Specialist in Pediatrics, Child Health and Human Development
Ministry of Social Affairs and Social Services
Medical Director, Division of Mental Retardation
Ministry of Social Affairs
Chairman, National Institute of Child Health and Human Development
Jerusalem, Israel

Professor, Department of Pediatrics
Kentucky Children's Hospital, University of Kentucky School of Medicine
Lexington, Kentucky

Ahsan Nazeer, MD
Assistant Professor, Department of Psychiatry
Michigan State University College of Human Medicine, East Lansing, Michigan
Division of Child and Adolescent Psychiatry
Psychiatry Residency Program
Michigan State University Kalamazoo Center for Medical Studies
Kalamazoo, Michigan

Alfonso Torres, MD
Assistant Professor, Department of Pediatrics and Human Development
Michigan State University College of Human Medicine, East Lansing, Michigan
Director of Pediatric Nephrology
Michigan State University Kalamazoo Center for Medical Studies
Kalamazoo, Michigan

Nickola W. Nelson, PhD, CCC-SLP
Director, PhD in Interdisciplinary Health Sciences
Professor, Department of Speech Pathology and Audiology
Western Michigan University, Kalamazoo, Michigan

Hatim A. Omar MD, FAAP
Professor of Pediatrics & Obstetrics and Gynecology,
Chief of Adolescent Medicine and Young Parent Program,
Department of Pediatrics, University of Kentucky,
Lexington, Kentucky

Vincent J. Palusci MD, MSc
Loeb Child Protection and Development Center

Bellevue Hospital Center
Department of Pediatrics
New York University School of Medicine
New York, New York

Dilip R. Patel MD
Professor, Department of Pediatrics & Human Development
Michigan State University College of Human Medicine, East Lansing, Michigan
Developmental-Behavioral Pediatrics and Neurodevelopmental Disabilities
Pediatric Residency Program
Michigan State University Kalamazoo Center for Medical Studies
Kalamazoo, Michigan

Mani N. Pavuluri MD, PhD
Associate Professor in Psychiatry
Director, Pediatric Mood Disorders Program
Institute for Juvenile Research and
Center for Cognitive Medicine
University of Illinois at Chicago
Chicago, Illinois

Helen D. Pratt PhD
Professor, Department of Pediatrics & Human Development
Michigan State University College of Human Medicine, East Lansing, Michigan
Director, Behavioral-Developmental Pediatrics
Pediatrics Residency Program
Michigan State University Kalamazoo Center for Medical Studies
Kalamazoo, Michigan

Cindee Quake-Rapp PhD, OTR
Director, Center for Allied Health Programs
Academic Center
University of Minnessota
Minneapolis, Minnessota

Vinay Reddy MD
Assistant Professor, Department of Pediatrics & Human Development
Michigan State University College of Human Medicine, East Lansing, Michigan
Inpatient Coordinator, Pediatrics Residency Program
Michigan State University Kalamazoo Center for Medical Studies
Kalamazoo, Michigan

William J. Reed MD
Director, Behavioral Pediatrics and Adolescent Medicine

Driscoll Children's Hospital
Associate Professor of Pediatrics
Texas A & M University College of Medicine
Corpus Christi, Texas

Lesley Reid, MD
Pediatric Resident, Pediatrics Residency Program
Michigan State University Kalamazoo Center for Medical Studies
Kalamazoo, Michigan

Antonio C. Sison MD
Clinical Associate Professor
Department of Psychiatry
University of the Philippines
Philippine General Hospital
Malate, Manila, Philippines

Erin Tentis-Berglund, Ph D
Licensed Psychologist
Gillette Children's Specialty Healthcare
St Paul, Minnessota

Artemis K. Tsitsika MD PhD
Lecturer in Pediatrics and Adolescent Medicine
Scientific Supervisor, Adolescent Health Unit
Second Department of Pediatrics
P & A Kyriakou Children's Hospital
University of Athens
Athens, Greece

Christopher K. Varley MD
Professor, Division of Child and Adolescent Psychiatry
Department of Psychiatry and Behavioral Sciences
University of Washington School of Medicine
Seattle, Washington

Amy West PhD
Department of Psychiatry
University of Illinois at Chicago
Chicago, Illinois

Index

A

AAC, 66
ABC, 90
abdomen, 149, 465
abdominal, 135, 142, 149, 212, 217, 389, 393, 408, 458, 466
aberrant, 282, 485
abnormalities, 44, 56, 84, 118, 135, 136, 152, 153, 172, 282, 306, 328, 349, 351, 352, 353, 354, 362, 365, 394, 399, 404, 410, 457
abortion, 285
ABS, 45
absorption, 79, 391, 408, 412, 424, 425
abstinence, 285, 289, 305, 308, 429, 445
abusive, 34, 62, 285, 455, 458, 461, 471, 475, 479, 487
academic, ix, xiii, 7, 9, 12, 13, 18, 28, 29, 32, 33, 34, 40, 51, 52, 53, 55, 56, 57, 58, 59, 61, 64, 69, 71, 72, 74, 75, 93, 133, 142, 162, 163, 166, 200, 208, 216, 272, 326, 356, 487, 497
academic progress, 12
academic settings, 75
academic success, 58
academic tasks, 33
Acanthosis nigricans, 409, 411
access, xi, 3, 4, 5, 31, 32, 51, 64, 66, 71, 91, 151, 229, 284, 289, 300, 303, 330, 331, 334, 390, 408, 417, 456, 466, 487, 489, 499
accessibility, 471
accidental, 141, 342, 354, 429, 439, 458
accidents, 67, 427, 440
accommodation, 58
accounting, 328, 330, 426

acculturation, 378
accuracy, 113, 209
ACE, 292
acetate, 437
acetylcholine, 423, 426
ACF, 483
achievement, 16, 18, 24, 32, 51, 52, 53, 55, 74, 137, 283, 460
achievement test, 55, 74
acid, 182, 198, 199, 251, 360, 418, 421, 428, 429, 437, 438, 441, 445
acidic, 221, 424
acidosis, 393, 398
acne, 275, 289, 409, 411, 420
acne vulgaris, 275
acoustic, 64
acquired immunodeficiency syndrome, 305
activation, 103, 104, 220, 222, 244, 249, 251
acts of aggression, 193
acute, 149, 225, 227, 232, 234, 258, 336, 353, 354, 355, 356, 358, 373, 374, 389, 398, 399, 401, 417, 436, 445, 446, 463, 465, 497
ADA, 32
Adams, v, 9, 22, 290, 342, 472
adaptation, 47, 103, 118, 395
adaptive functioning, 25, 39, 40, 48
addiction, 360, 422, 426, 427, 430, 431, 432, 433, 434, 435, 436, 437, 445, 446, 447, 448, 450
additives, 427
adenoidectomy, 137
adenoids, 137
adequate housing, 456
ADH, 141
ADHD-C, 160, 162, 166
adjudication, 468
adjunctive therapy, 154

adjustment, 34, 45, 67, 110, 136, 148, 307, 321, 324, 360, 490, 496, 497, 499, 500

administration, 13, 14, 15, 40, 89, 140, 145, 152, 250, 384, 412, 437, 496

adolescence, xv, 5, 7, 60, 61, 72, 92, 143, 148, 160, 163, 177, 179, 188, 207, 217, 240, 241, 242, 243, 255, 256, 266, 267, 270, 272, 276, 277, 283, 284, 289, 290, 293, 304, 310, 314, 320, 322, 324, 325, 326, 327, 328, 331, 344, 350, 351, 354, 364, 366, 367, 372, 373, 379, 388, 391, 408, 409, 423, 449, 459

adolescent behavior, 5, 455

adolescent boys, 322

adolescent female, 188, 282, 293, 295, 330, 405, 409

adolescent patients, 304, 335, 372, 402

adolescent sex offenders, 491, 492

adrenal gland, 272, 275

adrenal hyperplasia, 266, 299

adrenogenital syndrome, 266, 298

adult, 20, 21, 30, 47, 48, 68, 80, 133, 141, 208, 220, 225, 226, 227, 230, 232, 233, 265, 266, 268, 275, 276, 278, 280, 282, 284, 285, 291, 292, 301, 302, 303, 309, 312, 320, 325, 341, 343, 349, 350, 351, 352, 353, 360, 364, 365, 367, 369, 372, 379, 380, 387, 410, 411, 417, 420, 423, 426, 451, 453, 454, 458, 463, 474, 478, 485, 487, 488, 489, 490

adult obesity, 410

adult population, 284, 350, 369, 372, 380

adulthood, xv, 19, 21, 22, 23, 24, 25, 27, 159, 188, 200, 222, 256, 266, 267, 270, 272, 283, 284, 285, 304, 310, 323, 344, 351, 354, 362, 369, 371, 372, 379, 388, 391, 408, 410, 449, 451, 459, 482, 492, 495, 497, 499

adults, ix, 11, 49, 69, 71, 72, 122, 161, 177, 192, 206, 207, 208, 215, 217, 220, 221, 225, 230, 243, 244, 247, 249, 251, 253, 260, 265, 267, 270, 271, 275, 276, 280, 284, 292, 301, 302, 307, 308, 311, 320, 323, 324, 328, 329, 344, 345, 346, 351, 352, 354, 357, 358, 359, 362, 369, 394, 401, 403, 406, 409, 411, 412, 413, 417, 422, 426, 428, 429, 433, 434, 435, 440, 446, 449, 456, 458, 459, 461, 465, 469

adverse event, 224, 226

advertisements, 284, 411

advertising, 423, 448, 449

advocacy, xiii, 67, 94, 311, 464, 469, 471, 472, 476

aerobic, 387

aerosols, 444

affect intensity, 345

affective disorder, 57, 342, 363, 390

affective states, 380

Afghanistan, 435

Africa, 379

African-American, 278, 295, 408, 410, 422, 428

after-school, 228, 248

agent, 96, 127, 168, 169, 171, 214, 215, 226, 249, 260, 358, 401, 412

agents, 63, 96, 125, 126, 127, 129, 164, 170, 173, 182, 196, 197, 198, 213, 227, 229, 246, 249, 251, 259, 261, 271, 308, 357, 358, 392, 394, 399, 401, 412, 424, 478

aggression, 96, 97, 162, 171, 177, 185, 186, 187, 188, 189, 190, 192, 193, 194, 195, 196, 197, 198, 200, 201, 224, 225, 227, 268, 322, 379, 471, 497

aggressive behavior, 5, 96, 181, 185, 186, 188, 189, 190, 191, 192, 193, 194, 196, 197, 198, 221, 226

aggressiveness, 126, 192, 198, 431

aging, 177, 458

agnosia, 29

agonist, 105, 125, 126, 170, 196, 198, 199, 426, 436

agoraphobia, 179, 241

agrarian, 330

aid, 13, 443, 469

aiding, 87

AIDS, 290, 305, 306, 308, 429, 432, 433, 436

air, 462

Air Force, 474

Alabama, 470

Alaska, 476

albumin, 393

alcohol, 27, 44, 57, 108, 117, 164, 191, 192, 193, 197, 199, 210, 246, 284, 295, 303, 308, 309, 327, 343, 357, 376, 379, 391, 417, 418, 419, 421, 423, 427, 428, 429, 433, 434, 436, 440, 441, 442, 443, 445, 446, 447, 449, 450, 459, 470, 487

alcohol abuse, 210, 429, 434, 445

alcohol consumption, 379, 428

alcohol dependence, 193, 429, 436, 446, 450

alcohol problems, 193, 197, 449

alcohol use, 27, 164, 295, 309, 376, 418, 423, 428, 429, 446, 447, 459

alcohol withdrawal, 429

alcoholics, 428

alcoholism, 57, 451

alertness, 250, 462

algorithm, 128, 129, 174, 214, 224, 226, 228, 230, 234

alienation, 277

alkaline, 422, 429

alkaline phosphatase, 429

alkalosis, 393, 398

alleles, 352, 365

allergy, 137

alpha, 126, 132, 170, 171, 196, 198, 199, 426, 437, 439, 440

alpha2 adrenergic agonist, 126

alternative, 15, 32, 33, 66, 126, 171, 181, 198, 226, 227, 228, 230, 246, 260, 392, 393, 442

alternatives, 34, 227, 437

alters, 83

altruism, 370

ambivalence, 266, 298

ambivalent, 266, 298

amelioration, 127

amenorrhea, 383, 384, 398, 427

American Academy of Pediatrics (AAP), 47, 60, 87, 98, 291, 293, 310, 311, 312, 446, 447, 450, 470, 472, 473, 477, 478

American Heart Association, 415

American Psychiatric Association, 28, 35, 41, 48, 76, 98, 101, 116, 121, 129, 148, 155, 160, 173, 182, 195, 200, 216, 232, 240, 252, 299, 310, 311, 349, 360, 362, 402, 473, 491

American Psychological Association, 15, 252, 299, 332, 341, 345, 346

Americans with Disabilities Act, 32

amino acids, 463

ammonia, 422, 432

amnesia, 167, 441, 442, 443

amniotic fluid, 44

amphetamine, 168, 172, 228, 234, 429, 430, 431, 439

amphetamines, 164, 169, 210, 392, 427

Amsterdam, 313, 362

AMT, 438

amylase, 393

anabolic steroids, 440

anal fissures, 149

analgesia, 44

analgesics, 435

anatomy, 269, 270, 459, 488

androgens, 266

anemia, 165, 210, 393, 429, 496

anger, 95, 123, 136, 162, 171, 176, 186, 187, 188, 189, 190, 193, 194, 195, 198, 231, 269, 337, 375, 380, 421, 488, 489, 498

anger management, 188

anhedonia, 208, 321, 335, 353, 355

animal models, 388

animal studies, 133

animals, 75, 108, 178, 222, 288, 450

anorexia, 383, 384, 385, 386, 387, 388, 389, 390, 391, 393, 394, 395, 398, 399, 400, 401, 402, 403, 404, 407, 408, 431

anorexia nervosa, 383, 384, 385, 386, 387, 388, 389, 393, 394, 395, 399, 400, 402, 403, 404, 407

anoscopy, 305

anoxia, 67

antagonist, 105, 140, 401, 436

antecedents, 10, 11, 291, 381, 449

anterograde amnesia, 441

anthropology, 342

antibiotic, 259

antibody, 259, 426, 432, 434

anticholinergic, 141, 142, 143

anticholinergic effect, 141

anticonvulsant, 441

anticonvulsants, 128

antidepressant, 128, 129, 169, 196, 199, 212, 213, 216, 228, 235, 251, 261, 337

antidepressant medication, 213, 216, 251

antidepressants, 47, 128, 141, 196, 198, 253, 260, 261, 346, 401, 429

antidiuretic hormone, 143, 393

antihistamines, 437

antipsychotic, 96, 97, 98, 126, 127, 197, 198, 199, 233, 351, 357, 358, 364

antipsychotic drugs, 364, 380

antipsychotics, 47, 96, 97, 126, 127, 198, 224, 225, 226, 229, 261, 358, 364, 367, 429

antisocial, 188, 195, 323, 327, 372, 373, 378, 379, 490

antisocial behavior, 188, 327, 490

antisocial personality disorder, 195, 323, 327, 372, 379

antiviral, 196

antrum, 176

anus, 149, 154, 466

anxiety, xv, 5, 14, 26, 27, 28, 42, 43, 56, 83, 91, 92, 96, 97, 98, 123, 149, 166, 167, 171, 179, 191, 192, 195, 196, 197, 198, 199, 208, 211, 214, 223, 224, 228, 237, 239, 240, 241, 242, 243, 244, 245, 246, 247, 248, 249, 250, 251, 252, 253, 255, 256, 258, 259, 260, 261, 262, 268, 272, 275, 321, 322, 327, 353, 374, 376, 380, 388, 389, 390, 391, 396, 402, 418, 427, 430, 431, 433, 440, 442, 445, 459, 496, 497, 498

anxiety disorder, 5, 26, 56, 83, 91, 92, 98, 123, 149, 166, 167, 179, 191, 195, 211, 228, 239, 240, 241,

242, 243, 244, 245, 246, 247, 249, 252, 253, 255, 256, 258, 259, 260, 261, 321, 376
anxiolytic, 193, 211, 441
anxious mood, 239
aorta, 409
APA, 15, 35
apathy, 277, 429
apnea, 44, 409, 411, 414, 427
apoptosis, 272, 429
appetite, 97, 171, 205, 206, 209, 210, 212, 229, 383, 388, 401, 420, 439
apples, 386
application, xii, 47, 101, 424, 476
apraxia, 66, 73
Arctic, 400
arginine, 143
argument, 171, 189
aripiprazole, 127, 261, 358, 362
arithmetic, 24, 52, 54, 55, 91
Arizona, 473
armed robbery, 178
aromatic hydrocarbons, 423
arousal, 105, 108, 115, 133, 141, 221, 230, 266, 298
arrest, 299, 396, 436, 486
arrhythmia, 433
arrhythmias, 141, 172, 397, 429, 430, 440
arterioles, 423
artery, 409
arthritis, 210, 282
articulation, xi, 59, 61, 64, 66, 68, 71, 72, 84, 88, 90, 94
ASD, 74, 79, 80, 84, 85, 87, 194, 198, 199
ash, 225
Asian, 311, 447
asphyxia, 272
aspiration, 153, 435, 443
assault, 280, 281, 285, 290, 291, 292, 388, 441, 442, 458, 459, 460, 461, 464, 470, 472, 475, 479, 481, 487
assaults, 67, 188, 190, 280, 281, 308, 442
assertiveness, 27, 289
assessment, xiii, 3, 4, 7, 9, 10, 11, 12, 13, 14, 15, 16, 17, 18, 19, 21, 22, 24, 25, 28, 29, 30, 34, 40, 57, 60, 61, 62, 68, 70, 72, 73, 74, 76, 87, 88, 90, 91, 110, 113, 117, 130, 159, 173, 174, 182, 190, 194, 196, 201, 206, 220, 239, 245, 246, 252, 255, 261, 323, 326, 331, 332, 333, 334, 335, 336, 338, 339, 346, 353, 355, 356, 357, 358, 361, 392, 410, 451, 459, 461, 463, 467, 468, 469, 471, 481, 482
assessment procedures, 14, 25, 28, 34, 332

assessment techniques, 11
assessment tools, 18, 21, 22, 24, 28, 74, 246, 252
assignment, 452
assimilation, 287
associations, 75, 352, 353, 355, 387, 406
assumptions, 302
asthma, 246, 425, 452, 495, 496, 497
asymmetry, 135
asymptomatic, 142
asystole, 397
ataxia, 445
Athens, 506
atherosclerosis, 409
athletes, 387, 422, 442
Atlas, 477
atmosphere, 14, 33, 461
ATP, 397
atrophy, 420
attachment, 70, 83, 167, 279, 452, 456
attacks, 98, 195, 227, 240, 241, 242, 440
attention, xv, 4, 6, 7, 9, 10, 15, 21, 22, 29, 30, 31, 42, 51, 52, 53, 56, 57, 59, 60, 64, 67, 69, 70, 71, 74, 75, 83, 86, 96, 104, 107, 108, 114, 115, 117, 118, 124, 148, 149, 161, 162, 167, 173, 174, 180, 181, 192, 199, 220, 221, 223, 224, 228, 235, 256, 257, 261, 319, 321, 337, 370, 375, 389, 399, 401, 409, 423, 429, 430, 443, 446, 458, 471, 485, 490, 491, 495, 496, 498
Attention deficit hyperactivity disorder (ADHD), xv, 6, 13, 26, 34, 53, 56, 91, 98, 107, 118, 123, 124, 125, 126, 128, 129, 130, 159, 160, 161, 162, 163, 164, 165, 166, 167, 169, 171, 172, 173, 174, 178, 179, 180, 181, 182, 192, 193, 194, 195, 197, 198, 199, 208, 212, 214, 220, 223, 225, 227, 228, 230, 233, 234, 353, 417, 418, 427, 430, 431, 434, 450
attentional disorder, 24
attitudes, 59, 114, 147, 224, 230, 266, 270, 271, 283, 285, 286, 287, 293, 298, 301, 302, 320, 328, 343, 395, 403, 410, 451, 480
atypical, 73, 96, 97, 98, 127, 197, 199, 229, 269, 300, 354, 355, 357, 358, 363, 427, 489
atypical antipsychotic agents, 96
auditory hallucinations, 350
auditory stimuli, 108
Australia, 331, 345, 439, 480
authority, 176, 177, 194, 269, 370, 464, 470, 489
autism, xiii, 4, 32, 65, 70, 74, 75, 79, 80, 81, 82, 83, 84, 85, 87, 88, 89, 90, 91, 92, 93, 94, 95, 97, 98, 99, 104, 107, 108, 116, 117, 119, 356
autistic spectrum disorders, 118

autoimmune, 130, 257
autoimmune responses, 257
automobiles, 406
autonomic, 103, 131, 228, 230, 244, 409
autonomic nervous system, 103, 131, 244
autonomy, 268, 447, 456
autopsy, 327, 342, 343
autosomal dominant, 407
autosomal recessive, 407
availability, 59, 170, 223, 334, 345, 419, 432, 439, 445, 446, 452
avoidance, 98, 104, 208, 245, 247, 248, 257, 258, 309, 412, 497
avoidance behavior, 248, 257
avoidant, 253, 378, 379, 387
awareness, 12, 58, 66, 69, 71, 75, 82, 87, 93, 98, 107, 114, 132, 194, 219, 230, 244, 252, 277, 287, 300, 307, 308, 336, 440
axon, 272

B

babbling, 68, 70, 84
babies, 66, 70, 287, 288
BAC, 428, 429
bacteria, 308
bacterial, 357
bail-out, 181
baking, 432
bank account, 339
barbiturates, 445
barrier, 108, 434
barriers, 167
basic rights, 176
basketball, 283
batteries, 18, 20
battery, 23, 57, 102
Bayesian analysis, 468
Bayley Scales of Infant Development, 25, 45
beer, 428
behavior modification, 137, 359
behavior therapy, 32, 262, 335, 367, 380, 403
behavioral aspects, xiii, 7, 477, 492, 495
behavioral assessment, 3, 4, 11, 13, 25, 196
behavioral difficulties, 117, 353
behavioral disorders, xv, 6, 13, 67, 149
behavioral manifestations, 373
behavioral modification, 412

behavioral problems, xi, xii, 5, 25, 93, 102, 125, 143, 208, 220, 231, 244, 284, 322, 440, 459, 487, 496, 498
behavioral sciences, xv
behavioral theory, 28
behaviours, 403
beliefs, 285, 288, 305, 331, 342, 353, 354, 359, 380, 395, 442, 451
bell, 40, 41, 54, 145
beneficial effect, 335, 401
benefits, 96, 155, 227, 228, 249, 250, 260, 279, 359, 400, 448
benign, 192, 225, 242, 260, 275, 412, 427
benzene, 445
benzodiazepine, 441
benzodiazepines, 227, 228, 251, 427, 441
beta, 121, 196, 197, 199, 257, 258, 413, 426, 433
beta cell, 413
beta-blockers, 433
beverages, 392
bicarbonate, 398, 432
bile, 435
bilirubin, 429
binding, 364
binge drinking, 309, 428
binge eating disorder, 384, 388
bingeing, 376, 391, 401
biochemical, 394
biofeedback, 145, 150, 154, 155
biologic, 48, 244, 265, 266, 299, 311, 313, 386
biological, 3, 4, 5, 41, 82, 207, 223, 297, 299, 436, 486
biologically, 266
biology, xv
biomarkers, 357
biopsy, 149
bipolar, 5, 91, 92, 97, 166, 194, 196, 198, 219, 220, 221, 222, 223, 224, 225, 226, 227, 228, 230, 231, 232, 233, 234, 235, 249, 260, 354, 355, 362, 363, 366, 367, 368, 372, 427
bipolar disorder, 5, 91, 92, 97, 166, 194, 196, 219, 220, 222, 223, 224, 225, 226, 227, 228, 230, 231, 232, 233, 234, 235, 249, 260, 354, 355, 362, 366, 372, 427
bipolar illness, 166
birth, 42, 44, 57, 68, 86, 89, 107, 265, 266, 267, 268, 280, 283, 289, 352, 361, 364, 365, 366, 367, 423, 475
birth control, 283, 289
birth rate, 280

birth weight, 423
births, 66, 280, 455
black, 129, 162, 213, 227, 250, 260, 323, 337, 370, 395, 405
black hole, 162
black-box, 250, 260
blackouts, 441
bladder, 81, 86, 131, 132, 133, 134, 135, 136, 137, 141, 142, 143, 144, 145, 162
blame, 177, 206, 301, 449
bleeding, 44, 433, 458, 462, 474
blood, 11, 89, 126, 127, 134, 172, 196, 215, 226, 244, 308, 327, 358, 393, 409, 411, 428, 429, 431, 433, 434, 443, 445, 463
blood dyscrasias, 127
blood glucose, 127
blood pressure, 126, 127, 172, 196, 226, 358, 409, 411, 414, 429, 431, 443, 445
blood urea nitrogen, 393
blood-brain barrier, 434
BMI, 97, 127, 358, 406, 408, 409, 412
body dissatisfaction, 166, 403
body fat, 400, 408
body image, 281, 282, 371, 390, 400, 409, 414
body language, 31
body mass index, 127, 358, 384, 401, 408, 414
body shape, 385
body weight, 273, 384, 390, 394, 398, 407, 412, 414
boiling, 435
bonding, 95
bone, 141, 161, 393, 398
bone marrow, 141, 393
bone mass, 398
boot camps, 181
borderline, 194, 195, 346, 353, 372, 379, 381, 387, 390, 395, 403
borderline personality disorder, 195, 346, 372, 375, 376, 379, 381, 387, 391, 395, 403
boredom, 391
Boston, 20, 76, 482
bounds, 68
bowel, 81, 86, 142, 147, 149, 150, 151, 153, 155, 210, 393, 399, 462
bowel sounds, 149, 393, 462
boys, 65, 73, 81, 86, 118, 134, 148, 160, 178, 180, 188, 208, 243, 266, 267, 268, 276, 277, 287, 322, 374, 410, 414, 477, 486
BPD, 195, 380
bradycardia, 393, 396
bradypnea, 443

brain, 13, 19, 24, 42, 44, 52, 54, 59, 62, 63, 67, 89, 103, 108, 118, 127, 165, 191, 192, 196, 199, 221, 244, 272, 299, 311, 350, 351, 352, 353, 360, 362, 363, 364, 365, 367, 368, 388, 404, 423, 436, 455, 458, 463, 465, 473, 474, 476, 478, 481, 482
brain abnormalities, 362, 365
brain damage, 127, 474, 481
brain development, 118, 360
brain growth, 272
brain injury, 24, 62, 67, 165, 191, 192, 196, 199, 209, 455, 458, 465, 473, 476, 478, 482
brain tumor, 13
brainstem, 132
breakdown, 206, 440
breakfast, 154, 392
breast, 273, 274, 275, 288, 289, 423
breast cancer, 423
breastfeeding, 286
breathing, 42, 166, 240, 244, 411, 443
British, x, 340, 345, 346, 426
British Columbia, 426
brittle hair, 393
bronchitis, 427
bronchospasm, 427
bstinence, 284, 285, 295, 314, 426
buccal mucosa, 423, 425
Buddhism, 395
budding, 274, 275, 288
buildings, 178
bulimia, 383, 384, 385, 387, 388, 390, 391, 393, 394, 395, 398, 400, 401, 402, 403, 404, 407
bulimia nervosa, 383, 384, 385, 387, 388, 390, 391, 393, 394, 395, 400, 402, 403, 404, 407
bullying, 34, 208, 281, 370
bupropion, 129, 169, 170, 171, 172, 196, 214, 215, 424, 425, 426, 450
burn, 400, 445
burning, 330, 400
burnout, 422
burns, 161, 162, 457, 458, 462, 465, 480
business, 72
bypass, 58, 413

C

cachexia, 389
caffeine, 246, 412
calcium, 397, 398, 406, 429
caliber, 153
California, 22, 102, 116, 313, 443, 474

calluses, 398

caloric intake, 397, 405, 406, 410, 412

calorie, 229, 389, 399

campaigns, 335

Canada, 113, 201, 278, 331, 345, 426, 480

canals, 462

cancer, 165, 258, 422, 423, 447, 497

cancers, 423, 450

candidates, 250, 410

cannabis, 193, 195, 210, 356, 447

CAP, 212

capacity, 107, 132, 133, 136, 137, 138, 140, 141, 145, 265, 266, 298, 353, 374

capital, 409, 411

caps, 442

capsule, 427

carbohydrate, 406, 407, 412

carbon, 165, 422, 423

carbon monoxide, 422, 423

carcinogenic, 422

carcinoma, 423

cardiac arrhythmia, 141, 429, 440

cardiac dysrhythmia, 398

cardiac muscle, 400

cardiac risk factors, 172

cardiomyopathy, 172, 403

cardiovascular, 170, 172, 174, 408, 409, 440

cardiovascular failure, 440

cardiovascular function, 174

cardiovascular system, 170, 172

caregiver, 32, 45, 76, 105, 108, 111, 113, 167, 454

caregivers, 44, 68, 91, 105, 114, 162, 167, 168, 195, 207, 212, 219, 230, 240, 244, 258, 288, 356, 389, 391, 405, 489, 498

caregiving, 188

caretaker, 268, 465

Caribbean, 312, 379

CAS, 66, 73

case law, 468, 490

cast, 18

castration, 268, 271, 491

CAT, 458

catabolism, 400

cataplexy, 442

catatonic, 207, 350, 353

catechol, 351

catecholamine, 432

catecholamines, 437

categorization, 320

category a, 65, 81, 85, 384

Caucasian, 387, 422, 428

Caucasians, 278, 408

causal relationship, 279, 352

causation, 487

CBCL, 26

CBT, 212, 213, 214, 228, 231, 232, 336, 337, 359, 395, 400, 401

CCC, 503, 504

CDR, 471

Celexa, 249, 260

Celiac disease, 165

cell, 132, 210, 272, 358, 397, 496, 497

cell death, 272

cellulose, 153

Census Bureau, 7

Center for Disease Control and Prevention, 99

Centers for Disease Control (CDC), 48, 83, 87, 187, 193, 200, 278, 291, 308, 314, 340, 415, 426, 447, 454, 474, 483

central nervous system, 67, 76, 103, 104, 116, 121, 122, 131, 272, 357, 378, 425, 426, 428, 429, 430, 432, 433, 436, 439, 441, 443, 448

cereals, 399

cerebral palsy, 12, 66, 282, 496

cerebrospinal fluid, 399

cerebrovascular accident, 440

certainty, 92, 98, 165, 463, 468

certificate, xii

chancroid, 433

changing environment, 278

chaotic, 213, 355, 380, 436

cheating, 410

chemical, 29, 426, 430, 433, 441, 443

chemicals, 423, 431, 432, 438, 439, 440, 441

chemistry, 447, 450

chemotherapy, 165, 427

chewing, 423, 424, 425, 435

Chicago, 477, 478, 480, 505, 506

chicken, 386

child abuse, 5, 57, 334, 388, 451, 452, 453, 454, 455, 457, 458, 461, 463, 464, 465, 467, 468, 469, 470, 471, 472, 473, 474, 475, 476, 477, 478, 479, 480, 481, 482, 483, 484, 487, 489, 490

Child Behavior Checklist, 26

child development, x, 342, 464, 469, 470

child maltreatment, 451, 452, 455, 456, 457, 460, 461, 463, 464, 470, 473, 474, 475, 479, 481, 487

child mortality, 446

child protection, 464, 465, 469

child protective services, 455, 460, 464, 469, 472

child rearing, 147
child welfare, 458, 464, 469, 472
childbearing, 290
childcare, 470, 489
childhood, ix, xv, 4, 5, 7, 8, 39, 44, 45, 54, 58, 61,
    66, 67, 72, 73, 79, 81, 86, 117, 118, 129, 134,
    155, 160, 161, 192, 200, 201, 207, 217, 220, 228,
    235, 240, 241, 242, 243, 249, 252, 253, 255, 256,
    260, 266, 268, 272, 279, 283, 287, 292, 295, 299,
    304, 322, 323, 325, 329, 336, 340, 345, 349, 350,
    354, 359, 360, 361, 362, 363, 364, 365, 366, 367,
    372, 373, 379, 388, 390, 405, 409, 411, 413, 451,
    452, 456, 474, 475, 478, 480, 482, 483, 487, 489,
    492, 493, 495
childhood disorders, 350, 359
childhood history, 456
childhood sexual abuse, 388, 456, 487, 493
China, 331, 435
Chinese, 367, 440
chlamydia, 308
Chlamydia trachomatis, 305, 306, 308, 466
chloride, 144, 445
chlorpromazine, 127, 198, 199
chocolate, 152
cholelithiasis, 413
cholesterol, 409, 410, 412
cholinergic, 142, 423
cholinergic medications, 142
chromosome, 143, 299, 361, 367
chromosomes, 361
chronic, xiii, 4, 62, 89, 103, 108, 121, 122, 144, 149,
    150, 165, 212, 217, 219, 221, 223, 241, 242, 243,
    250, 255, 256, 260, 261, 281, 282, 295, 327, 353,
    357, 358, 364, 376, 391, 396, 399, 402, 421, 423,
    427, 440, 444, 446, 447, 452, 465, 470, 474, 495,
    496, 497, 498, 499, 500
chronic cough, 421, 427
chronic disease, 4, 452, 495, 496, 497, 498, 499
chronic illness, 256, 281, 282, 402, 495, 496, 497,
    498, 499
chronically ill, 282
cigarette smoke, 422
cigarette smokers, 422
cigarette smoking, 309, 379
cigarettes, 422, 424, 437
Cincinnati, 483
cingulated, 360, 365
circadian rhythm, 231
circumcision, 271
citalopram, 127, 215, 249, 260

citizens, 379
citrus, 406
classes, 57, 164, 275, 281, 350, 389, 470
classical, 221
classification, 64, 73, 80, 101, 106, 367, 483
classified, 17, 48, 61, 66, 79, 122, 280, 299, 406,
    439, 445, 453
classroom, 32, 33, 57, 59, 104, 161, 162, 163, 245
classroom management, 162
classrooms, 10, 32
cleaning, 444, 445
clients, 403
clinical approach, 131
clinical assessment, 332, 361, 461
clinical depression, 207, 211, 427
clinical diagnosis, 461
clinical judgment, 40, 125
clinical presentation, 51, 82, 147, 239, 353, 383, 477
clinical symptoms, 42, 43, 402
clinical syndrome, xiii, 27
clinical trial, 253, 262
clinically significant, 81, 113, 143, 172, 337
clinician, xv, 4, 6, 9, 57, 58, 59, 75, 134, 151, 154,
    165, 168, 169, 178, 179, 181, 185, 195, 209, 213,
    216, 223, 226, 227, 275, 282, 292, 302, 303, 304,
    308, 309, 310, 312, 314, 333, 347, 356, 379, 418,
    438, 442, 444, 445, 447, 461, 466, 468, 490
clinicians, xv, 3, 5, 6, 53, 59, 101, 131, 185, 188,
    211, 212, 219, 221, 258, 265, 275, 282, 284, 285,
    303, 304, 320, 355, 379, 417, 423, 428, 433, 434,
    446, 448, 451, 468, 471, 485, 489, 491
clinics, 13, 243, 283, 377, 471
clonidine, 125, 126, 129, 169, 170, 172, 196, 230
close relationships, 374
clothing, 134, 162, 266, 298, 389, 392, 460
clotting factors, 393
clozapine, 97, 197, 357, 358, 363, 367
clubfoot, 135
clusters, 80, 160, 198, 374
CMV, 209, 210, 306
CNS, 121, 126, 164, 193, 210, 217, 272, 291, 434,
    436, 440, 442, 445
coaches, 34, 176, 275
coagulation, 465
coagulation factors, 465
cocaine, 164, 193, 210, 284, 417, 421, 422, 427, 430,
    432, 433, 434, 435, 439, 441, 448
cocaine use, 193, 432, 434
Cochrane, 144, 155, 448
codes, 452, 467

coding, 32, 452, 467

coercion, 269, 453, 486, 489

cognition, x, 7, 39, 59, 60, 369, 372, 380, 427, 457, 496

cognitive, 4, 6, 7, 9, 12, 13, 18, 25, 26, 29, 34, 39, 40, 43, 45, 46, 48, 51, 52, 55, 56, 61, 62, 66, 67, 70, 72, 73, 74, 81, 85, 86, 91, 127, 129, 155, 162, 185, 194, 212, 219, 223, 225, 228, 231, 232, 234, 243, 249, 252, 253, 259, 266, 269, 275, 287, 323, 325, 332, 335, 336, 339, 346, 353, 354, 357, 359, 363, 370, 374, 393, 399, 404, 407, 412, 440, 460, 461, 470, 471, 474, 479, 486, 487

cognitive abilities, 45, 46, 73, 486

cognitive ability, 74, 479

cognitive capacities, 18

cognitive deficit, 39, 357

cognitive deficits, 39

cognitive development, 7, 46, 81, 275, 323, 325, 370, 460

cognitive dysfunction, 393, 440

cognitive function, 12, 13, 18, 48, 51, 72, 370, 399, 487

cognitive impairment, 67, 85, 86, 91, 127, 353, 404

cognitive level, 269, 287

cognitive process, 51, 55, 56

cognitive processing, 55

cognitive therapy, 335

cohesion, 323, 336, 496

cohesiveness, 497

cohort, 323, 367

coitus, 271, 277, 278, 281, 283

colds, 420

collaboration, 76, 114, 249, 261

collagen, 463

collateral, 395

college students, 281, 324, 326, 327, 329, 335, 341, 342, 345, 422, 439, 442, 449

colleges, 34, 342

colon, 153, 393

Colorado, 469

colposcopy, 459, 466

Columbia, ix, 294, 314, 426, 435

Columbia University, ix, 294, 314

coma, 261, 428, 437, 443, 445

commercial, 426, 444, 452

commissure, 299, 311

communication, 29, 30, 31, 33, 40, 46, 47, 56, 61, 62, 63, 64, 67, 68, 69, 70, 71, 72, 74, 75, 76, 79, 80, 81, 83, 84, 85, 86, 87, 88, 90, 93, 94, 95, 136,

192, 194, 196, 208, 230, 270, 283, 285, 302, 336, 395, 420, 456, 468, 496

communication abilities, 61, 64, 72

communication skills, 29, 64, 81, 230, 456

communities, 93, 94, 282, 429, 471

community, x, xii, xiii, 6, 34, 39, 40, 47, 48, 58, 93, 112, 116, 147, 160, 180, 182, 185, 206, 212, 220, 232, 247, 253, 258, 288, 295, 310, 321, 324, 357, 359, 377, 418, 422, 423, 451, 452, 456, 458, 459, 460, 461, 463, 464, 467, 469, 470, 471, 473, 474, 479, 483, 484, 486, 490

community service, 451, 460, 467, 486

community support, xiii, 359, 471

community-based, 418

comorbidity, 167, 173, 180, 182, 192, 195, 208, 212, 217, 221, 242, 345, 366

compensation, 384

competence, 61, 211, 241, 420

competency, 148

competition, 283

complement, 393

complete blood count, 89

complex partial seizure, 89

complexity, 66, 98, 114

compliance, 3, 6, 67, 167, 215, 250, 358

complications, 44, 46, 89, 141, 279, 282, 285, 297, 383, 385, 394, 396, 404, 405, 408, 410, 411, 412, 413, 423, 428, 429, 432, 433, 435, 444, 446, 450

components, 63, 73, 87, 114, 185, 231, 268, 301, 393, 436

composite, 363

composition, 406

compounds, 227, 422, 441

comprehension, 24, 52, 54, 58, 59, 60, 66, 71, 74, 370

compulsion, 492

compulsive behavior, 255, 256, 257, 259, 388, 401

compulsive personality disorder, 373

computer, 21, 32, 58, 154, 458

computers, 31, 85, 106

concentration, 138, 152, 206, 210, 211, 365, 399, 428, 434

conception, 266, 267, 342

conceptualization, 491

concordance, 299, 351

concrete, 63, 84, 188, 245, 248, 277, 323, 325

Concrete, 245, 276, 370

conditioning, 137

condom, 278, 285, 307

condoms, 283, 284, 289, 305, 308

conduct disorder, 4, 126, 183, 192, 194, 321, 327, 343, 379, 490

Conduct Disorder, vi, 175, 176, 177, 179, 181, 187, 418

conduct problems, 179, 211, 217

conduction, 260, 272

conductive, 66

confidence, 18, 32, 40, 106

confidentiality, 15, 285, 290, 292, 293, 308, 310, 464, 469, 490

confirmatory factor analysis, 118

conflict, xii, 3, 4, 163, 189, 190, 194, 220, 283, 305, 310, 329, 336, 370, 419, 454, 496

confusion, xii, 194, 195, 220, 275, 283, 290, 300, 427, 441

congenital adrenal hyperplasia, 266, 299

Congress, 66

congruence, 160

consciousness, 356, 441

consensus, 43, 49, 102, 221, 479

consent, 269, 453, 488, 490

constipation, 126, 135, 142, 144, 147, 148, 149, 150, 151, 152, 154, 155, 260, 399

constraints, 247

construction, 22, 23

consultants, 5

consumers, 213, 443

consumption, 229, 379, 406, 428

contamination, 257, 258

contingency, 30

continuing, 370, 417

continuity, 80, 220, 363

contraceptives, 283

contractions, 124

contracts, 154

control, 6, 31, 55, 56, 62, 66, 71, 72, 73, 76, 81, 86, 104, 105, 114, 115, 131, 132, 134, 137, 142, 147, 148, 150, 151, 154, 155, 162, 167, 179, 190, 223, 227, 230, 231, 248, 260, 268, 281, 283, 287, 289, 323, 327, 340, 342, 343, 345, 351, 369, 372, 374, 377, 380, 385, 388, 390, 391, 392, 403, 414, 419, 422, 430, 446, 452, 456, 482, 486, 497

control condition, 351

controlled, 14, 62, 126, 130, 137, 182, 190, 196, 198, 228, 230, 234, 253, 259, 262, 283, 321, 328, 337, 346, 358, 362, 366, 395, 400, 401, 412

controlled research, 182

controlled studies, 126, 137, 249

controlled trials, 228, 230, 358, 395, 400, 412

contusions, 462

convergence, 55

conversion, 310

convulsion, 145

cooperative learning, 71

coordination, 6, 23, 52, 55, 56, 57, 58, 66, 73, 85, 94, 106, 131, 485, 499

coping, 300, 496

coping strategies, 34, 359, 497

copyright, 14

correlation, 82, 163, 180, 189, 212, 387

correlations, 327

cortex, 119, 131, 132, 360

cortical, 63, 127, 133, 272, 351, 360, 362, 365

corticosteroids, 409

corticotropin, 428

cost-effective, 366

costs, 396, 413, 451, 455, 471, 486, 495, 497, 499

cough, 412, 417, 420, 421, 423, 425, 427

cough suppressant, 412

coughing, 425

counsel, xv, 285

counseling, xiii, 46, 137, 247, 294, 310, 400, 448, 452, 454, 460, 461, 470

coupling, 388

courts, 490

coverage, xi, xiii, 329

CP, 99, 437

CPS, 463, 469

CR, 145, 314, 339, 340, 345, 367, 447

crack, 432, 433, 441

cracking, 443

cranial nerve, 462

craniofacial, 362

craving, 105, 197, 425, 426, 435, 450

credibility, 34

credit, 178, 222

credit card, 178, 222

crime, 277, 305, 342, 406, 486, 490

crimes, 464, 486

criminal acts, 486

criminal behavior, 178, 490

criminal justice, 490

criminal justice system, 490

crisis intervention, 335

crisis management, 95

critical period, 266

critical points, 332

criticism, 188, 328, 343, 370, 377, 390

cross-cultural, 330, 331

cross-cultural differences, 331

CRS, 26
crying, 244, 479
crystal, 430, 441
crystalline, 432, 439
crystals, 431
cues, 20, 83, 114, 283, 423
cultural, x, xiii, 6, 55, 71, 266, 279, 298, 302, 330, 331, 379, 380, 385, 407
cultural differences, 331
cultural influence, x
cultural norms, 6, 380, 407
culture, xii, 15, 40, 95, 258, 259, 272, 300, 301, 386, 420
curiosity, 268, 269, 270, 287, 421
curriculum, 32, 346, 483
cycles, 223
cycling, 223, 232, 233
cystic fibrosis, 401
cystometry, 144
cystourethrogram, 135
cytogenetic, 352

D

daily living, 41, 105, 110, 257
dairy, 412
dances, 438
danger, 68, 74, 243, 279, 331, 333, 442
data base, 65
data collection, 151
data gathering, 57
database, 65, 479
dating, 187, 277, 279, 281, 285, 289, 295, 308, 371, 406, 428, 475
de novo, 352, 365, 368
DEA, 443
deafness, 192
death, 172, 178, 207, 265, 272, 292, 319, 320, 323, 324, 326, 327, 330, 334, 338, 339, 342, 343, 354, 383, 428, 429, 431, 433, 435, 437, 440, 442, 443, 445, 446, 455, 460, 471, 475, 477
deaths, 45, 126, 320, 324, 330, 345, 427, 428, 449, 455, 460, 471, 474, 479
decision making, xi, 272, 370
decision trees, 357
decisions, 31, 113, 246, 323, 326, 336, 377
decoding, 15, 54, 66, 69
decongestant, 439
deductive reasoning, 276, 370
defecation, 135, 142, 156, 457

defects, 135
defensiveness, 118
deficiency, 210, 266, 398, 407, 412
deficit, xv, 4, 6, 29, 33, 43, 53, 55, 59, 60, 67, 104, 107, 118, 123, 124, 130, 149, 159, 173, 174, 178, 179, 182, 191, 192, 199, 212, 220, 223, 224, 235, 257, 321, 357, 401, 409, 419, 423, 430, 446, 450, 490
deficits, 7, 16, 26, 32, 39, 40, 46, 48, 51, 52, 54, 55, 56, 58, 60, 67, 72, 74, 80, 83, 86, 87, 88, 89, 90, 91, 92, 93, 105, 107, 108, 113, 196, 353, 354, 356, 359, 364, 374, 375, 380, 460
definition, xii, xiii, 11, 14, 40, 41, 43, 65, 67, 86, 101, 122, 147, 173, 185, 240, 252, 384, 396, 459, 465, 496
deformities, 281, 282, 462
degradation, 299
degrading, 459
degree, 10, 71, 72, 91, 108, 159, 166, 171, 180, 181, 185, 189, 206, 208, 212, 215, 242, 266, 298, 303, 322, 323, 330, 332, 334, 338, 351, 354, 360, 419, 467, 468, 498
dehydration, 96, 153, 393, 440
delays, 42, 49, 55, 56, 57, 64, 67, 79, 81, 83, 84, 86, 87, 88, 91, 108, 162, 353, 457, 459, 460, 461
delinquency, 342, 379, 459
delinquents, 177, 490
delirium, 355, 357, 397, 429, 438, 443
delirium tremens, 429
delivery, xii, 44, 65, 75, 76, 89, 231, 282, 313, 433
delta, 426
delta-9-tetrahydrocannabinol, 426
delusions, 82, 92, 195, 221, 222, 233, 350, 353, 354, 355, 356, 359, 374, 430
demand, 10, 53, 114, 333, 397
demographic, 4
demographics, 479
denial, 269, 289, 309, 384, 422, 459
Denmark, 366
density, 409, 412
Department of Agriculture, 405
Department of Commerce, 7
Department of Education, 65, 77
Department of Health and Human Services, 60, 187, 296, 340, 381, 408, 413, 447, 449, 454, 476, 482, 483, 484
Department of Justice, 280, 291, 292, 479, 492, 493
dependent personality disorder, 379
depersonalization, 439
depressants, 421, 443, 445

depressed, 97, 166, 167, 171, 196, 205, 206, 207, 208, 211, 213, 216, 321, 323, 324, 327, 340, 341, 380, 391, 410, 431, 467

depression, xiii, xv, 5, 26, 91, 97, 98, 99, 136, 149, 166, 167, 171, 192, 196, 198, 205, 206, 207, 208, 209, 210, 211, 212, 213, 214, 216, 217, 221, 222, 223, 225, 227, 231, 232, 242, 250, 260, 270, 303, 304, 308, 313, 320, 321, 324, 327, 329, 334, 335, 336, 337, 340, 341, 343, 346, 354, 380, 401, 410, 421, 422, 425, 427, 428, 429, 435, 437, 442, 443, 445, 448, 451, 459, 467, 496, 497, 498

depressive disorder, 5, 56, 166, 179, 181, 191, 205, 206, 211, 215, 242, 340, 360, 379, 401

depressive symptoms, 206, 208, 217, 225, 321, 410

deprivation, 46, 107, 108, 119

dermatitis, 271, 275, 424

dermatologic, 275, 308

dermatological, 271, 445

descending colon, 393

desire, 46, 136, 222, 266, 306, 386, 391

desires, 177, 436

destruction, 178, 189, 207, 439

detachment, 437

detection, 59, 103, 116, 149, 335, 458, 495, 496

detoxification, 356, 436

devaluation, 375

developing countries, 160

developmental change, 325

developmental deficits, 460

developmental delay, 12, 25, 42, 49, 56, 65, 67, 72, 86, 87, 108, 357, 459, 461

developmental disabilities, 3, 5, 6, 48, 49, 90

developmental disorder, 3, 4, 43, 46, 56, 64, 79, 80, 86, 99, 123, 167, 179, 199, 212, 322, 350, 356, 357, 374

developmental factors, 207

developmental milestones, 4, 91

developmental process, 244, 320

developmental psychopathology, 350, 359

deviation, 16, 17

dextrose, 426

diabetes, 12, 28, 43, 165, 209, 226, 261, 352, 358, 362, 403, 406, 408, 409, 411, 412, 414, 428, 496

diabetes mellitus, 43, 226, 406, 408, 412, 428

diagnostic, 26, 58, 61, 62, 64, 67, 73, 80, 81, 82, 83, 85, 86, 97, 101, 102, 108, 160, 176, 178, 180, 205, 206, 209, 217, 221, 224, 246, 299, 350, 353, 355, 356, 357, 359, 363, 372, 384, 387, 408, 409, 458, 463, 471, 473, 480, 488

Diagnostic and Statistical Manual of Mental Disorders, 28, 35, 40, 48, 76, 80, 102, 121, 148, 155, 173, 182, 200, 216, 232, 252, 311, 360, 402, 473, 488, 491

diagnostic criteria, 80, 81, 82, 85, 160, 176, 178, 206, 350, 356, 359, 372, 384, 387, 409

dialysis, 429

diamond, 311

diamonds, 439

diarrhea, 229, 249, 260, 412, 438

diet, 150, 216, 229, 271, 389, 390, 391, 392, 398, 399, 400, 410, 412, 439

diet pill, 392

dietary, 137, 149, 150, 153, 389, 399, 406, 412, 443, 448, 497, 498

dietary fat, 399, 406

dietary fiber, 153

dieting, 391

diets, 389, 406, 411, 412

differential diagnosis, 46, 57, 79, 98, 124, 222, 243, 258, 280, 291

differentiation, 83, 102, 272

digestion, 399

dignity, 452

dilation, 433

dimorphism, 266, 298

diphenhydramine, 251

direct observation, 467

disability, xi, 29, 34, 39, 40, 41, 42, 43, 44, 45, 46, 47, 48, 49, 51, 52, 53, 54, 55, 57, 58, 59, 62, 65, 66, 67, 68, 74, 75, 76, 149, 292, 496, 497, 498, 499

disabled, 107, 282, 355, 496

disappointment, 277

disaster, 222

DISC, 246, 361

DISC1, 351, 352, 364

discharges, 89

discipline, ix, x, 4, 287, 471, 480

disclosure, 300, 455

discomfort, 178, 185, 288, 374, 377

discourse, 62, 69, 71, 353

Discovery, 268

discrimination, xiii, 104, 105, 106, 110, 300, 301, 309, 329, 496

disease model, 452

diseases, ix, x, 279, 284, 295, 297, 303, 304, 305, 308, 309, 310, 313, 314, 386, 433, 452, 458, 474, 477, 482, 483, 495, 499

disinhibition, 251

dispersion, 430
disposition, 15, 456
dissatisfaction, 166, 326, 403
disseminate, 116
distal, 124, 273
distortions, 374, 380, 438
distress, 44, 52, 92, 94, 137, 171, 205, 207, 208, 209,
     224, 240, 241, 242, 244, 248, 249, 256, 257, 259,
     324, 335, 336, 343, 369, 373, 384, 435, 438, 488,
     499
distribution, 16, 17, 40, 41, 274, 365, 404, 408
diuretic, 141
diuretics, 384, 385, 391, 392, 398
diurnal, 143
divergence, 102
divorce, xiii, 280, 284, 323, 329, 419, 459
dizygotic, 299, 351
dizygotic twins, 299, 351
dizziness, 126, 240, 260, 441
DMA, 439, 450
DNA, 427
doctor, xi, 68, 177, 285, 287, 310
doctor-patient, 285
doctors, xii, 33
dogs, 242
domestic violence, 282, 458, 459, 464, 465, 467, 470
dominance, 73, 283
doors, xi, 75, 221
dopamine, 96, 122, 126, 128, 170, 412, 428, 431,
     432, 442
dopaminergic, 434
doping, 447
dosage, 126, 127, 141, 170, 215, 431
dosing, 127, 196, 215, 229, 250, 251, 261, 436
Down syndrome, 47, 212
download, 26
drainage, 152
dream, 443
drinking, 151, 193, 309, 376, 389, 399, 428
drinking pattern, 428
drinking water, 151
dropouts, 277
drowning, 330
drowsiness, 126, 441
drug abuse, 303, 327, 417, 428, 446, 447, 449
drug addiction, 432, 436
drug dependence, 412, 436
Drug Enforcement Administration, 450
drug interaction, 225
drug treatment, 144

drug use, xi, 284, 343, 418, 419, 421, 422, 428, 429,
     434, 440, 442, 446, 448, 449, 450, 451
drugs, 44, 129, 142, 144, 164, 165, 193, 196, 225,
     303, 337, 344, 364, 379, 380, 412, 417, 419, 421,
     427, 428, 431, 433, 434, 436, 437, 440, 441, 442,
     443, 444, 445, 446, 447, 448, 450, 470, 491
drunk driving, 423, 428
dry, 12, 126, 133, 134, 135, 136, 137, 141, 142, 260,
     393, 426, 444
DSM, 5, 26, 28, 35, 40, 41, 64, 65, 67, 72, 76, 80,
     81, 82, 84, 85, 86, 98, 101, 116, 119, 121, 129,
     133, 148, 160, 163, 173, 179, 182, 183, 195, 205,
     206, 207, 220, 221, 222, 223, 224, 240, 246, 299,
     310, 311, 333, 349, 356, 360, 362, 372, 373, 374,
     375, 377, 381, 384, 387, 473, 488, 491
DSM-II, 80, 160, 299, 310, 362, 384
DSM-III, 80, 160, 299, 310, 362, 384
DSM-IV, 5, 26, 28, 35, 40, 41, 64, 65, 67, 72, 76, 80,
     81, 82, 84, 85, 86, 98, 101, 102, 116, 121, 129,
     133, 148, 160, 163, 173, 179, 182, 183, 195, 205,
     206, 207, 221, 222, 240, 299, 311, 333, 349, 356,
     360, 372, 373, 374, 375, 377, 381, 384, 387, 473,
     488, 491
duplication, 407
duration, 9, 11, 12, 31, 44, 57, 104, 105, 176, 181,
     205, 206, 207, 215, 220, 221, 223, 239, 250, 251,
     344, 350, 353, 356, 398, 438
dust, 437
duties, 282
dysfunctional, 135, 143
dyskinesia, 358
dyslexia, 53, 59, 66
dysmenorrhea, 434
dyspepsia, 425
dysphoria, 205, 353, 354, 355, 375, 389
dysplasia, 407
dyspnea, 423
dysregulated, 257
dysregulation, 220, 221, 222, 223, 225, 232, 388
dysthymia, 217, 321, 376, 427
dysthymic disorder, 5, 56

E

early warning, 98, 389
ears, 39, 58, 148, 243
Eastern Europe, 108, 117, 278, 284
eating, xv, 5, 6, 66, 166, 207, 208, 241, 257, 258,
     303, 384, 385, 386, 387, 388, 389, 390, 391, 392,

393, 394, 395, 396, 398, 399, 400, 401, 402, 403, 404, 409, 410, 425
eating behavior, 388, 389, 391
eating disorder, 166, 167, 386, 388, 404
eating disorders, xv, 5, 6, 303, 384, 385, 386, 387, 388, 389, 390, 391, 392, 394, 395, 396, 398, 399, 401, 403, 404, 410
ECG, 126
echolalia, 74
ecological, 118, 339
economic, 300, 308, 411, 460, 482, 485, 491, 497
economically disadvantaged, 406
economics, 455
economies, 330
economy, 30
ECS, 426
ecstasy, 439, 440, 446
edema, 393, 397, 435, 436, 440
education, ix, x, xiii, 4, 10, 28, 32, 33, 34, 39, 45, 48, 54, 58, 66, 74, 95, 106, 124, 127, 147, 150, 151, 156, 162, 247, 265, 270, 272, 275, 278, 282, 283, 284, 285, 288, 291, 292, 293, 294, 295, 304, 314, 330, 342, 359, 386, 446, 453, 455, 456, 469, 470, 475, 488
Education for All, 58
educational institutions, 270
educational programs, 476
educational psychology, 60
educational services, 39, 48, 74
educational system, 51
educators, xv, 58, 283
EEG, 89, 108, 117, 137, 141, 196
efficacy, 30, 114, 126, 130, 145, 167, 169, 182, 212, 224, 225, 226, 227, 228, 230, 249, 251, 259, 357, 401
egg, 154, 361
ego, 97, 310
ejaculation, 275
EKG, 97
elderly, 465
election, 198
electric circuit, 137
electrical, 458
electrodes, 154
electroencephalogram, 144
electroencephalography, 108
electrolyte, 153, 390, 394, 398
electrolyte imbalance, 398
electrolytes, 152
electrophysiologic, 109

elementary school, 112, 201
elementary students, 470
emancipation, 370, 371
emergency departments, 472
emotion, 67, 230, 243, 247, 334, 336, 349, 359, 496
emotion regulation, 336
emotional, xv, 4, 6, 7, 9, 13, 27, 32, 33, 51, 52, 56, 57, 59, 61, 65, 66, 67, 72, 93, 102, 108, 115, 137, 191, 193, 194, 207, 210, 219, 245, 246, 269, 279, 280, 290, 309, 322, 325, 326, 332, 336, 345, 355, 362, 370, 373, 380, 438, 440, 452, 453, 458, 459, 460, 461, 463, 464, 466, 467, 470, 471, 472, 487, 489, 497
emotional abuse, 280, 355
emotional disabilities, 32
emotional disorder, 362
emotional distress, 52, 137, 207, 438
emotional experience, 245
emotional health, xv, 66
emotional responses, 93, 108
emotional stability, 27, 325
emotional state, 193, 194, 245
emotional well-being, 459
emotionality, 375
emotions, 56, 68, 71, 84, 88, 95, 115, 149, 375, 377, 380, 437
empathy, 88, 375, 438, 459
emphysema, 423
employment, 39, 56, 95, 354, 456, 497
empowerment, xiii
encephalitis, 121, 124, 192, 196, 200
encopresis, 142, 144, 145, 147, 148, 149, 150, 152, 154, 155, 457
encouragement, 15
endocarditis, 429, 433
endocrine, 282, 398, 407, 409, 410
endocrine disorders, 282, 407
endocrinologist, 304
endogenous, 442
endophenotypes, 362
endoscopy, 149
endurance, 4, 105, 109
enemas, 150, 151, 152, 153, 384, 385, 391
energy, 10, 175, 206, 209, 210, 211, 250, 272, 276, 396, 398, 400, 408, 412, 440
engagement, 93, 110, 114, 115
engines, 88
England, 130, 144, 279, 295, 331, 448, 477, 479, 481
English, 14, 20, 25, 291, 292, 312
enlargement, 274, 411

enrollment, 412

enteritis, 308

enuresis, 131, 132, 133, 134, 135, 136, 137, 140, 141, 142, 143, 144, 145, 149, 155, 166

environment, 6, 9, 13, 31, 42, 83, 91, 96, 104, 105, 107, 109, 110, 115, 188, 190, 207, 208, 246, 248, 250, 259, 268, 278, 283, 294, 310, 352, 355, 369, 419, 420, 452, 456, 461

environmental, xiii, 3, 4, 5, 10, 11, 32, 34, 41, 51, 107, 108, 162, 207, 213, 246, 247, 252, 256, 319, 320, 332, 350, 351, 352, 407, 413, 456, 467

environmental change, 34

environmental factors, 5, 11, 256, 413

environmental influences, 319, 320

environmental issues, 213

Epi, 65

epidemic, 217, 405, 408, 450

epidemiological, 41, 65, 67, 90, 166, 344, 350

epidemiology, 40, 51, 60, 61, 82, 99, 131, 147, 173, 175, 183, 185, 219, 255, 342, 349, 365, 383, 405, 468, 476, 477, 478, 482

epidermis, 465

epigenetic, 352, 360

epilepsy, 192, 201, 425, 428, 495

epiphysis, 409, 411

episodic, 41, 193, 195, 221, 223, 333

Epstein-Barr virus, 165, 210, 306

equipment, 115, 154

equity, x

erosion, 393, 398, 404

escitalopram, 215, 228, 249, 260

esophagus, 398

estrogen, 275, 388, 398

ether, 444

ethical, 102, 285, 293

ethics, 377

ethnic background, 387

ethnic groups, 281, 301, 405, 419

ethnic minority, 301

ethnicity, 293, 300, 301

etiology, 41, 42, 107, 121, 122, 149, 150, 195, 299, 349, 361, 383, 492

euphoria, 193, 421, 427, 428, 429, 430, 431, 432, 433, 435, 436, 437, 438, 439, 442, 443, 445

Euro, 379

Europe, x, 117, 278, 284, 441

European, 108, 117, 155, 156, 160, 366

evacuation, 149, 150, 152, 153

evening, 137, 141, 154, 170, 215, 229

evidence, 5, 57, 66, 74, 75, 76, 95, 102, 105, 107, 109, 126, 133, 136, 149, 182, 196, 213, 216, 217, 221, 223, 224, 225, 226, 230, 232, 244, 247, 249, 251, 259, 261, 275, 319, 319, 320, 322, 325, 327, 335, 336, 345, 350, 351, 354, 355, 357, 359, 360, 361, 367, 374, 380, 387, 388, 394, 401, 403, 406, 422, 464, 465, 466, 468, 469, 475, 484, 485, 486, 490, 496

evolution, 39, 102, 103, 164

exaggeration, 104, 177

examinations, 57, 73, 283, 459, 464, 480

excitability, 223, 225

excitement, 178, 443

exclusion, 65, 106, 108, 195, 246

excuse, 490

execution, 24, 55

executive function, 21, 55, 62, 69, 91, 228

executive functioning, 21, 62, 91

executive functions, 55, 69

exercise, 229, 385, 389, 390, 392, 397, 398, 403, 410, 412

exercise attitudes, 403

expert, xi, 408, 413, 469, 487, 490

expertise, 44, 47, 74, 75, 259, 451, 459

experts, xi, 5, 128, 160, 171, 266, 300, 474

explicit knowledge, 71

exploitation, 268, 269, 291, 452, 453, 458, 488, 491

explosive, 105, 123, 191, 195, 199, 255

explosives, 330

exporter, 426

exposure, 3, 4, 15, 22, 44, 56, 75, 108, 117, 244, 248, 249, 259, 262, 283, 336, 358, 367, 386, 423, 448, 461, 467, 487

Exposure, 324, 370

expulsion, 421

ex-spouse, 454

external environment, 105, 107, 110

externalizing, 192, 497

externalizing disorders, 192

externalizing problems, 497

extinction, 180

extracellular, 397

extracranial, 465

extrapolation, 16

eye, 6, 23, 31, 64, 68, 70, 73, 80, 83, 84, 88, 93, 122, 135, 189, 207

eye contact, 31, 70, 80, 83, 84, 88, 93, 189, 207

eyes, 70, 83, 420, 423, 425

F

fabric, xiii, 444

facial expression, 63, 64, 88

factor analysis, 102, 118

faecal, 155

failure, xiii, 51, 52, 80, 106, 165, 198, 210, 243, 256, 265, 268, 270, 285, 325, 396, 397, 421, 440, 452, 453, 457, 459, 460, 464, 465, 484

failure to thrive, xiii, 459, 460, 484

fairy tale, 323

faith, 456, 464

false, 113, 177, 276, 333

false negative, 333

false positive, 333

familial, 224, 266, 298, 329, 361, 373, 383, 388, 405, 407, 409, 411

family behavior, xi, 323

family conflict, 3, 4, 496

family environment, 456

family factors, 496

family functioning, 8, 149, 230, 487, 497, 498

family history, 10, 34, 57, 97, 122, 172, 224, 245, 249, 328, 329, 333, 334, 352, 365, 410

family income, 278, 407

family life, 213, 498

family medicine, xv, 3, 5

family members, 45, 76, 92, 95, 97, 161, 166, 177, 185, 188, 195, 208, 359, 387, 390, 395, 420, 429, 495, 496, 498

family physician, 336

family planning, 289, 290, 307

family relationships, 244

family structure, 462

family support, 93, 232, 412, 456

family system, 220, 246

family therapy, xv, 336, 359, 362, 395, 399, 400

family violence, 464

famine, 352, 365, 367

farming, 147

FAS, 197, 199

fast food, 406, 407

fasting, 97, 358, 383, 385

Fasting, 89, 127, 385

fasting glucose, 358

fat, 384, 386, 389, 396, 399, 400, 406, 407, 408, 409, 412, 414, 415

fatalities, 452, 455, 458, 471, 475, 476, 477

fatigue, 97, 151, 171, 210, 411, 429, 432

fatty acid, 396

fatty acids, 396

FDA, 97, 125, 129, 171, 213, 215, 225, 251, 259, 260, 261, 337, 358, 426, 442, 443

FDA approval, 171, 260, 358

fear, 106, 108, 188, 240, 241, 242, 243, 247, 257, 258, 269, 271, 301, 377, 384, 396, 401, 427, 465, 487, 488, 489

fear response, 108, 247

fears, 150, 257, 258, 270, 277, 305, 370, 394, 437

fecal, 147, 148, 149, 150, 151, 152, 154, 412

feces, 135, 147, 148, 151, 152

feedback, 30, 75, 166, 287, 288, 374

feeding, 42, 44, 61, 65, 66, 68, 222, 399, 467

feelings, 64, 83, 84, 85, 88, 106, 186, 187, 197, 208, 209, 210, 245, 248, 268, 269, 270, 288, 289, 300, 301, 302, 306, 313, 377, 388, 438, 489, 496

feet, 109, 273, 423

felony, 486

females, 41, 134, 166, 188, 191, 193, 200, 207, 242, 243, 256, 268, 274, 275, 276, 278, 279, 280, 281, 282, 283, 293, 295, 301, 302, 308, 322, 328, 330, 331, 350, 376, 378, 379, 383, 384, 388, 405, 408, 409, 422, 428, 435, 442, 462, 486, 487

femininity, 266, 303

fertility, 275, 282, 285

fetal, 57, 133, 145, 199, 266, 272, 429

fetal alcohol syndrome, 57, 199, 429

fetus, 132, 266, 299, 427, 429

fetuses, 132

fever, 44, 438

FFT, 230

fiber, 150, 153, 399

fibers, 132

fibrinogen, 463

fibrosis, 209, 401

Fibrosis, 403

fidelity, 114, 116

fight or flight response, 104

film, 149

films, 345, 456

financial loss, 465

fine tuning, 131

fines, 465

Finland, 330

fire, 162, 400, 430, 441

firearm, 328, 330, 334, 339, 345

firearms, 328, 329, 330, 343, 345, 474

firewood, 400

first generation, 358

first responders, xii, 337

fitness, 414, 415

flashbacks, 421, 443

flatulence, 412

flexibility, 4, 59, 369, 462

flight, 104, 222, 243

flow, 73, 395

fluctuations, 92

fluid, 44, 137, 140, 141, 150, 229, 391, 397, 399, 444

fluoxetine, 127, 128, 198, 213, 214, 215, 249, 251, 259, 337, 401, 412

fluphenazine, 127

flushing, 142, 244

fluvoxamine, 127, 128, 249, 259

fontanels, 462

food, 151, 161, 162, 168, 169, 171, 229, 258, 354, 383, 384, 385, 386, 388, 389, 390, 391, 392, 396, 399, 406, 407, 412, 440, 460, 466

Food and Drug Administration, 129, 213, 249, 253, 337, 439

Food and Drug Administration (FDA), 129, 213

food intake, 151, 383, 384, 388, 389

football, 408

forceps, 44

Ford, 292, 296, 312

forensic, 459, 463, 464, 466, 475, 478, 482, 484, 485

forgetfulness, 163

formaldehyde, 427

fracture, 398, 457, 458

fractures, 161, 458, 462, 465, 471, 474, 479

fragile x syndrome, 57

fragile X syndrome, 104, 116, 118, 199

France, 278, 314, 345

freedom, 181

Freud, 267, 268, 271, 292, 299

Freudian theory, 277

friendship, 410

frontal lobe, 21, 22, 121, 192, 351

frontal lobes, 192

fruit juice, 406

fruit juices, 406

fruits, 399, 406, 412

frustration, 56, 67, 162, 163, 188, 192, 194, 195, 287

FSH, 275

fuel, 243, 400

fugue, 167

functional imaging, 357

funding, 39, 48, 226

fungus, 438

furniture, 400

FXS, 197, 199

G

GABA, 251, 442, 445

GABAergic, 360

gait, 29, 135, 411

games, 31, 68, 82, 83, 94, 106, 151, 163, 287, 288, 456

Gamma, 418, 441, 442, 443

gamma-aminobutyric acid, 445

gangs, 276

garbage, 395

gas, 445

gases, 444

gasoline, 444, 445

gastric, 399, 413, 429

gastritis, 428

gastroenterologist, 150, 153

gastrointestinal, 89, 171, 212, 240, 241, 244, 249, 260, 308, 398, 399, 423, 438, 441

gastrointestinal tract, 423

Gatekeeper, 334

gauge, 65, 161, 247

gay men, 301, 311, 312, 314, 344

gelatin, 427

gender, 11, 13, 16, 206, 265, 266, 267, 270, 276, 277, 286, 297, 298, 300, 301, 302, 303, 304, 306, 311, 322, 328, 333, 350, 371, 398, 410, 419, 456

gender differences, 350, 410

gender identity, 265, 266, 270, 286, 298, 303, 304

gender role, 265, 266, 300, 322, 371

gene, 351, 352, 360, 363, 364, 365

gene expression, 364

General Accounting Office, 295

generalized anxiety disorder, 98, 228, 241, 243, 253, 376

Generalized Anxiety Disorder, 241, 243

generation, 125, 198, 199, 224, 225, 226, 233, 339, 352, 357, 358, 364, 401, 426

generics, 168, 169

genes, 351, 352, 363, 366, 367, 387

genetic, 3, 4, 41, 43, 45, 49, 56, 57, 81, 89, 108, 242, 243, 245, 252, 282, 299, 322, 328, 344, 350, 351, 352, 353, 367, 383, 387, 407, 410, 412, 413

genetic disorders, 56, 353

genetic factors, 252, 351

genetic marker, 299

genetic syndromes, 42, 407

genetic testing, 43

genetics, 340, 344, 365, 366, 405
Geneva, 339, 450, 453
genital herpes, 477, 482
genome, 352
genomic, 352
genomic regions, 352
genomics, 361, 365
genotype, 407
geography, 24, 300
Georgia, 113, 442, 478
Germany, ix, 345
gestation, 44
gestational age, 44
gestures, 64, 83, 93, 189, 245
gifted, 16, 33
girls, 65, 73, 81, 86, 134, 148, 149, 160, 166, 178,
    180, 188, 208, 243, 266, 267, 268, 279, 281, 287,
    289, 291, 322, 374, 410, 414, 444, 477, 480, 481,
    482, 483
gland, 272, 275
glass, 430, 441
glasses, 15
glaucoma, 427
glia, 272
globus, 121
glucose, 89, 97, 127, 358, 397, 409, 410, 411, 412,
    429
glucose tolerance, 409, 412
glutamate, 352
glutamic acid, 360
glutathione, 439
glycemic index, 406
glycol, 152, 153
goal-directed, 221, 223
goal-orientation, 277
goals, 32, 71, 93, 94, 96, 137, 164, 196, 198, 230,
    277, 324, 326, 359, 371, 394, 395, 400, 411
going to school, 248
gold standard, 110
gonorrhea, 279, 308, 466, 481, 483
good behavior, 181
good faith, 464
government, 422, 446, 464
grades, 27, 53, 55, 66, 69, 187, 220, 420, 422
grading, 103, 106, 108, 129
graffiti, 178
grains, 406, 412
grandiose delusions, 233
grandparents, 245, 301
grants, 66

grass, 177, 426
gravity, 105, 152, 390, 392
gray matter, 132, 351, 360, 365, 367
Greece, 506
grey matter, 351
grief, 95, 337, 498
group therapy, 29, 400
groups, xiii, 16, 32, 34, 54, 67, 94, 105, 107, 124,
    161, 176, 196, 200, 231, 233, 270, 272, 276, 281,
    282, 288, 301, 305, 329, 337, 341, 358, 390, 399,
    405, 410, 412, 419, 429, 436, 481, 485, 491, 492
growth, ix, 3, 4, 39, 81, 105, 117, 149, 174, 266,
    272, 273, 274, 275, 285, 295, 303, 309, 388, 393,
    398, 401, 407, 409, 457, 461, 462
growth factor, 275
growth factors, 275
growth hormone, 275, 407
growth spurt, 275
guardian, 180, 454
guidance, xv, 188, 194, 282, 285, 286, 287, 288,
    289, 290, 294, 308, 470, 471
guidelines, 15, 32, 47, 196, 215, 229, 234, 250, 251,
    260, 268, 276, 314, 356, 430, 458, 465, 473, 474,
    489
guilt, 258, 269, 271, 289, 337, 421, 498
guilt feelings, 269
guilty, 148
guns, 330
gustatory, 24
gynecologist, 304
gynecomastia, 275

H

habituation, 103
half-life, 230, 251
hallucinations, 92, 195, 222, 350, 353, 354, 355,
    356, 359, 427, 429, 437, 438
haloperidol, 125, 127, 129, 130, 198, 358, 437, 438
Halothane, 444
handicapped, 95, 460
handling, 54, 439
hands, 54, 83, 106, 109, 162, 286
handwriting, 64, 105, 106
hanging, 30, 272, 330
haplotypes, 352, 360
harassment, 281
harm, 15, 34, 96, 177, 186, 213, 250, 328, 331, 332,
    335, 345, 346, 429, 452, 453, 459, 460, 462, 463,
    467, 469, 472

harmful, 178, 271, 272, 374, 451, 460
Harvard, 27
HDL, 409
head, 12, 15, 29, 44, 81, 85, 86, 89, 122, 192, 227,
    330, 365, 429, 455, 458, 462, 463, 465, 471, 475,
    476, 477
head injuries, 192
head injury, 12, 15, 429
head trauma, 455, 458, 465, 471, 475, 476, 477
healing, 337, 459, 466
Health and Human Services, 60, 187, 296, 340, 381,
    408, 413, 447, 449, 454, 476, 482, 483, 484
health care, x, xv, 39, 72, 110, 147, 265, 267, 270,
    285, 286, 290, 291, 292, 300, 302, 303, 307, 311,
    312, 314, 337, 413, 456, 460, 461, 463, 464, 467,
    468, 469, 470, 474, 481, 495, 497, 499
health care professionals, xv, 267, 270, 285, 464,
    468, 469
health care system, 467, 495
health clinics, 243, 377
health effects, 443, 455, 457, 478
health information, 279
health insurance, 495
health problems, 271, 322, 335, 379, 475, 483
health services, 45, 335, 342, 462, 471, 479, 499
healthcare, 58, 462
hearing, 42, 46, 52, 54, 56, 57, 61, 65, 66, 68, 70, 72,
    86, 186, 192, 196, 386, 392
hearing impairment, 42, 65, 70
hearing loss, 66
heart, 109, 165, 172, 240, 244, 393, 396, 397, 409,
    415, 423, 462
heart disease, 165, 423
heart failure, 396, 397
heart rate, 109, 172, 244, 393, 397
heat stroke, 440
heating, 142, 432
heavy drinking, 193
height, 14, 44, 97, 127, 149, 273, 274, 275, 384, 398,
    462
helplessness, 209, 377
hematocrit, 463
hematologic, 216
hematoma, 474
hemisphere, 19, 20, 63
hemorrhage, 440, 457
hemorrhages, 393
hemp, 426
hepatitis, 429, 432, 433, 466
Hepatitis A, 306, 308

Hepatitis B, 305, 307, 432, 433, 466
herbal, 216, 246, 392, 440
heritability, 322, 328
heroin, 284, 417, 418, 422, 427, 432, 433, 434, 435,
    436, 440, 442, 450
heroin addicts, 427
herpes, 279, 305, 308, 466, 477, 482
herpes simplex, 305, 308, 466
heterogeneity, 83, 367
heterogeneous, 70, 82, 350, 387, 487
heterosexuals, 299
high blood pressure, 226
high fat, 409
high risk, 71, 163, 189, 308, 309, 354, 376, 479, 489
high school, 24, 27, 33, 34, 48, 164, 193, 278, 280,
    281, 294, 302, 304, 324, 328, 344, 422, 426, 429,
    432, 435, 439, 442, 445, 447, 455, 459, 472
high scores, 328
high-fat, 406, 407, 412
high-frequency, 66
high-risk, 216, 290, 295, 327, 470, 475
hip, 408, 411
HIPAA, 465
hippocampus, 351
hips, 373
hirsutism, 409, 411
Hispanic, 278, 428
Hispanics, 278, 379, 405, 408
histamine, 401
HIV, 165, 209, 258, 279, 303, 305, 306, 308, 311,
    313, 357, 429, 432, 433, 436
HIV infection, 165, 306, 308
HIV test, 308, 311
HIV/AIDS, 308, 429, 432, 433, 436
hog, 437
holistic, 232, 296
holistic approach, 296
Holland, 313
homeless, 282, 291, 443
homelessness, 303, 309, 467
homes, 70, 464
homework, 33, 163, 177, 258
homicide, 283, 339, 345, 481, 490, 492
homolog, 430
homosexuality, 266, 285, 288, 297, 298, 299, 301,
    304, 305, 310, 314, 387
homosexuals, 299, 300, 301
honesty, 310
Hong Kong, 330
hopelessness, 206, 209, 321, 328, 335, 343

hormone, 141, 143, 229, 275, 288, 299, 384, 388, 391, 393, 396, 407, 428

hormones, 108, 266, 268, 272, 275, 299, 428

hospital, ix, 33, 66, 187, 233, 282, 345, 346, 400, 467, 469, 475, 483

hospitalization, 97, 154, 230, 321, 323, 336, 389, 396, 397, 399, 455, 472

hospitalizations, 45, 462, 482, 496, 497

hospitalized, 153, 233, 235, 280, 322, 336, 340, 396, 400, 473, 475, 476

hospitals, 464, 469

hostile environment, 283

hostility, 193, 220, 268, 426

House, 345, 346, 426

household, 286, 292, 444, 456

households, 5

housing, 456, 462, 467

HPV, 305, 306, 308

human, x, xii, 82, 105, 107, 145, 190, 205, 239, 243, 265, 268, 269, 270, 271, 272, 275, 279, 284, 285, 294, 299, 300, 305, 311, 362, 446, 466, 481

human behavior, x, xii

human brain, 311

human development, x

human experience, 239

human immunodeficiency virus, 305, 466, 481

human interactions, 82

human papilloma virus, 466

human papillomavirus, 305

humans, 10, 103, 105, 108, 265, 450

hunting, 244

hydrate, 442

hydro, 423, 445

hydrocarbons, 423, 445

hydrocortisone, 424

hydrogen, 152

hydroxide, 153

hygiene, 163, 231, 258, 270, 353, 354, 420, 460

hyperactivity, xv, 4, 6, 53, 60, 96, 104, 107, 118, 123, 124, 130, 149, 159, 160, 161, 162, 163, 164, 171, 173, 174, 178, 179, 182, 191, 192, 199, 212, 220, 223, 235, 257, 321, 322, 401, 423, 430, 446, 450, 457, 490

hyperactivity-impulsivity, 160

hyperandrogenism, 409

hyperarousal, 228

hyperglycemia, 391

hyperinsulinemia, 406

hyperlipidemia, 261

hypernatremia, 153

hyperplasia, 266, 274, 299

hypersensitivity, 104, 167, 377

hypersomnia, 206, 429

hypertension, 126, 172, 409, 411, 429, 430, 433, 438, 440

Hypertension, 409, 420, 430, 431, 440

hypertensive, 216, 409

hyperthermia, 429, 430, 440

hypnotic, 211, 441

hypokalemia, 153, 396

hyponatremia, 140, 141, 153, 440

hypophosphatemia, 396

hypotension, 126, 172, 393, 396, 433, 438, 441

hypothalamic, 272, 299, 413

hypothalamus, 132, 299

hypothermia, 438

hypothesis, 345

hypothyroidism, 225, 229, 407

hypovolemia, 153

I

iatrogenic, 96

ICD, 148, 300, 312, 453, 483

ice, 152, 430, 441

IDA, 448

IDEA, 32, 35, 65, 73

ideal body weight, 273, 398

idealism, 276

idealization, 277

identification, 4, 34, 66, 73, 74, 87, 93, 98, 114, 178, 212, 224, 252, 261, 266, 268, 298, 300, 302, 455, 457, 476, 484

identity, 265, 266, 269, 270, 275, 277, 286, 298, 300, 301, 302, 303, 304, 309, 311, 312, 314, 325, 326, 329

ideology, 279

idiopathic, 230

idiosyncratic, xiii, 353

Illinois, 65, 505, 506

images, 64, 154, 256, 466

imagination, 79

imaging, 44, 89, 136, 351, 357, 362, 364, 458, 461, 465, 473

imaging techniques, 458

imbalances, 398

imitation, 73

immigration, 367, 378

immunization, 305, 307

immunodeficiency, 209, 305, 306, 466, 481

Immunotherapy, 448
impaired glucose tolerance, 412
impairments, 29, 32, 42, 43, 46, 51, 55, 56, 59, 64,
    65, 67, 71, 76, 84, 85, 87, 91, 94, 191, 192, 196,
    198, 239, 248, 249, 255, 256, 257, 353, 360, 363,
    373, 399
implementation, 48, 413, 446, 470
impulsive, 105, 163, 164, 178, 190, 326, 334, 391
impulsiveness, 56
impulsivity, 56, 92, 96, 159, 160, 161, 162, 163, 164,
    166, 182, 190, 194, 376, 391
impurities, 439
in situ, 240, 251, 302
in utero, 268, 299, 435
in vitro, 443
in vivo, 443
inactive, 434
inattention, 34, 98, 159, 160, 162, 164, 166, 224, 228
incarceration, 57, 436
incentive, 151
incest, 270, 280, 487
Incest, 292
incidence, 108, 134, 197, 206, 299, 313, 324, 365,
    385, 387, 388, 391, 398, 412, 425, 452, 455, 456,
    473, 476, 479, 486
inclusion, 101, 102, 106, 489
income, 278, 290, 407, 462
incurable, 329
independence, 47, 57, 276, 290, 326, 370
India, 156, 292
Indian, 142, 147, 155, 292, 419, 420, 421, 449
Indiana, 474
indication, 212, 251, 261, 398
indicators, 53, 417, 420, 487
indices, 61
indigenous, 438
individual character, 160, 319
individual characteristics, 160, 319
Individuals with Disabilities Education Act, 32, 40
Individuals with Disabilities Education Improvement
    Act, 65
Indonesia, 422
induction, 289
industrial, 443
industrialization, 331
industrialized countries, 330, 339
industry, 282
inequality, 18

infancy, 39, 42, 44, 61, 79, 82, 83, 84, 86, 87, 107,
    117, 132, 135, 217, 223, 240, 266, 268, 455, 467,
    477
infant mortality, 271
infant mortality rate, 271
infants, ix, x, 4, 24, 66, 70, 75, 82, 87, 105, 108, 111,
    113, 117, 132, 144, 152, 153, 207, 267, 271, 369,
    459, 474, 475, 480, 483, 484
Infants, 68, 70, 82, 100, 110, 113, 117, 149, 207,
    268, 369, 478
infarction, 433, 440
infection, 121, 135, 149, 165, 258, 279, 306, 308,
    352, 361, 433, 457, 459, 464, 465, 466
infections, 42, 44, 89, 96, 130, 142, 144, 257, 258,
    259, 297, 304, 305, 306, 308, 311, 357, 429, 436,
    457, 463, 466, 471, 478, 481, 483
infectious, 56, 304, 357, 431, 433, 435, 452
infectious disease, 304, 357, 431, 452
infectious diseases, 357, 431, 452
inflammation, 192
influenza, 361
information processing, 62, 353
informed consent, 453
ingestion, 429, 442, 448
inhalation, 432, 444
inhaler, 424, 425
inheritance, 244, 387, 388, 407
inherited, 143, 243, 256, 388, 407
inhibition, 96, 260, 377, 391, 401, 437, 441, 442,
    444
inhibitor, 129, 169, 170, 196, 199, 214, 228, 401,
    412
inhibitors, 128, 138, 182, 217, 224, 249, 259, 412,
    426, 429, 437
inhibitory, 131, 251
initiation, 136, 141, 169, 295, 423, 447, 459
injection, 449
injections, 299
injuries, 67, 85, 161, 162, 192, 303, 344, 370, 420,
    434, 451, 453, 454, 455, 457, 458, 460, 464, 465,
    471, 473, 476, 477, 479, 480
injury, 12, 15, 24, 42, 57, 62, 67, 165, 177, 178, 187,
    189, 191, 192, 194, 195, 196, 199, 209, 320, 324,
    341, 396, 413, 429, 445, 452, 454, 455, 457, 458,
    462, 463, 465, 466, 473, 475, 476, 478, 481, 482,
    483
insecurity, 222, 266, 298
insight, 256, 394
insomnia, 171, 206, 210, 230, 241, 249, 260, 424,
    426, 427, 441

inspection, 305

inspiration, 62

instability, 29, 136, 144, 219, 332

instinct, 446

institutionalization, 117, 351

institutions, xiii, 4, 270, 469

instruction, 18, 20, 59, 66, 75, 285, 387

instruments, 40, 43, 45, 73, 101, 110, 151, 176, 246, 332, 423

insulin, 275, 391, 397, 403, 407, 408, 409, 412

insulin resistance, 407, 408, 409

insulin-like growth factor, 275

insults, 67, 351

insurance, 4, 167, 171, 495

integration, 23, 24, 91, 94, 101, 102, 103, 106, 110, 113, 114, 115, 117, 118, 119, 300, 309

integrity, 131, 132, 363, 465

intellect, 497

intellectual disabilities, 4, 48, 66

intellectual functioning, 6, 18, 40, 46, 194, 354, 357

intellectual potential, 52

intelligence, 39, 40, 41, 48, 53, 54, 55, 81, 84, 91, 194, 420, 456

intelligence quotient, 39, 40, 48

intelligence tests, 55

intensity, 9, 10, 11, 12, 33, 40, 41, 48, 57, 63, 88, 108, 151, 220, 221, 239, 241, 244, 245, 257, 258, 259, 345, 467

intentionality, 332

intentions, 63, 64, 66, 176, 189, 302, 446

interaction, 4, 64, 70, 72, 74, 75, 105, 107, 114, 265, 345, 350, 438, 439, 452, 459, 470, 471, 496

Interaction, 114

interactions, 62, 68, 69, 71, 74, 75, 80, 81, 82, 83, 84, 85, 86, 87, 88, 90, 91, 95, 215, 216, 225, 286, 291, 304, 352, 392, 395, 412, 491, 497

interdisciplinary, 47, 67, 74, 76, 464, 476, 479

interference, 62, 427

intermittent explosive disorder, 123, 199

internalizing, 497

international, 102, 470, 476

International Classification of Diseases, 148, 312, 452

internet, xi, 219, 279, 281, 293, 310, 441

Internet, 94, 283, 304, 309, 390, 404, 406, 450

interneurons, 132

internist, 394

internists, xv

interpersonal communication, 62

interpersonal conflict, 189, 329

interpersonal contact, 377

interpersonal relations, 3, 4, 64, 105, 275, 373

interpersonal relationships, 3, 4, 64, 105, 275, 373

interpersonal skills, 40

interpretation, 13, 40, 63, 103, 350, 359, 459, 468, 490

intersex, 266, 298

interval, 12, 127, 226

intervention, xv, 4, 5, 7, 10, 12, 16, 28, 31, 32, 34, 39, 45, 46, 47, 48, 51, 58, 59, 60, 62, 66, 67, 70, 73, 74, 75, 76, 87, 95, 96, 98, 101, 102, 103, 107, 110, 114, 115, 116, 118, 181, 187, 196, 197, 228, 229, 230, 232, 251, 282, 320, 332, 333, 334, 335, 336, 337, 340, 341, 342, 343, 346, 359, 389, 391, 414, 423, 466, 472, 485, 486

intervention strategies, 58, 60

interview, 25, 26, 91, 166, 206, 246, 302, 331, 332, 333, 336, 356

interviews, 151, 180, 206, 208, 357

intestine, 229

intima, 409

intimacy, 70, 277

intonation, 63

intoxication, 153, 193, 211, 355, 357, 428, 433

intracerebral, 440

intracerebral hemorrhage, 440

intracranial, 135, 474

intracranial pressure, 135

intramuscular, 443

intramuscularly, 437

intraocular, 427, 474

intraocular pressure, 427

intravenous, 429, 432, 433, 435, 437

intravenous fluids, 429

intravenously, 431, 432, 435

intrinsic, 115, 224

intrinsic motivation, 115

introspection, 326

invasive, 133, 154

investment, 284

Ipecac, 403

IQ, 16, 17, 18, 19, 20, 40, 41, 46, 48, 53, 57, 67, 73, 74, 81, 85, 95

IQ estimates, 19

IQ scores, 17, 19, 40, 48, 53, 67

irradiation, 165

irritability, 92, 96, 97, 162, 171, 190, 193, 194, 198, 208, 210, 211, 212, 219, 222, 226, 432

irritation, 153, 420, 425

isolation, 108, 148, 178, 208, 223, 241, 300, 327, 353, 354, 459, 470
isomers, 168
Israel, xi, 504
Italy, 331, 345

J

JAMA, 294, 296, 311, 313, 365, 367, 404, 414, 446, 448, 449, 450
January, 101, 443, 450
Japan, 331, 345
Japanese, 147
jaundice, 44
Jerusalem, xi, 504
Jews, ix
job skills, 47
jobs, xiii, 277, 421
joints, 393, 437
judge, 370
judgment, 40, 125, 220, 222, 309, 428
Jun, 174
junior high, 27
jurisdictions, 486
jury, 490
justice, 490
juvenile crime, 277
juvenile delinquency, 379, 459
juvenile delinquents, 177
juvenile justice, 490
juveniles, 217

K

karyotyping, 89
Kentucky, xi, 503, 504
keratosis, 423
ketamine, 440, 443
kidney, 144, 457
kidney failure, 457
kidneys, 135, 140
killing, 345
kindergarten, 71, 77, 116
kindergarten children, 77, 116
kindergartners, 71
kinesthetic, 105
King, 340, 342, 365, 448
Korean, 25
Kuwait, 330

L

laboratory studies, 394
labour, 453
lack of control, 283
Lafayette, 23
language, 4, 5, 6, 18, 19, 20, 25, 26, 31, 32, 43, 45, 46, 52, 53, 54, 55, 56, 57, 59, 61, 62, 63, 64, 65, 66, 67, 69, 70, 71, 72, 73, 74, 75, 76, 77, 79, 80, 81, 83, 84, 86, 87, 88, 89, 90, 91, 92, 93, 94, 98, 106, 108, 117, 188, 194, 198, 268, 353, 356, 370, 379, 457
language acquisition, 80
language delay, 56, 70, 71, 79, 81, 84, 86, 88
language development, 46, 66, 74, 75, 81, 83, 84, 92
language impairment, 46, 62, 64, 65, 66, 67, 70, 71, 73, 76, 77, 90
language processing, 63
language skills, 18, 19, 20, 54, 81, 188, 268, 370
large intestine, 229
larynx, ix
latency, 21, 270
later life, 321, 342
latex, 308
Latino, 314
laughter, 221
law, 10, 58, 181, 458, 464, 465, 468, 469, 486, 490
law enforcement, 181, 464, 465, 469, 486
laws, 39, 48, 58, 67, 176, 285, 331, 375, 453, 458, 464, 465, 474, 489, 490
lawsuits, 338
laxatives, 150, 151, 153, 384, 385, 391, 392, 399
LDL, 409
lead, 3, 4, 5, 6, 32, 55, 57, 62, 75, 82, 84, 95, 104, 108, 126, 127, 150, 151, 169, 178, 193, 194, 244, 248, 251, 268, 285, 290, 326, 335, 353, 383, 389, 406, 409, 421, 427, 428, 429, 430, 431, 433, 435, 438, 439, 440, 441, 443, 459, 468, 476, 499
leakage, 148
learners, 51, 53, 59
learning, x, 7, 10, 14, 22, 23, 29, 32, 33, 45, 51, 52, 53, 55, 56, 57, 58, 59, 60, 64, 65, 66, 71, 72, 73, 74, 75, 76, 91, 94, 95, 102, 106, 107, 108, 109, 116, 117, 149, 163, 166, 251, 259, 266, 285, 287, 299, 300, 353, 380, 389, 395, 409, 417, 443, 457
learning difficulties, 107
learning disabilities, 23, 29, 32, 34, 51, 52, 53, 55, 56, 57, 58, 59, 60, 65, 66, 73, 91, 102, 107
learning process, 94
learning skills, 300

left hemisphere, 63
legal issues, 319
legal systems, 458
legislation, 4, 66, 464, 465, 480
legislative, 58
legumes, 406
leisure, 40
leptin, 412
Lesbian, 307, 309, 311, 312, 314, 315
lesions, 149, 306, 357, 445, 465, 484
lethargy, 127, 422, 445
leukopenia, 393
Lexapro, 249, 260
libido, 249, 272
licensing, 464
life cycle, 320
life experiences, 334, 370
life span, 58, 60, 271
life stressors, 319
life style, 231
lifespan, 130, 220, 243, 319
lifestyle, 284, 285, 304, 310, 390, 400, 405, 409,
    411, 451, 498
lifestyle changes, 409, 451, 498
lifestyles, 278, 284, 329, 409
life-threatening, 390, 443
lifetime, ix, 39, 41, 193, 220, 257, 288, 323, 339,
    351, 385, 387, 422, 426, 428, 429, 431, 432, 435,
    439, 444
likelihood, 6, 14, 32, 189, 196, 213, 249, 321, 331,
    339, 379, 417, 496
limbic system, 426
limitation, 257, 496
limitations, 40, 48, 67, 107, 194, 249, 282
Lincoln, 35, 286, 293
linear, 300, 393
lingual, 398
linguistic, 63, 64, 71, 72
linguistic information, 63
linguistically, 64
linkage, 351
links, 73, 242
lipase, 393, 412
lipid, 86, 89, 97, 357, 358, 445
lipids, 127, 226, 411
lipophilic, 426
lipoprotein, 409, 412
liquids, 424, 431
listening, 52, 61, 64, 66, 68, 69, 74, 289
literacy, 67, 68, 72, 75, 76

literature, 49, 76, 105, 118, 129, 191, 192, 196, 199,
    201, 213, 220, 221, 247, 255, 280, 352, 359, 373,
    404, 408, 457, 485
lithium, 97, 196, 197, 198, 199, 225, 227, 229, 233,
    234
Lithium, 165, 182, 199, 216, 225, 226, 229, 234
litigation, 338
liver, 129, 225, 433, 440, 445, 457, 463, 466
liver function tests, 463
living conditions, 453
local community, 48, 490
location, 11, 31, 160, 458, 461, 465
locus, 114, 361, 364, 367, 456
London, x, 21, 145, 292, 293, 295, 345, 381, 403,
    477
long period, 12, 398
longitudinal studies, 244, 351
longitudinal study, 143, 182, 321, 325
long-term, 4, 46, 59, 87, 96, 226, 228, 232, 251, 295,
    349, 357, 358, 359, 362, 398, 400, 404, 409, 411,
    412, 471, 486, 499
Los Angeles, 116, 117, 118
loss of appetite, 97, 383
loss of control, 31, 385, 391
losses, 465
love, 88, 265, 266, 276, 279, 289, 290, 298, 438, 471
lover, 439
low risk, 308
low-density, 409, 412
low-density lipoprotein, 412
low-income, 290
LSD, 418, 421, 437, 438, 440, 441, 442
lumbar, 132
lung, 422, 423
lung cancer, 422, 423
lungs, 393, 422, 423
lupus erythematosus, 210
Luvox, 249, 259
lying, 177, 221, 258, 410, 421
lymph, 462
lymph gland, 462
lymphogranuloma venereum, 433
lymphoid, 273
lymphoid tissue, 273
lysergic acid diethylamide, 418, 437

M

macrocytosis, 429
magazines, 219, 448

magnesium, 398

magnetic, 362, 364, 465

magnetic resonance, 362, 364, 465

magnetic resonance imaging, 362, 364, 465

Magnetic Resonance Imaging, 463

maintaining attention, 71

maintenance, 47, 147, 153, 154, 225, 227, 232, 234, 235, 401, 471, 498

major depression, 221, 321

major depressive disorder, 5, 56, 379

malabsorption, 457

maladaptive, 26, 95, 103, 108, 159, 239, 241, 242, 247, 248, 256, 257, 259, 369, 372, 373, 380, 485, 491

malaise, 251, 422

males, 41, 52, 54, 81, 134, 166, 188, 191, 192, 193, 207, 241, 243, 256, 266, 268, 274, 275, 276, 277, 278, 279, 280, 281, 283, 284, 298, 301, 302, 307, 308, 309, 313, 322, 328, 330, 331, 350, 376, 379, 385, 387, 422, 428, 435, 456, 462, 486, 487, 491

malicious, 178

malignant, 127, 261, 358, 423, 440

malignant hyperthermia, 440

Mallory-Weiss tear, 398

malnutrition, 149, 391, 394, 396, 397, 399, 400, 460, 466, 467

malpractice, 338

malt extract, 153

maltreatment, 108, 323, 329, 345, 451, 452, 453, 455, 456, 457, 459, 460, 461, 463, 464, 465, 467, 468, 469, 470, 471, 472, 473, 474, 475, 476, 477, 478, 479, 481, 484, 487

management, xiii, 28, 29, 32, 39, 48, 58, 79, 91, 93, 95, 96, 98, 124, 127, 131, 136, 137, 142, 143, 144, 145, 150, 155, 162, 180, 188, 217, 224, 228, 229, 230, 232, 260, 297, 302, 304, 331, 332, 346, 347, 359, 362, 383, 390, 392, 394, 401, 402, 405, 409, 413, 417, 423, 429, 436, 441, 446, 450, 467, 484, 495, 496, 498

mania, 171, 196, 198, 221, 222, 223, 224, 225, 226, 228, 231, 233, 234, 249, 361, 367

manic, 97, 194, 221, 228, 233, 235, 249, 372, 376

manic episode, 249, 376

manic symptoms, 233

manic-depressive illness, 372

manipulation, 10, 268, 390

manners, 11

mannitol, 432

MAO, 426

mapping, 362

marijuana, 193, 210, 284, 417, 421, 426, 427, 432, 437, 440, 441, 442, 443

market, 426, 443

marketplace, 241

marriage, 280, 290

marrow, 141, 393

Maryland, xii

MAS, 168, 169, 172

masculinity, 266, 276, 283, 303

mask, 269, 320

mass media, 279

maternal, 44, 108, 268, 352, 407

mathematical, 53, 54, 74

mathematics, 52, 55

Matrices, 20

maturation, 4, 53, 108, 266, 272, 273, 325, 367

Mauritius, 330

MB, 143, 253

meals, 138, 140, 229, 390, 392, 396, 399

meanings, 63, 64, 69, 71, 74, 84, 486

measurement, 14, 40, 408

measures, 11, 12, 13, 15, 18, 20, 22, 24, 25, 73, 103, 108, 109, 110, 111, 112, 137, 150, 182, 224, 246, 258, 271, 328, 333, 365, 391, 436, 489

meat, 258, 412

mechanical, 88, 409

mechanical stress, 409

mechanics, 90

meconium, 435

media, 71, 219, 279, 283, 284, 291, 329, 341, 405, 406, 411, 417, 435

median, 82

medical care, 32, 33, 39, 47, 48, 86, 389, 455, 460, 462, 465, 470, 472, 499

medical school, xii, 271

medical services, 283, 469, 472

medical student, 313, 394

medication, 5, 11, 32, 34, 56, 97, 98, 126, 128, 141, 142, 143, 182, 196, 198, 199, 200, 201, 212, 213, 214, 215, 219, 224, 226, 228, 229, 230, 232, 246, 247, 249, 250, 251, 252, 259, 260, 337, 357, 358, 359, 394, 411, 431, 432, 491, 497, 498

medication compliance, 358

medications, xv, 44, 45, 47, 48, 96, 97, 98, 124, 125, 126, 127, 128, 129, 136, 137, 141, 142, 164, 166, 167, 171, 172, 174, 180, 182, 193, 196, 197, 198, 213, 215, 216, 224, 226, 227, 228, 229, 230, 231, 233, 246, 249, 250, 251, 259, 260, 261, 283, 351, 357, 385, 392, 398, 401, 417, 426, 429, 430, 436, 437, 462, 496 medicine, ix, x, xiii, xv, 3, 5, 75, 296, 394, 434, 463, 464, 480, 483

melatonin, 227, 230, 251

melting, 145

membranes, 44, 462

memorizing, 55

memory, 15, 18, 19, 21, 22, 29, 54, 55, 56, 64, 108, 210, 251, 356, 370, 393, 399, 409, 420, 421, 427, 439, 440, 441, 443

memory loss, 421, 440, 441

men, 287, 288, 292, 301, 302, 307, 308, 310, 311, 312, 313, 314, 344, 383, 385, 388, 483

menarche, 274, 275, 284, 288, 388

meningitis, 191

menstrual, 127, 226, 384

menstruation, 273, 275

mental actions, 256

mental age, 43, 46, 148

mental disorder, xi, 3, 4, 5, 42, 55, 98, 116, 327, 328, 335, 345, 379

mental health, xv, 4, 5, 29, 34, 57, 117, 242, 243, 247, 259, 271, 304, 309, 310, 321, 334, 335, 336, 338, 342, 344, 365, 377, 379, 452, 453, 461, 462, 463, 464, 467, 469, 483, 487, 499

mental health professionals, 4, 338, 461, 463, 464

mental illness, xiii, xv, 5, 56, 57, 205, 271, 299, 335, 372, 459, 482

mental retardation, 39, 40, 42, 49, 65, 67, 81, 82, 91, 92, 194, 199, 353, 456, 474, 491

mental state, 373

mental states, 373

mentorship, 34

messages, 63, 270, 286, 287, 289, 386, 396

meta-analysis, 114, 119, 206, 262, 322, 360, 361, 388, 402

metabolic, 13, 43, 89, 97, 152, 226, 357, 358, 391, 393, 397, 398, 399, 408, 462, 463, 467

metabolic acidosis, 398

metabolic alkalosis, 393, 398

metabolic changes, 399

metabolic disorder, 357

metabolic rate, 397

metabolic syndrome, 97, 226, 358

metabolism, 42, 44, 56, 122, 215

metabolite, 443

metaphors, 84

methamphetamine, 168, 193, 211, 284, 356, 360, 421, 430, 431, 432, 439, 441, 450

Methamphetamine, 169, 418, 430, 431, 441

methylphenidate, 126, 145, 168, 172, 228, 430, 434

Mexican, 435, 442

Mexico, 435, 438, 442

mice, 423

midbrain, 434

migraine, 434

migraine headache, 434

migrant, 350, 365

migration, 278, 361, 429

milk, 152, 153, 386, 399, 406, 439

milligrams, 215

Minnesota, 27, 482

minorities, 301, 302, 410

minority, 161, 173, 301, 312

minority groups, 301

minors, 330, 492

miosis, 445

mirror, 75, 392

misconceptions, 304, 395

misidentification, 471

misinterpretation, 6

misleading, 223

Missouri, 471, 476

misunderstanding, 69

MIT, 313

mitral, 242

mitral valve, 242

mitral valve prolapse, 242

mixing, 442

mobility, 47, 105, 268

Modafinil, 172

modalities, 61, 64, 69, 103, 104, 114, 116, 216, 337, 369, 380, 400, 491, 498

modality, 62, 115, 395

modeling, 75, 93, 94, 287, 419, 471

models, 75, 88, 107, 137, 216, 232, 277, 300, 309, 388, 420, 457, 492

modulation, 62, 103, 104, 105, 108, 116, 117, 118, 388

modules, 90

molasses, 152

molecules, 434, 438

money, 162, 178, 436

monoamine, 389

monohydrogen, 152

monotherapy, 225, 226, 227, 233

monozygotic twins, 299, 351, 387

Monroe, 448

mood, 3, 5, 15, 42, 47, 92, 104, 123, 167, 171, 179, 182, 194, 196, 199, 201, 205, 206, 207, 208, 210, 216, 219, 220, 221, 222, 223, 224, 225, 227, 228,

230, 231, 232, 234, 239, 242, 243, 320, 321, 325, 326, 327, 335, 340, 350, 353, 355, 356, 365, 372, 380, 388, 390, 391, 401, 419, 421, 422, 427, 431, 437, 490

mood change, 388

mood disorder, 3, 5, 104, 123, 179, 199, 201, 243, 320, 321, 327, 335, 350, 353, 355, 356, 365, 490

mood swings, 222, 223, 325, 422

Moon, 407

morality, 370, 420

morals, 377

morbidity, xi, 91, 192, 223, 283, 349, 376, 378, 410, 428, 458, 460, 487

morning, 140, 162, 163, 168, 169, 170, 171, 221, 229, 245, 250, 424, 438

morphemes, 63, 64, 69, 70

morphine, 433, 435

morphological, 69

morphology, 61

mortality, 192, 271, 283, 320, 354, 391, 402, 428, 429, 446, 449, 458, 460, 476, 477, 478

mortality rate, 271, 320, 391, 402, 458

mortality risk, 429

mothers, 147, 322, 323, 334, 341, 435

motion, 161

motivation, 15, 83, 114, 115, 151, 163, 210, 211, 266, 269, 298, 337, 432

motor activity, 62, 106

motor control, 55, 73

motor coordination, 55, 94, 106

motor function, 23, 29, 135, 443

motor neurons, 132

motor skills, 6, 23, 25, 42, 55, 86, 94, 108

motor system, 66

motor task, 106, 107

motor tic, 121, 122, 125

motor vehicle accident, 67, 428

mouth, 75, 126, 142, 260, 268, 425, 426

movement, 43, 54, 68, 96, 105, 106, 110, 124, 129, 130, 149, 151, 425, 431, 434, 452, 462, 471, 476

movement disorders, 96, 129, 130

MRI, 458, 463, 465

mucosa, 229, 393, 423, 425, 440

multidimensional, 464

multidisciplinary, xiii, 58, 87, 90, 98, 182, 403, 464, 469, 470, 471, 479, 484

multiple factors, 486, 499

multiplication, 55

mumps, 51

murder, 177

muscle, 105, 109, 123, 124, 128, 132, 138, 154, 251, 273, 393, 397, 400, 411, 438, 440, 441, 443

muscle mass, 411

muscle relaxant, 128

muscle relaxation, 138, 438

muscles, 124, 149, 154, 244, 400, 440

musculoskeletal, 135

mushrooms, 437, 438, 439

music, 420, 456

mutation, 81, 352

mutations, 352, 365, 368

myalgia, 443

myelination, 272, 396

myocardial infarction, 440

myopathy, 398, 403

N

NAA, 94

naloxone, 433, 437

naming, 71, 73, 270, 458

narcissistic, 276, 277, 284, 379

narcolepsy, 171

narcotic, 435, 436, 437

narcotics, 417, 434, 435

nares, 462

narratives, 166

nasogastric tube, 399

national, 32, 65, 102, 183, 187, 206, 292, 312, 314, 320, 324, 325, 344, 345, 422, 423, 449, 455, 456, 465, 470, 473, 476, 479, 483, 484

National Academy of Sciences, 480

National Health Interview Survey, 41, 496

National Institutes of Health, 60, 448, 449

National Research Council, 8, 66, 99, 480

Native American, 444

Native Hawaiian, 334, 346

natural, xv, 53, 105, 181, 188, 233, 258, 260, 270, 289, 400, 439

natural disasters, 258

nausea, 226, 249, 426, 438

NCS, 23

Nebraska, 23

neck, 272, 409

necrosis, 153, 436

negative attitudes, 283

negative body image, 409

negative consequences, 177, 190, 275, 279, 284

negative life events, 344

negative outcomes, 59, 380

neglect, 5, 57, 67, 91, 108, 118, 280, 323, 341, 342, 407, 451, 452, 453, 454, 455, 456, 457, 458, 460, 461, 463, 464, 465, 466, 467, 468, 469, 470, 471, 473, 474, 475, 476, 477, 478, 479, 480, 482, 483, 484, 490

negligence, 338

negotiating, 72, 495

negotiation, 231

neocortex, 294

neonatal, 479

Neoplastic, 210

nerve, 132, 272, 396

nerves, 63, 131, 132, 462

nervous system, 8, 67, 76, 94, 103, 104, 116, 121, 122, 131, 172, 244, 272, 273, 357, 378, 425, 426, 428, 429, 430, 431, 432, 433, 436, 439, 441, 443, 448

Netherlands, 331, 364

network, 6, 58, 231, 279

neural development, 364

neural systems, 63

neurobehavioral, 159, 192

neurobiological, 7, 272, 436, 487

neurobiology, 118, 344

neurodegenerative, 42, 357

neurodegenerative disease, 42

neurodegenerative diseases, 42

neurodegenerative disorders, 357

neurogenic, 136, 143, 144

Neurogenic, 138

neurogenic bladder, 136, 144

neuroimaging, 43, 109, 351, 357, 365

neuroimaging techniques, 365

neuroleptic, 127, 261, 357, 358, 362

neuroleptic malignant syndrome, 127, 261, 358

neurologic disorders, 179

neurological condition, 23

neurological deficit, 59

neurological disorder, 108, 357

neurologist, 29

neuromotor, 61, 65, 66

neuronal circuits, 108

neuronal migration, 429

neurons, 107, 132, 272, 439

neuropeptide, 389

neuropsychiatric disorders, 130

neuropsychological assessment, 15, 22, 29, 91, 357

neuropsychology, 12

neuroscientists, 102

neuroticism, 328

neurotransmitter, 108, 251

neutropenia, 393

New England, 279, 479, 481

New Orleans, 118

New World, 291

New York, ix, xiv, 7, 35, 60, 99, 118, 124, 173, 234, 252, 262, 291, 294, 312, 341, 342, 346, 381, 455, 464, 474, 476, 477, 480, 491, 499, 500, 501, 504, 505

New Zealand, 342

newsletters, 491

newspapers, 219

nicotine, 422, 423, 424, 425, 426, 447, 449, 450

Nicotine, 125, 423, 424, 425, 450

nicotine gum, 424

NIH, 60, 449

NIS, 482

nitrates, 444

nitrogen, 393

nitrosamines, 422

nitrous oxide, 444

nocturia, 411

nodules, 62

noise, 14, 94, 109

non-autistic individuals, 97

non-biological, 207

non-clinical, 206

non-invasive, 133

nonlinear, 73

nonverbal, 63, 64, 68, 70, 71, 74, 93

nonverbal communication, 70, 74

nonverbal signals, 63, 64, 68

norepinephrine, 129, 170, 228, 412

normal, xi, 8, 16, 17, 25, 62, 67, 68, 70, 72, 73, 74, 76, 81, 84, 86, 91, 92, 103, 105, 108, 113, 133, 137, 141, 144, 153, 177, 178, 194, 205, 207, 239, 243, 244, 247, 257, 265, 266, 267, 268, 270, 271, 275, 277, 282, 284, 285, 286, 287, 288, 291, 329, 355, 362, 384, 389, 391, 393, 398, 409, 421, 422, 428, 436, 467, 472, 485, 487, 488, 489, 496, 497

normal children, 108

normal curve, 16, 67

normal development, 25, 68, 72, 81, 177, 178, 244, 270, 291, 355

normal distribution, 16

norms, 6, 20, 57, 73, 83, 176, 245, 375, 379, 380, 407, 467

North America, 7, 60, 99, 155, 293, 340, 387, 473, 474, 477, 482

Northern Hemisphere, 361

NOS, 79, 80, 81, 82, 87, 160, 221, 223

novelty, 244, 391

nudity, 286

nurse, xi, xv, 32, 462, 479

nurse practitioners, xv

nurses, xii, 394, 464, 469, 471

nursing, 47, 464, 496

nursing care, 47, 496

nutrient, 396, 412

nutrients, 391, 395, 397, 400

nutrition, 389, 394, 395, 396, 397, 398, 399, 410, 441, 453

nutritional deficiencies, 396

O

obese, 389, 390, 405, 406, 407, 408, 409, 410, 411, 412, 413, 414, 415

obese patients, 406, 412

obesity, 390, 405, 406, 407, 408, 409, 410, 411, 412, 413, 414, 415, 460

obligations, 164, 427, 490

observable behavior, 178

observations, x, 11, 13, 15, 28, 57, 90, 102, 103, 110, 212

observed behavior, 180

obsessive-compulsive, 5, 97, 124, 195, 197, 257, 261, 262, 387, 388, 395, 400, 401

Obsessive-compulsive, 123, 128, 167, 373, 388

obsessive-compulsive disorder, 5, 97, 124, 195, 257, 261, 262, 388, 395, 400

obstructive sleep apnea, 409, 427

occlusion, 423

occupational, 29, 32, 58, 91, 94, 101, 102, 110, 116, 118, 119, 359, 373, 488

occupational therapists, 29, 58, 116

occupational therapy, 32, 58, 91, 94, 101, 102, 110, 118, 119

OCD, 92, 97, 125, 130, 255, 256, 257, 258, 259, 260, 261, 262, 378, 388, 401

oculomotor, 105

oedema, 403, 404

Oedipus, 268, 277, 278

offenders, 5, 281, 294, 461, 482, 485, 486, 487, 490, 491, 492, 493

Office of Justice Programs, 479, 492, 493

Office of Juvenile Justice and Delinquency Prevention, 292, 492

Office of National Drug Control Policy, 426

oil, 152, 153, 426

olanzapine, 97, 127, 233, 261, 357, 358, 364, 367

old age, 320, 323, 329, 330, 331

olfaction, 24, 114

omission, 21, 338, 460, 465

online, 117, 293, 294

openness, 279

operant conditioning, 137

ophthalmologist, 57

opiates, 164

opioid, 428, 433, 436, 442, 449

Opioid, 211, 436, 437

opioids, 445

opium, 271, 441

opposition, 285

Oppositional Defiant Disorder, 176, 177, 178, 180, 182, 418

optimism, 268

oral, 6, 62, 66, 69, 73, 114, 127, 129, 136, 145, 152, 153, 277, 279, 283, 285, 294, 399, 425, 426, 429, 450, 452, 453, 458, 466

oral cavity, 62, 466

oral contraceptives, 283

Oregon, 344, 346

ores, 370

organ, 42, 268, 457, 462

organic, 135, 148, 149, 150, 357, 427, 442, 463, 467

organic solvent, 427

organization, xii, 21, 23, 32, 59, 103, 115, 116

organizations, 87, 309, 469, 470, 489

orgasm, 266, 268, 272, 302

orientation, 266, 277, 285, 290, 297, 300, 301, 302, 303, 304, 309, 310, 311, 312, 313, 314, 323, 325, 326, 329, 344, 403, 461

Orlistat, 412, 414

orthostatic hypotension, 126, 393, 396

osmotic, 141, 229, 391

osmotic pressure, 141

osteodystrophy, 407

osteopenia, 398

osteoporosis, 398

OTC, 424

out-of-pocket, 495

outpatient, ix, 321, 338, 394, 396, 400, 403, 436, 468

outpatients, 340, 396, 399, 403

ovary, 409, 411, 414

overeating, 383, 384

oversight, 194, 489

over-the-counter, 216, 412

overweight, 384, 389, 407, 408, 409, 410

ownership, 498

oxide, 423, 444, 445
Oxygen, 445

P

Pacific, 35
PAF, 344
pain, 85, 89, 96, 109, 142, 149, 151, 178, 212, 217, 282, 370, 411, 420, 421, 462
paints, 379, 444
Pakistan, 435
palpation, 135
palpitations, 240
pancreatic, 412
pancreatitis, 428
panic attack, 98, 240, 241, 242, 440
panic disorder, 211, 240, 242, 243, 244
paper, 71, 79, 291, 292, 295, 312, 314, 362, 438
Papillomavirus, 305, 306
paradoxical, 251
parameter, 99, 143, 174, 182, 252
paranoia, 193, 421, 433, 440, 443
parasites, 306, 308
parental attitudes, 270, 410
parental influence, 277
parental involvement, 253
parent-child, 220, 454, 467, 470, 471
parenteral, 395, 399
parenting, 7, 220, 246, 456, 459, 464, 470, 471
parenting styles, 459
Paris, 291
Parkinson, 196
paroxetine, 215, 249, 253, 260
partial seizure, 89
partial thromboplastin time, 463
particles, 434
partnership, 394
passive, 86, 106, 114
paternal, 352, 364, 407
pathogenesis, 363
pathologist, 57, 65, 74, 90, 198
pathologists, 61, 72, 73, 74, 116
pathology, ix, 62, 86, 96, 166, 244, 301, 409, 488
pathophysiology, 130, 404
pathways, 7, 108, 352, 365, 367, 434, 451, 478
patient care, 394, 395
patient management, 58
pattern recognition, 106
Paxil, 249, 260
PCP, 211, 417, 418, 421, 427, 437, 441

pdgf, 447
pediatric, ix, x, xii, xiii, 3, 5, 7, 29, 51, 64, 91, 97, 98, 114, 128, 130, 142, 150, 153, 155, 159, 166, 175, 185, 188, 200, 205, 209, 212, 217, 219, 220, 222, 224, 226, 227, 230, 231, 233, 234, 235, 253, 262, 265, 278, 319, 335, 336, 337, 339, 350, 351, 358, 364, 366, 394, 408, 419, 420, 421, 449, 452, 455, 462, 464, 478, 479, 480, 482, 484
Pediatric care, 313
pediatric patients, 3, 7, 185, 209, 217, 265, 364
pediatrician, xi, xiii, 13, 98, 175, 180, 182, 185, 192, 219, 394, 446, 455, 459, 460, 464, 465, 466, 467, 469, 472, 473
peer, xiii, 6, 13, 75, 80, 94, 189, 213, 220, 230, 231, 244, 272, 281, 294, 295, 308, 325, 326, 421, 422, 456, 489, 491
peer group, 325, 326, 421, 422
peer rejection, 189
peer relationship, 80, 213, 244, 456, 489
peers, 11, 12, 34, 68, 69, 71, 84, 94, 162, 163, 188, 241, 257, 269, 275, 276, 277, 285, 288, 300, 321, 324, 325, 326, 329, 344, 370, 371, 386, 388, 410, 417, 419, 420, 422, 488, 497
pelvic, 132, 305
penalties, 464, 465
penis, 267, 268, 270, 287, 462
Pennsylvania, 343
peptides, 428
percentile, 17, 53, 398, 408
perception, 23, 54, 93, 106, 113, 277, 300, 349, 359, 379, 383, 384, 399, 410, 437, 439
perceptions, 27, 107, 116, 245, 293, 294, 322, 333, 347, 380, 427
perfectionism, 258, 342, 377
perforation, 153, 433, 457
performance, 13, 14, 16, 17, 18, 20, 28, 29, 40, 53, 85, 105, 113, 116, 117, 163, 228, 244, 283, 327, 353, 387, 388, 419, 421, 429, 446, 459, 497
perinatal, 57
perineum, 462
Peripheral, 433, 445
peripheral nervous system, 131
perpetration, 295, 461
perseverance, 84
personal, 47, 84, 109, 162, 163, 246, 266, 270, 278, 289, 290, 300, 302, 310, 326, 369, 371, 372, 373, 375, 420, 422, 452, 488
personal hygiene, 163
personal relations, 372, 375
personal relationship, 375

personal values, 289

personality, x, 5, 27, 28, 57, 191, 195, 200, 244, 265, 303, 323, 327, 328, 346, 353, 360, 365, 369, 370, 372, 373, 374, 376, 378, 379, 380, 381, 387, 390, 395, 403

personality characteristics, 328

personality dimensions, 27

personality disorder, 5, 191, 195, 200, 323, 327, 328, 346, 360, 365, 369, 370, 372, 373, 374, 376, 378, 379, 380, 381, 387, 390, 395, 403

Personality disorders, 191, 195, 200, 369, 378, 380

personality traits, 369, 373, 380

personality type, 354

perturbations, 64

pesticides, 330

pets, 176

pharmaceutical, 337

pharmaceutical companies, 337

pharmaceuticals, 441

pharmacologic agents, 129, 197, 412, 424

pharmacological, 228, 229, 335, 449

pharmacological treatment, 449

pharmacology, 446, 450

pharmacotherapy, 96, 126, 129, 130, 142, 168, 174, 180, 182, 200, 224, 232, 234, 249, 252, 259, 262, 357, 359, 447, 448

pharynx, 398, 462

phencyclidine, 417, 418, 421, 427, 437, 441

phenomenology, 223, 366

phenothiazines, 429

phenotype, 220, 221, 233, 363, 407

phenotypes, 220, 221, 234

Philadelphia, 7, 8, 42, 47, 49, 118, 130, 143, 234, 294, 296, 311, 313, 314, 447, 448, 475, 482

Philippines, 506

philosophy, 102, 272, 283

phobia, 167, 240, 241, 242, 243, 245, 252, 253, 378, 490

phone, 68, 486

phonemes, 63, 72, 73

phonological, 20, 53, 54, 62, 64, 66, 70, 71, 72, 75

phonology, 61, 72

phosphate, 152, 153

phosphates, 152

phosphorus, 397

phosphorylation, 397

photographs, 390, 465

physical abuse, 149, 280, 323, 388, 403, 452, 453, 455, 456, 458, 460, 465, 471, 472, 473, 474, 476, 483, 484

physical activity, 383, 405, 406, 407, 409, 412, 414, 431

physical aggression, 188

physical education, 106, 275, 386

physical fitness, 415

physical force, 486

physical health, 309

physical therapist, 29

physical therapy, 32

physicians, x, xv, 3, 5, 6, 74, 75, 87, 136, 168, 216, 225, 271, 335, 336, 389, 394, 399, 402, 459, 464, 468, 469, 472, 479, 480, 481, 484

Physicians, ix, 3, 6, 58, 392, 457, 458, 465, 468, 471, 478, 480, 485, 490, 492

physiological, 3, 4, 9, 154, 304, 374, 396, 432, 467

physiology, 131, 271, 289, 342

Piagetian, 323

Piers-Harris Children's Self-Concept Scale, 26

pilot study, 118, 230, 233

pituitary, 273

placebo, 126, 143, 213, 232, 233, 234, 249, 253, 262, 337, 358, 367, 401, 425, 426

placenta, 44, 433

placental, 108

placental barrier, 108

planning, 6, 21, 25, 46, 54, 55, 58, 70, 93, 94, 95, 106, 259, 289, 290, 307, 331, 353, 357, 359, 395, 462

plants, 438

plaques, 409

plasma, 389

plastic, 444

plasticity, 108, 272

platelet, 463, 465

platelet count, 463, 465

play, 10, 12, 42, 58, 68, 71, 74, 75, 81, 86, 87, 90, 91, 103, 107, 110, 115, 135, 161, 162, 163, 207, 208, 231, 249, 257, 266, 268, 282, 287, 299, 321, 327, 352, 392, 395, 406, 456, 467, 470, 471, 487, 488, 489, 496, 499

pleasure, 178, 206, 208, 266, 268, 269, 271, 321, 426, 443, 446, 489

PMA, 493

pneumonia, 436

pneumonitis, 435

poison, 330

poisoning, 57, 165, 324, 330, 345, 346

police, 190, 421, 464, 469

political, ix, 456

pollution, 258

polonium, 423

polycyclic aromatic hydrocarbon, 423

polycystic ovary syndrome, 409

polydipsia, 411

polyethylene, 152

polyhydramnios, 44

poor, 31, 52, 53, 54, 55, 56, 66, 85, 105, 106, 108,
    109, 142, 162, 163, 188, 194, 205, 206, 207, 211,
    213, 220, 222, 225, 284, 309, 321, 322, 323, 324,
    336, 349, 354, 358, 390, 393, 410, 459, 460, 467

poor performance, 85, 163

poor readers, 53, 66

population, 5, 16, 39, 40, 41, 56, 65, 66, 67, 82, 89,
    91, 97, 98, 107, 108, 117, 122, 159, 173, 176,
    179, 192, 211, 212, 220, 239, 242, 243, 255, 313,
    314, 322, 325, 326, 327, 329, 339, 345, 346, 350,
    351, 353, 367, 369, 372, 380, 387, 390, 405, 414,
    452, 467, 471, 476, 478, 483, 486

pornography, 303

ports, 387

positive attitudes, 230, 287, 328

positive behaviors, 180

positive feedback, 30, 287, 288

positive regard, 115

positive reinforcement, 30, 180, 287

positive relation, 388

positive relationship, 388

Post Traumatic Stress Disorder, 97

postmenarcheal, 384

postpartum, 479

postpartum period, 479

postsynaptic, 423

posttraumatic stress, 355, 475

post-traumatic stress, 126, 195

post-traumatic stress, 388

post-traumatic stress, 451

post-traumatic stress, 459

post-traumatic stress, 461

posttraumatic stress disorder, 355

post-traumatic stress disorder, 126, 195

post-traumatic stress disorder, 388

post-traumatic stress disorder, 451

posture, 457

potassium, 397, 398

potatoes, 406

poverty, 282, 330, 331, 350, 354, 408, 455, 457, 460,
    471

powder, 431, 432, 435, 437, 439, 443

power, 51, 340, 347, 352, 389, 452, 453

powers, 374

Prader-Willi syndrome, 191, 192, 197, 199, 407, 409

pragmatic, 62, 68, 84, 117, 346

praxis, 112, 113, 115

prayer, 271

prealbumin, 393

precedents, 95

predictive validity, 363

predictors, 117, 201, 343, 364, 373, 404, 449

prednisone, 225

pre-existing, 172

preference, 95, 208, 266, 290, 298

pregnancy, xiii, 46, 270, 277, 280, 284, 285, 290,
    423, 429, 432, 440, 459, 460, 461, 466, 467

pregnancy test, 290

pregnant, 283, 303, 311, 424, 427, 481

pregnant women, 311, 481

prejudice, 496

premature delivery, 433

prematurity, 467

prenatal care, 44

preparation, 14, 47, 75, 117, 168, 229, 390, 427

prepubertal, 221, 222, 233, 319, 320, 321, 322, 323,
    324, 329, 335, 336, 337, 341, 345, 346, 355, 459,
    472, 475, 480, 481, 483

preschool, 24, 65, 71, 87, 148, 160, 161, 162, 166,
    174, 176, 182, 200, 217, 240, 243, 266, 321, 335,
    340, 455

preschool children, 65, 87, 174, 182, 200, 217, 321,
    335, 340, 455

preschoolers, 75, 160, 161, 245, 269, 350, 475, 489

prescription drug, 421

prescription drugs, 421

pressure, 126, 127, 135, 141, 154, 172, 189, 196,
    222, 226, 269, 275, 289, 305, 308, 326, 358, 409,
    411, 414, 427, 429, 431, 443, 445, 489

presynaptic, 126, 423

prevention, xi, 46, 207, 249, 260, 262, 283, 285, 287,
    289, 290, 319, 320, 324, 334, 335, 336, 342, 344,
    346, 359, 362, 418, 423, 446, 452, 453, 464, 470,
    471, 472, 473, 479, 483

preventive, 47, 225, 339, 451, 460, 498

primary care, xi, xii, xv, 3, 5, 12, 13, 29, 58, 87, 89,
    90, 98, 195, 216, 239, 243, 247, 252, 255, 259,
    275, 292, 303, 304, 305, 310, 314, 335, 336, 346,
    390, 448, 468, 471, 472, 483, 485, 491

primary caregivers, 195, 390

primate, 107, 119

primates, 108, 294

privacy, 270, 276, 287, 288, 391, 469, 486

private, 15, 33, 287, 490

proactive, 187

probability, 4, 30, 189, 190, 321, 322, 327, 328, 452, 453

probation, 193, 356, 486

probation officers, 356

probe, 154

problem behavior, xiii, 57, 219

problem behaviors, xiii, 57, 219

problem drinking, 428

problem solving, 21, 24, 71, 91, 94, 220, 231, 232, 359, 370

problem-focused coping, 497

problem-solving, 21, 230, 343

procedures, 10, 13, 14, 25, 28, 34, 73, 75, 154, 167, 305, 332, 413, 463, 466

processing deficits, 55, 113

proctitis, 308

producers, 443

production, 23, 53, 62, 64, 65, 66, 70, 72, 73, 102, 145, 396, 397, 412, 431

profit, 59, 375, 422

prognosis, 6, 142, 165, 196, 211, 350, 354, 359, 361, 402

program, x, xii, 10, 12, 33, 34, 59, 95, 137, 142, 151, 194, 195, 231, 232, 266, 346, 398, 412, 423, 429, 436, 446, 475, 483

programming, 25, 299

progressive, 351, 389

prolactin, 127, 226

prolapse, 242

promote, x, xiii, 96, 193, 285, 399, 497, 498

pronunciation, 84, 88, 90

property, 177, 178, 185, 187, 189, 190

prophylaxis, 232, 307, 466, 481

proposition, 338

propranolol, 196, 229, 230, 433

Propranolol, 228

prostitution, 270, 281, 282, 453, 485, 486, 491

protection, 14, 284, 289, 308, 446, 461, 463, 464, 465, 469, 485, 491

protective factors, 332, 417, 456

protein, 389, 412, 466

prothrombin, 463

protocol, 14, 143, 230, 231, 392, 399, 472

protocols, 114, 180, 181, 358

provocation, 178, 195

proximal, 124, 273

Prozac, 249, 259

pruning, 272, 351, 429

pruritus, 271

psychiatric diagnosis, xi, 488

psychiatric disorder, 108, 136, 164, 165, 167, 171, 173, 178, 179, 182, 185, 189, 190, 194, 195, 196, 198, 200, 201, 205, 209, 211, 213, 280, 322, 334, 340, 353, 355, 363, 402, 427, 455, 497

psychiatric disorders, 108, 136, 164, 165, 167, 171, 173, 178, 179, 182, 185, 189, 194, 195, 196, 198, 200, 201, 209, 211, 213, 280, 334, 353, 355, 363, 455, 497

psychiatric illness, 239, 242, 335

psychiatrist, xii, xiii, 47, 79, 91, 97, 98, 216, 251, 261, 304, 394

psychiatrists, xii, xiii, 29, 338, 399

psychiatry, xii, xiii, xv, 4, 8, 99, 128, 195, 366

psychic energy, 272

psychoactive, 444

psychoanalysis, x

psychological, xi, 9, 10, 13, 14, 15, 16, 18, 20, 28, 29, 32, 33, 34, 59, 74, 94, 108, 142, 150, 180, 193, 206, 213, 272, 297, 299, 303, 304, 327, 335, 342, 359, 366, 400, 420, 427, 428, 432, 435, 436, 449, 452, 453, 459, 460, 461, 466, 467, 471, 478, 486, 487, 496, 497, 498

psychological assessments, 16

psychological distress, 335

psychological functions, 18

Psychological Perspective, 299

psychological problems, 459, 497

psychological well-being, 94

psychologist, 13, 29, 34, 57, 74, 167, 180, 395

psychologists, xii, xv, 13, 15, 58, 74

psychology, xiii, xv, 60, 231, 291, 312, 342

psychometric properties, 224

psychopathology, 27, 57, 79, 175, 192, 208, 268, 319, 323, 329, 336, 339, 343, 350, 359, 490

psychopharmacological, 89, 96, 337

psychopharmacology, xv, 5, 96, 253

psychoses, 363, 367

psychosis, 91, 127, 195, 196, 198, 221, 222, 224, 353, 354, 355, 356, 357, 360, 361, 362, 363, 364, 365, 366, 380, 417, 420, 427, 429, 430, 437

psychosocial, x, xi, 15, 57, 61, 96, 197, 220, 224, 230, 231, 232, 235, 247, 266, 268, 275, 276, 280, 297, 305, 322, 335, 339, 340, 355, 356, 357, 359, 392, 400, 405, 409, 411, 413, 414, 487

psychosocial development, 268, 276

psychosocial functioning, 96, 356

psychosocial stress, 275

psychosomatic, 403

Psychosomatic, 346, 414

psychostimulants, 182, 228, 356, 402

psychotherapeutic, 200, 228, 249, 259, 260, 261

psychotherapy, 98, 182, 197, 212, 213, 231, 247, 249, 252, 259, 361, 400, 404, 439

psychotic, 98, 167, 222, 226, 233, 322, 327, 350, 354, 355, 356, 357, 358, 360, 361, 362, 363, 364, 365, 374, 431, 438

psychotic states, 356

psychotic symptoms, 322, 350, 355, 356, 357, 358, 361, 363

psychotropic medications, 47, 48, 124, 167, 182, 197

PTSD, 97, 195

pubarche, 273, 274

pubertal development, 273, 288

puberty, 59, 207, 267, 268, 270, 272, 273, 275, 288, 289, 291, 292, 297, 300, 302, 325, 388, 391, 419

public, x, 14, 47, 69, 162, 176, 187, 194, 219, 241, 285, 287, 308, 319, 335, 341, 405, 413, 417, 426, 444, 464, 477

public awareness, 194, 219

public health, x, 319, 335, 341, 405, 413, 417, 464, 477

Public Health Service, 60, 341

public policy, 405

public support, 285

pulmonary edema, 393, 435

pulse, 126, 127, 172, 272, 431, 440, 462

pulses, 152, 462

pumps, 395

puncture wounds, 435

punishment, 30, 137, 149, 151, 389

punitive, 399

pupils, 438

pyruvic, 429

Q

QT interval, 226, 398, 437

QTc, 127, 261

quality of life, 261, 419

query, 245

questioning, 258, 297, 311

questionnaire, 25, 26, 90, 111, 112, 341, 345, 482

questionnaires, 166, 180, 181, 206, 208

quetiapine, 97, 127, 198, 233, 261, 357

quinine, 432

quinones, 439

R

race, 82, 293, 301, 341, 463, 466, 467

racial differences, 414

radiation, 44, 458

rain, 362

rales, 393

random, 189

range, 4, 17, 18, 40, 41, 42, 45, 51, 57, 82, 84, 90, 94, 104, 111, 124, 126, 147, 177, 215, 220, 244, 257, 259, 275, 282, 288, 302, 303, 320, 323, 330, 331, 335, 353, 356, 369, 373, 374, 383, 391, 397, 398, 411, 423, 428, 432, 436, 452, 458, 465, 487, 492, 497

rape, 177, 178, 280, 281, 290, 303, 388, 440, 441, 442, 458, 459, 470, 473, 486, 487, 490, 492

rapid-cycling, 232

rapists, 487

rash, 153, 225

rating scale, 89, 90, 112, 166, 180, 181, 224, 246

ratings, 116, 245, 303, 358, 456

reactivity, 104, 190, 332, 345, 375

reading, 24, 34, 47, 52, 53, 55, 56, 57, 58, 59, 61, 64, 66, 69, 71, 74, 75, 76, 91, 106

reading assessment, 53

reading comprehension, 66, 71

reading difficulties, 66

reading disability, 53, 58

reading disorder, 52, 56, 64

reality, 64, 79, 82, 102, 221, 308, 437

reasoning, 20, 21, 52, 55, 74, 114, 276, 370

rebelliousness, 326

recall, 22, 55, 189, 399

recalling, 51

reception, 54

receptor agonist, 125, 128

receptors, 126, 401, 423, 426, 436

reciprocity, 80, 82, 92, 93

recognition, xii, xv, 22, 42, 51, 53, 54, 71, 106, 220, 265, 291, 335, 477, 496

recollection, 14

reconciliation, 456

recovery, 24, 73, 223, 232, 233, 259, 353, 354, 399, 402, 404

recreational, 193, 394, 395, 417, 450, 496

rectal examination, 149

rectum, 148, 150, 151, 271

recurrence, 41, 193, 321, 472, 481

red blood cell, 463

red blood cells, 463

reduced bladder capacity, 136

reduction, xiii, 30, 68, 127, 210, 260, 305, 324, 358, 359, 409, 423, 427, 433, 434, 444

reflection, 39

reflexes, 9, 66, 135, 411, 427, 462

refractory, 97, 358, 364

regional, 312, 351, 368

regression, 97, 98

regular, 126, 147, 153, 225, 285, 355, 409, 412, 422, 423, 426, 442, 471

regulation, 5, 21, 62, 64, 69, 117, 147, 150, 231, 336, 380, 394

rehabilitation, 52, 93, 95, 359, 486, 490

rehabilitation program, 95

rehydration, 397

reimbursement, 28, 467

reinforcement, 30, 31, 75, 180, 287

rejection, 189, 222, 301, 309, 326, 370, 419

relapse, 137, 141, 150, 154, 230, 232, 233, 251, 260, 357, 359, 399, 401, 404, 435

relapses, 154

relationship, 14, 66, 102, 151, 177, 179, 183, 189, 269, 277, 279, 281, 284, 287, 301, 302, 310, 313, 327, 330, 338, 362, 388, 406, 415, 451, 452, 453, 454, 456, 464, 467, 483, 489

relationships, 3, 4, 34, 62, 63, 64, 69, 72, 79, 80, 82, 86, 105, 210, 213, 220, 244, 270, 275, 278, 279, 283, 284, 285, 290, 293, 300, 302, 305, 307, 308, 309, 312, 325, 326, 329, 352, 356, 370, 371, 373, 374, 375, 451, 456, 459, 497

relatives, 322, 323, 328, 334, 340, 351, 360, 387, 419

relaxation, 138, 154, 395, 438

relevance, 165, 187

reliability, 14, 17, 113, 182, 234, 262, 357, 361

religion, 276, 342

religions, 301

religiosity, 419

religious, 270, 271, 275, 284, 285, 305, 419, 456

religious belief, 305

religious beliefs, 305

REM, 227

remediation, 58

remission, 354

renal, 135, 144, 153, 165, 210, 215, 216, 440

renal dysfunction, 153

renal failure, 165, 210, 440

rent, 328

repair, 178

reparation, 168

repetitions, 22, 73

repetitive behavior, 80

replication, 352, 361, 365, 366

reporters, 460, 464

representative samples, 187

reproduction, 307, 436

research, x, xiii, 35, 81, 90, 102, 114, 115, 118, 119, 125, 126, 130, 136, 142, 181, 182, 183, 213, 220, 227, 253, 280, 292, 299, 302, 308, 319, 328, 334, 344, 346, 349, 351, 369, 380, 408, 423, 427, 432, 434, 436, 437, 438, 466, 469, 471, 484

research design, 126

researchers, 102, 271, 299, 300, 320, 405

resentment, 498

reserves, 81, 396

residential, 97, 394, 398, 400, 436

resilience, 6, 7, 476

resistance, 75, 176, 177, 227, 407, 409

resolution, 144, 145, 268, 278, 304, 313, 479

resources, 3, 4, 28, 34, 40, 59, 76, 93, 182, 188, 232, 288, 289, 290, 307, 309, 310, 332, 334, 339, 359, 395, 453, 460, 461, 464, 465, 499

respiration, 114, 462

respiratory, 62, 258, 259, 304, 409, 428, 429, 435, 437, 442, 443, 445

response time, 21

responsibilities, 178, 289, 338, 464

responsiveness, 109

restaurant, 68

restaurants, 162

restitution, 31

restless legs syndrome, 166

restoration, 401

resuscitation, 44

retardation, 39, 40, 42, 47, 49, 56, 65, 67, 81, 82, 91, 92, 167, 179, 194, 199, 206, 212, 353, 388, 456, 457, 474, 491

retention, 132, 137, 141, 143, 148, 149, 441

retina, 462

returns, 32, 396

rewards, 30, 95, 151, 248, 287

Reynolds, 27, 108, 118, 341

rhinitis, 425

rhythm, 73, 172, 231, 462

rhythmicity, 114

rhythms, 162, 207, 393

right hemisphere, 63

risk assessment, 331

risk behaviors, 187, 308, 309, 341

risk factors, 41, 48, 172, 190, 196, 292, 304, 308, 313, 320, 322, 329, 331, 332, 333, 334, 339, 340, 343, 350, 351, 352, 366, 383, 386, 390, 405, 406, 455, 456, 461, 466, 470, 474, 499

risk management, 347

risks, 71, 75, 109, 213, 227, 228, 249, 280, 290, 301, 303, 304, 308, 322, 327, 337, 340, 352, 358, 423, 427, 446, 455, 456, 461

risk-taking, 164, 222, 326, 461

risperidone, 97, 127, 182, 197, 198, 232, 234, 261, 357, 358, 362

robbery, 178

roentgen, 483

role playing, 93

romantic relationship, 293

Rome, 295, 314, 404

routines, 6, 80, 83, 85, 92, 114, 163

RTI, 74

rubber, 444

runaway, 270, 282, 291

rural, 147, 444

rural areas, 444

Russia, 278, 284

rye, 438

S

SAD, 240

sadism, 488

sadness, 205, 209, 269, 488, 489

safeguards, 58

safety, 34, 40, 91, 95, 96, 97, 115, 126, 145, 161, 173, 174, 196, 228, 230, 231, 241, 249, 257, 258, 259, 302, 357, 362, 463, 467, 471

saliva, 66, 422

salmonella, 308

Salmonella, 306

salt, 442

salts, 168, 172, 228, 234, 431

sample, 11, 12, 13, 16, 17, 18, 73, 107, 112, 160, 176, 183, 212, 222, 312, 313, 321, 322, 325, 327, 328, 337, 343, 352, 360, 364, 366, 417, 474, 483

sampling, 12

sarcasm, 63

satisfaction, 10, 291, 326, 389, 391, 499

SBA, 415

scabies, 308

Scandinavia, x

scheduling, 248, 259

schema, 463

schizoaffective disorder, 350, 367, 368

schizoid personality disorder, 378

schizophrenia, xiii, xv, 5, 79, 80, 82, 92, 116, 195, 234, 321, 349, 350, 351, 352, 353, 354, 355, 356, 357, 358, 359, 360, 361, 362, 363, 364, 365, 366, 367, 368, 372, 374, 376

Schizophrenia, vi, 46, 92, 116, 118, 167, 220, 234, 246, 349, 350, 353, 358, 359, 360, 361, 362, 363, 365, 366, 367, 374

schizophrenic patients, 362, 363, 366

school failure, 51, 256, 421

school performance, 327, 353, 419, 421, 497

schooling, 65

science, 24, 102, 436

scientific, xi, 39, 75, 288, 310, 470

scientists, 439

sclera, 462

sclerosis, 86, 89, 191, 192, 197, 199

scoliosis, 135

scores, 15, 16, 17, 19, 21, 22, 24, 25, 26, 27, 28, 40, 44, 48, 53, 55, 67, 90, 112, 113, 321, 327, 328

screening programs, 44, 67

scripts, 68, 94

scrotal, 274, 275

scrotum, 462

search, 43, 48, 102, 178, 437

Seattle, 361, 502, 503, 506

seborrheic dermatitis, 275

second generation, 224, 226, 357, 358

secret, 295, 300

secretion, 141, 143, 413

secrets, 14, 270, 287

security, 15, 267, 268, 286

sedation, 96, 126, 142, 171, 196, 225, 229, 249, 250, 260, 358, 442, 445

sedative, 227, 427, 435, 441, 445

sedentary, 109, 406, 409, 412

seeds, 426, 438, 439

seizure, 29, 89, 189, 191, 192, 196, 197, 198, 201, 357, 425, 430, 438

seizures, 44, 82, 89, 140, 141, 143, 153, 192, 196, 198, 199, 261, 425, 429, 434, 438, 442

selective attention, 6

selective mutism, 92, 242

selective serotonin reuptake inhibitor, 128, 182, 196, 199, 214, 224, 249, 259, 401, 412, 429, 437

Self, 12, 21, 26, 27, 35, 43, 71, 96, 114, 144, 155, 206, 246, 266, 271, 277, 286, 287, 288, 289, 298, 300, 302, 326, 347, 377, 385, 419, 448, 492

self esteem, 56, 106, 231, 269, 421, 497

self help, 90
self image, 370, 375, 419
self-awareness, 277
self-care, 40, 47, 81, 91, 107, 109
self-concept, 26, 56
self-control, 56, 190, 287, 390
self-doubt, 290
self-esteem, 56, 94, 136, 144, 206, 213, 220, 221, 222, 266, 281, 282, 287, 288, 289, 309, 325, 326, 390, 410, 419, 420, 456
self-help, 400, 429
self-identity, 309
self-image, 267, 277, 370, 407
self-interest, 277, 278
self-mutilation, 391
self-organization, 115
self-perceptions, 322
self-regulation, 64, 69
self-report, 11, 26, 27, 113, 206, 258, 321, 324, 342, 474
self-study, 341
self-worth, 206, 459
semantic, 71
semantics, 61, 90, 370
semi-structured interviews, 180
sensation, 112, 114, 123, 132, 137, 148, 154, 457, 462
sensation seeking, 112
sensations, 109, 117, 137, 151, 154, 240, 245, 427
sensitivity, 6, 90, 110, 112, 207, 212, 222, 272, 388
sensory experience, 11, 111
sensory functioning, 24, 112
sensory impairments, 59, 67, 192
sensory modalities, 103, 104, 116
sensory modality, 115
sensory systems, 107, 117
sentences, 54, 62, 63, 69, 71
separation, xiii, 102, 149, 195, 228, 240, 242, 243, 245, 323, 329, 419, 460
sepsis, 44
September 11, 144
septum, 433
sequelae, 4, 192, 200, 226, 258, 408, 424, 427, 433, 446, 463, 474
sequencing, 54, 55, 57, 73, 277
series, 17, 106, 114, 234, 247, 345, 389, 458, 464
serologic test, 466
serotonergic, 260, 344, 439

serotonin, 128, 182, 196, 197, 199, 214, 217, 224, 249, 259, 328, 388, 401, 412, 428, 429, 431, 437, 438
Serotonin, 336
sertraline, 127, 128, 215, 249, 253, 259, 262
serum, 11, 127, 229, 390, 397, 425, 429
services, 4, 12, 29, 32, 33, 39, 45, 46, 47, 48, 59, 65, 67, 73, 74, 95, 98, 282, 283, 307, 315, 335, 338, 342, 359, 451, 455, 456, 460, 461, 462, 464, 467, 469, 470, 471, 479, 485, 487, 499
SES, 3, 4
severity, 24, 40, 41, 42, 44, 48, 57, 82, 84, 90, 97, 129, 134, 141, 192, 209, 212, 223, 247, 252, 280, 328, 412, 463, 467, 476, 499
sex, 69, 72, 82, 87, 178, 222, 265, 266, 268, 270, 273, 275, 276, 277, 278, 279, 280, 282, 283, 284, 285, 286, 287, 288, 289, 290, 291, 293, 294, 295, 297, 298, 299, 300, 301, 302, 303, 304, 306, 307, 308, 312, 313, 314, 341, 342, 362, 364, 365, 374, 376, 408, 415, 486, 487, 489, 491, 492
sex hormones, 266, 275
sex offenders, 486, 487, 491, 492
sex ratio, 82
sex role, 266, 268, 286, 287, 298, 301
sexual abuse, 149, 222, 269, 275, 280, 282, 304, 323, 329, 387, 390, 407, 452, 453, 455, 456, 458, 459, 465, 466, 468, 469, 470, 472, 474, 475, 476, 477, 478, 479, 480, 481, 482, 483, 484, 485, 487, 489, 490, 493
sexual activities, 290, 303, 487
sexual activity, 222, 289, 303, 304, 308, 419, 428, 453, 458, 485, 488, 492
sexual assault, 280, 281, 285, 290, 291, 292, 388, 441, 442, 459, 461, 472, 475, 479, 481, 487
sexual assaults, 280, 281, 442
sexual behavior, 5, 34, 270, 275, 279, 280, 282, 292, 295, 297, 302, 303, 304, 308, 309, 310, 314, 374, 476, 485, 486, 488, 489, 491
sexual behaviour, 280, 294
sexual contact, 269, 458, 459, 465, 466, 470, 489
sexual development, 267, 282, 288, 299, 463
Sexual dysfunction, 292
sexual experiences, 374
sexual health, 268, 277, 279, 285, 296
sexual homicides, 281, 488
sexual identity, 269, 300, 302, 303, 329
sexual intercourse, 278, 294, 304, 458, 487
sexual offending, 485, 486, 487, 491
sexual orientation, 266, 285, 297, 301, 302, 303, 304, 307, 310, 311, 313, 329, 344

sexual pathology, 488

sexuality, 5, 265, 266, 267, 268, 269, 270, 271, 272, 275, 276, 278, 279, 282, 283, 284, 285, 291, 292, 293, 294, 295, 299, 300, 301, 303, 304, 305, 310, 314

sexually abused, 280, 388, 472, 473, 475, 477, 482, 484, 487

sexually transmitted disease, xiii, 270, 279, 282, 284, 285, 295, 297, 303, 304, 305, 308, 309, 432, 433, 458, 477, 478, 483

sexually transmitted diseases, xiii, 270, 279, 282, 284, 285, 295, 297, 303, 304, 305, 308, 309, 432, 433, 458, 477, 483

Sexually transmitted diseases, 310, 313, 314, 474, 482

sexually transmitted infections, 311, 457, 463, 471

SGA, 225, 226, 227, 229

shame, 377, 421, 498

shape, 384, 385

shares, 427

sharing, 15, 309, 392

shear, 459

shelter, 453, 460

shigella, 308

Shigella, 306

shock, 124, 287

short-term, 21, 41, 171, 230, 251, 356, 393, 420

Short-term, 22

short-term memory, 21, 356, 393, 420

shoulder, 122

shy, 6, 14, 134, 244, 377, 378, 379, 490

shyness, 27, 241

SIB, 45

sibling, 45, 220, 454, 487, 498

siblings, 95, 181, 222, 291, 301, 351, 363, 370, 374, 491, 497, 499

Sibutramine, 412

sickle cell, 496, 497

Sickle cell, 210

sickle cell anemia, 496

side effects, 96, 97, 126, 127, 137, 141, 142, 154, 171, 182, 216, 225, 249, 250, 260, 357, 358, 359, 374, 392, 394, 401, 412, 432, 440

sign, 62, 70, 83, 89, 94, 110, 389, 393, 397, 398, 409

signaling, 63, 352

signals, 63, 64, 68, 70, 71, 72

signs, 23, 42, 43, 46, 54, 68, 70, 71, 74, 83, 89, 98, 101, 107, 109, 127, 143, 149, 181, 205, 207, 208, 209, 249, 280, 281, 331, 332, 333, 334, 346, 351,

361, 362, 366, 370, 388, 389, 391, 396, 410, 411, 462, 470, 483, 499

Singapore, 404

sites, 310, 357, 386, 390, 408, 423, 434, 439, 466

skill acquisition, 6

skills, xiii, 5, 6, 11, 14, 18, 19, 20, 21, 23, 24, 25, 27, 29, 32, 40, 42, 47, 53, 54, 55, 56, 59, 60, 64, 69, 73, 75, 81, 83, 84, 86, 91, 94, 95, 98, 106, 108, 151, 180, 188, 207, 208, 220, 224, 230, 247, 253, 268, 276, 277, 281, 289, 300, 309, 310, 332, 334, 338, 341, 353, 359, 370, 371, 394, 456, 458, 459, 471, 497

skills training, 253, 359

skin, 222, 268, 393, 409, 423, 426, 435, 439, 462, 465, 473

slavery, 282

sleep, 92, 98, 133, 162, 166, 205, 206, 209, 212, 215, 220, 221, 222, 224, 227, 230, 231, 250, 271, 400, 409, 411, 414, 420, 427, 431, 441, 443

sleep apnea, 409, 411, 414, 427

sleep disturbance, 224, 250

sleep-disordered breathing, 166

sleeping problems, 251

smiles, 68, 83

smoke, 422, 423, 424, 426, 427, 435

smokers, 422, 423, 424, 426, 449

smoking, xi, 309, 379, 422, 423, 424, 425, 426, 428, 431, 432, 435, 446, 447, 448, 449, 482

smoking cessation, 426, 447, 448

smooth muscle, 132, 138

SMR, 273, 275

SMS, 197, 199

snakes, 242

snoring, 411

SNPs, 364

social acceptance, 456

social activities, 241

social adjustment, 136, 321, 324

social and emotional learning, 32

social anxiety, 98, 195, 241, 253, 374

social behavior, 243, 456

social change, 297

social class, 82, 281

social context, 189, 193

social costs, 497

social development, 46, 83, 219, 223, 452, 453, 487

social factors, 407, 456

social impairment, 79, 80, 86, 182

social integration, 309

social isolation, 327, 353, 354, 470

social learning, 163, 299
social norms, 375
social obligations, 427
social participation, 110, 112
social phobia, 179, 241, 243, 252, 253, 378
Social Phobia, 241, 243, 252
social problems, 276, 444
social relations, 79, 86, 210, 283, 325, 356
social relationships, 79, 86, 210, 283, 325, 356
social rules, 96
Social Security, 496
social services, 456, 461, 464, 469, 470
Social Services, 504
social situations, 83, 195, 373
social skills, 27, 32, 56, 81, 84, 220, 253, 268, 276,
   281, 309, 310, 359, 456, 459
social skills training, 253, 359
social status, 327
social stress, 459
social support, 6, 230, 309, 456
social support network, 6, 456
social transition, 200
social withdrawal, 353, 354, 497
social work, xv, 32, 58, 394, 395, 464
social workers, xv, 58, 464
socialization, 86, 87, 94, 194, 300
socially, 6, 63, 75, 83, 88, 163, 246, 287, 369, 375,
   377, 460, 490
society, x, 132, 266, 270, 275, 278, 280, 281, 282,
   283, 284, 290, 298, 301, 310, 370, 371, 422, 423,
   427, 428, 446, 452, 453, 456, 486
sociocultural, xiii, 39, 57, 299
sociocultural contexts, 39
socioeconomic, 5, 45, 71, 107, 242, 281, 294, 340,
   350, 383, 387, 406, 407, 408, 410, 456, 487
socioeconomic status, 5, 45, 242, 387, 406, 408, 456
sociological, 62
sociology, 342
sodium, 97, 152, 153, 225, 229, 233, 234, 432
sodomy, 490
soft drinks, 229, 406
soil, 135
solvent, 427, 443, 444
somatic complaints, 379
somatic symptoms, 208, 212, 217, 222
Somatoform, 212
somatosensory, 106, 107, 119
somnolence, 229, 411
sounds, 53, 54, 61, 62, 68, 69, 71, 73, 75, 83, 85,
   106, 109, 149, 209, 393, 462

South America, 432, 438, 439
Spain, 331
spatial, 57, 64, 91, 106
spatial analysis, 106
special education, 33, 39, 48, 59, 74
specialists, 29, 44, 58, 74, 205, 395, 399, 437, 446,
   463, 469, 472
species, 306, 466
specific gravity, 390, 392
specificity, 90, 208, 212, 334, 363, 466, 468
spectrum, 4, 65, 70, 74, 75, 79, 80, 81, 82, 83, 85,
   91, 93, 98, 99, 118, 191, 194, 198, 199, 200, 221,
   230, 234, 357, 358, 360, 363, 365, 455
speculation, 328
speech, 4, 32, 45, 52, 53, 54, 57, 58, 59, 61, 62, 64,
   65, 66, 67, 68, 69, 70, 71, 72, 73, 74, 75, 76, 83,
   84, 86, 88, 89, 90, 94, 96, 116, 194, 198, 222,
   350, 353, 354, 431, 445
speech sounds, 53, 61, 62, 69, 71
speed, 107, 272, 360, 427, 429, 439
spelling, 24, 54, 55, 57, 69, 74
sperm, 427
spermatozoa, 271
spheres, 453
sphincter, 132, 137, 148, 149, 151, 154
spin, 288
spina bifida, 12, 282, 497
spinal cord, 132
spine, 119
spiritual, 452, 453
sponsor, 470
spontaneity, 105
sporadic, 352, 368
sports, xiii, 67, 85, 304, 387, 429
spouse, 454
SRH, 343
SRIs, 128, 182, 224, 228, 249, 259, 401
St. Louis, 479
St. Petersburg, 294
stability, 27, 107, 220, 325, 363, 364
stabilization, 224, 227, 228, 230, 232, 234, 412
stabilizers, 47, 224, 226, 227, 380
stages, 70, 178, 216, 259, 265, 266, 267, 268, 273,
   300, 304, 309, 323, 389, 391, 400, 428, 497
standard deviation, 16, 17, 40, 41, 55
standard error, 40, 415
standardization, 16, 133, 145, 155
standards, 3, 5, 6, 14, 35, 102, 326, 338, 347, 463,
   468, 470
Staphylococcus, 436

Staphylococcus aureus, 436

starches, 406

stars, 30

starvation, 399

State-Trait Anxiety Inventory for Children, 27

statistics, 67, 187, 284, 302, 320, 324, 339, 341, 344, 455, 471, 480

statutes, 464, 486, 490

statutory, 465, 486

STD, 284, 290, 307, 313, 483

stereotypes, 86

steroids, 246, 272, 275, 440

stethoscope, 105

Stevens-Johnson syndrome, 171

STI, 466

stiffness, 251

stigmatized, 300

stimulant, 98, 127, 129, 167, 169, 170, 173, 197, 198, 199, 214, 227, 228, 233, 235, 429, 430, 432, 433, 439

stimulus, 6, 27, 75, 103, 104, 242, 333

STIs, 285, 297, 305, 307, 466

stomach, 138, 229, 398

storage, 86, 145, 155, 357

strain, 134, 151

strategic, 226

strategies, 19, 30, 31, 34, 46, 48, 58, 60, 93, 110, 147, 162, 197, 220, 228, 230, 239, 243, 245, 252, 255, 259, 292, 336, 352, 359, 370, 380, 466, 468, 469, 470, 474, 496

stratification, 410

strength, 4, 91, 170, 424, 462

stress, 84, 93, 95, 108, 117, 122, 126, 136, 149, 167, 191, 195, 275, 290, 326, 347, 355, 388, 409, 428, 437, 451, 459, 461, 470, 475, 498

stressors, 107, 178, 246, 250, 319, 320, 496, 497

stretching, 399

striatum, 121

stroke, 430, 440

strokes, 433

structural changes, 409

structuring, 94

students, 33, 55, 58, 59, 166, 187, 193, 278, 281, 313, 324, 325, 326, 327, 329, 335, 341, 342, 343, 345, 394, 422, 435, 439, 442, 445, 447, 449, 459, 470

subacute, 86

subdomains, 113

subdural hematoma, 474

subgroups, 85

subjective, 200, 205, 212, 229, 244, 333, 369, 373, 399, 410, 446

subpoena, 481

substance abuse, 5, 121, 166, 197, 282, 309, 323, 327, 329, 334, 343, 351, 353, 356, 359, 373, 376, 378, 379, 390, 417, 423, 428, 444, 446, 448, 455, 456, 459, 467, 487, 490

substance use, 34, 178, 179, 209, 210, 246, 304, 309, 327, 350, 356, 381, 428, 442, 446, 447, 449, 450

substances, 3, 4, 161, 164, 197, 210, 303, 308, 378, 391, 428, 438, 444, 445

substitutes, 443

substitution, 406

success rate, 137

sudden infant death syndrome, 477

SUDS, 210

suffering, 208, 211, 244, 248, 256, 474

sugar, 126, 200, 438, 441

sugars, 406

suicidal, 27, 34, 213, 222, 250, 260, 295, 302, 305, 319, 320, 321, 322, 323, 324, 325, 326, 327, 328, 329, 330, 331, 332, 333, 334, 335, 336, 337, 338, 339, 340, 341, 343, 344, 345, 376, 391, 410, 421

suicidal behavior, 222, 295, 319, 320, 321, 322, 323, 325, 327, 328, 329, 332, 333, 334, 335, 336, 339, 340, 341, 343, 344, 345, 376, 391

suicidal ideation, 27, 213, 222, 250, 260, 305, 320, 321, 322, 324, 332, 333, 335, 336, 340, 341, 410

suicide, 141, 171, 207, 210, 213, 222, 283, 303, 304, 308, 311, 312, 313, 314, 319, 320, 321, 322, 323, 324, 325, 326, 327, 328, 329, 330, 331, 332, 333, 334, 335, 336, 337, 338, 339, 340, 341, 342, 343, 344, 345, 346, 347, 354, 396, 422, 428, 451

suicide attempters, 321, 323

suicide attempts, 141, 303, 309, 312, 319, 320, 321, 322, 323, 324, 327, 328, 329, 330, 334, 335, 339, 343, 344, 345

suicide completers, 327

suicide rate, 324, 330, 331, 354

summaries, 344

summer, 240, 412

Sun, 233

Sunday, 240

superiority, 333, 357, 358

superstitious, 258

supervision, 47, 227, 394, 395, 419, 420, 460, 467, 477, 489, 491, 498, 499

supplemental, 24

supplements, 153, 397

supply, 397, 439, 444

support services, 39, 48, 359
suppository, 152
suppression, 122, 123, 127, 141, 172, 393, 413
Supreme Court, 496
Surgeon General, 319, 339
surgeons, 271
Surgeons, ix
surgeries, 45
surgery, ix, 271, 275, 411, 413, 441, 462
Surgery, 155, 271, 415, 476, 480
surgical, 409, 463
surprise, xii
surveillance, 311, 312, 341, 489
survival, 4, 271, 284, 301, 404, 452
survival rate, 4
survivors, 337, 338, 347, 402, 458
susceptibility, 351, 361, 364
susceptibility genes, 351
sustainable development, x
swallowing, 61, 65
Sweden, 292
swelling, 462
switching, 224, 227, 228, 229, 422
Switzerland, 339, 426, 441, 453
symbolic, 62, 68, 87
symbols, 55, 63, 64, 69, 370
symmetry, 257, 258
sympathetic, 104, 132, 438
sympathetic nervous system, 104
symptom, 26, 30, 65, 70, 80, 83, 85, 89, 92, 93, 110,
    122, 129, 160, 190, 194, 198, 205, 206, 207, 220,
    222, 230, 231, 250, 251, 260, 321, 335, 353, 355,
    356, 357, 358, 363, 364
symptomatic treatment, 181
synapse, 132
synapses, 108
synchronous, 63, 68
syndrome, 47, 57, 65, 81, 89, 99, 104, 107, 116, 118,
    121, 122, 124, 125, 126, 127, 128, 129, 130, 136,
    142, 144, 165, 166, 171, 191, 192, 195, 197, 199,
    205, 210, 212, 226, 257, 261, 266, 272, 298, 305,
    306, 352, 353, 358, 362, 364, 367, 397, 407, 409,
    411, 414, 427, 429, 430, 435, 445, 447, 453, 454,
    472, 477, 478, 479, 483
synergistic, 170
synergistic effect, 170
syntactic, 62, 71
syntax, 61, 90
synthesis, 76, 401
synthetic, 417, 440

syphilis, 279, 308
Syphilis, 306
systematic, 49, 82, 88, 174, 350, 358, 361, 364, 365,
    480
systematic review, 174, 361, 365, 480
systems, 24, 58, 61, 62, 63, 66, 70, 72, 80, 101, 107,
    117, 129, 137, 172, 205, 220, 231, 304, 305, 337,
    400, 410, 426, 452, 456, 458, 472, 499

T

tachycardia, 260, 393, 433, 437, 438
tactics, 230, 336, 390
tangible, 10
tanks, 444
tar, 422, 423
tardive dyskinesia, 261, 358
target behavior, 10, 11, 30, 31, 93
target organs, 409
targets, 423
task performance, 105
taste, 110, 114, 152, 153, 406, 424, 425, 442
taxonomy, 102
TBI, 192, 196, 199, 200, 455, 466
teachers, 10, 25, 33, 34, 52, 71, 85, 94, 110, 114,
    160, 161, 162, 166, 176, 208, 275, 280, 336, 342,
    356, 370, 386, 420, 464, 469
teaching, ix, x, 32, 76, 96, 151, 230, 272, 275, 283,
    285, 310, 359, 380, 417
team members, 394, 395, 464
technological, 76
technology, 117, 151, 458
teenagers, xv, 21, 137, 163, 295, 308, 309, 329, 346,
    459, 486
teens, 30, 33, 280, 282, 284, 285, 288, 289, 290, 301,
    302, 379, 418, 422, 423, 424
teeth, 62, 163, 393, 398, 423, 462
telephone, 151, 335
television, 12, 106, 219, 221, 279, 329, 345, 406,
    412, 413, 415, 456, 459
television viewing, 412, 415
temperament, 6, 7, 223, 235, 244, 419, 456, 486
temperature, 431
temporal, 15, 63, 69, 179, 191, 192, 196, 351, 355
temporal lobe, 191, 192, 196
tenants, 93
tendon, 411
tension, 62, 73, 148, 272
testes, 274, 462
testimony, 468, 474, 485

testosterone, 275

Tetanus, 436

Texas, 174, 217, 442, 506

textbooks, 162

thalamus, 121, 351

theft, 178

theoretical, 76, 102, 114, 116, 117, 170, 200, 231

theory, 18, 28, 75, 93, 94, 95, 102, 110, 121, 277, 334, 342, 474

therapeutic, 28, 115, 141, 154, 164, 181, 196, 217, 231, 232, 250, 260, 261, 272, 394, 399, 400, 414, 498

therapeutics, ix

therapists, 29, 33, 58, 94, 116, 395, 396

therapy, xiii, xv, 5, 29, 32, 53, 58, 90, 91, 93, 94, 95, 96, 101, 102, 110, 115, 118, 119, 124, 141, 143, 145, 154, 155, 212, 216, 226, 227, 228, 229, 230, 231, 232, 234, 249, 252, 262, 310, 311, 335, 336, 337, 346, 359, 362, 366, 367, 380, 394, 395, 399, 400, 401, 403, 409, 412, 446, 450, 470

thinking, xi, 64, 83, 137, 186, 187, 190, 206, 213, 231, 250, 276, 320, 324, 325, 326, 327, 335, 337, 345, 353, 354, 369, 370, 371, 372, 380, 431, 490

thioridazine, 127

threat, 178, 189, 243, 269, 308, 489

threatened, 188, 195, 243, 301

threatening, 177, 185, 208, 244, 245, 249, 383, 390, 443, 452

threatening behavior, 208

threats, 186, 333

threshold, 6, 53, 104, 196, 197, 220, 259, 426

thresholds, 85, 104

throat, 89, 153, 258, 393, 425, 462

thrombocytopenia, 225

thyroid, 216, 229, 246, 391, 462

thyroid stimulating hormone, 229

thyrotoxicosis, 242

tibia, 273, 409

tic disorder, 4, 121, 122, 124, 125, 126, 127, 128, 129, 166, 195, 198

tics, 121, 122, 123, 125, 126, 127, 129, 130, 171, 172, 198, 199, 257

TID, 229

tiger, 248

time commitment, 163

time consuming, 58, 85

time frame, 12, 393, 496

timing, 62, 106, 136, 273, 304, 459, 461, 466

tissue, 273, 274, 397, 400, 465

titration, 168, 169, 225, 228

tobacco, 44, 284, 417, 419, 421, 422, 423, 424, 425, 427, 432, 443, 446, 447, 449, 450

tobacco smoke, 422, 427

toddlers, 75, 105, 177

toilet training, 12, 150, 151, 155, 156, 287

tolerance, 56, 67, 162, 178, 188, 194, 215, 336, 409, 412, 427, 428, 429, 432, 435, 436

toluene, 444, 445

Tonsillar, 411

tonsils, 462

Topiramate, 125, 225

total costs, 451

total parenteral nutrition, 395

toxemia, 44

toxic, 56, 161, 261, 398, 428, 439

toxic effect, 261, 398

toxic substances, 161

toxicity, 129

toxicology, 450

toys, 31, 68, 83, 85, 303, 307

tracking, 12, 55, 181, 246

trade, 14, 221, 282, 390, 426

tradition, xiii

traditional gender role, 322

traffic, 33, 161, 330

training, x, xi, xii, xiii, 12, 13, 48, 89, 93, 94, 95, 96, 147, 150, 151, 154, 155, 156, 163, 180, 182, 185, 216, 231, 253, 268, 284, 285, 287, 334, 336, 337, 338, 346, 359, 395, 469, 471, 476, 477, 481, 482, 490

training programs, xii, xiii

traits, 6, 7, 118, 299, 343, 369, 372, 373, 380, 466

trans, 297, 455

transaminases, 429

transfer, 33

transference, 498

transition, 48, 71, 162, 325, 332, 371

transitions, 6, 34, 114, 200, 270

translation, 17

transmission, 89, 243, 466, 482

transplantation, 210

transport, 63

transportation, 47, 406, 495

trauma, 3, 4, 56, 116, 118, 355, 380, 398, 438, 455, 457, 458, 463, 466, 471, 472, 475, 476, 477, 479, 483

traumatic brain injury, 24, 62, 67, 199, 455, 458, 465, 473, 478, 482

travel, 131, 132

treatable, 46, 96, 178, 225, 247, 252, 255, 256

treatment methods, 230

treatment programs, 33, 394, 400, 455, 486, 492

treatment-resistant, 261

trees, 357

tremor, 124

trend, 85, 397, 447

trial, 95, 97, 126, 130, 143, 169, 197, 198, 216, 225, 230, 233, 234, 250, 253, 259, 260, 261, 262, 337, 346, 358, 401, 485, 490

triceps, 408

tricyclic antidepressant, 128, 169, 260, 429

tricyclic antidepressants, 261, 429

triggers, 137, 242, 248, 259, 332, 392

triglyceride, 410, 412

Trisomy 21, 407

truancy, 177, 421, 455

trucks, 287

trust, 3, 115, 163, 267, 268, 286, 374, 452, 453, 498

tryptophan, 389, 401

Tryptophan, 344

TSC, 197, 199

TSH, 229, 413

tuberous sclerosis, 86, 89, 199

Tuberous sclerosis complex, 191, 192, 197

tumor, 423, 426

tumors, 13, 357

turbulent, 471

tutoring, 33

twin studies, 242, 256, 322

Twin studies, 243, 328, 361

twins, 107, 299, 322, 351, 387

tympanic membrane, 462

type 2 diabetes, 358, 362, 408, 411, 412

type 2 diabetes mellitus, 412

type II diabetes, 406, 408

U

Ukraine, 278, 503

ulcer, 436

ultrasonography, 133, 135

ultrasound, 133, 141, 143

uncertainty, 220

underreported, 465

unemployment, 456

United Kingdom, 278, 314, 503

United Nations, 426

United States, ix, x, xi, xii, 39, 40, 41, 48, 67, 82, 108, 113, 124, 136, 147, 200, 272, 279, 280, 281, 282, 283, 284, 290, 291, 293, 294, 296, 302, 308, 311, 312, 314, 319, 340, 341, 342, 345, 372, 405, 406, 408, 412, 415, 417, 422, 426, 438, 441, 442, 444, 446, 447, 449, 450, 451, 455, 459, 464, 465, 474, 477, 478, 480, 481, 484, 485, 491

universe, 266

universities, 342, 469, 470

university students, 343

upper respiratory infection, 258, 259, 304

urban, 147, 321, 340, 350, 365, 406, 475

urban areas, 350, 406

urbanicity, 365

urbanization, 330

urea, 393

urea nitrogen, 393

urethra, 462

urethritis, 308

uric acid, 429

urinary, 96, 131, 133, 135, 141, 142, 143, 144, 145, 149, 155, 260, 441

urinary retention, 141, 143, 441

urinary tract, 96, 131, 133, 135, 141, 142, 144, 145, 149, 155

urinary tract infection, 96, 135, 142, 144, 149

urine, 133, 134, 135, 137, 141, 142, 145, 390, 392, 443, 445

URL, 293

urologist, 304

US Department of Health and Human Services, 340, 482

users, 63, 104, 117, 193, 210, 343, 392, 421, 426, 427, 429, 439, 440, 447

V

vacation, 240

Vaccination, 89

vaccinations, 89

vaccine, 305, 434

vagina, 267, 270, 462

vaginal, 44, 268, 275, 277, 293, 458

vaginitis, 483

validity, 14, 27, 102, 113, 114, 118, 182, 219, 234, 262, 350, 361, 363, 482

valproic acid, 182, 198, 199

values, 75, 90, 283, 288, 289, 325, 326, 370, 371, 386, 396, 408

varenicline, 426

variability, 16, 21, 160, 207, 244, 246, 323, 328, 352, 402

variable, 39, 136, 159, 162, 176, 188, 206, 274, 330, 333, 354, 358

variables, 14, 15, 321, 456, 486, 487

variance, 328

variation, 4, 7, 53, 56, 69, 208, 273, 299, 364, 427

variety of domains, 16

vascular, 409, 411, 440

vascular disease, 411

vasopressin, 136, 143

VDRL, 436

vegetables, 399, 406, 412

vegetarianism, 389

velocity, 273, 274

venereal wart, 308

venlafaxine, 215

ventilation, 44

ventricles, 351

ventricular, 261, 366, 433, 437

ventricular arrhythmia, 433

ventricular tachycardia, 437

Verbal IQ, 53

verbalizations, 20, 31

Vermont, 26

vertebrae, 389, 393

vibration, 124, 133

victimization, 295, 329, 451, 455, 461, 462, 463, 465, 466, 468, 469, 470, 471, 472, 473, 486, 488

victims, 178, 280, 281, 292, 328, 344, 428, 438, 451, 456, 461, 464, 466, 469, 470, 471, 475, 479, 481, 484, 485, 486, 487, 490, 492

Victoria, 49

video, 31, 284, 456

video games, 31, 456

Vigilante, 118

violence, xiii, 3, 4, 177, 178, 185, 187, 201, 281, 282, 283, 285, 292, 293, 294, 295, 301, 303, 304, 308, 309, 312, 324, 379, 422, 428, 451, 456, 458, 459, 461, 464, 465, 467, 470, 471, 473, 474, 481, 484

violent, 181, 188, 195, 200, 269, 281, 330, 338, 343, 379, 427, 431, 489, 492

violent behavior, 181, 379, 427, 431

violent offenders, 492

viral, 89, 121, 124, 304, 357

viral infection, 357

Virginia, 314

virus, 165, 192, 209, 210, 305, 306, 466, 481

virus infection, 165

visible, 279

vision, 29, 42, 43, 46, 56, 57, 86, 89, 106, 114, 142

visual, 4, 6, 11, 19, 20, 21, 22, 23, 24, 29, 52, 55, 56, 57, 58, 63, 64, 74, 91, 95, 106, 107, 108, 136, 154, 222, 355, 437, 438, 441, 496

visual attention, 74

visual images, 154

visual memory, 22

visual processing, 23, 24, 108

visual stimuli, 20, 22

visualization, 466

visuospatial, 20, 22

vitamins, 412

vocabulary, 20, 54, 58, 69, 71, 75, 84, 245, 286

vocational, 24, 48, 61, 69, 72, 359

vocational training, 48, 359

voice, 61, 62, 64, 93, 273, 350

voicing, 62

voiding, 132, 133, 134, 135, 137, 141, 142, 143, 145, 155, 392

voids, xi

vomiting, 43, 226, 383, 384, 385, 388, 391, 393, 397, 398, 411, 427

vulnerability, 256, 322, 367, 497, 498

vulva, 287

W

Wales, 331, 345

walking, 52, 85, 161, 221, 389, 406, 412

wants and needs, 47

war, 282

warrants, 319

warts, 306, 308, 476

Washington, 7, 8, 35, 48, 49, 76, 98, 99, 116, 119, 129, 173, 182, 200, 216, 232, 252, 291, 292, 295, 296, 311, 314, 315, 332, 339, 341, 342, 345, 346, 347, 360, 361, 363, 381, 402, 449, 475, 476, 479, 480, 482, 483, 484, 491, 492, 493, 502, 503, 506

water, 140, 148, 151, 152, 153, 169, 229, 242, 387, 389, 392, 425, 427, 432, 440, 442, 443

WCST, 21

weakness, 29, 32, 91

wealth, 51

weapons, 178

wear, 161, 164, 266, 389

web, 124

websites, 219, 284, 404

Wechsler Intelligence Scale, 19, 45

weight control, 392

weight gain, 127, 206, 225, 226, 229, 261, 357, 358, 385, 388, 389, 394, 397, 401, 406, 425, 426, 467

weight loss, 206, 383, 388, 389, 390, 391, 406, 407, 409, 410, 411, 412, 414, 420, 421, 431, 467
weight management, 229, 359, 409
weight reduction, 409
Weinberg, 311
welfare, 458, 464, 469, 472
welfare system, 472
well-being, 94, 193, 210, 308, 314, 439, 459
Western countries, 407
Western culture, 386
Western Europe, 284
Western societies, 386
wet, 134, 135, 137, 288, 427
wetting, 134, 135, 141, 142, 143
wheelchair, 32
white blood cell count, 358
White House Office, 426
white matter, 363, 399
whole grain, 406
Wikipedia, 296
windows, 178
wine, 428
winter, 240, 400
Wisconsin, 21, 503
wisdom, x, 70
withdrawal, 6, 31, 79, 97, 126, 164, 191, 193, 207, 210, 211, 212, 217, 251, 276, 353, 354, 356, 420, 425, 426, 427, 429, 435, 436, 447, 450, 497
witness, 490
witnesses, 459
women, 287, 292, 294, 302, 307, 311, 312, 313, 383, 385, 387, 390, 410, 472, 481, 483
wood, 400
word recognition, 53, 71

work ethic, 326
workers, xv, 47, 58, 356, 464, 465, 469
workplace, 58
workspace, 14
World Health Organization (WHO), 148, 331, 339, 450, 452, 453
worldview, 213
worry, 243, 244, 248, 256, 271, 272, 282, 301, 389, 392
writing, xi, 24, 52, 54, 58, 61, 64, 69, 71, 74, 91, 109, 258, 333

X

x-linked, 407
x-ray, 398, 408, 458, 463, 466
x-ray absorption, 408
x-rays, 463

Y

yield, 19, 22, 44, 98, 206, 359, 408, 412
young adults, 192, 311, 320, 323, 324, 328, 329, 345, 346, 362, 433, 440, 446, 449, 461
young men, 288
younger children, 160, 215, 242, 243, 257, 258, 323, 455, 485, 487, 489, 490

Z

Zen, 395
ziprasidone, 97, 127, 261, 357, 358
Zoloft, 249, 259